Legal Theory

Legal Theory

by

W. FRIEDMANN

LL.D.(London), DR.JUR.(Berlin), LL.M.(Melbourne)
Of the Middle Temple, Barrister-at-Law
Professor of International Law and Director of International
Legal Research, Columbia University

FIFTH EDITION

COLUMBIA UNIVERSITY PRESS

NEW YORK

Published in Great Britain by
Stevens & Sons Limited

SBN 0-231-03100-9
Library of Congress Catalog Card Number: 67-26509
Printed in the United States of America
10 9 8 7 6 5 4 3

CONTENTS

v

PART TWO

A CRITICAL SURVEY OF LEGAL THEORIES

Section One

Natural Law and the Search for Absolute Values

Section Two

Philosophical Idealism and the Problem of Justice

Section Three

The Impact of Social Development on Legal Theory

Section Four

Positivism and Legal Theory

PART THREE

LEGAL THEORY AND CONTEMPORARY PROBLEMS

Section One

Legal Theory of Modern Political Movements

Section Two

Legal Theory, Public Policy and Legal Evolution

Contents

Section Three

Legal Theory and International Society

PREFACE

FOR the present edition, the book has once again been subjected to substantial revisions. The major additions are in the introductory part which seeks to define the place of legal theory. The important discussions that since the publication of the last edition have taken place with regard to the structure of the legal order, and the revival of the discussions on the relation of law and morality that was provoked by the decision of the House of Lords in the "Ladies Directories" case form some of the background for a new chapter (Chapter 3) which discusses the concept of law in its relation to the structure of a legal system and the minimum "morality" of a legal order. At the same time, this chapter surveys the principal ethical theories in their relation to legal philosophy.

No contemporary jurist can ignore the impact of modern scientific thought on legal theory, as on the social sciences in general. The new chapter (Chapter 4) on "Science and Legal Theory" is a very tentative attempt to discuss some of the relevant problems. Lack of professional qualifications in the field of science would have prevented me from presenting these thoughts, had I not had the inestimable benefit of having the chapter checked by my friend and colleague Professor Ernest Nagel, of Columbia and Rockefeller Universities.

The robust law-making decisions of the House of Lords of recent years account for some of the rewriting of Chapter 31 of the Fourth Edition, now Chapter 32 and renamed "Legal Ideals, Public Policy and Judicial Law-Making." A major new section in that chapter entitled "Limits of Judicial Law-Making and Prospective Overruling" deals essentially with the—hitherto purely American—judicial doctrine of "prospective overruling," as part of the wider problem of the limits of the judicial function in legal changes. This section was published in the *Modern Law Review*, November, 1966. I am grateful to the editors for permission to reprint it. Other major revisions include the analysis of important new decisions bearing on the "higher law" interpretation of the American Constitution (Chapter 13); the analysis of Soviet and Social Democratic legal theory (Chapter 29); a new section on the role of law and the lawyer in developing countries (Chapter 31)—part of which was published in the *Vanderbilk Law Review*, December, 1963, and a more extended discussion of phenomenological and existentialist approaches to legal theory, especially of recent French writings (Chapter 17).

The chapter on state sovereignty and international order (Chapter 35) has been largely rewritten since I have modified my former view on the relation of national sovereignty and international law. This is more fully developed in "The Changing Structure of International Law" (1964).

In order to avoid an inordinate increase in the size of the book, two chapters contained in earlier editions, *i.e.*, "Fascist and National Socialist Legal Theories" and "Nationalist Interpretations of Legal and Political Philosophy," have been eliminated.

I am much indebted to Professor Ernest Nagel for his comments on "Science and Legal Theory," to Professor Charles Szladits for going over the chapter on "English, American and Continental Jurisprudence," and to Judge Charles D. Breitel for his comments on some of the new chapters of the book tested in a doctoral seminar in legal philosophy at Columbia which we have conducted jointly.

I am particularly grateful to Mr. Gabriel Wilner, LL.M., for his able assistance in the revision of this book, including the reading of new materials and the preparation of the Index and the Bibliography.

W. FRIEDMANN

New York
February, 1967

TABLE OF CASES

xv

AUSTRALIA

CANADA

UNITED STATES

TABLE OF STATUTES

xix

PART ONE

INTRODUCTORY
REFLECTIONS

CHAPTER 1

THE PLACE AND FUNCTION
OF LEGAL THEORY

ALL systematic thinking about legal theory is linked at one end with philosophy and, at the other end, with political theory. Sometimes the starting-point is philosophy, and political ideology plays a secondary part—as in the theories of the German classical metaphysicians or the Neo-Kantians. Sometimes the starting-point is political ideology, as in the legal theories of Socialism and Fascism. Sometimes theory of knowledge and political ideology are welded into one coherent system, where the respective shares of the two are not easy to disentangle, as in the scholastic system or in Hegel's philosophic system. But all legal theory must contain elements of philosophy—man's reflections on his position in the universe—and gain its colour and specific content from political theory—the ideas entertained on the best form of society. For all thinking about the end of law is based on conceptions of man both as a thinking individual and as a political being.

This dual aspect will facilitate an understanding of the development of legal thought, as traced in this book. Some legal philosophers have been philosophers first and foremost, and jurists for the sake of the completeness of their philosophical system. Others have been politicians first and foremost, and jurists because they felt the need to express their political thought in legal form. A third group —mainly in recent times—has been driven to consider the ultimate ends of law, by the professional study and practice of the law. They have been nonetheless compelled to accept one or the other philosophical or political premiss.

This may account, to some extent, for the difficulty of assigning to legal theory a place of its own. It must, however, gain such a place; for, as will be apparent throughout this book, the lawyer, whether as legislator or magistrate, whether as citizen or as professional craftsman, is always consciously or unconsciously guided by the principles which legal theory formulates for him in pro-

3

fessional form, from the precepts of philosophy and political theory. In Radbruch's formulation, its task is "the clarification of legal values and postulates up to their ultimate philosophical foundations."

To the further question of the relation of law to religion, ethics, economics and science, no general answer can be given. These are the sources from which a particular legal theory may be nourished. Religion determines the philosophical and political outlook of the scholastics, ethical principles determine the legal philosophy of Kant, economics underlie the legal thought of Marxism, scientific fact study inspires the functional approach of the realist movement. The answer to these questions must therefore be given in conjunction with any particular legal theory which is discussed. But all these sources contribute, though in varying strength and combination, to form the philosophical and political valuations from which a legal theory is built up.

The present book cannot attempt to give a full analysis of these philosophical, political and other non-juristic premises of legal theory. It must be content to point them out in general terms. This should suffice, however, not only to link a legal theory with the religious or ethical principles, the political philosophy, the economic theory by which it is inspired; it should also help to bring out a significant shift in the development of legal thought.

Before the nineteenth century, legal theory was essentially a by-product of philosophy, religion, ethics or politics. The great legal thinkers were primarily philosophers, churchmen, politicians. The decisive shift from the philosopher's or politician's to the lawyer's legal philosophy is of fairly recent date. It follows a period of great developments in juristic research, technique and professional training. The new era of legal philosophy arises mainly from the confrontation of the professional lawyer, in his legal work, with problems of social justice.

It is, therefore, inevitable that an analysis of earlier legal theories must lean more heavily on general philosophical and political theory, while modern legal theories can be more adequately discussed in the lawyer's own idiom and system of thought. The difference is, however, one of method and emphasis. The modern jurist's legal theory, no less than the scholastic philosopher's, is based on ultimate beliefs whose inspiration comes from outside the law itself.

CHAPTER 2

GREEK PHILOSOPHY AND THE BASIC PROBLEMS
OF LAW

THE Romans laid the foundations of modern analytical jurisprudence, but their contribution to legal philosophy has been slight.
What there is of it is mainly eclectic and secondhand, such as the
writings of Cicero and Seneca. From the Greeks, on the other hand,
we can learn little for the modern law of contract, tort or property,[1]
but all the main issues of legal theory were formulated by Greek
thinkers, from Homer to the Stoics. The rise and development of
the Polis, the Greek city state, was the persistent background of
Greek speculative thought on law and government, from the descriptions of life in a city state on the shield of Achilles—in Homer's
Iliad—to the reflections of Plato and Aristotle. But only the combination of two factors could produce the abundance of mature
thought on the function and problems of law in a community. The
social disorders, internal conflicts, the frequent changes of government, the many periods of tyranny and arbitrariness, provided the
external stimulus to speculation about the relation of higher justice
to positive law. But only a unique gift of speculative insight and
intellectual perception, a sense of tragedy and human conflict
which is apparent in Greek philosophy and poetry, made possible
the Greek contribution to legal philosophy, and in particular to
the problem of eternal justice and positive law.

The following sketch of the main problems, as formulated by
Greek philosophers, is no more than a brief introduction to the
problems of modern legal theory with which this book is primarily
concerned.

---

[1] The failure of the Greeks to reduce their law to a system is no doubt connected with the absence of a trained legal profession—but both facts are probably
attributable to more basic approaches to life and society. For a valuable study of
Greek legal thought and institutions, see J. W. Jones, *The Law and Legal Theory
of the Greeks* (1956).

FROM HOMER TO PERICLES

In Homer's work law has an essential but unproblematical place. Law is embodied in the Themistes which the kings receive from Zeus as the divine source of all earthly justice and which are based on custom and tradition. Justice is still identical with order and authority. An awareness of the conflict between positive law and justice becomes more and more pronounced from the eighth century onwards. It arises against a background of social trouble, of discontent with the rule of aristocracy and frequent abuse of power. The problem of justice ($\delta i \kappa \eta$) becomes articulate in the poems of Hesiod and of Solon, the great Athenian law-giver.[2] Both appeal to Dike, the daughter of Zeus, as a guarantor of justice against earthly tyranny, violation of rights and social injustice. Solon sees Dike as rewarding civil unrest and injustice with social evils while she rewards just communities with peace and prosperity.

The problem of the relation between justice and positive law dominated Greek thinking, as indeed all legal thought ever since. The nature philosophers of the Milesian school turned to external nature as a source of law more permanent than human laws. The process by which Heraclitus found the law of nature in the rhythm of events and subsequent thinkers came to conceive of nature ($\phi \acute{\upsilon} \sigma \iota \varsigma$) as opposed to reason ($\nu \acute{o} \mu o \varsigma$) is described in the following chapter. This development led Greek thinkers to a contemplation of the relation between the outer world of the universe and the inner world of man. In the first phase the main theme is the tragic antithesis between the need to obey the positive law of the state and the higher moral claims of the unwritten and unaltering divine law. The classical expression of this is found in the tragedies of Æschylus and Sophocles: both Æschylus' *Eumenides* and Sophocles' *Antigone* end in the appeal to the respect for law as the main guardian of order, peace and harmony in the state. Both are still dominated by the sense of accomplishment which preceded the decline of Athenian democracy, a belief in the progress which a civilised and ordered community dominated by wise laws had made over the anarchy and tyranny of earlier days. The last classical expression of this phase of Greek legal thought is Pericles' Funeral Oration:[3]

---

[2] His great political poem, *Our City*, was probably composed between 600 and 590 B.C.

[3] Thucydides, *The Peloponnesian War*, Book 2, 37, 38 (Everyman's Library, ed. Rhys).

If we look to the laws, they afford equal justice to all in their private differences; if no social standing, advancement in public life falls to reputation for capacity, class considerations not being allowed to interfere with merit; nor again does poverty bar the way; if a man is able to serve the state he is not hindered by the obscurity of his condition. The freedom which we enjoy in our government extends also to our ordinary life. There, far from exercising a jealous surveillance over each other, we do not feel called upon to be angry with our neighbour for doing what he likes, or even to indulge in those injurious looks which cannot fail to be offensive, although they inflict no positive penalty. But all this ease in our private relations does not make us lawless as citizens. Against this fear is our chief safeguard, teaching us to obey the magistrates and the laws, particularly such as regard the protection of the injured, whether they are actually on the Statute Book, or belong to that code which, although unwritten, yet cannot be broken without acknowledged disgrace.

PLATO'S APPROACH TO LAW

It is the subsequent decline of Athenian democracy, in the Peloponnesian war and after, which provided the background for the preoccupation with justice that dominates the legal philosophy of Plato and Aristotle. As in our own time, the decline in the standards of government and society stimulated the yearning for justice. Faced with the disintegration of Athenian society and the disruption of the very values and accomplishments which Pericles had praised, both devoted a considerable part of their work to a more concrete definition of justice and to the relation between justice and positive law. But as Kelsen has pointed out,[4] they approached the problem from two different angles, contrasted by him as the metaphysical and the rationalistic approach. Plato attempted to derive his conception of justice from inspiration; Aristotle developed it from a scientific analysis of rational principles developed against a background of existing types of political communities and laws. The connecting link between them is concept of virtue ($\dot{\alpha}\rho\epsilon\tau\acute{\eta}$), the all-embracing idea of which justice is a necessary part and aspect. From this flows the conception of balance and harmony as the test of a just commonwealth and a just individual. But here the ways part. Harmony for Plato is a state of inner balance of mind not capable of rational analysis. To Aristotle it is the mean ($\mu\epsilon\sigma\acute{o}\tau\eta s$) between extremes, deduced by quasi-

---

[4] Kelsen, "The Metamorphoses of the Idea of Justice," in *Interpretations of Modern Legal Philosophies*, 390, 398 *et seq.* (Sayre ed. 1947).

mathematical principles from a blend of extremes in government and human relations.

In his attitude towards the necessity and importance of law for the community, Plato's later message differs from that of his earlier work. In the commonwealth pictured in the *Republic*, the law as an organised and formulated system of rules binding upon the community has no place. That work is mainly devoted to an analysis of the functions of the different classes in the state and in particular to the philosopher-kings who are to control the state. The execution of justice is entirely entrusted to these rulers whose education and inspired wisdom are a guarantee of just government. It is the task of the rulers to see to it "that man should do his work in the station of life to which he is called by his capacities."[5]

Plato's later work is, on the contrary, dominated by the problem of law as a formulated system of positive rules governing the whole of the state. If the *Republic* was a reflection of Plato's ideal state, experience and disillusionment—particularly his work as adviser to the Sicilian tyrant Dionysius—had brought him to consider the necessity of a "second best state." Plato's great work of his old age, *The Laws*, is entirely devoted to a discussion between an Athenian, a Spartan and a Cretan on the principles and subject-matter of laws in a state.[6] There are few activities which the later Plato did not consider as in need of legal regulation. In *The Laws* he discusses, through the mouth of the Athenian, in minute detail, such divers matters as marketing regulations, community meals and the legal aspects of every kind of agricultural activity. But the law is meant to regulate further the most intimate personal relations, the emotions of infants, conduct in marriage, and divorce, no less than the types of funerals or the scale of earnings in different occupations. A detailed scale of sanctions—both civil and criminal—cements these laws. There are still state-appointed supervisors, but

[5] Barker, *Greek Political Theory: Plato and His Predecessors*, 149.

[6] In a recent essay (*Studies in Jurisprudence and Criminal Law*, p. 48 *et seq.* 1958), Jerome Hall has challenged the generally held theory that there is a major divergence between Plato's views on law as between the *Republic* and *The Laws*. In Hall's view, these two works (linked by an intermediate work, *The Statesman*) had entirely different objectives. The *Republic* was intended to outline Plato's ideas of state and government, but not to give a practical code of laws, as was the case in *The Laws*, and, to some extent, in *The Statesman*. Be that as it may, the emphasis in the two works is basically different. Granted that there is no evidence of change in Plato's basically authoritarian and anti-democratic views of justice, law and government, it is to *The Laws* that one must turn for Plato's mature views of law in action.

they now take their knowledge and guidance from the written law. As Cairns has pointed out,[7] Plato anticipates Bentham[8] in his faith in the omnipotence of laws made by an omniscient legislator. But his philosophy resembles the philosophy of the modern authoritarian welfare state—Communist or Fascist—in the extent to which it subjects individual life to the legal and administrative control of the state.

Law now appears as a golden stream, the embodiment of "right reasoning" ($\dot{o}\rho\theta\dot{o}s$ $\lambda\dot{o}\gamma os$). As to the content and sources of this right reasoning, Plato is, however, silent. His conception of justice is still essentially the same as in the *Republic*.

Justice, namely, virtue in the sense of inner harmony and balance, is not knowable or explicable by rational argument. In several of his *Letters* Plato has in fact made this observation. On the knowledge of the good, that is of justice, there are no writings of his, "for it does not at all admit of verbal expression like other branches of knowledge."[9] The progress from the *Republic* to *The Laws* lies in the insight that a class of aristocratic philosopher-kings, wise enough to apply justice without written laws, cannot be hoped for, but the knowledge of justice which directs the laws of the state is still a matter of mystical inspiration.

The nearest approach to an explicit formulation of the conflict between justice and legality is contained in a short dialogue which, if it cannot be ascribed with certainty to Plato himself, certainly emanates from one of his disciples. In *Minos* Socrates and a pupil discuss the definition of law and move from the original definition of law as something stipulated in proper form by the proper authority, to the necessity of relating law to the revelation of truth and good. While the problem is stated with dialectic pungency, the dialogue ends inconclusively with a discourse by Socrates on "Minos" who, as a wise law-giver, received his inspiration from Zeus himself. This does not lead beyond the Platonic conception of justice, as the revelation of good received by the select few and communicated by them to the community in the form of laws.[10]

[7] Cairns, *Legal Philosophy from Plato to Hegel*, 48 *et seq.* (1949.)
[8] Below, p. 312 *et seq.*
[9] *Epistle* VII, 341c.
[10] This interpretation of justice serves, however, Plato's political ideal, which is that of a rigidly stratified anti-equalitarian society, in which nobody must attempt to change his status and everybody is told what is good for him. See, in particular, Popper, *The Open Society*, Chap. 6. (Rev. ed. 1950.)

B*

ARISTOTLE'S CONTRIBUTION TO LEGAL THEORY

Aristotle's contribution to legal theory, inspired as it was by an encyclopedical study of existing laws and constitutions, is a more definite one.

The most fundamental of Aristotle's doctrines is that which has since inspired not only legal theory but Western philosophy in general, *i.e.*, the dual character of man as part and master of nature. Subject, as part of the universe, to the laws of matter and all creation, man, at the same time, dominates nature by his spirit which enables him to will freely, to distinguish between good and evil. This, the mature consolidation of Greek philosophy, underlies the legal thought of scholastic as of rationalist natural law philosophy; of Kant as of Hegel; of John Stuart Mill and Herbert Spencer as of Del Vecchio and Kohler.

The second great contribution of Aristotle to legal thought is his formulation of the problem of justice. His distinction between "distributive" and "corrective" or "remedial" justice still forms a basis of all theoretical discussions on the subject. The first directs the distribution of goods and honours to each according to his place in the community; it orders the equal treatment of those equal before the law. This stresses the fundamental fact, always true, but so often ignored by legal philosophers eager to prove the truth of their political conviction, that no ideal of justice can be at once theoretically valid and have a specific content. It is for positive law, based on specific ethical and political principles, to say who is equal before the law.

The second form of justice is essentially the measure of the technical principles which govern the administration of law. In regulating legal relations a general standard of redressing the consequences of actions must be found, without regard to the person, and for that purpose actions and objects must be measured by an objective standard. Punishment must redress crime, reparation must redress civil wrong, damages must restore wrongful gain. The conception of Themis, the goddess, who balances the scales without regard to the person, underlies this form of justice. But it must be understood subject to distributive justice.

Aristotle's third major contribution is the distinction between legal and natural justice, or, as we would put it, between positive and natural law. The former derives its force from being laid down as law, whether just or unjust; it explains the diversity of positive laws; the latter derives its force from what is based on human nature everywhere and at all times.

This tension between positive and natural law is one of the basic themes of all natural law philosophy.

Aristotle's fourth great contribution is the distinction between abstract justice and equity (νόμος and ἐπιείκεια). The law is necessarily general and often harsh in application to the individual case. Equity mitigates and corrects its harshness by considering the individual case. All discussions of the problem of equity, of the proper interpretation of statute or precedent, are derived from this fundamental statement of the problem.

Aristotle's fifth great contribution is his definition of laws as a body of rules binding upon the magistrates as well as the people:

> Laws are something different from what regulates and expresses the form of the Constitution; it is their office to direct the conduct of the magistrate in the execution of his office and the punishment of offenders.[11]

It is to this definition that some modern jurists appeal in opposing unfettered administrative discretion.[12]

Much of Aristotle's work is devoted to the definition and study of the state. In his definition, the continuity of the state is linked with the type of constitution which governs it:

> For if a city is a community, it is a community of citizens; but if the mode of government should alter and become of another sort it would seem a necessary consequence that the city is not the same; as we regard the tragic chorus as different from the comic, though it may probably consist of the same performers.[13]

While Aristotle's particular views on the state were fashioned by his political views and the social conditions of his time, largely formulated in controversy with his master Plato, some general formulations underlie all subsequent discussions of principles of government. In developing Plato's thoughts Aristotle classified the principal forms of government into (1) Monarchy, (2) Aristocracy, (3) Polity. Each of these degenerates when they are no longer exercised for the common good but for the selfish interest of him or them who govern. The forms of degeneration are in this order: (1) Tyranny, (2) Oligarchy, (3) Democracy.

[11] *Politics*, Book 4, Chap. 1, 1289a.
[12] *Cf.* Goodhart in *Interpretations of Modern Legal Philosophies, op. cit.* at 297.
[13] *Politics*, Book 3, Chap. 3, 1276b.

Aristotle also developed the theory of the "mixed state," originally adumbrated by Plato, in which stability is attained by a balancing of diverse forces and tendencies, of the oligarchical element in particular, arising from wealth, birth, education, and the democratic element based on weight of numbers. This principle foreshadows the modern theory of the Separation of Powers.

If Aristotle thus gave classical expression to the great and abiding issues of legal thought, he also showed the limitations of speculation on the ideas of justice and he is not altogether free from the widespread fault of legal philosophers, namely concealing the lack of fundamental solutions by ambitious-sounding formulas. Aristotle's formula for distributive justice was the model for the classical Roman formula: *"honeste vivere, neminem laedere, suum cuique tribuere."* But it failed to give any direction as to what is just or unjust.

Aristotle's formula of distributive justice says only, that *if* rights are allotted, and *if* two individuals are equal, equal rights shall be allotted to them. According to this formula, a capitalistic as well as a communistic legal order is just, and a legal order which confers political rights only to men who have a certain income, or who belong to a certain race or are of noble birth is as just as a legal order which confers the same rights to all human beings who are of a certain age without regard to other differences. Any privilege whatever is covered by this formula. When a legal order reserves all possible rights to one single individual, the ruler, so that all the others—the ruled—have only duties, such a legal order, too, is just, since the difference between the ruler and the ruled is considered to be so decisive that the ruled cannot be considered as equal to the ruler.[14]

Nor is Aristotle's attitude towards the respective authority of natural justice and positive law unambiguous. In his *Rhetoric*, which is mainly a manual of the art of litigation, he advises the parties to appeal to universal law if the written law tells against them, but to urge the superiority of positive law over any unwritten law where it is a positive law that supports a party. In his *Politics*, probably a more reliable indication of Aristotle's own beliefs, he seems to identify justice and positive law. "For justice is a political virtue, by the rules of it the state is regulated and these rules are the criterion of what is right."[15] In other words, Aristotle seems to stress the justice of legality or positivity in preference to any eternal principles of good.

[14] Kelsen, *Interpretations of Modern Legal Philosophies, op. cit.* at 405.
[15] Book 1, 1253a.

Aristotle's work thus anticipates all the major themes and conflicts of modern Western legal thought: the conflict between the search for absolute values and the necessity to strengthen the authority of laws even if they are unjust; the conflict between the definition of law by reference to ideals, and by reference to the source of authority; the need to supplement any system of written laws however comprehensive, by flexible and creative individual justice, that is, by equity.

In nearly two and a half thousand years of subsequent controversy the scope and the social setting as well as the technical elaboration of these issues have developed and expanded together with the evolution of society. But the fundamental issues have not changed nor has their solution greatly advanced beyond the problems and conflicts as the Greek thinkers stated them.

CHAPTER 3

LAW, JUSTICE, ETHICS, AND SOCIAL MORALITY

THE present chapter is an attempt to appraise the interrelationship between concepts and disciplines which are obviously closely connected. The analysis of their interrelationship has been the subject of countless discussions, by philosophers, jurists, theologians, and others. It will nevertheless be apparent from the subsequent discussion that recent contributions to this age-old problem, from jurists and philosophers alike, as well as some important recent judicial decisions, have cast new light on the nature and function of the legal order.

In the following discussions the concept of Law, as a characteristic type of social norm, will be distinguished from that of the Legal System. The concept of Justice will be surveyed in its dual relationship to Law and Ethics. A distinction will be made between Ethics, as a system of values governing individual conduct, and Social Morality, as a system of norms which governs the social conduct of a community.

THE CONCEPT OF LAW

All definitions or characterizations of law veer between two extreme positions: One extreme emphasizes its coercive character; the other lays stress on the social acceptance, the actual observance of law by the community to which it is addressed. The coercive aspects of the legal norm rest both on the source of authority (sovereign command, hierarchical order) and on the enforceability by sanctions —which may be civil, criminal, or administrative. Both elements are pivotal to the theories of Austin and Kelsen, which will be analysed in some detail later in this book.[1] Whether the "ought" aspects of the legal norm are conceived as an actual command flowing from a sovereign (Austin) or as a hierarchical structure of norms attributed to an ultimate "depersonalized" sovereign (Kel-

[1] See below, pp. 258 *et seq.*, 275 *et seq.*

14

sen), it is the authoritative aspects of the legal norm that are singled out as its essential characteristics. By contrast, the concept of law as reflected by the theories of Savigny and Ehrlich[2] emphasizes the actual observance, the growth of customs, the "living law" of groups and communities, as the decisive element. Such law may receive authoritative confirmation from the sovereign, but it is not created by him. However, the differences between these two approaches are relative rather than absolute; they are essentially matters of emphasis. The "positivist" definition cannot dispense with the acceptance of the legal norm by the community, as shown by the inclusion, in Austin's definition, of "habitual obedience," and, in Kelsen's analysis, of the "minimum effectiveness."[3] On the other hand, at least in the context of a modern legal system, no social behaviour, however steady and supported by conviction on the part of the observing group, can dispense with the recognition bestowed upon it by the legislator, the administrator, or the judiciary, or a combination of all these organs of the modern state.

A third essential element in the concept of law is a degree of generality. The first desideratum of a system for subjecting human conduct to the governance of rules is an obvious one: there must be rules. This may be stated as a requirement of generality.[4] Here, as in so many other fields, John Austin's distinction was basically right, but too rigidly drawn: "where it obliges generally to acts or forbearances of a class, a command is a law or rule, but where it obliges to a specific act or forbearance, or to acts or forbearances which determine specifically or individually, a command is occasional or particular.[5] In the legal systems of modern societies, legal norms, resulting from a constant interplay of legislative, executive, and judicial pronouncements, cover the whole spectrum from extreme generality to great particularity. They range from Constitutional Bills of Rights to Orders prohibiting the sale of a particular commodity in a specific district on certain days. The relativity and even elusiveness of the distinction between general and particular command is brought out clearly in the doctrine of the "Stufen-theorie," which will be discussed later.[6] On the other hand, it is equally obvious that a community which had no general prescription

---

[2] See below, pp. 209 *et seq.*, 247 *et seq.*
[3] See further below, pp. 260, 278.
[4] Fuller, *The Morality of Law*, 46 (1964).
[5] Austin, *Province of Jurisprudence Determined*, Lecture 1, 19 (Library of Ideas Ed. 1954).
[6] See below, p. 282.

at all, but only an infinite multitude of individual commands, would not be regarded as having a legal order. It would dissolve into millions of individual relationships. Taking these three essential elements into consideration, we may say, without an attempt at "definition" of the term, that the concept of law means a norm of conduct set for a given community—and accepted by it as binding —by an authority equipped with the power to lay down norms of a degree of general application and to enforce them by a variety of sanctions.[7]

THE CONCEPT OF A LEGAL SYSTEM

Modern jurists have paid increasing attention to the general concept and minimum requirements of a "legal system" as distinct from the individual legal norm. A legal system "constitutes an individual system determined by 'an inner coherence of meaning,' . . . an integrated body of rules . . ."[8] A multitude of individual legal norms may not amount to a legal system unless they are linked with each other in an integrated structure. An analysis of the minimum requirements of the legal system, which greatly preoccupies contemporary jurists, such as Kelsen, Ross, Hart, and Fuller, has therefore a very different perspective from the attempt to define or characterize a legal norm in isolation. The awareness of a legal system as a structure in which the different organs, participants, and substantive prescriptions of the legal order react upon each other, is essentially the corollary to the increasing complexity of modern society, in which millions of individuals depend on the functioning of a complicated network of legal rules of many different types, and the interplay of public authorities of many different levels. In primitive societies the reach of law is generally weaker, and the institutionalization of the legal structure much less developed than in a more advanced and complex society.[9] Not as a

---

[7] This description is fully applicable only to municipal systems, and not to contemporary international law, which lacks both a clearly defined sovereign and effective sanctions. Whether international law is recognized as law, "or merely as positive morality" (Austin) depends on the relative importance one attached to *customary observance* of a rule or a system, as against the requisites of command and enforceability. See further below, p. 259.

[8] Ross, *On Law and Justice*, 32, 34 (1958).

[9] Modern anthropologists have, however, corrected the impression that primitive societies are generally devoid of legal institutions. Quite elaborate adjudication procedures exist in many primitive societies. See, *e.g.* Hoebel, *The Law of Primitive Man*, 22 (1954).

matter of conceptual definition, but as a basis for meaningful inquiry into the nature of a legal system, we may accept the suggestion of Graham Hughes[10] that "for many purposes it will be useful to reserve the description 'legal system' for those types of social order characterized by a high degree of institutionalization in the creation of general prescriptions, in the apparatus for adjudicating disputes, and in ordering the disposition of force." A similar conception underlies H. A. L. Hart's rationalization of the differences between primitive and advanced legal systems through the distinction between "primary rules of obligation" and "secondary rules of recognition."[11] Hart's "primary rules of obligation" correspond very closely to what are usually described as "customary" rules. Such rules, which generally are concerned with restrictions on the free use of violence, and other elementary forms of co-existence, are adequate for primitive communities, but inadequate for a more developed society because they are uncertain, static, and inefficient. Hart's "secondary rules of recognition" are in effect a shorthand description for the major aspects of a modern institutionalized legal system, which develops machinery for the formulation of legal rules, for orderly change, and for adjudication.[12]

It is a concept of stratified legal order which forms the model of Kelsen's legal analysis, and in particular of the "Stufentheorie." This analysis reflects a *mature* legal system in which there is a definite relationship between constitution-maker, legislator, administrator, judge, and private legal subjects. But the analysis of a modern legal system will also include that of other institutions such as the family, the church, or the trade union, which enjoys law-making and sanctioning powers in varying degrees (*e.g.*, through the very powerful sanction of expulsion of union members by union procedures which, until recently, have been almost entirely immune from control by the courts, *i.e.*, the state).[13]

The range of a legal system in a modern state—which he prefers to call "legal order"—is aptly summarized by Julius Stone[14] in the following four requisites:

---

[10] Hughes, *The Existence of a Legal System*, 35 N.Y.U.L. Rev. 1029 (1960).
[11] Hart, *The Concept of Law*, 89 *et seq.* (1961).
[12] The distinction is, however, too categorically formulated, since the studies of legal anthropologists, such as Hoebel, Gluckman, Llewellyn, Diamond and others, have shown that judicial authority—though not legislative institutions or rules of change—is often very strongly developed in primitive societies.
[13] See, in this sense, Ross, *op. cit.* at 60; Hughes, *op. cit.* at 1029.
[14] Stone, *Legal System and Lawyer's Reasonings*, 178 *et seq.* (1964).

First, a legal order arises in the general range of modern states, unitary or federal and regardless of its particular ideology; second, a legal order must somehow be distinguishable from a moral and social order; third, the concept of law is a class concept, *i.e.*, it must apply to the members of a given class; and fourth, a legal order is an "experienced single entity," something distinct from the "individual norms which are a part of it."[15]

All the above-mentioned descriptions and analyses of a legal order or legal system have abstained from linking the essence or existence or basic structure of a legal system with certain minimum requirements of justice or morality. An exception is the recent attempt of Professor Fuller to deduce eight requirements of "inner morality" of law from the very nature of a legal system.[16] These eight principles are not conceived as maxims of substantive natural law, *i.e.*, as a summary of the ideals inspiring a particular society as worthy of attainment. They are instead seen as a kind of "procedural natural law." The eight principles are: (1) generality; (2) promulgation; (3) prospective legal operation, *i.e.*, generally prohibition of retroactive laws; (4) intelligibility and clarity; (5) avoidance of contradictions; (6) avoidance of impossible demands;[17] (7) constancy of the law through time, *i.e.*, avoidance of frequent changes; (8) congruence between official action and declared rule.

It is difficult to see in what respect these eight requirements do more than spell out the minimum components of an efficiently functioning modern legal system. As such they are applicable to any legal system, regardless of ideology, whether totalitarian or democratic. Even the one requirement that might be thought of as expressing a particular—liberal—philosophy, *i.e.*, the general— though not absolute—prohibition of retroactivity, is essential to the functioning of any legal system. No totalitarian legal order could survive for any length of time if all or a great majority of its laws were made retroactive; legal order would break down in confusion. On the other hand, as Fuller himself says, democratic legal

---

[15] For an interesting presentation of various structural models of a legal system in a modern state, as applied respectively to developed, less developed, federal and unitary states, see Akzin, "State and Law Structure", in *Law, State and International Legal Order*, Essays in Honour of Hans Kelsen, 1, 8 (1964).

[16] Fuller, *The Morality of Law*, 6 *et seq.* (1964).

[17] This is illustrated by the problem of strict liability in tort and crime, although it does not become very clear what the learned author regards as "impossible," since strict liability is clearly, in the author's admission, a frequent and justifiable phenomenon of modern law. The internal morality of law demands only "that it define as clearly as possible the kind of activity that carries a special surcharge of legal responsibility." *Id.* at 75.

systems may sometimes have to admit retrospective legislation. In this context, Fuller mentions the difference between, e.g., *ex post facto* criminal statutes (unjustifiable) and retroactive tax laws that impose taxes on earnings received before the date of their enactment (justifiable).[18] The Nazi system, at the height of its effectiveness, complied with all the eight requirements, except, to some extent, that of promulgation.

The Nazi extermination decrees, for example, whose "orderly" and systematic brutality has more than anything else inspired the many postwar discussions on the invalidity of the Nazi legal system as incompatible with basic principles of humanity—were certainly general, insofar as they applied to a tragically large but clearly definable class of victims; they were made known to them with cynical brutality; they were prospective, clear, and free from contradictions; and they were, unfortunately, far from being impossible of execution. Nor was there any lack of congruence between the law and official action, because the exterminations took place within a hierarchic structure derived from the supreme legislative authority of the *Fuehrer*. It is only by means of a *petitio principii*, namely that barbarous "laws" should not be qualified as such, that we can circumvent this conclusion. In the earlier debate which clearly inspired Fuller's book,[19] he maintains "that a dictatorship which clothes itself with a tinsel of legal form can so far depart from the morality of order, from the inner morality of law itself, that it ceases to be a legal system." The illustration given by Fuller, and also earlier by Gustav Radbruch, in his moving attempt to find some criterion of illegality with regard to the greatest enormities of the Nazi system, referred to the *chaotic* features of the final Nazi period, a period when the shouts of Hitler, pronounced in epileptic fits, could be taken as overruling previously published legal orders. Such a state of affairs is "anarchy" in the strictest sense. It will collapse simply because it can no longer maintain minimum legal order in a complex society. Use of the term "morality" in connection with this galaxy of requirements is misleading. They are "essentially principles of good craftsmanship."[20]

---

[18] *Id.* at 59 *et seq.* By a somewhat strained reasoning, Fuller seeks to show that the latter are not really retroactive, because "men are in effect penalized for what the law originally induced them to do." For the contrary, and more persuasive interpretation of such tax laws as retroactive, see Hart, Book Review, 78 Harv. L. Rev. 1284 (1965).
[19] Fuller, "Positivism and Fidelity of Law," a reply to Professor Hart, 71 Harv. L. Rev. 660 (1958).
[20] Hart, Book Review, *op. cit.* at 1284.

Nor do they offend against the characterization of law as a "purpose-ful enterprise dependent for its success on the energy, insight, intelligence, and conscientiousness of those who conduct it," and which "displays structural constancies."[21] The legal system of the Nazi period, dominated by the ideology of racial discrimination, was extremely successful, in terms of its stated purpose: the degra-dation and extermination of "inferior" races, especially of the Jews. No order in human memory has achieved its purpose more swiftly and efficiently; none achieved a greater result in so little time, with comparable economy (including the utilization of the remains of the victims for the production of fertilizers). The use of the term "morality," however qualified, instead of the term "structure," which characterizes the anatomy of a legal system, regardless of ideology, is therefore unfortunate. Underlying Fuller's thesis that the institutionalized structure of a legal system as a purposeful enterprise implies a degree of morality, is his conviction that humanity is progressing in moral insight through growing "partici-pation in institutional procedures" through "human beings con-fronting one another in some social context, adjusting their relations reciprocally, negotiating, voting, arguing before some arbiter. . . ."[22] But this is a picture of pluralistic society, in which groups and individuals can argue and bargain freely, not of a society in which there is no such give and take, at least in the major conditions of political and social life. There is also ambiguity in Fuller's use of the term "conscientiousness"[23] with regard to the administration of legal institutions and precepts. An Eichmann applied the norm set for him, *i.e.*, the efficient disposal of the greatest possible number of Jews, with supreme conscientiousness. Hence his failure to understand why he should be prosecuted.[24] The conscience of a Nazi differs from that of a Christian or a pacifist. He is directed by the basic values of the order he seeks to obey and administer.

The structural analysis of a "legal system" is indeed more com-plex than that of a primitive legal order. It denotes any cohesive order of norms that purports to govern a community through the use of "posited" authority, whether oppressive or liberal, socialist or capitalistic in character. The structural requirements of a legal

---

[21] Fuller, *The Morality of Law, op. cit.* at 145-151. The conviction that purpose in law imparts to it certain moral characteristics, also underlies Fuller's earlier discussion with Ernest Nagel: *Human Purpose and Natural Law,* 3 Natural Law Forum 68 (1958).

[22] Fuller, *Irrigation and Tyranny,* 17 Stan. L. Rev. 1021, 1033 (1965).

[23] Fuller, *The Morality of Law,* 145.

[24] See Hannah Arendt, *Eichmann in Jerusalem,* (1964).

system must be accepted by the analytical positivist as much as by the advocate of a natural law philosophy. It is only by a consideration of the related but distinct concepts of "Justice," "Ethics," and "Morality" that we can elucidate the relation of the legal order to the values of life.

THE RELATION OF JUSTICE TO LAW AND ETHICS

Every legal system is oriented towards certain purposes which it seeks to implement. In this sense, every legal system is of necessity a "purposeful enterprise." But in this universal sense the concept of justice is also of necessity devoid of ideological content. The "justice" of a given legal system may be a *laissez faire* economy, or the public ownership of all productive enterprise; it may be a parliamentary multi-party system or a one-party state; the system may be built upon the ideology of separation of powers, or on the subordination of administration and the judiciary to the will of the legislator. It may aspire to the equality of all citizens, or to a hierarchical structure of superior and inferior citizens; it may implement the supremacy of international over national law or— as is the case with almost all contemporary legal systems—the inverse.

The classical definition of "distributive justice" is that of Aristotle: "Injustice arises when equals are treated unequally, and also when unequals are treated equally."[25] Does this mean anything beyond the proposition, stated earlier, that every legal order is directed toward some ideal of justice? Certainly it cannot lead to any specific political philosophy of equality. It is compatible with legal systems that discriminate between free men and slaves, between blacks and whites, between "Aryans" and Jews, between nationals and foreigners, between rich and poor, between men and women. For all of these are "class concepts," groups which the legal order may consider as being equal or unequal in relation to each other. Some legal philosophers have attempted to extract substantive meaning from the very idea of justice, notably Stammler and Del Vecchio. The failure of both in their attempts to extract from Kant's "practical reason" substantive ideals of justice is analysed later in this book.[26]

The difficulty of extracting any substantive principle from Aris-

[25] *Nicomachean Ethics*, see above, p. 10.
[26] See below, pp. 179 *et seq.*, 186 *et seq.*

totle's "distributive justice" is increased by the fact that the number and types of classes which a legal order can establish for purposes of differential treatment is almost infinite. For this or that purpose property owners may be distinguished from tenants, local residents from out-of-town residents, high school graduates from elementary school graduates, and so forth. It is common sense and the practical needs of administration rather than principles that tend to limit class distinctions. Yet, there is a procedural residuum in the notion of "equality for equals" which makes it more than a meaningless formula. It implies a minimum machinery of justice, some procedure for the determination of treatment as equal or unequal in a particular case. This carries the implication of a third party procedure, and thus some minimum concept of "due process."[27] Thus Ginsberg is right[28] in deducing from the concept of "general" justice "the control of power relations and more particularly the exclusion of arbitrary power."[29] Some concept of impartiality is inherent in the very process of determination of equality, even in the most hierarchical society. But since there are no theoretical limits to the ways in which a particular legal order chooses to determine and subdivide classes of "equals," "arbitrariness" can become a very elusive criterion. When Ginsberg deduces that because "differential treatment requires justification in terms of relevant differences," arbitrary discriminations, "such as those based on race, colour, religion, sex," must disappear and "equality in political rights is extended to equality in social and economic rights," he slides from a formal and procedural notion of equality to a substantive and political one. To one legal order differences of race, colour, religion, sex, or wealth may appear "relevant" and far from "arbitrary," whereas to another they may not.[30] Nor has

---

[27] "Due process" must, of course, be understood here in a purely procedural sense and not in the substantive sense given to it by the U.S. Supreme Court in the interpretation of the Fifth and Fourteenth Amendments. See below, p. 138.

[28] Ginsberg, *On Justice in Society*, 63 *et seq.* (1965).

[29] *Id.* at 71.

[30] The difficulty of finding agreement on "relevancy" or "arbitrariness" is illustrated by the following statements reported by Calvin Trillin in the *New Yorker*, December 4, 1965, at p. 144—in a report on racial discrimination in Britain:

"Some labor-exchange managers . . . insist that a company's refusal to hire colored people represents neither personal prejudice nor racial discrimination:

'It is true that there are some firms that do not hire over a certain percentage of colored workers,' says a Youth Employment Officer.

'But isn't that color discrimination?'

'No. The employer may know that if the balance is tipped his white workers will leave.'

history shown a continuous evolution in the sense indicated by Ginsberg. While the belief in steady progress towards democracy and equality was popular in the nineteenth century, the twentieth century has shown, in the most brutal manner, how powerful the philosophies of racial, national, and religious discriminations are. Concepts of justice contrary to the democratic idea of equality govern the majority of the world's states, while in the relations between nations equality has barely begun to compete with the ideologies of nationalism, racialism, and power politics. Another attempt—similar in result, though not in method, to that of Ginsberg—to demonstrate the possibility of rational justification of values of justice, is that of Chaim Perelman. In his *Idea of Justice*[31] Perelman had demonstrated that the only factor common to various conceptions of justice was "formal justice." This consists in equality of treatment for all the members of one and the same essential category. "The only requirement we can formulate in respect of a rule is that it should not be arbitrary, but should justify itself, should flow from a normative system."[32] But, "the only claim one could rightfully make would consist in eliminating everything arbitrary save what is implied in affirming the values at the base of the system." In other words, no values and aspirations can be rationally deduced, the ultimate values and aspirations themselves are non-rational. This approach is essentially similar to Aristotle's concept of distributive justice, and to the more modern philosophy of relativism as developed by Max Weber, Gustav Radbruch, Kelsen and others.[33] More recently, Perelman has, however, attempted to find some rational justification for values and norms.

'Color discrimination.'
'No. It's not that they're white workers. It's that they're the experienced workers, the ones who have been there long enough to know the business.'
'But the reason they leave—isn't that color discrimination?'
'Oh, no. It might be any number of things. The white workers might not want to work next to someone who smells of garlic. It's not a matter of color.'
'Wouldn't assuming that a man smells of garlic because he's colored be color discrimination?'
'It's not the employer's color discrimination.' "
. . .
"An honest and progressive English journalist who believes that people must be taught to regard immigrants as individuals also believes that an automobile-insurance company's charging higher premiums for all colored people is no different from its charging higher premiums for all journalists."
[31] *L'Idée de Justice* (1949), *The Idea of Justice and the Problem of Argument,* (English ed. 1963).
[32] *Id.* at 60.
[33] See below, pp. 191 *et seq.*, 275 *et seq.*

In a work devoted to the theory of argument[34] Perelman took the
Topics of Aristotle as a starting point for the use of dialectical,
in contrast to analytical, proof of legal argument. Juristic argument
aims at justification, not demonstration, of truth. The justification
of an action, a kind of behaviour or decision is not concerned with
truth or falsehood. Justification can deal only with debatable things.
It is concerned with arguments of morality, legality, regularity,
usefulness or opportuneness.[35] It follows that "assertions which
represent the systematic formulation of an ideal cannot be judged
the way we judge factual judgment. Their role is not to conform
to experience, but to furnish criteria for evaluating and judging
experience and, if necessary, for disqualifying certain aspects of
it."[36] How can legal argumentation be made "rational"? Perelman's answer is that, in conformity with Kant's "Categorical Imperative," the characteristic of rational argumentation is "the aim
for universality"; its postulates must be "valid" for the whole of
the human community." This does not mean that the criteria and
values of rational argumentation constitute "absolute and impersonal values and truths." Rather do they express "the convictions
and aspirations of a free but reasonable man, engaged in a creative,
personal and historically situated effort: that of proposing to
the universal audience as he sees it, a number of acceptable
theses."[37]

The difficulty with this approach is that we must assume there is
a "universal audience" which shares common values. This is possible on the basis of the philosophy of the Stoics, which appeals to
universal reason, or of the scholastics who deduce the rightness of
human institutions from the will and reason of God. In other
words, it must base itself on a natural law philosophy. On any
other assumption, the universality of the audience dissolves itself
into a number of conflicting values, ideas and policies.[38]

The impossibility of deriving specific legal ideals from the "sense
of justice" is expressed by another contemporary jurist[39] in the distinction between "justice" and "justness." Varied as these judgments on justness will "always be, they respond to emotion which,

[34] (With Albrechts-Tyteca), *Traité de l'Argumentation* (1958).
[35] Perelman, *Justice and Justification,* 10 Natural L. F. 1, 6 (1965).
[36] *Id.* at 16.
[37] *Id.* at 20.
[38] For an excellent critique of Perelman, see Stone, *Human Law and Human Justice,* 346 *et seq.* (1965).
[39] Ehrenzweig, "Psychoanalytical Jurisprudence: A Common Language for Babylon," 65. Colum. L. Rev., 1331 (1965).

insofar as language permits a verification, . . . flows from a sense of morality" or "justice" or "value." Ehrenzweig, basing himself on the work of Bienenfeld,[40] looks to psychoanalysis for the answer to the various concepts of justice, which "follow the youth through adolescence to adulthood when their conflict will determine and threaten the very coexistence of families, communities and nations. Yet they coexist. If in need he leans towards communism; if efficient to socialism; if attacked to conservatism; and if attacking to liberalism [and] if in the nationalist dogma of the nursery that is exhibited in the instinctive presentation of a united front against the outsider.[41] The conflict of values is here transferred from the outside world to the psyche of the individual.

We conclude that "justice," as a generally valid concept, is formal, in the sense that it is the goal to which every legal order aspires as a "purposeful enterprise," and procedural, in the sense that the Aristotelian notion of "equality for equals" implies a minimum machinery of justice and third party determination.

Beyond this, it is necessary to turn to the field of ethics and morality for a determination of the values that may give the idea of justice a specific substantive content.

ETHICS AND SOCIAL MORALITY

The great majority of writers use the terms "ethical" and "moral" interchangeably.[42] Although the choice of terms is largely a matter of preference, it is submitted that the distinction recently suggested by P. F. Strawson between social morality and ethics is more than a matter of terminology, because it clarifies the relationship of individual values to those of the social and, from there, the legal order. In an article entitled "Social Morality and Individual Ideal,"[43] Strawson suggests that "the region of the ethical . . . is a region of diverse, certainly incompatible and possibly practically conflicting ideal images or pictures of human life. . . ."[44] Ethics is thus the sphere of ideal forms of life set by *individuals* for themselves.

---

[40] Bienenfeld, *The Rediscovery of Justice* (1946); *Prolegomena.*
[41] Bienenfeld, *Prolegomena* 22 ff.
[42] See, among many others, Broad, *Five Types of Ethical Theory,* 276 *et seq.* (1930); Frankena, Ethical Theory, in *Philosophy* 347 (1964): "The main concern of ethical theory or moral philosophy in our period has been a so-called meta-ethical question rather than normative or practical ones."
[43] 37 *Philosophy,* 1 (1961).
[44] *Id.* at 4.

It is further implicit in his suggestion that these ideal images of man's life—generally called values—conflict, and that "the multiplicity of conflicting pictures is itself the essential element of one's picture of man." By contrast, the sphere of morality denotes "rules or principles governing human behaviour which apply universally within a community or class." A "minimal conception of morality" limits itself to those rules which are "a condition of the existence of society," whereas a more comprehensive conception of morality would embrace the entire body of rules governing a community or class.

The merit of this approach is that it illuminates the tripartite relation between (*a*) the values that individuals, as conscientious and responsible human beings, set to themselves, (*b*) the moral norms governing a society—which reflects a social balance and choice between conflicting individual values, and (*c*) the legal order, which must reflect the current social morality but is far from identical with it. In the completely master-minded and conditioned society depicted in Huxley's *Brave New World* or Orwell's *1984*, the distinction between social morality and individual ethics, and ultimately that between law, morality and ethics, might altogether disappear. The norms of social behaviour would be set by "Big Brother," who exercises complete legislative authority, and whose law-making power is used to direct and control every aspect and corner of social behaviour. The individual in turn is conditioned to accept the socio-legal norms as controlling his entire life and precluding the formation of individual values—which in Orwell's terminology would be "ungood."

In contemporary societies the relative spheres of law, morality, and ethics, as defined here, differ, of course, considerably. But in every contemporary society there is some tension between these three orders of conduct. In the pluralistic and relatively individualistic society which characterizes the value system of modern democracy, the tension between these three spheres is and must be considerable. There is liberty left for the individual to form and live by one of the many conflicting "pictures of life"; this is limited by the many constraints of social morality, which flow from the necessities of social life, as well as ideological restraints imposed by society on the individuals living within it. Finally, there is an increasingly active reciprocal interrelationship between the legal and the moral order. On the one hand, moral values press upon the legal system, and on the other, the modern law-maker can to an increasing extent influence and modify the social habits of the community.

Another advantage of the tripartite classification would appear to be that it bypasses the ancient and rather age-worn characterization of law as being concerned with external conduct, and morals as concerned with internal conduct. This is, of course, the classical distinction drawn by Kant in the *Critique of Practical Reason,* which has been adopted by many moral and legal philosophers.[45] Clearly such a distinction, even if generally valid, is greatly dependent upon the reach of law in society, which is vastly greater in the fairly concentrated and manipulated modern society than it is in primitive communites. A legal system that makes punishment or civil obligation dependent upon malicious intention or capacity to control one's actions reaches into the inner mind of man, and modern psychology has refined and enlarged the interrelationship between the inner workings of the mind and external conduct. Even more barren is the converse proposition that morality is only concerned with internal conduct. The distinction between ethical, *i.e.,* individual value judgments, and social conduct, *i.e.,* morality, helps to clarify this matter. Instead of the watertight and artificial division into three distinct spheres, we should think of a fluid interrelationship, variable with regard to the separation and interpenetration of the three spheres according to the character of the society in question.

ETHICAL THEORIES AND VALUATIONS

There have been innumerable classifications of ethical theories.[46] The most important and recurrent division is that according to the sources of knowledge of ethical values, into naturalistic, intuitionistic, and noncognitive. Very briefly, naturalism (a term coined by G. E. Moore in his *Principia Ethica,* 1903) denotes any view that holds that ethical properties can be analysed into or defined in terms of natural ones."[47] Intuitionism holds that ethics is an autonomous discipline with its own peculiar subject matter. In contrast to

---

[45] See, for example, among recent writers, Kantorowicz, *Definition of Law,* 43 (1958).

[46] See, among many other surveys, Frankena, Ethical Theory, in *Philosophy* at 347 *et seq.* (1964); Frankena, Ethics *(Foundation of Philosophy Series* 1963); Broad, *Five Types of Ethical Theory* (1930); Nakhnikian, *Contemporary Ethical Theories and Jurisprudence,* 2 Natural L. F. 4 (1957); Ginsberg, *On Justice in Society,* Chap. 1 (1965).

[47] See Frankena, *op. cit.* at 356.

the naturalists, "intuitionists" believe that the basic propositions of normative ethics are intuitive or self-evident insights of a unique kind, which cannot be inferred from any other discipline.[48]

The link between these two types of ethical theory—which can be almost infinitely subdivided—is that they hold ethical values to be capable of objective determination. By contrast, the "noncognitive" theories regard ethical values as incapable of any objective analysis, because they are purely emotive, or at least not verifiable.[49]

ETHICAL AND LEGAL THEORY

As will be apparent from the following observations, all three types of theory have had considerable influence on legal theory and correspond to distinct types of jurisprudential thinking. The perspective from which ethical theories are best considered in the light of legal theory is that of "validity." As a convenient point of departure we may take a definition of "validity" that embraces both formal and substantive theories, by abstracting the validity of a legal system from the content of its basic norms. According to Kelsen[50] "a legal norm is valid . . . because it is created in a specific manner, ultimately determined by a presupposed (vorausgesetzt) basic norm." In the formulation of Alf Ross, "a system of norms is 'valid' if it is able to serve as a scheme of interpretation for a corresponding set of social actions, in such a way that it becomes possible for us to comprehend the set of actions as a coherent whole of meaning and motivation, and within certain limits to predict them."[51] From this perspective it may be convenient to divide ethical theories into those that postulate the *objective validity* of the ethical postulates and those that deny such objective validity. In the former category there are:

(*a*) The type of ethical theory that is based on metapositive values, either of a religious or a non-religious order. In legal theory this type of ethical approach is reflected in the main body of natural

---

[48] Frankena, *op. cit.* at 349.

[49] Another distinction—in terms of end values—is that between teleological and deontic ethical theories. In the former, the "good" is the end value, while duties and rights are derivative (Aristotle). For the latter, rights and duties are primary, and "good" is derivative (Kant).

[50] *Reine Rechtslehre*, 200 (2nd ed. 1960).

[51] Ross, *On Law and Justice*, 34 (1958). For other discussions of validity, see Stone, *Legal Systems and Lawyer's Reasonings*, 202-205 (1964); Hart, *The Concept of Law*, Chap. VI; Christie, The Notion of Validity in Modern Jurisprudence, 48 Minn. L. Rev. 1049 (1964).

law philosophy, whether of a theological or a rationalistic character.[52]

(*b*) Those that postulate ethical values of an objective, and therefore compelling, but instinctively felt character. To this approach there corresponds, in legal philosophy, the type of theory that bases postulates of justice on a *Rechtsgefühl* (Krabbe), or a *sentimento giuridico* (Del Vecchio), or "intuitive" law (Petrazhitsky). A more rationalized version of this approach is Edmond Cahn's "sense of injustice." In this category there is also Gény's "creative intuition" as a source of legal evolution through juristic action. The philosophical godfather of most of these theories is the French philosopher, Henri Bergson, whose work *Evolution Créatrice* has been one of the most influential of the present century.[53]

(*c*) *Empirical theories.* A contemporary American philosopher has described empiricism in the following terms:

> It is characteristic of "empiricism," as a philosophical tradition, to assume that we have certain criteria of evidence, or that we can identify a certain "source" of our knowledge, and then to apply these criteria, or to refer to this source, and thus determine what it is that we can know.[54]

In this wide sense, "empiricism" is contrasted with all theories that derive principles of ethical conduct from *a priori* metaphysical premises. In a broad way, "empiricism" corresponds, in legal theory, to "positivism," and metaphysical ethical theories are reflected in legal idealism.[55] In ethical theory, empiricism, to a large extent, coincides with naturalism, since one of the fundamental theses of the latter is that "the truth or falsehood of ethical sentences is established by methods of experimentation and observation characteristic of the natural sciences."[56]

From the perspective of relevance to corresponding legal theories, we may distinguish three major types of ethical empiricism: First, the approach that derives ethical maxims from historical and social experience. Second, the approach that tests ethical values in the light of social facts and realities. This type of empiricism, commonly known as "pragmatism," is a specifically American contri-

[52] See below, Chaps. 7-11.
[53] See further below, on the intuitionist theories of jurisprudence, p. 84 *et seq.*, and on Gény's legal philosophy, p. 328 *et seq.*
[54] Chisholm, in *Philosophy,* 244 (Princeton Studies, 1964). Empiricism is contrasted with "commonsensism" and "skepticism".
[55] See further on this distinction below, p. 87 *et seq.*
[56] Nakhnikian, *op. cit.* at 7.

bution to modern philosophy and ethics. It is linked with the names of Charles Saunders Peirce and John Dewey. Third, there is "logical positivism," *i.e.*, the approach to philosophical statements which excludes from scientific study anything that is not "verifiable," by either logical deduction or experimental observation. In ethical theory this approach leads to "noncognitivism," on which some further observations will be made below. Noncognitivists exclude ethical maxims from scientific enquiry as being essentially "emotive" and not subject to scientific verification.

LEGAL THEORIES BASED ON OBJECTIVE ETHICAL CRITERIA

In jurisprudence, the first approach is represented by those theories that regard certain basic principles of conduct as essential to a satisfactory legal order, not as a matter of *a priori* postulates set by God or reason (natural law) but as a matter of social experience. Generally we can group under this approach all the "social contract" theories, which are predicated on the assumption that men need to restrain their appetites for violence, greed, and domination, in order to achieve a minimum of mutual protection and security.[57] A logical continuation of the "social contract" approach could be Kant's *Categorical Imperative* and its derivative definition of law as "the aggregate of the conditions under which the arbitrary will of one individual may be combined with that of another under a general inclusive law of freedom."[58] But in Kant's philosophical scheme these principles are not empirical; they are given *a priori*, as an essential basis of man's volition as a free and rational being.

Similar or even identical ethical postulates can thus be derived either from *a priori* judgments or from empirical observations. A corollary to this duality of approaches in ethical theory can be found in legal philosophy. Thus, throughout the long history of natural law philosophy, many postulates such as the absolute integrity of private property, the supremacy of the law-making authority of the Church over the State, or vice versa, the equality or inequality of men, nations, or races, and many more, have been deduced from metaphysical principles of a God-given universe or universal reason. But a contemporary jurist[59] has formulated five

---

[57] See, for an account of the various social contract theories, and their very divergent views on the restrictive functions of government and individuals, below, Chap. 11.
[58] See further below, p. 59.
[59] H. L. A. Hart, in *The Concept of Law*, 189 *et seq.* (1961).

principles of what he describes as "the minimum content of natural law" not as *a priori* principles but as necessary to "the minimum purpose of survival which men have in associating with each other."[60] They are thus essentially a continuation and modernization of the "social contract" philosophy. The five principles are: (1) human vulnerability, which makes it necessary for a legal order to restrict the use of violence; (2) approximate equality, which makes it necessary for a legal system to develop rules of mutual forbearance and compromise; (3) limited altruism, which makes necessary some provisions to restrain tendencies to aggression;[61] (4) limited resources, which makes necessary some system of exchange or joint planning of services and goods; and (5) limited understanding and strength of will, from which follows the need for a system of voluntary cooperation in a coercive system. Thus, maxims of conduct which many of the older natural law philosophers have presented as flowing from the immutable nature of man, are here presented as having been shown by experience and history to be necessary to the survival of man in civilization.

PRAGMATISM IN ETHICS AND LAW

Pragmatism, as a particular type of empirical philosophy, has had a direct and traceable influence on modern jurisprudence, in the American realist movement, of which a detailed account is given below.[62] Its intellectual fathers are William James and John Dewey. The characteristic feature of Dewey's pragmatism, as applied in the realist movement, is the method of enquiry. An enquiry into an ethical proposition may start with the formulation of a value hypothesis;[63] but this value postulate is only provisional, and has to be tested by the means of its possible realization. A study of such means—which include the legal, social, and economic environment of a society—may influence and modify the value postulate. A convenient illustration of this approach[64] might be the question of

---

[60] *Id.* at 189.
[61] This principle could easily be contained in the first.
[62] See below, Chap. 25.
[63] There have been many definitions of the concept of "value" which, as observed by a contemporary philosopher of ethics (Frankena, Ethical Naturalism, in *Philosophy*, 360), has become central in present-day thought. Generally acceptable definitions would be those of Everett, *Moral Values*, 611 (1918): "The principle which determines the subordination of one end to another" or of Perry, *Realms of Value*, 3, 1954: "A thing—anything—has value, or is valuable, in the original and generic sense when it is the object of an interest—any interest."
[64] The present writer's illustration, not Dewey's.

prohibition of alcohol, which deeply influenced American legal, economic, and social life for more than a decade after the First World War. Absolute prohibition could be stated as a value goal. Means of its execution consist in the appropriate Constitutional amendments, statutory prohibitions, administrative regulations, and the policing of the legal prohibitions. An enquiry into the means of execution may show that the purported enforcement of prohibition leads—as in fact it did—to a vast increase in the consumption of illegal and often lethal alcohol, bootlegging, gang warfare, murder, and a general increase in criminality. The results of such enquiries may lead to an abandonment or the modification of the original value postulate. Abandonment of the ethical postulate, in the light of practical experience, is expressed in the repeal of the Constitutional amendment in the U.S. Constitution. An alternative solution is that of the institution of state-controlled liquor boards, which prevails in Canada.

ETHICAL AND LEGAL THEORIES DENYING OBJECTIVE VALIDITY

Whereas all the previously mentioned types of theory assert that ethical values can be objectively ascertained—whether they be deduced from natural law foundations, from *a priori* principles predicated on the rationality of man, from empirical data based on history, from generally accepted principles of good and right, or from pragmatic enquiry, the "non-objective" theories of ethics deny that ethical values can be objectively—ascertained. To them, ethical values are a matter of conviction. They must be believed in but cannot be proved.

RELATIVISM IN ETHICS AND LEGAL PHILOSOPHY

There are, however, two major types of this kind of approach to ethical norms. One trend of thought is best described, in ethics as in jurisprudence, as "relativism"; the other is "noncognitivism." While both agree on the non-provability of values, the relativists believe that rational argument can and must support the choice of a particular value, by comparison with, and often in opposition to, another value. The noncognitivists reject all study of ethical values as purely emotive, and therefore not within the realm of science. Probably the most influential of the relativists in modern times is Max Weber, to whose celebrated essay on "Der Sinn der Wertfreiheit der soziologischen und okonomischen Wissenschaften" reference is made later in this book.[65] His most important disciple in the field of legal theory is Gustav Radbruch, whose legal philosophy —which in recent years has become the subject of attention far beyond the borders of Germany and Europe—is a profound and important application of the relativistic approach. For it is not content to state the antinomies of legal ideas, but follows the major antithetic values of legal philosophy into particular legal institutions and concepts.[66]

Among contemporary ethical philosophers, we may list as relativists Dewey, Russell, and Ginsberg. Dewey's entire work[67] is permeated by the thought that value statements are prescriptions or recommendations for action based on alternative convictions, but that "it is morally necessary to state grounds or reasons for the course advised and recommended. These consist of matter-of-fact sentences reporting what has been and now is, as conditions, and of estimates of consequences that would ensue if certain of them are used as means."[68]

Bertrand Russell has, in his many writings, veered from the conviction that ethical statements are purely emotive to one that holds that truth can be discovered by the use of reason. The former view is expressed, for example, in his *Science and Religion*,[69] where he says that: "Since no way can even be imagined for deciding a difference as to value, the conclusion is forced upon us that the difference is one of tastes, not one as to any objective truths." But in his more recent work in *Human Society in Ethics and Politics* of 1954, Russell stresses the role of reason.

Reason has a perfectly clear and precise meaning. It signifies a choice of the right means to an end that you wish to achieve. It has nothing whatever to do with a choice of ends. But opponents of reason do not realize this, and think that advocates of rationality want reason to dictate ends as well as means.[70]

The essence of his reasoning[71] is that a concept such as "good" has an intrinsic value of its own. Intrinsic value is "the property of being a state of mind desired by the person who experiences it."

[65] See below, p. 191.
[66] See, for a detailed discussion of Radbruch's philosophy, below, p. 192 *et seq.*
[67] *E.g.*, Dewey, *Theory of Moral Life*, or in particular one of his last papers, "Ethical Subject Matter and Language," 12 in *Journal of Philosophy*, (1945).
[68] Dewey, "Ethical Subject Matter and Language," *op. cit.*, at 711.
[69] Russell, *Science and Religion*, 238 (1938).
[70] *Human Society in Ethics and Politics*, Preface, pp. vi-vii.
[71] See particularly *op. cit.*, Chapter IX, "Is There Ethical Knowledge?"

"Good" is the property of arousing an emotion of approval, "bad" that which arouses disapproval. Thus "good" is linked with pleasure or desire on the part of the actor and approval on the part of the community. "Right" conduct is that which is likely to produce "good" effects. This position is very close to that of Henry Sidgwick, who in his *Methods of Ethics* argued that generally recognized moral rules can be deduced from the principle that we ought to aim at maximizing pleasure. Russell's later theory thus comes close to that of the "naturalists."

Like the former, and like that of the utilitarian legal philosophers —of which an account is given later in this book[72] this approach is full of ambiguities. Even if we accept that the "good" is the end desired by an individual, the test of "approval" is highly ambivalent. Does it mean approval by the entire community, by a select avant-garde, approval by the greatest number or by the wise? Is not the highest ethical conduct sometimes that which is in revolt against the majority and therefore arouses intense disapproval? Ethical pioneers, like the early Christians, the early fighters for women's rights or labour organizations, or pacifists, have had to pursue their values in intense opposition to the overwhelming majority of their fellow countrymen. A similar criticism can be raised against the essay by S. E. Toulmin,[73] which accords with Sidgwick and Russell in the assertion that "to say that X is right is to say that X is worthy of approval."[74] For Toulmin, to be "worthy of approval" means that "there is a valid reason for approving X." It is not the fact of acceptance but the worthiness of acceptance which gives an argument validity. But here the same question arises, namely, what the criteria for worthiness of approval are. One answer given by Toulmin[75] is that there is a valid reason for doing something when it can be shown to be in accordance with rules or maxims accepted in our society. Where there is conflict between rules or norms within a society, it is reasonable to appeal to an "overall" principle, that "preventable suffering shall be averted." "The notions of 'obligation,' 'right,' 'justice,' 'duty,' and 'ethics' apply in the first place when our actions and institutions may lead to avoidable misery for others; but it is a natural and familiar extension to use them also when the issue concerns a chance of deeper happiness for others and even for ourselves."[76] This appears

---

[72] See below, Chap. 26.
[73] *The Place of Reason in Ethics* (1950).
[74] *Id.* at 71.　　　[75] *Id.* at 69.　　　[76] *Id.* at 160.

to gloss over the deep conflicts which may arise between conflicting values, and in particular between the ethics of an individual and the prevalent morality of a society. Here we can see again the value of the distinction between individual ethics and social morality which has been adopted at the outset of this section. There simply is no necessary equivalence between the avoidance of misery, happiness for others, and happiness for oneself. These emotions or purposes may coincide, but they may also starkly conflict with each other.

The value of the aforementioned attempts does not lie in their somewhat simple version of utilitarianism, but rather in the emphasis on the use of reason and rational argument in the clarification of ends. This appears to be the position of Morris Ginsberg,[77] who describes the task of ethics as being: "(a) to bring out what is implied in the notion of a norm or principle of action, and (b) to survey the major or dominant goods or values and the norms or injunctions they entail."[78] Ginsberg accepts that there is a plurality of values and of conflicting ways of life. He does, however, assert that "there is . . . in every society a general framework, the maintenance or furtherance of which comes to be conceived as an overriding obligation, though this may come into conflict with the demands of particular ideals."[79] It is in an attempt to spell out the principal legal values of a contemporary Western-type society rather than absolute values that Ginsberg, in subsequent chapters, elaborates such matters as economic and political rights, the modern status of association and contract, the ethics of punishment, and freedom of thought. How important rational arguments can be, not in the determination of ends, but in the clarification and concretization of given values, as applied in the legal life of a community, may be illustrated by the problem of freedom of contract. A general catalogue of basic rights and values in a democratic society is likely to enumerate both "freedom of contract" and "equality," as values to be protected by the law. As long as these values remain abstract and general, there appears to be no contradiction. But when we follow the implications of freedom and equality of contract, in the context of modern industrial society, such conflicts and tensions become readily apparent and may compel the subordination of one end to another. In the earlier stages of industrial capitalism, free-

---

[77] *On Justice in Society* (1965).
[78] *Id.* at 40.
[79] *Id.* at 46.

dom of contract led to an increasing inequality between the entre-
preneur and the unorganized worker, due to stark differences in
their economic power. This led to a counter-move by the organization of trade unions, which increasingly, through collective organization, compensated for the weakness of the individual worker.
In contemporary industrial society, unions tend to face employers
as equals, but at the expense of the freedom of bargaining of the
individual worker, who has surrendered it for the sake of equality,
expressed in better terms and the improvement of his standard of
living. Individual freedom of contract here gives way to the more
important goal of economic equality. The two values cannot be
implemented simultaneously.[80]

It is thus only by following basic ethical values into their implementation in a given social content that their true meaning and
ranking can be ascertained. This is indeed a matter of reasoning,
supported by factual data.[81] It is only with this qualification that
we may accept the attempts of such writers as Russell, Dewey,
Perelman, Ginsberg and Toulmin, to emphasize the place of rational
argument in the ascertainment of values.

NONCOGNITIVIST ETHICAL THEORIES

David Hume is generally regarded as the father of ethical non-
cognitivism. His celebrated statement that reason "is and ought
only to be the slave of the passions and can never pretend to any
other office than to serve and obey them" not only undermined
the foundations of natural law but also implied that reason is
essentially the servant of emotions, which latter set the goals of
action. But Hume may also be cited in support of the relativist
position since, in his *Enquiry Concerning the Principles of Morals*,[82]
he says:

> The hypothesis which we embrace is plain. It maintains that morality
> is maintained by sentiment. It defines virtue to be whatever mental
> action or quality gives to a spectator a pleasing sentiment of approba-
> tion; and vice the contrary. We then proceed to examine a plain matter
> of fact, to wit, what actions have this influence; we consider all the
> circumstances, in which these actions agree; and thence endeavour to
> extract some general observations with regard to these sentiments.

[80] For a more detailed analysis of the evolution of the law of contract see
Friedmann, *Law in a Changing Society*, Chap. 4, 1959.
[81] In the matter of contracts, by wage statistics collective agreements and other
relevant aspects of the terms of employment.
[82] Appendix 1, "Concerning Moral Sentiment."

Be that as it may, modern ethical noncognitivists have asserted emphatically that normative concepts are purely emotive. For the most radical of the noncognitivists, A. J. Ayer,[83] all normative words are "pseudo-concepts." All genuine concepts must be either empirical or logical. The empirically verifiable and the logically certifiable exhaust the cognitive dimensions of meaning. Everything else, such as a simple command, a blush, a yawn, but also words like "good," "bad," "ought," "worthy," are purely emotive, and there cannot be such a thing as ethical or moral science.

An important modification of this position is Charles L. Stevenson's influential *Ethics and Language* (1944). Whereas Ayer argues that "What we do not and cannot argue about is the validity of these moral principles. We merely praise or condemn them in the light of our own feelings,"[84] Stevenson distinguishes between *attitudes* and *beliefs*. Only disagreements in attitude—which comprise the basic values—are genuine and irreducible. You cannot argue about purposes or preferences. But a value judgment such as that a certain person is "good" has a complex meaning which is partly emotive and partly cognitive. A full picture of ethics must recognize both factors. To illustrate his position, Stevenson gives as an example the choice before trustees for the estate of a philanthropist who have been instructed to forward any charitable cause that seems to them worthy. They argue as to whether to provide hospital facilities for the poor or to endow universities. The choice between these alternatives is an irreducible choice between different "attitudes." But "the discussion is almost certain to involve disagreement in belief. Perhaps the men will disagree . . . about the present state of the poor, and the extent to which hospital facilities are already provided for them. Perhaps they will disagree about the financial state of the universities, or the effects of education on private and social life."[85] On the latter type of question, agreement can be reached through the investigation of facts, which may confirm the one or other position.

In essence, this position is very close to that of Dewey's pragmatic "logic of enquiry." The need to test legal values in the light of reality, by factual evidence, would be regarded by contemporary lawyers as almost too trivial to require demonstration. In part this is due to the efforts of the American legal realists, who themselves

---

[83] Ayer, *Language, Truth and Logic* (2nd ed., 1946).
[84] *Id.* at 111-112. [85] *Id.* at 14.

are strongly influenced by Dewey. But it is today—and has been for some time—part and parcel of the administration of justice in modern society. An outstanding and familiar example is the so-called "Brandeis Brief" to which reference is made elsewhere. This brief consisted of a short "value statement," *i.e.*, the proposition that an Oregon statute fixing a ten-hour maximum day for women was in accordance with the Constitutional values embodied in the Fourteenth Amendment, and a very elaborate factual brief as to the conditions actually prevailing in the relevant industries, and their relevance to the state of women's health, safety, and morals.

Among contemporary legal theorists, Alf Ross is clearly a "non-cognitivist." For Ross[86] such terms as "just" or "unjust" are entirely devoid of meaning. They are merely expressions of like or dislike. "To invoke justice is the same thing as banging on the table, an emotional expression which turns one's demand into an absolute postulate. . . . It is impossible to have a rational discussion with a man who mobilizes 'justice,' because he says nothing that can be argued for or against." It seems that this position differs sharply from that of relativists like Radbruch or Ginsberg, for whom there is very much to argue about in respect to conflicting values, even though they accept that the ultimate ends cannot be proved but must be believed in.[86a] Although Kelsen could also be described as a "noncognitivist" for the purposes of legal science, insofar as he denies that the prescription of values of any kind, including ethical ideals, can be the proper subject of legal science, he regards the cognition (Erkenntnis) and description (Beschreibung) of the law as a system of norms constituting legal values as the proper realm of legal science.[87] But such values are, for Kelsen as for Radbruch, relative not absolute.[88]

The influential contemporary school of Oxford "ordinary language philosophers" is sometimes linked with the ethical noncognitivists.[89] But it would appear that the Oxford philosophers' emphasis on the analysis of the meaning of language has no particular ethical connotation, positive or negative. It seeks to elucidate the meaning of legal terms and concepts in the context of legal

---

[86] Ross, *On Law and Justice*, at 274.

[86a] In a criticism of R. M. Hare's *Freedom and Reason* (1963), Ross appears to concede a somewhat larger function to reason in moral argument: see Danish Yearbook of Philosophy, vol. 1 (1964), 120 *et seq.*, 132.

[87] *Reine Rechtslehre*, 89 *et seq.*

[88] See further on Kelsen, Chap. 24.   [89] *E.g.*, by Nakhnikian, *op. cit.* at 23.

language.[90] An illustration is H. A. L. Hart's "Definition and Theory in Jurisprudence,"[91] where he investigates the meaning of such concepts as a legal right or corporate personality in the legal context in which they are used. By contrast, Hart's principles of "minimum natural law" are, as shown earlier, not connected with the "ordinary language philosophy" but state an ethical philosophy of an essentially empiric character.

ETHICAL THEORIES AND THE SOLUTION OF LEGAL PROBLEMS
AN ILLUSTRATION

It may be useful to test both the relevance of various ethical theories and the differences between them by applying them to the solution of a legal problem with deep ethical implications. No contemporary problem has shaken the consciences of lawyers more deeply, and revealed more pungently the tension between conscience and legal order, than the problem of disobedience to Nazi laws—a problem that could be transposed to other, comparable situations of conflict between an inhuman legal order and the ethical conscience of the individual. This problem has been at the heart of the revival of natural law thinking after the Second World War, it has inspired the post-war thinking of Gustav Radbruch, and it has been the main subject of a now famous debate between Professors Hart and Fuller.[92]

How would the different ethical theories approach the problem posed for an officer or a civil servant by an order to draft one of the Nazi extermination decrees or to organize a transport of Jews to an extermination camp? How would they react to the problem of the "informer wife" who, utilizing a wartime decree authorizing —or perhaps commanding—the denunciation of family members for utterances hostile to the regime, volunteered information to a special tribunal about anti-Hitler utterances made by her husband

---

[90] In this respect, the "language philosophers'" approach may be compared to Dewey's "logic of enquiry." Dewey's work and American pragmatism have, however, been all but completely ignored by English philosophers. See the recent admission by A. J. Ayer (*The Listener*, Nov. 4, 1965): "My conception of philosophy as an activity of analysis owed a great deal to Moore, as well as to Wittgenstein. Only the emotive theory of ethics, the idea that moral judgments were expressions of feeling and so neither true nor false, was relatively new. I recently discovered that my synthesis of these ideas was similar to the position taken by William James, under the heading of pragmatism, or radical empiricism, thirty years before me."
[91] 70 L. Q. Rev. 37 (1954).
[92] See below, p. 350 *et seq.*

within the four walls of the home, refusing the even then existing privileges of the wife not to testify against her husband, because she welcomed this opportunity to dispose, under the cover of legal authority, of her husband and to carry on her own love affairs?[93]

The first possible approach is that of transcendental or "supernatural"[94] ethics, which corresponds to the orthodox natural law approach in legal philosophy. This approach would regard the type of decrees that led to Auschwitz and Belsen as contrary to a natural law of respect for human dignity, as an emanation either of the law of God or of universal reason. It would conclude that a law clearly offending against these elementary principles was void and therefore not binding. From this premise flows the right to punish those who offended the higher law by obeying the positive law. In technical terms, this means that a subsequent legal order such as that expressed by the Nuremberg Charter or by postwar German legislation is made applicable retroactively.[95]

A second approach would be that of the intuitionist ethics. The rightness or wrongness of a conduct would be determined by an objectively but intuitively known feeling of right or wrong, a *Rechtsgefuhl* or a *sentimento giuridico*. The difficulty with this approach is that an intuitive evaluation can lead the individual concerned to very different decisions. He may intuitively feel the wrongness of an extermination decree, and derive from this his duty to disobey it, or he may on the contrary accept the injunction of the Nazi law of 1935 which empowered judges to inflict punishment "in accordance with the sound instincts of the people," interpreting such sound instincts as dictating the persecution and even extermination of Jews, Slavs, and other inferior races. Or he may be inspired by the feeling: "Right or wrong, my Country." Intuition may help to inspire marginal decisions in the sense indicated by Gény,[96] but if asked to guide in the basic choice of values it yields nothing.

Third, there are the various relativistic approaches. One of these, that of Dewey, would be based on a pragmatic "logic of enquiry, directed to the exploration of a given value." Such an approach would tentatively appraise the Nazi laws that "legalized" racial

---

[93] See also, on these problems, p. 352 *et seq.* below. For a brilliant dialectical presentation of five alternative approaches, see Fuller, "The Problem of the Grudge Informer," in *The Morality of Law, op. cit.* at 187.

[94] In the terminology of Frankena in *Philosophy, op. cit.* at 446.

[95] See further below, p. 354 *et seq.*

[96] See below, p. 330.

oppression, degradation of the human personality, and mass murder, as evil. It would, however, study the question of subsequent punishment of those who obeyed the Nazi laws in the light of feasibility. Such a study might show that a complete implementation of the goal of punishing everybody who participated in the making and execution of such laws was simply not feasible.[97] The result of such a pragmatic enquiry might be that a more modest goal, *i.e.*, the selection for punishment or other sanctions of those prominently associated with the Nazi regime through their high position or known deeds, would implement more adequately the objective of disapproval of the Nazi values, and of treating equals equally.

While pragmatic ethics are compatible with a relativistic approach, the basic attitude of relativistic ethics would be that whether to obey or disobey the Nazi laws was essentially a question of choice between the religious, humanistic, hedonistic, and other values relevant to the problem. One possible value—which indeed was chosen by the great majority of Germans—was that of obeying the positive authority of the State, at the expense of the principles of human dignity, compassion, and charity. The rationalistic ethics that is usually combined with the relativistic approach would demand a careful study of the means by which the different values would have to be implemented. It would show, for example, that the necessary implication of legal discrimination between "Aryans" and Jews would lead not only to the undermining of the family but also to a profound modification of the principles of equality, in contract, in criminal law, and in other fields. Such clarification of the goals might at least articulate and underline the severity of the choice between values.

"Noncognitivist" ethics would dismiss the entire problem as beyond the reach of rational discussion. It would regard the punishment of Nazi criminals, or their non-punishment, as expressions of conflicting emotions, be they the retribution imposed by an outraged humanity, a sophisticated version of the traditional exercise of the

---

[97] Something approaching 100% execution was attempted in the immediate postwar Allied legislation that proposed a great variety of sanctions, for virtually the entire German nation, in the light of a questionnaire comprising 132 questions designed to show the degree of participation in the Nazi regime. As was to be foreseen, this system broke down under its own weight, in view of numerous exceptions made for those who were important enough to be necessary in the postwar administration, the cooling off of revenge sentiment which set in after the first year or so had elapsed, and the sheer impossibilities of fair administration. See on the entire problem Friedmann, *The Allied Military Government of Germany* (1947), especially Chap. 7.

C*

rights of victors over vanquished, or on the other hand a sceptical or even cynical acquiescence in the man's cowardice.

The solution suggested later in this book[98] for these problems is predicated on the belief that no legally compelling solution can be found for this type of problem. Whatever the technical device, a subsequent and differing set of values has to be substituted for the values governing the offensive action. Whether, and to what extent, to punish the soldier, the civil servant, or the "grudge informer" for the actions described earlier is a metalegal problem.

Social Morality and the Legal Order

Although, following Strawson, we have distinguished individual ethics from social morality, it is obvious that there is no complete separation between the two. The social morality of a community will be determined by the balance of the thousands or millions of individual ethical "pictures of life" within it. This will not, of course, be necessarily an arithmetical median. The relative impact of the multitude of individual ethics upon social morality—and in turn, the impact of social morality upon the legal order—will greatly depend on the character of the society. In the pre-democratic age, the ethical values of a greater or smaller group of leaders had infinitely greater impact than that of the inarticulate masses. The evolution of many societies, from a stage of kingly or aristocratic leadership to the rise of the middle class, and from there to the participation of the "common man," clearly produces a progressive widening of the basis for the impact of individual ethics upon social morality. But whatever the relative weight of the different groups within a society may be, the social morality of a community at any given time will be the composite of a multitude of ethical values. The variety of the latter depends in turn upon the degree of moral freedom. A liberal and pluralistic society will more easily reflect a variety of ethical values than an authoritarian one. The same number of pacifists may, in one society, produce a legal procedure for exemption of conscientious objectors from military service, while in another they may have no impact at all upon the social morality and the legal order. Ultimately, a completely conditioned society may reduce or eliminate this fear of individual ethics. If, as is now no longer a fantasy, the increasing control over reproduction, through the selected implantation or

---

[98] See below, p. 356 *et seq.*

substitution of certain genes, will be under the control of the masters of a society, individual values—as forecast in Huxley's *Brave New World*—will become an automatic and standardized reflection of officially controlled genetics. The cultural counterpart is the all-pervasive control by "Big Brother" over the individual movements and actions of all individuals. All that we have said so far on the impact of ethics, and the variety of ethical theories, is conditioned upon the survival of social conditions in which individuals can still be produced, grow, and develop with a degree of uniqueness.[99]

In any society there is a close connection between social morality and the legal order. There cannot be—and there never has been—a complete separation of law and morality. Historical and ideological differences concern the *extent* to which the norms of the social order are absorbed into the legal order. And while, in the traditional, more or less custom-bound society, the flow was essentially in one direction, the gradual transformation of social behaviour into legal custom, and from custom into legislative prescription, in the contemporary, highly articulate and organized society, the law becomes in turn increasingly a major factor in the formation of social morality.

This interrelationship cannot be bypassed by any legal theory which maintains that law is a self-contained order of enforceable prescriptions. The difference between certain "positivist" theories, such as those of Austin or Kelsen, and others which in one way or another incorporate ethical postulates into the concept of law and the legal order, lies mainly in the question whether the metalegal foundations of a legal order should be sought inside it or outside it. The "habitual obedience" which forms part of Austin's definition of law, or the "minimum of effectiveness" which is the condition of the continuing validity of a legal system in Kelsen's theory, but also "rules which contain patterns of conduct for the exercise of force" (Olivecrona), or the "peaceful co-existence of masses of individuals in social groups and their cooperation for other ends than mere existence and propagation" (Lundstedt)—all incorporate into the law a certain body of social norms, whether the latter be stated as hypotheses or "facts" or parts of the legal definition itself. In the words of one of the most strongly anti-idealistic Scandinavian realists, "The study of law must in the final analysis be a study of social phenomena, the life of a human community; and jurisprudence must have as its task the interpretation of the 'validity' of

[99] See further, below, p. 67.

the law in terms of social effectivity, that is, a certain correspondence
between a normative idea content and social phenomena."[1]

LAW, MORALITY, AND SOCIAL CHANGE

Unless a minimum of conformity between legal order and social
effectiveness is maintained by the various processes of legal evolution, a revolution will ultimately destroy the existing legal order and
substitute a new one. When the feudal order that tied peasant serfs
to the land was no longer acceptable, the peasants fled to the free
cities and eventually the feudal order collapsed. When a majority
of Negroes no longer accepts legal, economic, or social inferiority
to a white minority within a legal order, and the change of the
legal system through legislative, administrative, and judicial reforms
fails to keep pace with the change of moral pressure, a revolution
will ultimately displace the former order. Sometimes the revolution
will come from outside, as in the destruction of the Nazi order by
the majority of nations that were willing to fight against it.

The normal process of interrelation between social morality and
legal order is one of evolution, *i.e.*, the use of the instrumentalities
of legal change for the reduction of tension between the two types
of normative order. The intensity of this process of interaction is
decisively determined by the degree of organization of a society.
Generally in primitive societies the reach of authority, and therefore of law, is limited by physical conditions and social tradition.
Most of the social life moves beyond the law, which is concerned
with minimum order—defence, a rudimentary system of justice and
police, and a minimal revenue system sufficient to maintain government. It is only against this background of undeveloped and slow-
moving societies that the theories of Savigny, Ehrlich, and other
advocates of custom as against law-making can be understood.[2] In
contemporary society, the reach of the law is far greater, and there
are correspondingly closer relations between the legal order and
social morality. The transition can, in our time, be closely observed
as the many new states of the postwar world seek to transform
themselves from traditional static and agricultural societies into
societies that aspire at economic development, diversification, and
social change. The legal machinery becomes the paramount instrument of social change. In the process it often becomes necessary

---

[1] Ross, *On Law and Justice,* 68 (1958).
[2] See further below, Chaps. 18, 20.

for the law to impose new patterns of social behaviour upon the society.

Thus it may become necessary for the state that seeks economic and social development to destroy existing patterns of land ownership, especially where they are linked with tribal custom and family tenure. In order to become a modern society, India found it necessary to legislate the abolition of the caste system and of the polygamous marriage. The fact that the legislation has hitherto been far from effective, especially with regard to the abolition of the caste system as a continuing pattern of social life, shows that the power of the law to influence and change social morality is as yet far from unlimited.

The majority of legal systems move between what Strawson has called "maximum" and "minimum" morality, *i.e.*, they vacillate between the incorporation into law of those moral conditions which are crucial to the survival of the legal structure, and the transformation of all or most of the social norms of the community into legal norms. The question will often arise: What in fact are the minimum moral conditions essential for the survival of society and therefore requiring their hardening into legal norms?

LAW AND THE ENFORCEMENT OF MORALS

This question has been the subject of sharp controversy in recent years, against the background of two important aspects of the relation between law and morality, one contained in a decision of the House of Lords,[3] the other in the report of the Wolfenden Committee published in 1957. In Shaw's case, the defendant had composed and procured the publication of a magazine called *The Ladies' Directory* which gave the names and addresses, as well as nude photographs, of prostitutes, supplemented by a coded indication of the sexual practices. Although Shaw was clearly guilty of two statutory offences, *i.e.*, publishing an obscene libel and living on the earnings of prostitutes, the House of Lords, with only one dissent, also convicted him of a "conspiracy to corrupt public morals." The House of Lords here emphatically asserted "a residual power, where no statute has yet intervened to supersede the common law,

---

[3] *Shaw* v. *Director of Public Prosecutions* [1962] A.C. 220. For a study of the question in the United States see Henkin, "Morals and the Constitution: The Sin of Obscenity," 63 *Colum. L. Rev.* 391 (1963). For the development of the issue of obscenity in publication see *Roth* v. *U.S.*, 354 U.S. 476 (1957); *Ginzburg* v. *United States*, 383 U.S. 463 (1966).

to superintend those offences which are prejudicial to the public welfare" (Lord Simmonds). The subsequent discussion, to which the most prominent contributions are Professor Hart's *Law, Liberty and Morality* (1963) and Lord Devlin's *The Enforcement of Morals* (1965), centred around the question of how far the law should go in legislating on morality, beyond the elementary needs of public order.[4] The same problem was raised, in a socially more serious context, by the report of the Wolfenden Committee which recommended, by a majority of twelve to one, that homosexual behaviour between consenting adults in private should no longer be treated as a criminal offence. The crucial issue of the relation between law and social morality is put in the words of the report itself:

Unless a deliberate attempt is made by society acting through the agency of the law to equate this fear of crime with that of sin, there must remain a realm of private morality and immorality which is, in brief and crude terms, not the law's business.

The question what the proper sphere of law is, in relation to morality, was the main subject of the debate between Professor Hart and Lord Devlin. The former based himself essentially on John Stuart Mill's essay *On Liberty*, in which Mill said that "the only purpose for which power can rightfully be exercised over any member of a civilized community against his will is to prevent harm to others." By contrast, Lord Devlin maintained that the State may claim on two grounds to legislate on matters of morals. It could function to promote virtue among its citizens—the Platonic ideal—and therefore claim "the right and duty to declare what standards of morality are to be observed as virtuous and must ascertain them as it thinks best."[5] This conception of the State, which invests it with the power of determination between good and evil, destroys freedom of conscience and paves the road to tyranny, is unacceptable to Anglo-American thought. Alternatively, "society may legislate to preserve itself." In Lord Devlin's judgment, the House of Lords in Shaw's case had done just this when it sought to indict the defendant, *inter alia,* for corruption of the moral welfare of the State. And it was a jury of twelve reasonable men, expressing the moral values of the common man rather than the

---

[4] The further question, to what extent the law courts, as distinct from the parliamentary legislator, should do what the House of Lords did in Shaw's case, need not be discussed in the present context. On this question, see below, p. 500 *et seq.*

[5] Devlin, *The Enforcement of Morals,* 89 (1965).

educated elite, that best represented the moral standards of a society.[6]

While this debate is highly relevant to the question whether and to what extent a law should, in contemporary British society, interfere with actions that, however contrary to predominant sexual morality and practice, are carried on in private and therefore do not directly affect the public, it does not elucidate the theoretical question of the relation between law and social morality. As we have seen, the dimensions of public order vary greatly from one type of society to another, both historically and ideologically. In a theocratic or totalitarian society, the regulation of sexual practices or of freedom of discussion, even in private, may be eminently a matter of "public order," whereas in a liberal contemporary democracy, influenced by modern psychological, criminological, and sociological studies, male homosexuality carried on in private may be regarded as being of no concern to public order.[7] The Spartans approved of homosexuality because they believed that it promoted courage in battle.[8] A Spartan type society might well legislate for the promotion of homosexuality, private or public, as being an important aspect of "public order."

The essential theoretical lesson of the discussion that has arisen from Shaw's case and the Wolfenden Committee report is that modern, articulate, and highly organized society, equipped with a multitude of media of communication and information, has the means and the power to transform preferred moral standards into law, but that the question how much of social morality should be regulated and promoted by law is a question deeply dependent upon differing social ideologies and ethical valuations.

The only general conclusion to be drawn is that, in any society that preserves a modicum of individual responsibility, there is a tension between individual ethics and social morality on the one part, and social morality and the legal order on the other part. How much these three spheres of normative order influence and modify each other is a question that cannot be answered in absolute terms.

---

[6] *Op. cit.*, 89.

[7] For an excellent discussion of these questions, see Ginsberg, *op. cit.*, at 230 *et seq.*

[8] Russell, *Human Society in Ethics and Politics,* 99.

CHAPTER 4

SCIENCE AND LEGAL THEORY

THE nature of scientific inquiry has been described by an eminent contemporary philosopher of science as being "a systematic explanation of facts, by ascertaining the conditions and consequences of events, by exhibiting the logical relations of propositions to one another. . . ."[1] Further, "The conclusions of science are the fruits of an institutionalized system of inquiry which plays an increasingly important role in the lives of men."[2]

For the student of the theory of a social science—law—the first question is whether the same system of inquiry can be applied to the natural sciences—namely, to the study of matter and its behaviour in the world around us—and to the social sciences, which are concerned with the patterns of human behaviour, and their interactions, in society. The scope and complexity of this question have been immensely widened by the enormous expansion of the objects and processes of inquiry in both areas in our time. From the relatively simple study of the behaviour of visible objects and clearly ascertainable forms of energy, on the earth and—since the birth of modern astronomy—in the solar system, the objects of study by the natural sciences now extend, on the one hand, to constellations billions of light-years away, and, on the other hand, to the nature, movements and interactions of immeasurably minute subparticles of the atom. This has produced not only a greatly widened area of study, but also many new, different and constantly changing methods of inquiry. On the other hand, the field of the social sciences has widened, from the study of the relatively simple and static patterns of rural and earlier urban societies, to the enormously larger, more complex and constantly changing structures of modern industrialized societies. These societies are not only vastly greater in area and density of population, but formed by an ever more complex interaction of factors that mould the shape and structure of

[1] E. Nagel, *The Structure of Science*, 6 (1961).
[2] *Id*. at 14.

such societies. "Those who are engaged in a course of decision-making soon become aware that each decision is conditioned not only by the concrete situation in which it is taken but also by the sequence of past decisions and that their new decisions in their turn will influence future decisions not only by their effect on the history of events but also by the precedents which they set and the changes which they make in the way decision-makers in the future will see, interpret and respond to events. . . ."[3] That there is a fundamental difference between the scientific methods of the natural sciences and the social sciences has been a basic tenet of the various neo-Kantian schools of thought. Kant had made a general distinction between man as part of nature—and to that extent subject to the laws of causation—and man as a reasonable being which regulates conduct by imperatives. But whereas Kant himself had confined this distinction to the theory of knowledge, the neo-Kantians applied it to construe a basic difference in the methods and purposes of natural and social sciences. This is a reflection—particularly strong in the nineteenth century—of the growing belief in the accessibility of all human phenomena to scientific knowledge. Neo-Kantian philosophers, such as Dilthey, Rickert and Windelband, apply scientific method not just to the theory of knowledge, *i.e.*, to the perception and the ordering of phenomena outside the human individual, but to the whole of human nature in its different manifestations, thinking, feeling and willing. The chief result of this is the methodological separation of the natural and cultural sciences. The former are concerned with the perception of the phenomena of nature and they apply a process of investigation different from the cultural sciences. The latter are concerned with the manifestation of human volition in man's social organization expressing itself in ethics, law and history. These sciences, different in their object, require different principles of approach, and the one which is paramount in Neo-Kantian legal theory is the contrast between causality as dominating natural science, and of volition (or purpose) as dominating social sciences.

METHODS OF INQUIRY

The dichotomy of the methods of inquiry governing the natural and social sciences, respectively, has been applied to legal theory by

[3] Vickers, *The Art of Judgment*, 15 (1965).

modern neo-Kantian legal philosophers, notably Stammler, Del Vecchio and Kelsen. The differences between the theories of these jurists are analysed elsewhere in this book.[4] They share the basic assumption that law is a normative, not a natural, science, concerned with *sollen*, not with *sein*.

Doubts have been cast upon the validity—or at least the absoluteness—of this methodological distinction by both natural and social scientists. For more than a generation, leading scientists and philosophers of science have questioned the purely causal and deterministic character of the natural scientists. Thus, in *Science and Hypothesis*, Henri Poincaré has shown that the choice between alternative hypotheses in the natural sciences is often one of convenience and that the same conclusions may be derived from different premises. It is impossible to make experiments without preconceived ideas, and no experiment gives scientific results without generalizations which serve as prediction for other experiments. Since then, continuous inquiries and changing theories about the structure of the atom, the theory of relativity, the interchangeability of matter and energy according to Einstein's celebrated formula $e = mc^2$, the dual "wave" and "corpuscular" character of the electron, and in particular the quantum theory have led to an interaction between speculative assumptions and experiments in physics. Modern quantum mechanics, and in particular the uncertainty formula of Heisenberg, are the chief bases for assertions of indeterminism in contemporary physical theories, implying at least a partial abandonment of the deterministic principle of causality in the natural sciences. Heisenberg's uncertainty formula asserts that, in the subatomic world, owing to the growing precision of the instruments of observation, the relation between the "momentum" and the "position" of a given subatomic particle at any given moment cannot be precisely determined. The unpredictable variations in the momentum and position of subatomic particles are produced by the interaction of the latter with the instruments used in measuring these features. ". . . [I]n general, every experiment performed to determine some numerical quantity renders a knowledge of others illusory, since the uncontrollable perturbations of the observed system alter the value of previously determined quantities."[6] The principle of causality—so it is maintained—can be

---

4 See below, Chaps. 16, 24.
6 Heisenberg, *The Physical Principles of the Quantum Theory*, 3 (1930).

retained in the subatomic world only by ignoring the wave-particle duality of electrons. If, on the other hand, the traditional notions of space and time are preserved for subatomic particles, a deterministic, causal explanation of their movements and interactions is not possible.[7]

To the doubts cast by modern physical theory on the principles of causality and determinism, there corresponds, in the social sciences, an increasing emphasis on certainty and measurability. Behavioural research, *i.e.*, in particular the use of quantitative techniques in the analysis of factual data, as utilized in mathematical equations, is held by a growing number of contemporary sociologists, political scientists and jurists, to provide a far greater degree of certainty of analysis of legal phenomena, especially of the judicial processes. Thus the question—highly relevant for interpretation of the Constitution by the U.S. Supreme Court—whether Negroes have been discriminated against in the selection of jurors, can be accurately determined by precise statistical inquiries and mathematical computations. The probability calculus is said to permit the determination whether and to what extent the exclusion of Negroes is due to chance or to intentional policy, a vital factor in the legal decision.[8] Even before the recent revolutionary expansion in the categorization and analysis of complex factual data made possible by the advent of the computer, the realist movement in legal theory, a generation ago, drew attention to the importance of fact research and analysis in the process of legal decision.[9] Modern behaviourists accept the same premise but use modern computer programming to obtain more precise predictions of legal behaviour. They seek "to obtain *a precise and exhaustive* distinction between combinations of facts that lead to decisions in favour of one party and combinations of facts that lead to decisions in favour

---

[7] See, for a concise description and analysis of this argument, Nagel, *op. cit.*, at 293-298. It should be noted that this reasoning is applied only to the microcosm of the subatomic world, whereas it can be neglected in the measuring of what for the physicist are large-scale objects, *i.e.*, for all matter larger than subatomic particles. And for the latter it applies only insofar as each subatomic particle is considered as an individual. In the interrelation of billions of them, as they constitute the objects of human experience, statistical probabilities confirm the results of traditional physics. See Bridgman, *Determinism in Modern Science, in Determinism and Freedom in the Age of Modern Science*, 57 *et seq.* (Hook ed. 1958).

[8] See, for example, Ulmer, "Quantitative Analysis of Judicial Processes," 28 Law & Contemp. Prob., 164 ff. (1963); Berns, Law and Behavioural Science, 185, 195, *ibid.*

[9] See, on the realist movement, below, Chap. 25.

of the opposing party. This distinction can be obtained with the aid of mathematical models."[10]

There has thus been a considerable softening of the once rigid distinctions between the methods of enquiry in the natural and social sciences. By stressing the importance of hypotheses, of uncertainty, and the possibility of articulated or unarticulated value assumptions, the natural scientists let in an element of indeterminism. The social sciences have widened the area of causality, by extending the uses of fact research, statistics and mathematical computations in the determination of legal decisions.

But is doubtful whether the contemporary approaches to the relation of the natural and social sciences indicate a change in substance rather than a growth in self-consciousness about methods of enquiry. Natural scientists have always started from hypotheses which they have sought to verify by experiment. These hypotheses may have been caused by chance observation—like the fall of an apple or the movement of the water in a pail that is swung around —or by a sudden inspiration, or by a philosophical speculation on God and Nature. It is the articulation of hypotheses and value premises that has grown. On the other hand, it is doubtful whether such theories as the "uncertainty" principle, however important in physics, represent more than another phase in the unending interplay of theory and experiment in the observation of physical phenomena. They do not affect the basic difference between the objectives of natural and social sciences. The former are exclusively concerned with the study of matter, the latter with the purposive behaviour of human beings. Modern sciences—anthropology, blood chemistry, genetics, psychology—have greatly widened the material component, and therefore the deterministic factors in human behaviour. But there remains an indeterministic element in the human decision, which is not of the same order as the indeterminism of the movements of sub-atomic particles. As long as men do not become purely chemically and genetically predetermined conglomerations of chemical substances—as pictured in Aldous Huxley's *Brave New World* —they will differ in their ideas, their goals, their conceptions of good and bad which direct their objectives. The arbitrariness or inarticulateness of the choice between competing and conflicting values can be significantly reduced by behavioural research, and the utilization of behavioural data has been immensely advanced

[10] Kort, *Simultaneous Equations and Boolean Algebra in the Analysis of Judicial Decisions*, 28 Law & Contemp. Problems at 143 (1963).

by modern computer programming which can handle data of infinitely greater quantity and complexity than the human brain.[11] As long as man does not become a mere product of chemical compounds, but retains a uniqueness of mind which enables him to be an individual, to distinguish between good and evil, to choose between alternative courses of action, the main use of modern scientific, technical, mathematical advances must be to widen the area of rationalization in the choice between alternative values. This means not only the articulation of values and interests cardinal to a given legal decision—as it has been attempted in the work and the philosophy of Holmes, Pound, Radbruch, Scheler and others —but also a greatly extended use of modern methods of fact research, as a basis for value decisions. Thus the vast area of value choices described by the general term of "public policy" can be made far more precise by modern opinion research and statistical inquiries, on such vital issues of public policy as the legitimacy of birth control or the criminality of homosexual practices. There are beginnings of a theory of rational decision in which the respective roles of values and quantitative factors are sorted out.[12] On the other hand, modern statistical—computer-aided—research methods can be used and may be essential to implement a legal policy decision.[13]

FACTS, VALUES AND JUDGMENTS IN THE SOCIAL SCIENCES

The foregoing discussion implies that, while, with regard to the recognition of the interdependence of value hypotheses and empirical evidence, the natural and the social sciences have come closer together, a basic distinction between values and facts remains. Such

[11] See Kort, *Id.* at 150: "The solution of simultaneous equations with twenty or more unknowns, which must be expected in the analysis of decisions in the indicated areas of law, would be prohibitive without the aid of a computer. Moreover, the particular method of factor analysis which is recommended here involves such extensive iterative matrix multiplications that a computer becomes indispensable."

[12] See *Rational Decision* (ed. Friedrich) Nomos VII (1964), especially Kaplan, "Some Limitations on Rationality," 55 *et seq.*

[13] For an illustration, see Silva, "Reapportionment and Redistribution," *Scientific American*, 20 *et seq.* November, 1965, on the implementation of the principle of *Baker* v. *Carr*, 369 U.S. 186 (1962) that state legislative districts must be approximately equal, by use of the demographic concept of compactness. "The aim of the computer programme is to construct legislative districts by combining smaller areas of known population—such as census enumeration districts if total inhabitants are the population base or voting precincts if the number of voters is the base—into a given number of contiguous districts of approximately equal population and relatively maximum compactness."

a view is, however, challenged by many outstanding social scientists. Ernest Nagel has summarized the principal types of critique as follows:[14]

The first, and most prominent, critique is that which holds that a "value orientation" is inherent in the very choice of material for investigation by the social scientist. The best known exponent of this view is Max Weber.[15] A variant of this approach is, second, the view that, since the social scientist is himself affected by considerations of right and wrong, of his own notions of a satisfactory social order, these personal standards enter into the analysis of social phenomena (e.g., into the appraisal of the physical and psychological "needs" of a particular culture).

A third approach maintains that the distinction between fact and value is untenable with regard to the analysis of purposive human behaviour, since value judgments inextricably enter into what appear to be descriptive of factual statements. A prominent exponent of this approach is the Swedish economist and social philosopher Gunnar Myrdal.[16] Myrdal distinguishes between "beliefs," *i.e.*, a person's knowledge, to be objectively judged as true or false, and "valuations," *i.e.*, a social situation or relation adjudged to be "just, right, fair, desirable, or the opposite, in some degree of intensity or other. . . ." "Opinions" are usually composite of beliefs and valuations. The difficulty, according to Myrdal, is that, in an appraisal of any particular social problem, beliefs tend to be biased, *i.e.*, twisted in the direction of a person's desired hierarchy of valuations.

Valuations are seldom overtly expressed except when they emerge in the course of a person's attempts to formulate his beliefs concerning the facts and their implications in relation to some section of social reality. Beliefs concerning the facts are the building stones for the logical hierarchies of valuations into which a person tries to shape his opinions. When the valuations are conflicting, as they normally are, beliefs serve the function of bridging illogicalities. The beliefs are thus not only determined by available scientific knowledge in society and the efficacy of the means of its communication to various population groups but are regularly 'biased,' by which we mean that they are systematically twisted in the one direction which fits them best for purposes of rationalizations.[17]

From Myrdal, who has written a classical study on "An American

[14] Nagel, *The Structure of Science*, 485 *et seq.*
[15] Weber, *The Methodology of the Social Sciences* (1947).
[16] See in particular "Valuations and Beliefs," Appendix I in An American Dilemma, reprinted in *Value in Social Theory*, 71 *et seq.* (1958).
[17] *Id.* at 76-77.

Dilemma: The Negro Problem and Modern Democracy," this twisting of beliefs is principally illustrated in the "systems of popular beliefs concerning the Negro and his relations to the larger society."

> There is an emotional load of valuation conflict pressing for rationalization, creating certain blind spots—and also creating a desire for knowledge in other spots—and in general causing conceptions of reality to deviate from truth in determined directions.[18]

In the field of jurisprudence, Professor Fuller appears to be of this persuasion:[19]

> When we are dealing with purposive action projected through time, the structure that we observe, recall, and report lies, not in any instantaneous state of affairs, but in a course of happening, which can be understood only if we participate in a process of evaluation by which the bad is rejected and the good retained.

The movements of a boy digging in the sand cannot be understood until we know that he is searching for clams. In this action "descriptive and evaluative efforts cannot at the outset be considered as being carried on simultaneously because we do not at first know what the boy is trying to do.[20] Transferring this to the wider framework of legal inquiry, Professor Fuller asserts that "in disposing of controversies and issuing directives we may operate within a framework of purposes which conditions our decisions, even though only certain of these purposes are called into consciousness by the facts of the case at hand."[21] The legal process is "the collaborative articulation of shared purposes."

A fourth critique maintains that a value-free social science is impossible, because value commitments enter into the very assessment of evidence by social scientists. Thus, the modern science of theoretical statistics seeks to rationalize the evidence for so-called "statistical hypotheses," *i.e.*, hypotheses concerning the probabilities of random events. To take an example given by Nagel,[22] tests may have to be performed to determine whether a new medicine has toxic effects because of certain impurities in its manufacture. The medicine is tested by being introduced into the diet of 100

---

[18] *Id.* at 85.
[19] See in particular Fuller's debate with Professor Nagel. Fuller, "Human Purpose and Natural Law" 68; Nagel, "On the Fusion of Fact and Value: A Reply to Professor Fuller" 77, 3 *Natural L. Fo.* (1958).
[20] *Id.* at 86.
[21] *Id.* at 95-96.
[22] *Id.* at 496 *et seq.*

guinea pigs, and only three of the animals become gravely ill as a result. The experimenter must decide between two alternative hypotheses: one, that the drug is toxic; and the other, that it is not toxic. The decision between these two alternative hypotheses cannot be made according to strictly mathematical-statistical principles; it involves certain judgments of value, such as a decision of preference on the respective importance of preservation of human lives that might possibly be endangered by the drug proving to be dangerous, as against the financial loss incurred by the manufacturer through the abandonment of the product. Statistical theory appears to support the thesis that value commitments enter into the rules for assessing the evidence of statistical hypotheses.

Some social philosophers go further and maintain that the connection between the social perspective of a student of human affairs and his standards of competent social inquiry is not merely contingent but necessary. This is based on the assumption that social institutions and their cultural products are constantly changing, and that the intellectual apparatus required to understand them must change correspondingly.

With regard to all these critical approaches, it may be readily admitted that the element of valuation, and of other uncertainties, in the selection and appraisal of evidence of social phenomena is generally far greater than in the natural sciences. Yet, "these admissions do not entail the conclusion that, in a manner unique to the study of purposive human behaviour, fact and value are fused beyond the possibility of distinguishing between them."[23] A distinction must be made between "value judgments" as expressing estimates of the degree to which certain types of actions, objects, or institutions are contained in a given process of assessment, and "value judgments" as expressing approval or disapproval of a certain moral or social or legal ideal. In all types of science the attempt must be made to distinguish between the characterizing and the appraising aspects. It is generally more difficult to do so in the social sciences, but not inherently impossible, and much of the difficulty lies in the relatively undeveloped character of complex fact analysis in the social sciences.

POLICY DECISIONS AND THE ART OF JUDGMENT

The growing complexity of modern social and legal planning pro-

[23] Nagel, *op. cit.* at 491.

cesses has made the simple distinction between facts and values insufficient. In industrialized, and in developing, societies, any decision of major social significance, such as the planning of a road system in a densely settled area, or a government grant for the construction and staffing of a number of new universities, entails a multitude of complex and inter-related factors. Some of these are constants, such as the size of a given area of land, or—at least within a limited period—the rate of growth and composition of the population within a given community.[24] The great majority of the relevant factors are variables, such as the density rate of traffic— influenced by many different factors such as the rate of production of motor vehicles, urban zoning legislation, farming subsidies, technological changes as well as changes in social habits, which may deeply influence patterns of life, or national and local tax policy.

The complexity of the policy judgments involved in such major planning projections may be illustrated by the Buchanan Report of 1963.[25] The terms of reference of the Buchanan Committee were "to study the long-term development of road and traffic in urban areas and their influence on the urban environment." The report begins with a general factual estimate of the expected increase in the number of motor vehicles in Britain over the next few decades, and of the more obvious consequences of such increase in various aspects of social life. It assumes that at a certain point Englishmen will react negatively against a state of affairs which will bring motor traffic itself to a standstill and at the same time drastically impair other basic amenities of life. As against this assessment of a value judgment by citizens, the report also assumes that they will continue to value and desire motor traffic rather than to abolish it in what would be a kind of Erewhonian revolution.

Most of the report is devoted to an analysis of the quantitative and qualitative aspects, and to the interaction of the different variables relevant to the situation. This implies an analysis of the types of traffic, moving from buildings to buildings, the minimum accessibility to buildings required in any environment, the functional nature of streets in towns—still multi-purpose streets used for

---

[24] While the use of constants and variables corresponds to the use of these factors in the mathematical equations of physical laws, it is one of the characteristics of the social as distinct from the natural sciences that absolute constants are relatively few, because of the interaction of human beings. Thus, population estimates can be given with fair though not precise accuracy for a strictly limited, but not for a long period.

[25] *Traffic in Towns*, London, HMS. (1963).

traffic, trade, personal intercourse and parking—and the relation between the minimum of environmental value and the upper limit accessibility. The report also analyses traffic flows with relation to the needs and habits of people as they move from home to work and back.

In a pioneer study on "The Art of Judgment," in which the Buchanan Report figures as one of the principal illustrations of the complexity of factors involved in policy judgments, Sir Geoffrey Vickers[26] analyses the various aspects of this, and of other reports, in terms of: (a) reality judgments; (b) value judgments; (c) instrumental judgments. Reality judgments are concerned with the appreciation of the reality factor which have a relatively high degree of certainty—although one generally lower than empirical observations in the natural sciences. They include such elements as the number, size and projected development of towns, of arable land, the use of streets, and the proportion of the national product invested in motorcar production.

The second factor is the value judgment, which concerns the hierarchy of values and priorities, such as the relative weight attached to good environment as against the conveniences of travel in motor vehicles. The later is a variable in so far as an increase of motor traffic beyond a certain point will defeat the objective of fast and convenient movement from place to place—as is already apparent in the movement of traffic in and out of major towns in most Western countries. Value judgments are also deeply influenced by the economic and social philosophy prevailing in the community. In a centrally directed system, the choices for the individual will be rigidly limited by the planners, whereas in a liberal society the choice between the different values is, to a far greater extent, left to individuals and groups.

There is, third, the "instrumental" judgment. This is the judgment which assesses a problem in its full complexity. It is shaped by what Kenneth E. Boulding has called "the image."[27]

. . . As we proceed from lower to higher levels of organization, the concept of the image becomes an increasingly important part of any theoretical model, and the image itself becomes increasingly complex. . . . A rudimentary image is exhibited in simple control mechanisms. It is clearly present even at the very earliest stage of life. It grows in

---

[26] Vickers, *The Art of Judgment: A Study of Policy-Making* (1965).
[27] Boulding, *The Image* (1961). See especially Chap. 2 (The Image in the Theory of Organization).

importance and complexity as we ascend the biological ladder. It is of overwhelming importance in the interpretation of human behavior and of the dynamics of society.[28]

The instrumental judgment is based on the skill "which produces apt solutions to the problems set by such surveys of 'reality,' calculated to change the pattern of expected relationships by responses perhaps never tried before."[29]

It is the combination of reality, value, and instrumental judgments which is involved in the process of "appreciation." These processes of appreciation are not confined to public policy and planning decisions. They also occur in private business where, in an age of rapidly changing technology, a new chemical invention may produce a revolution in needs affecting manufacturing equipment and causing a change from one line of production to another. The larger the enterprise involved, the closer the analogy of the policy judgment to that of public authorities.

It is obvious that the complexity of the various types of appraisal involved, and of their interdependence, will involve close integration between scientific methods of inquiry and policy judgments. Because of the dynamics of changing societies, "reality" judgments will to a large extent be estimates of probability in which the mathematician, the statistician and the economist, aided by computer techniques, will have to supply many of the reality estimates —such as of the increase in the population over a given period expected to seek university education, or the interaction between social stratification, income distribution, local taxation, urban amenities and traffic density in a given area, or the estimated effect of slum clearance and provision of community facilities on juvenile criminality and the consequent need for the building of prisons as against reform institutions.

It follows from the above—highly tentative and condensed— observations that there will have to be developed a science as well as an art of policy judgment, and that the two will be closely interlocked. The estimate of probabilities, and of the interrelation of different variables in a given social planning process, will to a large extent be a matter of scientific computation, but subject to the uncertainties that—as we have already seen—are inherent in any probability calculus involving human and social behaviour. But there will remain value judgments, as between technological pro-

---

[28] *Id.* at 31.
[29] Vickers, *op. cit.* at 73.

cess and aesthetic factors, between cultural values and economic progress, between the degree of individual choice and the degree of public control, which will deeply affect the total picture. Ultimately the decisional process will be deeply affected by the "image" of the kind of society that will be shaped by all these factors.

SCIENCE, DETERMINISM, AND LEGAL RESPONSIBILITY

Our enquiry so far has been concerned with the extent to which scientific enquiry—be it by the use of natural science processes of enquiry for the purposes of social science, or by the use of scientific methods specific to the social sciences—can help to clarify and implement social (including legal) value goals.

The present section will be concerned with the more fundamental question to what extent the enormous progress and broadening of the psychological, physiological and genetic analysis may affect established distinctions between right and wrong, and therefore the elements of legal responsibility. In philosophical terms, the question is whether the increasing knowledge of the causes of human behaviour—through the analysis of mind, through the study of social environment by which the behaviour of an individual is conditioned, or through the knowledge of the genetic makeup of a given individual—makes human behaviour predetermined and thus diminishes or excludes the freedom of choice on which moral and legal responsibility is founded.

PSYCHOLOGY AND CRIMINAL RESPONSIBILITY

Modern psychology has dissolved the—formerly somewhat simple —assumptions about the capacity of an individual to choose between right and wrong, into a multitude of factors. Until recently, legal theory generally assumed that a person was free to choose and act, unless his freedom was excluded by certain conditions of physical or mental compulsion. "The individual is not liable to punishment if at the time of his doing what would otherwise be a punishable act he is, say, unconscious, mistaken about the physical consequences of his bodily movements or the nature or qualities of the thing or persons affected by them, or in some cases, if he is subjected to threats or other gross forms of coercion or is the victim of certain types of mental disease."[30] Mental disease was

---

[30] Hart, "Legal Responsibility and Excuses," in *Determinism and Freedom in the Age of Modern Science* 95 (Hook ed.)

generally defined narrowly, as insanity, and the test of insanity was, in the classical formulation of the M'Naghten rules,[31] "that, to establish a defence on the ground of insanity, it must be clearly proved that, at the time of the committing of the act, the party accused was labouring under such a defect of reason, from disease of the mind, as not to know the nature and quality of the act he was doing, or, if he did know it that he did not know he was doing what was wrong."

This test assumes that a person who intellectually apprehends the distinction between the right and wrong of a given conduct must be held criminally responsible. This identification of knowledge and the power to control one's action was attacked as early as 1883 by the great British criminal lawyer Sir Fitzjames Stephen,[32] and although the M'Naghten test was adopted throughout the British Commonwealth and almost universally in the United States,[33] contemporary psychiatry and criminology have almost universally rejected it as scientifically untenable. The gravamen of the criticism is that knowledge is not the sole guide of conduct and "that the capacity of knowing right from wrong can be completely intact and functioning perfectly even though a defendant is otherwise demonstrably of disordered mind."[34]

Since all contemporary societies continue to have in their midst a considerable number of individuals whose propensities and actions are so dangerous that society must be protected from them, they can only have two alternative responses to the challenge posed by modern scientific analysis of the human mind. First, they can abandon any test of guilt and moral responsibility in favour of a purely utilitarian and socially determined elimination or confinement of persons dangerous to society.

> The suggestion has sometimes been made that the insane murderer should be punished equally with the sane, or that, although he ought not to be executed as a punishment, he should be painlessly exterminated as a measure of social hygiene.[35]

Such a philosophy can lead to the exposure of weakling children— as in ancient Sparta—or to the extermination, confinement or

[31] (1843) 4 St. Tr. (N.S.) 847.

[32] *History of Criminal Law*, II, 157 (1883).

[33] See the survey in the Report of the Royal Commission on Capital Punishment, 1949-53, H.M.S.O., Cmd. 8932.

[34] Sheldon Glueck, "Psychiatry and the Criminal Law," 12 Mental Hygiene 575, 580 (1928).

[35] Report of the Royal Commission on Capital Punishment, note 31 above.

sterilization of entire nations, races or other groups of people as hostile or obnoxious to society—a philosophy largely practised in National Socialist Germany.

The second alternative—adopted by the overwhelming majority of modern legal systems—is to modify the concepts of guilt, fault and the moralistic basis of criminal law, in the light of modern science. One such modification is the test of "irresistible impulse."[36] But this is now generally rejected, on the ground that a criminal act of an emotionally or mentally disturbed person may be coolly and carefully prepared, and yet be the act of a madman.[37] Another test, adopted in a much discussed decision of the United States Court of Appeals for the District of Columbia,[38] is "that an accused is not criminally responsible if his unlawful act was a product of mental disease or mental defect." The majority report of the Royal Commission on Capital Punishment adopted a similar test.[39] The Model Penal Code of the American Law Institute holds a person not responsible for criminal conduct "if at the time of such conduct as a result of mental disease or defect he lacks substantial capacity either to appreciate the criminality of his conduct or to conform his conduct to the requirements of law."[40] The Penal Code of Switzerland, the law of Scotland, and more recently the British Homicide Act of 1957 have adopted the test of "diminished responsibility" as justifying a modification of punishment for a criminal act, including detention, treatment or confinement to hospital as possible alternatives.[41]

The importance of all these different responses to modern psychiatry is that, as against the simple antithesis of sanity and insanity, they recognize a whole spectrum of mental disturbances, including in particular psychopathic disturbances, that they consequently distinguish between intellectual apprehension and emotional control, and, as a result, correlate the degree of legal—in particular,

[36] Adopted, *e.g.*, in *Smith* v. *United States*, 36 F. 2d. 548 (1929).
[37] Report of the Royal Commission, Section 314.
[38] *Durham* v. *United States*, 214 F. 2d. 862 (1954).
[39] ". . . [T]he jury must be satisfied that, at the time of committing the act, the accused, as a result of disease of the mind or mental deficiency, (a) did not know the nature and quality of the act or (b) did not know that it was wrong or (c) was incapable of preventing himself from committing it." Report, para. 317. The New York Penal Code as revised in 1965 adopts the same criteria (a) and (b), see 1150.
[40] This test was adopted by the U.S. Court of Appeals for the Second Circuit in a decision rendered on February 28, 1966 as the formulation most conducive to "an inquiry based on meaningful psychological concepts." 358 F. 2d. 459 (2d. Cir. 1966).
[41] See Penal Code of Switzerland, Article 17.

criminal—responsibility to the degree of emotional control of which the individual is capable.

But the findings of modern psychiatry and neurology are only part of the widening process of inquiry into the circumstances which make an individual behave in a particular way. Where these modern branches of medical science inquire into the structure of the individual human mind, modern sociology investigates the social antecedents of antisocial and illegal behaviour. The two join hands where, for example, psychopathic behaviour or abnormal sexual proclivities can be traced to social conditions, such as deeply disturbed domestic circumstances, or upbringing in a social environment conducive to criminal behaviour. Generally, urbanization and industrialization, with all the social disruption they entail, have a demonstrated effect on the rate of crime. The wider the range of inquiry, the more difficult does the simple equation of right and wrong with sin and innocence, good and evil become. A consequence, in the modern science of criminology, is the increasing emphasis on reformation rather than deterrence as the reaction to crime—which is more and more seen as a particularly grave form of unsocial behaviour. This has gone furthest in the treatment of juvenile offenders. In all the advanced countries of our time, the juvenile offender is now subjected to a special procedure, before separate tribunals, and such measures as probation, approved schools, or supervision by welfare authorities have increasingly replaced punishment as the normal sanction for juvenile crimes.[42] This process has, in some states, (*e.g.* California) been extended to the adult offender.

MORAL GUILT, DETERMINISM AND LEGAL RESPONSIBILITY

The widening challenge of both natural and social science to traditional notions of the causes of criminal behaviour poses grave problems for legal theory. Does it altogether destroy the moral basis of criminal law? Some distinguished contemporary jurists emphatically deny that anything but the moral wrongness of an act can form the basis of criminal law. Among them are Jerome Hall, who asserts that *mens rea* is "the ultimate summation of the moral judgments expressed in the voluntary commission of numerous

---

[42] See, among many others, for an authoritative analysis, Sheldon and Eleanor Glueck, "Unraveling Juvenile Delinquency," 3 Brit. Journ. of Delinquency, 289 (1953).

social harms"[43] and Lord Denning, who, in his evidence before the Royal Commission on Capital Punishment, said that

". . . The ultimate justification of any punishment is not that it is a deterrent, but that it is the emphatic denunciation by the community of a crime. . . ."

A similar conception is that of Thurman Arnold, who, in two important decisions rendered during his brief membership in the U.S. Court of Appeals for the District of Columbia,[44] expressed the view that the M'Naghten test should be retained because

"In the determination of guilt, age-old conceptions of individual moral responsibility cannot be abandoned without creating a laxity of enforcement that undermines the whole administration of criminal law."[45]

But the major trend of contemporary legal theory, in particular with reference to the reaction of the law to the defence of insanity in the light of modern science, appears to point towards a utilitarian approach. This is essentially a modernization of Bentham's philosophy, according to which the sanctions of the criminal law are to be measured in terms of their efficiency in securing the maintenance of law at the least cost in pain.[46] Among the contemporary exponents of this theory are Professors Glanville Williams and H. L. A. Hart. The former has stated that:

Normal people may be punished for the sake of general or particular deterrence, and mentally ill or subnormal persons may perhaps be given some punishment if it is thought that this may have an effect upon their future conduct. . . . Mentally ill or subnormal persons whose conduct is unlikely to be influenced by the threat of punishment must be cared for; to punish them for the sake of general deterrence is unnecessary, because normal persons are not influenced by what happens to the insane.[47]

H. L. A. Hart has criticized the doctrine of criminal responsibility based on the "economy of threats" as misrepresenting "the character of our moral preference for a legal system that requires mental

---

[43] Hall, Principles of Criminal Law, 146 (2nd ed. 1960).

[44] *Holloway* v. *U.S.*, 148 F. 2d. 665 (App. D.C. 1945); *Fischer* v. *U.S.*, 149 F. 2d. 28 (D.C., 1945).

[45] *Id.* at 28. And see, on the wider question of the function of law as a guardian of morality, above, p. 45 *et seq.*

[46] See below, p. 316, and specifically Bentham, *Principles of Morals and Legislation*, Chap. XIII.

[47] Williams, *The General Principles of Criminal Law*, 2nd ed. at 467 (1961).

conditions of responsibility over a system of total strict liability or entirely different methods of social control such as hypnosis, propaganda, or conditioning."[48] Hart accepts the utilitarian criterion of the cost to an individual "of obeying the law—and of sacrificing some satisfaction in order to obey—against obtaining that satisfaction at the cost of paying 'the penalty.' "[49] But he suggests that the purpose of a system of criminal law not totally based on strict liability, and the freedom of the choice of the individual, can be preserved by a system of "excusing conditions to criminal responsibility." These include the usual defences against criminal responsibility, such as mistake, accident, provocation, duress or insanity, and they are parallel to the conditions that invalidate civil transactions, such as wills, contracts or marriages. In the light of a knowledge of these excusing conditions, an individual can determine his choice. The difference between this and the Benthamite approach is that, in Hart's view, "Excusing conditions are accepted as something that may conflict with the social utility of the law's threat; they are regarded as of moral importance because they provide for all individuals alike the satisfactions of a costing system."[50]

The foregoing discussion underlines the fundamental dilemma with which legal theory is faced, as a result of modern scientific inquiry into the conditions of both individuals and society. Once the assumption of the human being as one who is either moral or immoral and chooses freely between lawful and illegal action is undermined, there is no theoretical limit to the tracing of causes of human behaviour to an infinite chain of antecedent causes. The emotional disorders of a sex criminal may be traced to the slum conditions under which he grew up, or to exposure to the brutality of his father. But the latter is in turn the result of his genetic make-up, or of the conditions in which he grew up. And so it goes on in infinite regression. In philosophical theory, the analysis of the increasingly complex interweaving of physical and social factors which determine a given individual is incompatible with "freedom of will," since the actions of murderers as well as of the most selfless and law-abiding members of society are determined by pre-existing—physical, mental or social—conditions. Yet the great

---

[48] Hart, "Legal Responsibility and Excuses," in *Determinism and Freedom in the Age of Modern Science*, 108 (Hook ed. 1957).
[49] *Id.* at 111.
[50] *Id.* at 113.

majority of modern legal systems and of legal philosophers reject
the total abandonment of individual responsibility as a criterion of
criminal—and to a lesser extent of civil—liability. Modern utilitarians like Hart and Williams agree with "moralists" like Hall or
Denning, and with most psychiatrists,[51] on the continuing necessity
of retaining some form of punishment related to responsibility.
Philosophers appear to agree that the philosophical question of
freedom of will must be kept separate from the criteria of responsibility essential to law as a social discipline. In a recent symposium
on the subject of "Determinism and Freedom,"[52] one discussant
suggested that "when we judge a person morally responsible for a
certain action, we do indeed presuppose that he was a free agent at
the time of the action. But the freedom presupposed . . . is nothing
more than . . . the ability to act according to one's choices or
desires."[53] Another suggestion[54] is that the degree of moral responsibility is dependent on the level of "reflectiveness" achieved by a
particular person. The simplest, and also the most convincing,
answer to the dilemma is the admission that "we have to recognize
clearly that there are two levels of operation. There is the level of
daily life and social interaction, *i.e.*, the level of 'free will,' and
there is the deterministic level. So far as the deterministic level has
concrete reference beyond the purely verbal, it is the level of scientific activity. At this level . . determinism has the status merely of
a programme to direct inquiry, a programme applicable to the overwhelming majority of the phenomena of the world about us. . . . The
other level is the common sense level of everyday life, the level
of 'free will.' . . . On this level we have to devise a practical
method of dealing with situations in which we cannot control or
predict."[55]

A legal system must assume freedom of choice between alternative courses of action and direct its sanctions accordingly. It is concerned with the practical ordering of social life in a given community.
It does not purport to answer the philosophical question of "free
will." And insofar as a legal system must reflect the general attitudes of the society which it regulates, it must accept that the
torturers of children or the killers of Auschwitz are not regarded

---

[51] See, *e.g.*, Flügel, *Men, Morals and Society*, 168 *et seq.* (1945).
[52] *Op. cit.*, note 46 above.
[53] Edwards, *op. cit.* at 119.
[54] Campbell, "Is Free Will a Pseudo-Problem?" *Mind*, 1951; Edwards, *op. cit.*
at 122 *et seq.*
[55] Bridgman, "Determinism and Punishment," *op. cit.* at 155.

with moral indifference. This is reflected in the views of such experienced trial judges as Lords Devlin and Denning.

What modern scientific analysis can teach us is two things: First, that the simple dichotomy of good and evil, of moral reprehensibility and innocence, must give way to a much subtler gradation of shades of responsibility. This has, as we have seen, already deeply influenced modern criminal law and criminology. Second, the growing knowledge of the biological and social complexities that determine a person's behaviour should teach humility and a sense of perspective. The men who, as legislators, judges or administrators, lay down the conditions of legal responsibility can and should do so, not from a posture of moral superiority, but as executants of a social and legal order which has not yet found any alternative to the criterion of free choice between right and wrong as a basis of legal sanctions. And it is at least possible that, at some time in the future, such insights may modify the collective relations between nations, which still operate in their mutual intercourse on a psychological level that civilized societies have long abandoned in their internal affairs, and that mature individuals would feel ashamed to apply in their personal relations.

GENETICS AND RESPONSIBILITY

The foregoing discussion—and indeed the entire discussion of legal theory in the present book—assumes a human society based on individuals different from each other in a multitude of ways but all capable, to a greater or lesser extent, of reasoning, and of choosing between different courses of action. The borderline between freedom and necessity must always be somewhat arbitrary, and for the purposes of legal science it is, as suggested here, determined by social necessity rather than philosophical speculation. But certain developments in modern genetics suggest that a society is now conceivable in which the moral makeup of human beings is predetermined by genetic selection. This was foreshadowed in Aldous Huxley's *Brave New World*, a generation ago. It is now within the realm of scientific possibility.

A leading geneticist[56] suggested a few years ago that reproduction should be regulated by the fertilization of stored genes collected from outstanding individuals, and that such genes should be substi-

---

[56] H. J. Muller, *New York Times*, December 2, 1959.

tuted for the female genes in the fertilized ovum. In this way, mankind could in the future be increasingly populated by the likes of Beethoven, Lincoln, or Einstein. Shortly after, in a symposium on "Evolution and Man's Progress"[57] this same geneticist suggested a coordination of cultural and biological evolution, and a general extension of artificial insemination to human reproduction. The fertilization of selected female eggs with chosen sperm, subsequently implanted in selected female hosts, "would permit the multiple distribution of eggs of a highly selected female into diverse recipient females, yet when so desired it would enable the child to be derived on its paternal side from the recipient's husband. Possibly, too, techniques involving mature eggs could be combined with deep freezing to allow indefinitely prolonged storage." Though admitting that it was impossible to "proceed in humans according to principles governing simple Mendelian differences," Professor Muller believes that, through the control of reproduction by selected genes, mankind will progress towards a higher intellectual and moral level. A majority of the commentators—all eminent authorities in the field of biology, zoology, sociology, and paleontology—were sceptical. Underlying their doubts was the uncertainty about the results of man's interference with the concept of the pluralistic society, "in which no one way of life is considered absolutely better than several others,"[58] and doubt that certain genes and mutations were in all circumstances good or bad.[59] Above all, we do not know who may do the genetic planning for the future society. As a result of the growing concentration of power in a few hands, "Big Brother" may decide on a genetic selection stressing physical prowess, obedience, and low intellectual capacity. "We may soon find that the doctrine of 'clearly deleterious' is no easier to apply in practice than is Holmes' doctrine of clear and present danger in a realm of free speech."[60] The power of genetic determination by

[57] Daedalus (Journal of the American Academy of Arts and Sciences), Summer, 1961.

[58] R. S. Morison, *op. cit.* at 453.

[59] "Usefulness and harmfulness are not the intrinsic properties of a variant gene; genes are useful, neutral, or harmful only in a certain environment; and the relevant environments are of two kinds: the external or secular, and the internal or genetic environment. . . . It is possible that the genius of Dostoevsky was in some way conditioned by his suffering from epilepsy. Shall we deny that in Dostoevsky's genotype the gene that made him liable to epilepsy was perhaps of some value to the rest of mankind? . . . We know far too little about human biology to equate the genetic leads with the sociological burdens of human populations." (Dobzhansky, *op. cit.* at 461, 463.)

[60] Morison, *op. cit.* at 452.

preselection will include the determination of the level of moral responsibility. People will increasingly be made to behave according to certain predetermined patterns of conduct. In such a society, the concepts of good and evil, freedom and coercion, the imputation of a free choice between right and wrong, will have ceased to have any meaningful application.

CHAPTER 5

LEGAL THEORY AND SOCIAL EVOLUTION

LAW AND SOCIAL CHANGE

A CRISIS of society challenges the law more directly perhaps than any other branch of social activity. The profession of the lawyer, and the values dear to the law, are threatened by an upheaval in the foundations of society. Though the law is obviously concerned with politics, economics, social life and ethics, it is its function to give them form and order. From this relation of law to the matters which it regulates, there develop three characteristic features, all sound in principle and indeed fundamental to the idea of law, yet all apt to divorce law from social reality in a time of crisis.

The first of these characteristics is stability. Stability is a paramount object of law, and indeed a vital incentive to its development. But the desire of the lawyer to preserve stability of conditions may, and often does, blind him to social changes and developments, with the result that the law eventually becomes a mere phantom or is defied by forces stronger than itself.

The second character is formalism. Since law is a method of ordering social relations in a specific manner, the form gains paramount importance in the legal system and legal training. One of the principal controversies in legal theory is between those who emphasise form and those who emphasise substance. But there is little doubt that, for the average lawyer, the form of regulating a specific social relation becomes more important than the social relation itself. It is extremely difficult for a lawyer working under any modern legal system not to be overwhelmed by technique.

The distinction of precedents, the interpretation of statutes, the tracing of the historical development of a particular clause or notion, matters of evidence and procedure—all these preoccupations tend to overshadow the social stuff behind them.

Thirdly, and perhaps most important in its effect, there is the desire for security from disorder. This, indeed, is a universal human

70

desire, the more cherished because of the frequency of disturbance. However, for the law, security has assumed an overwhelming importance, heightened by the development of social conditions and legal education in the positivist era of the nineteenth century. Under the protection of settled conditions, a steadily growing power of state organisation and an increasing prosperity of the middle class, the background of social and political struggle became dimmer and dimmer for the lawyer, while his technical training became more and more complex. Encouraged by the method of legal education, law developed into a skilled craft, a professional technique, pursued with less and less regard for the social matter which it was to regulate.

This world of comparative security, comfort and self-sufficiency is crumbling everywhere, though in many degrees of speed and intensity. Political revolution, social strife and war are laying bare the roots of law, its close and inevitable link with the ethical political and social foundations of the community in which it operates. Communist and Fascist revolutions alike have brought the lawyer face to face with fundamental political issues; but in every country a continuous though less abrupt social revolution affects the law in its principles as well as in its daily routine work. Such matters as the growth of a publicly directed and state controlled economy, from Fascism to Communism, with many intermediate stages; the universal delegation of powers from a legislative assembly to the executive; the standardisation of industry, business and employment; the growing predominance of collective bargaining with different degrees of state supervision; the development of transport in its effects upon the civilian, the standardisation of housing, building, insurance; the increase of "administrative" or "public welfare" offences—these and many other developments permeate not only the fundamental issues of individual liberty, but every technical rule of contract, tort, property. They demand a new legal technique which cannot be developed without reference to, and consciousness of, the political issues involved.[1]

The challenge is particularly evident in the sphere of international law. For, whereas the municipal lawyer can seek delusive protection behind a rigid division of is and ought, the separation of legislation and application of law, the international lawyer lacks even this comfort. The absence of legislative authority and machinery

[1] This is developed in detail in the writer's *Law in a Changing Society*, 197 *et seq.* (1959).

exposes him, without any protective curtain, to the perpetual changes in international society and should compel him to test his rules perpetually in relation to social reality.

Only too often vital social developments have found the lawyer ill-prepared. The abject prostitution of lawyers in Nazi Germany, Fascist Italy and Soviet Russia, the prolonged blocking of social progress by the legal interpreters of the American Constitution, or the predominantly hostile attitude of English judges towards the inevitable predominance of statute in modern law, have had a profound and, on the whole, negative effect on social and political development.

On the other hand, the many important developments in the English common law of the last decade, or in the interpretation of the American Constitution, would have been impossible without a remarkable change in the legal ideology of the judiciary.[2]

What part has legal theory to play in the reshaping of society? In the past, it appears, jurists and legal philosophers have either claimed too much or too little. Some legal philosophies, like that of Hegel, have purported to give a complete solution to all problems; on the other hand, legal positivism, prevalent during the nineteenth century, as well as Marxist thought have denied to the law any constructive function and reduced it to the role of the obedient servant.

The many different trends of legal thinking can be divided into three principal types: first, there is legal philosophy proper, comprising all those theories which formulate legal ideals as the basis of a system. Second, there is analytical jurisprudence, which is essentially concerned with legal technique. Third, there are sociological theories, which are essentially concerned with the examination of the relations between legal principles and their functioning in society. These three principal trends of legal thinking have usually been in opposition to each other. Both analytical and sociological theories have opposed legal idealism, while also fighting each other. Yet each of these three principal approaches to the law is necessary. Each requires the others in order to give to the law its proper place in society.

Even the non-lawyer cannot fail to be impressed by the vital part played by legal philosophy in political developments. The ideology of natural law is generally considered to be the essential

[2] *Cf.* below, Chap. 12, especially p. 142 *et seq.*

and characteristic basis of Western civilisation.[3] The relations between God, Nature and Man; the conflicting theories of government; the standards which govern the relations between nations—are all formulated in terms of natural law. A number of the most powerful political philosophies have been put forward in the form of legal philosophies. Hobbes, Kant, Fichte and Hegel have developed their doctrines of state and their whole political ideology as legal philosophy. If these are part of a general philosophical system established by thinkers not trained in the law, there are in modern times no less important legal philosophies developed by jurists, as part of their legal teaching. Among them are Savigny's doctrine of the *Volksgeist*, a vital part of the romantic exaltation of the nation;[4] Gierke's organic theory, a forerunner to modern doctrines which claim the absolute merger of the individual in the state;[5] Ihering's doctrine, which firmly establishes the coercive power of the state as the basis of law;[6] Duguit's doctrine of social solidarity, which forms an essential basis of collectivist economic theory;[7] Hauriou's doctrine of the *institution* which prepares the way for corporate supremacy in modern France, on a Catholic basis;[8] Pashukanis's doctrine that in socialist society all law becomes merged in administration.

Nor is this vital importance of legal philosophies an accident. The complex structure of modern society and the extending machinery of government makes for organisation and the formulation of principles in terms of law. But it is vital to recognise that no legal philosophy can be anything but a formulation of political ideals through the medium of law. The attempts of so many philosophers, politicians and jurists to give their ideals the appearance of objective truth by clothing them in legal terminology have brought nothing but confusion and hypocrisy into the perpetual struggle of conflicting ideals. Legal theory formulates political ideals in terms of justice. But it cannot give a magic formula of justice which can say once and for all what is just and unjust.

Aristotle said that justice demanded the equal treatment of those equal before the law. But it remains for each political order to determine whom to treat as equal or otherwise. All legal philoso-

---

[3] *Cf.*, among others, *Troeltsch*, Append. to Barker, Gierke's *Natural Law and Theory of Society* (1934); Cobban, *The Crisis of Civilisation* (1941); Butler, *The Roots of National Socialism* (1941).

[4] See below, p. 209 *et seq.*

[5] See below, p. 236 *et seq.*

[6] See below, p. 260 *et seq.*

[7] See below, p. 229 *et seq.*

[8] See below, p. 239 *et seq.*

phies, which, in one way or another, have attempted to establish absolute ideals, reveal themselves as pure political ideologies.[9] As Radbruch[10] has said:

> All great political changes were prepared or accompanied by legal philosophies. At the beginning there was legal philosophy, at the end revolution.

Having formulated its basic principles, legal idealism can further follow up the expression of these principles in legal institutions. At the peak, there may be such principles as the inalienable rights of man, or the supremacy of the will of the people, or the will of the leader, or the duty to work for the community, or the unity of the working people of the world. Such legal ideals must be translated into more concrete principles, such as separation of powers, freedom of contract, socialisation of the means of production, or political control of the judiciary.

LEGAL IDEALISM AND THE SOCIOLOGICAL APPROACH TO LAW

At this point legal idealism needs the support of the functional or sociological approach to the law. Legal idealism left alone is dangerously theoretical. It falls an easy victim to the political purposes of skilful perverters. It is the lasting merit of the Marxist analysis to have first revealed the discrepancy between legal form and economic reality. On this basis, a number of sociological investigations have shown how the legal ideology of individual freedom and inviolability of private property has been put into the service of a systematic exploitation by the few of the many. The story of the development of natural law ideology in the hands of the American law courts has been told by Pound, Haines, Frankfurter and others. Thurman Arnold[11] has exposed the myth of corporate personality, by which a protection meant for the pioneer colonist was extended to monopolistic corporations. The realist movement has supplemented legal ideology by making use of statistics, psychology, criminology, business practice, administrative practice, etc., in order to demonstrate the working of law in

---

[9] See, *e.g.*, the discussion of the ideals of justice of Hegel and Stammler, below, pp. 164 *et seq.*, 179 *et seq.*
[10] *Rechtsphilosophie*, p. 9.
[11] Arnold, *The Folklore of Capitalism* (1937).

society.[12] The investigations, by Continental as well as American
jurists, of the ways in which judicial discretion has developed,
altered or killed legal principles laid down in constitutions or
statutes, give a corrective to the abstract approach inherent in the
formulation of general principles. The functional method must, in
fact, supplement the idealistic approach, by laying bare possible dis-
crepancies between legal ideology and social reality. Thus, Renner's
analysis of the change in the function of property[13] has shown
how the legal notion of property becomes an empty shell, while the
real function of property is exercised by complementary institutions.
Modern English and American jurists have pointed out how, under
the cover of the rule of law and of constitutional principles, the
power of bureaucracy, big business and trade unions develops and
alters the structure of the constitution. Students of banking, insurance, transport or housing law have shown how little the
principle of autonomy of will and of freedom of contract comes to
mean in the modern standard contract, in which equality of bargaining is a mere fiction, while the terms of the contract are fixed
once and for all for millions of people by the more powerfully
organised side.[14] A decision by Denning J. (as he then was) supplies
an excellent—though unfortunately rare—example of the sociological interpretation of a legal concept. A firm of builders had
challenged a compulsory purchase order made by the city of Bristol
under the Housing act of 1936 for a municipal housing scheme.
The challenge was on the ground that the Act used the formula
"Houses for the Working Classes," whereas the proposed houses
were open to members of all classes, including doctors, engineers
and salesmen. Denning J. refused to quash the order and his
reasoning included the following characteristic passage:

"Working classes" fifty years ago denoted a class which included men
working in the fields or the factories, in the docks or the mines, on the
railways or the roads, at a weekly wage. The wages of people of that

---

[12] In constitutional cases this method of presenting evidence is known as the
"Brandeis Brief." In 1908, Mr. Brandeis, who later became a justice of the
Supreme Court, appeared in a Supreme Court case *Muller* v. *Oregon*, 208 U.S.
412 (1908) to defend the validity of an Oregon statute fixing a ten-hour maximum
day for women. The legal part of Brandeis's brief covered only two pages, but
over 100 pages were devoted to evidence drawn from committee reports, statistics,
factory inspectors' reports and other material showing that long hours of work
had been proved dangerous to women's health, safety and morals. The Supreme
Court accepted this revolutionary technique, which has since become established
in constitutional cases.
[13] See below, p. 292 *et seq.*
[14] See Friedmann, *Law in a Changing Society*, Chap. 3.

class were lower than those of the other members of the community, and they were looked upon as a lower class. That has now all disappeared. The social revolution in the last fifty years has made the words "working class" quite inappropriate today. There is no such separate class as the working class. . . . Nor is there any social distinction between one or the other. No one of them is of a higher or lower class.[15]

To resolve this tension between legal ideal and social reality is a matter of legal policy. Functional analysis only prepares the way for a political decision to be made by the legislator. He may attempt to come to the rescue of the exploited individual, by abolishing abuses, for example, by anti-trust legislation. He may, on the other hand, decide to attack the power of the "over-mighty subject" of modern times by socialisation of the means of production. He may choose to protect equality of bargaining and liberty of contract by means of restrictive covenants, or by an official recognition of collective bargaining. He may decide to fight the power of administrative authorities by rigid judicial supervision (English and American system) or by a system of adminstrative tribunals (French system) or by the complete merger of all law in administration (totalitarian systems). Whatever the jurist may have to say of this he does so as a politician, not as a lawyer, though legal experience and knowledge may lend weight to the argument.

Once the choice is made, legal ideology must once more ask for the support of functional analysis, in order to ensure the adequacy of the means chosen to realise the ideal. Many legislative ideals have failed through inadequacy of means. The noble ideals of the German Republican Constitution of 1919 were frustrated, because the basis of economic, administrative, judicial and military power remained unaffected. A modern charter of the rights of men would be futile without the provision of conditions of society which make their realisation possible. In the light of experience gained by legal developments of the past, for example, the development of fundamental rights in the legal interpretation of the American, German or Soviet Constitutions, the legislator will have to consider how far an ideal such as individual liberty of contract may demand a machinery of collective bargaining, compulsory powers of state arbitration or even a socialisation of all industry. Again, the results of sociological analysis help the legislator to decide how far judicial supervision and administrative discretion are likely to help or

---

[15] *Green & Sons* v. *Minister of Health* [1948] 1 K.B. 34, 38.

hinder the furtherance of the principle adopted. The degree of latitude given to the judge in inflicting a greater or smaller penalty may be a small point in the ideology underlying a particular reform of criminal law, but it may be a decisive factor in practice. Unsympathetic magistrates may completely foil, by trifling fines, the best enactment designed to fight food profiteering. This again points to the importance of the personal element in the administration of law, to the methods of choosing judges, administrators or juries.

The legal experience of the period of the industrial revolution has taught us not the futility of ideology in the shaping of the law and thus of the conditions of society—the ultimate direction given to the law must depend on the underlying political ideology—but the fatal consequences of an ideology left unsupported by solid social foundations.

Analytical jurisprudence plays, on the whole, the part of a servant. Any modern legal system, whatever its ideology, depends for certainty, clarity and efficiency on an adequate legal technique, provided by a coherent system of concepts and classifications. Yet analytical jurisprudence has no mean part in the clarification of some vital political issues of our time. One of the principal problems before mankind is the alternative between international order and international chaos. In terms of law, it means the clarification of the hierarchical relation between national sovereignty and international legal order.[16] The choice is a political one, but legal theory can do much to help or hinder it, by a clear and consistent definition of law. The definitions of law vary according to the philosophy of their authors. Some emphasise the element of coercion, others that of usage and popular conviction. But no one will dispute that a definition, once chosen, must be consistently used. That indeed is the principal function of the analytical science of law: to develop a system logically and clearly from its foundations. A grave, and sometimes not unintended, confusion has been created by the use of the identical concept of "law" for the type of rule ordering the conduct of individuals within the modern state on one hand and that regulating the relations between the states on the other hand. While the former is characterised by a central law-making authority and the sanction of enforcement, the latter lacks both. The analytical distinction has been developed by Austin with exemplary clarity. But many important tasks remain for con-

[16] See further below, p. 574 *et seq.*

temporary analytical jurisprudence. The weaknesses of the compromises between national and international sovereignty attempted in the Covenant of the League of Nations and the United Nations Charter, the implications of the partial transfer of sovereignty attempted in the European Communities Treaties, the problem of the division of sovereignty envisaged by the federal form of government, these, among others, are vital preliminaries to a reconstruction of international life.

A particularly important part in the development of future international society will have to be played by comparative jurisprudence. Whether a new international society will develop as a world-wide community, or centre round groups of nations closely linked by military, economic and political ties, the assimilation of legal institutions is a necessary part of closer association. The intensity of legal relations expresses the degree of social cohesion achieved between different nations. It is indeed possible and necessary to classify international relations according to the extent to which they depend upon a community of social values. The preparatory work must be done by comparative jurisprudence, combining the ideological, the functional and the analytical approach. A comparison of legal ideals must form the foundation. It will reveal, for example, the impossibility of any but the most superficial relations between legal systems based on rights of man and those based on unrestricted omnipotence of the state. This was illustrated long before the war, by the withdrawal of Germany, Japan and Italy from the International Labour Conventions, their refusal to join the International Broadcasting Convention of 1937 and, in general, their refusal to submit to decisions of international tribunals. Similar difficulties have arisen, more recently, over the tripartite representation in the ILO of the U.S.S.R. and Yugoslavia, because of the alleged identity of state, employers and workers in these states. An understanding of the dependence of law on community of values leads, in contemporary international law, to a general distinction between the international law of coexistence— regulating the essentially formal diplomatic and jurisdictional relations between states—and therefore independent of their political and social structure—and the international law of cooperation, dependent upon community of values and interests, and therefore much more sensitive to internal structure.[17] The science of com-

---

[17] See for an elaboration of this distinction, Friedmann, the *Changing Structure of International Law*, Chap. 6 (1964).

parative law has hitherto been chiefly concentrated on an analytical comparison of different legal institutions, such as commercial law, family institutions or criminal law. But a comparison of codes, statutes, decisions may give a misleading impression of either affinity or diversity unless it is checked by a functional comparison.

Legal theory cannot provide a magic escape from the need for decision between alternative ideals and ways of life. But it is not condemned to the purely passive and subordinate function which both analytical positivism and early Marxist theories ascribe to it.

To formulate political ideals in terms of justice and to ascertain the means by which these ideals can be translated into social reality, through the agency of a legal order, is the vital function which legal theory must fulfil.

The reasons why the lawyer must open his eyes to the issues of legal theory may be summed up in the following four propositions:

(1) There is no escape for the law from the struggles of life. Each legal philosophy, each legal system, each judgment is necessarily related, though possibly remotely, to a political ideology. The self-sufficiency of law is an illusion. It is, to use a well-known phrase by Moltke, "a dream, but not even a beautiful one."

(2) Legal technique is always subordinate to social ideals. The technically most divergent legal systems can attain similar social ends if inspired by similar purposes; on the other hand, the closest affinity of legal technique gives no basis for harmony and co-operation where the purposes differ.

(3) The study and practice of law provides one avenue to a diagnosis of social crisis, no less so than any other social science Consequently the lawyer, not only the legislator, is just as much concerned with social change as the politician, the economist, the sociologist, or the preacher. It follows that there is no reason why the lawyer should not play a leading part in social reform. Among the great social reformers of history there have not been many lawyers (although exasperated lawyers, like Bentham, have sometimes turned into ardent reformers). But only a misunderstanding of the function of the law can disable the lawyer from taking his part in the evolution of society. In the first place, the lawyer may discover that the law as it stands is inadequate to fulfil the legislative or social ideals which inspire it. Thus, both English and American law of today are inspired by the ideal of freedom of contract. A minority of American judges saw that the transformation of the United States from a state of pioneer farmers to a state

of large-scale industry meant a re-interpretation of this ideal in contracts, executive and legislative measures. English judges have seen that at some point freedom of contract may become a travesty of freedom and have accordingly adjusted the law of restraint of trade and of the employer's duties towards employees; but they have not yet adapted freedom of contract to the standardised conditions of modern mass employment, and a legal doctrine of collective bargaining hardly yet exists. In the second place, the lawyer has ample opportunity to assist social progress by developing and interpreting a widely framed legal principle in accordance with changing conditions. Thus, "a reasonable and fair price," or a "fair and equitable" restitution means nothing, except in conjunction with the social conditions of the time. Finally, the lawyer, whether as legislator, judge, advocate or administrator, may discover, through his particular way of contact with social reality, that a law fails to achieve its ostensible social purpose and brings misery instead of welfare. It may be the law of blackmail, or of defamation, or of divorce. When that happens the lawyer can and often does draw the legislator's attention to the need for a change in the law.[19] An even wider function devolves on the lawyer in the planning and regulation of the process of transition from static and primitive, to evolving and diversified economies that characterises the many new developing societies.[20]

(4) The respective shares of legislator and practical lawyer in the evolution of society through law are, however, determined both by the political structure of society and by the extent to which the legislative machinery can satisfy the need for social change.[21] The dependence of judicial creativeness on the political function of law is discussed in a later chapter.[22] Recent developments in Great Britain for example indicate that the courts vacillate between a desire to take an active share in social evolution, through an elastic interpretation of precedent, a socially conscious and helpful interpretation of statutes, or the use of general principles of equity and public policy, and a tendency to judicial aloofness from social reform, as a reaction to increased legislative activity. Differences in

---

[19] For example, see the observations of MacKinnon L.J. in *Speed* v. *Thomas Swift & Co.* [1943] 1 All E.R. 539, on the doctrine of common employment (since abolished).

[20] See further below, p. 429 *et seq.*

[21] This is discussed in far greater detail in *Law in a Changing Society*, Chap. 1.

[22] See below, p. 440 *et seq.*

judicial temperament add another element of uncertainty.[23] There remains, beside, the increasingly vast and complex task of statutory interpretation, through law courts, administrative tribunals and other agencies. The interaction of legislator and the various law-applying agencies is even more complex in federal systems. In such countries as Australia, Canada, India, West Germany and the United States, the highest constitutional court has an arbitral function which is also to a high degree law-making. As the years go by, the constitutions of these states are less and less understandable in terms of the text rather than of successive interpretations. Almost any political issue becomes also a legal issue, and vice versa, the lawyer has, through his interpretation, a major influence on the balance of power between federation and states, and on the very structure of the federal system.

The share of the law in social evolution is thus a matter for constant re-examination, in the light of changing political, social and legislative conditions. But two general conclusions emerge:

First, the creative function of the lawyer in the social process shifts from a primary, law-making, to an ancillary, supporting role, as modern states develop from mainly passive and protective into active instruments of social service, and legislative articulateness increases accordingly.

Secondly, the lawyer cannot afford to isolate himself from the social process. His independence can never be more than relative, and it is only a clear awareness of the political, social and constitutional foundations of his function in general as well as of particular legal problems that enables him to find the proper balance between stability and progress.

[23] See, for a detailed discussion below, p. 463 *et seq.*

Chapter 6

THE PRINCIPAL ANTINOMIES
IN LEGAL THEORY

LEGAL theory stands between philosophy and political theory. It therefore is dominated by the same antinomies.

Legal theory takes its intellectual categories from philosophy, its ideas of justice from political theory. Its own specific contribution consists in formulating political ideas in terms of legal principles. The specific terminology of law has at times obscured this position of legal theory and created an illusion of self-sufficiency.

"What is the purpose of life?" is the fundamental question to be answered by legal theory as by philosophy, political theory, ethics, religion.

In the many endeavours to give an answer the principal movements in legal thought veer between certain fundamental values of life. Western civilisation at any rate has hitherto been unable to agree even theoretically on the ultimate values and purposes of life. So persistently has the pendulum swung backwards and forwards between certain antinomic values that we cannot but register a tension which perpetually produces new efforts and a search for harmony.

With some diffidence a brief classification of the principal antinomies in legal theories may be attempted. Each legal theory, while perhaps indifferent to some of them, has taken a stand in regard to others. Jurists bitterly opposed to each other on one issue might stand together on another.

It follows from the position of legal theory between philosophy and political theory that the issues concern in part philosophical, and in part political, controversy.

INDIVIDUAL AND UNIVERSE

Legal theory reflects the fundamental philosophical controversy

---

* Some readers may prefer to read this chapter as a conclusion rather than an introduction to the discussion of legal theories.

whether the universe is an intellectual creation of the ego or the ego a particle in the universal order of things. Natural law theories of all kinds have placed an objective order of things above the individual. This is true of the old Greek philosophers, who first discovered an order of things outside man, of scholastic and of rationalist natural law theory. Aristotle sees man in his dual character as part of nature and distinct from nature as a reasonable being. But man is still part of the universal order of things.

The intellectual priority of the ego over the world, first established in modern philosophy by Descartes: *"Cogito, ergo sum,"* is developed by Kant, who establishes the individual as the creator of the intelligible world of phenomena. It is continued by Fichte's apprehension of the world as the result of the self-consciousness of the individual. Hegel's projection of the individual into the universe prepares the way for the supremacy of will which his own philosophy still disguises, but which modern Fascist philosophy brings out uncompromisingly.

VOLUNTARISM AND OBJECTIVE KNOWLEDGE

It is an issue intimately connected with the first, whether will directs knowledge or knowledge directs will. This question determines the further question whether objective values are possible or whether will creates its valuations. The extreme opposites are represented by the philosophies of St. Thomas Aquinas and Nietzsche. For St. Thomas, will is necessarily determined by the knowledge of good. For Nietzsche, all knowledge is a technique used in the service of the will to power.[1] Between these extremes every philosopher has faced the problem. For legal philosophy it has become articulate through the attempts of Neo-Kantian jurists to establish an objective legal science, uncontaminated by political ideals. For Kelsen, every legal ideology is the expression of subjective will. "The manner in which, in the realm of knowledge, the subject is seized by the object, is, for a more profound analysis, very much like the question of domination which is the theme of politics. In either case, there is an implacable antagonism between a limited number of problems and their solution."[2]

It is going too far, however, to say that every legal ideology must go together with a subjective outlook on the world. Where, as in

---

[1] Nietzsche, *Der Wille zur Macht.*
[2] Kelsen, *Staatsform und Weltanschauung.* 7.

the philosophy of the schoolmen or the rationalists, knowledge comprises ethical values such as the truth and the good, the objective legal order can be given a metaphysical basis. Thus the natural law ideas of the schoolmen can be derived from the divine order of things, and those of the rationalists from the principles of reason. Where, on the other hand, knowledge is restricted to an intellectual apperception of the world, an objective legal order can be no more than a formal legal science such as Kelsen's pure theory of law.

In Kant's own philosophy, the domain of will is practical reason, the domain of knowledge is pure reason. Ethical and legal ideals are therefore a matter of will, not of thought, although the categorical imperative attempts to give them an absolute direction.

Hegel has attempted to overcome the dualism of will and knowledge, as he has denied any dualism. But his legal philosophy establishes in fact the supremacy of the will of the state.[3]

Relativist legal philosophy as developed by Jellinek[4] and in particular by Radbruch,[5] on the other hand, acknowledges the subjective character of legal ideologies by stating the principal ideological issues and leaving the choice between them to individual decision, that is to will.

Intellect and Intuition

Time and again belief in the power of reason has been followed by distrust of reason and corresponding faith in instinct. Intellect is pitched against intuition, reflection against life. In philosophy, the rationalism of the eighteenth and the positivism of the nineteenth century analysing life and thinking intellectually, according to the principle of causality, have been followed by a widespread revolution. Its battle cry is instinct rather than intellect, the inner meaning of things rather than their intellectual classification, the totality of life in its meaning and value rather than the analysis of individual phenomena according to cause and effect.

Schopenhauer's antithesis of *Wille* (will) and *Vorstellung* (apperception), the phenomenology of Scheler, and the vitalism of Driesch, Bergson, Klages, the study of the specific methods and purposes of *Geisteswissenschaften* by Dilthey and others all take part in that

---

[3] Hegel, *Philosophie des Rechts*, 257.
[4] Jellinek, *Allgemeine Staatslehre* (1905).
[5] Radbruch, *Rechtsphilosophie* (3rd ed., 1932).

revolt which is but a sophisticated return to a more elementary state in the relations between man and universe.

Legal theory shows a corresponding cyclical movement. The "charismatic" law finder of primitive communities[6] finds the law intuitively. Plato's philosopher-king knows and applies justice because the balance and harmony of his personality give him insight and virtue. Systematisation of the law goes parallel with a more rational attitude. When a disappointed generation, dissatisfied with the self-complacency of positivism, becomes doubtful about the power of reason, instinct and intuition come again to the fore. The *Freirechtslehre* of the early twentieth century, tired of purely analytical and logical interpretation of codes and statutes, invokes the free unfettered discretion of the judge, his feeling of right and wrong, as a true guide to justice. The Dutch jurist Krabbe appeals to the *Rechtsbewusstsein* in order to limit the unfettered legislative sovereignty of the state. The Russian Petrazhitsky opposes a variable and subjective "intuitive" law to an objective, patternised and intellectually ascertainable "positive" law. Del Vecchio establishes a theory of juristic sentiment of right as being able to "weigh" specific grades of truth.[7] More recently, Edmond Cahn has written of the "sense of injustice" as the motive force which, concretised in specific demands for equality, desert, "human dignity, conscientious adjudication, confinement of government to its proper function, and fulfilment of common expectations"—drives the law forward.[8] The most elaborate application of the philosophical issue between instinct and reason to legal theory is contained in Gény's system.[9] Gény, who is a follower of Bergson, allocates the principles of reason to the facts of law (*donnés*). These facts of law are the object of intellectual perception, while juristic action moulds these facts in accordance with the needs of life through a creative intuition equipped with legal technique. The most elaborate attempt to bridge the antinomy between intellect and instinct is that of the phenomenologists, who merge intuition and understanding in the "immediate" apprehension of the object (Husserl, Scheler, Hartmann). From this, jurists have derived certain values as objectively inherent in legal institutions.[10]

---

[6] *Cf.* M. Weber, "Rechtssoziologie," in *Grundriss des Sozialoekonomik.* Below, p. 245 *et seq.*

[7] Del Vecchio, *Il sentimento giuridico* (2nd ed., 1908).

[8] *The Sense of Injustice* (1949).

[9] Gény, *Science et Technique en Droit Privé Positif*, 4 vols. (1914-24). See below, p. 328 *et seq.*

[10] See below, p. 203 *et seq.*

STABILITY AND CHANGE

Law must be stable and yet it cannot stand still. Hence all thinking about law has struggled to reconcile the conflicting demands of the need of stability and of the need of change.[11]

In these words Roscoe Pound has summarised another of the perpetual antinomies which the tension between law and life creates.[12]

Legal theory reflects the struggle of law between tradition and progress, stability and change, certainty and flexibility. In so far as the object of law is to establish order, it emphasises the need for stability and certainty. On the whole, legal theories and lawyers are inclined to stress stability rather than change. Kelsen has suspected all natural law theories of being a device for strengthening existing authorities and suppressing change.[13] Max Weber, on the other hand, has stressed the revolutionary aspect of certain natural law ideologies.[14] In fact, natural law theories have served reaction as well as revolution.

The scholastic theory of natural law stands out as the most comprehensive attempt to stabilise the existing order of things by anchoring it in the divine order acting through natural law. The same theoretical foundation makes modern scholastic natural law philosophers, like Le Fur and Cathrein, oppose socialist revolution. From a different angle, Savigny's historical school opposes legal change. For this school the task of a jurist and the legislator is to verify and formulate existing legal customs; the function of law is essentially to stabilise, not to be an agent of progress. Analytical positivism, by its emphasis on logic and obedience to written law,

---

[11] *Interpretations of Legal History, op. cit.* 1.

[12] Mephistopheles, in Goethe's *Faust*, speaks on the same problem in more vigorous terms:
"All rights and laws are still transmitted
Like an eternal sickness of the race,—
From generation unto generation fitted,
And shifted round from place to place.
Reason becomes a sham, Benificence a worry:
Thou art a grandchild, therefore woe to thee!
The right is born with us, ours in verity,
This to consider, there's alas! no hurry."
Dialogue between Mephistopheles and the Student, Scene IV Faust, (Modern Library Ed., B. Taylor trans. 1950).

[13] Kelsen, *Naturrechtslehre und Rechtspositivismus* (1928). On the conflict of conservative and progressive trends in law, see also Virally, *La Pensée Juridique*, 22 (1960).

[14] Welser, *Rechtssoziologie* (rev. ed. 1960).

tends to regard stability and certainty as the paramount objects of legal interpretation. On the other hand, all utilitarian and socio-logical theories tend to emphasise the changing content of law because they see it against its social background and the needs of life. The ways to attain pleasure and avoid pain change with social circumstances, so the law must change with them. Bentham, there-fore, was an ardent legal reformer. Ihering rejects the idea of a universal law for all nations and times as being "no better than that medical treatment should be the same for all patients."[15] Duguit's social solidarity implies that the needs of the community, which it is the absolute duty of the individual to obey, change with social circumstances. Again, all those theories which see the task of law in a balancing of conflicting interests, consider the interests themselves as changing according to time and circumstances. The respective claims of employers and employees, of landlords and tenants, etc., change as the life and organisation of the community change and the law must be elastic and create a just balance in accordance with the social needs and ideals prevailing at the time. This is well expressed in Pound's formula of "Social Engineering." Modern totalitarian theories, no less than Marxist legal theory, make the law changeable at will by making it entirely dependent on outside agencies and depriving it of any autonomy. In order to facilitate legal change, the constitutional machinery of totalitarian states makes legal change as swift and unencumbered as possible.

By way of contrast the complex machinery of the American Constitution is designed to keep legal change within bounds, although the extent to which this is done largely depends on the spirit in which the courts interpret the fundamental clauses. Tech-nically, a written constitution tends to stabilise law, while a machinery like that of the British constitutional system and even more that of totalitarian states, facilitates legal change. Technique, however, is always subordinate to the mind which directs it. The ultimate legal ideals decide the use to which the machinery is to be put.

POSITIVISM AND IDEALISM

Legal theories again follow an elementary antagonism in philo-sophical thought by being either positivist or metaphysical. The

---

[15] Ihering, *Law as a Means to an End*, 328 (1913).

opposition between idealism and materialism, although not identical, runs on closely parallel lines. Idealistic legal theories deduce the law from first principles based on man as an ethical and rational being. Positivistic legal theories consider law as necessarily determined by the subject-matter.

The two principal types of positivism in legal theory are "analytical" and "functional," or "pragmatic" positivism. The former takes the basic legal norms—as set by the legislator—as given and concentrates on the analysis of legal concepts and relations on the basis of a strict division of "is" and "ought." The latter regards social facts as determining legal concepts. An extreme form of social realism is Marxism, which regards all law as a "superstructure" determined by the economic substratum, *i.e.,* the ownership of the means of production.

Some professedly materialistic legal theories are, in fact, idealistic, deducing legal rules from *a priori* principles. Thus, Duguit is an idealist disguised as a materialist, an empiricist by profession, an *a priori* philosopher at heart. His "social solidarity," alleged to be an observable fact, is in reality a modern natural law idea. Similarly, Spencer's legal theory, put forward as an application of his biological positivism, is in fact the expression of metaphysical principles, namely, the belief in the evolution of man towards greater freedom through industrial organisation.

The struggle never ceases. Tired of ideals and abstractions, man turns towards concreteness and positive fact, towards action and power. Disillusioned he turns back again to ideals and metaphysical principles.

COLLECTIVISM AND INDIVIDUALISM

Every ideal of justice must be taken from political theory. The fundamental controversy of political thought in the history of Western civilisation has been that between collectivist and individualist ideals. Whether the individual or the community is the ultimate value, is a problem which was studied in all its principal aspects by Greek philosophers. To the issues as formulated by Plato, Aristotle and the Stoics thousands of years have added an infinite number of illustrations and variations but little that is essentially new; nor has the task, which confronted philosophers, jurists and politicians alike, of resolving the conflict by a harmonisation of the claims of individual and community, been solved.

Legal theories assume one of three attitudes: Either they subordinate the individual to the community, or they subordinate the community to the individual, or they attempt to blend the two rival claims.

(1) Seldom has the supremacy of the community over the individual been more radically formulated than by Plato. In the *Republic* that supremacy is so marked that there is not only no room for private rights but not even any for private institutions such as family and property. In the *Laws,* the work of his old age, these institutions are recognised, but are still under strict state supervision. It is mainly the cultural background of Greek civilisation and education which distinguishes Plato's ideal state from that of modern totalitarian systems of government.

The Greek conception of life is inseparable from the development of personality, whereas modern totalitarianism asserts the supremacy of the community by the complete destruction of individual rights. This is achieved through the abolition of the separation of powers and judicial independence, the overriding competence of a secret police, state supervision of all public and private activities, and a strict machinery of political control.

In a different manner, the Catholic theory of society makes the community supreme over the individual. He has to accept the place and function into which he is born. Authority over him is divided between Church and state, but the Church is supreme as the authoritative interpreter of divine and natural law. For the divine order of things, the modern scholastic Duguit substitutes the social discipline of modern industrial society. To this society the individual owes absolute service and obedience. There is no room left for private rights. The form of community, which is thus extolled, is not the state, but the social group, which forms the most effective unit in the organisation of social solidarity through division of labour.

(2) The Stoics first developed a coherent legal philosophy based upon the individual as a reasonable being detached from the community in which he lives. Apart from the partial application of this philosophy under the Antonine Emperors, individualistic legal philosophy reappears only with the doctrine of inalienable rights.

Hobbes must be classed with the individualists, although his doctrine leads to political absolutism. Individualism is the clear basis of Locke's political and legal theory. It is put on a new basis in Kant's moral and legal philosophy. The individualism of Kant and the early Fichte underlies the legal philosophy of their disciples, Stammler and the young Del Vecchio. Bentham's utilitarianism, Spencer's theory of evolution, Gény's *donné rationnel*, all embody in different ways an individualistic philosophy. The most powerful expression of an individualist philosophy of law is the American Constitution.

(3) The purpose of Hegel's legal philosophy is the combination of the idea of individual autonomy with the superior power of the community, which for him is expressed in the state. As Hegel professes to overcome the dualism of thought and will, of matter and idea, so he seeks to abolish the dualism of individual and state. But the apparent solution is a delusion. Hegel's individual must will the state or else his will is not considered as rational. He is not armed with individual rights which he can put against the will of the state; the latter, Hegel imagines, will always protect individual liberty. Hegel has disguised, not overcome, the choice between alternatives. No wonder that the path leads straight to the unmitigated glorification of state and community by Neo-Hegelians. Del Vecchio's synthesis is no more successful. He does not admit the definite break between his earlier Kantian ideals, dominated by the autonomy of the individual as the goal of legal development,[16] and his later Hegelian ideology, which praises the Fascist state.[17]

The nearest approach to a genuine synthesis of individual autonomy and the needs of the community is perhaps the legal philosophy of the younger Fichte. Individual liberty, the basis of that philosophy, is considered in the framework of the social and economic life of the community. More recently, Radbruch has developed similar ideas as the principal features of a democratic-socialist legal philosophy.

The subordination of the individual to the collective can be theoretically justified by Marxism—at least for the revolutionary phase, which can be indefinitely prolonged. Such individual rights as are laid down in the Soviet Constitution of 1936 are not capable of legal enforcement. The more recent British experiment in partial socialisation, on the other hand, is based on the principle of preservation of essential individual freedoms, and attempts to blend it with superior claims of the community to economic and social services.

[16] Del Vecchio, *Formal Bases of Law* (trans. Lisle, 1921).
[17] Del Vecchio, *Justice, Droit, Etat* (1938). See further, below, p. 189.

It is because conflict in the world of politics that legal philosophers, according to their sympathies, put community or individual first. But the solution of the conflict is less a problem of legal theory than of human conduct.

DEMOCRACY AND AUTOCRACY

Legal theories seldom fail to come down on the side of either democratic or autocratic principles of government. The choice is usually, but not necessarily, parallel with that between individualist and collective principles. If democracy and individualism are, in the struggles of our own days, usually ranged together against autocracy and collectivist ideas, this is mainly due to the historical association of those ideas, especially in the rise of the middle class, but not to theoretical necessity. The theories of both Locke and Rousseau suffer from their failure to explain how the supreme right of the majority can go together with the inalienable rights of the individual. The same conflict is clearly illustrated in American legal development, where the judiciary has backed individual rights, often against the will of the majority expressed through legislation. Hobbes' individualism is associated with absolutism; on the other hand, Duguit's collectivism is also strongly autocratic, as it subjects governors and governed alike to an objective principle. It is possible to affirm individual rights without vesting political control in the people. Social developments may demand a form of government different from parliamentary democracy without touching the issue of individual development or omnipotence of the community as the goal of political life. An oligarchy of rulers, for example, may be chosen from the community on the basis of full and equal education for all.

NATIONALISM AND INTERNATIONALISM

Individualist legal theories are often cosmopolitan, collectivist theories nationalist, but again the connection is not a necessary one. Historically the assertion of natural rights has often been linked with a revolt against state, authority and a humanitarian belief in the equality and dignity of all men. This is true of the legal philosophy of the Stoics or of Kant. The ideal of equality of men often causes democrats to be internationalists. On the other side the principal exponents of collectivist ideals, like Fichte, Hegel,

Binder, have been nationalists who glorify the national state. But this need not be so. Hegel's essentially anti-individualistic legal philosophy would not have been affected if it had continued the dialectic development from the state to an international league of states or some other international organisation. On the other hand, the scholastic conception of society, while anti-individualistic and authoritarian, is an international one. In present-day schemes of future international society, the supremacy of some international authority is often combined with collectivist features. Politically, the issue between nationalism and internationalism is one of clashing political ideals. Juristically, however, it is merely a question of the entity to which legal sovereignty is to be attributed.

PART TWO

A CRITICAL SURVEY OF LEGAL THEORIES

Section One

Natural Law and the Search for Absolute Values

CHAPTER 7

THE PROBLEM OF NATURAL LAW

THE history of natural law is a tale of the search of mankind for absolute justice and of its failure. Again and again, in the course of the last 2,500 years, the idea of natural law has appeared, in some form or other, as an expression of the search for an ideal higher than positive law after having been rejected and derided in the interval. With changing social and political conditions the notions about natural law have changed. The only thing that has remained constant is the appeal to something higher than positive law. The object of that appeal has been as often the justification of existing authority as a revolt against it.

Natural law has fulfilled many functions. It has been the principal instrument in the transformation of the old civil law of the Romans into a broad and cosmopolitan system; it has been a weapon used by both sides in the fight between the medieval Church and the German emperors; in its name the validity of international law has been asserted, and the appeal for freedom of the individual against absolutism launched. Again it was by appeal to principles of natural law that American judges, professing to interpret the Constitution, resisted the attempt of state legislation to modify and restrict the unfettered economic freedom of the individual.

It would be simple to dismiss the whole idea of natural law as a hypocritical disguise for concrete political aspirations and no doubt it has sometimes exercised little more than this function. But there is infinitely more in it.[1] Natural law has been the chief though not the only way to formulate ideals and aspirations of various peoples and generations with reference to the principal moving forces of the time. When the social structure itself becomes rigid and absolute, as at the time of the Schoolmen, the ideal too will take a static and absolute content. At other times, as with most modern natural law theories, natural law ideals become relative or merely formal,

[1] See Virally, *La Pensée Juridique*, 76 *et seq.*, especially 84-87 (1960).

95

expressing little more than the yearning of a generation which is dissatisfied with itself and the world, which seeks something higher, but is conscious of the relativity of values. It is as easy to deride natural law as it is to deride the futility of mankind's social and political life in general, in its unceasing but hitherto vain search for a way out of the injustice and imperfection for which Western civilisation has found no other solution but to move from one extreme to another.

The appeal to some absolute ideal finds a response in men, particularly at a time of disillusionment and doubt, and in times of simmering revolt. Therefore natural law theories, far from being theoretical speculations, have often heralded powerful political and legal developments.

Many distinctions of natural law theories are possible, depending on the criterion adopted.[2] They may be divided into authoritarian and individualistic, into progressive and conservative, into religious and rationalistic, into absolute and relativist theories. For a juristic consideration the most important distinction would appear to be that between natural law as a higher law, which invalidates any inconsistent positive law, and natural law as an ideal to which positive law ought to conform without its legal validity being affected. Broadly speaking, ancient and medieval law theories are of the first type, modern natural law theories of the second. This change coincides on the whole with the rise of the modern state and its claim to absolute sovereignty.

Natural law has, at different times, been used to support almost any ideology; but the most important and lasting theories of natural law have undoubtedly been inspired by the two ideas, of a universal order governing all men, and of the inalienable rights of the individual. When used in the service of either of these ideas, natural law has formed an organic and essential part in a hierarchy of legal values. As the basis of an international order, it has, in a continuous line of development, inspired the Stoics, Roman jurisprudence and philosophy, the Fathers of the Church, the legal order of medieval Western society and Grotius' system of International Law. Through the theories of Locke and Paine, it has provided the foundation for the individualist philosophy of the American and other modern constitutions. The growing supremacy of the national state, on the

---

[2] The many different meanings of "nature" and their relation to different concepts of natural law have recently been analysed by Erik Wolf, *Das Problem der Naturrechtslehre* (1955).

one hand, and the growth of collective discipline on the other, have not favoured natural law ideology, nor has an effective combination of these two main trends of natural law thinking been as yet achieved. This remains a challenge to be taken up by a society which would combine an effective international legal order with the protection of individual rights.

At the same time, closer social and legal organisation means an increasing measure of incorporation of natural law principles into positive law. The natural law principle of scholastic philosophy became the highest positive law within the Church; the natural law ideas of Locke and Paine became the highest positive law of the United States through their incorporation in the Bill of Rights of the Constitution. Moreover, the general clauses of the Constitution came to be interpreted in the light of natural law principles which thus became part of positive law.

The interlocking of an unwritten higher law and "posited" fundamental principles becomes particularly complex when certain principles of a written constitution are held to be higher in rank than other parts of the same constitution. In a basic decision of 1953, the West German Constitutional Court held that the principle of separation of powers and the principles governing the relations between husband and wife on the basis of general equality were "suprapositive" ("uebergesetzliche") principles governing the Constitution, and could be declared by the Constitutional Court to invalidate a "simple" constitutional norm.[3] Again, the modern controversy between theories of national and international sovereignty reduces itself juridically to an endeavour to transform certain natural law principles binding all nations into positive law. If and when the whole of mankind becomes legally organised, certain principles described by Grotius and others as natural law, and today described by more modest names such as "general principles of law," will become the foundation of the highest positive law emanating from the international sovereign.

[3] BGZ vol. II, Appendix, p. 34 *et seq.*

CHAPTER 8

ANCIENT THEORIES

THE conception of natural law as an order which commands human respect, becomes possible only when man becomes conscious of his position in the universe, when law is no longer just a part of magic or religious rites, but emerges as a separate concept.

GREEK THEORIES OF NATURAL JUSTICE

Greek thinkers laid the basis for natural law and developed its essential features. First among its forerunners is Heraclitus. Trying to find the essence of being, Heraclitus found it in the rhythm of events. This he called destiny ($\epsilon\iota\mu\alpha\rho\mu\epsilon\nu\eta$), order ($\delta\iota\kappa\eta$), and reason ($\lambda o\gamma os$) of the world. Here, for the first time, nature is not just substance, but a relation, an order of things. This provided the basis for the Greek school of enlightenment (Sophists). The movement developed in the fifth century B.C. when the high state of political, social and spiritual development of the Greek city states and the resulting problems of political and social life forced upon thinking people a reflection on law and order. Laws changed frequently in the democratic republic, and the human and changing elements behind the laws became visible. Philosophers began to think about the reason for and validity of laws. At such a point the conception of nature, as an order of things, could be utilised. With a generation sceptical of itself, weary of the arbitrariness of human government, conscious of oppression and injustice, nature came to be opposed to the tyranny of men. $\Phi\nu\sigma\iota s$ is opposed to $\nu o\mu os$ or $\theta\epsilon\sigma\iota s$. In Sophocles' *Antigone,* natural "divine" law is opposed to written law. The former is wise, the latter arbitrary. From this arise demands for justice which anticipate the principal demands for social justice, raised and disregarded again and again in modern history. Nature demands equality for all, and from this spring demands for the abolition of privileges and slavery and for equality of possession.[1] Nature for the Sophists is still something external, outside man; the order of things which embodies reason. Aristotle, whose *Logic* prepared the decisive change in the conception of natural law adopted by the Stoics substantially adhered to their point of view, in his ideas on natural law. In his *Nichomachean Ethics* he distinguishes between natural and legal or conventional justice. "Natural justice is that which everywhere has the same force and does not exist by the people thinking this or that. Legal justice is that which is originally indifferent but when it has been laid down is not indifferent; *e.g.*, that a prisoner's ransom shall be a mina or that a goat and not two sheep shall be sacrificed and again all the laws that are passed for particular cases."[2]

With the Stoics, over a century later, nature and the law of nature have assumed a very different meaning. Nature is now not only the order of things, but also man's reason; it is not only outside but at the same time inside him. Man's reason is now part of nature. This decisive change had become possible through the revolution in thinking which Socrates, Plato and Aristotle brought about in the ancient world and which, especially in the form given to it by Aristotle, has remained the basis of practically all subsequent philosophy. Socrates had found that man's intelligence and insight were the measure of the good and it was this insight which tested the reason and goodness of laws.

Aristotle, in his *Logic*, sees the world as a totality comprising the whole of nature. Man is part of nature in a twofold sense: on the one hand he is part of matter, part of the creatures of God and as such he partakes of experience; but man is also endowed with active reason which distinguishes him from all other parts of nature. As such he is capable of forming his will in accordance with the insight of his reason. This doctrine of Aristotle has inspired philosophers throughout the history of Western civilisation. Such differing thinkers as Kant, Hegel, Kelsen, Del Vecchio, Stammler, and also Ihering and Mill have based their legal theories on this Aristotelean thesis. It is this recognition of human reason as part of nature which provided the basis for the Stoic conception of the law of nature. The Stoics developed this principle into an ethical one. Reason governs the universe in all its parts. Thus man, a part of universal nature, is governed by reason. Reason orders his

---

[1] Lykophron, Alkidamos, Phaleas, Hippodamos and others. *Cf.* Windelband, *Geschichte der Philosophie*, 62.
[2] Book 5, Chap. 7, 1134b.

faculties in such a way that he can fulfil his true nature. When man, who is destined to be a social being and citizen, lives according to reason, he lives "naturally." The law of nature thus becomes identified with a moral duty.

The duality of the concept of natural law—as a way of life common to all creatures, such as the laws of reproduction on the one hand and, as a body of principles of conduct accessible only to man as a higher being uniquely endowed with reason and the capacity to distinguish between good and evil on the other—has continued to plague the philosophy of natural law throughout its long history.[3] Thus a passage in the most celebrated of the classical Roman jurists,[4] *Jus naturale est quod natura omnia animalia docuit,* suggests the wider, biological conception of natural law. This passage, though regarded as not very important by both Pollock[5] and Bryce,[6] exercised a considerable influence upon medieval writers who understood *jus naturale* as comprising the lowest type of rule—common to all animals. While, from the Stoics onward, the alternative or "spiritual" concept of natural law as the embodiment of higher reason and the guide to moral conduct undoubtedly displaced the biological interpretation, the dilemma of the duality broke through again in such acutely controversial questions as the legitimacy of artificial insemination. In the unconditional condemnation by the Catholic Church of artificial insemination, even between husband and wife,[7] a description of artificial insemination as a process which would convert the "sanctuary of the family into a biological laboratory" recalls Ulpian's formulation and a, perhaps unintended, return to the biological concept of natural law.

To the Stoics the postulates of reason are of universal force. They are binding on all men everywhere. From this the Stoics develop the first great cosmopolitan philosophy of Western thought. Men are endowed with reason, irrespective of nationality and race. The difference of city states, of Greek and barbarian, is rejected, and a universal world-state postulated in which men live as equals. The Stoics couple this ideal with a distinction between absolute and relative ideals of natural law. In the golden age of absolute

---

[3] See Fechner, *Rechtsphilosophie*, 179 *et seq.* (1957).
[4] Ulpian (Digest I, 1).
[5] Pollock, *Essays in the Law*, 36 *et seq.* (1922).
[6] Pollock, *Essays in Jurisprudence and History*, 150 (1882).
[7] See the address given by Pope Pius XII on October 29, 1951, to the Congress of Italian Catholic Midwives, see further below, p. 391.

natural law there was neither family nor slavery nor property nor government. But all these institutions became necessary with the moral deterioration of mankind. "Relative" natural law demands, from the legislators, laws which, guided by reason, approximate as closely as possible to absolute natural law.

NATURAL LAW AND ROMAN JURISPRUDENCE

It was not given to the Greek philosophers to see their philosophy turned to practical account. Alexander's empire, had it lasted, might well have found in this conception of natural law the foundation of a common law for orient and occident. Centuries later, the practical genius of Roman jurisprudence used this conception of nature based on reason to transform a rigid system into a cosmopolitan one fit to rule the world. Long before natural law became a part of philosophical and juristic teaching, the practical lawyers, who in Rome and in many parts of the empire had to administer the law to hundreds of non-Roman peoples and tribes living under different customs, had turned the idea of natural law to practical account. The ancient idea of citizenship made it impossible to apply Roman civil law to foreigners. Nor could Roman magistrates apply foreign laws as such. But they could take, from the material supplied by foreign laws and customs, those which appeared capable of general application, such as maritime and other commercial usages, greatly developed among the seafaring people on the Mediterranean, and they could mould them into general legal principles. Roman magistrates developed these general principles of justice and reason empirically from case to case, not by deduction from any general idea. What they created was not directly a body of natural law principles, but the *jus gentium* as the embodiment of the law and usages observed among different peoples, and representing general good sense. Gradually not only the sphere of application, but the meaning of *jus gentium* widened. It was described as *jus quod apud omnes populos peraeque custoditur* (Just. I, 1), and finally as *jus quod naturalis ratio constituit* (Dig. XII, I, 1).[8]

---

[8] As Jolowicz points out (*Historical Introduction to Roman Law*, 103 *et seq.* [1939]) this "theoretical" sense of *jus gentium*, as being law common to all peoples, is closer to natural law than the "practical" sense, as understood by Roman jurists. In the latter sense it means only "that part of the law which we apply to both ourselves and to foreigners." Even in its theoretical sense *jus gentium* and *jus naturale* did not become fully identified. Slavery was the principal point of difference.

The creative period as usual precedes the philosophical period. After the *jus naturale* has exercised its creative function through the agency of *jus gentium* it became explicit when, at a later period, Stoic philosophy was received by a civilised and disillusioned generation which dictators had ousted from politics, and which found its refuge in philosophy. Natural law, apart from transforming the old *jus civile*, now created the basis on which Roman and foreign people could live together under a common rule of law. Under the emperor Caracalla (A.D. 212-217) Roman citizenship was extended to all but a very few classes of people living in the empire. Civil law and *jus gentium* became one. But as slaves remained excluded, both still fell short of the ideal of *jus naturale*.

At no other period has the ideal of natural law exercised as creative and constructive an influence. The only parallel is perhaps the development of the English Law Merchant in the eighteenth century. The law of persons, of things, of obligation were all profoundly modified. The emancipation of slaves, the definition of things which could not be the object of private property (sea and air), the development of family relations, the children's right of succession, above all the various actions for restitution of unjust benefit (with the possible exception of the *condictiones*), all these were based on natural law, mostly through the medium of *jus gentium*.

Was *jus naturale* for the Romans a higher law by which the validity of positive law was measured? For Cicero it emphatically has that function: "It is not allowable to alter this law nor deviate from it, nor can it be abrogated. Nor can we be released from this law, either by the Senate or by the people."[9]

Theories on this question were, however, not much indulged in by Roman jurists. Roman legal development, as later English legal development, was a gradual adaptation to new needs and the infiltration of new ideas through practical experiment. The development occurred through the judicial process. Judges and magistrates introduced new conceptions, when necessary, by reference to such notions as *justum, aequum et bonum, natura*. Moreover, through being part of *jus gentium*, most natural law precepts were part of positive law. On the whole, the problem of *jus naturale* as a higher law invalidating incompatible positive law did not trouble Roman lawyers much since there was no conflict of law-giving authorities

---

[9] *De Re Publica*, Book 3, 22.

as there was later. A primitive and strict legal system was transformed into a highly refined and flexible one. *Jus naturale* "expresses a tendency in the trend of legal thought, a ferment operating all over the law."[10]

Thus slavery, though contrary to natural law, was not an illegal status, but under the influence of *jus naturale* and *aequitas* it was gradually modified.

[10] Buckland, *Textbook of Roman Law*, 55.

CHAPTER 9

THE MIDDLE AGES

FOUNDATION OF MEDIEVAL, POLITICAL AND LEGAL THOUGHT

DURING the dark and long period between the collapse of ancient civilisation and the emergence of the medieval order, the Fathers of the Church, of whom Ambrose, Augustine and Gregory are the most notable, preserved the continuity of the idea of natural law and, at the same time, began to give it a different meaning and foundation.[1] The Stoics' distinction between an ideal absolute and a second best relative natural law was now linked more definitely with original sin. Only the fall of man from Christian love makes human institutions necessary. They can never become good; but it is the task of the Christian Church to require the utmost approximation of human laws to eternal Christian principles. For this purpose, the Church is given absolute supremacy over the State, which is bad, but which can justify its existence by protecting the peace and the Church and striving to fulfil the demands of eternal law. The other-worldiness of a pessimistic doctrine is thus ingeniously coupled with a philosophical justification of the claim of the Church for sovereign political authority.

In the traditional theory the great institutions of human society, coercive government, slavery and property, were the results of the vicious desires and impulses of men, not of the original character of their true nature; but they were also the means by which these vicious impulses might be restrained or limited. In the terms of the Christian Fathers they were at the same time the results of sin and the divine remedies for sin.[2]

Medieval political and legal thought, which developed from the twelfth century to the beginning of the fourteenth century and reached its climax in the scholastic system of St. Thomas Aquinas, broke decisively with this tradition. Five major trends of thought

---

[1] St. Augustine defines eternal law as "the divine order or will of God which requires the preservation of natural order, and forbids the breach of it" (Reply to Faustus the Manichaean, XXII, 27).

[2] Carlyle, 5 *Medieval Political Theory in the West*, 10 (1950).

run through the innumerable writings and disputations of the period.

First, and most important of all, political society and the state cease to be considered as institutions of sin. They become instead the embodiment of moral purpose and instruments in the realisation of justice and virtue. This transition was prepared in the *Policraticus* written by John of Salisbury in 1159, which derives much of its thought on the state as an instrument of general good from the writings of Cicero and Seneca. But it received its main impetus from the revival of the study of Aristotle. The blend of Aristotelean teaching on the nature of state and society with Christian principles, in the work of Albert the Great and St. Thomas Aquinas, gave scholastic philosophy its most characteristic aspect.

Closely related to this first principle is, secondly, the medieval emphasis on law as the highest principle of society, binding rulers and ruled alike. This emphasis on the supremacy of law, in conjunction with the natural law philosophy of the ancients and the new emphasis of the Christian teaching as the embodiment of the highest law, led to the scholastic doctrine of natural law summarised later in this chapter. The conception of an objective and immutable law separates medieval legal theory from the subsequent age of national sovereignty.

At the same time, however, medieval philosophers, jurists and politicians were confronted with a third problem, the authoritative interpretation of the supreme law. This brings the abstract principle of the rule of an objective law down into the political arena. The doctrine of the two swords, propounded by Pope Gelasius at the end of the fifth century, had established a temporary balance by distinguishing between spiritual and temporal power, each having its proper sphere. As both Pope and Emperor grew more powerful and ambitious, it became increasingly difficult to maintain the balance. The main controversy was provoked by two historic political conflicts: the first was the struggle between Pope Gregory VII and the Emperor Henry IV, at the end of the eleventh century, over the rival claims of Church and Emperor, of spiritual and temporal power. Through Pope Gregory, the Church, as the appointed guardian of religion, claimed not only the right of investiture of bishops but also moral and legal authority over the Emperor. The Emperor, on the other hand, claimed the right of appointment of the clergy and the right to hereditary succession, as aspects of imperial power.

As the German Empire disintegrated, the struggle was taken up by the new temporal rulers. A great stimulus was given to legal and political thought by the controversy between Pope Boniface VIII and King Philip the Fair of France (1296-1303). The most important presentation of the case for supremacy of the Church was written about 1302 by Egidius Colonna (*De ecclesiastica potestate*). The gist of his argument is the uniqueness and supremacy of the spiritual power vested in the Pope. From the intrinsic superiority of the spiritual over the temporal follows the right of the Church to judge all temporal authority. On the other side, John of Paris (*De potestate regia et papali*, 1302-03), in defence of the autonomy of the king, put forward the first great argument for the division of spiritual and secular power. The necessity of political and civil government was established as a good thing in itself, independent from its sanction by the Church, not inferior to the spiritual power. It is in pursuance of this line of thought and action that the unity of European society held together by the supremacy of a Christian order and authority, gave way to the dualism of Church and state until, with the steadily growing power of the modern national state, law increasingly became an instrument of the state. Together with this went the gradual undermining of the doctrine of natural law.[3]

Fourthly, the question of the source of legal authority within civil society arose. Most medieval writers stated a principle denied by the subsequent era of absolutism in state government but revived from the end of the seventeenth century onwards against a different background: the principle that law and government derive from the people. This theory was stated clearly by John of Paris, but as early as 1159 John of Salisbury justified tyrannicide by the cognate principle that ruler and ruled alike are bound by the law. According to John of Paris all power is derived from God and from the people. Thomas Aquinas denies the right to murder a tyrant who usurps the law but he too[4] asserts the right of the people to appoint the ruler and deduces from it the right of the people to depose a tyrant who violates their faith. He also derives from Aristotle a general advocacy of the mixed state in which not only are rulers elected by the people but the people participate in government.[5] It is from these foundations that the later theories of social contract are developed.[6]

[3] See Chap. 12.

[4] Both in the *Summa Theologica* and in *De Regimine Principum* (I,6).

[5] Professor O'Rahilly, 10 *Irish Quarterly Review*, No. 37 (1921), emphatically claims that the overwhelming majority of scholastic writers, from the early fourteenth to the seventeenth century, have advocated the doctrine of popular supremacy and government by consent.

[6] See below, Chap. 11.

Lastly, the attitude of the medieval writers to private rights and in particular to the right of property, marks the transition from the early Christian principle that all private property is bad, to the paramountcy and integrity of the right of private property which reached its climax in the nineteenth century and which is now challenged by the modern growth of collectivism and planning. To the Fathers of the Church and to the canonic lawyers, private property was still an evil institution arising from the vicious and greedy appetites of men.[7] The influence both of Aristotle and of Roman jurisprudence probably accounts for the different attitude to private property evident in the writings of St. Thomas Aquinas. It marks the growing strength of a secular and utilitarian outlook towards civil society and law.[8]

Natural Law and Divine Order

The new European civilisation which began to take shape in the ninth century was built on the dual foundations of feudalism and the Christian Church. Politically and socially, Europe was not yet divided into national states; it was a hierarchical and international society, in which the social scales were determined by the conditions of land tenure. At the bottom of the scale was the serf-like tenant who tilled the soil; at the top was the emperor, who claimed the loyalty of the nobility by virtue of the grant of land made to them. The same ties linked every tenant with the one immediately above him.

The Christian religion, once the faith of the persecuted, had become the universal religion of Europe; it was organised in the Church, an international institution built on as strict a hierarchical pattern as political society, with the Pope in Rome as its acknowledged head, to whom clerics of all countries owed obedience, from archbishop to priest.

The spiritual and the worldly order both professed Christianity. This pointed to a theory of law in which Christianity was the supreme spiritual and legal value, superior to all other laws. The Stoic conception of natural law provided a basis; the Fathers of the Church had already begun to substitute the Christian faith for reason, as the supreme law of the universe. It remained to provide the new hierarchical medieval society with a hierarchy of laws. This proceeded in several stages.

[7] *Cf.* Carlyle, *op. cit.* at 14.
[8] See further below, p. 109 *et seq.*

Early medieval writers derived from the above-quoted passage, in Ulpian, a hierarchy of laws: *Jus naturale*—common to all animals, *jus gentium*—common to all mankind, *jus civile*—particular law of a commonwealth.

DECRETUM GRATIANUM

The *Decretum Gratianum* of the twelfth century initiated a new turn in natural law thinking. The law of nature is now exalted further than by identification with reason. It becomes part of the law of God. As such it is immutable and prevails over custom and any positive law. It is implied that the Church is the authentic exponent of the law of nature, which is thus coextensive with the rule of Scripture.

With this growing emphasis on the Church as the authentic interpreter of Christianity—a development prepared by Augustine's indictment of the state as an institution of sin—the latent conflict between the spiritual and the secular law-giving authorities, between Pope and Emperor, became more threatening. This controversy,[9] which lasted for centuries, provided a powerful incentive for the development of the doctrine of natural law, which was invoked by both parties. Its greatest product, the scholastic system of law, buttressed the claim of the Church to legal supremacy; but it expressed, beyond the political controversies of the time, the aspirations and legal conceptions of a society which was about to give way to a society of nation states.

ST. THOMAS AQUINAS (1226-74)

The derivation of natural law from the law of God provides the basis for the scholastic thought of St. Thomas Aquinas.

St. Thomas defines law as "an ordinance of reason for the common good made by him who has the care of the community and promulgated."[10]

Since the world is ruled by divine providence, the whole community of the universe is governed by divine reason. Divine law is supreme. But the whole of divine law is not accessible to men. Such part of it as is intelligible to man reveals itself through eternal law as the incorporation of divine wisdom, which gives direction

---

[9] See above, p. 106.
[10] *Summa Theologica*, Part 2, vol. 8, p. 8. (English ed., London, 1927).

to all actions and movements. Natural law is a part of divine law, that part which reveals itself in natural reason. Man, as a reasonable being, applies this part of divine law to human affairs, and he can thus distinguish between good and evil. It is from the principles of eternal law, as revealed in natural law, that all human law derives. But St. Thomas establishes a fourth category, which seems to stand in a similar relation to human law as eternal law does to natural law. This is the *lex divina*, the positive law, enacted by God Himself for all mankind, in the Scripture. All law enacted by human authority, that is positive law, must keep within these limits. In a hierarchy of legal values, *lex divina* is perhaps the least necessary of the categories. But it served to cement the position of the Church as the authoritative interpreter of divine law laid down in the Scripture. One might perhaps say that divine law is the written, and natural law the unwritten, exposition of God's eternal reason. Lowest comes positive law, which is valid only in so far as compatible with natural and thus with eternal law. Human law is part and parcel of divine government; there is no schism between faith and reason; on the contrary, reason is a partial manifestation of faith.

In St. Thomas's system, the state is a natural institution, born from elementary social needs of men. In making the social life of men secure, and serving the general good, it is an imperfect reflection of God's realm, not an evil as St. Augustine had taught. The strong influence of Aristotle upon scholastic thinking shows itself in this much more positive attitude towards the state.

Moreover, the lowest category of laws, human laws, are recognised to be variable according to time and circumstances. Their purpose is—an interesting anticipation of utilitarianism—to be useful to men, to further the commonwealth, whilst at the same time being a part of divine and natural law. Human laws are thus valid within their province, within the limit of justice as ordained by the higher law. This leads us to Thomas's conclusions in regard to the practical relation between human laws and higher laws. The state, the worldly authority, has a legitimate function and sphere: to regulate social life justly, that is to the common good, within the limits of the authority of the law-giver. State laws must not be tyrannical. When a law is unjust either in respect of the end (that is, laws conducive not to the common good but to the cupidity and vainglory of the law-giver), or in respect of the author (as when a law is made that exceeds the power given to him), or in respect of form (as when burdens are imposed unequally on the community) such law is unjust and therefore in contradiction to natural and divine law. It is consequently invalid. In regard to the first two requisites St. Thomas is adamant. They are invalid because: "We ought to obey God rather than man." In regard to the last he recommends obedience despite injustice. For, "In order to avoid scandal or disturbance . . . a man should even yield his right."

Thus St. Thomas's system clearly upholds the supreme authority of the Church, gives the state or rather the Emperor his due share and at the same time discourages civil revolution by opposing to the injustice of oppressive laws the beneficial effect of order as against disturbance.

On the right of property, St. Thomas's teaching stands between the unconditional rejection of private property by the Fathers of the Church and the later elevation of the right of property into a natural right, by Locke and his followers as well as by the modern Catholic Church. St. Thomas starts from the contention that by natural law all things are common, but he answers by making a distinction between the acquisition and the use of property. He justifies the power to possess individual property as follows:

First because every man is more careful to procure what is for himself alone than that which is common to many or to all: since each one would shirk the labour and leave to another that which concerns the community, as happens where there is a great number of servants. Secondly, because human affairs are conducted in more orderly fashion if each man is charged with taking care of some particular thing himself, whereas there would be confusion if every one had to look after any one thing indeterminately. Thirdly, because a more peaceful state is ensured to man if each one is contented with his own. Hence it is to be observed that quarrels arise more frequently when there is no division of the things possessed.[11]

St. Thomas maintains that the use of things must be not by man for his own benefit but for the common good. He justifies the difference between rich and poor by saying that it is not unlawful to anticipate someone else in taking possession of something which at first was common property provided others get a share, but complete exclusion of others makes property unlawful.[12] The theoretical justification for this distinction by St. Thomas is the distinction between natural and positive law. He considers the right to

---

[11] *Summa Theologica*, Part 2, Q. 66, Art. 2.
[12] This foreshadows some modern doctrines on the social function of property.

the acquisition of property as one of the matters left by natural law to the state as a proper agency for the regulation of social life. Thus there is no foundation whatsoever, in St. Thomas's teaching, for the elevation of the right of private property into a principle of natural law. Even some three and a half centuries later, Suarez, one of the most influential of Spanish-Catholic natural law philosophers,[13] substantially agreed with St. Thomas. As against Duns Scotus, who maintained that natural law demands community of property, Suarez argued that neither division nor community of property was postulated by natural law: "just as, conversely, the advantages which show that a division of property is better adapted to a man's [human] nature and the fallen state, are proof, not that this division of ownership is a matter prescribed by natural law, but merely that it is adapted to the existing state and condition of mankind." It is only in the modern reformulation of scholastic philosophy by the Catholic Church, in the latter half of the nineteenth century, that the right of private property is classed among the natural, God-given rights. But while the modern Church doctrine professes to be guided by St. Thomas, it has never admitted that, in regard to the philosophy of property, it deviates decisively from the master, and the scholastic tradition.

In St. Thomas's system the austere ecclesiasticism of the Fathers of the Church and the political philosophy of Aristotle are blended in a system of great logical power which, at the same time, has elasticity. In the struggle of political forces his system vindicated the right of the Church to control the ecclesiastical appointments made by the Emperor. It was inevitable that the double-edged character of the law of nature would be exploited not only by defenders but also by antagonists of the Church. The most famous champion of the supremacy of the Holy Roman Empire of the German nation was Dante Alighieri.[14] He pictured a universal order without the interposition of the Church. In its place, he put the German Emperor (traditionally crowned in Rome) as the legitimate successor of the Roman people, chosen by God to rule the world. Again, at a time when the struggle for supremacy between the Pope and the General Council was not yet decided, their struggle was carried on in the name of natural law. Just as modern codes may be silent on important questions, thus necessitating decisions according to justice and reason, so the law of God as revealed in

---

[13] *Treatise on Laws and God the Law-Giver* (1612), Book II, Chap. XIV.
[14] *De Monarchia*, written about 1312.

Scripture might be silent or ambiguous, and thus the authority of the law of nature would be invoked in the service of whatever cause the learned interpreter wished to support. For St. Thomas himself the law of nature was not merely a matter of expediency; but it often deteriorated to that function in the innumerable controversies which accompanied the bitter struggle for supremacy between rival powers, above all between Pope and Emperor. The law of nature also served as a powerful weapon in the later struggle between Catholics and Protestants, when either side invoked it for the true interpretation of Scripture or the right of the state in regard to spiritual jurisdiction.

Once the medieval structure of Europe and the claim of the Church for universal leadership had collapsed under the onslaught of new ideals and social forces, the scholastic doctrine of natural law was bound to be relegated to temporary oblivion. But the Catholic Church survived and continued to command not indeed the universal allegiance of Christendom, but still that of hundreds of millions all over the world. After the tremendous social changes of the industrial revolution, the Catholic Church found itself faced with the necessity of redefining its belief and views in the light of modern social conditions. Towards a solution of that problem St. Thomas's system and his doctrine of natural law provided a starting point and strong guidance. From it some great Popes, above all Leo XIII, have developed modern principles of Catholicism. This shows the greatness as well as the elasticity of the Thomistic system.[15]

DUNS SCOTUS (1265-1308) AND WILLIAM OF OCCAM (1290-1349)

In St. Thomas's system reason is superior to will. Only in God are will and reason one. From divine reason an objective system of values is derived. While this has remained the foundation of all orthodox natural law thinking, two Franciscan monks, very shortly after St. Thomas, taught the supremacy of will over reason. With a boldness that anticipates certain aspects of Hume—and of modern existentialism—Duns Scotus[16] asserts that the freedom of man— to love or to hate—to do good or evil—means, of necessity, the

---

[15] The legal theory of the contemporary Catholic Church, though based on Thomistic principles, is so much concerned with modern political and social problems that it will be discussed in a later part of this book, which deals with problems of legal theory and political order.

[16] *Opus Oxoniense.*

will's independence from reason. And it is not intellectual insight that directs will, but, on the contrary, *"voluntas imperat intellectui."* [17] In God alone, power and justice coincide, since there is no law above God, and His will is therefore absolute. But because God's will is love, and He is in His essence goodness (*bonitas*), God's absolute freedom can never be evil. For the Franciscan Duns Scotus there is only one principle of natural law: to love God. All other norms of behaviour, including most of the Ten Commandments, are only derivative and relative (thus the prohibition to kill is not absolute), in so far as consonant with the love of God. Some norms, such as the regulation of property, can only be laid down by authoritative decision. These doctrines were developed further by a contemporary, William of Occam, who eliminated Duns Scotus's one remaining natural law precept: the impossibility of hating God, because of God's essential goodness.

William of Occam lays down a hierarchy of rules of conduct which foreshadows some modern doctrines[18]:

(1) Universal rules of conduct, dictated by natural reason.
(2) Rules that would be accepted as reasonable and therefore binding in a society governed by natural equity without any positive law.
(3) Rules which may be deduced from general principles of the law of nature but, not being of a fundamental character, are liable to modification by authority.

The revolutionary significance of the teachings of Scotus and Occam lies in the identification of law with the absolute will of God, which is not identical with the essential nature of things. God's will is subject only to His own arbitrary decree. This, according to some neo-scholastic philosophers, prepares the way for the supremacy of will over intellect, and, politically, for the acceptance of the absolute power of the sovereign (Machiavelli, Hobbes, Hitler).[19] Such an interpretation ignores, however, the other aspect of Scotus's and Occam's teaching, that is the emphasis on the individual's moral responsibility, his freedom of choice between good and evil. Voluntarism is not Nihilism.

---

[17] Ox. IV d. 49 q. 4.
[18] *e.g.*, Gény's *"donnés,"* below, p. 330.
[19] *Cf.* Rommen, *Natural Law,* 57 *et seq.* See also Welzel, *Naturrecht und materiale Gerechtigkeit* 67 *et seq.* (1951).

Chapter 10

REASON AND THE LAW OF NATURE

The spiritual, social and political revolution which is marked by the Renaissance, the Reformation and the rise of the national state, was bound to bring new problems and new answers. The Renaissance broke down the medieval order under which the individual was a minute part of a universal organism, and from it emerged the individual as an end unto himself, critical, sceptical, thirsty for knowledge and conscious of his power. At the same time the Reformation struggled for individual freedom of conscience. Both contributed powerfully to the emergence of the modern state, absolute and sovereign, no longer bound by allegiance to either Church or Emperor. At the same time the aftermath of the Crusades and the discovery of new continents helped to destroy the economic basis of the medieval order and laid the foundation for the era of commercial expansion. These changes brought with them new legal problems and postulates. The absolute rulers demanded the legitimation of their claims to omnipotence over their people. On the other hand, the individual, now seeing himself without the bonds of an authoritative order, demanded rights to safeguard and protect his personality and interest. The rising commercial middle class wanted protection of its rapidly increasing property interests. They all appealed to general principles of natural law in justification of their claims.

For the spiritual authority of divine law the intellectual authority of reason was now substituted. It was Hugo Grotius who gave classical expression to the new foundations of natural law as well as to the principles of modern international law in his celebrated work, *De Jure Belli ac Pacis* (1623-25).[1] To him, as to St. Thomas and to many generations of philosophers, Aristotle's system was the fountain of wisdom, but Grotius turned it to different account.

According to Grotius, the property peculiar to man is his desire

[1] Grotius could build on the work of distinguished forerunners, in particular Gentilis' *De Jure Belli* (1598).

for society, for a life spent tranquilly in common with fellow men and in correspondence with the character of his intellect. From the nature of the human intellect which desires a peaceful society, principles of natural law are derived. They are independent of divine command. "Natural law is so immutable that it cannot be changed by God Himself." These principles of reason can, according to Grotius, be deduced in two different ways: *a priori,* by examining anything in relation to the rational and social nature of man, and *a posteriori,* by examining the acceptance of these principles among the nations. The former, Grotius says, is the more subtle method.

The rationalist shares with the schoolman the doctrine that any law contrary to the principles of natural law is invalid. Natural law is not yet the rather vague guide to the right path, which it has become in modern times. It is the superior law. On his principles of natural law Grotius built his system of international law. The most fundamental of his principles is *"Pacta sunt servanda,"* the respect for promises given and treaties signed. Other rules of natural law are the respect for other people's property and the restitution of gain made from it, the reparation of damage caused by one's fault and the recognition of certain things as meriting punishment. All these principles are still recognised in international law, although no longer under the name of natural law. Natural law also supplied once again the basis of more concrete political controversy. While the Dutchman Grotius, at a time when the Dutch were the first maritime nation, stipulated the freedom of the seas as a principle of natural law,[2] the Englishman Selden sought to demonstrate that natural law permitted private and public dominion over the seas.[3]

In Grotius' work the idea of natural law assumed once more a constructive and practical function, comparable to that which it had exercised at the time of the growth of Roman law towards a cosmopolitan system. In both cases, principles partly deduced, partly observed as being of general acceptance, gave the basis. In international law, natural law was gradually and subtly reduced from a position of superiority over state practice to an empty formula good enough to give resonance to claims put forward by states, but too weak to interfere with them effectively.

Pufendorf, like Grotius, bases natural law on the two sides of human nature, which bid him, on the one hand, to protect his

---

[2] *Mare liberum* (1609).
[3] *Mare clausum seu de dominio maris* (1635).

person and property, but, on the other hand, not to disturb the peace of society. From these Pufendorf derives a maxim remarkable for its anticipation of Kant's Categorical Imperative: "Let no one bear himself towards a second person so that the latter can properly complain that his equality of right has been violated in his case."[4]

Chr. Wolff, a follower of Leibniz, sees in the duty of self-perfection the principal command of natural law. But the conditions of such perfection are, to him, only provided by a benevolent sovereign who promotes peace and security. In none of these systems is the sovereign bound by effective obligations. But natural law is still a living force.

Pufendorf, Thomasius, Christian Wolff and Selden still reassert, in their general theory and for the law of nations in particular, the supremacy of the law of nature. A decisive change comes with the work of Vattel.

Vattel, popularising certain distinctions made by Wolff, emphatically reasserts that "the law of nations is originally no other than the law of nature applied to nations."[5] Natural law is thus necessary law; all nations are bound to observe it. It cannot be changed or abrogated. But this apparently sweeping assertion is deprived of all meaning by the distinction which Vattel makes between an internal law (law of conscience) and an external law (law of action). For all practical purposes only the latter counts. Natural law is relegated to the unfathomable depths of the conscience of a state, whereas all real international law is held by Vattel to have derived from the will of nations, their presumed consent expressing itself in treaties or customs. Thus, while lip-service is still paid to natural law, international law has in fact started on its positivist career which accompanies a growth of nationalism and ultimately leads to the international anarchy of today. Only when in our own days the conflict between national and international sovereignty arose afresh, did natural law ideas begin to assert themselves again in a modified form, in the science of international law.[6]

---

[4] *Elementa jurisprudentiae* (transl. Oldfather), Book 2, Obs. IV, 4.
[5] Preliminaries to *Droit des Gens*, para. 5.
[6] *Cf.* above, p. 91 *et seq.*, and below, Chap. 35.

CHAPTER 11

NATURAL LAW AND SOCIAL CONTRACT

GROTIUS and the rationalists shared with the medieval theorists of natural law the aim of establishing an objective order. Natural law ideas were used for a very different purpose by the new rising tide of individualism which culminated, in different ways, in the English Revolution of 1688, the French Revolution of 1789 and the American Declaration of Independence. The Renaissance and Reformation paved the way for the spiritual emancipation of the individual; the expansion of commerce gave economic prosperity to the new middle class which became the moving spirit in the struggle for individual emancipation. On the other side, political absolutism, while anxious to dissociate itself from the theocratic order of the Middle Ages, looked for a justification of its claim to unlimited authority over the people. The legal construction used by both sides in that new political struggle was that of social contract. The principle of social contract is found in Plato's *Republic*:

> Therefore when men act unjustly towards one another, and thus experience both the doing and the suffering, those amongst them who are unable to compass the one and escape the other, come to this opinion: that it is more profitable that they should mutually agree neither to inflict injustice nor to suffer it. Hence men began to establish laws and covenants with one another, and they called what the law prescribed lawful and just.[1]

The contention that legal authority comes from the people—not from the arbitrary will of a ruler—is put forward by many of the greatest medieval writers, such as John of Salisbury, John of Paris, St. Thomas Aquinas.[2]

But the use of social contract as a definite concept in political and legal controversy can be traced back to the Italian Marsilius of Padua (1270-1343), who fought, like his English contemporary William of Occam, against the supremacy of the Church in other than spiritual matters. Against the claim of the Church to worldly

---

[1] Book 2, 358 (Lindsay trans.).
[2] See above, Chap. 9.

power Marsilius stressed the autonomy of the prince and his right of jurisdiction over anything within his territory including ecclesiastical appointments; but at the same time he first developed the idea that the people are the source of all political power and government is by mandate of the people, and with their consent. The prince is therefore under an obligation to the people to observe the law and can be punished if he violates it.[3] This truly revolutionary proposition contains the elements of the construction of a social contract which was resumed some time later, both by Catholic and Protestant writers, and gained an ever-increasing importance until the end of the eighteenth century.

The essential features of the doctrine of social contract are these: From a state of nature, in which they have no law, no order, no government—this state of affairs appears to some writers as a paradise, to others as chaos—men have at some time passed to a state of society, by means of contract in which they undertake to respect each other and live in peace (*pactum unionis*). To this contract is added simultaneously or subsequently a second pact by which the people thus united undertake to obey a government which they themselves have chosen (*pactum subjectionis*). During the first phase of the use of social contract it is treated as an historical fact, although with little actual historical research and mixed with constructions; in the second phase it is used entirely as a construction of legal reason, not as an historical fact. The transition is a gradual one. Grotius treats social contract as an historical fact, Kant treats it purely as a postulate of reason.

What links all protagonists of the social contract theory is that they find the source of political power in the people and are unanimously opposed to the deduction of political authority from above, whether from divine law or the grace of God. In that sense the whole theory of social contract is a forerunner of democratic theory. The other common aspect of all social contract theories lies in the individualistic and indeed atomistic conception of society which it implies. The state is seen as the legal creation of individual will; contract is the suitable legal form for such a conception, although the construction of social contract has, of course, little to do with modern legal rules on private contract. It follows that social contract theories are quite incompatible with an organic view of society and corporate personality. Apart from these common features, however, the theory of social contract like that of natural law in general

[3] *Defensor Pacis* (1324).

has served the most divergent political purposes. In particular it has been used to justify absolutism on one hand and democracy on the other.

In one form or another many different writers have used the construction of social contract while it was fashionable. It is neither possible nor necessary to discuss them all here. The principal aspects of the social contract theory are well represented by four eminent political and legal thinkers: Grotius, Hobbes, Locke and Rousseau.

GROTIUS (1583-1645)

Grotius[4] uses the construction of social contract for a twofold purpose, internally for the justification of the absolute duty of obedience of the people to the government, internationally to create a basis for legally binding and stable relations among the states.

Grotius puts forward social contract as an actual fact in human history. The constitution of each state, he thinks, had been preceded by a social contract, by means of which each people had chosen the form of government which they considered most suitable for themselves. Whatever opinion one might hold about the excellence of the one or the other form of government, each people has the right to choose the government it prefers. But once the people have transferred their right of government to the ruler—whether in order to find a protector against danger or because they preferred auto-cratic rule to liberty, or as a result of war—they forfeit the right to control or punish the ruler however bad his government. In order to justify this thesis Grotius goes so far as to deny that all govern-ment is for the sake of the governed. Grotius appears strangely vacillating on the question how far a ruler is bound by promises to his subjects. On the one hand, his sovereignty must not be impaired, at least in any case where authority has not been merely temporarily conferred upon him. On the other hand, Grotius is bound to admit from his philosophical premise that the ruler is bound by natural law which is valid even without promise. And the keeping of promises is, as we have seen, a paramount principle of natural law. From this dilemma Grotius has not indicated any satisfactory way out.[5] His main concern is the stability and orderliness of inter-

---

[4] In *De Jure Belli ac Pacis* (1625).

[5] Gierke, *Natural Law and Theory of Society*, 55 (Trans. 1957) explains the inconsistency of Grotius by his lingering attachment to the individualism of the school of natural law, while he also tends towards an organic conception of the state.

national society. His social contract theory served this purpose, first by stressing, against medieval conceptions, the equivalence of different forms of government established by different peoples, secondly by freeing the ruler or government which conducts foreign relations from any internal restriction or fetters, thirdly by stressing the absolute force of a promise once given. It is in regard to the last point that Grotius becomes involved in contradictions.

HOBBES (1588-1679)

Thomas Hobbes in many respects improved the social contract theory and made it an essential part of a system of extraordinary logical power.

Like Grotius and later Locke, Hobbes wrote his principal books, *De Cive* (1642) and *Leviathan* (1651), with a definite political purpose. Living during the civil wars in England, Hobbes was convinced of the overwhelming importance of state authority, which he thought ought to be vested in an absolute ruler. In the struggle between Long Parliament and Charles I, Hobbes defended the cause of the King. In theory Hobbes, like most writers of his time, acknowledges the authority of natural law. But he understands it in a sense fundamentally different from those writers for whom natural law constitutes a definite objective order superior to positive law. Hobbes shifts the emphasis from natural law as an objective order to natural right as a subjective claim based on the nature of man and thus prepares the way for the later revolution of individualism in the name of "inalienable rights." Thus far Hobbes still acknowledges objective rules of natural law of an immutable character, but he divests them of any practical significance by depriving them of sanctions. At the same time Hobbes understands by natural law no longer certain ethical precepts but laws of human conduct based on observation and appreciation of human nature.

The chief principle of natural law for Hobbes is the natural right of self-preservation. This is connected with his view of the state of nature in which—

men live without a common Power to keep them all in awe, they are in that condition which is called Warre; and such a warre, as if of every man, against every man.[6]

In this natural state man pursues solely his own advantage with-

[6] *Leviathan*, Part 1, Chap. 13.

out regard for anyone else and recognises no limitation of his rights. Hence a state of perpetual and devastating warfare which threatens everyone. But natural reason dictates to man the rule of self-preservation, in pursuit of which man tries to escape from this state of permanent insecurity. He does so by transferring all his natural rights to the ruler, whom he promises henceforth to obey unconditionally. Hobbes does not, like Grotius, recognise an unlimited variety of social contracts by which the people may surrender a greater or smaller proportion of their rights. There is only one kind of pact, an unconditional *pactum subjectionis* by which the whole of the natural right is transferred to the ruler, who thus obtains absolute power.

Hobbes emphatically rejects any contractual or quasi-contractual right by which subjects could demand the fulfilment of certain obligations by the ruler. His "social contract" is therefore no true contract but a logical fiction. There is only one condition attached to the absolute power of the ruler: that he can govern and keep order. Hobbes naturally discourages civil disobedience. But he clearly states in *Leviathan* that where resistance is successful the sovereign ceases to govern, the subjects are thrown back upon their original position and may now transfer their obedience to a new ruler.

The Obligation of Subjects to the Sovereign, is understood to last as long, and no longer, than the power lasteth, by which he is able to protect them.[7]

Hobbes' conception of sovereignty is thus entirely rational and utilitarian. It is purely the result of rational individual self-interest which supersedes the unrational and thus self-destructive lust for power as man pursues it in the state of nature. From this fundamental thesis follow a number of rather revolutionary propositions:

(1) Natural law, though still given a place of honour—Hobbes enumerates no fewer than nineteen principles—is shorn of all power. For all law is dependent upon sanction. "Governments without the sword are but words, and of no strength to secure a man at all."[8] All real law is thus civil law, the law commanded and enforced by the sovereign.

---

[7] *Leviathan*, Part 2, Chap. 21.
[8] *Leviathan*, Part 2, Chap. 17.

(2) There is no society as distinct from the state. Without the state, which is government, there is only the shapeless and anarchist multitude. Consequently there is no law between sovereign and subjects, no autonomy of corporation. All social and legal authority is concentrated in the sovereign. In him rest all necessary powers of government.

(3) With Hobbes the Church is definitely and unconditionally subordinated to the state. It has the same legal status as any other corporation, all of which have the same head, the sovereign.

(4) Hobbes' sovereign—he prefers monarchy, but the form of government is of minor importance as long as it does its job, to govern—is in no way instituted and legitimated by superior sanction whether of divine right or of natural law, or of anything else. He is purely and solely a utilitarian creation of the individuals who institute him in order to prevent them from destroying each other.

Thus Hobbes destroys all that was left of medieval conceptions of authority and law. The Church is deprived of the authority of divine law, natural law is no longer a superior law, the autonomous corporation, essential to medieval society, is eliminated, and there remains the human individual, a strange mixture of animal and rational being. For his protection alone, there is law and authority. Hobbes is individualist, utilitarian and absolutist. Each of these different aspects of his teaching has had a powerful influence upon the legal and political thought of the next few centuries. He has shaken himself free from medieval society and medieval ideas. He completes the revolution of the Renaissance. From his political and legal theory emerges modern man, self-centred, individualistic, materialistic, irreligious, in pursuit of organised power. Hobbes' individualism links him with Locke, his utilitarianism with Bentham and Mill, his absolutism with all the theories which cement the growing power of the state.[9]

LOCKE (1632-1704)

Locke contributes to the emancipation of the individual in a differ-

---

[9] Spinoza (*Tractatus theologico-politicus*, 1670; *Ethica*, 1677) develops a theory of striking similarity, in constructions and conclusions, to that of Hobbes. But he deduces from the physical limitations of the state's power an indestructible freedom of thought which is closer to the liberalism of his contemporary, Locke.

ent manner. His political theory gave powerful expression to the aspirations and interests of the class which was destined to lead and to profit most from that emancipation for a long time to come. Locke was the theoretician of the rising middle class, individualistic, acquisitive, but ethically minded in a way which avoided conflict between ethics and profit. A theory which would express the beliefs, interests and aspirations of this class, could not be, like that of Hobbes, of ruthless and uncompromising logic. Locke formulated ideas, which appealed to his generation and the following century, by an extremely skilful, if eclectic, combination of ideas from different sources. Locke restored the medieval conception of natural law in so far as he made it superior to and immutable by positive law. At the same time, he placed the individual in the centre and invested him, in the name of supreme ethical principles, with inalienable natural rights, among which the right of private property occupies a prominent place. He used the notion of social contract, not, like Hobbes, in order to demonstrate the transfer of all natural rights to authority, but on the contrary, to justify government by majority and to show that governments hold their power in trust, with the duty to preserve the individual rights whose protection the individuals have entrusted to them.

Thus Locke became essentially the great opponent of Hobbes, to whose theory of absolutism he opposed his theory of the individual's inalienable rights. The struggle between their opposite political ideals—authority and liberty—has been a dominant theme of political history ever since.

Writing after the Glorious Revolution of 1688, at a time when constitutional ideals began to take shape, Locke takes over, mainly from Hooker, some medieval ideas of the superior and binding force of certain moral principles upon governments. But Locke modernises these ideas by adopting many of Hobbes' individualistic premises and stating those values in terms of inalienable natural rights. The individual has a natural inborn right to "Life, Liberty, Estate," and it is to the latter, the right of private property, that Locke devotes his chief attention. Like Hobbes, Locke goes back to a state of nature, but his state of nature is Paradise Lost, a state "of peace, good will, mutual assistance and preservation." In this state men have all the rights that nature gives them; they mainly lack the organisation. The essential contribution of Locke in this field is his elaboration of the natural rights of man to that with which he has mixed the labour of his body, for example, by tilling land.[10] By his labour a man projects his personality into the objects of his work. This right of property exists prior to and independent of any social contract. The function of social contract is to preserve and protect this and other natural rights. Locke uses social contract in its double function. There is first a *pactum unionis,* "the original compact by which men agree to unite into one political society, which is all the compact that is, as needs to be, between the individuals that enter into, or make a commonwealth."[11] At the same time, Locke states[12] that a majority agreement is identical with an act of the whole society, as the consent by which each person agrees to join a body politic obliges him to submit to the majority. Thus majority vote can take away property rights and other supposedly inalienable rights. To the *pactum unionis* is added a *pactum subjectionis,* by which the majority vests its power in a government whose function is the protection of the individual. As long as it is faithful to this pledge, the government cannot be deprived of its power. Locke here stops short of later democratic theories, and this is an important point in which he differs from Rousseau.

There are many logical flaws in Locke's theory, such as the incompatibility of inalienable individual rights with majority rule, of the supremacy of the individual with his inability to recall a government which is only his trustee, not to speak of the inconsistency of his theory of knowledge with his political theory.[13] But it is seldom logical consistency that has decided the success of theories and movements.

Locke's theory admirably expressed certain ideas which were in the ascendant at his time and about to develop continuously throughout the eighteenth century and most of the nineteenth century. It gave theoretical form to the reaction against absolutism and the preparation of parliamentary democracy; to the emphasis

---

[10] Locke's justification for private property is emphatically that of a pre-capitalistic age. It is entirely based on the value of personal labour, "which puts the greatest part of value upon land, without which it would scarcely be worth anything" (*Second Treatise of Civil Government,* s. 43), and to Locke it was still inconceivable that a man would "value ten thousand or a hundred thousand acres of excellent land, ready cultivated . . . where he had no hopes of commerce with other parts of the world . . ." (*op. cit.* s. 48). Locke also admits the power of government to regulate the use of property, where it has been turned from land into money (s. 50). Thus, ironically, Locke's ideology of property is taken from pre-commercial conceptions, while it was destined to have its greatest influence in an increasingly industrialised society, where the function of property came to depart further and further from Locke's pre-supposition.

[11] *Of Civil Govt.,* Book 2, s. 99.

[12] s. 96.

[13] On this, see Sabine, *A History of Political Theory,* 530.

upon the inalienable rights of the emancipated individual; and last, but not least, the struggle of the rising middle class for giving its acquisitive aims the solid legal sanction of natural law. Trade expansion and the enclosure movement were both fortified by Locke's theory. His greatest effect was to be upon the French and, in particular, upon the American revolution. The characteristic combination of noble ideals and acquisitiveness, of natural law philosophy and protection of vested interests, in American history owes much to Locke.

ROUSSEAU (1712-88)

Rousseau's great influence upon the French and American revolutions and subsequent political theories is to be ascribed to the sweeping emotionalism of certain doctrines which appealed to his contemporaries, rather than to any consistent theory, such as the scholastics Bodin, Hobbes or Locke had put forward. Rousseau's work simply abounds in contradictions; it would be easy to quote him as a champion of inalienable individual rights as well as of the absolute supremacy of the community; as a nationalist—or as a cosmopolitan; as a defender of reason—or as the apostle of instinct and sentiment; as a democrat—or as an autocrat. But, as said before, it is not logical consistency which determines success or failure.

Rousseau contrives to justify the people's sovereignty, the *"volonté générale"* on the one hand and the original and inalienable freedom and equality of all men on the other. The construction used by Rousseau for the proof of these contentions is once again the social contract, used more clearly than with previous writers as a hypothetical construction of reason, not as an historical fact. Rousseau's deduction of the natural freedom and equality of men differs fundamentally from that of either Hobbes or Locke. The latter both base their systems on the egoism of the self-centred individual, and it is that very contention which Rousseau opposes with his emotional enthusiasm for the primitive self-contained community in which people live harmoniously together, satisfied in their contact with nature through their hard but contenting work and the simplicity of their life. His whole *Contrat Social* labours under the difficulty of proving the superiority both of the organic community and of natural rights of man. Essentially Rousseau's argument is that freedom and equality of men were the basis of their happiness, existent in primitive communities and lost in modern civilisation. Now that the blissful natural state of society has gone, the task is to find a form of social organisation which guarantees those natural rights of freedom and equality. By a social contract men unite in order to guarantee their rights of freedom and equality by the state. (The social contract is not an historical reality but a postulate.) The state derives its existence and its justification solely from the guarantee of freedom and equality. Having received these from men, it restores them not as natural but as civil rights to all. The state and the state law thus remain subject to the general will which creates the state for the better protection of freedom and equality. Rousseau never develops the implications of "general will" to consistent conclusions. He extols the direct sovereignty of the people, as against the representative democracy of Parliament. Rousseau always had in mind the small city state existing in his own Swiss homeland at that time. Sovereignty belongs to the people as a group, but Rousseau never makes it quite clear whether this means majority judgment or not. That would have compelled him to face the possibility of compulsion of the individual by majority will. This would not have gone well together with the inalienable freedom of each.

It has been said that if Hobbes recognises only a *pactum subjectionis,* Locke both the *pactum unionis and subjectionis,* Rousseau knows only a *pactum unionis*[14] and that of a mystical kind, little connected with contract. What Rousseau has in mind is what German jurisprudence calls a *"körperschaftlicher Gesamtakt,"* a corporative collective act creating a new mystic entity, but not a contract of individuals with mutually dependent obligations. Rousseau's thesis, in fact, brings out clearly the incompatibility of any organic conception of a society with the notion of social contract which, whether in its absolutist or its democratic form, whether used as an historical explanation or a hypothetical construction of reason, is an atomistic and individualistic conception. Rousseau does not attempt to solve this or many other problems inherent in the contradictions of his teachings. The most immediate and far-reaching influence of Rousseau's doctrine, which "was so vague that it can hardly be said to point in any specific direction,"[15] was on the makers of the French Revolution, who took up his theory of popular sovereignty to justify revolution without end or measure Furthermore, Rousseau's doctrines of liberty and equality, added

[14] Pollock, *Essays in the Law,* 80-112 (1920).
[15] Sabine, *op. cit.* at 523.

to those of Locke, exercised a strong influence upon the formative era of American independence and the rights of man. But another side of Rousseau's writing may well be said to have had an influence no less great. His hymn on the community did not bring back to life the primitive city state of which he dreamt. But it gave stimulus to the rising tide of nationalism, and was really incompatible with the cult of reason which had formed the basis of natural law doctrines since Grotius. It glorified the collective will as the embodiment of what is good and reasonable, a line of thought which it was left to the later Fichte and Hegel to develop to a dangerous climax.

CHAPTER 12

TWILIGHT OF NATURAL LAW IDEOLOGY

ROUSSEAU'S approach to the problem had in substance, if not in name, abandoned natural law. The era of natural law as developed from Grotius onwards was coming to an end. The doctrines of natural law and social contract are prominent in the legal philosophies of Kant and Fichte which are discussed elsewhere in this book. As shown there, both operate with certain fundamental rights of the individual which the law must satisfy, and thus continue the tradition of Locke and Rousseau. They both use, in connection with the individualistic conception of society, the construction of social contract as an hypothesis of reason, not as an historical fact. Fichte's social contract is largely based on Rousseau's, with whom he shares the difficulty of combining an individualist construction with leaning towards an organic conception of the community. In his later work Fichte openly develops organic ideas of the state.[1]

For three reasons above all, the social contract theory did not survive the eighteenth century:

First, an individualistic conception of society as put forward by the rationalism of the eighteenth century was giving way to a collectivist conception, stimulated by the rising tide of nationalism.

Secondly, the stupendous growth of natural science gave strength and emphasis to empirical methods against deductive methods.

Thirdly, the new and increasingly complex European society demanded a comparative and sociological approach to problems of society, rather than an abstract one.

If Rousseau helped to promote the transition from individualism to collectivism, two other thinkers of much greater intellectual power destroyed the foundations of natural law from other angles.

MONTESQUIEU (1689-1755)

With Montesquieu's famous doctrine of Separation of Powers we

[1] *Cf.* below, p. 164.

are not here concerned. In his *Esprit des Lois*[2] Montesquieu introduced, although tentatively and with many imperfections, a new approach to law. Like all writers of his time, Montesquieu still superficially adhered to the doctrine of the law of nature. Law means "the necessary relations arising from the nature of things," and he also emphasises that there is a standard of absolute justice prior to positive law. But the natural laws which he enumerates, such as knowledge of God, bodily appetites and fundamental conditions of society, are so vague as to mean very little. The really important idea of his *Esprit des Lois* is the thesis that law, although vaguely based on some principles of natural law, must be influenced by environment and conditions such as climate, soil, religion, custom, commerce, etc. It was with this idea in his mind that Montesquieu embarked upon his comparative study of laws and governments, a study in many ways incomplete, unsystematic and incorrect,[3] but nevertheless of the greatest significance as an essay in comparative sociological jurisprudence. This approach in substance undermined the doctrine of natural law to which Montesquieu still paid lip-service.

HUME (1711-76) AND MODERN SCEPTICISM[4]

It was David Hume, a thinker of exceptional analytical power and penetration, who destroyed the theoretical basis of natural law. The theory of natural law was based upon a conception of reason as a faculty inherent in all men and producing certain immutable norms of conduct. Hume showed that "reason" as understood in the systems of natural law confused three different things:

(1) Inevitable and necessary truths, of which there are very few, such as certain mathematical axioms. They do not exist in the realm of human behaviour.

(2) Relations between facts or events which are normally described by "cause and effect" because they are usually associated in a particular way, as a matter of experience and observation. But there is no logical necessity in such association; it is merely a matter of empirical correlation and the

---

[2] (1748).

[3] As, for example, in the assertion that England was a model for separation of powers.

[4] *Treatise of Human Nature* (1739-40); *Inquiry Concerning the Principles of Morals* (1751).

observation of these correlations is the object of empirical science.

(3) "Reasonable" human conduct. Natural law theories assume that there are rational principles of behaviour which are as such of universal and necessary validity.

But reason in itself dictates no way of acting. It can only show what means will lead to a desired end. The guides of human action itself are certain values inspired by human motives and propensities to action. Reason "is and ought only to be the slave of the passions and can never pretend to any other office than to serve and obey them." It is merely a matter of convention based on utility if human actions follow certain patterns.

This analysis undermines the basis of natural law and, at the same time, lays the foundation for the distinction between the aims and methods of natural and social science which was taken up in our own time by Neo-Kantianism. Hume can also be described as the first of the utilitarians. Having rejected reason as the guide to action, he constitutes the moral sense "as the force which establishes" moral distinctions. "The moral sense is guided by pleasure and pain. An action, or sentiment, or character, is virtuous or vicious. Why? Because its view causes a pleasure or uneasiness of a particular kind. . . . To have the sense of virtue is nothing but to feel a satisfaction of a particular kind from the contemplation of a character."[5] This anticipation of the felicific calculus has had great influence on Bentham. For Hume the moral sense is not the source of justice, which he regards as an artificial though a necessary creation of society for the establishment of peace and order. It guards the public interest, though often, and inevitably, at the expense of individual equity.

His analysis heralds a new era, an era which is predominantly anti-metaphysical, scientifically minded and utilitarian.

The "social contract" theory was too much connected with metaphysical and natural law ideas of the state to survive the onslaught of positivist and utilitarian movements. But it also suffered from a juristic inadequacy which an age of refined and specialised juristic science was bound to find out. Moreover, most adherents of the social contract theory had twisted the function of contract as the embodiment of mutually dependent and basically equivalent obli-

---

[5] Hume, 2 *Treatise,* 179 (Everyman ed.).

gations in favour of the definite superiority of either individual or authority, in accordance with their particular ideology.

It was left to the Germanistic school of jurisprudence—a product of the romantic movement—to elaborate a different juristic conception, the corporate *Gesamtakt* as distinct from the individualistic *Vertrag* and thus to create a new juristic basis for public law, corporate personality and the state.

Chapter 13

NATURAL LAW THEORIES IN ANGLO-AMERICAN LEGAL DEVELOPMENT

On the whole, the nineteenth century was hostile to natural law theories. The rival movements of historical romanticism, utilitarianism, scientific positivism and economic materialism were united in their opposition to natural law. On the Continent, the natural law tradition was continued, but with decreasing force and without essential new contributions, by Ahrens, Krause and others. The Scottish jurist Lorimer, in his *Institutes of Law,* vigorously restated the orthodox natural law theory as determining the ultimate objects of positive law and elaborated a catalogue of rights revealed by nature.

The revival of natural law theories, towards the end of the nineteenth century, came as a reaction against some of the most powerful trends of nineteenth-century thought and cannot be understood without them.

Nowhere was the derision of natural law more complete than in English and American legal thinking of that period. To the then fashionable polemics against natural law was added the much stressed and often exaggerated emphasis on the difference between the metaphysical, deductive and abstract Continental approach to legal problems and the empirical, inductive and individualising approach of Anglo-American law. In fact, at least two Englishmen, Hobbes and Locke (not to speak of Hooker and others influenced by the medieval doctrines) have had a very great influence upon natural law thought.

It is true that utilitarianism and positivism had a particularly strong influence upon England in the nineteenth century. But at the same time natural law thinking declined on the Continent, and the only substantial difference is perhaps that positivist thinking has persisted longer in England (hardly in America) than on the Continent, and English jurisprudence remained, for a certain time, unaffected by the Continental revival of natural law theories.

Anglo-American legal thinking has, on the whole, indulged much less in theoretical discussions on natural law. Much of its own theory is inarticulate, absorbed in judicial law-making. But the actual moulding force of natural law ideas has probably been greater in English and, particularly, in American legal development than anywhere on the Continent.

Paradoxically, natural law celebrated its greatest triumphs in American judicial developments when it seemed philosophically at its lowest ebb.

NATURAL LAW IDEAS IN ENGLISH LAW

The use of natural law ideas in the development of English law revolves around two problems: the idea of the supremacy of law, and, in particular, the struggle between common law judges and Parliament for legislative supremacy on one hand, and the introduction of equitable considerations of "justice between man and man" on the other.

The first ended in a clear victory for parliamentary supremacy and the defeat of higher law ideas; the latter, after a long period of comparative stagnation, is again a factor of considerable influence in the development of the law.

Coke, as Chief Justice, vigorously asserted the supremacy of common law over Acts of Parliament in his famous dictum in *Bonham's* case,[1] having, in his previous career as a Crown lawyer, magnified the state and the prerogative with equal vigour.

It appears in our books that in many cases the common law will control Acts of Parliament and sometimes judge them to be utterly void, for when an Act of Parliament is against common right or reason or repugnant or impossible to be performed the common law will control it and adjudge such Act to be void.

Here, as in other cases, higher law is invoked for the legitimation of a bitter political struggle, which has its parallel, although with very different results, in the struggle between the American legislature and the Supreme Court. Coke's dictum is generally recognised as having had little basis in the actual administration of law,[2] and Professor Holdsworth asserts that from the sixteenth century onwards—and beyond any shadow of doubt after the revolution of

[1] (1610) 8 Co.C.P. 114a.
[2] Pollock, *Expansion of Common Law*, 121, 122 (1904).

1688—supremacy of law and supremacy of Parliament had merged,[3] not to be challenged again until the present day. Lip-service continued to be paid, however, to the idea of natural law. The following passage in Blackstone's *Commentaries*[4] might well have come from St. Thomas himself:

> This law of nature being coeval with mankind and dictated by God Himself is, of course, superior in obligation to any other. It is binding over all the globe, in all countries, and at all times; no human laws are of any validity if contrary to this. . . . Upon these two foundations the law of nature and the law of revelation depend all human laws. . . .

This statement does not prevent Blackstone from asserting the absolute legislative supremacy of Parliament. Since then higher law doctrines have fallen into disrepute in England. In some branches of modern English law, principles of natural justice are openly invoked as the test of validity of legal acts, although that test cannot, of course, be applied to any Act of Parliament. The most important examples are the supervision of administrative acts and decisions by the law courts, the recognition of foreign judgments and the recognition of custom.

(1) A custom will not be admitted by the courts if it is unreasonable, and the test is "whether as such it is fair, proper, and such as a reasonable, honest and fair-minded man would adopt,"[5] or, with more direct reference to natural law, "whether it is in accordance with the fundamental principles of right and wrong."[6]

(2) By means of an order of *prohibition* or *certiorari* the High Court can control administrative acts and quasi-judicial decisions of administrative bodies which are contrary to rules of natural justice.[7] These rules are mainly two: (a) *Nemo judex in causa sua,* and (b) *Audiatur et altera pars.*

(3) A foreign law applicable or a foreign transaction recognised in a case before an English court under private international law will not be enforced if certain principles of natural justice, such as fair trial, freedom of person, freedom of action, would be disregarded by such application or recognition.[8]

Of greater significance is the working of natural law ideas

---

[3] Holdsworth, 4 *History of English Law*, 186 (1924).
[4] 2, 41-43.
[5] *Produce Brokers* v. *Olympia Oil and Coke Co.* [1916] 2 K.B. 296.
[6] Brett J. in *Robinson* v. *Mollett* (1875) L.R. 7 H.L. 802.
[7] Dicey, *Law of the Constitution* 523 (10th ed. Wade 1959).
[8] Cheshire, *Private International Law*, 154 *et seq.* (5th ed. 1957).

through equity in the sense in which Aristotle conceives ἐπιείκεια, *i.e.*, as an aspect of justice, and, at the same time as a corrective, in individual cases, of the severity and rigidity of the justice of the general law.

In this sense, natural law ideas have exercised great formative influence upon English law, in various phases of its development.

First, they seem to have operated upon common law courts in the thirteenth and fourteenth centuries when legislative interference was scant and the common law had not yet developed that rigidity which led to the growth of a separate equity jurisdiction. The influence of natural law ideas upon equity itself is less prominent, as equity is conceived as a matter of conscience between individuals, but Maitland thinks that natural law ideas borrowed from canonists or civilians were of considerable importance.[9]

It is as guiding principles in law-making that natural law ideas have exercised the most profound and enduring influence upon English law. Sometimes natural justice was openly invoked (as by Lord Mansfield). For the greater part the common law preferred matter-of-fact expressions such as "reasonable," "fair," *"ex aequo et bono,"* etc.

Of the open invocation of principles of natural justice the most important example is Lord Mansfield's famous attempt[10] to introduce the doctrine of unjust enrichment in English law. From the existing counts for money had and received he sought to deduce a general principle, an obligation based on ties of natural justice, to refund; an attempt energetically repudiated by the subsequent century and a half of positivism,[11] only to be revived, more cautiously but unmistakably, by present-day judges and jurists.

Thus Professor Winfield finds the common basis of quasi-contractual obligations in *"aequum et bonum"*[12] and Lord Wright has said[13]:

The obligation is imposed by the court simply . . . on defendants who would be unjustly benefited at the cost of the plaintiffs if the latter . . . should be left out of pocket by having to discharge what was the defendant's debt.

[9] *Equity*, p. 9.
[10] In *Moses* v. *Macferlan* (1760) 2 Burr. 1005.
[11] *Cf.* Hamilton L.J. (later Lord Sumner) in *Baylis* v. *Bishop of London* [1913] Ch. 127: "Whatever may have been the case 146 years ago we are not now free in the twentieth century to administer that vague jurisprudence sometimes attractively styled 'justice between man and man.'"
[12] Winfield, *Province of the Law of Tort*, 133 *et seq.* (1931).
[13] *Brook's Wharf and Bull Wharf* v. *Goodman* [1937] 1 K.B. 534.

An important example of "reasonableness" as the criterion for what is just is the law of restraint of trade, since the *Nordenfeldt* case[14] made reasonableness between the parties and towards the public the test of the validity of restrictive covenants. In a wider sense the notion of the "reasonable man" on which the law of negligence is built may be said to be an application of principles of natural justice to the standard of behaviour expected of the citizen.[15] Decisions like *Haynes* v. *Harwood*,[16] which recognise to a limited extent the duty to save life, as a factor not merely of moral but of legal relevance, are based on similar considerations. But two observations apply to this modernised version of natural justice.

In the first place, the reasonableness or fairness is not a rigid or absolute one, as in former natural law theories. It is essentially another word for public policy; it means the application of the underlying principles of social policy and morality to an individual case.[17]

What is "reasonable" restraint of trade, for example, is a matter to be decided in accordance with the economic conception dominating the society of the day.

In the second place, the function of "reasonableness" is to enable the judge to be creative where a gap in the law, conflicting authorities, or a widely framed provision of a statute allows him to be creative. The test of reasonableness thus is nothing substantially different from "social engineering," "balancing of interests," or any of the other formulas which modern sociological theories suggest as an answer to the problem of the judicial function.[18]

NATURAL LAW IN AMERICAN JURISPRUDENCE

At no period of legal history and in no other legal system has the law, and through it social life, been moulded with greater effect by higher law principles based on a specific interpretation of natural

---

[14] [1894] A.C. 535.

[15] Professor Goodhart, in his review of the first edition of *Legal Theory*, in 8 Mod. L. Rev. 229 (1945), has doubted any connection between these developments of modern English law and natural justice. But the modern conception of natural law is essentially a relative and evolutionary one, and there is at least as much "natural law" evolving in the developments noted above as in the Continental theories noted in Chap. 14, below.

[16] [1935] 1 K.B. 146.

[17] For a further discussion of "public policy," and "general equity," see below, pp. 479 *et seq.*, 490 *et seq.*

[18] See further below, Chap. 27.

justice than American law. Compared with English law there has been infinitely wider scope for judicial control of positive law. This is due both to the existence of a Federal and fifty state constitutions, all framed under the influence of natural right concepts formulated in general and sweeping terms, and to the position of a Supreme Court which since 1803[19] has asserted its right, under the Constitution, to test the validity of any legislative or administrative act in the light of the Constitution. The courts fully seized the opportunity of using this power by infusing their particular conceptions of society into the general clauses of the Constitution.

The Declaration of Independence, strongly influenced by the ideas of Locke, Paine and Rousseau, had spoken of man's inalienable rights of life, liberty and the pursuit of happiness, and these ideas are amply reflected in many American state constitutions. We must confine ourselves to a brief consideration of some provisions including the 5th and 14th Amendments of the Federal Constitutions, the most important sources of judicial review of legislation.

Initially, the principle of the limitation of legislative power by certain basic principles of justice, whether laid down in written constitutions or not, had been deduced (in an *obiter dictum*) by Chase J. in *Calder* v. *Bull* (1793), from the principles of social contract. Subsequently, eminent judges, notably Marshall C.J., Kent C., Story J. asserted the same principle. Professor Haines[20] has well summarised the principal motives of such dicta as being:

(1) Distrust of legislative power.
(2) Protection of minorities.
(3) Protection of property rights.

The protection of vested rights was particularly favoured by judicial pronouncements in the early 19th century. A landmark in this development is *Dartmouth College* v. *Woodward*,[21] when the Supreme Court held that the clause in the Federal Constitution prohibiting a state from impairing the obligation of contracts was intended to restrain state legislatures from passing any law interfering with "contracts respecting property under which some individual could claim a right to something beneficial to himself." This

---

[19] *Marbury* v. *Maddison*, 1 Cranch 137 (1803).
[20] Haines, *The Revival of Natural Law Concepts* (1929).
[21] 4 Wheat. 518 (1819).

was held to apply to the property of corporations and prepared the way for two developments of the gravest importance for the future of American political and social life. It asserted the sanctity of vested rights against social legislation and it extended the "indestructible right of the individual" to the corporation, thus creating the "myth of personality" which Thurman Arnold has so pungently described in his *Folklore of Capitalism*. About the same time Story J. expounded the doctrine that a grant of title to land by the legislature was irrevocable upon principles of natural law as well as of the American Constitution.[22]

But the main impact of judicial review of legislation, based upon a combination of eighteenth-century natural law principles with the Constitution, did not come until the second half of the nineteenth century. For several decades in the period of so-called "frontier democracy" popular government had a free hand. The consolidation of capitalist interests which later on were to press for immunity from interference in the name of natural right had not yet sufficiently proceeded. It was after the civil war, with the supremacy of the new financial and industrial interests established, that judicial supervision of legislation began to assume ever-increasing proportions. The technical instruments chosen were the "Due Process" clauses of the 5th and 14th Amendments.[23] These clauses had originally had a purely procedural significance with the object of preventing arbitrary administration of justice. Under the impact of the developments which turned the United States from a country of colonising farmers into a powerful industrial and trading power and produced an unparalleled competition for the control of mineral resources, finance, transport and trade, its meaning was changed.

Towards the middle of the nineteenth century, financial and industrial states began to take an increasing share in transport developments. They embarked upon public financing of many private enterprises supported by popular vote. These often resulted in failure and bankruptcy. Often public money was squandered and it may well have appeared necessary to many people that some check should be imposed upon legislative recklessness. It was

---

[22] *Ferret* v. *Taylor*, 9 Cranch 430 (1815).

[23] 5th Amendment: "No person shall . . . be deprived of life, liberty or property without due process of law."

14th Amendment: "No state shall deprive any person of life, liberty or property, without due process of law nor deny to any person within its jurisdiction the equal protection of the laws."

under such circumstances that Cooley, in his *Constitutional Limitations* (1868) and *Principles of Taxation* (1879) established principles of judicial supervision of legislation by a wide extension of the meaning of "inalienable rights," "due process" and "eminent domain" provisions. As developed by Cooley, Dillon and others, these constitutional clauses were the expression of certain inalienable natural rights and, in practice, had a threefold aspect:

(1) On the lines previously foreshadowed by Marshall, Kent and others, vested property interests were held to be inalienable rights and immune from legislative interference.

(2) The power to impose taxes was restricted to "public purposes" and public purposes were what the judges understood them to be. Under the influence of Cooley's doctrines, taxes for the purpose of purchasing railway stock[24] or for granting aid to private enterprises or for the development of the natural advantages of a city for manufacturing purposes[25] were held invalid.

(3) Under clauses in most American constitutions the inviolability of private property was mitigated by the power of expropriation for public purposes, by virtue of "eminent domain." Here the court imposed, in the name of natural justice, a similar limitation. Eminent domain can only be exercised for public purposes, and with adequate compensation.

It would be unjust to assert that all these judicial doctrines were a deliberate support of the existing distribution of property. The motives, in many cases, were legitimate anxiety lest legislation or administration might abuse their position. But, deliberate or not, the attitude taken has had far-reaching consequences.

In the first place, by restricting the power of states and public authorities to participate in economic development, the courts did not check recklessness but cleared the road for the exclusive development of economic resources through private interests, which they protected with the help of the natural right of the individual and the sanctity of vested interests.

In the second place, the courts extended the protection given to the individual to the corporations (which are juristic persons and thus in law "individuals"), many of which came to control immense assets, and they thus encouraged the growth of capitalist monopoly which has faced the United States with a social problem of the

[24] *People* v. *Salam*, 20 Mich. 452 (1870).
[25] *City of Ottawa* (1885) 184 Sec. 659.

greatest gravity and, indeed, compelled it to launch a complex and costly system of anti-trust legislation.[26]

In the third place, they arrogated to themselves the ultimate decision as to what was "public use" and hence what was the state's function. Now in every country the state has been compelled to extend its function with the growing complexity of social problems, such as in matters of public health, housing, insurance, industrial protection, labour hours, etc. Judges are likely to be influenced by the conceptions prevalent in their youth and among their class. Where the legislature is supreme, there is but limited scope for the application of their conceptions. But where they are the ultimate arbiters—responsible to no one, protected by judicial independence—of what the state's function should be, they can retard vital social legislation for decades, and American courts have done so.

A further significant stage in the development of judicial control of legislation in the name of higher law was reached when "due process" of law was extended to protect unrestricted liberty of contract. In several judgments[27] Field J. deduced from the natural rights of man, as laid down in the Declaration of Independence, and from the 14th Amendment, the right to pursue any business or selling unhindered, and although he emphasised "that all persons should be equally entitled to pursue their happiness and acquire and enjoy property," the actual effect was to produce in the state courts a line of decisions interpreting this in the sense of absolute freedom of contract.[28] This doctrine was subsequently accepted in the Supreme Court and the 5th and 14th Amendments were given an interpretation which placed new limits on legislative powers of both the Federal and state Governments.

The results were most far-reaching. Again and again the courts invalidated legislative attempts by which maximum hours or minimum wages were stipulated. Prominent examples are the *Adkins* case,[29] in which the Minimum Wage Act passed by Congress for the District of Columbia was invalidated, and the *Lochner* case,[30] where a New York law limiting employment in bakeries to ten

---

[26] On this, *cf.* below, p. 407 *et seq.*
[27] *Butcher's Union Co.* v. *Crescent City*, 111 U.S. 746 (1883); *Barbier* v. *Connolly*, 113 U.S. 27, 31 (1885).
[28] Pound, "Liberty of Contract" 18 Yale L.J. 454 (1909); 23 Yale L.J. 472 *et seq.* (1913).
[29] (1923) 261 U.S. 525.
[30] 198 U.S. 45 (1904).

hours per day was held invalid as depriving an employer of liberty without due process of law. In many other cases, however, regulation of wages and labour conditions were declared justified by the exercise of police power.[31]

Under art. 1 section 8 of the United States Constitution, Congress has power to regulate commerce with foreign nations, and among the several states. In *Hammer* v. *Dagenhart*,[32] a Congressional Act discouraging child labour in interstate commerce transactions was held unconstitutional, as the main purpose of the Act was not the regulation of interstate commerce but of social conditions. On the other hand, the court in a series of decisions sustained national tariffs as a legitimate exercise of the Federal power to collect duties even though the main purpose of the legislation was not the collection of revenue but the discouragement of certain imports.[33] The difference in the approach of the court to the protection of economic interests on the one hand, and to the establishment of minimum social standards on the other hand is striking.

The climax of this development appears to have been reached with the two leading decisions of the Supreme Court condemning important parts of the New Deal legislation, although neither decision is directly based upon the "natural law" interpretation of the 5th or 14th Amendment.

In the *Schechter* case[34] the defendants had been charged with a violation of the live poultry code, which under the N.R.A. imposed a minimum rate of wages and working hours.

The Supreme Court held that the relevant clause of the Act was (a) an unconstitutional delegation of legislative power, and (b) an unconstitutional attempt to regulate intrastate commerce, but thought it unnecessary to pronounce on the third complaint that the Act violated the due process clause of the 5th Amendment.

In *U.S.* v. *Butler*[35] the court decided that certain taxes imposed by the Agricultural Adjustment Act to provide benefit payments for farmers curtailing production in the national emergency were part of an unconstitutional plan to regulate agriculture, in violation of the 10th Amendment, by using economic coercion of alternatively financial inducements to make farmers contract for restriction of production.

---

[31] *Cf.* quotations in Haines, *op. cit.* at 186.
[32] 247 U.S. 251 (1918).
[33] *e.g., Hampton* v. *U. S.* 276 U.S. 394 (1928).
[34] *Schechter Poultry Corporation* v. *U. S.* 295 U.S. 495 (1935).
[35] 297 U.S. 1 (1936).

Both decisions brought to a head an approach to the interpretation of fundamental rights guaranteed by the Constitution which had dominated the Supreme Court for the greater part of a century. Its most effective aspect was the elevation of the "due process" clauses and of the right of property into the natural law principles immunising the individual—including, of course, the most powerful corporations clothed with legal personality—from interference by regulative economic and social action. The court was less effective in preserving what was undoubtedly the underlying principle of the 5th and 14th Amendments, *viz.*, the effective civil and political equality of persons, races and classes within the United States. The most obvious violation of this principle, the poll tax, and other enactments effectively disenfranchising the negro population in many of the southern states, remained unchecked.

The reconstitution of the courts during Franklin Roosevelt's second presidency brought a far-reaching and dramatic reversal in the outlook of the court and in its scale of values. The approach first outlined by Holmes, and developed in particular by Brandeis and Cardozo, won the upper hand with the appointment of several new justices. Its most important aspect was a greater consciousness of the limitations of the non-elected organ of the Constitution, and a correspondingly greater deference to the function of the elected legislature in matters of economic and social legislation. At the same time the court came to abandon the doctrine that economic activities of the state are necessarily "non-governmental." The number of economic and social statutes declared unconstitutional declined drastically, and the court has on the whole maintained this attitude, which agrees with the substance of Holmes' dissenting judgment in the *Lochner* case.

In *Steward Machine Company* v. *Davis*[36] the Supreme Court declared by a majority for the constitutionality of the unemployment scheme of the Social Security Act, 1935. A decision in 1937 upheld the constitutionality of the National Labour Relations Act of 1935[37] The *West Coast Hotel* case[38] explicitly overruled the *Adkins* case. This was made possible by a dramatic change in the position of Justice Roberts, which converted the former minority into a majority. This decision opened the door to legislative action on the control of wages, hours and child labour. This was

---

[36] 301 U.S. 548 (1937).
[37] *N. L. R. B.* v. *Jones & Laughlin Street Corporation*, 301 U.S. 1 (1937).
[38] 300 U.S. 379 (1936).

implemented by the Fair Labour Standards Act of 1938. In subsequent decisions, notably the *Darby* case,[39] the court upheld the provisions of the Act which protected employees engaged in interstate commerce and in the production of goods for such commerce, as a legitimate exercise of Congressional power to legislate on interstate commerce, even though the main object was not commerce as such but the improvement of social conditions for the increasingly wide part of industry which is concerned in interstate commerce.[40] This decision reverses *Hammer* v. *Dagenhart* and the philosophy underlying it.

A series of fundamental decisions illustrates the new and on the whole unanimous bid of the court for a more effective protection of the equality of races guaranteed in particular by the 14th Amendment.

In *Smith* v. *Allwright*[41] the Supreme Court held that the action of the Texas Democratic Party State Convention in excluding negroes from the vote in primary elections was so related to the state regulations of primary elections as to make it a state action repugnant to the 15th Amendment.[42] In *Shelley* v. *Kramer*[43] the court refused to enforce a "racial covenant" purporting to enjoin purchasers of real property from selling it to members of "non-Caucasian" races. In *Sweatt* v. *Painter*[44] the court condemned as unconstitutional the establishment of a separate law school for negroes at the University of Texas. Most important of all, in *Brown* v. *Board of Education*,[45] the court declared segregated public schools for negroes to be in violation of the 14th Amendment and thus overruled its own doctrine of "separate but equal" facilities established in 1897.[46]

Any "higher law" philosophy implies a hierarchy of values. If the Supreme Court formerly gave priority to the right of economic self-assertion and the protection of private property, the court has increasingly come to regard these matters as within the purview of the legislator—save only for obvious infringements of clear

[39] *U. S.* v. *Darby*, 312 U.S. 100 (1941).
[40] For a survey see Stern, "The Commerce Clause and the National Economy, 1933-46," 59 Harv.L.Rev., 645, 883 (1946).
[41] 321 U.S. 649 (1944).
[42] "The right of citizens of the United States to vote shall not be denied or abridged by the United States or by any state on account of race, colour or previous condition of servility."
[43] 334 U.S. 1 (1948).
[44] 339 U.S. 629 (1950).
[45] 347 U.S. 483 (1954).
[46] *Plessy* v. *Ferguson* 163 U.S. 537 (1897).

constitutional provisions—while it has tended to regard the protection of individual rights, equality of educational facilities, and non-discrimination in matters touching the person as more fundamental.[47]

In acting in such problem areas of individual rights as privacy involved in the dissemination of birth control information, voting and the broad issues of procedural rights in the administration of criminal justice the Supreme Court has articulated a number of arguments to justify the extension of the scope of the Bill of Rights so as to restrict the power of the states over their own citizens. The notion that the Bill of Rights was limited in application to the Federal government was announced by Chief Justice Marshall in an 1833 case, *Barron* v. *the Mayor and City Council of Baltimore*[48] which held that the Fifth Amendment prohibition of the taking of property for public use without just compensation did not apply to the states.

This principle has been eroded, in the area of individual rights, through the use of the Due Process and Equal Protection Clauses of the subsequently enacted Fourteenth Amendment.[49] The general tendency of the Court has been towards a selective incorporation of the first eight Amendments as demonstrated by several well-known decisions of the 1930s in the areas of criminal procedure. Cardozo J. justified incorporation on the ground that certain "immunities that are valid as against the Federal government by force of the specific pledges of particular amendments have been found to be implicit in the concept or ordered liberty, and through the Fourteenth Amendment, become valid as against the states."[50] This approach was taken up by Frankfurter J. in subsequent cases[51] and has to a large extent laid the foundation for what may be a return to substantive due process, this time in the area of individual rights.

It is perhaps ironic that Black J. who has steadfastly maintained the motion of the complete incorporation of the first eight amendments, essentially natural law principles, by the Fourteenth

---

[47] A survey of this development and its underlying philosophy is given in the concurring judgment of Frankfurter J. in *A. F. of L.* v. *American Sash Co.* 335 U.S. 538 (1949). In this case the court affirmed the constitutionality of an Amendment to the Arizona Constitution forbidding the exclusion of any person from employment because of non-membership in a labour organization.

[48] 7 Pet. 243 (1833).

[49] Amendment XIV was enacted in 1868.

[50] 302 U.S. 319, 324 (1937).

[51] *Wolf* v. *Colorado*, 338 U.S. 25 (1949); *Rochin* v. *California*, 342 U.S. 165 (1952).

Amendment should attack the majority of the Court as he did in *Adamson* v. *California*:[52]

> This decision reasserts a constitutional theory . . . that this Court is endowed by the Constitution with boundless power under "natural law" periodically to expand and contract constitutional standards to conform to the Court's conception of what at a particular time constitutes "civilized decency" and "fundamental liberty and justice."

The Supreme Court, in cases such as *Mapp* v. *Ohio*[53] (extension of Fourth Amendment privilege against unlawful search and seizure), *Malloy* v. *Hogan*[54] (extension of the Fifth Amendment privilege against self-incrimination) and *Gideon* v. *Wainwright*[55] (extension of the Sixth Amendment right to counsel) has greatly expanded individual protections within the limits of rights specifically enunciated in the United States Constitution. However, the acceleration of the Court's pace in the protection of individual rights has resulted in a splintering of views in areas more difficult to resolve within the already announced limits. In *Griswold* v. *Connecticut*,[56] where the constitutionality of a Connecticut statute making it a crime to give information on birth control was challenged, the Court divided into several groups. Douglas J., writing for the Court, but in a minority in his reasoning, firmly attached his argument to his conception of the Due Process Clause and sought to demonstrate that rights not specifically mentioned in the Constitution or the Bill of Rights exist since, "specific guarantees in the Bill of Rights have penumbras formed by emanations from those guarantees that help give them life and substance."[57] Involved here was one of those rights, the right of privacy: "We deal here with a right of privacy older than the Bill of Rights— older than our political parties, older than our school system."[58]

Harlan J. put the issue in terms of whether the statute infringed the Due Process Clause because its enactment violated the basic values "implicit in the concept of ordered liberty." He held that, "While the relevant inquiry may be aided by resort to one or more of the provisions of the Bill of Rights, it is not dependent on them or any of their radiations. The Due Process Clause of the Fourteenth Amendment stands, in my opinion, on its own bottom."[59] Goldberg J. joined by Brennan J. and Warren C.J.

[52] 332 U.S. 46, 69 (1947).
[53] 369 U.S. 643 (1961).
[54] 378 U.S. 1 (1964).
[55] 372 U.S. 335 (1963).
[56] 381 U.S. 479 (1965).
[57] *Id*. at 484.
[58] *Id*. at 486.
[59] *Id*. at 500.

sought to base their finding of unconstitutionality on the almost never used Ninth Amendment.[60] Goldberg's conclusion was that, "the Ninth Amendment shows a belief of the Constitution's authors that fundamental rights exist that are not expressly enumerated in the first eight Amendments and an intent that these rights be included there not be exhaustive."[61] As to the specific issue: "The entire fabric of the Constitution and the purposes that clearly underlie its specific guarantees demonstrate that the rights to marital privacy and to marry and raise a family are of a similar order and magnitude as the fundamental rights specifically protected.[62] White J.[63] used the specific language of the Fourteenth Amendment by holding that the Connecticut law deprived married couples of "liberty" without due process of law. Black J. joined by Stewart J. based his dissent on his views of the limits of Constitutional protections: [64]

I cannot rely on the Due Process Clause or the Ninth Amendment or any mysterious and uncertain natural law concept as a reason for striking down this state law. The Due Process Clause with an "arbitrary and capricious" or "shocking to the conscience" formula was liberally used by this Court to strike down economic legislation in the early decades of this century. . . . That formula, based on subjective considerations of "natural justice" is no less dangerous when used to enforce this Court's view about personal rights than about economic rights.[65]

In a subsequent case, this time involving the constitutionality of a Virginia poll tax for state elections,[66] Douglas J. writing for a majority of six found that such a tax violated both the Due Process and Equal Protection Clauses. He observed:

We agree, of course, with Justice Holmes that the Due Process Clause of the Fourteenth Amendment "does not enact Mr. Herbert Spenser's Social Statics" . . . likewise the Equal Protection Clause is not shackled to the political theory of a particular era. . . . Notions of what constitutes equal treatment for purposes of the Equal Protection Clause do change.[67]

[60] Amendment IX states: "The enumeration in the Constitution, of certain rights, shall not be construed to deny or disparage others retained by the people."
[61] 381 U.S. 479, 492 (1965).
[62] *Id.* at 495.
[63] *Id.* at 502.
[64] *Id.* at 509.
[65] *Id.* at 522.
[66] *Harper v. Virginia State Board of Elections,* 383 U.S. 663 (1966).
[67] *Id.* at 1082.

Justice Harlan had expressed a similar view in Griswold, although prefaced by a comment on the need for judicial self-restraint:

> "Specific" provisions of the Constitution, no less than "due process", lend themselves as readily to personal interpretations by judges whose constitutional outlook is simply to keep the Constitution in supposed "tune with the times." Need one go further than to call up last Term's reapportionment cases.[68]

The ideological conflicts and pressures of the present time have caused other problems. The First Amendment lays down that: "Congress shall make no law respecting an establishment of religion, or prohibiting the free exercise thereof; or abridging the freedom of speech, or of the press; or the right of people peaceably to assemble, and to petition the Government for a redress of grievances." In days of social and international stability this provision caused no major problems but the First and Second World Wars as well as the tensions of the post-war period have brought out sharply the latent conflict between individual freedom and public security. In *Schenck* v. *U.S.*,[69] Holmes J. formulated the test of "clear and present danger" as a yardstick by which lawful though unpopular political opposition had to be distinguished from criminally subversive behaviour against which the state could act without infringement of the Constitution. The statute in question was an Espionage Act of 1917 whose validity the court confirmed. The test laid down by Holmes J. was as follows:

> The question in every case is whether the words used are used in such circumstances and are of such a nature as to create a clear and present danger that they will bring about the substantive evils that Congress has a right to prevent. It is a question of proximity and degree.

In *Gitlow* v. *New York*,[70] Holmes went so far as to read the right of free speech into the due process provision of the 14th Amendment. In a long series of decisions the Supreme Court has laboured to clarify the "clear and present danger" doctrine which inevitably leaves a great deal of room for different opinions. During the Second World War the Court was frequently split over the legality of compulsory parades and public school flag salutes,

[68] *Griswold* v. *Connecticut*, 381 U.S. 479, 501 (1965). Harlan J. was referring to *Baker* v. *Carr*, 369 U.S. 186 (1962) and *Reynolds* v. *Sims*, 377 U.S. 533 (1964). For a discussion of the cases see below, p. 505 *et seq*.
[69] (1919) 249 U.S. 47.
[70] (1925) 268 U.S. 652, 672.

both of which were attacked by Jehovah's Witnesses as infringements of the First Amendment.[71] In recent years the point at which propaganda for Communist doctrines becomes a subversive action against the Constitution has been the court's most vexing problem. Here again it is impossible to dissociate the judgments of the court from the changing climate and pressures of public opinion and the international situation. At the height of the "Cold War" tension, in upholding the conviction of Communist party officials for violation of the Smith Act[72] the court, in effect, equated the advocacy of Communist doctrine with conspiracy to overthrow the constitutional government.[73] Six years later, a differently composed court in a less tense atmosphere, virtually abandoned the doctrine, by reversing the conviction of fourteen Communist leaders, for similar reasons, under the same Act.[74] A minority which was for some years represented by the two surviving members of the "left wing" of the court[75] has consistently given a radical interpretation of freedom of speech, while it deprecates any attempt of the court to interfere with legislative measures imposing economic and social controls. For this minority the propagation of Communist doctrine is clearly protected by the constitutional guarantee of free speech and therefore outside the regulatory power of the legislator. In the *Dennis* case Black J. said:

> I have always believed that the First Amendment is the keystone of our government, that the freedoms it guarantees provide the best insurance against destruction of all freedom. . . . So long as this court exercises the power of judicial review of legislation, I cannot agree that the First Amendment permits us to sustain laws suppressing freedom of speech and press on the basis of Congress of our own notion of mere "reasonableness."

But the majority, led by Vinson C.J., held in *Dennis* that the legislator should determine the proximity of the danger created by a conspiratorial organisations.[76] The concurring judgment of Frank-

---

[71] *e.g., West Virginia* v. *Barnette*, 319 U.S. 624 (1943).

[72] Sec. 2 (a) It shall be unlawful for any person—
　　(1) to knowingly or wilfully advocate. . . . overthrowing or destroying any government in the United States by force or violence . . .
　　(3) to organize or help to organize any . . . group who teach, advocate, or encourage the overthrow or destruction of any government in the United States by force or violence . . . 18 U.S.C. §2385.
　　See *Scales* v. *United States*, 367 U.S. 203 (1961) and *Noto* v. *United States*, 367 U.S. 290 (1961).

[73] *Dennis* v. *U. S.*, 341 U.S. 494 (1951).

[74] *Yates* v. *U. S.*, 353 U.S. 346 (1957).

[75] Black and Douglas JJ.

[76] *Dennis* v. *U. S.*, 341 U.S. 494, 509 (1951).

furter J. pours cold water on the idea that some constitutional protections are more fundamental than others.

> In no case has a majority of this court held that a legislative judgment, even as to freedom of utterance, may be overturned merely because the court would have made a different choice between the competing interests.

Regardless of the point at which the delicate balance between security and freedom may be struck at different times, this controversy brings out a more fundamental problem of a hierarchy of values within the basic principles of the Constitution. The proposition that there was such a hierarchy was first tentatively mooted by Chief Justice Stone, in 1938.[77]

> Regulatory legislation affecting ordinary commercial transaction is not to be pronounced unconstitutional unless in the light of the facts made known or generally assumed it is of such a character as to preclude the assumption that it rests upon some rational basis within the knowledge and experience of the legislators. There may be narrower scope for operation of the presumption of constitutionality when legislation appears on its face to be within a specific prohibition of the Constitution, such as those of the first ten amendments, which are deemed equally specific when held to be embraced within the Fourteenth.

This was developed into a consistent doctrine by Justices Black and Douglas joined, more recently, by Chief Justice Warren, in a number of decisions or dissents, among them *Dennis* and *Yates*. The preferred freedom doctrine was repudiated with increasing fervour by Frankfurter J.[78] It has also been condemned by another eminent judge:[79]

> I can see no more persuasive reason for supposing that a legislature is *a priori* less qualified to choose between "personal" than between economic values; and there have been strong protests, to me unanswerable, that there is no constitutional basis for asserting a larger measure of judicial supervision over the first than over the second.

Even if one accepts a priority of personal over economic freedom, there may be a conflict between different personal freedoms, *e.g.*, between freedom of association or contract and racial non-

---

[77] *U. S.* v. *Carolene Products Company*, 304 U.S. 144, 152 (1938).
[78] See his doctrine in *Dennis* above, p. 96; also *Kovacs* v. *Cooper* 366 U.S. 77 991 (1949); *A. F. of L.* v. *American Sash and Door Co.*, 335 U.S. at 555 (1949).
[79] Judge Learned Hand, *The Bill of Rights* 50-51, (1958).

discrimination.[80] The plea for a "neutral" and "principled" approach to constitutional interpretation[81] may clarify, but it cannot eliminate, the conflict of values.

The foregoing brief survey shows the full extent to which changing ideas, pressures and personalities influence the scale of legal values, however clearly it may appear to be prescribed in constitutional documents. It is this conclusion which is of importance to legal theory. One of the ablest of modern natural law philosophers[82] points to the natural law thinking in the United States as a guarantee against ethical relativism and legal positivism. The example is not happily chosen. Natural law thinking in the United States undoubtedly inspired the fathers of the Constitution, and it has dominated the Supreme Court more than any other law court in the world. Such thinking has not prevented the court from vacillating, from the unconditional condemnation of legislative regulation of social and economic conditions to its almost unrestricted recognition, from the recognition of almost unrestricted freedom of speech and assembly to the virtual outlawing of a political party, and, on the other hand, from the toleration of the most blatant discrimination against negroes to the strong protection given in recent judgments. Yet the American Constitution gives as near an approach to the unconditional embodiment of "natural" rights as can be imagined. It is not the weakness or the vacillations of the court which in the face of such provisions have created so much uncertainty. The generality of "Bills of Rights" and similar provisions can disguise but not eliminate the conflict of values and interests which is ever present.[83] Neither the Australian nor the pre-1960 Canadian Constitution—both more easily comparable to the United States Constitution than any other—contains a Bill of Rights, yet the conflict between economic freedom and state regulation, between the freedom of the individual and the power

---

[80] *Shelley* v. *Kramer* 334 U.S. 1 (1948) (non-enforceability of covenants restricting land transfers to persons of designated race). See also *Pennsylvania* v. *Board of Trustees* (1957) 353 U.S. 230 (illegality of refusal by City Board as trustees of a will establishing a college for "poor white male orphans," to admit negro orphans). See also the cases on extension of the principle of non-discrimination to private organisation with monopoly powers, such as labour unions (*Steele* v. *Louisville & NRR* 323 U.S. 192 (1944)); and recent state statutes, *e.g.*, of New York, prohibiting race discrimination.

[81] Wechsler, "Toward Neutral Principles of Natural Law," 73 Harv.L.Rev. 1, 26 *et seq.* (1960).

[82] Rommen, *Natural Law* 41 (1947).

[83] The continuing tensions and vacillations between conflicting values and interests, in the interpretation of the American Constitution, have recently been analysed by Walter Gellhorn, *American Rights*, 1960.

of self-protection of the state, and other basic conflicts have arisen in much the same manner, though in a different legal form.[84]

Conflicting principles, of private enterprise and social control, of racial equality and racial discrimination, of tolerance and intolerance, will continue to battle for legal recognition. Where the battle is fought in terms of fundamental rights embodied in the written Constitution—and especially in a federal framework, with its delicate system of balances and counter-balances—the natural law appeal will be more direct and powerful than in a system which, like the British constitutional system, allows for changing ideologies through the simple interaction of legislative change and public opinion.

[84] *Cf.*, for Canada, Laskin, *Constitutional Law* (1952), *passim*; for Australia, Sawer, in *Federalism in Australia* (1949). For a comparative survey of the problems of interpretation in federal constitutions, *cf.* Freund, "A Supreme Court in a Federation," 53 Colum. L. Rev. 597 (1963).

In August 1960, Canada enacted the Canadian Bill of Rights, which embodies the basic human freedoms as well as principles of statutory construction designed to prevent arbitrary interference with these freedoms in criminal or other investigatory proceedings. The Bill has not so far been incorporated in the British North America Act, and it has also been criticised as not offering protection against invasion of rights by the provinces. See Dawson, *The Government of Canada*, rev. ed. 1964.

CHAPTER 14

REVIVAL OF NATURAL LAW THEORIES

THE predominant forces in nineteenth-century legal thinking, nationalism, materialism and the scientific outlook, while of dynamic significance for the political, economic and technical evolution of modern Western society, contributed to the sterility of legal philosophy. From different angles they all arrived at a philosophy of certainty which was likely to last just as long as the certainty of the social conditions in which it prospered. Savigny's and Hegel's theories led straight to absolute faith in the protector state cemented by a host of theories of national sovereignty. Materialism resulted in an unquestioned belief in mankind's salvation through economic progress. The scientific outlook in law ended in the rigid formalism of a scientific, analytical jurisprudence.

Even before Western society was shattered by the First World War and its aftermath, a reaction set in, a deep-seated dissatisfaction with material prosperity, with self-assurance, with Victorian bourgeoisie and many other things. Once more the human mind grew restless, revolted against the accepted standards of the day and, as in previous generations, searched for an ideal of justice.

The sources of this restlessness were many. Science began to become doubtful about itself and the certainty of scientific facts. Youth rebelled against the self-satisfaction of the bourgeoisie, against cities, money worship and the flatness of modern life. Social reformers and socialists attacked the social inequalities hidden under legal formalism, and the authority worship of positivists. Lawyers began to find that the law was not simply a matter of applying statute or precedent to any given case or situation, by means of pure logic, that more and more unsolved problems presented themselves, problems the solution of which demanded a guide higher than the positive law.

As the faith of certainty wavers, idealistic philosophy revives; in the field of law this means once more a search for ideals of justice. Most of the legal theories which are thus preoccupied are usually characterised as "reviving" natural law.[1]

But there are, in fact, at least three widely different ways in which natural law re-entered the field in the late nineteenth and early twentieth century. The first leads straight back to the scholastic conception of natural law and is little more than a modernisation of the Catholic theory of law, in connection with which it has been treated.

The second and third trends both show, as against the absolute ideals of schoolmen and rationalists, the scepticism of a world which feels that all values are relative and that no absolute ideal of justice can hope for universal recognition and validity.

But two different types of alternative solutions are offered. Stammler's "Natural Law with Changing Content" shares with genuine natural law theories nothing but the yearning for a legal ideal, which it formulates, however, in a purely formal sense.

A more genuine revival of natural law ideas can be detected in different modern theories which conceive natural law as an evolutionary ideal, and thus as a directive force in the development of positive law.

Underlying these theories is the scepticism of modern thinkers against a static ideal, coupled with a relativist outlook and, in most if not all cases, a belief in the progress of mankind.

The most representative of these modern natural law theories —apart from the neo-scholastic ones—are those of Gény and Del Vecchio. Of both, a detailed account is given in connection with the general theory of these two legal philosophers.[2] For both, natural law serves essentially as a guide to positive law.

Del Vecchio conceives natural law as the principle of legal evolution which guides mankind, and law with it, towards greater autonomy of man.

Gény asserts the idea of natural law against the positivist theory of law. His own natural law ideas are contained in the third and fourth of his "*donnés*," the "*donné rationnel*" and the "*donné idéal*." The former is static, comprising a number of principles of reason, interpreted in accordance with the ideals of Western Liberalism, and the latter is dynamic, comprising the ideas and values predominant in a given community at a given time.

---

[1] *e.g.,* Charmont, *La Renaissance du Droit Naturel* (1910); Haines, *Revival of Natural Law Concepts* (1929).
[2] See below, pp. 186 *et seq.,* 328 *et seq.*

A modern natural law theory, rather akin to that of Gény, but with a theological flavour and close to neo-scholastic natural law theories is that of Le Fur.[3]

Le Fur considers the conception of natural law as necessary, because given with the very idea of justice. It rests on human nature which, being that of a reasonable being, demonstrates to man that he is the creation of a superior will and intelligence, that is of God.

But natural law supplies only the general framework of legal principles. They are three: sanctity of obligations, duty to repair unlawfully done harm, and respect for authority. This tripartite division is not far from the famous three principles of the *Institutes*. The framework is filled in by "*le droit rationnel ou scientifique*." This is the result of reason applying the facts (donnés) of history and economics, and thus harmonises tne law with the needs of different peoples and circumstances. From these sources positive law is derived, both in its foundations and its objects. Positive law, the object of which is the common good, must have a moral basis. Its function is to determine, make precise and provide with a sanction the general commands of natural law developed by rational law.[4]

Natural law terminology thus adopted by some modern legal philosophers, but not by others, may disguise the fundamental affinity between all those modern legal theories which, in opposition to positivism, stress the need of legal ideals. Spencer's principle of evolution, Duguit's social solidarity, Kohler's evolution of "*Kultur*," Pound's "social engineering," Ripert's "*règle morale*," these and a host of others are natural law ideals in the modern relativist and evolutionary sense, whether they choose to adopt the term or not. The Norwegian jurist Castberg[5] speaks of natural law in the sense of rules of ideal laws which are adapted to the constantly changing conditions of life. Professor Fuller,[6] speaks of natural law as essentially "a way of thinking." Another contemporary American jurist[7] goes somewhat further. He believes that there are objective and absolutely valid ethical values. "The objective validity of moral judgments is known intuitively or, as regards problematic situa-

---

[3] *Les grands problèmes du droit* (1937).

[4] For all practical purposes, this natural law theory is almost identical with the positivism of G. Ripert (see below, p. 215 *et seq.*). The two theories start from opposite ends and mcet in the middle.

[5] *Problems of Legal Philosophy* 112 (2nd ed., 1957)

[6] *The Law in Quest of Itself* (1940).

[7] Jerome Hall, *Living Law of Democratic Society* (1949).

tions, it is established by analysis, discussion and reflection, coherence with wider experience, the consensus of informed unbiased persons, and the universality of the solutions among diverse cultures."[8] But Hall does not believe that the correct answer to the most difficult ethical problems can be found by conscience, intuition or the law of God. Reason must aid in the choice between conflicting principles. To Hall, democracy is part of modern natural law because the values incorporated in democratic law "represent the most stable policy decisions which it is wise and feasible to implement by compulsion."[9] Such an estimate will be accepted by democrats and rejected by others. It leads no further than to the assertion that democracy is a good society and should be accepted by everybody.

Apart from neo-scholastic Catholic doctrine, the most significant revival of natural law thinking in our time is to be found in contemporary German legal philosophy. This revival is, in large measure, not merely one of the periodic intellectual cycles. It springs directly from the reaction against the excessive and, in the later phases of the Nazi régime, nihilistic manifestations of legal positivism. Trying to rebuild not only new cities and factories, but also a new order of values from the material and spiritual débris of the Second World War, German legal philosophers as well as the law courts have sought to rethink and reformulate the relation of "higher law" principles and positive law. The signal was given by Gustav Radbruch, whose legal philosophy,[10] though imbued with high ethical purpose and a sense of values, had denied the possibility of a scientific and provable choice between alternative values. In a much discussed post-war article[11] Radbruch, deeply moved by the excesses of absolute state sovereignty perpetrated by the Nazi régime, stated that, since law was, in its very nature, destined to serve justice, certain types of positive law could not be defined as law, and this applied to whole portions of National Socialist "law." The implication of Radbruch's challenge—which has stimulated a great revival of natural-law thinking in Germany—will be discussed later in the context of the problem of absolute ideas of justice.[12]

---

[8] *Id*. at 80-81.
[9] *Id*. at 96.
[10] See below, p. 192 *et seq*.
[11] "Gesetzliches Unrecht und übergesetzliches Recht," *Süddeutsche Juristenzeitung* (August 1946); reprinted in Radbruch: *Rechtsphilosophie* (4th ed., Erik Wolf, 1950).
[12] See below, p. 350 *et seq*.

Philosophically, the predominant type of natural law revival in post-war German philosophy has been a coupling of natural law with *"Wertphilosophie"* and existentialism. A number of contemporary German legal philosophers have attempted to re-establish an objectively valid scale of higher values as a realisation of man's true struggle for existence.[13] To name but a few, Johannes Messner[14] regards it as essential to rejoin hedonistic and intuitional thinking which have been artificially separated. He sees in the institution of the family the basic community order, from which all elements of the nature of law can be demonstrated. In particular it embodies the constant tension between the welfare and peace functions of law and the egoistic tendencies. Von der Heydte[15] sees any positive norm of law as a simultaneous realisation of a timeless moral postulate and a time-conditioned and time-limited political objective. Law exists in the tension between the moral and the political. The postulates of justice are not only principles of order existing independently of man, but also the will of the individual, a measure of his moral justification and destination.

Coing[16] thinks the establishment of "highest principles" of law is the phenomenological insight into the structure and essence of certain institutions such as contract, family, or commercial transactions.

It is apparent that with the exception of neo-scholastic theories, modern natural law theories have lost the distinctiveness of earlier natural law philosophers. They become part of the never-ending search for ideas of justice which many other jurists prefer to express in terms shorn of natural law phraseology.

---

[13] On the modern movements in phenomenology and existentialism, see below, p. 197 *et seq.*

[14] Messner "Naturrecht ist Existenzordnung," 42 *Archiv für Rechts- und Sozialphilosophie*, 187 (1956).

[15] Von Der Heydte "Vom Wesen des Naturrechts," *Archiv für Rechts- und Sozialphilosophie, id.* 211.

[16] *Grundzüge der Rechtsphilosophie* (1950).

Philosophical Idealism and the Problem of Justice

CHAPTER 15

GERMAN TRANSCENDENTAL IDEALISM

THE comparatively brief period during which Germany produced an abundance of great philosophers, poets, musicians and scholars has also profoundly influenced the further development of legal thought.

The three great philosophers, Kant, Fichte and Hegal, of whose legal philosophy an account is to be given, do not nearly exhaust the intellectual fecundity of that period. But they are the outstanding figures, and each of them has devoted a considerable part of his philosophy to the law.

Widely as Kant, Fichte and Hegel differ in their systems and conclusions from each other, they share some fundamental ideas. They all deduce their legal philosophy from certain fundamental principles, which they discover through an inquiry into the human mind; in studying the human mind they start from one fundamental Aristotelean principle: That man is a rational free willing being distinct from nature. Man as an animal is indeed part of nature, and as such he is subject to the physical laws of nature. But being endowed with reason, he is at the same time distinct from nature and capable of dominating it.

While this identical point of departure provides a substantial community of outlook among the three philosophers, their conclusions in the field of legal philosophy are nevertheless widely different.

KANT (1724-1804)

Kant, embodying and developing in a comprehensive and profound system the results of centuries of philosophical thought, gave modern thinking a new basis which no subsequent philosophy could ignore. The "Copernican Turn" which he gave to philosophy was to replace the psychological and empirical method by the critical method, by an attempt to base the rational character of life and world not on the observation of facts and matter but on human consciousness itself. This Kant did by a systematic inquiry into the functions of human reason. His main work consists of three principal parts, in accordance with the three functions of human consciousness, thinking, volition and feeling. The first part, the *Critique of Pure Reason*, deals with perception, the second, the *Critique of Practical Reason*, with morality, while the third, the *Critique of the Power of Judgment*, deals with aesthetics. Of these, only the first two need concern us. For an understanding of Kant's own legal philosophy we could be content with the second. Kant himself did not apply his discoveries on the theoretical possibilities of human knowledge to his principles of morality (which includes his legal philosophy). For him the realms of perception and volition were derived from entirely different principles. The Neo-Kantian philosophers, of whose theories an account will be given later, have based their legal theories on Kant's theory of knowledge, not on his theory of law. Thus a brief introduction to Kant's theory of knowledge is indispensable.

Kant, in his *Critique of Pure Reason*, set himself the task of analysing the world as it appears to human consciousness. Absolute reality as such, the "*Ding an sich*," Kant, like Plato, holds to be unknowable to men. Kant draws a fundamental distinction between form and matter. The impressions of our senses are the matter of human experience, which is brought into order and shape by the human mind. Emotions become perceptions through the forms of space and time, perceptions become experience through the categories of understanding, such as substance and causality, quality and quantity, etc.; the judgments of experience are linked with each other by general principles (ideas). Formal categories therefore bring order into the chaos of emotions and sensations, and they are constant while matter changes. This approach is based on a fundamental opposition between nature and mind. Nature follows necessity, but the human mind is free because it can set itself purposes and have a free will. This opposition Kant himself develops by distinguishing strictly between the realm of knowledge and that of volition. The human mind brings order into the chaos of things as they appear to man, but he cannot make them or determine their course. But man can freely set his aims to himself. To realise them is not a matter of necessity but of belief.

Kant then inquires whether there are any general principles which can be laid down as a basis of man's volition and thus of all ethical action. Such basis cannot be gained from experience. It must be given *a priori*, but not as logical necessity; it can only be stated as a postulate for man, as a free and rational being. The freedom of man to act according to this postulate and the ethical postulate itself are necessary correlatives. No ethical postulate is possible without this freedom of self-determination, and the ethical postulate is a necessary condition of freedom. The substance of this ethical postulate is Kant's famous *Categorical Imperative*. It is categorical as distinguished from a hypothetical imperative which says: "If you want this do that." The *Categorical Imperative* commands: "Do this without any regard to any particular end to which you may or may not be inclined."

This is what Kant's *Categorical Imperative* says: "Act in such a way that the maxim of your action could be made the maxim of a general action." This imperative is the basis of Kant's moral as well as his legal philosophy. But the spheres of morality and law are clearly distinct. Morality is a matter of the internal motives of the individual. Legality is a matter of action in conformity with an external standard set by the law. Thus it is not the principle but the kind of command issuing from the common principle which distinguishes law from morality. It must be emphasised that Kant's legal philosophy is entirely a theory of what the law ought to be. A discrepancy between the law that is and the law that ought to be is not discussed. His is the legal philosophy of a philosopher, not of a lawyer. From the *Categorical Imperative* Kant deduces his definition of the law.

Law is the aggregate of the conditions under which the arbitrary will of one individual may be combined with that of another under a general inclusive law of freedom.

This is the way in which man as a rational being can achieve harmony of all beings and things with each other under a principle of reason. It is in accordance with the principle of freedom that an individual should act in such a way that he leaves it open to all others (who are equally rational beings) to act alike.

It follows from Kant's sharp distinction between morality and law that compulsion is essential to law and a right is characterised

---

[1] Only in this sense is Kant's ethical postulate a fact. Brecht 54 Harv. L. Rev. 818 (1941) quotes a passage from the *Critique of Practical Reason*: "the objective reality . . . of a pure practical reason, is given in the moral law *a priori*, as it were by a fact . . . ," for an alleged link between Is and Ought. To fuse pure with practical reason would shatter the whole structure of Kant's philosophy.

by the power to compel. Kant distinguishes between legal duties and legal rights. As for legal duties he is content with Ulpian's three principles: *Honeste vivere, neminem laedere, suum cuique tribuere*. As to rights, he distinguishes between natural rights and acquired rights. But he recognises only one natural right: the freedom of man in so far as it can co-exist with every one else's freedom under a general law. Equality is implied in the principle of freedom. From this follow a number of rights pertaining to the individual, in particular the right to property, considered by Kant (as by Locke, Hegel and many others) as an expression of personality. By projecting his will into certain objects, the individual makes them partake of his inviolability. Since the earth is in common possession of all, each can establish a claim to a part of it, in so far as he grants equal liberty to others to establish exclusive possession of parts appropriated by them against him. Kant also discusses marriage, through which an individual acquires a right over another. But the other person, by acquiring a similar right in return, recovers his personality. Logic, however, deserts Kant and prejudice comes in, when he further proclaims wide patriarchal rights of the head of the household over the family.

It follows from Kant's primary assumption of the freedom of the reasonable individual, that he considers political power as conditioned by the need of rendering each man's right effective, while limiting it at the same time through the legal right of others. Only the collective universal will armed with absolute power can give security to all. This transfer of power Kant bases on the social contract, which is to him not an historical fact but an idea of reason. The social contract is so sacred that there is an absolute duty to obey the existing legislative power. Rebellion is never justified for Kant, although he is no authoritarian, but considers a republican and representative state as the ideal. Only the united will of all can institute legislation. But once more prejudice thwarts logic, when Kant proceeds to argue that there are active and passive citizens and that the latter who include not only women and children, but also house-servants and day-labourers, are only potential citizens, and have not yet acquired any political right. In principle, however, Kant thinks that law is just only when it is at least possible that the whole population should agree to it. He favours separation of power and is opposed to privileges of birth, an established Church and autonomy of corporations; he also favours free speech.

But since the subject has no right to revolt under any circumstances, all these principles are only directions to the legislator. The function of the state is for Kant essentially that of protector and guardian of the law. It is not, as for Hegel, the integration of the individual, its rational self, nor does it have to undertake comprehensive functions in order to ensure the maximum liberty of the individual, as with Fichte. It is not the state's task, says Kant, to make the subject happy according to its own judgment. "When the sovereign limits himself to his proper task of maintaining the state as an institution of the administration of justice, and interferes with the welfare and happiness of citizens only so far as is necessary to secure this end, when, on the other hand, the citizen is allowed freely to criticise acts of government but never seeks to resist it—then we have this union of the spirit of freedom with obedience to law and loyalty to the State which is the political ideal of the state."

Kant's individualistic conception of society is logically developed in his theories of international law. His aim is a universal world state. The establishment of a republican constitution based on freedom and equality of states is, for Kant, a step towards a League of States to secure peace. He sees it as a phase in a development which should eventually lead to a world state of which the individual is an immediate citizen and where the state can disappear.

On the other hand, Kant appears to be doubtful of the practical possibility of a "State of Nations." In his *Perpetual Peace* he envisages at times a Federation of Nations (p. 129), at times a State of Nations which would embrace all the peoples of the earth (p. 136). The same doubt appears in his *Rechtslehre* (2, s. 61). On the whole Kant's idea seems to have been to ensure peace through a process as close as possible to that by which a people becomes a state.[2] Kant saw no possibility of international law without an international authority superior to the states. This view, derided by nineteenth-century positivists, is again accepted today under the bitter experience of modern history.

FICHTE (1762-1814)

The comparison between Kant's and Fichte's legal philosophies demonstrates how, from a common theoretical standpoint, it is

---

[2] Kant, *The Philosophy of Law* 189 (trans. Hastie (1887)), *Cf.* note by Hastie.

possible to reach the most divergent conclusions where political ideals differ.

Fichte's legal philosophy[3] is deduced, like Kant's, from the self-consciousness of the reasonable being. No reasonable being can think himself without ascribing free activity to himself. But this he cannot do without ascribing it equally to others. Freedom is of necessity mutual. The sphere of legal relations is that part of mutual personal relations which regulates the recognition and definition of the respective spheres of liberty, on the basis of free individuality. It only refers to actions, not to motives. On the relation of law and morality, Fichte develops Kant's doctrine. Whereas there is a moral duty to respect the liberty of others absolutely, a legal duty to do so is dependent on reciprocity. Unless my liberty is recognised in turn, the law gives me a right of compulsion to enforce my fundamental rights. The conditions of that right, however, must be fixed by a third power. This third power is the law which can govern only by and in the state. This justifies the existence of the state. Fichte proceeds to state those elementary rights of the individual which must be protected by the state, as they are the necessary condition of personal existence; these are the integrity of body, property and self-preservation, and the law must regulate the measure of their protection. The law must realise justice and the state must be a *Rechtsstaat*. To ensure this, Fichte postulated an institution comparable to what a little later became reality in the United States of America, an institution independent of state-power, with the object of examining the legality of the actions of the state (*Ephorat*). Fichte did not, however, demand a written constitution to fix the fundamental rights. Fichte's *Social Contract* is divided into a property contract and a protection contract. Through property one becomes a citizen, but the correlative of this is that every one must have property, since no one must be excluded from the legal community.

The relation between individual and state is defined in three principles: (1) Through fulfilment of civic duties the individual becomes a member of the state. (2) The law limits and assures the rights of the individual. (3) Outside this sphere of civic duties the individual is free and only responsible to himself. He is man, not citizen.

The right to punish is part of the social contract and based on

---

[3] The account is based on Fichte's *Grundlage des Naturrechts* (1796) and *Der geschlossene Handelsstaat* (1800).

retaliation. But the aim of reforming the criminal modifies retaliation. Criminal law embodies and ensures the protection of rights guaranteed by the *Rechtsstaat*.

Fichte, with professorial solemnity, propounds some amazing theories on marriage and family. Marriage is unity of will and excludes separation of property. Like other idealistic philosophers, Fichte sees property as an emanation of personality. But although a woman through marriage becomes a full citizen, she still remains represented by her husband in the public sphere. This difference is carried into the private sphere. Male self-consciousness, Fichte teaches, may find an object in the satisfaction of sexual impulse. But woman must never confess to such a purpose, although she must have the same impulse. Her nature demands giving herself to a man. Man replies by generosity. Adultery of the wife destroys marriage, that of the husband destroys it only if it kills the wife's love. As for children, Fichte asserts that the state, which may, in general, influence the relations of parents and children, is not interested in the preservation of incapacitated children. It does not order their killing, but does not forbid it either.

Much more important is Fichte's application of his legal philosophy to principles of state life.[4] His work gains new significance in our time.

The rights to be protected by the state are: (1) the right to live; (2) the right to work. Without the latter there can be no duty to recognise the property of others. The state has therefore the duty to see:

(a) That the necessities of life are produced in a quantity proportionate to the number of citizens.
(b) That every one can satisfy his needs through work.

There are three main branches of public work: (1) Natural production; (2) Trade; (3) Manufacture.

The products of nature, which are won by man's labour, are his property. But those products which are only produced by nature (minerals) should be state property. Fichte also urges that there should be a constant readjustment of the proportion between money and goods. If the state is to protect property it must also regulate labour and trade. This leads to the rejection of free trade and business internally as well as externally. Fichte's aim is the creation of a closed economic entity based on national production, which is

[4] *Der geschlossene Handelsstaat* (1800).

possible only if the state has natural frontiers. Foreign trade which is thus reduced to subordinate importance must be a state monopoly.

As for international law, Fichte's legal philosophy stands half-way between Kant and Hegel. Fichte denies the possibility of a universal state because of the distinction of races. But as human self-consciousness demands mutual recognition of men as reasonable beings, so states must recognise each other and form a legal community.

War, the means of asserting legal rights between states, is based on force, not on law. The law can assert itself only in a League of Nations with a federal tribune endowed with authority to judge, and military executive powers to enforce the judgment.[5]

The subsequent era of liberal nationalism rejected or ignored Fichte's system of legal philosophy while paying much attention to his theory of knowledge. Today the main outline of the way in which Fichte applies the principles of his legal philosophy to political reality has a far more realistic and, indeed, prophetic aspect than the opinions of most of his critics. The freedom of man as a reasonable being was the starting point for Fichte as for Kant and Hegel, but he thought more deeply about the implications of this premise, and anticipated by almost a century the criticism expressed by modern jurists against the formal conception of liberty which dominated the nineteenth century.

HEGEL (1770-1831)

Hegel's philosophy is the most comprehensive and ambitious attempt ever undertaken to give a complete theoretical explanation of the universe. Hegel is not content to analyse knowledge or will or natural sciences or logic or history or law. All are welded by Hegel into a gigantic unity in which not only the whole universe is contained, but in which all antinomies or conflicts, dualism of ideas all real forces are eliminated. The Idea, which is Reason and Spirit, contains them all. Hegel's system is a monistic one. The idea unfolds from the simple to the complex by means of the dialec-

---

[5] This account refers to Fichte's legal philosophy, and leaves out the purely political work of his later years, which, inspired by the Napoleonic suppression and the wars of liberation, shows an increasingly fervent nationalism and the preaching of the mission of the German nation in the world—a dangerous idea which was destined to produce disastrous political consequences in the subsequent century.

tical process. Thus there can be no dualism of any kind; for any phase of reality is based on reason.

"What is reasonable is real, and what is real is reasonable."[6] The whole task of philosophy is to Hegel the vindication of that conviction, and consequently he emphatically rejects any antinomy between idea and experience or reason and reality.

What matters is to perceive in the appearance of the temporal and transitory, the substance, which is immanent, and the eternal, which is actual. For the reasonable, which is synonymous with the idea in that it assumes external existence in its actuality, appears in an infinite variety of forms, phenomena and surrounds its kernel with the shell in which consciousness dwells first, and which the Notion then penetrates to find its pulse and to feel it in its manifold appearance.

The Absolute Spirit contains and comprises all previous stages of development, and therefore is at the beginning of all things as well as at the end. This means and implies that every phase in the development of the world must follow as a matter of necessity from a previous one, that there is nothing between elementary logical conditions of existence and the most comprehensive edifice of philosophy which is not, of necessity, connected. The link is provided by the dialectical method. It means that any concept contains its own opposite hidden away within itself. Thus the conception of being, abstracted from any content, contains in itself, as its opposite, the conception of nothing. The passage from being into nothing or vice versa implies a third category, that of becoming. There is thus a triad composed of thesis, antithesis and synthesis. Becoming is the synthesis of being and nothing. To take an example of another part of the system: Essence and Appearance are opposites, actuality is their synthesis. Each synthesis forms again the starting point for a new triad, and thus the universe, in all its aspects, unfolds by a process which Hegel considers as being strictly logical and in which each part is in a necessary logical connection with any other. Logic, morality, religion are all linked with each other in this way. Legal philosophy finds its place in this process. The idea, which comprises all reality, unfolds by a dialectical process in which the idea "itself," the logical idea, contains as its antithesis the idea outside itself, nature. The synthesis of logic and nature is the idea in and for itself, spirit. Spirit unfolds in a dialectical process in which subjective spirit (the categories of feeling, thinking and consciousness) is the thesis,

[6] *Rechtsphilosophie* 40.

objective spirit (legal and social institutions) the antithesis, and the absolute spirit—Art, Religion and Philosophy—constitutes the synthesis and, at the same time, the full realisation of the idea. Legal institutions are within the sphere of objective spirit. This in Hegel's system covers the spheres of legal, ethical and political institutions. All these institutions are the expression of the free human mind, which wishes to embody itself in objectivity, in institutions. The human spirit which projects itself in the human world, is therefore governed by itself, and is consequently free. Hegel emphatically rejects the dualism of thought and will. That is possible only because mere instinctive will is to Hegel no free will, and only free will he considers as will.

Only as thinking intelligence, will is free will. The slave does not know his essence, his infinity, his freedom. He does not know himself as a being—that is, he does not think himself. Self-consciousness which perceives its own essence by thinking and thus frees itself of the accidental and untrue, makes the principle of law and morality.[7]

The free will, that is the rational will, thinks in institutions, in which it projects itself.

Hegel does not divide the creations of the objective spirit into ethics, laws and politics. His triad is abstract right, morality and social ethics. This sphere of abstract right is the sphere of those rights and duties which belong to human beings as persons simply, not as citizens of the state. Morality is the sphere of the inwardly directed human will, and social ethics, which comprises family, civil society and state, is the synthesis of abstract right and morality.

Of abstract right Hegel knows three categories: property, contract and wrong (composed of tort and crime).[8]

A thing may be appropriated by the person as a means to his own satisfaction:

To appropriate is at bottom only to manifest the majesty of my will towards things, by demonstrating that they are not self-complete and have no purpose of their own.[9]

Since this will inheres in the single individual person, property must be private property. Hegel considers private property as

[7] *Rechtsphilosophie*, Introduction (4th), § 21.

[8] In this conception of abstract right, Hegel relapses into natural law theories which were contrary to his whole philosophical system, as segregating the sphere of inborn private rights from the general legal position of the individual, which for Hegel can be conceived only in the community. See the criticism of Lasson, *Einleitung zu Hegels Rechtsphilosophie*.

[9] *Rechtsphilosophie*, § 44.

inevitable in the nature of things, with the remarkable argument that food, for example, can be eaten and therefore appropriated only by individuals. If exceptions are to be made the state alone must make them. Now Hegel must face the problem of every legal philosopher that, if the right to property is an outcome of the free human will and each human being is a free person, property should be equally divided among men. This Hegel denies. Individuals are all equals inasmuch as they are all persons; but they have in addition certain definite capacities and abilities. The question of the amount of property which each may appropriate is determined by these differences.

Contract is the antithesis of property. Two persons owning property have each the right to relinquish their property in favour of the other, and this is contract. It brings to life the capacity, the right of the individual, to acquire and dispose of property by voluntary acts.

To that extent the individual acts as part of the universe. But in so far as the individual is a being of impulses, private interests, etc., he may oppose himself to the universal will. This results in a wrong, of which the greatest is crime. By committing a crime, the individual openly negates the right, and right must restore itself by negating the negation. This is done by punishment, the object of which is to restore the true will of the criminal, that is the will which is in accordance with the universal. Hegel therefore rejects the deterrent theory of punishment. The object of punishment is to restore right. Since the state is a higher aim than the individual, Hegal advocates capital punishment but advises moderation.

Morality, the antithesis of abstract right, has only a rather narrow field in Hegel's system.[10]

The dialectic transition from abstract right to morality is provided by a wrong revealing the possibility of the individual will, different from what it ought to be in order to be universal. This tension produces morality. The will turns back into itself, to discover—by means of a further dialectical process—that the indivi-

[10] This is no accident, as the leading German interpreter, Lasson, has shown, *Einleitung zu Hegels Rechtsphilosophie*, xli, xlvii. Hegel strongly opposed Kant's and Fichte's separation of law and morality on the one hand, and the romantic tendency of his period to seek morality in subjective sentiment on the other. Morality to him is a rational factor, a stage of the reflection of the individual. So strong was Hegel's aversion against the subjective tendency, that morality became completely submerged in the objective institution of the state which embodies morality. This has largely contributed to Hegel's reputation as a protagonist of a deified state.

dual must act with a purpose and that any will opposing itself to the universal will is wicked. Morality therefore consists in doing the universal, the rational.

Social ethics, unfolding through family, civil society and the state, is a synthesis of abstract right and morality. We are now in the realm of institutions, in which the particular will finds itself at one with the universal will. The family is the first stage of the objective will, an institution based on feeling. Its first phase is marriage, where two persons give up their independent personality to become one person. Hegel emphatically rejects the idea that marriage is essentially a contrivance for benefiting the individuals who marry. In that case it might be dissolved like a contract. Marriage, he asserts, is an institution based on reason, and "being in love" is not its essential side. Were it otherwise, the merely subjective and particular would be exalted above the objective and universal. To Hegel the rational consists in a marriage wisely arranged upon rational considerations and accepted by parents and family, instead of being based purely on romantic love. Because the family is one, property becomes common possession, but is held in trust by the husband and father.

Civil society arises through the members of the family acquiring an independent status and being no longer part of the family. All these people now stand towards each other in a state of mutual independence, but each working for his own end. Hegel here has in mind the society which for many of his contemporaries was the ultimate goal, a society of individuals each pursuing his intelligent self-interest. What for many other philosophers would mean the state, is for Hegel merely a stage leading towards a state. The individuals, living together in a mutually dependent society, have not yet been identified with the universal purpose. They work for the satisfaction of their wants which Hegel analyses as consisting in mutual dependence, labour and wealth. Accordingly he divides society into estates, of which again he only knows three,[11] the agricultural class depending mainly on nature, the industrial and commercial class depending more on its own work and reflection, and the universal, that is the governing class, depending on reason. Birth, except in the case of monarchy, is not an essential factor in determining to which class an individual belongs. Rather is this a matter of free choice and ability.

The fabric of civil society demands an administration of justice,

[11] The figure is not accidental, but again an instance of the dialectic triad.

defining the mutual relations of individuals. This implies promulgated laws and law courts, both upholding the universal will against capricious acts of particular wills. Civil society also demands the protection of the individual right to wellbeing. This gives rise to the police. The true wellbeing of the individual further demands a formation of groups of individuals into associations which, although pursuing in the first instance their own interests, nevertheless promote the universal end of society since their aims are relatively wider and more universal than those of the individual.

Hegel has now arrived at the state which forms the synthesis of family and civil society. The state is a unity in difference of the universal principle of the family and the particular principle of civil society. It is an organism in which the life of the parts is embodied. The state is not—this is a very important point—an authority imposed from outside upon the individual. It is the individual himself, which thus realises his true universal self. The state thus is freedom. Hegel did not want to glorify an existing state as such, but his deductions led others to assert the definite supremacy of the state over the individual.

The state again has three phases: (1) its constitution or internal polity, the relations to its members; (2) international law, the relation of the state to other states, (3) its passing into world history. The constitution of the state Hegel considers as embodying individual freedom and interest as much as the universal. The state preserves the citizens' liberty and rights, fosters and advances their interests, their property and persons. The state, in accordance with the notion, has three aspects: the universal, the particular and the individual. In its universal function it is a sort of law, in its particular functions it applies laws to special cases, and its individuality is embodied in the monarch. . . . Hegel does not approve of the doctrine of separation of powers because he thinks that different powers checking each other will lead to the dissolution of the state. They should all be taken within the organic life of the state, and Hegel therefore approves the English system (which Montesquieu regarded as a model of separation of powers). Hegel rejects democracy and universal franchise. For the state is not the embodiment of the common will, the will of the majority, but of the rational will. The multitude becomes organised and rationalised by institutions within the state, that is the corporations and the classes. These, not the people as such, should be represented in legislation. To rule is the function of the universal class, to which merit, not birth or wealth, should give access. Finally, the monarch embodies the individual function of the state, and in the following astonishing passage Hegel attempts to prove that hereditary monarchy is a philosophical necessity.

> This ultimate self of the state's will is, in this, its abstraction, an individuality which is simple and direct. Hence its very conception implies that it is natural. Thus the monarch is appointed to the dignity of a monarch in a directly natural way by natural birth.[12]

In his views on state and international relations Hegel differs fundamentally from both Kant and Fichte. The state has an external side in its relation to other individuals of the same type, that is other states. States have no authority above them, there is no objective sphere of universal right between them. Their relations are perpetually shifting, and the ultimate settlement is by war.

The world's spirit is the final tribunal or judge on nations. In history the idea unfolds in various phases, and the dominant phase at any time is embodied in a dominant people. Its state embodies a particular phase of universal history.

Criticism

The influence which Kant, Fichte and Hegel have exercised as the most prominent exponents of German idealism in European legal philosophy has been very great.

Kant's contributions to legal philosophy stands between the rationalist natural law theories of the seventeenth and eighteenth centuries and the liberalism of the nineteenth century. His critical philosophy of knowledge, however, has been applied to the law by the Neo-Kantian jurists whose theories will be analysed below.[13] Fichte, as a legal philosopher, has not had much influence in the nineteenth but greater importance for the twentieth century. His general philosophy, however, has inspired much of Del Vecchio's teaching. Hegel has exercised the greatest influence of all. His philosophy of the relations of individual and state has laid the foundation for the ascendancy of the state over the individual and, in combination with his ideas on the intermediate function of the corporation between individual and state, has directly inspired modern Fascist ideas on the corporative and totalitarian state.

---

[12] *Rechtsphilosophie*, § 280.
[13] See Chap. 16.

Another aspect of Hegel's teaching, his philosophy of history in its bearing upon the law, is discussed elsewhere.[14]

In view of modern distortions of the teaching of all those philosophers it must be emphasised that their common starting point is the free rational individual, and that they all see the object of the legal order in the greatest possible realisation of this freedom.

Much as they differed in their outlook and conclusions none of them would have eliminated the individual in favour of the state, although Hegel's philosophy lent itself very well to such an interpretation. Both Kant and Fichte emphasised that the individual was man, apart from being citizen, and the state was bound to conform to the law built upon this foundation. Kant, however—contrary to Fichte—provided no guarantee for this postulate and his absolute denial of any right to revolt made this assertion rather theoretical. The chief danger in Hegel's theories of the individual discovering his true rational self in the state could lead, and has led, to the absorption of the individual in a deified state. Moreover, the use of the notion "rational" introduced under the cover of logic an element of valuation which could easily be distorted to fit the purpose of autocracy.

All three philosophers have mixed with their general philosophy some astonishing doctrines which are sheer expressions of personal opinions and prejudices. All three were not only great thinkers but also Prussian professors. Kant taught and lived all his life in East Prussia amidst aristocratic landowners, and this explains his distinction between actual and potential citizens, the latter, including day labourers, being excluded from political rights. The learned observations of Kant, Fichte and Hegel on marriage are not without a touch of unintended humour, giving as they do the views of respectable nineteenth-century bourgeoisie rather than philosophical deductions.

The most blatant example of political opinion disguised as philosophy is Hegel's deduction, quoted above, of the necessity of hereditary monarchy. These extravagances are important mainly in so far as they keep awake a critical spirit in a reader who might well be overawed by minds so much greater than his own.

They do not, however, affect the basic conclusions drawn by Kant, Fichte and Hegel on the relations between individual and state. On this question Fichte thought more clearly and logically than either Kant or Hegel. Where the latter were content with

[14] See below, p. 213.

vague phrases and assertions on such matters as the right to property and sometimes resorted to rather dishonest subterfuges, as Hegel did in his distinction between quantity and quality of property, in order to justify differences of wealth, Fichte saw, at a time when the industrial revolution had not yet assumed any noticeable proportions, that the right to property is empty without an opportunity to acquire property, and that this entails the right to work and state ownership of objects of a monopolistic character, like minerals. This right to work is entirely absent from the legal codifications of the nineteenth and twentieth centuries, and it first appears again in the Soviet Russian Constitution while it is also recognised, although from a different angle and with the emphasis on duty rather than right, in Fascist systems of government. Between Fichte and these modern developments there lies over a century of tremendous social development and a science of jurisprudence which preferred, on the whole, a formal and legalistic interpretation of such concepts as the right to equality before the law.

Kant's definition of the law has remained the basis for all those conceptions of law and state which might be described as atomistic, which denies the state any organic character and definitely sees a paramount object of life in the development of the individual. Kant's definition contains, however, the germs of social reformism, in so far as the necessity for each individual to live in accordance with the maximum freedom of any other individual, can and must be interpreted in the light of social circumstances, a factor which Kant ignored but Fichte realised. Kant's conception of the law will regain ascendancy whenever individualist and cosmopolitan ideas prevail over organic and nationalist ideas.

It is due to the very gigantic dimensions of Hegel's philosophic system that his place cannot be as easily assessed and that different movements of rather divergent tendencies have taken up some of Hegel's thoughts and adapted them to their particular purposes. Hardly any other philosopher has provoked as fervent admiration on the one hand and as bitter condemnation on the other as Hegel. In particular, Hegel's ideas on the relation of state and individual and on the purpose of history have inspired different political and legal philosophies. Whether one accepts or rejects his basic ideas is essentially a matter of political conviction. This main criticism must be directed against Hegel's use of the dialectical method as a means of proving the logical and necessary character of his deductions in the field of the law and other social sciences. With the correctness of his use of the dialectic method stands and falls his whole attempt to establish a monistic system in which natural and social sciences, freedom and necessity, will and thought, individual and nation are all linked and welded into unity. Now the dialectic method may or may not be a valid one for other parts of philosophy; but the way in which Hegel has applied it to the law shows patently the arbitrary use to which it has been stretched in order to justify certain conclusions. In other cases the actual relation between social and legal institutions has been distorted by Hegel beyond any justifiable limits in order to prove to his own satisfaction the validity of the dialectic triad in all spheres of life. For any lawyer the analysis of private law as an antithesis of contract and property, and above all tort and crime as the synthesis of property and contract, does not deserve serious discussion. The dialectic relation of administration of justice, police and corporations is equally difficult to understand, and few people would think of considering the police as an institution of civil society rather than of the state. To arrest the dialectic development with the state rather than international organisation is equally arbitrary. Hegel undoubtedly became the slave of his system, and he was forced to cling to it if he wanted to prove the unity as well as the necessity of all parts of human life. The fallacy of his use of the dialectic method in application to historical and social development has been most clearly demonstrated by Benedetto Croce,[15] who has pointed out Hegel's fundamental logical error in confusing opposites and distincts. The conception of being may be the logical opposite of nothing, but contract is not the logical opposite of property, nor is police the logical opposite of administration of justice. Rather are all these institutions and conceptions different aspects of the social life of mankind which one may, according to predilections, arrange so as to show a progressive development from one to another. The arrangement of all these developments in triads is an unnecessary and artificial complication to which Hegel is forced by his own preconceived system.

Had Hegel clearly perceived the difference between dialectic opposite in the field of logic and the very different dialectic antithesis in historical and political development, his legal philosophy would have gained in value. For in a different sense, in so far as it shows how any development in social life tends to produce a reaction out of itself, legal history provides abundant evidence of dialectic development. Marx has used it for his theory of the development

---

[15] Croce, *What is Living and what is Dead in Hegel's Philosophy?* (1912).

of capitalistic society, which leads to its own annihilation. His system is still tainted, however, by the false aspect of necessity inherent in Hegel's philosophical system. There are equally interesting illustrations of antithetic developments in the law, such as Dicey's analysis of the transition from Bentham's Liberalism to State Socialism.[16] Such developments in social life may be described as dialectic, but in a sense very different from the way in which Hegel uses the term. It is, however, Hegel's very method in the use of dialectic which his most fervent disciples in legal philosophy have admired and imitated. What modern Fascism has adopted and developed is Hegel's teaching of the function of the individual in this state, and in particular his thesis that true freedom is gained only through the individual's integration in this state. Because of this identification of the state with freedom and the "reality of the moral idea" Hegel finds it easy to subordinate the individual to any claim of the conservative nationalist monarchy which he revered.[17] This is, of course, clearly a political philosophy. But Neo-Hegelian philosophers like Binder and Larenz have disguised the political assumption behind Hegel's conclusions by representing it as a necessary development, and the means to prove this necessity is the same spurious use of the dialectic method as Hegel had taught.

Thus it is understandable that, where as to some Hegel must appear as the greatest of philosophers, other condemn him as one of the greatest as well as one of the most dangerous dilettantes in philosophy. Those who accept Hegel's political and legal principles will derive added satisfaction from the impression of necessity created by the dialectic method. Others, like Marx, may use the dialectic method to prove the phases of historical evolution while completely rejecting Hegel's political assumptions. Those who believe that the cardinal task of philosophy is to distinguish between objective truth and belief will condemn Hegel's influence as dangerous in the extreme.

NEO-HEGELIANS

The disastrous effect of Hegel's spurious proof of the dialectical necessity in the relation of the individual and the national state is borne out by the development of Neo-Hegelian philosophy. It has

---

[16] Dicey, *Law and Public Opinion in England* 130 *et seq.* (2nd ed. 1914).
[17] For this reason, I am unable to accept Professor Friedrich's defence of Hegel in his *Philosophy of Law in Historical Perspective* (1958).

overwhelmingly been directed towards the increasing glorification of the state as the embodiment of the spirit of world history. The meaning of that spirit mysteriously coincides with the aspirations of whatever nation the writer happens to belong to.

The Italian Gioberti[18] proclaimed the greatness of Italy, as the centre of European civilisation, as the culmination of history. The modern Fascist Gentile[19] has taken up this line and stressed the culmination of national development in Fascism, the embodiment of the strong state in the devotion to which the individual finds his fulfilment.

The modern German Neo-Hegelians, among whom Binder and Larenz are prominent,[20] demand the almost unqualified abandonment of the individual to the state, in the name of dialectic integration. It is characteristic that in the cases of both the German legal philosopher Binder and the Italian legal philosopher Del Vecchio, the turn towards the strong state of Fascist complexion corresponds to a change from Neo-Kantianism to Neo-Hegelianism.[21] The English Neo-Hegelian Bosanquet[22] arrives at slightly more moderate conclusions by a similar and equally dangerous argument, in which some of Rousseau's *"volonté générale"* is mixed with Hegelian dialectics. According to Bosanquet the real will "of an individual is what he would desire if he were, morally and intellectually, fully developed." And to him as to most Neo-Hegelians, the state embodies this purified intellectual and moral conduct of which the average individual is incapable. No doubt Bosanquet would have shuddered at the elaboration of this conception by the German and Italian Neo-Hegelians of our own days. But the fallacy is in his own thought too, as in that of Hegel himself. It is the indiscriminate identification of "the state" as an abstract ideal with any of the many existing types of state which the particular Neo-Hegelian wishes to elevate into an absolute. Thus, "the state" signifies an idealisation of moral and national conduct which is never realised in any existing society, while contrariwise individual judgement is identified with "ordinary trivial moods."[23]

It is significant to contrast with this development towards the unmitigated idolatry of state and power the very different conclu-

---

[18] Gioberti, *Del Primato Morale e Civile degli Italiano* (1843).
[19] Gentile *Che cosa e il Fascismo* (1925).
[20] *Cf.* below, p. 189 *et seq.*
[21] *Cf.* below, pp. 189, 190.
[22] Bosanquet, *The Philosophical Theory of the State* (1899).
[23] Sabine, *History of Political Theory*, 678.

sions of two thinkers who, though influenced by Hegel, discovered the decisive weakness in his system. T. H. Green[24] adopted from Hegel the opposition of positive and negative freedom, but turned it to a very different account. To the purely negative conception of freedom of contract—often resulting in economic slavery—he opposed a positive freedom which should mean "a positive power or capacity of doing or enjoying something worth doing or enjoying." Green also emphasised the character of any individual right, such as property, as a social institution, recognised not for its own sake, but limited by its usefulness in contributing to the common good. The reduction of the formal freedom of contract to a mere means, to be modified when in conflict with this "positive freedom," was a powerful and fertile contribution to juristic thought. For though, owing to social developments and the work of numerous thinkers and politicians, the relativity of formal freedom of contract is now almost a commonplace truth, this was not so in Green's days, when political liberalism and Maine's thesis of the evolution from status to freedom of bargaining as a characteristic of progressive societies dominated current thought. The opposition of positive and negative freedom, and of individual right and social community, shows the influence of Hegel. But Green saw the pitfalls of Hegel's deification of the state, and of his identification of a particular state with the state as an absolute ideal. That is why his legal philosophy leads to Fabianism and social democracy, not to Fascism. In Italy the adoption of Hegel's state philosophy has led Gentile and Del Vecchio, among others, to a Fascist philosophy, closely akin to that of their German fellow Neo-Hegelians. But Benedetto Croce[25] discovered the flaw in Hegel's confusion of logical opposites and historical or political antinomies, and this discrimination has led the greatest of Neo-Hegelian philosophers towards a strongly anti-Fascist political and legal philosophy.

[24] Green, *Liberal Legislation and Freedom of Contract.* Lectures on the Principles of Political Obligation (ed. Nettleship)
[25] Croce, *op. cit.*

CHAPTER 16

NEO-KANTIAN PHILOSOPHY AND
SCIENTIFIC LEGAL IDEALISM

THE great German idealistic philosophers of the late eighteenth and early nineteenth centuries marked the twilight of one phase in legal thinking and the dawn of another. They belonged to the twilight of a period which by believing in God or Nature or Reason upheld certain absolute values. But they belonged to a new age in so far as they established a new theory of knowledge, based on a critical examination of the faculties of the human mind. It is this latter side of German idealistic philosophy which was to become the source of a revival of legal theory many years later.

The Neo-Kantian legal philosophers resume, on the whole, Kant's theory of knowledge but not his moral and legal philosophy. They continue the line of thought developed in his *Critique of Pure Reason* but not that of the *Critique of Practical Reason*. For Kant, to be sure, the two are essential parts of one philosophical system. Pure Reason orders the perception of the senses by means of the formal categories of the human intellect. This is the realm of knowledge. But Practical Reason sets to man certain purposes which he must believe, and will. They are not logically necessary, not an inevitable result of thinking. Kant himself tries to overcome this dualism to some extent in his theory of aesthetics, with which we are not here concerned.

The nineteenth century, the century of science, technique and industry, was a period of almost limitless growth of self-confidence of a generation which seemed to produce miracles and which looked like mastering nature for ever. This self-confidence found extension in a philosophical positivism which spread from natural science to other sciences.[1]

The new idealism of the Neo-Kantians opposes this self-sufficiency of positivists, but it shares with them the faith in the

---

[1] On Positivism, see below, Chaps. 21-25.

power of science to explore the whole of human life, without leaving anything aside as being beyond knowledge. It denies the existence of the *"Ding an sich,"* the reality of things not recognisable to man. It rejects the distinction between knowledge and belief, between thinking and postulates. Everything is thought capable of being known and being grasped by the human mind. Human consciousness is the centre and measure of things. But at the same time philosophy now begins to analyse further the different ways in which the human consciousness can know and order the world; having before them the tremendous development of the natural sciences as well as that of historical study, ethics, sociology, law, Dilthey, Rickert, Windelband and others attempt a methodology of knowledge. They do not, like Kant, detach from the totality of the human individual one part, his perception and the ordering of phenomena outside him, but they take the individual in his totality, as a being which not only thinks but also feels and wills.[2]

Scientific thought is to be applied to the whole of human nature in its different manifestations. The chief result of this is the methodological separation of the natural and social sciences. The new methodology which has been the object of much criticism from many quarters[3] gave a new impetus to legal theory, at a time when there was a widespread desire for a general legal theory distinct from the mere classification of materials. But it was possible for legal theory once again to develop very different conclusions from similar premises. The new idealistic legal philosophy represented by Stammler, Binder, Del Vecchio[4] and the new critical positivism of Kelsen and the Vienna school[5] all have a Neo-Kantian basis. But the attempt of Dilthey and others to bridge the antinomy between will and knowledge, instinct and understanding, has also inspired the new *Wertphilosophie* (Scheler and Hartmann) and its important application in contemporary legal philosophy.

Yet another aspect of Neo-Kantianism, the distinction between the methodology of cultural and natural sciences, leads to the conception of law as a *Kulturwissenschaft,* elaborated in the legal philosophy of Lask and Radbruch.

The common purpose of these different theories may be said to be

---

[2] See, in particular, Dilthey's Foreword to *Einleitung in die Geisteswissenschaft.*
[3] For a further discussion of the methodology of the natural and social sciences, see above, p. 49 *et seq.*
[4] *Cf.* below, pp. 179-90.
[5] *Cf.* below, Chap. 24.

the attempt to distil from legal material those elements of legal knowledge which are of universal validity.

STAMMLER[6]

Stammler's legal philosophy is most closely related to the whole of Kant's system, including his legal philosophy. Stammler takes as fundamental the distinction between human experience as being either perception or volition. Law clearly is volition. Volition sets itself an object as something not present in perception but to be attained in the future. Law is not concerned with the perception of the external physical world. It relates means and purposes to each other. To find a common determining characteristic of the ways of relating means and ends in the law, is one part of the task of legal theory. In this way the concept of law is found, as the universally valid element common to all legal phenomena whatever their content. Stammler thus seeks to discover a scientific notion of law as a specific realm of human volitions. This universally valid element, which constitutes the essence of law, can only be a formal one, a method of ordering the variety of legal materials.

This corresponds to Kant's pure reason. What Kant did in regard to the ordering by the human mind of all natural phenomena Stammler set out to do in regard to the law as a special kind of volition. But there is, for Stammler, another task for legal theory. That is the realm of practical reason. Where as pure reason (the concept of law) contains the principle of perception (in the case of law the perception of means to pursue certain ends) practical reason sets purposes. For Stammler practical reason is the idea of law, the task of which is to set those purposes.

The Concept of Law

Stammler's aim in searching for the concept of law is to find a definition of universal logical validity. To be universally valid it has to be pure form, to be composed entirely of elements which apply independently of experience or the diversity of social matter,

---

[6] Stammler's principal works are: (1) *Wirtschaft und Recht*, setting out the relations of law and economics as one of form and matter; (2) *Die Lehre vom richtigen Recht* (1902), translated in the Modern Legal Philosophy Series as *Theory of Justice*, in which there is the most detailed elaboration of the idea of justice; (3) *Theorie der Rechtswissenschaft* (2nd ed., 1911); (4) *Lehrbuch der Rechtsphilosophie* (1923).

which at any given time determines a legal precept. Therefore the concept of law cannot be taken from history or from any empirical elements. Although no search into the essence of law can abstract from legal experience, it must not itself be a mere generalisation of legal material. It must detect those elements in the law which apply to every legal phenomenon in all time and space, and which are necessary because deduced from the nature of law itself. These elements can only be form, not matter, if legal theory is to be really scientific. In every actual legal phenomenon form and matter make a unit.

Stammler emphasises that one cannot pour legal matter into legal forms as into a container. But logically the method of ordering must be separated from the material which is ordered.

What, we may ask, is the use of a universally valid concept of law? The use is twofold, a philosophical and a practical one. Philosophically the quest for a universal concept of law is a manifestation of the desire of the human mind to reduce all phenomena, natural or social, to that unity which only the human mind can provide:

> The idea of unity, as the highest condition of all imaginable scientific knowledge is not a sum of legal details, but a peculiar ultimate way of ordering the contents of our consciousness. Thus the concept of law has also a pure conditioning mode for the ordering of our willing consciousness, on which depends the possibility of determining a particular question as a legal one.[7]

The practical aim is a clear distinction from religion, morality, history, etc., a task which every jurist and legal philosopher has tackled in some way or other.

Stammler defines law, in his heavy and unattractive style, as: (1) combining, (2) sovereign, and (3) inviolable volition. Law is first of all volition, because law is a mode of ordering human acts according to the relation of means and purposes. Combining volition signifies volition of men in their mutual relation; sovereignty distinguishes law from arbitrary volition of an individual, but must not be understood in the sense of political sovereignty of one will over another. The permanency of the tie created by law is indicated by its inviolability. All these elements have formal, not material significance. In plainer language this definition is not far from the current definition of the analytical school; it contains the elem-

[7] Stammler, *Theorie der Rechtswissenschaft* 12 (2nd ed. (1911)).

ents of mutuality, compulsion and sovereignty. Stammler naturally rejects such conceptions as the "Spirit of the People." Nor does he admit that the state determines the law. The state is nothing but a particular type of legal order. Stammler can therefore conceive the logical possibility of a world law co-ordinating and combining all particular and limited legal orders.

The Idea of Law

The idea of law is Stammler's counterpart to Kant's practical reason, the realm of purposes realised by volition. But while Kant's critical knowledge (pure reason) of the things perceived by the senses is opposed to purposes set by belief and volition (practical reason), for Stammler the critical knowledge of law is not the knowledge of a physical phenomenon. It is the analysis of purposes to which the idea of law gives a unifying direction. The purpose of Stammler's idea of just law is to help in building up a fundamental conception of life. As put by Stammler in the concluding chapter of his *Theory of Justice*:

(1) Just law is the highest universal point in every study of the social life of men.
(2) It is the only thing that makes it possible to conceive by means of an absolutely valid method, of social existence as unitary whole.
(3) It shows the way to a union with all other endeavours of a fundamental character which aim likewise at right consciousness.

The concept of law gives the formal and universal elements of law. The idea of law directs all possible means and purposes towards one aim. But to be of scientific value the idea must be a merely formal one, it cannot have any particular content like a precept of natural law. It must give expression to the idea of free will. This formal ideal is the social ideal of a free willing community of men. Stammler continues the tradition of Kant in considering the idea of freedom as the basic law of volition. The social ideal must therefore be an expression of the idea, of free will. But Stammler does not stop there, he becomes more specific. He establishes certain maxims of right law, deduced from the idea of a community of free willing men. This idea implies: (1) the community of purposes; (2) the fact that man, as a reasonable being, is an end in himself. From this Stammler derives his famous four maxims:

(1) Principles of respect—(a) No one's volition must be subject to the arbitrary desire of another: (b) Any legal demand must be of such a nature that the addressee can be his own neighbour.
(2) Maxims of participation—(a) No member of a legal community must be arbitrarily excluded from the community; (b) A legal power may be exclusive only in so far as the excluded person can still be his own neighbour.

To make these maxims better applicable to the division of actual cases, Stammler introduces an auxiliary fiction. In the Special Community (*Sondergemeinschaft*) each individual is taken as a centre of a circle, the circumference of which comprises the whole sphere of his legal relations with others. These circles cut each other at certain points in this special community; each individual invests in it, as it were, his own volition, and the adjustment is made with the help of the maxims of right law. This community, however, is conceived merely as a construction, not as a living entity.

Stammler is not content with formulating these principles. A large section of his *Theory of Justice* is devoted to an attempt to apply these maxims, formal as they are meant to be, to the solution of actual problems, most of them taken from the German Civil Law. Stammler examines the principles of just law under five headings: (1) The right exercise of legal relations; (2) Limits of freedom of contract; (3) Duties of just law; (4) Determination of a just transaction; (5) Justified termination of legal relations.

Examples taken from these different sections will illustrate Stammler's methods.

A celebrated anecdote in Prussian history is the dispute of the miller Arnold at the time of Frederick the Great. The neighbour of this miller intended to construct fish ponds on his land and filled them from the water of the millstream. The miller complained that this would prevent him from getting enough water to drive his mills. The Supreme Court upheld the right of the neighbour to use the water flowing through his land whatever the purpose for which he wanted it. Stammler attempts to solve the problem with the help of the principles of just law. His solution is as follows: The party excluding the other and the party injured thereby must be imagined as united in a separate community according to the principle of participation, each party must be treated so that he may remain his own neighbour. Thus, neither of the parties must alone be the entire sufferer from the construction of the ponds, nor must the other party simply refrain from constructing them. Therefore the disadvantage accruing by the construction to the other party must not be out of all proportion to the loss which the person entitled to do it avoids by the exercise of his right. These two losses must first be computed and the combined loss divided in proportion to the amount contributed by each side.

Under "Freedom of Contract" Stammler discusses the legal position of cartels, syndicates, trusts, etc. On the one hand, he says that these achieve a social purpose by

opposing the anarchy of production and sale in the sphere of their activity. . . . They can lend protection and defence to the individual who, under conditions of unrestrained freedom, would not be able to realise his proper activity in the social economy, but on the other hand, they are a combination for personal ends and may become the means of abuse.[8]

The court, armed with the principle of participation, must examine how far on the ground of mutual responsibility objective volition is possible for both sides. No party must be excluded from social activity by the arbitrary judgment of the other. This is apparently as far as the principles of just law can guide towards the solution of the problem.

A contract has to be regarded as void, which, instead of aiming to be a means for just co-operation endeavours to exploit the other members of the community by arbitrary demands of the members of the ring.[9]

For a final example, Stammler invokes both the principles of participation and of respect to show that there is a legal obligation for a good swimmer to come to the rescue of a drowning man, where it is possible without any particular danger. To decide otherwise would be "opposed to the fundamental idea of all law that all should carry the struggle for existence in common."

Apart from the concept of law and the idea of just law, Stammler considers a third factor, which is usually overlooked in accounts of Stammler's theory, as essential to a theory of law, the validity of

[8] Stammler, *Theory of Justice, op. cit.* at 345 *et seq.*
[9] *Id.* at 346.

law, *Geltung des Rechts*. This introduces, of course, a factual element into pure formal theory. Stammler admits that critical investigation here needs a psychological supplement. Into the details of his psychological examinations we need not enter here, but the fact itself is important.

Criticism

The importance of Stammler's theory can be gauged from the flood of controversy which it has provoked.[10]

Before 1914, in a world overwhelmed by the mass of new discoveries, new material for observation and classification, Stammler expressed the urge for scientific clarity and unity on one hand and a new idealism on the other. This new scientific idealism was both more arrogant and more diffident than the natural law ideologies of previous centuries. More arrogant in that it thought everything knowable; more diffident in that the nineteenth-century idealism was too sceptical to establish absolute ideals. Nor did it possess the unity of moral values backed by one predominant authority, such as the medieval Church, which absolute ideals presuppose. Accordingly Stammler's contribution to legal theory has two aspects: to put the law scientifically on its own feet and to revive legal idealism against the sterility of positivism. Both these aspects have been of great influence on modern legal theory. Until the rise of the new irrational forces which have resulted in modern Fascism and National Socialism, the need for a true science of law came to be all but universally recognised. This does not mean that Stammler's particular conception of law as pure form applied to changing economic matters was scientifically unchallengeable. Neo-Kantianism itself has produced a very different philosophical appreciation of the law as a cultural phenomenon, which partakes in the complex pattern of social life as a social value of a special character, and which cannot therefore be abstracted as form from any given content.[11]

The most detailed criticism of Stammler's conception of legal science as pure form came from Max Weber,[12] who has shown that the alleged formal categories are, in fact, categories of progressive generalisation, the more general ones being relatively more formal

[10] For a compilation, see Wu, Appendix 2 to *Theory of Justice*.
[11] This line leads from Rickert, Windelband, Max Weber, to the legal philosophy of Lask, M. E. Mayer and Radbruch.
[12] In *Gesammelte Aufsätze zur Wissenschaftslehre*.

than the less general ones. But even if a purely formal concept of law could be imagined, it remains incomprehensible how Stammler can maintain throughout his work the illusion that a purely formal idea of law is capable of material guidance to the lawyer. Philosophically his fallacy is that he adopts the different parts of Kant's philosophy, but destroys the basis of Kant's system.[13]

Law for Kant was never an object of critical knowledge, but part of practical reason. Stammler forced it into pure reason and within it made the idea of law into something analogous to Kant's practical reason. Law and justice were for Kant not accessible to critical understanding, but a matter of belief which he reduced to certain fundamental ethical principles. One may contest these without touching Kant's theory of knowledge. Stammler, less wise than the master, makes his practical reason a matter of theoretical insight. It can be such only if it is formal in character. But Stammler wanted his idea of justice to be of practical guidance, and it therefore never was and never could be purely formal, but in fact became an anaemic version of Kant's categorical imperative. It is certainly not devoid of an ethical premiss. That premiss is the rational free individual. Stammler was apparently torn between his desire as a philosopher to establish a universal science of law and his desire as a teacher of civil law to help in the solution of actual cases.

The result is an "Idea of Justice" which is a hybrid between a formal proposition and a definite social ideal, kept abstract and rather vague by the desire to remain formal. Stammler therefore produces solutions dependent on very specific social and ethical valuations which it was his chief endeavour to keep out of an idea meant to be universal.

In the case of the miller Arnold, Stammler's solution is one of several possible ones. According to English law the miller would probably win, since the construction of a fish pond would hardly be a riparian use. But no English lawyer would claim that this is more than one of several possible solutions. Stammler's solution is based on the following assumptions: (1) recognition of private property, however unequal in value and amount, subject to certain limitations in the use of that property; (2) equivalence of all uses of property regardless of their economic and social importance.

Now Stammler's first principle of respect might very well be interpreted to mean that inequality of property, especially under

---

[13] On this aspect, see particularly E. Kaufmann, *Kritik der neukantischen Rechtsphilosophie* (1921).

modern industrial conditions, demands a redressing of the balance with the help of the idea of justice. This idea has been developed among others by Ficht and Radbruch. Stammler takes it for granted that property cannot and need not be equally distributed. More remarkable still is Stammler's tacit assumption that the construction of a fish pond and the running of a mill are of equal value to the law. Both Fascist and Socialist communities would emphatically subordinate the private luxury of a fish pond to the productive use of a mill for the livelihood of the miller and the provision of food for the community. They would oppose to Stammler's social valuation a different valuation.

Again, the legal position of cartels, a question of paramount economic policy which every legal system solves according to certain basic political principles, cannot be judged by formal tests. Each solution must evaluate the rival claims of monopolies, free trade and public control. Stammler's own solution is not formal but vague. The difficulty is glossed over, not resolved, by such phrases as "objective volition" and "arbitrary judgment." Stammler's own position is characteristic of a widespread tendency towards social reform by a limitation of the exercise of individual rights, but with emphasis on the individual as the basic measure of things.

If we reject as untheoretical the whole part of Stammler's theory which attempts the solution of practical problems with the help of formal ideas of justice, the latter remains only a shadow, and the only practical result is that law is always valid, whether good or bad, but must always strive to attain certain ideals.

Del Vecchio[14]

How much Stammler's position is representative of a widespread trend of thought of his period, is shown by the work of the Italian Del Vecchio who, independently of Stammler, about the same time developed a theory of law on essentially similar foundations. Del Vecchio, a jurist of much greater elegance and universality than Stammler, whose writing displays a profusion of philosophical, historical and juristic learning, is also Neo-Kantian, although an important part of his theory is based on Fichte rather than on Kant.

---

[14] Principal works. *Formal Bases of Law* (Mod. Legal Philosophy Series, 1921, a collection of monographs); *Il Sentimento Giuridico* (3rd ed., 1908); *Justice, Droit, Etat Etudes de Philosophie Juridique*, 1938; *Justice* (English ed., 1952, with notes by A. H. Campbell, translated from Del Vecchio's *La Giustizia*, 1951), and a textbook on legal philosophy, *Philosophy of Law* (English ed. tr. Martin, 1954).

The critical approach of Del Vecchio to the problem of legal theory is so akin to Stammler's that the very occasional reference to Stammler's works is rather surprising. The basis of Del Vecchio's theory is again the opposition between an objective and universal formal concept of law and an idea of law. The concept of law

must have reference only to its form, to the logical type inherent in every case of juridical experience. The logical form of law is more comprehensive than the sum of juridical propositions.[15]

In connection with this definition Del Vecchio demonstrates the error of theories which have defined the law from history, ethics, religion or generalised contents. Whereas the concept of law is juridically neutral, cannot distinguish between good and bad, just and unjust law, the idea of law can. Del Vecchio's idea of law differs from Stammler's. It is not meant to be formal. It is based on ideas which can be traced from Aristotle to Vico, Leibniz, Kant, Fichte and Bergson. Man has a double quality. He is at once physical and metaphysical, both part and principle of nature. As part of nature he cannot distinguish between good and bad, but as an intelligent being he has the possibility of free decision in himself. As this intelligent being which transcends and comprehends nature, man has in himself the "eternal seed of justice."[16] This seed of justice is an idea as well as a sentiment.[17] As an idea it springs from the necessity of the individual to conceive himself as an ego in antithesis to a non-ego. Individuality can only be conceived as a reciprocal notion in relation to another being equally conceived as individual (Fichte). The essence of justice therefore is its inter-subjectivity (*alterità*), that is the simultaneous consideration of several subjects on an equal plane; from this follows the element of parity and of reciprocity, that means personality and law can only be conceived through the interrelation of individuals. This idea of *alterità* further means an objective evaluation of each juridical act. All these formal elements justify, again in a purely formal sense, such maxims as: *honeste vivere, neminem laedere, suum cuique tribuere.*

But justice has for Del Vecchio not only a formal, but also a substantial meaning and an implicit faculty of valuation. Human

[15] *Formal Bases of Law, op. cit.* at 81.
[16] *Cf. Il Sentimento Giuridico* (1908).
[17] It is a little confusing that Del Vecchio speaks both of a concept of law and of the form of justice as distinguished from the content of justice. The form of justice is apparently the same as the concept of law.

consciousness postulates not only reciprocity in a formal sense, but instinctively it also emits a definite valuation, a conception of justice which discriminates between various forms of juridicity, for example, between a society of thieves living under certain rules and a society pursuing a recognised aim within a state. In this sense justice demands the equal and perfect recognition of personal quality in oneself as in every one else, and for all possible relations between different individuals. Del Vecchio here appears to go back to Kant and Fichte, but in a manner different from Stammler. Law, like the human being, has an empirical and metempirical aspect. As an empirical phenomenon law is a phenomenon of nature and collected by history. But it also is an expression of human liberty which comprises and masters nature and directs it to a purpose. As such, law is the object of a qualitative progress of phenomena from mere formless matter to progressive organisation and individualisation. The aim is perfect autonomy of the spirit. Del Vecchio leans on Vico for deducing from this the necessity for development of law in history, towards the goal of natural law which means human autonomy. Sometimes, however, there is a distinctly Hegelian flavour in his argument, as when he describes the "circular life of law, which born of the spirit returns to the spirit through history."[18]

For Del Vecchio justice has thus an ideal content which, stripped of all technicality, is the "absolute value of personality" or the "equal freedom of all men." This ideal content is postulated by the inner conscience of men. It explains the ever-recurring quest for natural law. Not any specific content but the evolution of mankind towards an increasing recognition of human autonomy appears to Del Vecchio to be the basis of natural law. Partial expression of this is given by the development from status to contract (Maine), from aggregation to association (Tönnies). In conformity to this necessity, world-wide human law or juridical co-ordination of all mankind tends to positive formation.[19] Thus the feeling of justice, springing from the introspective conscience of man, is not only able to evaluate where the formal conception of justice cannot do so, but it also bound to realise itself in history. It follows from this that, like Kant and Stammler, Del Vecchio considers the state as only one of several possible juridical orders; and that the development of law towards the goal of natural law means a tendency towards a universal world law. In a lecture delivered in 1931 Del

---

[18] *Justice, Droit, Etat, op. cit.* at 103.
[19] *Formal Bases of Law, op. cit.* at 331.

Vecchio definitely asserted the superiority of international over national law.

Just as Del Vecchio's master, Fichte, developed from the legal individualism and liberalism of his main legal philosophy towards the passionate nationalism and collectivism of his later work, so Del Vecchio's more recent work shows a definite move from the Kantian to the Hegelian way of thinking, and consequently to Fascist ideals. In his former work Del Vecchio advocated solutions of legal problems which definitely had Kantian individualism as their basis. Thus the right of privacy excluded the right of a photographer to take the picture of any one, and although there is the right to work, the right to be given work (as postulated even by the earlier Fichte) was rejected by Del Vecchio. But after the advent of the Fascist régime in Italy, Del Vecchio devoted much of his work to a juristic justification of Fascism. The corporative system is praised as giving true expression to the multiplicity of individual forces. The State becomes "the harmoniser of dissonances," a proper *Rechtsstaat,* "thanks to this dialectic synthesis of liberty and authority."[20] It is not without irony that as late as 1934, shortly after Mussolini's brutal invasion of Abyssinia, Del Vecchio still saw a parallel between the new synthesis of state and individual and the growing co-operation of states, tending towards a universal community which alone would satisfy the thirst for justice.

The principal original contribution of Del Vecchio is his *sentimenti giuridico,* which he credits with being able intuitively to valuate legal phenomena. The philosophical basis for this appears to be Henri Bergson's vitalistic philosophy.[21] No concept lends itself better to mysticism and serves better to justify any given legal institution.

BINDER

Del Vecchio's turn from a Neo-Kantian to a Neo-Hegelian legal philosophy finds a close and revealing parallel in the development of a contemporary German jurist. The political purpose is the same in both cases: the justification of an anti-democratic Nationalism.

In an early work[22] Binder distinguishes, very much like Stammler, between the concept and the idea of law. The latter has

---

[20] *Justice, Droit, Etat, op. cit.* at 365.
[21] *Cf.* Levy-Ullmann in *Preface to Justice, Droit, Etat, op. cit.*
[22] *Rechtsbegriff und Rechtsidee* (1907).

no specific content but, being part of general reason, acts as a guiding value. Such guiding force is given to it by the idea of freedom of man as the ultimate principle. Freedom is, however, imaginable only in relation to other individuals, that is within the community. So far Binder's theory is essentially a mixture of Kant and Stammler.

In his principal work, eighteen years later,[23] Binder justifies a violent nationalism by considering the nation as the only form of community within which the individual ought to realise his freedom. The argument, including the derision of an international community, has become Neo-Hegelian. In his last work[24] Binder justified Fascism almost without reserve by granting the individual "reality" only in so far as he acts and thinks the universal, that is the state and, needless to say, that means the Fascist state.

Any right to question the power of the state, for example, by granting the courts the power to question the constitutionality of state acts, is denied.

[23] *Rechtsphilosophie* (1925).
[24] *Rechtsphilosophie* (1935-37).

CHAPTER 17

MODERN VALUE PHILOSOPHIES AND THE LAW

RELATIVISM

A DEVELOPMENT of Neo-Kantian premises, quite different from the theories of Stammler, Del Vecchio and Binder, leads Kelsen and his followers to a formal science of law, which excludes any ideology or philosophy of values from the realm of legal science. The affinity of this school with the analytical positivism of Austin and his successors is, however, so strong that it is better dealt with in this context.[1] We now turn to another important development in contemporary legal philosophy, which, unlike Kelsen, seeks to utilise Neo-Kantian insight for a philosophy of values instead of a formal science. While the human mind searches for knowledge, it also wants action; it is will as well as perception, faith as well as knowledge; it wants to order life, not only to understand it.

Scientific relativism seeks to do justice to both these aspects of human nature and to see them in their proper perspective. Its cardinal point was developed by Max Weber in a celebrated essay written in 1917 in the midst of the hatred of war which tainted thinkers and scientists in all belligerent countries.[2] With supreme detachment from the blindness of these passions and a deep conviction of the true task of science. Weber developed the thesis that no value in the field of sociological and economic sciences could be scientifically proved. He showed that such allegedly scientific demonstrations as "tendencies of progress," "right economic

[1] See below, Chap. 25.
[2] Weber, "Der Sinn der Wertfreiheit der soziologischen und ökonomischen Wissenschaften," in *Gesammelte Aufsätze zur Wissenschaftslehre*.

191

behaviour" and similar formulas covered ethical valuations. The true task of social science was the intelligent explanation of social phenomena up to the point of ultimate valuations between which it is not the task of science to choose.

From this relativism on the one hand and the studies of some Neo-Kantian philosophers, notably that of E. Lask, which see law as a *Kulturwissenschaft* necessarily endowed with purpose and meaning, Gustav Radbruch has developed a legal philosophy.[3] It shares with Kelsen's pure theory of law the emphasis on the necessity of distinguishing between valuation and science in law. But to Radbruch, who follows the philosophy of Lask, the essence of law as a *Kulturwissenschaft* is not, as it is to Kelsen, a formal ordering of norms. All *Kultur* aims at the realisation of values, not merely at perception. It is thus practical, not pure reason. Law must thus be conceived as a totality of facts and relations, whose purpose it is to realise justice. It is the task of legal science to analyse the law as a factual unity of cultural values. It is the task of legal philosophy to analyse the law in its specific valuations. Radbruch's legal philosophy therefore sees its proper task as starting where the pure theory, concerned with legal science only, stops. Its task is threefold:

(1) The clarification of the means appropriate to reach a given legal object.
(2) The clarification of legal values and postulates up to their ultimate philosophical foundations.
(3) The analysis of possible legal systems in their affinities and antinomies.

This legal relativism is therefore concerned with the ultimate meaning of legal systems but does not see its task in suggesting a choice between opposite values. This choice is a matter for personal decisions; a matter not of science but of conscience. Relativism does not evade political decisions, but does not wish to give them a scientific cloak. "I have no fear of irreconcilable antinomies, to decide oneself is to live!"[4] Legal science and philosophy can

---

[3] *Lehrbuch der Rechtsphilosophie* (3rd ed., 1932). This work has now been translated into English (*Legal Philosophies of Lask, Radbruch and Dabin*, Twentieth Century Legal Philosophy Series).
[4] Radbruch, in 3 *Annuaire de l'institut international de philosophie du droit*, 162.

show these antinomies, but not indicate a choice between them. Radbruch further concludes that relativism, because it refuses to decide between conflicting political ideals, must concede to every political opinion which succeeds in securing the majority in the state the right to assume political responsibility. In other words, it shares democracy's belief in political tolerance.[5]

The notion of law, according to Radbruch, as a cultural notion cannot be formal. but must be directed towards the idea of law, which is justice. But justice as an idea—as already Aristotle found out—can say no more than that equals shall be treated equally, unequals unequally. To fill this ideal of justice with a concrete content, we must turn to utility as a second component of the idea of law. The question of what is utility can only be answered by reference to different conceptions of state and law. To supplement the formality of justice and relativity of utility, security comes in as a third component of the idea of law. It demands positivity of law. The law must be certain. The demands of justice and of positivity are invariable parts of the idea of law, they stand above conflicts of political opinion. Utility provides the element of relativity. But not only utility itself is relative, the relation between the three components of the idea of law is relative too. How far utility should prevail over justice, or security over utility, is a matter to be decided by each political system.

Between these three pillars of the idea of law there is bound to be tension. Justice demands equality, that is generalisation. But utility demands individualisation. Thus the executive tends to make decisions in accordance with the individual situation, and administrative justice as represented by the administrative tribunal of Continental countries tends to equalise by seeing administrative problems from the point of view of justice.

Again, positivity of law often means certainty at the expense of justice or the consideration of the individual case. Even patently unjust decisions continue to be recognised in the interest of legal

[5] In a lecture given abroad during his period of intellectual exile under the Nazi régime, and published in a posthumous collection of essays (*Der Mensch im Recht*, 1957, VI), Radbruch went further, in claiming that relativism, because of its postulates of liberty of thought, science, faith and expression, is bound to lead to liberalism, and that its postulate that the state itself should be bound by law leads to a system of separation of powers. Finally, the free struggle of ideas would inevitably lead the most powerful social force, *i.e.*, socialism, to victory. It may well be doubted that, apart from the postulate of tolerance, these postulates can be reconciled with the essence of relativistic philosophy.

stability.[6] In history the authoritarian police state tends to make utility the dominant element; the natural law period emphasises the element of justice and tries to give it substance; legal positivism considers nothing but certainty of the law and neglects both justice and utility. But the freer judicial interpretation advocated by modern theories emphasises again utility rather than certainty.

Radbruch also considers the possible contents which may be given to utility as determining the end of law. He finds that there are three possible objects of valuation in life: individual personalities, collective personalities, works. Accordingly social and therefore legal systems can emphasise either individualism, collectivism or what Radbruch styles transpersonalism. The first values the individual and his integrity higher than the needs of either the community or of any cultural, scientific, technical or other achieve-

[6] In a short Introduction to Legal Philosophy (*Vorschule zur Rechtsphilosophie*), published in 1947, Radbruch tentatively departs from this position. Obviously under the impact of the perversion of law by the Nazi régime, he suggests that where the injustice of positive law reaches monstrous proportions the unjust positive law would have to yield to justice. The problems and implications of Radbruch's tentative approval of "higher law" principles justifying disobedience to positive law are analysed further (p. 350 *et seq.*). So is his apparent turn from the Kantian dualism of "is" and "ought" to the phenomenological deduction of certain legal values from the "essence" of things (below, p. 203). In the decade following Radbruch's death in 1949, numerous interpretations have been given of his apparent conversion from a strict relativism to a natural law philosophy. Among those closest to Radbruch's thinking, some (see Erik Wolf, *Umbruch oder Entwicklung in Gustav Radbruchs Rechtsphilosophie, Archiv fuer Rechts- und Sozialphilosophie*, 481 *et seq.* (1959), and Barata, *ibid.* p. 504 *et seq.*; Engisch, *Gustav Radbruch als Rechtsphilosoph*, 1949) believe that Radbruch did not abandon the basic postulates of his relativistic legal philosophy. But others (notably F. von Hippel, *Gustav Radbruch als rechtsphilosophischer Denker* (1957); see also Fuller, "The Legal Philosophy of Gustav Radbruch," 6 *Journal of Legal Education*, 481 (1954), believe that there had been a major change in Radbruch's thinking. For both views there are substantial arguments. Radbruch himself in 1949 included in a posthumously published selection of his essays a reassertion of his relativistic philosophy (*Der Mensch im Recht*, 1957, Chap. VI), even though some of the assertions made in that essay cannot be reconciled with the approach of his principal work. It is also abundantly clear from all of Radbruch's work that the antinomy of values does not mean indifference or even equivalence. At times justice is more important than security or utility. But all this does not lead to the assertion of the invalidity of "evil" positive law unless the further assumption (justifiable by some of Radbruch's writings) is made that the unspoken basis, the *Grundnorm*, of any legal philosophy, is the treatment of the individual as a human being with ethic autonomy. With such a postulate a system that like the Nazi régime treats classes of human beings as "subhuman," as things to be tortured or exterminated in masses, is not compatible. But even if we accept this as a basic postulate of order in civilised humanity (see p. 356 *et seq.*), the question of the border-line between absolutely invalid and merely objectionable law remains vague, as it does in all fundamental philosophies. An appraisal of Radbruch's work must end with this question mark, which reflects the tension between faith and scepticism that accompanies the life and work of this noble man and philosopher.

ment of civilisation. This is typified by the American Constitution. The second sees that individual life as well as achievements of civilisation culminate in community life. This is typified by Hegel's philosophy. The third would consider an Egyptian pyramid or a modern road through fever-stricken country as more important than the thousands of lives sacrificed for this work.[7]

The slogans corresponding to these three paramount valuations are: Liberty, Nation, Civilisation.

The individualistic conception uses the legal concept of contract (social contract theories), the second uses the notion of organism (German theories of corporate personality), the third uses the symbol of an edifice erected by the common work of all. Whereas legal and political history provide abundant illustration for both individualistic and collectivist systems, the transpersonal valuation has, according to Radbruch, hardly yet found adequate expression in social life. The syndicalist idea comes nearest to it. But in the existing forms of syndicalism, notably in the Fascist State, Radbruch sees but a perversion of the transpersonal idea used to bolster up the power of the state.[8]

Radbruch examines the principal political ideologies in relation to these basic values and shows how liberalism emphasises the individual as an abstract autonomous unit and idealises it in the "Rights of Man." whereas democracy sees the individual as citizen in relation to others from the angle of equality. Social reformism and socialism, by inquiring into social and economic reality, reveal the rigidity of formal equality and aim at mitigating formal justice by equity while still considering the individual as the ultimate value. Conservatism on the other hand adheres to the organic conception of a political community. Radbruch follows up these basic values throughout various legal institutions and systems such as property, marriage, corporate personality, the relations of state and law, the possibilities of international law, etc. In the conception of a world state, the citizens of which would be the individuals of the whole world, Radbruch sees an application of the individualist ideal; in the nationalist state he sees an application of the collectiv-

---

[7] The discussion early in 1944, of the respective value of the preservation of Italian monuments of culture on one side, and thousands of soldiers' lives on the other, vividly illustrates this antinomy.

[8] It would seem that Duguit's postulate of social solidarity as the guiding fact of a legal order would come nearest to what Radbruch calls a transpersonal system. The political and legal philosophy of the U.S.S.R. seems to stand between the second and third type, emphasising the collective against individual values, but putting the achievement of social works above life.

ist idea, and in a society of states, organised in international law, an application of the transpersonal idea.

The quintessence of relativism has also been expressed, from a very different philosophical standpoint and in different language, by Oliver Wendell Holmes, in his essay on natural law[9]:

Deep-seated preferences cannot be argued about—you cannot argue a man into liking a glass of beer—and therefore, when differences are sufficiently far reaching, we try to kill the other man rather than let him have his way. But that is perfectly consistent with admitting that, so far as appears, his grounds are just as good as ours. . . .

It is true that beliefs and wishes have a transcendental basis in the sense that their foundation is arbitrary. You cannot help entertaining and feeling them, and there is an end of it.[10]

[9] Holmes' "Natural Law," 32 Harv.L.Rev. 40 (1918).

[10] Holmes J. ought, therefore, to have been included among the "give-it-up philosophers" whom Roscoe Pound attacked in his *Contemporary Juristic Theory* (1940). Dean Pound lumps together Marxian determinism and sceptical realism with Neo-Kantian relativism. All these philosophies, according to Pound, eliminate the "ought" from jurisprudence and are indifferent to values. Whatever the merits of this attack upon the first two of these movements in legal thought (on this, see below, Chaps. 25, 29) it seems misconceived as far as the relativism of Max Weber and Radbruch is concerned. As Pound himself states (at 37), relativism merely says—like Holmes J.—that judgments of value cannot be scientifically proved. This is radically different from the proposition that they do not matter. On the contrary, the legal philosophy of Radbruch—who, like Max Weber, was an active politician with definite and consistent ideals—is dominated by the conviction that legal philosophy means the linking of ultimate political valuations with the legal order. Kelsen, on the other hand, tries to make jurisprudence immune from political conflict by eliminating values from jurisprudence. Though Radbruch states the principal legal values in terms of antinomies—and do the struggles of our time not show beyond doubt that the antinomies of basic political and juristic values are real and deep?—he nowhere states, as Pound implies, that a legal order is or must be exclusively built upon one or the other. For Pound's further deduction that, according to this relativism, "there is nothing more to politics or jurisprudence than force or threats" (p. 38), there is no foundation. Radbruch specifically rejects the over-emphasis on force and threats (*Rechtsphilosophie*, 10). In the end, Pound himself concedes that "there is no absolute value; that value in jurisprudence is relative to civilisation" (p. 82).

Kelsen, on the one hand, Lask and Radbruch, on the other, represent different aspects of Neo-Kantian relativism. The latter give, in fact, strong support to Pound's main argument that legal ideals cannot be eliminated from jurisprudence. For a further discussion of Pound's own position, see below, p. 336 *et seq*. For a recent vindication of "Scientific Value Relativism" see Brecht, *Political Theory*, Chap. 3 (1959). For a criticism of the relativist position, especially of Max Weber, see Strauss, *Natural Right and History* (1953). Strauss apparently shares Pound's misconception when he writes (p. 63) that Weber assumes that "there is no hierarchy of values." As Brecht has pointed out (*op. cit.* p. 263, he says that the hierarchy of values is not scientifically demonstrable—a very different thing. Strauss' further criticism that Weber apparently regarded "the quest for truth as valuable in itself" (*op. cit.* p. 72) may be conceded. The search for truth is the *Grundnorm* of scholarly criticism.

PHENOMENOLOGY, EXISTENTIALISM AND CONTEMPORARY
LEGAL PHILOSOPHY

One of the most important aspects of Neo-Kantian thinking has been the attempt to bridge the tragic gap between action and knowledge, between intuition and understanding.[11] One of the most significant applications of this new approach to the theory of knowledge has been the movement that is generally, and loosely, described as phenomenology, from the basic work of Edmund Husserl.[12] While this general description covers a great variety of trends in modern philosophy, the common theme of the many variations is the postulate that the Kantian antinomy between the individual and the world, between the categories of thinking and the object which it apprehends, can be overcome by the apprehension of the "immediately Given" in the world of consciousness, by the concrete and underivative experience of the phenomena, as they confront man in their total, undivided fullness and immediacy.

While it is beyond the scope of this book to pursue the implications of this approach for theoretical philosophy, it is important for the philosophy of law for two reasons:

First, it has directly inspired[13] certain phenomenological theories of law. Second, it has been the intellectual godfather of the philosophy of values (*Wertphilosophie*) established by Max Scheler[14] and Nicolai Hartmann.[15] The attempt of these two German thinkers to establish objectively valid—though not invariable—values has in turn, been a major inspiration for contemporary legal philosophy, especially in Germany and Latin-America.

SCHELER AND HARTMANN

The basic thought of the philosophy of values is the conviction that "values" are real, objective and autonomous essences (*Wesenheiten*) which can be intuitively experienced and apprehended by man and therefore constitute a source of obligations. Scheler and Hartmann have combined the philosophical approach of the phenomenological movement with a reappraisal of Aristotle's scale of values, as devel-

[11] See above, Chap. 16.
[12] *Ideen zu einer reinen Phenomenologie*, I (1913).
[13] See below, p. 205 *et seq.*
[14] *Formalismus in der Ethik und die materiale Wertethik* (3rd ed. 1927, first published in 1913).
[15] *Ethik* (3rd ed., unchanged from first ed., 1925, 1949).

oped in his *Nicomachean Ethics*. Aristotle had established, on the one hand, a scale of "virtues,"[16] of which the σωφροσυνη, the Greek concept of wisdom, is the best known. On the other hand, he had a scale of value intensities, from "not bad" to "worthy of love," "worthy of admiration," and "worthy of sublimation." To this corresponded a scale of "non-values" from "failure" to "odiousness."

In an Aristotelean vein, Scheler established five criteria to determine rank in the hierarchy of values: First, the durability of values is determined by the degree of detachment from a temporal, transitory situation. This gives spiritual values a higher rank than material values.

Secondly, values are the higher the less they increase by quantitative extension and decrease by division. This again distinguishes spiritual from material values.

Thirdly, Scheler regards lower values as founded in higher values.

Fourthly, there is a relationship between the rank of the value and the "depth of satisfaction" which accompanies the consciousness of realisation of a value.

Lastly, the rank of a value is determined by its relation to a specific experience. Thus, moral values have a more general quality than sense and lust experiences.

Hartmann has partly developed and partly modified this attempt of Scheler. Perhaps his most important contribution has been to demonstrate, in a development of Aristotle's tables of values, that the acceptance of a hierarchy of values does not mean the acceptance of an invariable and absolutely valid "Good." "The Good . . . is solely the teleology of values in the real world."[17] There is a choice between a Good and an Evil for everybody. The potentiality of acting for certain purposes, the choice between what for the individual is a whole range of actions between Good and Evil, is the essential aspect of human freedom. "The possibility of the Good is necessarily, at the same and in equal measure, the possibility of the Evil. The highest potentiality is at the same time the highest danger. It is of the nature of man to stand in this danger. The danger itself is a basis of his ethos. Through it he is a moral being."[18]

For both Scheler and Hartmann an "experience"[19] is not a matter

---

[16] Virtue is a "mean" (μεσότης) between extremes.

[17] Hartmann, *op. cit*, at 380.

[18] *Id*. at 381 (the present author's translation).

[19] The German term *"Erleben,"* which implies a fusion of emotional and intellectual apprehension, is not properly translatable into English.

of reaction to physical experience (such as fear of punishment for a criminal action); it is an emotional and spontaneous *a priori,* which "immediately, intuitively and emotionally permeates our practical conscience, our entire conception of life."[20] This *a priori* consciousness of values is a matter of the "logic of the heart,"[21] an adaptation of Pascal's *ordre du cœur.*

This approach to values rejects both empiricism and rationalism. since values have an objective existence prior to all experienced reality, and since they can be emotionally and intuitively apprehended. At the same time, at least in Hartmann's version, there is a clear differentiation of the ethic of values from natural law philosophy, in so far as it constitutes an absolute and immutable hierarchy of values. There is a strong link with relativism, in Hartmann's insistence that the "Good" is the realisation, for each individual, of the utmost of which he is capable, in the attainment of the highest in his scale of values, in the choice of which he is, apparently, guided by the *Rechtsgefühl.*[22]

The agony and nobility of the choice which human freedom imposes on the individual, gives to both the ethics of Hartmann and the relativism of Max Weber and Radbruch an "existentialist" aspect.[23] It is from a combination of the phenomenological value philosophy and existentialist teaching that modern legal philosophy derives much of its inspiration.

EXISTENTIALISM

Existentialism—perhaps the most widely discussed philosophical movement in the post-war world—does not, by itself, contribute much to the philosophy of law, since it is essentially concerned with the existence, the struggle to become, of the individual in a world into which he is "thrown" (*"geworfen"*). Heidegger, Jaspers and Sartre, the main exponents of this philosophy, have all, though in different ways, been concerned with the ways in which the individual can overcome his loneliness by realising himself in a hostile world. But there are attempts, especially in the philosophy of

---

[20] Hartman, *Id.* at 116.

[21] Scheler, *op. cit.* 59 (4th ed., p. 84).

[22] The key position given to the intuitively felt sense of values clearly links this aspect of the *Wertphilosophie* with the *"Rechtsgefühl"* of Krabbe, and the *sentimento giuridico* of Del Vecchio. See on these pp. 85, 186 *et seq.*

[23] Radbruch has indeed described his own legal philosophy as one of "existentialism," *Rechtsphilosophie* 102 (4th ed., 1950).

Jaspers, to see law and the evolution of the legal order not merely as an external compulsion imposed by a hostile world upon the individual, but as part of his self-realisation. "Just as nature cannot be denied without man destroying himself, . . . so man cannot reject society, profession, state, marriage and family, without being blown to the winds, and he can find himself only if he enters into them."[24] Since existence can only realise itself in communication (with one another) the law is conceded at least a protective function, in so far as it gives man a minimum of social security and protects the individual from the fear of the "invasion of the uncertain." In non-existentialist terminology, this apparently means that the individual, however much he may struggle with the realisation of his self, can do so only within the framework of a social order and minimum rules for the living together of numerous individuals, under conditions that permit each of its members to realise himself without the fear of chaos. This insight is, of course, one that legal philosophers, for all their differences in the respective evaluation of individual and community values, have held, from Aristotle to Kant, from Fichte to Del Vecchio, from Bentham and John Stuart Mill to Stammler.

An important attempt to develop a legal philosophy of existentialism is that of Maihofer[25] who seeks to overcome the isolationist individualism of existentialist philosophy by conceiving man as a being not by and for himself, but as "sujet-objet, monde-homme . . . homme particulier dans ce monde particulier qui est le sien. . . ." His existence is, in Sartre's words, the conquest of his self (être), "dans la somme des relations dans lesquelles il vit." Man has not only an individual vocation as judge, physician, brother, husband, buyer or seller (être en tant que Alssein), but he is also "homme en général" with a universal vocation. The dereliction of man does not derive from his own anti-social nature but from the "antagonistic, antinomic, paradoxical structure of the world." An illustration of such irresolvable conflict is the choice between killing the mother by refusing abortion, or killing the embryo by procuring it, where the mother would not survive the birth of the infant.[26] Man's existence, while subject to certain natural laws, is not predetermined, but guided by the criteria of human decision which man shapes himself. Natural law becomes an existential law,

---

[24] Karl Jaspers, *Philosophie*, 838 (2nd ed., 1948), (the author's translation).
[25] Maihofer, "Le Droit naturel comme dépassement du droit positif," 8 Archives de Philosophie du Droit, 177 (transl). Poulantzas and Mavrakis, 1963).
[26] See on this problem below, p. 391.

an instrument for the implementation of a human order "digne d'être vécu," an order of the greatest possible satisfaction of human needs and the greatest possible development of human faculties.[27]

That law is both the realisation of values given to man from a *Wertordnung,* in the sense of Scheler and Hartmann, and existentialist realisation of the individual, that it is through the agony of decision between alternatives that he contributes to the shaping of the world and community around him, is the conclusion of another contemporary German jurist,[28] although this theory has yet to be elaborated in its application to specific legal problems. Meanwhile, the value philosophy of Scheler and Hartmann has become the dominant trend of contemporary Latin-American legal philosophy.

MODERN LATIN-AMERICAN LEGAL PHILOSOPHIES

The Spanish-Mexican jurist Luis Recasens-Siches has been principally concerned with an attempt to reconcile the objectivity of juridical values, on the basis of Scheler's and Hartmann's theories, with the historicity of juridical ideals.[29] He distinguishes five sources of historicity: (1) the fact that social reality is diverse and changing; (2) the diversity of obstacles which in each situation must be overcome in order to materialise the requirements of value in such situation; (3) the lessons drawn from practical experience as to the adequacy of the means to materialise a value in a concrete situation; (4) the priorities raised by the gradations of urgency of the social needs which historical events bring up; and (5) a multiplicity of values, some of which refer to universal human qualities and needs, whereas others are attached to specific historical conditions, which engender particular norms for each community and each situation. As to the hierarchy of values, Recasens-Siches seeks to demonstrate that humanism or personalism, which regards the state and the law as means in the service of the individual, is

[27] This importation of the ideology of human liberty—apparently on a universal scale—into existentialism is accepted and developed by Poulantzas in an as yet unpublished thesis, *Le Concept de Nature des Choses dans la philosophie et la sociologie contemporaines du droit,* according to the account given by Villey, "Deux Théses de Philosophie du Droit," 10 Archives de Philosophie du Droit, 157 (1965).

[28] Erich Fechner, *Rechtsphilosophie* 223 et seq. (1956).

[29] The principal of Recasens-Siches has been translated, under the title *Human Life, Society and Law in Latin-American Legal Philosophy* (20th Century Legal Philosophy Series, 1948). See also his own account of his legal philosophy in *Natural Law Forum,* 148 (1958).

superior to transpersonalism, which regards the individual human person as a mere means in the service of the state, because individual consciousness is the centre and proof of all other realities, and because human life, in its relation to the world is a first point of departure for all philosophy.

Another Mexican jurist, Eduardo Garcia-Meynez,[30] while accepting the objective validity of juridical values, declares that they have various forms of relativity, which he classifies into three groups: (1) relativity to persons; (2) relativity to concrete situations; (3) relativity to space and time.

The Uruguayan jurist, Juan Lambias de Asevedo,[31] who also accepts the juridical axiology of the *Wertphilosophie*, distinguishes between "validity" and "positivity" of law. Positive law is seen as mediation between the values of the community and human conduct.

One of the most influential of the Latin-American legal philosophers, who has sought to combine the Neo-Kantian thinking of Kelsen with Heidegger's existentialism and phenomenological philosophy is the Argentinian Carlos Cossio,[32] who has given his theory the high-sounding name of "egological theory of law." Law is an "egological object," *i.e.*, human conduct in its intersubjective interference. The judicial decision consists of three elements: the logical structure given by a framework such as a constitution; the contingent contents of a situation, which are supplied by the circumstances of the case; and the juridical evaluation which the judge imposes on these two elements in a given situation. Because a judge deals with human conduct, he cannot be an automaton. To illustrate his theory, Cossio quotes some Argentine decisions in which the court points out the need to make decisions in accordance with principles of justice and public utility. "In absence of any norm, they are obliged to endeavour by following the principles of the legislation in force or basic norms of what may be considered just, to arrive at a decision founded on a conception of justice."[33] Despite the high-sounding name of "egological theory," which Cossio gives to his approach, it seems to tell us little more than what Article 1 of

---

[30] Garcia-Meynez, *Introduction a l'estudio del derecho* (6th ed., 1956).

[31] de Asevedo, *La objectividad de los valores ante la filosofia de las existencias* (1952).

[32] Some of Cossio's work (*Phenomenology of the Decision*) has been translated in *Latin-American Legal Philosophy* 345-400. (20th Century Legal Philosophy Series, 1948).

[33] *Id.* at 385.

the Swiss Civil Code, or jurists like Gény, Pound, Cardozo and Radbruch have presented as the problem of the judicial process in simpler language.

The above-mentioned theories have a distressing tendency to build up some elementary truth about the inevitable tension between individual and community claims, and the function of the law in mediating between them, into ambitious philosophical systems. Much of what is valuable in the elaboration of the juridical axiology was, in fact, said many years earlier by the French jurist François Gény in his theory of the *donnés*—developed from Bergson's vitalistic philosophy, of which an account is given elsewhere in this book.[34]

THE "NATUR DER SACHE"

A rather more fruitful juristic development of the phenomenological value philosophy may be found in some of the post-war German legal thinking on the "nature of the thing" (*Natur der Sache*). This approach means translating the reality of phenomena, which have certain immanent values, into the world of legal institutions. The nature of the legal order, as expressed in the varying number and interrelation of legal institutions, has certain immanent qualities which legal science must recognise. Radbruch has described the *Natur der Sache* as the moving force in the transformation of legal institutions, in response to social change.[35] As an illustration, Radbruch gives the new discipline of Labour Law. Whereas the civil law only knew persons, legal subjects supposed to conclude contracts by mutual free resolutions, the development of combinations and associations of employers and employees demanded a new institution, the collective agreements of Labour Law, to represent and shape the new type of social relationship. To Radbruch, the *Natur der Sache* thus means a dynamic concept, by which law, as an instrument of social change, responds to the manifoldness of life and changing social relationships.

A more static element has been stressed by Helmut Coing, who seeks to derive certain "highest principles of law" from basic values and institutions. Unlike Radbruch, who sharply distinguishes the philosophy of the *Natur der Sache* from natural law thinking,

---

[34] See below, p. 328 *et seq.*
[35] Radbruch: "Die Natur der Sache als juristische Denkform," in *Festschrift zu Ehren von Rudolf Laun*, 157 (1948).

Coing seeks to combine the two.[36] There are certain basic values such as the elementary feeling of justice, which leads to the familiar principles of the Roman jurists: *Honeste vivere, neminem laedere, suum cuique tribuere.* But certain other moral values as well as changing social data influence the basic principles of justice. Personal dignity supplements justice, with the demand of respecting the autonomous value of personality. Institutional values are represented by the state as the protector of material existence, the economic institutions as the representatives of values of utility, the universities as the exponents of truth and free inquiry, etc. The legal institutions have certain immanent values. Contract is based on the principle of reciprocity, marriage implies a minimum of permanence and community between the spouses.

As another German jurist has pointed out,[37] a large element in the *Natur der Sache* are the physical factors which determine, for example, the legal rules on the period of gestation, on paternity, or, one might add, the often detailed rules in civil codes governing the respective rights in regard to escaped swarms of bees. Again, it seems that the essentials of the philosophy of the *Natur der Sache* have been put most clearly by Gény in his theory of the *donné naturel.*[38] An essentially similar integration of phenomenological and natural law thinking is found in Werner Maihofer's "Konkretes Naturrecht."[39]

In his approach, the *Natur der Sache* is a suprapositive yardstick of rightness and justice, an extra-statutory source of law, which serves to bring the abstract imperatives of the law in accord with the norms of conduct prescribed by the social situation of a concrete legal condition. This is exemplified by the infusion of such concepts as "good faith" (*Treu und Glauben*) or reasonableness in the provisions of the civil code.[40] Thus, the *Natur der Sache* is not something remote from the positive law, but part of the legal life of every day.

The main merit of the new legal approaches derived from phenomenology and existentialism is the new perspective it puts on the

---

[36] Coing, *Die obersten Grundsätze des Rechts* (1947); *Grundzüge der Rechtsphilosophie* (1950).

[37] Fechner: *Rechtsphilosophie*, 146 *et seq.* (1956).

[38] Below, p. 328 *et seq.*

[39] Maihofer, "Die Natur der Sache," 44 Archiv für Rechts-und Sozialphilosophie, 145-174 (1958).

[40] A practical illustration of the use of the "Treu und Glauben" clause of the German Civil Code for the adjustment of contract obligations is given below, p. 506.

age-old conflict between the demands of the community and the claims of the individual. No less important is the attempt to bridge the apparently insoluble conflict between a permanent and fixed hierarchy of natural law values, and modern relativism, which leaves the decision between conflicting values entirely to the individual as a matter of choice and conviction, to which philosophy can give no guidance. It has, in particular, been Hartmann's merit to show that an order of values is not identical, and indeed opposed to, a natural law philosophy. If Radbruch said that "to live is to decide,"[41] Hartmann and, following him, Fechner can say that to decide means also to have a part in the implementation of a real though not an unchangeable order of values.

But the limitations of this approach are equally evident. Even if the conflict of values is put on a new philosophical basis, the conflict still remains. The immanence of values may demand a respect for human personality, as it requires marriage as a permanent and necessary social institution. But whether the permanence of marriage implies its indissolubility or dissolution only in cases of grave fault, such as adultery, or whether, on the other hand, the autonomy of the individual requires the dissolubility of a marriage that has become irretrievably disrupted, is a question that a concrete legal order can only decide in the light of the balance of the values and interests, as it prevails in a given community at a given time.

PHENOMENOLOGY AND LAW

Edmund Husserl's work directly inspired an attempt published in 1913 to interpret the institutions of the German Civil Code from a phenomenological perspective.[42] It seeks to isolate the *a priori* "essence" of legal institutions, such as contract or property, in terms of legal and ideological premises which, half a century later, show the degree to which values or "essences" are subject to historical and ideological change. The studies of Gerhard Husserl[43] show more awareness of the problem of how to reconcile the "eiditic" essence of legal norms with their historical relativity.

In recent years, phenomenological jurisprudence has become a major preoccupation of French jurisprudence, from a positivist and

[41] See above, p. 192.
[42] Reinach, Phänomenologie des Rechts. Die apriorischen Grundlagen des bürgerlichen Rechts. (1953).
[43] *e.g.*, Husserl, Rechtskraft und Rechtsgeltung; Recht and Zeit. (1925).

existentialist standpoint. The most ambitious effort to develop a contemporary phenomenological theory of law is that of Amselek.[44] It seeks to establish an anti-metaphysical phenomenological positivism. The "phénomène juridique" is the application (*mise en oeuvre*) of a norm to an object. The Ought (*devoir-être, Sollen*) is nothing but a way to express the structure of the norm model. Any order of values, as an external model to which the specific norm must conform, is rejected. The science of law reposes on the hypothesis that there exist objectively observable juridical norms. These formulated norms are "syntactic propositions constituting models."[45] They are instruments of judgment, obligatory in the sense that they are assigned the vocation of having to be compulsorily (*obligatoirement*) respected and executed.[46]

The lawyer must accordingly conceive law not only as an object of cognition and deductive reflection (homo sapiens) but as artisan (homo Faber) who engages in technical activities (politique juridique), *i.e.*, the forging of legal instruments and institutions, and technological activities (art juridique), *i.e.*, an effort to make the technical instruments more relevant, more systematic, more rational.[47] Amselek's message is that legal science must seek to observe, objectively, the "intersubjectivity" of juridical norms instead of being content like classical technological theory, with "prediction" or "certainty." A phenomenological positivism must study the reasons for a particular legal institution, and it must develop a psychological and sociological theory of law. It must have historicité, mondanité, facticité, temporalité, as against the classical views which made of the "sujet connaissant, un simple réceptacle négligeable, du monde extérieur . . ."[48]

CRITIQUE OF PHENOMENOLOGICAL AND EXISTENTIALIST LEGAL THEORY

Phenomenological and existentialist approaches are linked: One concentrates on the concreteness of legal phenomena, the other on the existential experience of man thrown into a world of conflicts. They meet, in particular, in man's appraisal and conquering of

---

[44] Amselek, Perspectives Critiques d'une Réflexion Epistémologique sur la Théorie du Droit (Essai de Phénoménologie Juridique) (1964).

[45] *Op. cit.* at 144.

[46] *Op. cit.* at 275.

[47] Amselek criticises Gény's distinction between "science" and "technique" as inadequate.

[48] *Op. cit.* at 447.

concrete legal phenomena. The emphasis on law and legal institutions as "Gestalt," as concrete and developing phenomena, in a world of conflicts and antimonies, is valuable, but far less original than its proponents pretend. Stammler, Radbruch, Gény, Pound, the American realists, the German exponents of Interessenjurisprudenz, Stone, Hart, and even some of the contemporary natural law philosophers, are among those who have studied legal values and concepts in their relations to concrete legal problems—of obedience to immoral legal orders, of the conflict between stability and freedom in modern family law, of the clash between moral fault and psychological or social determinism in the contemporary treatment of criminal responsibility. Sociologists, economists, psychologists and demographers have joined with lawyers in the study of the impact of legal aid and of more liberal divorce grounds on the stability of the family, or of insurance on the fault principle in tort liability.[49] The "phenomenological" relativity of corporate personality—which Amselek appears to regard as an original discovery—has been the subject both of theoretical studies by Kelsen, Kocourek, Berle, Hart and others, and of application in countless judicial decisions (lifting the veil) both Anglo-American and Continental.[50] These approaches do not usually bear the "etiquette de phénoménologie"[51] but they have done what Amselek postulates, in a study characterised by a high degree of abstract theorising, and an almost total absence of concreteness. The rejection of any external order of values—going far beyond Austin, Kelsen, Hart and other analytical positivists who merely seek to separate the "Is" and "Ought"—has been convincingly criticised by two contemporary French legal philosophers.[52] The rejection of natural law is is in no way to be confused with the rejection of the dependence of legal norms on a given hierarchy of values that change in time and space. Can it be seriously denied that such problems as the legitimacy of birth control and abortion, the liberalisation of divorce, the propriety of judicial condemnation of immoral behaviour regardless of its effect on public order,[53] and, most tellingly, the choices that faced the soldier, the civil servant and the informer wife under the Nazi regime, cannot be decided without

---

[49] See for a discussion of these matters, *e.g.*, Law in a Changing Society, Chaps. 5, 7.
[50] See below, Chap. 34, especially p. 559 *et seq.*
[51] Villey, *op. cit.*, at 162.
[52] Virally, *La Pensée Juridique*, 31 *et seq.* (1960), Villey, *op. cit.*
[53] See above, p. 45 *et seq.*

reference to the basic values of the legal system—as distinct from a multiplicity of individual legal norms each comporting its own value?

Existentialist legal philosophers, like Reinach, Maihofer, Poulantzas[54] do recognise the tension of fact and value but they deceive themselves by regarding what is in fact a species of natural law philosophy as "existentially immanent in the human destiny. Reinach[55] postulates for example, as inherent in the essence of property, its indivisibility—other than by quotas—and its transferability by consent between assignor and assignee. This not only excludes non-civilian concepts of property but is totally at variance with the function and treatment of property half a century later.[56] Maihofer sees both the need for an existential choice between conflicting values and demands, and the danger of a static acceptance of specific existential relations. But in postulating the development of human freedom and human faculties as the existential goal he adopts a plain, old-fashioned natural law ideal, vague enough to embrace innumerable contradictions[57] but specific enough to exclude numerous legal orders, past and present.

[54] See Poulantzas, "Notes sur la phénomélogie et l'existentialisme juridiques," .8 Archives de Philosophie du Droit 213 (1963).
[55] Reinach, Phanomenologie des Rechts 95 *et seq.* (1913).
[56] See Law in a Changing Society, Chap. 3.
[57] On some of these, see below, p. 356 *et seq.*

The Impact of Social Development
on Legal Theory

CHAPTER 18

HISTORICAL EVOLUTION AS A GUIDE TO LEGAL THOUGHT

THE term "historical jurisprudence" is usually associated with the particular movement in legal thought of which Savigny is the most famous exponent. That movement represents, however, but one particular aspect of the association into which law and history may enter. There is at least one other major movement in legal theory which is based upon an interpretation of the meaning of history in relation to law. Whereas Savigny and his followers invoke history in the name of tradition, custom and nation against the belief in conscious and rational law-making, the second movement, which one might call philosophical historism, develops a definite legal philosophy from the evolution of history. Vico, Montesquieu, Hegel, Kohler, Spengler, all have developed in different ways a legal philosophy from a philosophy of history.

SAVIGNY'S HISTORICAL SCHOOL

The teaching of such men as Hugo, Savigny, Puchta on the function and development of law can hardly be described as a theory of law. For that it is too negative in its conception and remains too general. The implications of this approach to law have, however, been very far-reaching. In large measure it has been responsible: (1) for the powerful development in the study of legal history; (2) for the emphasis placed more recently upon a "people's feeling of right" against the dead letter of statute or precedent, apparent in modern sociological and "free law" theories; (3) for the mystical throb of national socialist law.

This historical school represents a determined reaction against two powerful forces of the time: (1) The rationalism of the eighteenth century with its belief in natural law, the power of reason and first principles, all of these combining to establish a legal theory by means of general deduction and without regard to historical fact, national peculiarity and social conditions. (2) The beliefs and the spirit of the French Revolution, with its revolt against authority and traditions, its faith in reason and the power of human will over circumstances, its cosmopolitan message.

Before the German jurists who form the nucleus of the historical school, Edmund Burke[1] had formulated its principal political and philosophical beliefs. He ridiculed the attempt to deduce a constitution from abstract principles and asserted that it could only be the product of a gradual and organic development. Hugo[2] also insisted on the irrational elements present in every growing body of law, which were bound to reduce the importance of legal concepts and deliberately made rules. But the concrete issue, which produced the principal formulation of the thesis of the historical school,[3] was the question of codification of German law after the Napoleonic wars. A Heidelberg professor, Thibaut, inspired by the French Code Civil and impressed by the movement for German national unification, had advocated the rationalisation and unification of the innumerable laws then ruling in the different parts of Germany.[4]

Behind the practical issue of codification stood the larger issues of reason against tradition, history against renovation, creative and deliberate human action against the organic growth of institutions.

The essence of Savigny's thesis may be summed up in his own words:

In the earliest times to which authentic history extends, the law will be found to have already attained a fixed character, peculiar to the people like their language, manner and constitution. Nay, these phenomena have no separate existence, they are but the particular faculties and tendencies of an individual people, inseparably united in nature and only wearing the semblance of distinct attributes to our view. That which binds them into one whole is the common conviction of the people. The kindred consciousness of an inward necessity excluding all notions of an accidental and arbitrary origin . . . law grows with the growth, and strengthens with the strength of the people and finally dies away as a nation loses its nationality . . . the sum therefore of this theory is that all law is originally formed in the manner in which in ordinary, but not quite correct, language customary law is said to

---

[1] *Reflections on the Revolution in France* (1790).
[2] *Lehrbuch des Naturrechts.*
[3] Savigny's *Vom Beruf unserer Zeit zur Gesetzgebung und zur Rechtswissenschaft* (1814).
[4] *Über die Notwendigkeit eines allgemeinen bürgerlichen Rechts für Deutschland* (1814).

have been formed, *i.e.*, that it is first developed by custom and popular faith, next by jurisprudence, everywhere therefore by internal silently operating powers, not by the arbitrary will of a law-giver.[5]

The principal doctrines of the historical school, as expounded by Savigny and some of his followers, may thus be summarised:

(1) Law is found, not made. A pessimistic view is taken of the power of human action. The growth of law is essentially an unconscious and organic process; legislation is therefore of subordinate importance as compared with custom.

(2) As law develops from a few easily grasped legal relations in primitive communities to the greater complexity of law in modern civilisation, popular consciousness can no longer manifest itself directly, but comes to be represented by lawyers, who formulate the technical legal principles. But the lawyer remains an organ of popular consciousness, confined to the task of bringing into shape what he finds as raw material. Legislation follows as the last stage; the lawyer is therefore a relatively more important law-making agency than the legislator.

(3) Laws are not of universal validity or application. Each people develops its own legal habits, as it has its peculiar language, manners and constitution. Savigny insists on the parallel between language and law. Neither is capable of application to other peoples and countries. The *Volksgeist* manifests itself in the law of the people; it is therefore essential to follow up the evolution of the *Volksgeist* by legal historical research.

Savigny deprecated the admiration bestowed upon the then modern codifications of law in Prussia, Austria and France. Against it he stressed the need for the scientific study of a particular system of law in its continuous development, by which each generation adapts the law to its needs. Savigny was inspired by his profound study of Roman law, whose development was to him the model of wise juristic guidance moulding the law through gradual adaptation for centuries before the *Corpus Juris* gave the final form of codification. This explains Savigny's preference for the jurist rather than the legislator as the medium of legal progress. A somewhat strained blend of Savigny's two convictions, first that legal science is better than legal reform, and second that popular consciousness is the source of all law, is his contention that, in advanced civilisation, the jurist represents and formulates popular consciousness.

---

[5] Savigny *op. cit.*, English translation by Hayward (1832) pp. 24, 27, 30.

It is an ironical aspect of the teaching of Savigny and Puchta that, while emphasising the national character of all law, they should themselves have taken their inspiration from Roman law and devoted their main work to its adaptation to modern conditions. In Germany, indeed, the reception of Roman law had for centuries all but completely displaced the older Germanic law, and much of Savigny's work[6] was devoted to an attempt to show how genuine Roman law had been perverted by the many changes of the *Gemeine Recht*. But sooner or later the growth of the new German national consciousness was bound to produce a call for a revival of Germanistic influences in the law. Beseler, Eichhorn and Gierke led the fight. Beseler[7] opposed to Savigny's romantic conception of the jurist as the agent of popular consciousness the law of the people as being, on the contrary, divergent from the technical and artificial science of the jurist. Gierke[8] much later, when controversy was raging round the draft of the new German Civil Code, strongly opposed the prevalence of Romanistic influence in it, with the result that many Germanistic ideas were introduced into the second draft and the final draft became a mixture of Germanistic and Romanistic influences.

Although not immediately concerned with general ideals of law, and despite its outward rejection of first principles, the historical school is far from being anti-ideological. For the *Volksgeist* is, in substance, an idea, an abstraction from facts, quite capable of serving as basis for an idealistic philosophy. Schelling and Hegel, in fact, made of the *Volksgeist* an aspect of the Spirit, which unfolds in the universe. By praising, on the whole, instinct against reason, and gradual evolution against deliberate action, the historical school did not encourage creative energy and law reform.[9] The mystical and emotional element in its doctrine lent itself, however, to different interpretations.

---

[6] Savigny, *Geschichte des Römischen Rechts im Mittelalter* (7 vols.); *System des Heutigen Römischen Rechts* (8 vols.).

[7] *Volksrecht und Juristenrecht* (1843).

[8] *Deutsches Privatrecht* (1895).

[9] Twenty-five years after the publication of his pamphlet, Savigny, in the introduction to his *System des Heutigen Römischen Rechts*, defended himself against the charge of fatalism: "The existing matter . . . will be injurious to us so long as we ignorantly submit to it; but beneficial if we oppose to it a vivid creative energy—obtain the mastery over it by a thorough grounding in history, and thus appropriate to ourselves the whole intellectual wealth of preceding generations."
This belated defence could not mitigate the effect of the doctrine which, at a time when social developments made the use of legislative energy more important than ever, looked backwards rather than forwards.

As Fascism took over from Duguit the doctrine of social solidarity, but eliminated his rejection of state sovereignty, so National Socialism took over from the historical school the doctrine of the *Volksgeist*, but substituted for the scepticism against legislative activity the most ruthless and efficient machinery of law-making ever devised.

Another link exists between the historical school and those modern sociological theories which, after a period of intense legislative activity and corresponding analytical activity of the lawyers, once more stress the "living law" of the people against the unmitigated supremacy of legislative command.[10]

HEGEL, MAINE AND ETHNOLOGICAL INTERPRETATIONS OF LAW

Hegel sees in world history the gradual unfolding of the Idea, from its unconscious state of nature, in primitive communities, to the self-reflecting realisation of freedom. Each nation contributes something to the making of the road which leads to that goal. The notion of the *Volksgeist* is here utilised.

Hegel's conception contains the germs of a comparative and historical philosophy of law, which would ascertain law in its relation to the particular spirit or function of the specific nation, but Hegel himself did not develop that aspect of his philosophy. His own philosophy of law is of a metaphysical and essentially unhistorical character; but his philosophy of history has inspired further studies on the relation between national character, the spirit of history and the law.

The idea that law is the manifestation of a particular "spirit" is capable of applications different from that of Savigny's school. The increasing interest in detailed legal research combined with the belief in progress of mankind through history, characteristic of the nineteenth century, to produce different theories of legal evolution.

Montesquieu had not only collected a wealth of comparative material on the laws and constitutions of different peoples, but he also deduced from it the dependence of law on many natural and social factors, fourteen in all, only one of which is the *esprit de la nation*. The nineteenth century, with its greater international horizon, study of history and eagerness for knowledge in all fields, saw many further attempts in the direction of a comparative legal

---

[10] Notably Ehrlich and the Freirechtsschule, below, p. 342 *et seq.*

science. Most of these followed the predominant empirical trend and refrained from developing their conclusion to a philosophy.

Thus Post[11] undertook a comprehensive comparative investigation of the legal institutions of many different peoples and periods and came to the conclusion that there is a large measure of community between them. In particular, he deduced from comparative legal history the general existence of a tension between the dual forces working in a biological individual: the egoistic forces which make him demand rights, and the moral forces which make him feel bound by duties, as a member of a social group. This is reminiscent of Kant and Hegel, but also prepares the biologico-sociological legal philosophies later advanced by Spencer or Duguit. But Post is emphatic in rejecting anything like a general idea of law which would be prior and superior to the variety of legal experience.

Dahn[12] postulated a legal philosophy which

must begin with speculative valuation of the results of the historical school and with the setting up of a legal philosophical edifice on the basis of comparative legal history, folk psychology and ethnology.

A specific application of this line of thought is Fouillée's comparative analysis of the laws of different nations in terms of guiding ideas.[13] To Fouillée, German law represents the power idea in law, English law represents the utilitarian interest idea, and French law, in contrast to these two essentially realistic principles, realises the idealistic element; it belittles success and interest for the sake of the universal principles of liberty, equality and fraternity, expressed in declarations of right.

The danger of such interpretations of legal history is obvious. Not only do they tend to take a particular phase in comparative national development as permanent—fifty years later Fouillée's analysis which, in 1878, had some elements of truth, had no longer any relation to reality—they also tend to degenerate into a coarse national apotheosis at the expense of other nations.

It is Sir Henry Maine's work which stands out as the most important and fruitful application of comparative legal research to a legal theory inspired by principles of historical evolution.

[11] Post, *Bausteine für eine allgemeine Rechtswissenschaft* (1880); *Die Grundlagen des Rechts* (1884).
[12] Dahn, *Rechtsphilosophische Studien* (1878).
[13] Fouillié, *L'idée moderne du droit* (1878); transl. in *Modern French Legal Theory*.

This is not the place to discuss either the many fruitful suggestions which Maine had made in the field of comparative legal
research as such (as, for example, on the historical priority of the
family group over the individual, or the origin of private property
in land), or his political views on democracy. His great contribution
to legal theory lies in the combination of what is best in both
Montesquieu's and Savigny's theories, without the dangers involved
in both. Maine's theory avoids the danger of an excessive disintegration of theoretical laws of legal evolution, inherent in Montesquieu's comparative and factual approach to the development
of legal institutions; but it is equally free from the abstract and
unreal romanticism which vitiates much of Savigny's theory about
the evolution of law.

The comparative study of the development of different legal
systems—in particular the contrast between Hindu law and Roman
law—leads Maine to a fundamental distinction between static and
progressive societies and their legal evolution. The former, both
in their methods of law-making and the development of their legal
institutions, do not proceed beyond a certain stage. They move
from law-making by personal command, issuing from rulers
believed to be acting under divine inspiration (such as the Themistes·
in the Homeric poems), to a gradual crystallisation of habits into
custom. Concurrently with this, the theocratic power of the original
royal law-makers weakens and gives way to the dominion of an
aristocratic minority, which formulates the legal customs. The
epoch of customary law, and of its custody by a privileged order,
is followed by an era of codes, such as Solon's Attic Code or the
Twelve Tables of Rome. The great majority of human societies
never proceed beyond this stage, which marks the end of spontaneous social and legal development.

It is indisputable that much the greatest part of mankind has never
shown a particle of desire that its civil institutions should be improved
since the moment when external completeness was first given them by
their embodiment in some permanent record.[14]

Their legal condition—which is arrested at this stage—remains
characterised by what Main sums up as Status: that is a fixed legal
condition dominated by family dependency. The member of a
family household, wife, child or slave, remains tied to the family
nexus dominated by the *paterfamilias*.

[14] Maine, *Ancient Law*, 22 (ed. Pollock 1906).

But the few progressive societies of history—notably the Romans and the nations of modern Europe—move beyond the phase of codes and status relationships because they are propelled by a conscious desire to improve and develop. Three agents of legal development are brought to bear upon the primitive codes. They are, in historical sequence, Legal Fiction, Equity and Legislation. By the use of legal fictions the law is, in fact, changed in accordance with changing needs, while it is pretended that it remains what it was. Maine's favourite example is the extension of the Roman *familia* by adoption; the whole history of both Roman and English law is, in fact, deeply marked by the use of the fiction for this purpose. Equity—again particularly prominent in Roman and English legal development—is then used to modify the law, "as a set of principles, invested with a higher sacredness than those of original law." Finally, legislation represents the most direct comprehensive and systematic method of law-making, expressive of an enhanced law-making power of the state.

The corollary to these agencies of legal development, in progressive societies, is the

gradual dissolution of family dependency and the growth of individual obligation in its place. The individual is steadily substituted for the family, as the unit of which civil laws take account.

The Roman family, the slave, the caste, the medieval guilds, the feudal nexus, are typical instances of status. Gradually this rigid position, into which the individual is born and which he cannot leave, gives way to more freedom of will and movement. The authority of the *paterfamilias* loosens, the slave can be emancipated; he can, as slave, contract to the extent of the *peculium*, the medieval serf can become free by escaping into the town, and eventually slavery and serfdom are abolished; they give way to a free contractual relation between employer and employee. Thus progressive societies are characterised by the increasing legal freedom of movement of the individual. The development is summed up in a celebrated phrase:

If then we employ Status . . . to signify these personal conditions only, and avoid applying the term to such conditions as are the immediate or remote result of agreement, we may say that the movement of the progressive societies has hitherto been a movement from status to contract.[15]

15 *Id.* at 170.

Unlike Savigny, Maine did not reject this rationalising development of the law. He accepted it as inevitable for the small number
of progressive societies. His theory of the development of personal
legal conditions from status to contract was, in fact, a theoretical
corollary to the freedom of labour and contract demanded by a
vigorously expanding industrial and capitalist society. The effect
of Maine's principal thesis was thus liberalising, despite his personal
bent towards a conservative interpretation of history and the insistence on the fundamental stability of human institutions, which he
shared with Savigny, the historical school and, it may be added, the
great majority of legal historians.

Maine's theory, more constructive and less vague than the
Volksgeist theory, commended itself to a society which had wit-
nessed the American Civil War. That war resulted in the triumph
of the industrial, commercial and progress-minded North over the
agricultural, feudal and status-minded South. This meant, in terms
of legal development, the victory of the "free" contract, indispensable to an industrialised and capitalist society, which wanted—
at that time—mobility of labour and capital. It meant the eclipse
of status conceptions which tie the worker to an estate by an
unchangeable slave status.

In Europe, too, many peasant communities still living in a feudal
condition were transformed into an industrial proletariat, the
members of which enter into "free" contractual agreement with
an employer. As long as the liberal and expansive phase of capitalism lasted, legal developments went to prove Maine's thesis; the
abolition of the legal prohibitions against labour and trade unions;
the development of the legal position of married women in English
law, from the original merger in the husband's personality to the
complete legal independence achieved by the Act of 1935, or the
gradual abolition of Catholic and Jewish civic disabilities.

The position might be summarised by saying that, within the
sphere of Western civilisation and up to the spreading of modern
totalitarian systems, the abolition of differences in personal status
and capacities had proceeded far. Wives have emerged from the legal
tutelage of husbands; servants have ceased to be bound to master
and household;[16] infants have acquired, in most modern laws, a
considerable degree of commercial and professional freedom. But,

---

[16] Although there still are such archaic survivals as the action for damages by a
master for the seduction of his servant. See Winfield, *Law of Torts*, Chaps. 10, 24
(2nd ed. 1943).

on the other hand, Maine's thesis was always—as he himself recognised—subject to important limitations.[17] It was never meant to apply to personal conditions imposed otherwise than by natural incapacity. It did not apply to the development of feudalism which moved from contract to status rather than the other way round.

But far more significant than these qualifications is the dialectic development by which the very removal of the fetters imposed by status conditions on freedom of contract has created the conditions for a new "status." T. H. Green opposed a "positive" conception of freedom to the merely negative and formal conception of early liberalism which had, often enough, led to a new slavery founded not on legal incapacity, but on the economic helplessness of the worker.

The counter-move came, on the one hand, with the association of workers in trade unions which gradually succeeded in creating a more equal bargaining position and, on the other hand, with a growing amount of state interference in unmitigated freedom of contract, designed to remedy some of the worst consequences of the formal and "negative" freedom of contract. Both movements developed with increasing momentum, though with greatly differing speed, in all countries affected by industrialisation. In the development of trade unionism England took the lead, and the abolition of the Combination Acts, greatly accelerated the development. In the field of protective social legislation, Bismarck's Germany, with the object of weakening the growing Socialist movement, took the lead with a series of Social Insurance Acts which served as a model for the English health insurance reforms of 1911. In the United States, where the doctrine of freedom of contract was most firmly embedded, both developments were retarded until social and economic crises drove home the negative aspects of a purely formal and legal conception of freedom of contract.[18]

The result has been, in many ways, a recoil from contract to status, of which Dicey gave, in 1898, a classical analysis.[19]

Dicey perceived, long before most of his contemporaries, the significance both of the growing trade union movement and of the inevitable increase of social legislation. He saw all this as a dialectic development from the removal of inequalities which the Benthamites had fought for by reforming legislation. They, indeed,

---

[17] *Ancient Law, op. cit.* at 385.
[18] Of which the twin doctrines of *volenti non fit injuria* and common employment are typical examples.
[19] Dicey, *Law and Public Opinion in England* (2nd ed., 1914).

had hoped that with the removal of rotten boroughs and numerous other inequalities, the legislative machinery could be set at rest, for the benefit of free competition. But, once created, it had to be used for the mitigation of the very consequences of such freedom.

Social legislation leads to such "status" fetters on freedom of contract, as Workmen's Compensation, Minimum Wages Acts, Factory Acts, National Insurance Acts. The principle of social insurance, based on compulsory contributions from employers and employees and thus limiting the freedom of fixing the terms of contract, has now led to the comprehensive British National Insurance Act, 1946, which covers the whole population.

The growth of trade unions and business associations leads to the replacement of individual bargaining by collective group agreements which move and curtail the freedom of the individual on both sides by penalising the outsider and compelling the member to submit to collective terms.[20] The sacrifice of freedom is brought in exchange for considerable advantages; but the worker who joins the trade union, the industrialist who joins the cartel, certainly does sacrifice this freedom in substance. In return, the industrialist who joins a cartel, and the worker who, through his union, adheres to a long-term collective agreement, gains security of price, production, employment or pension.[21]

Another factor has greatly modified the freedom of contract which Maine had in mind: the standardisation of contract terms which substitutes, for freedom of bargaining, status-like conditions in the great majority of modern transport, insurance, mortgage or landlord and tenant contracts.[22] Terms are largely fixed, and the parties face each other as members of social classes rather than as individuals. In form they bargain freely, in substance they do not. Another type of contract which differs considerably from the free contract between equal parties is the increasingly important standard contract between government departments and private firms, which normally contains a unilateral "break" clause.

Finally, the rise of modern totalitarian government has produced a far-reaching return to a more direct status condition: Fascist labour legislation proceeded to tie workers to their jobs and to create several classes of citizens, from a master class to a slave class.

---

[20] For a detailed analysis, see *Law in a Changing Society*, Chaps. 4, 11.

[21] For a fuller discussion of this whole problem, see *Law and Social Change in Contemporary Britain*, at 44-72.

[22] See Prausnitz, *Standardisation of Contracts* (1937); Symposium on Compulsory Contracts, 43 Colum.L.Rev. 565 *et seq.* (1943).

Non-Fascist countries have resisted this return to medieval conceptions; but the last war compelled them to accept severe limitations of the freedom of labour and contract which, for good or evil, constituted one of the most distinctive achievements of modern times.

The present position is well summed up by a modern critic:

> On the one hand the movement in domestic status is away from dependence on the head of the family, with its corollary of vicarious liability, towards full individual legal capacity; on the other, state interference in the terms and conditions of employment in industry has given rise to a new type of personal legal condition which bears many of the features of a status.[23]

A conception of status which includes, but is not limited to, the restrictions put by public law upon freedom of contract, enables us to use it as a helpful and illuminating notion in the wider context of "social engineering," the clash and adjustment between public and private interests that is at the core of every modern legal system. In modern industrialised Western society—and increasingly in non-Western societies—where there are no fixed classes of slaves or feudal serfs, or underprivileged castes, we must conceive of status, *i.e.*, the sum of public-law restrictions, as relative, as attaching to persons in certain but not in other capacities. Every legal subject in modern society, individual or corporate, has a multiplicity of legal relations, and status restrictions may attach to him in certain capacities but not absolutely.

"Status" thus becomes a convenient shorthand description of the shifting balance between freedom of will and freedom of movement —which is essentially the province of private law—and the public policies of the modern welfare state expressed in terms of public law. Such an approach will make it possible for the contemporary jurist to reevaluate the essentially political significance of Maine's dictum, which was that freedom of contract, *i.e.*, private law, was the avenue to political and social freedom, and to progress in society, whereas status meant immobility, tradition and servitude. Only if we understand that, at least in contemporary industrialised society, status is a many-sided thing, that the interrelations of private freedom and public regulation are infinite and complex, that no individual or group in modern society is either "free" or "status bound," can we begin to reevaluate the validity of Maine's dictum for our own time.

[23] Graveson, "The Movement From Status To Contract," 4 Mod.L.Rev. 267 (1941).

Maine's theory, though careful in its generalisations, reflects the belief in progress through the emancipation of the individual which reached its climax in the first half of the nineteenth century. Hegel's philosophy of the unfolding of history through different phases is, however, capable of a different development. Kohler's legal philosophy infuses into the Hegelian philosophy of history the relativity of values and progress, a conception foreign to both Hegel and Maine. This relativism characterises a later period, which has begun to experience the negative aspects of freedom of contract and of uncontrolled capitalist development.

Kohler[24] asserts that all laws are relative and conditioned by the civilisation in which they arise. But the idea of law has to follow the universal idea of human civilisation, and the meaning of civilisation is the social development of human powers toward their highest possible unfolding. The evolution of civilisation (*Kulturentwicklung*) results from the struggle between the human mind, distinguishing itself from nature, and the object-matter of nature. The values of civilisation which result from this struggle are: Apperception, Creation and Dominion through Technique.[25] The degree of domination achieved over nature thus seems to be the test of civilisation. The task of law—following the evolution of civilisation—is both to maintain existing values and to create new ones for the further development and unfolding of human powers. The adjustment of these two functions—the protective and ordering functions on the one hand and the creative on the other—must depend on the time and place. It would be different in a primitive agricultural as compared with an industrialised society. It is only the relation of law and civilisation which is constant; the contents must vary "with the infinite variety in the conditions of human cultivation."[26] Every civilisation has certain jural postulates, that is ideas of right to be made effective by legal institutions. Legal materials must be shaped so as to give effect to those postulates and legislators; judges, jurists, must mould the law in accordance with them. The link between this conception of jural postulates conditioned by time and place, and the relativist philosophy of Radbruch or the "initial hypothesis" of Kelsen, is evident. But Kohler's

---

[24] Kohler, "Rechtsphilosophie und Universalrechtsgeschichte" in Holtzendorff's *Encyclopædie d. Rechtswissenschaft*; *Moderne Rechtsprobleme*, 1907 (2nd ed., 1913); *Lehrbuch der Rechtsphilosophie*, transl. as *Philosophy of Law* (Albrecht, 1914).

[25] *Erkenntnis, Schöpfung, Herrschaft durch Technik.*

[26] *Moderne Rechtsprobleme*, para. 1.

approach seems to have been more immediately fruitful in inspiring Roscoe Pound's theory of social engineering and the balancing of social interests.[27] The Hegelian form of Kohler's theory obscured— not least to the author himself—its affinity with the modern socio- logical turn of legal theory. Kohler bitterly assailed the many jurists who seemed to him to develop theories without proper philosophy. Ihering was the chief object of his very considerable powers of vituperation. Yet Ihering's linking of law to a social purpose fulfils essentially the same object as Kohler's linking of law with changing jural postulates. Both have inspired modern sociological theories of the end of law, and neither is far from modern theories of law which are essentially relativist and pursue an idea of justice to be interpreted in accordance with the changing needs of time and circumstance.

Over two centuries ago, the great Italian philosopher, Vico, wrote about the *Corsi e ricorsi* of human history and the different types of epochs to which certain political forms correspond. In our own days, Spengler[28] has resumed this line of thought and put forward a comparative morphology of civilisations, which all go through certain phases of growth and decay, but all have a par- ticular spirit of their own. There are two ideas inherent in Spengler's rather amateurish and often incorrect observations on the comparative characteristics of Roman, Arabic and Western Law.

The one is that, just as every civilisation goes through certain stages of youth, adolescence and decay, so every law is spontaneous and practical experience until, in a late unproductive stage, it is petrified into a system of law.[29] The other idea is that every civilisa- tion has a particular spirit, which does or should find expression in this law. Spengler bitterly attacks modern legal science for having aped, in a superficial manner, the technique and notions of Roman law. The latter is a static law centring round the concept of a tangible thing,[30] whereas Western (Faustian) civilisation is dynamic and should revolve round a functional notion of law, like the capacity to work, the spirit of invention, creative talents, etc.

A juristically much more fruitful application of the comparative

---

[27] See Pound, *Interpretations of Legal History*, Chap. 7.

[28] Spengler, *The Decline of the West*.

[29] The best illustration of this development, English equity, has escaped the author's attention.

[30] Elsewhere Spengler says, however, that it centres round the notion of the person seen as the member of a community.

and historical approach to legal theory can be found in the work of Lord Bryce.[31] From a comparative study of Roman and English legal evolution Bryce draws a number of important conclusions. He considers as the law of best scientific quality "that which is produced slowly, gradually, tentatively, by the action of the legal profession." The high quality of the Roman system of private law is largely due to the existence of "an organ of government specially charged with the duty of watching, guiding and from time to time summing up in a concise form, the results of the natural development of the law." (The Praetor.) The law more directly influenced by political changes, on the other hand—including administrative law—is most successfully created "by the direct action of the sovereign power in the State, whether the monarch or the Legislative Assembly acting at the instance of the Executive." Bryce's studies serve as a corrective to Savigny's over-emphasis on the law, as shaped by the juristic profession, as compared with the "spontaneous and irregular" development of law due to economic and social phenomena.[32]

---

[31] Bryce, *Studies in History and Jurisprudence*, Vol. 2. (1901). See, in particular, the essays on: 'Methods of Law-Making in Rome and England"; "The History of Legal Development at Rome and in England."

[32] Vinogradoff, 2 *Historical Jurisprudence*, 158 (1923), tentatively outlines a theory of legal evolution, in the following six principal stages: Totemistic Society, Tribal Law, Civil Law, Medieval Law in its combination as Canon and Feudal Law, Individualistic Jurisprudence, Beginnings of Socialistic Jurisprudence. Although not elaborated, this theory seems to combine the thought of Maine (for the earlier stages) with that of Dicey (for the later stages).

Chapter 19

BIOLOGY, SOCIETY AND LEGAL EVOLUTION

The New Social Discipline

One of the most significant aspects of the crisis of modern society is the emergence of a new social discipline which replaces the individualism prevalent in the nineteenth century. The causes are manifold and their exposition is a matter of social rather than of legal philosophy.[1] They can be chiefly traced to the consequences of the Industrial Revolution: the urbanisation and standardisation of the life of the masses; the disastrous effects of an uncontrolled capitalism supported by a philosophy of economic liberalism; the rising revolt of the dispossessed masses, forcing the state to intervene in order to mitigate the worst injustices; the growing international friction leading to a new militant imperialism which demands the absolute and thorough military, economic, social and mental organisation of the masses; these factors combine to produce a thoroughly disciplined society. Nor is this a phenomenon confined to the so-called totalitarian states. As regards the ultimate purposes towards which this discipline is used, there is, indeed, an irreconcilable conflict between rival philosophies of life; but the technique of modern life, as a consequence of the Industrial Revolution, demands social discipline, the co-ordination of individuals as the only alternative to chaos. Legal theory has played an important part in the development of these new ways of social life. The most representative of these theories have been developed by an Englishman, two Frenchmen and a German. They differ widely in their philosophy, political outlook, training and purpose. Worlds separate the Darwinian and liberal principles of Spencer from the nationalism and collectivism of Gierke, or the neo-scholastic background of Hauriou from the sociological positivism of Duguit. But they are

[1] *Cf.* among others, Ortega y Gasset, *Revolt of the Masses*; Spengler, *Decline of the West*; Juenger, *Der Arbeiter*; Berdiaev, *Destiny of Man*; Mumford, *The Culture of Cities*.

all deeply impressed with the rise of a new collective consciousness and social responsibility, which they strive to make more articulate and to put on a scientific basis.

The scientific basis is biology applied to the evolution of society, conceived as a quasi-biological organism. Every one of these legal philosophers is anxious to prove that his theory is scientific; but no theory of society[2] has as yet been able to dispense with certain political assumptions which science cannot prove.

BIOLOGY AND HUMAN PROGRESS

Darwin and Spencer[3]

Utilitarian principles, as established by Bentham and developed by John Stuart Mill,[4] are put by Spencer on a different basis, by his application of the biological discoveries of Darwin to ethics and law. Added to those are individualistic and ethical ideals which, *a posteriori*, arrive at results very similar to those which Kant had formulated *a priori*.

Charles Darwin, in his work *On the Origin of Species* (1859) had developed this theory of the struggle for life which compels the species, man as well as animal, to adapt itself continuously to the conditions of existence, in order to survive. Those of the human species who develop a stronger social instinct are better suited for survival than the peoples which remain purely an aggregation of individuals.

Spencer's system is, above all, based on this theory of biological evolution. Life is a gigantic rhythmic process, in which there is a development from the uniform and amorphous to the diversified and specialised. In human society a shapeless association of individuals develops into a community in which specialisation of functions and activities produces a higher unity. This living entity Spencer likens to the texture of a biological organism. To the different groups of cells correspond the three principal classes which, in the social organism, look after the feeding, the distribution of feeding stuffs and the protection of the organism. The elaboration of these ideas would have led Spencer to an organic theory of

[2] This does not include the descriptive sociology of M. Weber and his followers.
[3] Spencer, *Principles of Sociology*; *Principles of Ethics*; *Justice*; *Negative and Positive Beneficence* (1891); *The Man versus the State* (1916).
[4] On these, see below, pp. 312-321.

law and society with the effect of complete absorption of the individual, a result reached in different ways by Plato, Gierke, Duguit and modern Fascism. From this Spencer refrained as he was, in his political and ethical views, a strong individualist and liberal.

Spencer explains the way in which the individual adapts himself to social conditions by the principle of heredity. The species acquires, in adaptation to the needs of social life, certain experiences which are inherited by the next generation. What is accumulated experience in one generation becomes instinct in the individuals born in the next one. Morality, duty, justice thus become instincts based on the experience which has taught a previous generation the most useful way of life, in the sense that it has enabled it to survive. This is, in essence, the way in which Spencer puts utilitarianism on a new, biological basis.

As conditions of existence vary among different peoples and times, so do the principles of ethics and law. So far, Spencer's theory of ethics and law appears to be entirely positivist and relativist, dependent upon the matter presented from outside. Yet Spencer's conclusions in the field of legal theory are very far from this. The reason is that Spencer, like so many positivists, like Comte and Duguit for example, is an idealist *malgré lui*, and is deeply influenced, like those two thinkers, by the belief in the progress of mankind through the gradual perfection of social life. As with Comte, this belief is largely disguised under the appearance of biological and sociological principles of evolution. Human society, Spencer teaches, evolves from the primitive stage of military hierarchy to an industrial organisation, in which the individual lives and works more freely, more dependent upon his initiative than on order and discipline, and with the object of peace instead of war.

In accordance with this evolution, alleged to be the result of scientific (biological) laws, the individual acquires (heredity gradually transforming experience into instinct) a deepening feeling of social duty.

At this point Spencer's ethical ideals mitigate, deflect and indeed annul his biological positivism and relativism. Spencer envisages a time in the future when the individual will have adapted himself perfectly to the needs of social life. In other words, his sense of social duty mitigates and transforms his former individualistic utilitarianism. Here the link with John Stuart Mill is evident. But as already foreshadowed by the development of Bentham's principles through Mill, an amazingly complete identity of ideas is also established between the positivist Spencer and the meta-physicist Kant. Spencer's maxim of law is:

> Each man may do what he likes, provided he does not injure the equal freedom of others.

This, of course, is Kant's definition of law, at which Spencer arrived, without knowing of Kant's formula, and from entirely different premises.

In the end Spencer deduces from this maxim a number of "natural rights" on familiar lines (right of property, freedom of trade, religion, speech, etc.) which reveal the influence of the ideas of the French and American revolutions as developed by nineteenth-century liberalism. This liberalism entirely prevails in Spencer's theory of state. The state's sole function is the protection of individual rights, and the need for this diminishes as the individual develops towards ever greater responsibility and initiative. Spencer abhors social activity by the state.[5] Instead, he tempers the individual's right by certain principles of "corrective equity" in the sense developed by Aristotle (expounded by Spencer in his *Negative and Positive Beneficence*). Beneficence compels the individual to mitigate certain consequences of justice by helping the weak. Freedom is paired with a sense of responsibility.

This in outline is the essence of Spencer's legal philosophy.

Few legal theories demonstrate more strikingly the impossibility of determining the fundamental values of life scientifically. The evolution of the human species from lower species of animals may be a scientific fact. The conclusions derived from it as to the future social organisation of mankind are no longer scientific facts, but hypotheses based on certain value assumptions.

As for these value assumptions Spencer's theory combines a number of ideals which other legal theories propound simply in opposition to each other.

(1) With Kant, Spencer shares the appeal to man's social duty. (He deduces it, however, from biological not from metaphysical principles.)

(2) With Maine, Comte, Durkheim and Duguit, Spencer shares

---

[5] Spencer, in his *Social Statics*, Chap. 28 (1850), goes so far as to assert that it is better that smallpox should decimate a community than that an individual should be made to vaccinate. In *The Man versus the State*, 33 (1884) he pours contempt and ridicule upon the beginning practice of public authorities to supply gratis food and clothes to needy children.

the belief in the progress of society through increasing social organisation and specialisation.

(3) With Comte and Duguit, Spencer shares the belief in the supremacy of social duty over egoistic impulse as a matter of biological evolution.

(4) On the other hand, Spencer shares with Kant, Bentham and Humboldt the aversion against any active social function of the state.

(5) With a host of exponents of the "natural right" theory, from Locke to Gény and the American Constitution, Spencer shares the postulate of certain fundamental individual rights.

(6) As later Duguit, Spencer is inevitably led by his biological conception of society towards an organic idea of the community, but shrinks from thinking it out to the end, owing to his individualistic faith.

COMTE, DURKHEIM AND DUGUIT

The extension of scientific study to many new fields, and the belief, so strong in the nineteenth century, that scientific progress would ultimately determine human behaviour, influenced legal thinkers in different ways. While Spencer deduced his theories about law from laws of biological evolution, the scientific positivism of Auguste Comte leads to a different line of thinking which culminates in the legal theory of Duguit.

Comte's scientific positivism[6] is based on the empirical as opposed to the metaphysical method. All reflections must, according to Comte, be derived from experience and observation, from facts, not preconceived ideas. Applying this method to the evolution of mankind, Comte divides human history into three phases: a theological phase in which the human mind explains the forces of nature by personified deities; a metaphysical phase, in which the forces of nature are still personified, but put into causal relations; and the scientific or positivist phase in which man regards nature objectively, experimentally and without personification. By a parallel division of the branches of human knowledge—all of which go through these three phases—Comte ascribes to sociology the task of building up a real science of human society, based purely on observation of facts and excluding all metaphysical ideology. Like

---

[6] Comte's. His principal work is, *Cours de philosophie positive*, 6 vols. (1830-42).

his followers and most positivists, Comte was unaware of the meta-physical and ideological element in his interpretation of human evolution, which, like Spencer's, is dominated by the belief in the inevitability of human progress.

The manifold aspects of Comte's teaching and its influence on different fields of science and philosophy cannot be discussed here. In the field of legal theory its most important result was the work of Durkheim, which, in its turn, inspired Duguit. Durkheim,[7] by his distinction between collective and individual consciousness, came to investigate some of the factors of social needs and action.

Durkheim distinguishes between two kinds of needs and apti-tudes of men living in society. Both hold them together and ensure that they remain united in national societies. There are, on the one hand, common needs satisfied by men lending each other mutual assistance and by putting together their similar aptitudes (solidarity by similitude or mechanical solidarity). On the other hand, men have different aptitudes and diverse needs. They are satisfied by an exchange of services, each using his own aptitudes to satisfy the needs of others.

This division of labour is, according to Durkheim, the pre-eminent fact of social cohesion (solidarity by division of labour or organic solidarity). But the social solidarity will be the greater, the more energetically and freely individual activities develop.

This discovery of social solidarity as a fact and necessity of social life served Léon Duguit as the basis of a legal philosophy which, however, he was most anxious not to have termed "philosophy." For the great inspiration was, to Duguit, the scientific establishment of social cohesion as an indisputable fact, beyond controversy, beyond ideology, beyond religious or metaphysical speculation. At last, so it seemed to him, the age-old controversies about ideals of justice could be left alone. The "constant realisation of the social fact which is quite simply the interdependence of indi-viduals,"[8] could at last replace ideological quarrels by observable facts.

Duguit rejects an idealistic tendency in Durkheim's work, the assertion that, immanent in the experience of social community there are objective ideals which surpass experience and manifest themselves in objective realities.

As biological laws are founded in the fact that constitutes the

[7] Durkheim, *La division du travail social*, 1891 (3rd ed., 1911).
[8] Duguit, *Traité de Droit Constitutionnel*, xviii. (2nd ed. 1921-1925).

organism, so social norms are based on "the fact that is society." Duguit

transposes into the social, the idea of biological finalities and, as a result, biological values. In effect, he envisages as a factor of social values that finality of human activity which consists in realising solidarity. . . . But that solidarity is, according to him, the law of the social body, the law according to which the life of that body is maintained and developed. Consequently, these finalities consist in the adaptation of individuals to the maintenance and to the development of social life.[9]

How does Duguit translate these premises into terms of law?

Law, as an aspect and requisite of social solidarity, is a fact. It is

a rule which men possess not by virtue of any higher principle whatever—good, interest, or happiness—but by virtue and perforce of facts, because they live in society and can only live in society.[10]

The duty to maintain social solidarity is also a fact, beyond discussion.

From this maxim disguised as fact, Duguit deduces many juristic conclusions. The conviction of its unassailability supports him in the boldest attempt made by any modern jurist to assail, at the same time, the sovereignty of the state and the rights of the individual.

As a jurist Duguit has one object above all; to establish a rule of law absolute and incontestable, and at the same time objective, freed from the arbitrariness of human will and lust for power, which so often assumes the mantle of state sovereignty. A large part of his work is devoted to an attack on the myth of state sovereignty and the theories which personified and sometimes deify the state. To Duguit the state is not a person distinct from individuals. The only thing in existence is the individual will of those who govern. They do not act for any supposed collective. Since those in government are just those who exercise preponderant force, they have a corresponding duty of fulfilling a social function: to organise certain services, to assure their continuity and control their operation. Thus, government and the state lose their towering status and become part of the social organism with a particular function in the division of labour which serves the attainment of social solidarity. *"L'état est mort,"* exclaims Duguit.

---

[9] Bonnard, in *Archives de Philosophie du Droit et de Sociologie juridique*, 7 (1932) (transl. Greenburg), quoted from Hall, *op. cit.* at 223-224.

[10] Duguit, in *Modern French Legal Philosophy*, 251 (1921).

From this general point of view follow a number of conclusions of great constitutional legal and social importance.

First, Duguit is in favour of a strong check on the abuse of state power through the establishment of strict principles of state responsibility. For the growth of those he sees abundant evidence in the principles of state responsibility for *excès* or *détournement de pouvoir,* as developed by the French *Conseil d'Etat,* and similarly in other countries which have developed an independent system of administrative law. Further, Duguit's mistrust of an all-powerful state combined with his belief in the advisability of the greatest possible division of labour leads him to emphasise decentralisation and group government as the best way of government. From this Duguit develops a syndicalism strongly opposed to the revolutionary syndicalism of Sorel. Duguit defines it as

a movement which tends to give a definite juristic structure to the different social classes, that is the groups of individuals who are already combined by community of task in the division of social labour.[11]

These different classes co-operate with each other and at the same time protect the individuals belonging to them against the excessive claims of other classes and against arbitrary action of the central power. This side of Duguit's theory, which is, of course, radically opposed to the Marxist conception of perpetual conflict between capital and labour, has provided much of the theoretical basis for the corporative theory of Fascism. At the same time Fascism and national socialism have radically altered the basis of Duguit's system, by subordinating syndicalism to a state even more powerful, godlike and arbitrary than any that Duguit had in mind and abhorred.

A further consequence of Duguit's minimisation of the state's function is the rejection of the intervention of the state as the decisive factor in turning a social into a legal norm. Duguit's conclusions in this respect thus tally with those of the historical and some of the sociological theories.

It is not the intervention of the state which gives the character of juridical norm to the rule; it would be powerless to prove it if the rule did not already possess it itself. An economic or moral rule becomes a juridical norm when there has penetrated into the consciousness of the mass of individuals composing a given social group, the notion that the group itself, or those in it who constitute the greatest

[11] Duguit, *Droit social,* 122 (1922).

force, can intervene to suppress violation of the rule; in other words, a rule of law exists whenever the mass of individuals composing the group understands and admits that a reaction against the violation of the rule can be socially organised.[12]

The legislator is consequently not the creator of law, but merely gives expression to a juridical norm formed by the consciousness of the social group. This is an almost exact restatement of Savigny, despite the vast differences in the approach and social creed of these two thinkers.

It further follows that Duguit radically rejects any division between public and private law. This division, all-important on the Continent and of growing significance in English and American law, stands and falls with the distinction between public authority and private subject. Both are, however, in Duguit's system, parts of the social body with certain functions to fulfil. "The notion of public service replaces the conception of sovereignty as the foundation of public law."[13] Duguit's position is, in this respect, similar to Kelsen's. Both distrust the arbitrariness of authority disguised under the special status of public law and both therefore deprecate the distinction. The same ideal underlies the English constitutional tradition so strongly praised by Dicey: that there can only be one law to which all, government and governed alike, are subject.

In yet another direction Duguit reaches conclusions similar to those of Kelsen. Viewing all individuals, whether exercising public functions or not, as parts of a social organism with the function of helping the weal of others as well as their own, by public service, he rejects the whole conception of private right. The idea of social function "crowds out" the conception of subjective right. Duguit often repeats a saying by Comte:

The only right which any man can possess is the right always to do his duty.[14]

The necessity of individual right disappears with the absence of any one that can and must exercise it. Since all co-operate for a common end by exercising a certain function the conception of a subjective right either of the state or the individual becomes superfluous and dangerous.

---

[12] Duguit, 2 Colum.L.Rev. 22.
[13] Duguit, *Transformations du droit public*, 33 (1913).
[14] *Système de politique positive*, 361.

Criticism

Duguit attacked so many positions at once that his work was bound to stir up great controversies. It touches many problems of modern society.

Aware of the growing complexity of modern social life Duguit attacks individualism as reflected in the conception of inalienable individual rights. But he equally rejects the alternative, suggested by most other theories which take this line, of strengthening the central power of the state. Instead he advocates decentralised group government and the link between the different groups is to be an objective rule of law, the principle of social solidarity. This savours of natural law although Duguit emphatically rejects any such metaphysical conception as incompatible with scientific positivism; yet his ideal of social solidarity is as strong a natural law ideal as any ever conceived. It is as absolute and austere as the natural law of Thomas Aquinas or Kant's categorical imperative.

Despite Duguit's insistence on the scientific and factual character of his rule of social solidarity, his three rules of conduct are framed in terms of imperatives[15]:

(1) Respect every act of individual will determined by an end of social solidarity. Do nothing to prevent its accomplishment. Co-operate as far as possible toward its accomplishment.
(2) Every individual ought to abstain from any act that would be determined by an end contrary to social solidarity.
(3) Do nothing to diminish solidarity by similitude, or social solidarity through division of labour. Do everything materially practicable for the individual to increase social solidarity in both its forms.

This problem is necessarily linked with the question which authority would decide when the superior law has been infringed. In the scholastic system the Church is the interpreter of eternal law. In the United States the Supreme Court is guardian of the Constitution and enforces the superior law against legislation and Executive. Duguit was aware of the possibility of conflict between positive law and the higher objective law of social solidarity. In the absence of a higher tribunal he sympathised with the idea of granting judges the right to refuse recognition to statutes not in accordance with social solidarity, but it is understandable that

[15] Duguit, "Theory of Objective Law Anterior to the State," in *Modern French Legal Philosophy*, 290-296 (1921).

Duguit found it difficult to make up his mind about it. For the judicial right to invalidate statutes as being incompatible with so general a principle would have given full play to judicial prejudice and would impair what certainty the law possesses. Even in the United States, where a complicated mechanism of checks and balances is designed to ensure the rule of law, where a written Constitution lays down principles much more concrete than Duguit's principle, and where the ultimate word rests with a court composed of carefully selected judges of high integrity and great experience, the fact that the ultimate word rests with a court composed of nine men has led to a judicial despotism which for many decades, in the name of the rule of law and under the protection of judicial independence, has retarded vital social legislation. A judicial control exercised without such elaborate safeguards and in the name of a principle as vague as it is high sounding would be more dangerous still. Duguit himself saw clearly that the state is an instrument of those who have power to govern. This human weakness exists equally in judicial personnel.[16]

And what exactly does social solidarity mean? We may admit that the mutual interdependence of men in society and the need to collaborate for the functioning of social life is a scientific fact. But as many of those who have examined the comparative precision of facts in the social and the natural sciences have observed, social facts are much less clearly determined than natural facts, and Duguit's social facts are, as one critic has observed, "facts of a highly metaphysical order."[17] Duguit's principle of social solidarity is what Kelsen would call an "initial hypothesis." Duguit's *Grundnorm* is not, however, hypothetical but categorical. And it is capable of very diverse interpretations. It can stand for social progress or for social reaction, for liberty or for suppression. It may be and has been used by whatever individuals hold power to be interpreted for their convenience. Thus Duguit's ideas have had considerable influence on Soviet jurisprudence but particularly on Fascist jurisprudence. The former derived from Duguit's notion of function and duty the exclusion of individual right, the elimination of private law and the assimilation of all law to administration; the latter used

---

[16] The creation, in the Constitution of the Fifth Republic (1958), of a *Conseil Constitutionnel* with power to pass on the constitutionality of laws, may, in a sense, be regarded as a belated victory for Duguit's ideas. It is, however, at most a certain counterbalance against the drastic reduction of parliamentary powers, in a constitution that, quite contrary to Duguit, greatly strengthens the authority and prestige of the state, symbolised by the President.

[17] Elliott, 37 Pol.Sc.Q. 639 (1922).

Duguit's anti-revolutionary syndicalism as an effective weapon again Marxist conceptions and the organisation of the working-class in trade unions, while superimposing upon it an all-powerful state.

While Duguit saw clearly one social fact of modern life, namely the growing complexity of society, with a corresponding increase of social task and needs, he neglected another, namely the trend towards a strengthening of central authority, as being alone capable of mastering the vital social problems of a modern community.

It is therefore not surprising that the least successful of all Duguit's doctrines is his belated revival of theories which minimised the function of the state and made group-consciousness the test of the legal norm. It is a pious illusion to assume that "the rising of an active group against the author of an act attacking social solidarity"[18] would be a good proof of the existence of a legal norm. This "rising" appears to be a poor relation of a sanction and its weakness lies in the indistinct character of a social group as compared with an order issuing from a legislative or executive authority and binding the entire community. How, for example, can one define "the working class" today with sufficient accuracy? Does it include the highly skilled and paid in industrial work, the occasionally employed and the permanently employed, is it to centre round the manufacture of a certain product or round a working unit, such as a factory? Will managing directors, office clerks and skilled workers rise in union?

In this respect more than in any other, Duguit was a romantic. By a strange irony of history, this romantic aspect of his theory was destined to become extremely useful for the most unromantic, cold-blooded and cynical attempt to use this alleged social solidarity for the suppression of the rights of the citizen, and ultimately for the satisfaction of the unlimited power lust of a few.

Another paradox in Duguit's system is his attack on the myth of collective personality, while his conception of social solidarity and the close analogy of his ideas to Claude Bernard's biological values savours strongly of the same organic theories of state and corporate personality which Duguit detested. Never, perhaps, has a more sincere effort been made in jurisprudence to reconcile antinomies, the supremacy of the community with the highest development of the individual, the rule of law with the will to power,

[18] 2 Colum.L.Rev. 22, 31 (1902).

justice and efficiency. In this attempt Duguit has failed, but no one else has succeeded either.[19]

GIERKE

As the atomistic conception of society fades before the growing claims of the community, as the Industrial Revolution, in its later stages, demands a reorientation of the relations between individual and collective, legal theory helps to prepare the way for the new technique of living which, in our time, under the name of "Totalitarianism," has placed undreamt of powers and functions in the hand of the state as the supreme collective organisation.

An important part in this process has been played by certain theories of corporate personality.[20]

Gierke's theory of corporate personality is familiar to the Anglo-Saxon legal world, above all through its introduction and championship by Maitland.[21]

Its basic theme is the reality of the group personality as a social and legal entity, independent of state recognition and concession. It goes together with a general theory of law.

The fundamental distinction which Gierke draws is between *Sozialrecht* and *Individualrecht*. The former is concerned with the claims of society, the latter with those of the individual. As a legal historian Gierke found the latter exclusively stressed, at the expense of the former, in the Romanistic tradition, prevalent in Germany and predominant in the first draft of the new Civil Code.

For a true appreciation of the former, Gierke sought his inspiration in the old Germanic conception of *Gesamte Hand* which pervaded the old "Germanic community," the *Genossenschaft*, before the reception of Roman law overgrew it.

The principal points of Gierke's *Genossenschaftstheorie* developed from these premises are these:

(1) The life of an association does not depend upon state recognition. The legal statute which bestows legal personality merely has declaratory significance, in so far as it declares the general conditions of juristic personality to be applicable to a particular associa-

---

[19] Duguit's principal works are: *The Law in the Modern State* (transl. Laski); "Theory of Objective Law Anterior to the State" (in *Modern French Legal Philosophy*); *Les Transformations Générales du Droit Privé depuis le Code Napoléon*; *Traité de Droit Constitutionnel*.

[20] *Cf.* also below, Chap. 34.

[21] Introduction to Gierke, *Political Theories of the Middle Ages* (1900).

tion. But it does not create that association, either socially or legally.

Thus far, the parallel of Gierke's thought with that of Savigny and Ehrlich is obvious.

(2) A juristic person comes into being not by a multitude of individual contracts, but by a collective unilateral act directed towards the creation of the juristic personality. Its juristic form is the corporate constitution (*Verfassung*), not contract (*Vertrag*). A plurality of individual wills becomes merged in a collective unit through this joint action directed towards a purpose. Out of this arises a corporate personality with a will and capacity to act of its own. It is the *reale Gesamtperson*. This capacity to will and act is the basis of legal personality. Legal recognition follows upon it, but does not create it. Within this corporate life of the corporate unit the respective claims of the collective and the individuals must be adjusted, but it is wrong to conceive the individuals as standing outside the corporate unit in any of their membership relations.

(3) The life of the corporate body is, however, limited by its purpose.[22] This leads Gierke to his theory of the relations between the state and corporate bodies within it. He solves the problem by a kind of *Stufentheorie,* in which the state is the highest corporate unit, the only one not to be limited by a will above it. All other corporate bodies are placed, in their sphere of life and action, under the superintendence of the state. By a piece of very strained reasoning Gierke attempts to reconcile three apparently irreconcilable ideas:

(1) The sovereignty of the state.
(2) The *Rechtsstaat* idea.
(3) The autonomy of corporate life within the state.

The state is sovereign, subject to no superior will. But it is supreme only in the sense in which every legal order must have a sovereign legislator. It is thus an expression of reason, and its own unlimited will is bound by this objective idea of reason. As Hallis puts it,[23] Gierke is thus, on his own ground, an adherent of the theory of the *Rechtsstaat.* At the same time its power over other corporate bodies is not that of giving them legal existence—this would be contrary to Gierke's main theory—but merely that of superintending the purposefulness and legality of their activities.

---

[22] *Cf.* the Anglo-American *ultra vires* doctrine.
[23] Hallis, *Corporate Personality,* 148 (1930).

For the state, as the highest corporate unit, itself the collective will of the whole community and as such a real person, merely comprehends the totality of corporate life within it and must thus watch that they keep within their respective spheres. But apart from this supervision, corporate bodies retain their freedom of self-administration as an expression of their freedom of personality.

There is thus a double organic conception of corporate personalities. The state comprises, as a living unit, all corporations as members, and it also exercises the sovereign right of supervision over other corporate bodies which, in this respect, are conceived as independent organic entities within the limits of their corporate purpose.

The great contribution which Gierke has made to the theory of corporate personality has been discussed by eminent jurists of many countries.

No less important, however, is Gierke's contribution to legal philosophy and political theory. Gierke is, first of all, foremost in the development of organic conceptions of the community which are first apparent in Rousseau's theory and have been developed by German romanticism and by Savigny in particular. Gierke is at pains to emphasise that his conception of the corporate unit is not a biological one; but it is almost impossible to conceive of a corporate personality as a living being, acting through organs, without using at least biological analogies. This aspect of Gierke's teaching, strengthened in the eyes of German nationalists by its deduction from Germanistic origins, has formed an important stepping stone towards that merger of the individual in the collective, which is an essential and vital aspect of modern totalitarian government. On the other hand, Gierke was a genuine champion of corporate autonomy as well as a good German patriot of the Second Reich, and his theory is an unsuccessful attempt to reconcile both. Genuine corporate autonomy is incompatible with state sovereignty. To solve this dilemma Gierke introduces a second organic conception, superimposed upon the first, which forms a kind of sociological parallel to Kelsen's formal hierarchy. But from the absolute supremacy thus given to the state Gierke shrinks, first by limiting state will in a quasi-Hegelian way through the idea of reason which it represents as an expression of right, and second by emphasising the autonomy of corporate personality within the state. This is, however, dependent upon what Jellinek calls more clearly a self-limitation of the state. It means no real check upon sovereignty, as shown elsewhere.[24] The same applies to the check imposed upon state arbitrariness by the rule of right which it embodies. Like Jellinek, Triepel, Duguit, Stammler and many others, Gierke attempts to reconcile irreconcilables: to have it both ways. In the end the result is absolute obedience to the positive law imposed by the state, tempered by an expression of respect for the idea of right or natural law.

> We have to accept together both the external experience which affirms that all valid law is positive, and the internal experience which affirms that the living force of law is derived from an idea of right which is innate in humanity.[25]

It was easy for more unscrupulous successors to discard such pious aspirations to limit the power of the state, and to develop its supervising function over corporate bodies to its logical conclusion: the abolition of corporate autonomy. This Fascism has done, while the Vienna school was substituted for Gierke's half-hearted hierarchy a strictly logical and uncompromising one which shows that the state cannot be half sovereign nor corporate bodies half autonomous.

Within the more strictly juristic field Gierke's theory has done much, in particular for the understanding of the unincorporated association. As an explanation of the basis of society it has not solved the essential antinomy between basic ideals any better than other theories.[26]

HAURIOU

The organic theory of society is often described as a specifically German contribution to political and legal thought. But some of its principal exponents are Frenchmen. Rousseau's interpretation of the *Contrat Social* started the organic conception of society. Hauriou has developed conceptions in his theory of the institution, in a way which has earned him the praise of a modern National Socialist German jurist.[27]

---

[24] Below, p. 278.
[25] Jellinek, *Natural Law and the Theory of Society*, 226.
[26] Gierke's principal works:
  (1) *Das deutsche Genossenschaftsrecht* (4 vols., 1868-1913); parts of the third and fourth volumes have been translated into English and edited as Gierke's *Political Theories of the Middle Ages* (ed. Maitland, 1900), *Natural Law and the Theory of Society* (ed. Barker, 1934).
  (2) *Die Genossenschaftstheorie* (1887).
  (3) *Das Wesen der menschlichen Verbände* (1902).
[27] C. Schmitt, *Drei Arten des rechtswissenschaftlichen Denkens* (1934).

Hauriou's theory[28] which, in its sociological and political effect, is best appreciated in conjunction with the theories of Gierke and Duguit, widely as these three differ in their beliefs as well as their conclusions, centres round the conception of the institution. It has three essential elements.

(1) The idea of an undertaking or enterprise which is realised and persists juridically in a social *milieu.*

(2) For the realisation of this idea, a power is organised, which gives it organs.

(3) Between the members of the social group interested in the realisation of the idea, manifestations of communion arise which are directed by the organs and regulated by rules of procedure.[29]

There are two types of institutions, *"institutions-personnes"* and *"institutions-choses."*

Only the former type is seriously developed by Hauriou. Hauriou approaches the problem of the institution as a sociologist. He sees in it the synthesis of subjective will and objective reality; the institution is to him not only an analysis of social facts, but also apparently a juristic ideal as the best combination of sovereignty and liberty. In the institution, individuals communicate through combined action. This will to engage one's self in a common cause makes the institution something more than an intellectual creation. It is the embodiment of action.[30] From the three elements which constitute the essence of an institution, results the personification of an organised group bent on realisation of a common purpose. The objective reality of this institution, whose directing idea gives it continuity despite the discontinuity of the subjective wills which go to its formation, is not only a social reality, but also the source of legal personality. Like Gierke, Hauriou considers the formal incorporation of an institution as of subordinate importance. Through the participation of all its members in the government of the institution, and the consequent passing of the idea of the institution into the consciousness of all its members, moral personality is achieved. This moral personality seems to be the essential factor, but Hauriou recognises the need for juristic fixation of this somewhat indeterminate status, and considers the granting of juristic personality as a sort of formal acknowledgement of moral personality operated according to the directives of the judicial order in

[28] Hauriou, "La théorie de l'institution et de la fondation," in *Cahiers de la nouvelle journée,* No. 4 (1925).

[29] *Id.* at 10; Hauriou, *Précis de droit administratif* (4th ed., 1938).

[30] Hauriou calls his study *Un essai de vitalisme social.*

which it develops.[31] He thus compromises between fiction and realist theory.

There is an affinity between this idea and the theory of integration of the German jurist Smend,[32] which sees the relations between the citizens and the state as one of perpetual mutual inspiration. Citizens live in and through the state, and the state in and through the citizens.

Hauriou himself is a pluralist. He does not integrate the *institution* in the state as the highest type of institution. But it is easy to see how, like Gierke's organic theory or Duguit's social solidarity principle, Hauriou's *"idée directive"* could be used to strengthen the collective as against the individual, and how close it comes to the mysticism of Fascist theory which subordinates the individual to the idea of service to something higher than himself. It is not far, from this conception, to the National Socialist conception of labour embodied in the law of 1934, which deprives the employee of all collective rights and substitutes for these a personal, quasi-feudal duty of allegiance to the undertaking, *i.e.*, the "institution" by which he is employed. But as the *Führer* is the expression of the state, so the owner or director of the undertaking is its soul and expression. Thus the mystical idea of service to an institution becomes in practice the duty of obedience by one class to another.

Hauriou repudiates the organic theory. But his definition of an institution as a social organism in which those who have the power have to submit to the idea which inspires the enterprise[33] is, in fact, an organic theory. Whether the institution be a commercial company, a political party, a trade union or the state, the myth of its super-personal purpose demands obedience and subordination.

Another line of development leads from Hauriou's theory of institution to a Catholic conception of the corporate state. It combines the scholastic conception of an objective order of the universe with the corporate theory always inherent in Catholic doctrine and openly advocated in the modern teaching of the Catholic Church.[34] The institution becomes the medium through which individual activity serving a higher cause fulfils the divine purpose. In the doctrine of Renard and Delos the institution becomes thus the basis of a neo-scholastic doctrine of natural law.

Its political result is eventually a Latin, Catholic, depersonalised

[31] Hauriou, *Précis de droit administratif, op. cit.*
[32] Smend, *Verfassung und Verfassungsrecht* (1928).
[33] *Précis de droit administratif*, 23.
[34] *Cf.* below, p. 392.

counterpart of the Germanic, irreligious and personalised authoritarian state of German theory.

Seen in perspective and with reference to their social and political effect, the theories of Spencer, Gierke, Hauriou, Duguit all lead to a similar result: the subordination of the individual to a new social discipline and service to a collective. All these jurists were strongly inspired by the idea of corporate autonomy. In different ways they abhorred the idea of the state-leviathan. But their theories were fated to lead to a new state despotism, which cunningly used the idea of devotion to a collective for the glorification of individual power.

CHAPTER 20

MODERN SOCIOLOGICAL THEORIES OF LAW

MEANING AND DEFINITIONS OF SOCIOLOGICAL JURISPRUDENCE

AN accurate definition of scope and meaning of sociological jurisprudence meets as yet with insuperable difficulties. A vast variety of divers approaches to the study of law is held together by little more than a common tendency to "look more for the working of law than for its abstract content."[1]

To a number of recent authors the study of the relation of actual law to ideals of justice is a legitimate and essential part of a sociology of law. Thus Horvath[2] sees its task in the discussion of the relations between the "facts of life" and "judicial rules of evaluation," a programme that looms large in the work of the American realist movement. Sinzheimer[3] goes further, by interpreting sociology of law as a practical science showing the law-makers the better way to proceed in their task. Ginsberg[4] considers the study of the relations between actual law and ideals of justice as one of the four principal objects of the sociology of law. J. Hall[5] defines the sociology of law as a theoretical science consisting of generalisations regarding social phenomena, in so far as they refer to the contents, purposes, applications and effects of legal rules.

The most comprehensive attempt to define the place of sociology of law[6] includes in its survey as different theories and systems as the comparative ethnological approach of Post or Vinogradoff, the teleological approach of Ihering, the psychological analysis of Tarde

---

[1] Pound, "The Scope and Purpose of Sociological Jurisprudence" 25 Harv.L.Rev. 489 (1911).

[2] *Rechtssoziologie*, 1934.

[3] *De Taak der Rechtssoziologie*, 1935.

[4] Ginsberg, Book Review, 1 Mod.L.Rev. 169 (1937).

[5] Hall, "Criminology and a Modern Penal Code," 27 *Journ. Criminal Law.*

[6] Timasheff, An introduction to *The Sociology of Law* (1939) and by the same author, "Growth and Scope of Sociology of Law" Modern Sociological Theory 444 (1957). For a more recent critical survey of the scope and nature of sociological jurisprudence, see Stone, *Social Dimensions of Law and Justice*, Chap. 1 (1966). See Friedmann, "Sociology of Law," 10/11 Current Sociology No. 1 (1961-62).

or Petrazhitsky, the free law theory of Kantorowicz, the American realist movement and Max Weber's study of the mechanism of legal evolution. But it rightly draws a clear distinction between scientific study and valuations. "The sociology of law can formulate propositions in which the ends of positive legal regulations would be stated. But whether one or another of these ends should be pursued by the law, whether within the competition of ultimate end systems (for instance, those of conservatism, liberalism, socialism or fascism) this or that system should be preferred, can never be decided by scientific methods, such questions being beyond the scope of science."[7] This does not mean, of course, that legal theory is only concerned with theory, and sociology of law only with practice. There is an intimate relation between ultimate valuations and the practical working of the law.[8] Theory of law and sociology of law must co-operate in the science of legislation.

The sociology of law will procure the best means to the ends; but ultimate ends will forever depend on philosophical, and not on scientific considerations.[9]

Many of the sociological or functional studies of law are mixed with valuations and have therefore been discussed in this book—concerned with the ends and purposes of law—from this latter angle.[10]

One trend of sociological jurisprudence should, however, be kept altogether distinct from the sociology of law, as defined before.

The host of theories for which Ihering's *Zweck im Recht* provides the starting point indicate a new ideological trend in jurisprudence; but they formulate their valuations and ideals in terms of social force and interests, not in metaphysical terms like the older legal philosophers. The theories of Gény, Pound, Cardozo or Ernst Fuchs continue the long line of theories of justice; but they are the theories of modern jurists expressed in terms of social interests.[11]

If these modern theories of justice and the many sociological studies which are blended with legal theory are separated, there remain a number of rather diverse attempts, largely concerned with methodology, of explaining the law as it functions. Of these the

---

[7] Timasheff, *op. cit.* at 30.

[8] *Cf.* in particular, Part 6.

[9] Timasheff, *An Introduction to the Sociology of Law* (1939).

[10] *e.g.*, the theories of Post, Durkheim, Duguit, the free law school and the realist movement.

[11] See Chap. 27, below.

American realist movement, because of its importance and its link with the positivist philosophy of law, will be discussed separately.[12] Of the remaining analyses we select with some diffidence what appear to be the three most important attempts made so far to state the principles of legal evolution in terms of social forces.[13] They are the studies of E. Ehrlich, M. Weber and K. Renner. Each of these gives theoretical generalisations on the interrelation of social forces and legal evolution.

SOCIOLOGICAL THEORIES OF LEGAL EVOLUTION

Renner's work, based as it is on certain Marxist premises, will be discussed in connection with socialist thought on law.[14] The two other attempts, differing widely from each other as well as from Renner's study, indicate the tentative and experimental character of the sociological study of legal evolution.

Weber's *Sociology of Law*[15] has for its main theme the analysis of the transformation of law from a "charismatic" finding of law to a state of rationalisation. This transformation is followed up in various legal phenomena: in the gradual distinction of public from private law, which is, however, a distinction shifting with the development and principles of government; in the evolution from the decision of individual cases to general principles and eventually a systematisation of law; in the development from the early formal status-contract to the elastic and formless purpose-contract; from the autonomous legal personality of the Middle Ages to the modern state monopoly of the creation of legal personality.

All these are legal developments closely linked with social, political and economic factors. Thus a development of an exchange economy with its increasing use of money leads to the development of modern contract with its free assignability.

The most interesting part of Weber's analysis is concerned with the influence of legal professionalism and of different forms of political government on the development of law.

When belief in irrational powers of law-finding has gone and

[12] See below, Chap. 25.
[13] Apart from Maine's work, which has been discussed at p. 214 *et seq.*
[14] See below, p. 368 *et seq.*
[15] Weber, "Rechtssoziologie," in *Grundriss der Social-Oekonomik*; *Dritte Abteilung, Wirtschaft und Gesellschaft, Zweiter Band.*
This work is now available in English under the title: *Max Weber on Law in Economy and Society* (transl. Shils, 1954), with an excellent introduction by Max Rheinstein.

rational reasoning takes its place, the administration of justice becomes more and more a regulated procedure to decide a conflict of interests. A class of persons of high social standing, half-way between the law-finder of earlier and the professional jurists of later days (*Rechtshonoratioren*), develops and largely influences a rationalisation of legal procedure, although it is often interested in retarding the material rationalisation of law.[16] This process Weber traces comparatively in the development of Roman, English, German, Islamic and many other systems of jurisprudence.

The tendency towards rationalisation of law is powerfully stimulated by the ascendancy of modern absolutist governments with their apparatus of permanent officials and machinery of administration. Where the absolute monarch, for political reasons, establishes direct contact with his subjects through a special administration of justice, an equitable jurisdiction (as in England) arises and helps the government in its fight, first against feudal and later against autonomous corporate interests.

But the fullest degree of rationalisation of law is reached only where rulers, who want rationalisation for the sake of order and central authority, combine with modern middle class interests, which favour rational organisation of legal procedure and transactions because this naturally favours the better organised and economically more powerful side. Another impulse towards modern systematic rationalisation of law, of which the French Civil Code is an expression, is provided by modern revolutionary natural law ideas.[17] These natural law ideas are used in the service of the aspirations of new social class movements and disintegrate in modern times with the progress of juristic rationalisation and the scepticism of modern intellectualism. In this struggle, the professional juristic classes are on the whole solidly ranged on the side of legal positivism which strengthens their own position. In its name they fight both social ideals rising from below and governmental welfare aspirations from above.

Writing shortly before the war of 1914, Weber detected a recent tendency to replace the rational administration of law by a new anti-formalism (*Freirechtslehre*), but he believed that such reactions would not affect the increasing professional specialisation of law

---

[16] *Cf.* the attitude of the English legal profession towards the rationalism of real property law, land registration, fusion of law and equity, etc.

[17] This emphasis on the revolutionary tendency of natural law ideas corrects Kelsen's one-sided assertion that natural law ideology has always covered reactionary interests.

with its growing technical apparatus, the necessary result of modern technical and economic developments.

The theoretical conclusions which Weber derives from his comparative sociological investigations are that law in general develops from a charismatic revelation by "prophets of law" to an empirical creation and administration by a special class of legal advisers, further to a law imposed by worldly or theocratic powers and eventually to a rationalised system of law-giving and professional administration of justice by experts. Correspondingly, legal technique develops from a magically rooted formalism through the utilitarian rationalisation sponsored by modern absolutist government towards the logical rationality of modern law.

Weber qualifies these theoretical conclusions by pointing out that neither have these different stages succeeded each other everywhere in that particular order, nor does every community or legal civilisation reach them all. The difference of political conditions, the relations between theocratic and worldly authority, the divergences in the structure of the classes of jurists, all these factors produce differences which Weber traces by a comparison, not only between different Western legal systems, but also between these and the legal systems of other civilisations (Islamic, Chinese, Buddhist, Jewish, etc.). Of particular interest are Weber's observations on the difference between the empirical and the rational type of legal thinking. Parallel to this is the contrast between a practitioner-made law and a university-made law. Anglo-Saxon law is essentially a product of juristic practice; the systems based on the reception of Roman law are a product of legal university education; the Code Civil is a product of rational legislation.

This very summary account of Weber's sociology of law reveals an approach which, without preconceived valuations, has points of contact with Maine's historical jurisprudence on one hand and the Marxist approach to law on the other. It demonstrates the interdependence of law with political, economical and social forces.

Had Weber lived longer (he died in 1920) he might have been less confident of the inevitable process of rationalisation of law. But his work, as a whole, brings out the relative character of any particular legal development.

EHRLICH

Of a very different character is Eugen Ehrlich's study of the sociology of law. Unlike Weber's study it is out to prove a theory, namely that:

> The centre of gravity of legal development lies not in legislation nor in juristic science, nor in judicial decision, but in society itself.

Ehrlich resumes the old controversy about the juristic supremacy of authority or custom and in this issue he is very definitely on Savigny's side. But for the mystical conception of the *Volksgeist,* interpreted by the historical school in terms of the past, he substitutes the more realistic and specific notion of "facts of law" (*Rechtstatsachen*) and of the "living law of the people." Moreover, in a series of essays grouped round the central theme,[18] Ehrlich makes an important contribution to the method of a sociological study of law.

The central point in Ehrlich's approach is his minimisation of the differences between law and other norms of social compulsion. The difference is relative and smaller than usually asserted because the essential compulsion behind legal no less than other social norms is social compulsion not state authority. Tribal allegiance, family, religion provide motives of obedience to social norms including most legal norms. Many legal norms never find expression in legal provisions even in developed systems. In other words, the law is something much wider than legal regulation. The state is but one of a number of legal associations, others being the family or the Church, or corporate bodies with or without legal personality. On the other hand, there are certain typically legal norms of compulsion such as punishment or execution of civil judgments. These specific means of compulsion the state develops in the first place in order to secure its main original purposes, to wit, military organisation, taxation and police administration. The state, as the principal source of law, is to Ehrlich historically a much later development, and the state remains, for him, at all times essentially an organ of society, although an increasingly predominant one in modern conditions, and absolutely predominant in the socialist state. Even then the specifically legal (state) norms of compulsion have principally the function of protecting norms formed in society (apart from their function of protecting primary state institutions,

---

[18] Collected as *Grundlegung der Soziologie des Rechts* (1912). (Translated by Moll as *Fundamental Principles of the Sociology of Law.*)

such as state constitution, military, administrative, financial organisation.)[19]

Basically the legal norm is always derived from social facts anchored in the conviction of an association of people. State protection through specific means of compulsion is never essential, even where it is provided. The essential body of legal rules is always based upon the social "facts of law" (*Tatsachen des Rechts*). The "facts of law" which underlie all law are usage, domination, possession and declaration of will. These four facts either give enforcement to legal relations, or they may control, hinder or invalidate them, or they may attach legal consequences to them other than those which follow directly from them. Within the total body of legal norms only a certain group, the so-called "norms of decision" (*Entscheidungsnormen*) are state-made and dependent upon the state. These norms of decision are necessarily part of official law. But whether they develop into a fundamental legal norm (*Rechtssatz*) depends on the extent to which judicial, administrative, legislative or scientific jurisprudence moulds it and succeeds in making it part of living law. Whereas American realists place the judicial decision in the centre of law as it functions in life, Ehrlich reduces it to a more restricted function in relation to the whole of the law as it lives in society; for litigation shows law as an order of war, not of peace; and only a small fraction of law finds its way to the courts. Ehrlich sees the difficulty of drawing a clear border line between the different legal norms. Rules of interpretation are *Juristenrecht,* special privileges granted by statute (*e.g.,* exemption from liability) are always official law. Either apparently may, but need not necessarily, become "living law." Ehrlich faces the fact of ever-increasing state activity and a parallel increase of state norms by distinguishing between three types of legal norms. All legal norms regulate in some way the relation between command or prohibition and the underlying "facts of law." They do so in different ways:

(1) The protection may simply be given to legal norms purely based on facts of law, such as by-laws of associations and corporations, or contracts. Closely connected are norms directly derived from social facts, such as the remedies for damage, unjust enrichment, etc.

---

[19] The principles of Ehrlich's thought have been restated, with a much more elaborate though abstrusely formulated typology of law, by Gurvitch, *Sociology of Law* (1942).

(2) Legal commands or prohibitions (imposed by the state) may create or deny social facts as in the case of expropriation or nullification of contracts.

(3) Norms may be entirely detached from social facts, such as imposition of taxes or the granting of trade concessions and privileges.

Where the social facts of law are clear, the function of the jurist is mainly a technical one, but to the extent that conflicting interests in society demand a solution his task becomes a more active one. Ehrlich here arrives at the problem of *Interessenabwägung*, which occupies all modern sociological theories. The lawyer must find his guidance in the principles of justice.[20] Ehrlich distinguishes between static and dynamic principles of justice. Thus such institutions as contract, succession, the interest in one's own labour, have certain ideal forms. Justice demands the perfect economic contract or the legal prohibition to enrich oneself by someone else's labour (a principle very imperfectly realised by the existing positive law of most countries). But this static justice which tends to consolidate existing conditions of society is mitigated by "dynamic justice," whose main rival propelling forces are individualist and collectivist ideals. Thus Ehrlich arrives at a less elaborate formulation of the political foundation of antinomic ideals of justice, which Radbruch has developed in greater detail.[21] All the help that sociology can give in the solution of these problems is to show to jurisprudence the laws of development of human society and the effect of legal norms upon it. The "living law," that is the law as it actually lives in society, Ehrlich insists, is in permanent evolution, always outpacing the rigid and immobile state law. The great task of jurisprudence is to solve this eternal tension. Like Renner, Ehrlich sees jurisprudence as standing between the application and the making of law, both product and stimulus of social developments.

The practical impact of Ehrlich's teaching has been the stimulus given to fact-study in law. The Austro-Hungarian empire provided an inexhaustible variety of local customs, jealously guarded among the dozens of races, Germans, Czechs, Slovaks, Croats, Serbs, Slovenes, Hungarians, Rumanians, Poles, Jews, Russians, etc., which composed that extraordinary state. Ehrlich's own seminar for "living law" was designed to study these manifold rules.

---

[20] In his *Freie Rechtsfindung* (1905), Ehrlich has advocated the principles of the *Freirechtslehre*.

[21] See above, p. 192 *et seq.*

The chief field of investigation is that of family relations, including rules of succession. For in no other sphere of law do habits and traditions persist more independently of or even in spite of statutory regulations. That is especially the case in peasant communities which form a large proportion of the people of the former Austro-Hungarian empire. Ehrlich is particularly insistent on the need for the study of documents predominant in commercial law, and in other spheres of law such as succession.

Criticism

Ehrlich's work is full of stimulating suggestions for a scientific approach to law which relates the law more closely to the life of society. It has played a leading part in the reaction of legal thinking, towards the turn of the century, against the surfeit of analytical jurisprudence which had characterised legal thinking of the preceding generation. If Ehrlich resumes Savigny's line of thinking, he does so with a much more practical and active purpose, with his eye on the present much more than on the past. Whenever legal science becomes too self-sufficient, too exclusively preoccupied with its technique as an end in itself, it is necessary to remind it of its social function. Ehrlich's effort in this direction is parallel to that of sociological and functional jurisprudence in America with the characteristic difference that the latter centres round litigation, whereas the former concentrates on law outside the courts.

Theoretically Ehrlich's works show three main weaknesses, all caused by his desire to minimise the function of the state in the making of the law.

First, it gives no clear criterion by which to distinguish a legal from any other social norm. The interchangeability of both, which is an historical and social fact, does not diminish the need for a clear test of distinction. Accordingly, Ehrlich's sociology of law is always on the point of becoming a, necessarily sketchy, general sociology.

Secondly, Ehrlich confuses the position of custom as a "source" of law with custom as a type of law. In primitive society as in the international law of our time custom prevails both as source and the chief type of law. In modern state society it is still important in the first, but less and less important in the second, role. Modern society overwhelmingly demands articulate law made by a definite law-giver. Such law will always, in varying degree, depend on these facts of law, but it does not derive its validity as law from this factual observance. This confusion permeates the whole of Ehrlich's work.

Thirdly, Ehrlich refuses to follow up the logic of his own distinction between specific legal state norms and legal norms where the state merely adds sanction to social facts. If the former protect specific state purposes, such as its constitutional life, military, financial and administrative organisations, it was obvious a few decades ago and is even more obvious now that these specific state purposes, and with them specific state law norms, continually increase and expand. As modern social conditions demand more and more active control the state extends its purposes. Consequently custom recedes before deliberately made law, mainly statute and decree. At the same time, law emanating from central authority as often moulds social habits as it is moulded itself.

The breaking-up of nomad life in Soviet Russia, the educational system of National Socialism, the new relations of employer and employee created by Fascist legislation powerfully modify the social habits of the people. Instead of examining this shifting relationship between state norms of compulsion and the social "facts of law" Ehrlich ever-emphasised one aspect only, the one which was characteristic of a former age much more than of the society of his own time.

Section Four

Positivism and Legal Theory

CHAPTER 21

POSITIVISM IN MODERN PHILOSOPHY

THE conflict between those thinkers who construct the world from *a priori* concepts and ideas, and those who regard matter as prior to ideas, accompanies the history of philosophy.[1]

In this sense "positivism" is as old as philosophy. But as a definite movement in general philosophy, sociology and jurisprudence it is essentially a modern phenomenon, accompanying and reflecting the scope and heightened importance of science on one hand, and—in political philosophy and legal theory—the rise of the modern state on the other hand.

The development of modern science was bound to affect deeply the philosophers' conception of the relation between man and universe. The revolution in astronomy, symbolised by the names of Copernicus, Kepler and Galileo—which would not have been possible without the recently opened up technical ability of observing the movements of the stars—reduced the earth, and all on it, to a minor, and after the discoveries of modern astronomy totally insignificant, part of an inconceivably vast universe, of which neither earth nor man is the centre. The development of physics and chemistry—again made possible through the perfection of technical instruments permitting more observation—came to centre more and more around the study of matter, particles, movements and compounds. At the same time, the study of forms of life (botany, biology and zoology) eventually led to theories of evolution in which man ceased to be the ready-made centre of life, but emerged on the contrary as a, provisionally final, product of a long process of evolution of plant and animal life.

Although modern science proceeds through a constant interaction of hypothesis (theory) and verification (experiment), the study of matter and of phenomena outside the realm of pure ideas is an inevitable, and indeed a dominant, aspect of modern science.

The philosophical counterpart of the rise of modern science is a

[1] See above, p. 87 *et seq.*

253

method generally described as "empiricism." Its first major exponent was Locke.[2] Locke in the first book of the *Essay* argued, against Plato, Descartes and the scholastics, that there are no innate ideas or principles. He considered that ideas are derived from experience, and that the operations of the human mind, which Locke called "perceptions," presuppose experience.

Locke's empiricism was pushed further by David Hume, whose scepticism destroyed even the principle of causality as one of necessity, as distinguished from habitual observation of certain sequences in the world of nature.[3]

Empiricism has exercised a decisive influence on modern philosophy, especially in its negative aspects, namely the downgrading of metaphysics in philosophy. The rejection of metaphysics as the pre-eminent—or even as a relevant—preoccupation of philosophy is common to both "pragmatism" and "logical positivism." Both these movements have exercised considerable influence on modern legal theory, but from very different angles. While pragmatism emphasises the importance of fact study, as against concepts, for law, logical positivism[4] is principally interested in the method of verification. Its basic data are those of mathematics and science, from which it develops a mathematical logic of language. In the *Principia Mathematica* of Russell and Whitehead mathematical logic is expressed in language symbols. This form of positivism has, through various metamorphoses, led to a renewal of the study of legal concepts in modern analytical jurisprudence.

Empiricism became important for the law when the scientific study of the external world was extended from the phenomena of nature to the social order. The study of laws governing social behaviour—in the family, in groups, in the state—became increasingly the object of science (sociology). An early exponent of this new preoccupation of political philosophy and jurisprudence with

---

[2] Not as a political philosopher or an advocate of inalienable human right (on which see above, p. 122 *et seq.*), but as a theorist of knowledge (*Essay concerning Human Understanding*).

[3] Although Kant adopted much from both Locke and Hume, especially the emphasis on sense impression as given to the human mind, he restored the priority both of the idea over matter and of the human mind over the outer world by reducing sense data to the raw material which is shaped by the categories of human understanding. He thus initiated the idealistic movement in philosophy which has been discussed earlier (see above, Chap. 15).

[4] A description commonly given to the so-called Vienna school, initiated by Schlick and continued by Carnap and others. it also includes Bertrand Russell and such English sympathisers as Ayer. See Ayer, *The Revolution in Philosophy* 41 *et seq.*, 70 *et seq.* (1956).

the laws of social behaviour was Auguste Comte's *Cours de philosophie positive*.[5] A more important offspring of the various modern trends is the way of thinking described as "pragmatism" or "realism."[6]

In so far as they are concerned with the response of law to certain social facts, these pragmatic or realist movements in legal thought must be sharply differentiated from the theories which from Bentham and Ihering onwards orient the law towards certain purposes. Even though these theories are not based on metaphysical ideals or natural law but state the ends of the law in terms of social purposes and human want, they are in essence ideological. They are therefore different in conception and orientation from the pragmatic or sociological interpretations of law, which treat law as a resultant of certain social facts and forces.[7]

Thus, the word "positivism" in philosophy,[8] while far from having a generally accepted meaning, appears to comprise at least three different trends: empiricism, pragmatism and logical positivism.

It is in modern legal theory that "positivism" has acquired major significance and come to symbolise the dominant trends in contemporary legal thinking. Much its most important manifestation has been "analytical positivism," scientifically established by Austin and his successors, and modified in our time by Kelsen and the Vienna school.[9]

It should, however, be properly understood as comprising at least two major trends in legal thinking: analytic and pragmatic positivism, both related, though in different ways, to philosophical empiricism.[10]

---

[5] See above, p. 228 *et seq.*

[6] See p. 292 *et seq.* A link between empiricism and theoretical philosophy, and pragmatism and social science, is provided by John Dewey's *Logic of Inquiry*, an attempt to link methods of thinking with social environment and purposes.

[7] For this reason they are treated in this book as part of the "idealistic" theories of law.

[8] It is interesting to note that Bertrand Russell in his *History of Western Philosophy* (1945) does not use the word at all but deals instead separately with empirical and pragmatist movements in philosophy.

[9] This appears to be identified with "positivism" in general by H. L. A. Hart, "Positivism and the Separation of Law and Morals," 71 Harv.L.Rev. at p. 601, n. 25 (1958).

[10] See in this same sense Helen Silving: "Positive Natural Law" 3 *Natural* L.F. 24 (1958). Later in the same article, the learned author comprises under "positivistic jurisprudence" the following: "juristic positivism, pragmatism, realism and functionalism" (*Id.* at 30).

Chapter 22

ANALYTICAL LEGAL POSITIVISM

Different Aspects of Analytical Legal Positivism

As the shift in emphasis from metaphysical to empirical trends in theoretical philosophy corresponds to the displacement of speculation by observed phenomena and their interpretation in the world of nature, so the rise of analytical positivism in jurisprudence accompanies the displacement of a loosely organised secular or ecclesiastical-international order by the modern national state. The emergence of the modern state as the more and more exclusive repository of political and legal power not only produced a professional class, of civil servants, intellectuals and others, which increasingly gave its loyalties and its talents to the modern national state rather than to an international church or to a distant and impotent emperor; it also demanded more and more organisation of the legal system, a hierarchical structure of legal authority, and the systematisation of the increasing mass of legal material.

In a recent article,[1] H. L. A. Hart has differentiated five meanings of "positivism," as they are "bandied about in contemporary jurisprudence": (1) the contention that laws are commands of human beings; (2) the contention that there is no necessary connection between law and morals or law as it is and ought to be; (3) the contention that the analysis (or study of meaning) of legal concepts is (a) worth pursuing and (b) to be distinguished from historical inquiries into the causes or origins of laws, from sociological inquiries into the relation of law and other social phenomena, and from the criticism or appraisal of law whether in terms of morals, social aims, "functions," or otherwise; (4) the contention that a legal system is a "closed logical system" in which correct legal decisions can be deduced by logical means from predetermined

---

[1] Hart, See Shuman, *Legal Positivism*, 12 *et seq.* (1963) for arguments on the differences between analytical jurisprudence and legal positivism. "Positivism and the Separation of Law and Morals," 71 Harv.L.Rev. 593, 601, n. 25 (1958).

legal rules without reference to social aims, policies, moral standards; (5) the contention that moral judgments cannot be established or defended, as statements of fact can, by rational argument, evidence, or proof ("non-cognitivism" in ethics).

The last of these appears to equate relativistic and non-cognitivist philosophies. Both share the belief that values cannot be proved, but the former, not the latter, hold that there can and must be rational argument about moral values and judgments.[1a] Of the other four, the contention that a legal system is a "closed logical system" is closely connected with the more general proposition of a strict separation between is and ought. Subject to this simplification, the differentiation of the various aspects of analytical positivism is valuable and important.

The separation, in principle, of the law as it is, and the law as it ought to be, is the most fundamental philosophical assumption of legal positivism. It represents a radical departure both from the scholastic hierarchy of values in which positive law is only an emanation of a higher natural law, and from the fusion of the philosophy of law and the science of law as it is most notably represented in Hegel's system. Separation of "is" and "ought" does not imply any contempt for the importance of values in law, as is evident from the work of Austin, Kelsen and others. It does assign both to strictly different fields.

With the elimination of the values underlying the legal system, as essentially irrelevant to analytical jurisprudence, analytical positivists can concentrate their attention on the structure of a "positive" legal system. This leads positivists to the elaboration of the structure of law in the modern state, from Austin's "command of the sovereign" to Kelsen's hierarchy of norms derived from a hypothetical *Grundnorm.*

In the construction of a modern legal system, tools of legal science are elaborated, and one of the principal preoccupations of analytical jurists has therefore been the elaboration and classification of legal concepts. With some, as with Austin, this only forms part of a general analysis of the province of jurisprudence, whereas for a large number of nineteenth and twentieth century jurists the definition and classification of legal concepts became an exclusive preoccupation.

In recent years, a new turn has been given to this preoccupation with legal concepts by an essentially English trend in jurisprudence,

[1a] See above, p. 38.

which seeks to link the interpretation of legal concepts with the analysis of ordinary language, as it has preoccupied modern— especially English—philosophers since the work of the Vienna school, Russell and Wittgenstein.

AUSTIN'S THEORY OF LAW

The work of the English jurist John Austin (1790-1859) remains the most comprehensive and important attempt to formulate a system of analytical legal positivism in the context of the modern state.

Austin's most important contribution to legal theory was his substitution of the command of the sovereign (*i.e.*, the state) for any ideal of justice in the definition of law. Austin defines a law as

a rule laid down for the guidance of an intelligent being by an intelligent being having power over him.[2]

Law is thus strictly divorced from justice and, instead of being based on ideas of good and bad, is based on the power of a superior. This links Austin with Hobbes and other theorists of sovereignty; but it was left to Austin to follow up this conception into the ramifications of a modern legal system.

The first division of law is that into laws set by God to men (law of God), and laws set by men to men (human laws). The former class of laws is of no real juristic significance in Austin's system, compared, for example with the scholastic teaching which establishes an organic relation between divine and human law. In Austin's positivist system, which refuses to relate law to goodness or badness, the law of God seems to fulfil no other function than that of serving as a receptacle for Austin's utilitarian beliefs. The principle of utility is the law of God. This proclamation of Benthamite faith has no influence whatsoever on the main principles of Austin's doctrine.[3]

Human laws are divisible into laws properly so called (positive law) and laws improperly so called. The former are either laws

---

[2] I *Lectures on Jurisprudence* 86 (4th ed., Campbell 1876).

[3] Austin himself apologises for introducing the principle of utility as "that which not only ought to guide but has commonly in fact guided the legislator," *Province of Jurisprudence* 59 (Library of Ideas (1954)). Austin's formulation is a stylistic improvement on the substantially similar definition by Bentham (*Limits of Jurisprudence Defined*, p. 88) of law as ". . . a volition conceived or adopted by the sovereign in a state, concerning the conduct to be observed in a certain case by a certain person or class of persons."

set by political superiors (either "supreme" or "subordinate") to political subordinates (such as statutes and by-laws), or laws set by subjects, as private persons, in pursuance of legal rights granted to them. As an example, Austin gives the rights of a guardian over his ward. But since the legal nature of such rights derives from the indirect command of the superior who confers such right on the guardian, it is obvious that every enforceable private right must fall within this category.[4] Laws improperly so called are those which are not set—directly or indirectly—by a political superior. In this category are divers types of rules: rules of clubs, laws of fashion, laws of natural science, the rules of so-called international law. To all these Austin gives the name of "Positive Morality," thus describing both their closeness to and their difference from positive law.

The positive law, or "law properly so called," which remains, is characterised by four elements, command, sanction, duty and sovereignty:

> Laws properly so called are a species of commands. But, being a command, every law properly so called flows from a determinate source . . . whenever a command is expressed or intimated, one party signifies a wish that another shall do or forbear; and the latter is obnoxious to an evil which the former intends to inflict in case the wish be disregarded. . . . Every sanction properly so called is an eventual evil annexed to a command. . . . Every duty properly so called supposes a command by which it is created . . . and duty properly so called is obnoxious to evils of the kind. . . .[5]

> The science of jurisprudence is concerned with positive laws, or with laws strictly so called, as considered without regard to their goodness or badness.[6]

All positive law is deduced from a clearly determinable law-giver as sovereign.

> Every positive law, or every law simply and strictly so called, is set by a sovereign or a sovereign body of persons, to a member or members of the independent political society wherein that person or body is sovereign or supreme.[7]

The sovereign is thus defined by Austin:

---

[4] This idea has been developed fully by the Vienna school which, consequently, denies any distinction between public and private law, relating all norms to the ultimate sovereign norm (which Austin calls "command"). *Cf.* p. 281 *et seq.*

[5] Austin, I *Lectures on Jurisprudence, op. cit.* at 182-183. *Province of Jurisprudence, op. cit.* at 133.

[6] *Lectures on Jurisprudence, op. cit.* at 176.

[7] *Id.* at 225.

If a determinate human superior, not in a habit of obedience to a like superior, receive habitual obedience from the bulk of a given society, that determinate superior is sovereign in that society, and the society (including the superior) is a society political and independent.[8]

Austin explains that the superior may be an individual or a body or aggregate of individuals.

The sovereign is not himself bound by any legal limitations, whether imposed by superior principles or by his own laws. Any higher principles or self-limitations are merely guides which the sovereign may discard.

Austin's conception of sovereignty as an element of law clearly presupposes a pre-legal element, which cannot be deduced, but must be assumed or proved as existing in fact: the habit of obedience from the bulk of a given society.

GERMAN POSITIVISTIC THEORIES OF LAW AND STATE

In so far as Austin's theory is based upon the command of the sovereign—the sovereign being the modern state—his teaching was accepted and further developed by the leading German nineteenth-century jurists, notably Rudolf von Ihering and Georg Jellinek.

Ihering, apart from being the forerunner of sociological juris-prudence, is also the principal German exponent of the coercive or imperative theory of law. A substantial part of his *Law as a Means to an End*[9] is devoted to the demonstration that law is dependent upon coercion and that the right to coerce forms the absolute monopoly of the state.

Ihering's influence is apparent in the dominant trend of the German doctrine of the state as represented by Jellinek, Zorn, Laband and others. Thus Jellinek[10] gives the following three essential marks of a rule of law:

(1) They are norms for the external conduct of men towards one another.

(2) They are norms which proceed from a known external authority.

(3) They are norms whose binding force is guaranteed by external power.

---

[8] *Id.* at 226.

[9] This title, chosen in the Modern Legal Philosophy Series, is a poor translation of "*Zweck im Recht*," which means "Purpose in the Law."

[10] Jellinek, *Allgemeine Staatslehre* (1905).

To this purely imperative conception of law Jellinek gives, however, a psychological turn by adding to these three requisites the effectiveness of the rule in action. The authority which has prescribed it must be so backed by social and psychological power as to be in a position to give effect to it.

The particular theory of state sovereignty which Jellinek combines with his definition of law is discussed elsewhere.[11]

Altogether, Ihering's insistence on force, concentrated in the state as the essential element of law, combined with the state glorification and anti-internationalist bias of Hegel to give German doctrines of public constitutional and international law an intensely nationalist turn.

ANALYTICAL POSITIVISM IN FRANCE AND THE "CODE CIVIL"

In the main, French nineteenth-century legal thinking participated in the positivistic trend. It produced some of the most uncompromising modern positivists such as Roguin[12] who pleads for a pure judicial science confined to the authoritatively established precepts and excluding all interpretation and application of the law as outside the realm of legal science,[13] or Jéze[14] who reaffirms the absolute distinction of law and politics and confines the law to a purely technical function. To Jéze the "sentiment of justice" is not so much an agent in the creative development of the law as an act of political revolution against the law. It was natural that the jurists of the country that, early in the nineteenth century, with the Napoleonic Codes, had started the era of modern codifications, should be preoccupied with systemisation and classification of materials, and with the principles of legal analysis. For the same reason, however, it was in France that towards the end of the century—Italy had only recently codified its civil law and Germany was preparing for it—French jurists began to doubt the sufficiency of logical analysis, and of analytical positivism, altogether.

The growing bulk of judicial decisions interpreting the Code made it apparent to French jurists earlier than elsewhere that a mere self-contained body of logical rules failed before the infinite

[11] *Cf.* below, p. 575.
[12] Roguin, *La Science Juridique Pure* (1923).
[13] In this respect, Roguin is closer to Bentham who deeply distrusted all judicial law making than to Austin who acknowledged the necessity and desirability of the judicial development of the law.
[14] Jéze, *Principes généraux du droit administratif* (3rd ed. 1925).

variety of problems which progressing industrialisation in particular raised in France as everywhere else.

The most powerful and successful attack upon this *réseau d'abstractions* is that of Gény.[15]

To this, French analytical positivism has responded by modifying the rigid analytical method of earlier days by a cautious admission of extra-analytical factors.

Among the many attempts along this line the most notable are, perhaps, those of Saleilles and Ripert.

Saleilles, while insisting on the fundamental advantages of certainty and objectivity presented by the analytical approach, supplements this *méthode raisonnante* by a *méthode rationnelle*,[16] that is, a more synthetic and comprehensive view of the Code, a view more in accordance with equity and practical needs. Since he also insists on the nature of law as a social science, this theory clearly foreshadows the more openly independent sociological approach of Gény. Saleilles himself formulates the difference, with French elegance, by characterising his own approach as, "*Au-delà du Code civil, mais par le Code civil,*" and that of Gény as "*Par le Code civil, mais au-delà du Code civil.*"[17]

By a different method Ripert[18] reaffirms a modified positivism.

A strong opponent of natural law theories, ancient or modern, Ripert stresses the clear separation of legal authority which is entirely and purely based on positive law, and the *règle morale*, which intervenes both to assist the legislator in framing rules which are not likely to be disobeyed and the judge, where the law is silent, obscure or insufficient.

This intervention Ripert pursues in the law of civil obligations, where it appears as a supervising force in such rules as those about *bonnes mœurs*, equality of parties, judicial intervention in contract through the *clausula rebus sic stantibus*, the principle of *abus de droits, etc.*

The legal sanction of moral duties Ripert sees in three paramount principles of modern civil obligation:

(*a*) The duty not to harm others.
(*b*) The duty of restoration of unjust enrichment.
(*c*) The duty to assist your neighbour.

---

[15] *Cf.* below, p. 328 *et seq.*
[16] Preface to Gény, *Méthode d'interprétation*, xviii (1919).
[17] *Id.* at xxv.
[18] Ripert, *La règle morale dans les obligations civiles* (3rd ed., 1935).

On the whole Ripert considers the separation of the legal command from the moral rule as a technical necessity. Only by means of a legal rule can a moral rule gain the necessary precision.

In short, Ripert maintains the formal position of positivism, but abandons its substance. When all is said and done, his position is not so very far from that of Gény and other representatives of a modified natural law ideology which, in its turn, is close to the idealistic trend in sociological jurisprudence.

AUSTIN'S SUCCESSORS AND CRITICS

Austin's principal theories have deeply influenced legal thought to the present day.

The challenge to natural law theories and metaphysical idealism has, in its general conception, remained the basis of all subsequent legal thought. With the exception of some adherents of the *Freirechtslehre* and of extreme totalitarian jurisprudence, no serious legal theory has since denied the basic distinction of the law as it is and the law as it ought to be. In its extreme and rigid form this principle became the gospel of analytical positivism, which denied that legal ideals were of any concern to the lawyer as such. A radical exponent of strict separation is the German Bergbohm[19] who insists on a rigid exclusion of any consideration of the law as it ought to be from a scientific study of the law. It is true that Austin himself repeatedly emphasises, against Bentham, the need for judicial law-making, as an essential supplement to statutory legislation, in the development of the law. But he did not analyse the ways in which judicial law-making was bound to qualify, if not to destroy, the rigid separation of Is and Ought, of Science and Value, in legal theory. The relativity of their distinction has become the major preoccupation of modern analyses of the judicial process.[20]

The insistence on command and sanction is opposed by those theories which maintain the independence of law from authority and command. Their principal exponents are the historical school and the sociological jurisprudence of Ehrlich. Most of the controversy in this field seems to be based upon a confusion between historical and logical argument. Once the question of legal authority is clearly separated from the question of the social source

[19] *Jurisprudenz und Rechtsphilosophie* (1892).
[20] See below, Chap. 32.

of such authority, it appears that little has been said or written that would effectively impair this part of Austin's theory.[21]

From analytical jurists opposition has come both to the association of law with sovereignty and to its definition as a command.

The association of law with sovereignty has been reaffirmed and put on a new scientific basis by the pure theory of law of the Vienna school.[22] But it has been opposed by other analytical jurists.

The opposition is thus formulated by John Chipman Gray:

> The idea of the state is fundamental in jurisprudence; but having postulated the state, we can turn at once to see what are its organs, legislative, judicial and administrative, and to consider the rules in accordance with which they act. . . .
> The real rulers of a political society are undiscoverable. They are the persons who dominate over the wills of their fellows. In every political society we find the machinery of government, king or president, parliament or assembly, judge or chancellor. We have to postulate one ideal entity to which to attach this machinery, but why insist on interposing another entity, that of a sovereign? Nothing seems gained by it, and to introduce it is to place at the threshold of jurisprudence a very difficult, a purely academic, and an irrelevant question.[23]

The characterisation of all law as command has been criticised from different quarters. Kelsen has condemned it as introducing an inadmissible psychological element into the pure norm of law.[24] Bryce, Gray, Dicey and others have criticised the description of such legal relations as legal powers, rights, privileges as sovereign commands. These writers think that private rights, administrative acts, declaratory laws cannot be characterised as commands. In this matter, however, Austin is powerfully supported by the Vienna school, whose theory of concretisation of law (*Stufentheorie*) considers that all kinds of legal acts, whether statutes, decrees, by-laws, contracts, administrative and judicial acts, represent different stages in the unfolding of the law and acquire the character of legal acts by the sanction of the ultimate law-giving authority.[25]

In the analysis of municipal law the essential features of Austin's theory have established themselves beyond serious challenge. Controversies between analytical and other schools of jurisprudence affect this issue but little. It is only the rigid separation of law

---

[21] See on this point, above, p. 251 *et seq.*
[22] *Cf.* below, p. 279 *et seq.*
[23] Gray, *Nature and Sources of Law*, ss. 182 and 183.
[24] See below, p. 277.
[25] See below, p. 282.

from the ideals of justice which has been effectively attacked by modern development and theories.

In the sphere of international relations, however, the majority of jurists, often the same who have accepted the Austinian thesis for law within the state, have opposed the Austinian theory by maintaining the legal character of international law despite the absence of both sovereign authority and sanction. This particular issue is discussed elsewhere.[26] It would be difficult to deny that Austin's conclusion on the character of international law follows necessarily from his definition of law. Austin, as a jurist, has kept himself free from the rival political ideologies of nationalism and internationalism. This is more than one can say of the majority of the modern writers who have discussed the character of international law. The assertion of one definition of law for municipal law and of another for international law is confusing unless it is made clear that the term has different meanings in the different contexts[27] and to be explained only on political and ideological grounds. In this respect, too, Austin's thesis retains its value.

Austin's command theory of law became the starting point for subsequent analytical theories of great importance.

Holland accepts the command theory in principle, but substitutes enforcement for the command of the sovereign:

A law, in the proper sense of the term, is therefore a general rule of human action, taking cognisance only of external acts, enforced by a determinate authority.[28]

This leads to the very substantial modification of analytical positivism, of which John Chipman Gray in America and John Salmond in England are the principal representatives.

Gray agrees with Austin's main contribution to analytical jurisprudence, which he describes as being

the recognition of the truth that the law of a state, or another organised body, is not an ideal, but something which actually exists. It is not that which is in accordance with religion, or nature, or morality, it is not that which it ought to be, but that which it is.[29]

---

[26] *Cf.* below, pp. 279, 574 *et seq.*
[27] See Glanville Williams, "International Law and the Controversy Concerning the Word 'Law'" in *Philosophy, Politics and Society*, 134 *et seq.* (ed. Laslett, 1956). See also Kantorowicz, *The Definition of Law* (ed. Campbell, 1958) on the practical importance of choosing a definition of law which, without inconsistency, can include international law. See further below, p. 578 *et seq.*
[28] Holland, *Elements of Jurisprudence*, 41 (10th ed.).
[29] Gray, *op. cit.* s. 213.

But Gray emphatically disagrees with the function which Austin attributes to the sovereign law-giver. To him the statute, together with precedent, equity and custom, is but a source of law, and the law itself is what the persons acting as judicial organs of the state lay down as rules of conduct.

To determine rights and duties, the judges settle what facts exist, and also lay down rules according to which they deduce legal consequences from facts. These rules are the law.[30]

Very similarly, Salmond says:

Law may be defined as the body of principles recognised and applied by the state in the administration of justice. In other words, the law consists of the rules recognised and acted on by the courts of justice.[31]

Gray proves the correctness of his definition by numerous examples taken mostly from American law, which purport to show that it is impossible to fix the law before a court lays it down one way or another. The rule in *Rylands* v. *Fletcher*, adopted judicially in some American states, rejected in others, is a case in point. Gray denounces the "childish fiction" that common law judges only state the law as it is, but do not make it. Thus Gray introduces a new element into analytical positivism which has greatly inspired American realists in their opposition to analytical positivism. Gray devotes much attention to the personal factor in legal development. The history of the United States, with the important function exercised by the courts in the political development, provides him with a wealth of material.

Suppose Chief Justice Marshall had been as ardent a Democrat (or Republican as it was then called) as he was a Federalist. Suppose, instead of hating Thomas Jefferson and loving the United States Bank, he had hatred for the United States Bank and loved Thomas Jefferson, how different would be the law under which we are living today.[32]

Another example is the majority decision in *Pells* v. *Brown*,[33] which laid it down that future contingent interests can be created validly by will, and thus settled the fate of vast estates for hundreds of years. Thus Gray sees law much more than Austin as law in action, an approach full of potentialities. The shift of emphasis from legislative command to judicial decision has, in fact, been

---

[30] *Id*. at s. 231.
[31] Salmond, *Jurisprudence*, 41 (10th ed. Williams, 1946).
[32] *Id*. at s. 477.
[33] (1620) Cro. Jac. 590.

a major contributing factor in the rise of legal pragmatism, which largely substituted for the study of legal logic that of social facts.[34]

Lastly, through his insistence on the distinction between necessary and general concepts of law, Austin initiated a development which culminated, almost a century later, in Kelsen's pure theory of law. Holland contributed to this development by teaching that jurisprudence

deals rather with the various relations which are regulated by legal rules than with the rules themselves which regulate those relations,[35]

and by comparing the relation between jurisprudence and actual law to the relations between the science of grammar and specific languages.

[34] See below, Chap. 25.
[35] Holland, *Op. cit.* at 6-8.

CHAPTER 23

POSITIVISM AND THE ANALYSIS OF LEGAL CONCEPTS

ANALYTICAL positivists from Austin onwards not only greatly influenced legal theory by shifting the emphasis from theories of justice to the national sovereign state as the repository and source of legal power; they also concentrated—and some of them exclusively so—on the elaboration of legal concepts and categories, *i.e.*, on the tools of legal science. The legal theory underlying this preoccupation with legal concepts is generally an implicit rather than an expressed one. The larger task is seen in the ordering and clarification of the legal structure, in the elaboration of the forms of law rather than in preoccupation with ideals and values. Hence, the accounts of this aspect of analytical positivism can be dealt with briefly in a book devoted to legal theory.

Austin held that

of the principles, notions and distinctions which are the subjects of general jurisprudence some may be deemed necessary. . . . For we cannot imagine coherently a system of law (or a system of law evolved in a refined community) without conceiving them as constituent part of it.

For Austin there were six necessary principles, notions and distinctions: [1] the details of these six categories are not now important, except for the attempt to establish the outline of a general system of rights and obligations. In the first of the six groups, Austin lists the notions of duty, right, liberty, injury, punishment, redress; with their various relations to one another, and to law, sovereignty and independent political society. Austin regards rights and obligations as well as delicts and crimes as necessary principles, as distinct from certain other classifications which were merely matters of scientific arrangement (*e.g.*, Justinian's *Institutes*).

---

[1] *Lectures on Jurisprudence*, 1072-1075. (Campbell, ed. 1885).

Many years later a Hungarian jurist, who was among the first continental jurists to study Austin carefully,[2] took Austin's distinction between essentials and incidentals in the law, and he reduced Austin's six necessary notions to four: right, duty, sovereignty and state. All these are logically presupposed by the idea of the legal order.

The logical classification of legal concepts, not merely as an aid to the teaching and application of law, but generally as a substitute for legal philosophy, generally prospered in continental jurisprudence during the nineteenth century. This "Allgemeine Rechtslehre" was first stimulated by the development of the received Roman Law (*Gemeines Recht*), and later by an analytical approach to the new codifications of law which, in the twentieth century, gave way to the new legal idealism and to sociological approaches to legal interpretations.[3]

As regards the basic legal concepts of a civilised legal order, Austin and before him Bentham pointed the way. In an only recently discovered early book[4] Bentham distinguishes not only rights and duties but makes a distinction between "rights," "liberties" and "powers," which was revived and developed by twentieth-century analytical jurists. He illustrates this distinction in the analysis of the permission to walk over someone else's field coupled with the command to plough it for the owner. He shows that contained in this operation there are rights as well as liberties and powers.[5]

Austin took up the distinction between liberty and right,[6] but his dicta on the subject are not very precise, and the subject is to Austin of minor importance as compared with the basic concepts of "right" and "duty" which are closely linked with Austin's theory of state and sovereignty.

In 1883 the German jurist Bierling developed the Benthamite approach by distinguishing between *Anspruch* (claim), *Dürfen* (liberty) and *Können* (power).[7] In the common law world, Salmond, in the first edition of his *Jurisprudence* (1902) developed this classification by distinguishing between legal advantages and legal burdens. In the former class Salmond distinguishes between rights in

---

[2] Somló, *Juristische Grundlehre* (2nd ed., 1917).
[3] See below, Chap. 27.
[4] *Limits of Jurisprudence Defined* (ed. C. H. Everett, ed. 1945).
[5] *Id.* at 77.
[6] 1 *Lectures on Jurisprudence*, 356.
[7] 2 *Zur Kritik der juristischen Grundbegriffe*, 49 *et seq.* (1877-83).

the strict sense, and liberties, power and immunities; the latter includes duties, disabilities and liberties. In 1923 the American jurist Hohfeld[8] constructed a more elaborate scheme of opposites and correlatives in which right is opposed to duty, liberty to no-right, power to subjection and immunity to disability. This scheme was subsequently modified by Kocourek, whose own scheme of concepts was closer to Salmond's distinction between legal advantages and burdens.[9] From the point of view of legal theory, the elaboration of legal concepts and categories is essentially an ancillary function. Implicit in it is the rejection of a higher unwritten legal order. The various rights, duties, permissions and prohibitions follow from the sovereignty of an ordered positive legal system.

ANALYTICAL JURISPRUDENCE AND THE "MEANING" OF LEGAL CONCEPTS

The analysis of legal concepts has been carried by Hohfeld, Kocourek and others to a point of refinement where, in Roscoe Pound's words, "Occam's razor may well be applied to the hypertrophy of categories which analysis . . . produced for a time."[10] The limitation of this type of juristic analysis lies in the assumption that such concepts as "right," "property," "corporate personality," "possession," and hundreds of others have a fixed and static meaning. A challenge to this approach to the analysis of legal concepts has come both from the modern science of semantics and from certain trends in contemporary philosophy. In their classic work on *The Meaning of Meaning,* first published in 1923, Ogden and Richards challenged the widely held assumption[11] that words have a real existence in themselves. They are, in fact, a special class of symbols, the most important class of signs used in thinking and communication. Words and verbal analysis therefore receive meaning only by reference to an object or a situation in the real world (called "referent" by Ogden and Richards).

As we shall see, this apparently simple theory, from which modern semantics has developed into an elaborate science, has in

---

[8] Hohfeld, *Some Fundamental Legal Conceptions as Applied to Judicial Reasoning* (1913).

[9] For a lucid brief survey of this field see Pound: "Fifty Years of Jurisprudence" 50 Harv.L.Rev. 571 (1937).

[10] *Id.* at 573.

[11] Related to the old philosophical controversy between nominalists and realists.

recent years begun to be fruitfully applied to legal analysis and interpretation. Another, though similar, change in the approach to legal analysis has come from certain trends in contemporary philosophy. "Logical positivism" or "logical atomism" as represented by Bertrand Russell and the so-called "Vienna school" could, as such, yield little of value for jurisprudence. Its strong opposition to any kind of metaphysics only reaffirmed the philosophy of analytical legal positivism, in a strict separation of Is and Ought. Its affirmation that statements of value are emotive, and therefore neither true nor false,[12] is essentially a development of Hume's position and implies a philosophy of relativism. The basic tenet of the logical positivists is that the meaning of any statement is the method of its "verification." Verification can be obtained either through experiment or through mathematical-logical deduction.[13] A representative view is that of the English philosopher Ayer,[14] for whom the only genuine concepts are either empirical or logical. The empirically verifiable and the logically certifiable exhaust the area of the cognitive. All other statements are "emotive." All ethical "concepts" are in this category. Hence, the validity of ethical disputes is not a matter of argument. "We merely praise or condemn them in the light of our own feelings."[15]

This comes close to Kelsen's "pure science of law" and to the relativism of Max Weber, Gustav Radbruch and Oliver Wendell Holmes.[16] The difference is that the last-named thinkers do regard the elaboration of conflicting sets of values as intensely relevant to the theory and practice of law.

Whatever its place in the history of philosophy, logical positivism had little to contribute to legal theory, which is concerned with the ordering of social facts.

A break in this position came when Wittgenstein, originally close to the Vienna school, in his later work—which has deeply influenced contemporary English philosophy—came to think about the analysis of language. This had become a major concern of English philosophers since Moore and Russell. But Wittgenstein, in his later work, departed from his teacher Russell by relating language to the world of which language speaks, by saying that the

---

[12] *Cf.* Ayer, "The Vienna Circle" in *The Revolution in Philosophy*, 78 (1958).
[13] For a brief but illuminating discussion see Warnock: *English Philosophy since 1900*, Chap. IV (1958).
[14] Ayer, *Language, Truth and Logic* (2nd ed., 1946).
[15] *Id.* at 112.
[16] Above, p. 191 *et seq.*

forms and uses of language are infinitely flexible and various. "To imagine a language means to imagine a form of life."[17] The exploration of the meaning of language thus becomes a kind of adventure. Language cannot be understood without the things we do.

It is easy to see the link between this approach to the meaning of language by emphasis on its use, and the "social engineering" approach of modern jurists. Both make it possible to resume the analysis of legal concepts from a different angle. Only tentative beginnings have been made in this direction by contemporary jurists, but it seems possible to outline both the possibilities and the limitations of this approach.

The analysts of "meaning" do not challenge the basic philosophy of analytical positivism, which is one of unconcern with "values," *i.e.*, of a strict separation of "science" and "philosophy" of law.[18] There are two ways in which this analysis may aid jurisprudence throughout the analysis of legal concepts and statements: one is essentially negative. It is concerned with the discovery of the deception and confusion caused by the use of one and the same legal term for a multitude of different meanings. This approach is admirably represented by Dr. Williams' important essays on "Language and the Law."[19] Williams analyses the frequent ambiguities in the use of such important legal concepts as "ownership," "property," "condition," "possession," "malice" and the like. The tendency to use these terms as if they had either one fixed meaning or a "true" meaning is linked with the work of modern logicians who dispute the old assumption that a thing must be either black or white and cannot have degrees of both.[20] The same tendency to ignore "fringe" meanings is inherent in the classifications that abound in statutory or judicial definitions, of such terms as "carriage," "vessel" and the like. From the point of view of legal theory, perhaps the most dangerous aspect of confusion in legal language is the attribution of a "proper" meaning to certain words, for it usually disguises inarticulate legal philosophy. An example is the confusion reigning in the definition of "ownership," both in regard to the objects that may be owned and the degree of control that is

[17] Wittgenstein: *Philosophical Investigations*, 19 (1953).
[18] *Cf*. Hart: "Positivism and the Separation of Law and Morals" 71 Harv.L.Rev. 593 *et seq.* (1958).
[19] Williams, "Language and the Law," 61 L.Q.Rev. (1945). 71, 179, 293, 384; and 62 L.Q.Rev. p. 382 (1941). See also Williams, "International Law and the Controversy concerning the Word Law." Brit. Y'b Int'l L. 148 (1945).
[20] *Cf., e.g.,* Stebbing: *Thinking to Some Purpose* (1939).

exercised.[21] Closely linked with this is, in Dr. Williams' analysis, the "emotive" function of words, *e.g.*, in the statement that laws enacted for a sectional or class interest are "false to the nature of law."[22] We may add to this the even more important example of the term "rule of law" in which both ambiguities and emotive functions abound, with the result that the apparent clarity of the phrase hides deeply clashing political philosophies.[23]

An important conclusion drawn from this approach is that the attempt to define the term "law" is a useless endeavour. As in Humpty Dumpty's famous answer to Alice's question "whether you can make words mean different things," "the question is which is to be master—that's all."

A more positive approach to the possibilities of gaining legal insights from the meaning of legal concepts and phrases in their context is taken by Professor Hart.[24] Hart seems to agree with Williams and the semanticists in stating that words are vague and ambiguous, and that such words may stand for a variety of different things. The vagueness of words can be clarified by distinguishing a core of settled meaning from a penumbra of border-line cases. In the latter area there can be no deductive reasoning and "the criterion which makes a decision sound in such case is some concept of what law ought to be."[25] In an analysis of the meaning of "corporate personality," Hart seeks to demonstrate that the well-known controversy between the adherents of a "realist" and a "fiction" theory is irrelevant because it ignores the difference in the use of ordinary expressions developed for individuals, when transferred to corporations (*e.g.*, in the use of the term "residence"). Instead of asking "What is a corporation?" we should ask "Under what types of conditions does the law ascribe liabilities to corporations?"[26]

The usefulness of an analysis of "meaning" as briefly portrayed here, for the clarification of legal language in statutes, court decisions and legal treatises is obvious. In this respect, the new analyti-

[21] For a detailed analysis of the meaning of the words "property" and "ownership" see *Law in a Changing Society*, Chap. III.
[22] Quoted by Williams from MacIver: *Community*, 143 (3rd ed., 1924).
[23] *Law in a Changing Society*, Chap. 16.
[24] Hart, "Definition and Theory in Jurisprudence," 70 L.Q.Rev. 37 (1954). See also his review of "Dias and Hughes on Jurisprudence" (1958) *Journal of the Society of Public Teachers of Law*, 144.
[25] Hart, "Positivism and the Separation of Law and Morals," 71 Harv.L.Rev. 608 (1958).
[26] Hart, *Definition and Theory in Jurisprudence, op. cit.* at 56.

cal jurisprudence opens up the impasse in which traditional analytical jurisprudence had landed itself.[27] But its contribution to legal theory, *i.e.*, to the study of the relation of law to values, is limited. An analysis of meaning can uncover hidden ambiguities or inarticulate value assumptions, but it cannot indicate directions.[28] Implicit in this new analytical approach is a philosophy of relativism. Words and concepts have no pre-established meaning. It varies according to context and purpose. What these purposes are, under what conditions it is, for example, appropriate to impute criminal liability to a corporate person, remains open. And even if we accept the distinction of a settled "core" and a less certain "penumbra" as valid for purposes of interpretation, this is only another way of stating the choice that confronts the interpreter, a choice that can never be decided by linguistics but only by a purposive decision. It seems that the analysers of "meaning" are not far from Dewey's "logic of inquiry," the "experimental and flexible logic" which seeks to clarify a confused situation by sorting out an interplay of questions and possible solutions.[29] We are thrown back to the problem of interpretation which traditional analytical jurisprudence could not answer and which, as we shall see, provides the bridge between Is and Ought, between science and philosophy of law.

[27] It is, however, possible to deduce the relativity of legal concepts such as that of corporate personality and the "emotive" character of the theories of corporate personality from different premises, such as the formal structure of the legal order (this is the approach of Kelsen and the Vienna school, see below, p. 280) or from a consideration of the social purposes of attribution of legal personality (see the discussion of corporate personality below, p. 571 and the identical statements in all earlier editions).

[28] See C. L. Stevenson's *Ethics and Language*, 2-3 where problems of ethics are characterised as "disagreements in attitude," involving "an opposition of purposes, aspirations, wants, preferences, desires and so on". See further above, p. 37.

[29] See below, p. 294 *et seq.*

CHAPTER 24

KELSEN'S PURE THEORY OF LAW

ANALYTICAL positivism has been restated, developed and put on a theoretical philosophical basis in our own time, by the very influential theory of Kelsen and his followers collectively known as the "Vienna school."[1] Basically, Kelsen's thought is remarkably akin to that of Austin, although Kelsen, when he began to develop his theories[2] was, as he later acknowledged, quite unaware of Austin's work. The philosophical parentage of the "Vienna school" differs, however, greatly from Austin's utilitarianism. The philosophical basis of Kelsen's thought is Neo-Kantianism. This links Kelsen with the Neo-Kantian inspiration of Stammler and Del Vecchio, but the conclusions drawn by Kelsen and the "Vienna school" from Neo-Kantian premises are radically opposed to those of these two jurists.

Stammler becomes involved in insuperable difficulties when he attempts to establish a pure theory of law, universally valid, cleansed of all that is changeable, and yet able to give ideals which guide the lawyer in search of justice.[2a] Kelsen clearly sees the weakness of this attempt as much as the open or hidden political or ethical ideology in other legal philosophies. His cure is a more radical one. No theory of justice can form part of a pure theory of law. Ideals of justice must be a matter of political science. A pure theory of law must be uncontaminated by politics, ethics, sociology, history. Its task is knowledge of all that is essential and necessary to law and therefore freed from all that is changing and accidental in it. The Vienna school represents within the realm of legal theory the quest for pure knowledge in its most uncompromising sense, for knowledge free from instinct, volition, desire. Both Stammler and Del Vecchio had combined the Kantian distinction of form and matter with a legal ideology: Stammler with a pseudo-formal ideal of law derived from Kantian ethics, Del Vecchio with his

[1] It must, of course, be distinguished from the "Vienna Circle" which is generally identified with logical positivism, although there are many affinities of thinking between the two.

[2] His first major work, *Hauptprobleme der Staatsrechtslehre*, was published in 1911.

[2a] See above, p. 185 *et seq.*

intuitive idea of justice based on the conscience of man. Kelsen and his followers reject any such legal idealism as unscientific. The theory of law must be purely formal. On the other hand law is different in essence from nature.

The science of law is a hierarchy of normative relations, not a sequence of causes and effects, like natural science. This, the most important foundation of Kelsen's theory, is essentially Neo-Kantian, in so far as Kant had made the fundamental distinction between man as part of nature—subject to the laws of causation—and as a reasonable being which regulates its conduct by imperatives. This produces the essential difference between "Ought" and "Is" (*Sollen und Sein*).

Whereas Kant himself had confined this distinction to his theory of knowledge, Kelsen and his school extend this theoretical knowledge to law. Kelsen does not, like Stammler, attempt to extend a theory of law to what the law ought to be. Science, according to Kelsen, can never be volition, it is only knowledge.

His sole object is therefore to determine what can be theoretically known about law of any kind at any time and under any conditions. The essential foundations of Kelsen's system may be enumerated as follows:

(1) The aim of a theory of law, as of any science, is to reduce chaos and multiplicity to unity.

(2) Legal theory is science, not volition. It is knowledge of what the law is, not of what the law ought to be.

(3) The law is a normative not a natural science.

(4) Legal theory as a theory of norms is not concerned with the effectiveness of legal norms.

(5) A theory of law is formal, a theory of the way of ordering, changing contents in a specific way.

(6) The relation of legal theory to a particular system of positive law is that of possible to actual law.

From these premises it is comparatively easy to follow the cardinal points of Kelsen's pure theory. In his determination of the legal as distinguished from the moral norm, Kelsen is in agreement with the principal teaching of the analytical school. The legal norm derives its validity from an external source, and the particular "ought" of the legal, as distinguished from the moral norm, is the sanction. The threat of a sanction which shall be imposed if a certain thing is done or not done characterises the legal relation.

Such sanction must be threatened by an authority, and thus the question of the source of the legal norm arises. This is Austinian, but there is a significant difference. For Austin, law is a command, for Kelsen, the imperative would introduce a psychological element, foreign to the law. The legal norm does not constitute a command, but a relation of condition and sequence. "If A is done, B ought to happen." Only in this sense is the law an "ought." The relation thus constituted is one of subordination, and any given legal system constitutes a hierarchy of norms, each of which must be derived from a superior source. Now all knowledge is the endeavour to establish unity out of chaos. In the realm of natural knowledge it is also established that there must not be contradiction. If A is equal to B, A cannot also be equal to non-B. The same applies to the normative sciences, including law. Legal norms cannot be derived from conflicting authorities. A judgment, for example, derives its authority from an Order in Council, the Order from an Act of Parliament, the Act of Parliament from the Constitution; between these sources of legal authority there is a relation of subordination. Ultimately every legal norm in a given legal order deduces its validity from a highest fundamental norm (*Grundnorm*). This fundamental norm itself is not capable of deduction, it must be assumed as an "Initial Hypothesis."[3] That Parliament is sovereign in England is a fundamental norm, no more logically deducible than that the command of the Führer was the supreme legal authority in Nazi Germany or that native tribes obey a witch-doctor.

The task of legal theory is to clarify the relations between the fundamental and all lower norms, but not to say whether this fundamental norm itself is good or bad. That is the task of political science, or of ethics, or of religion.

---

[3] Recently, Kelsen has modified his concepts of the Grundnorm and of the general character of the legal norm. The Grundnorm he no longer regards as a hypothesis but as a fiction—distinguished from a hypothesis by the consciousness that reality does not correspond to it. This modification is the consequence of the new insight that there is an essential correlation between Sollen and Wollen. The Sollen, the norm, is the essence (Sinn) of an act of will, *i.e.*, of an act "the sense of which is that another should conduct himself in a certain manner." (Zum Begriff der Norm, Festschrift für H. C. Nipperdey, at p. 59). "One may describe the Grundnorm as a constitution in the transcendental-logical sense, as distinct from the constitution in the positive legal sense. The latter is the constitution posited by human acts of will, the validity of which is based on the assumed (vorausgesetzte) basic norm." "Die Funktion der Verfassung", 11 Forum 583 (1964)). For Kelsen's most recent brief restatement of the pure theory of law see 'Recht und Logik," 12 Forum, 421 *et seq.*, 495 *et seq.*, October 1965. None of these modifications affects the basic structure of Kelsen's theory.

Between conflicting fundamental norms, as between the legal sovereignty of dictatorship or representative assembly, a choice must be made. Kelsen's legal theory thus leads to a relativism which he and his followers have not pursued any further, but which has been made the basis of an elaborate legal philosophy by Radbruch.[4] Theoretically it thus does not matter for the pure theory of law which fundamental norm is adopted, but at one point it cannot help facing political reality. Can the pure theory of law take note of a revolutionary change which establishes a new *Grundnorm* in defiance of the former one? Could a legal command for instance still be based, with any claim to theoretical validity, on the Czarist Constitution or on the German Weimar Constitution? Neither has ever been abrogated by a legal process, reducible to anything but a conflicting *Grundnorm*. Kelsen here is forced to introduce an element which is neither formal nor normative. No fundamental norm can be recognised which has not a minimum of effectiveness, that is, which does not command a certain amount of obedience. "The efficacy of the total legal order is a necessary condition for the validity of every single norm of the order." How this minimum of effectiveness is to be measured Kelsen does not say, nor could he do so without going deep into questions of political and sociological reality.

The thesis that there must be unity of legal authority has been applied by Kelsen and some of his followers[5] to the problems of international law and state sovereignty. If norms of international law are to be binding upon the states, they can be binding only as norms put by an international order superior to the legal authority of the states, even if that international order is only loosely organised. Thus a recognition of the principle, *pacta sunt servanda*, means recognition of a legal authority limiting state sovereignty. All attempts made by Jellinek and others to compromise by their theory of self-limitation of the state are mercilessly denounced by Kelsen. Such theories all amount in effect to the negation of international law. If a state is sovereign it is bound to subordinate every other system of law to its own. As long as there are some ninety sovereign states in the world there is an equal number of legal orders each of which must claim to be all comprehensive and none of which can acknowledge the superior or even the equal authority

---

[4] See above, p. 192 *et seq.*

[5] In particular, Verdross, *Einheit des rechtlichen Weltbildes* (1923), and *Verfassung der Volkerrechtsgemeinschaft* (1926).

of any other, except by *de facto* toleration. The recognition of only two states as being equal in law to each other implies necessarily the recognition of a higher legal authority which can bestow upon them the attribute of equality. As soon as one recognises any principle, such as *pacta sunt servanda,* as binding upon the states, one recognises the supremacy of international law over national sovereignty. At this point, however, Kelsen has introduced an element of confusion. It is of vital importance to distinguish between the legal character of international law in present-day international society and the authority of international law as a logical alternative to the present era of state sovereignty. Logically Kelsen should have been led to deny the character of law to international law in present international society. But in contrast to his usual method he proceeds[6]:

(1) To draw an analogy between present-day international law and the primitive law of early uncivilised communities preceding the modern state;
(2) to see the sanction of international law in war and reprisal.

Kelsen is aware that this theory is arguable only on the supposition that war and reprisals are forbidden, as instruments of national policy, and permitted only as reactions of the international community against a delict committed by a state. The weakness of the theory—now admitted by Kelsen[7]—is that international law does not altogether outlaw war as an instrument of national policy, and that the international community has no tribunal to decide, authoritatively and compellingly, whether the action of a state is to be interpreted as a sanction or as a delict.[8]

The principal efforts of the Vienna school are, however, devoted to theoretical consideration of legal norms within the state. On the character of the state the Vienna school has developed some of its most characteristic theories. State and law it declares to be identical, for the state is nothing but a system of human behaviour and order of social compulsion:

This compulsive order is not different from the legal order, for the reason that within one community only one and not two compulsive orders can be valid at the same time.[9]

---

[6] *Cf. Legal Process and International Order* (1934); *General Theory of Law and State,* p. 328 *et seq.* (1946).

[7] *General Theory of Law and State,* 328 *et seq.* (1946).

[8] See further, below, p. 284 *et seq.*

[9] Kelsen, "Pure Theory of Law" in 51 L.Q.Rev. 517, 534 (1935).

It is impossible to distinguish between law and state, because an act of state can be such only by virtue of a legal norm which qualifies it as such. Source and contents of this norm are, of course, irrelevant for the pure theory. The uncontrollable will of a despot is as valid a legal norm as a democratic form of government. Only in so far as an act can be deduced from such a superior norm can it be legally qualified as a state's act.

Thus the Vienna school rejects any dualism, such as follows from subordinating either the law to the state or the state to the law. The former would be the deification of a personified state, the latter a natural law ideology. Nor does Kelsen admit any distinction between a legal and a sociological notion of the state.[10]

This at first may seem surprising in view of the sharp distinction drawn between law and sociology. But to Kelsen the state is nothing but a legal construction, and to admit a sociological side of it would open the door to biological conceptions of the state which he rejects, like any personification of the state. This leads to the next part of his theory, the denial of any legal difference between physical and juristic persons. Law is a system of norm-relations and it uses personification merely as a technical device to constitute points of unification of legal norms. The difference between natural and artificial persons is irrelevant, since all legal personality is artificial and derives its validity from superior norms. It is remarkable how the pure theory of law here reaches conclusions similar to those reached by modern sociological theories and modern judicial treatment of the problem of corporate personality.[11]

It follows also from the conception of law as a system of norm-relations that Kelsen and his followers recognise no individual right, except as a technical device which the law may or may not adopt in order to carry out legal transactions. Legal duties are of the essence of law, for law is a system of "oughts," but legal rights are only an incident, and the law may dispense with them. This detaches the law from any association with political theory of the law, such as those which affirm inalienable rights of the individual. Another consequence of this system of a formal hierarchy of norm relations is Kelsen's attack upon the distinction between public and private law, much more familiar and important to Continental systems than to Anglo-American law, where it has only begun to develop as a consequence of recent constitutional and social evolution. Public

---

[10] As developed by Jellinek, *Der juristische und soziologische Staatsbegriff.*
[11] See below, Chap. 34.

law regulates the relations between the state and public authorities on the one hand and the subject on the other, private law regulates relations between subjects. Public law is therefore fundamentally a relation between superior and inferior, and it is only through a process of self-limitation that the state submits to a kind of legal relation between itself and a subject, a development which has produced administrative law and corresponding systems of tribunals in Continental countries. This very division of law into spheres is attacked by the Vienna school as emphatically as by Duguit, but from an entirely different angle. The attack is made on theoretical grounds and follows naturally, once the theory of the law as a system of relations, all deducible from an ultimate superior authority and each subordinate to the next higher one, is accepted. But the attack is supported by examples from social and political reality. The traditional division is based on the twofold argument: (1) that obligations in public law arise from a unilateral command,[12] but obligations in private law arise from mutual agreement; and (2) that the organs from which the order is issued can also enforce it, whereas a sanction in private obligations is provided by the state which stands above the parties.

The Vienna school objects (1) that the will of the parties never constitutes of itself a legal obligation, but is only the condition which the legal order stipulates for giving it legal sanctions; and (2) that administrative organs which create legal relations must appeal to a higher state organ for legal sanction.

Behind the division of public and private law Kelsen suspects, not without reason, a political ideology which wishes this sphere of private law to appear as being beyond politics, whereas in reality private law institutions embody political ideology as strongly as public law institutions and relations.[13] In this respect the Vienna

[12] Although administrative tribunals such as the French Conseil d'Etat have imposed certain limitations on the exercise of such unilateral command.

[13] There is a certain link between this criticism and the reasons which caused Dicey to be so profoundly and mistakenly distrustful of *droit administratif*. The methodological point of departure of the two jurists is, however, entirely different. Kelsen sees in the dichotomy of public and private law an improper splitting up of law into two separate streams, instead of the monistic pyramidal structure which his school sets up. Dicey sees administrative law in the light of the English legal tradition and of the ideologies inherent in the common law. For this reason it might be said that the controversies of continental jurists on the dualism of public and private law have no significance for the Anglo-American legal sphere. But present-day Anglo-American law has an elaborate system of administrative law, as distinct from private law, and such problems as the delegation of legislative powers or the legal position of public authority in relation to the citizen are at least as acute as in continental jurisprudence. (*Cf. Law in a Changing Society*, Part Four.)

school is impressed by the Marxist thesis, developed in particular by Karl Renner, of the delegation of public powers, under the form of private law, to the owner of the means of production.[14]

For the division of law into private and public law the Vienna school substitutes a different theory, first established by A. Merkl[15] and later adopted by Kelsen. This theory of the "concretisation" of law (*Stufentheorie*), sees the legal system as a pyramidal structure. The law unfolds in a gradual process from the highest norm, which is also the most abstract, general and purely norm-giving, to the lowest, which is completely individualised, concrete and executive. Between these two poles each norm does not only give law, but also applies and thus partakes in the process of concretisation of the law. Thus if a statute establishes a general norm, it concretises the general legislative principle established by the *Grundnorm*, but it is abstract in relation to the private contract or to the company by-laws which are made between individuals or groups of them within the framework of the statute. Each such transaction not only applies law, but also creates law by individualising the general terms of a superior norm in relation to particular circumstances and parties. The judgment, which authoritatively interprets the terms of the transaction, marks a further stage in the process of concretisation. It at once applies and creates the law. The freedom of creative function is progressively narrowed down in each successive stage, although it never quite ceases. Every judgment contains an act of creation in choosing one of several possibilities of interpretation which the statute, or whatever the superior norm in question may be, permits. In that process the whole of public administrative law takes part. That each administrative act, such as the assessment of rates, concretises the general authority given by the law is obvious. Administration is thus necessarily law. But it further follows that the distinction between judicial and administrative acts is relative. The administrative organ usually has a wider amount of discretion, but also acts within the framework of a superior norm. But it regulates a particular legal situation as does the judicial organ. If the creative function is often more marked with an administrative act and the deciding function more marked with judicial acts, this lies mainly in the difference of the subject-matter.

This point is well illustrated by the increasing assimilation in

---

[14] For an account of Renner's theory, *cf.* below, p. 386 *et seq.*
[15] Merkl, *Die Lehre von der Rechtskraft* and *Allgemeines Verwaltungsrecht.*

totalitarian states of administrative and judicial functions. Both judges and administrators take their orders from superior personalities, and the difference between public and private law becomes correspondingly more and more meaningless. The Soviet Russian jurist Pashukanis can argue that in socialist states all law becomes a matter of administration for the benefit of the public. It might also be noted that similar conclusions as to the relation between judicial and administrative law are reached by Jennings, from the point of view of the British constitutional lawyer,[16] and by Duguit.[17]

The Vienna school sees a similar process of creative concretisation in the application of "law" to "facts" in the judicial process. Facts in any legal case are not self-evident, but are sifted, weighed, stated and subsumed. They are thus as much part of the law as the rules which are applied to them. This not only gives some theoretical foundation to the widely practised art of distinguishing precedents on "facts"; it also stresses the element of selective and normative law-making in the weighing of evidence and other "fact" findings which American realists, above all Jerome Frank,[18] have so often stressed. For example, a statute makes disorderly conduct or driving under the influence of drink an offence, and lays down maximum and minimum punishments. The practices which magistrates develop in regard to the scales of punishment are not only an application of the law but part of the law-making process.

As for the position of the judge and the process of concretisation of law, the pure theory comes, from very different premises, to conclusions similar to those of American realist jurisprudence and the German *Freirechtslehre*, that the judge has a choice between different interpretations of the higher norm. But Kelsen and his followers refuse to give any indication about the way in which the choice should be exercised. All this, as a matter of justice, morality, ideology, is no concern of a pure theory of law.

CRITICISM

The merciless way in which Kelsen has uncovered the political ideology hidden in the theories which profess to state objective truth has had a very wholesome effect on the whole field of legal

---

[16] Jennings, *Law and the Constitution* (5th ed. 1959), Chaps. 6 and 7.
[17] *Cf.* above, p. 230 *et seq.*
[18] *Cf.*, apart from numerous earlier writings, his *Courts on Trial* (1949).

theory. Hardly a branch of it, whether natural law theories, theories of international law, or corporate personality, of public and private law has remained untouched. Even the bitterest opponents of the Vienna school have conceded that it has forced legal theory to reconsider its position.

Genuine criticism should keep two questions clearly distinct: (1) The question how far Kelsen's theory is consistent with its own assumptions; (2) the question how far legal theory can be content with the task that Kelsen has outlined for it.

The distinction, between natural science as dominated by causation, and social science as dominated by volition, has been criticised from many quarters.[19] It would, however, be possible to justify the specific definitions of the Kelsen school for legal science, even if its theory about natural science were not absolutely correct.

As for this particular legal theory, strong opposition has been raised against the thesis of the *Grundnorm* as being a fiction incapable of being traced in legal reality. Thus Allen points out that there are concurrent sources of law, like custom, statute, precedent, none of which can be said to have supremacy over the other.[20] Similar criticism has been voiced against Austin's search for the sovereign. But surely the fact that the ultimate authority in any given legal order may be a composite one, as in the United States of America or in Great Britain, does not alter the fact that such ultimate authority must exist. Otherwise we might be driven to limit legal sovereignty to those systems which have a single political peak, such as dictatorships. The only other criticism against this particular side of Kelsen's theory comes from those who see the essence of the law not in the authority which sanctions it but in the sources which make it. This leads to the general controversy between historical and analytical jurisprudence, in which the Kelsen school stands on the side of Austinian positivism. Once one adheres to the concept of legal sovereignty, Kelsen has shown that the need of an alternative between national and international sovereignty is inescapable. Nor is the criticism formulated, for example, by Allen justified that Kelsen accepts with the principle of *pacta sunt servanda* a natural law norm. Kelsen does not express any preference for this or any other principle, but puts it as a possible basis of international order. He has, however, greatly obscured the matter in introducing historical factors into his plea for the characterisa-

[19] See above, p. 50 *et seq.*
[20] *Law in the Making* 49 (5th ed.).

tion of the present international structure as a legal order. To see a legal sanction in such institutions of self-help as reprisals and war which are the outcome of the denial of superior legal norms, is incompatible with the whole basis of Kelsen's doctrine. In his most recent work, Kelsen seems to have become increasingly doubtful about the soundness of this part of his doctrine.[21]

That absolute purity of any theory of law is impossible Stammler had to admit when discussing the question of validity of the law. Kelsen must similarly acknowledge defeat when it comes to the question of conflicting fundamental norms. The question which is the valid fundamental norm his pure theory cannot avoid, for without it the whole structure would collapse. The "Minimum of Effectiveness" which according to Kelsen must decide is at bottom nothing else but Jellinek's *Normative Kraft des Faktischen,* although the formula chosen by Kelsen is much more nebulous. How can the minimum of effectiveness be proved except by an inquiry into political and social facts? And this implies the necessity of a further political choice: Does the obedience of the majority, of an enlightened minority or sheer physical force decide? Whatever the answer, purity here ceases.[22]

The chief merit of Kelsen's pure theory would seem to lie in the elucidation of the relation between the initial hypothesis (which might less abstractly be described as the basic political faith of the community) and the totality of legal relations derived from it. The conception of the law as a dynamic process of concretisation is a very fruitful one, and it gives a logical justification to conclusions which Gray and American realists on the one hand and continental exponents of the modern sociological theories on the other hand have reached from very different angles. Modern political and juristic developments have lent point to the relativity of the distinction between justice and administration, of physical and juristic personality, of public and private law, of the creative and executive function of the judge. Jurists working in as different fields and from as different angles as Gray, Holmes, Ehrlich, Duguit, Jennings, Barker and others have reached conclusions similar to those reached by the *Stufentheorie.* Many of the accepted juristic distinctions are thus disclosed as particular to political and social conditions of the nineteenth century which do not form any necessary

[21] *Cf.* above, p. 279.
[22] Austin was both more forthright and more logical in defining as sovereign a "determinate human superior" who "receives habitual obedience from the bulk of a given society" (*cf.* above, p. 260).

part of the law. But what may indeed be questioned is the pure formality of the *Stufentheorie*. That it does itself assume a certain political structure may be shown by the constitution of the modern totalitarian states. Under National Socialism and Fascism the will of the leader is the fundamental norm from which the legal order derives its validity. But below this norm there is no clear hierarchy between statute, administration, judicial decision, etc. Law courts are directed to disregard the expressed norm of a statute, if it seems incompatible with the political ideals of National Socialism. Administration, judicial decision and other manifestations of law are all supposed to be inspired by the will to realise National Socialism as personified by the leader. In this task they rival with each other, but are not superior to one another. The very notion of a fixed formal structure is anathema to this conception of state and society.[23] If that is so, it is clear that the *Stufentheorie* cannot express the pure and universal form of law. For were it so, no possible legal system could fall outside it. The hierarchy of the Kelsen system implies, in fact, a minimum of rationality in the structure of law.

From another angle, Lauterpacht,[24] a follower of Kelsen, has questioned whether the theory of hierarchy of legal norms does not imply a recognition of natural law principles, despite Kelsen's violent attacks upon natural law ideology. Most modern natural law theories do not establish absolute ideals but affirm the principle of a higher norm superior to positive law. In the same degree as mankind would become legally organised, natural law principles would become positive norms of a higher order, and the difference between Kelsen's theory and many modern natural law theories would disappear. The very conception of a definite rank between different manifestations of legal will, such as statutes and judicial decisions, implies itself a certain social valuation of state activity.

In another criticism Hägerström[25] has uncovered the natural law ideology hidden in Kelsen's assumption of the unconditional authority of the supreme power or in Verdross' "constitution of the law of Nations" as the formulation on which the basic principle of international law (*pacta sunt servanda*) is supposed to rest.

There remains the second question: what value has the pure

[23] See further below, p. 352.
[24] Lauterpacht, "Kelsen's Pure Science of Law" *Modern Theories of Law*, p. 131 *et seq.*
[25] Hägerström, *The Nature of Law and Morals*, Chap. IV (ed. Olivecrona, 1953).

theory to the lawyer assuming it to be correct within its own premises? It will help him to clear his mind of crypto-ideologies and inarticulate major premises, though it must share the credit for such education with the teaching of Austin, Holmes, Radbruch and others. While the pure theory of law points out the situations which leave a choice between alternative ideologies, such as conflicting interpretations of statutes, it refuses to give any guidance for the solution of such conflicts. At this point, the lawyer must turn to legal philosophy.[26]

CONTEMPORARY MODIFICATIONS OF ANALYTICAL POSITIVISM

Through the closer analysis of legal concepts, and particularly through the distinction between "rights" and "powers", Salmond and Hohfeld had already laid certain foundations for a subtler analysis of the concept of law than was inherent in the simple antithesis of "right" and "duty." A more comprehensive reformulation of analytical positivism—which both builds on, and in certain respects, importantly modifies the theories of Austin and Kelsen— is H. L. A. Hart's "The Concept of Law" (1961). Two aspects of Hart's analysis of the concept of law are of special importance: in the first place, he bridges the age-old conflict between the theories of law emphasising recognition and social obedience as the essential characteristic of a legal norm, and those that see the distinctive characteristic of law in the correlated elements of authority, command and sanction. The former approach is notably represented by Savigny and Ehrlich—neither of whom is mentioned in Hart's book; the latter by Austin, Kelsen and their various disciples and successors. Social acceptance predominates in primitive societies; organised authority predominates in more developed societies. This distinction is expressed in terms of a contrast between primary rules of obligation and secondary rules of recognition.[27] The main defects of rules of behaviour controlling primitive societies are their uncertainty, their static character and their inefficiency. In Hart's analysis the remedy for the uncertainty of a regime of primary rules is "the rule of recognition." This means acknowledgment of the rules of behaviour as authoritative, "*i.e.*, as a proper way of disposing of doubts as to the existence of the rule." The remedy for the

[26] *Cf.* Laski's criticism (*Grammar of Politics*, 4th ed., p. vi): "Granted its postulates, I believe the pure theory to be unanswerable, but I believe also that its substance is an exercise in logic and not in life."

[27] *Op. cit.* pp. 91 *et seq.*

static quality of primary rules consists in "rules of change," *i.e.*, some form of empowering an individual or a group of persons to introduce new primary rules for the conduct of the life of the group. The remedy for inefficiency consists of secondary rules empowering individuals to make authoritative determinations of the question whether on a particular occasion a primary rule has been broken.

Both historically and logically, the primary rules of obligations generally give way to secondary rules, in which the forms of recognition, change and adjudication are systematised, usually through the centralisation of authority, the articulation of definite procedures for the making, application and execution of law, and a system of official sanctions.

In the contemporary world, international law is the conspicuous illustration of a system of "primary" rules. Hart ranges himself with the majority of the theorists of international law, who see the basis of obligation in international law as that of all customary law, in the fact that the rule "is observed, not because it has been consented to, but because it is believed to be binding. . . ."[28]

This approach to international law is of course possible only by detaching the concept of law from the punitive sanction regarded as an essential characteristic of the legal norm by both Austin and Kelsen. While law, as an order backed by threats, is perhaps a correct characterisation of criminal law, it ignores the principal function of law as a means of social control, outside the spheres of private litigation or prosecution. It is through the conferring of powers, not through orders backed by threats, that law makes its great contribution to social life. It enables individuals to mould their legal relations with others by contracts, wills, marriages and other legal actions.

Although, analytically, this approach to law is not original with Hart, and has, in different terms, been used by both Continental and Anglo-American jurists, such as Salmond, Hohfeld, Kelsen and Ross, the emphasis on the socially constructive function of law is important.[28a] The demotion of the punitive sanction has great importance for contemporary international law—although Hart himself fails to apply his own approach to international law. Although

---

[28] Brierly, *The Law of Nations,* 52 (6th Ed. Waldock, 1963).

[28a] Hart appears to be unaware that Ehrlich developed this contrast between the socially constructive and the state-sanctioned (decisional) aspects of law more than half a century earlier. See above, p. 248 *et seq.*

it lacks effective punitive sanctions, there is another important area of modern international law—which we may term "co-operative" international law. It regulates the pursuit of common endeavours by international organization and treaties. The "sanction" in this area of international law is exclusion from participation, and not punishment.[29]

ANALYTICAL POSITIVISM—SOME CONCLUSIONS

The analytical lawyer takes the law as a given matter created by the state, whose authority he does not question. On this material he works, by means of a system of rules of legal logic, conceived as complete and self-contained. In order to be able to work on this assumption, he must attempt to prove to his own satisfaction that legal ideology can be excluded from the lawyer's province. Therefore the legal system is made watertight against all ideological intrusions, and all legal problems are couched in terms of legal logic. Such conceptions as "public policy," in English and American law, clauses of good faith in Continental codes, grounds of invalidity of contracts, the standard of the "reasonable man," are shorn as far as possible of their extra-legal significance. The result is, for example, the tendency of English courts to consider the categories of public policy as closed, on the strength of old precedents, an attitude invariably shattered in times of great crisis. The Continental analytical positivist disguises the problems of "social engineering" (Pound) which face the lawyer in many situations by the use of allegedly logical arguments such as analogy or *argumentum e contrario*. He discreetly glosses over the fact that whether, in a given case, an unregulated problem has to be considered as analogous or opposite to one regulated in a statute, is not a matter of logic. As discussed in more detail in another chapter[30] the choice between conflicting interpretations of a statute or of precedent, the reasonableness of a custom or of combined action taken in pursuit of economic interests (blackmail, conspiracy) depends on certain ethical, political and economic theories upon which the lawyer acts. The certainty which the analytical positivist pursues as the chief end of law was largely provided by the political and social background against which it could develop.

---

[29] See in more detail Friedmann, *The Changing Structure of International Law*, 88 *et seq.* (1964).
[30] *Cf.* below, Chap. 32, p. 451 *et seq.*

The predominance of analytical positivism in jurisprudence corresponded to the consolidation of the modern state into a highly organised instrument of political organisation, claiming absolute authority (through the legal concept of sovereignty) in matters political, while leaving considerable autonomy to the citizen in other matters. This combination of state nationalism and liberalism above all made legal positivism possible. The nineteenth-century state left economic and cultural activities, on the whole, to the individual. Consequently the enormous development of the law concerning these matters, in particular of the law of property, contract, tort and commerce, could take place in comparative remoteness from political issues, or as it would be better put, with little consciousness of the issues involved. The lawyer, and the private lawyer in particular, could concentrate on legal technique, on craftsmanship rather than design. This neat division of spheres was strengthened by the constitutional principle of separation of powers, which provided judicial independence as protection for individual rights. This protection was further strengthened by judicial control of administrative acts, either by a separate system of administrative tribunals (French model) or by the application of a common rule of law to authority and subject alike (Anglo-American model). Under either method state interests were balanced against private interests in a manner which, on the whole, would not hamper the state's political action, while protecting the individual against arbitrariness.

When the state began to invade the spheres hitherto left to the individual, the precarious balance was disturbed. The state became directly interested in economics, family, education, and consequently could not leave the administration of justice as much alone as before. Thus the political foundations of analytical positivism were upset, while such juristic foundation as it possessed disappeared with the realisation that the law could not be interpreted without reference to ideals. Lastly, the mental attitude which analytical positivism demands was bound to be deeply affected by the profound social crisis in the midst of which we live. The faith in certainty and self-sufficiency which characterises the analytical positivist is disturbed by a society in revolution.

The nineteenth century produced, together with the Industrial Revolution, the seeds of social unrest and such powerful critics of contemporary Western society as Marx, Carlyle, Ruskin and Nietzsche. But to the class which provided the bulk of the legal profession, the nineteenth century was, on the whole, a period of progress, prosperity, liberty and comparative peace. There was no vital inducement for them to do more than a skilled specialist's job.

When, nationally as well as internationally, the balance of forces was upset and self-satisfaction gave way to doubt and revolt, analytical positivism was bound to give way to a new preoccupation with social justice.

CHAPTER 25

PRAGMATIC POSITIVISM

THE AMERICAN REALIST MOVEMENT

THE healthy scepticism which, towards the end of the nineteenth century, assailed the complacency of analytical jurisprudence took two very different forms. A new legal idealism, partly of a metaphysical, partly of a sociological, bend, set out to fight the assumption of analytical positivism and turned to investigate the realities of modern society in their relation to modern law. The first and greatest attempt in this approach to social problems had been the Marxist analysis of society, but it did not have much immediate effect upon legal science, owing to a number of factors analysed elsewhere.[1] The realist movement in jurisprudence is of much later origin, and its principal home is the United States although certain Continental movements show rather similar tendencies. Nowhere was the discrepancy between the form of the law and its theoretical logic on the one hand and its sociological reality on the other hand more blatant than in the United States at the beginning of this century. No country could offer richer material for the study of the law as it worked in fact than the United States, with a Federal and forty-eight state jurisdictions, together producing innumerable precedents; with the function which the Supreme Court exercised in the political and social life of the country; with the contrast between the theoretical and practical aspects of constitutional principles; with the development of powerful corporations protected by the same individual rights as the pioneer farmer in the Wild West; with the manifold political machinations within the judicial system. These and many other factors contributed to develop a scepticism symptomatic of the crisis which affected the nineteenth century's outlook on life in the law no less than in other fields.

In the field of law two great American jurists above all may be

[1] *Cf.* Chap. 29.

considered as the mental fathers of the realist movement: John Chipman Gray and Oliver Wendell Holmes.

Gray, although a distinguished exponent of the analytical tendency in jurisprudence, with his insistence on sharply defined notions in the law and his opposition to any infusion of ideologies into the science of law, had begun to shake the position of analytical jurisprudence by relegating statutory legislation from the centre of the law to one of several sources and placing the judge in the centre instead. Although Gray himself still considers the making of the law from those sources as an essentially logical process, his own definition as well as his comments admit and emphasise the great influence of personality, prejudice and other non-logical factors upon the making of the law. The illustrations which Gray gives from English and American legal history show how political sympathy, economic theories and other personal qualities of particular judges have settled matters of the gravest importance for millions of people and hundreds of years.[2]

Gray prepared the ground for a more sceptical approach, which proceeded to deprecate the logical factors and to turn to the non-logical factors with correspondingly greater emphasis.

This tendency was made articulate by Oliver Wendell Holmes who, in an essay published in 1897, gave an entirely empirical and sceptical definition of the law:

Take the fundamental question, what constitutes the law. . . . You will find some textwriters telling you . . . that it is a system of reason, that it is a deduction from principles of ethics or admitted actions, or what not, which may or may not coincide with the decision. But if we take the view of our friend, the bad man, we shall find that he does not care two straws for the action or deduction, but that he does want to know what Massachusetts or English courts are likely to do in fact. I am much of his mind. The prophecies of what the courts will do in fact and nothing more pretentious are what I mean by the law.

Here was, coming from a distinguished judge and thinker, a definition of law, in terms of consequences, and one which seemed to demolish not only any analytical certainty, but also any connection between law and ethical ideals. As has been pointed out by many competent critics, Holmes himself, neither as a jurist nor as a judge, adhered to this statement which, taken by itself, is one-sided, exaggerated and patently incorrect. In fact no one has stressed the need for legal theory with greater force or eloquence

[2] See above, p. 266.

than Holmes himself, in the same essay.[3] But this particular phrase came to be something like a gospel for the followers of realism in jurisprudence who, however great their scepticism and sarcasm in regard to other jurists and their doctrines, followed this and some similar statements of Holmes J. with almost religious fervour.

The tendency thus developed by American lawyers found philosophical support in the new version of positivism, called "Pragmatism," which became popular in the U.S.A. about the same time.[4]

Pragmatism is, as its principal exponent William James said, "a new name for some old ways of thinking."[5] Its outlook is emphatically positivist:

A pragmatist turns away from abstraction and insufficiencies, from verbal solutions, from bad *a priori* reasons, from fixed principles, closed systems and pretended absolutes and origins. He turns towards completeness and adequacy, towards facts, towards actions, towards powers. That means empiric temper regnant, and the rationalist temper sincerely given up, it means the open air and the possibilities of nature as against dogma, artificiality and the pretence of finality in truth.[6]

Pragmatism is thus indeed a new formulation of a very old philosophy. It has stimulated a new approach to law, that "of looking towards last things, fruits, consequences."[7]

No less important a foundation of legal realism than the teaching of James is that of John Dewey.[8] The essence of Dewey's teaching

---

[3] "We have too little theory in the law, rather than too much. . . . The danger is that the able and practical-minded should look with indifference or distrust upon ideas the connection of which with their business is remote. . . . To an imagination of any scope, the most far-reaching form of power is not money, it is the command of ideas. If you want great examples, read Mr. Leslie Stephens's *History of English Thought in the Eighteenth Century*, and see how 100 years after his death the abstract speculations of Descartes had become a practical force controlling the conduct of men. Read the works of the great German jurists, and see how much more the world is governed today by Kant than by Bonaparte." Holmes, 'The Path of the Law," 10 Harv.L.Rev. 457, 476 (1897).

[4] The coexistence of the fundamentalist and the pragmatic strain is a fascinating aspect of contemporary American jurisprudence. The former is exemplified in constitutional interpretation and the anti-trust philosophy, the latter in "social engineering" and the realist approach to law.

[5] James, *Pragmatism* (1925).

[6] *Id.* at 51.

[7] *Id.* at 55.

[8] The most concise statement of Dewey's theory of law is found in his article on "Logical Method of Law," 10 Cornell L.Q. 17 (1924). See also his *Logic, the Theory of Enquiry*, Chaps. 6 and 7 (1938), and Dewey's contribution in *My Philosophy of Law* (1941). For a full account of Dewey's logical and ethical theory, see Patterson, *Jurisprudence*, ss. 4.53, 4.54 (1953).

is that logic is not a deduction of certainties from theoretical principles such as the syllogism, but a study of probabilities. Logic is a theory of inquiry into probable consequences, a process in which general principles can only be used as tools justified by the work they do. As applied to the legal process this means that "the sanctification of ready-made antecedents universal principles" must be abandoned for a "more experimental and flexible logic." The lawyer does not derive his conclusions from general principles. He starts with a problematic and often confused situation; the process of clarification involves the sorting out of certain questions. With the determination of the problem, a possible solution suggests itself to the inquirer (such as the judge). As the lawyer "learns more of the facts of the case, he may modify his selection of rules of law upon which he bases his case." Premises and conclusions are two ways of stating the same thing. Law then is an experimental process in which the logical factor is only one of many leading to a certain conclusion. Dewey also stresses the social importance of substituting this approach for that of logical positivism. Only experimental and flexible thinking in law can turn it into a steady, secure and intelligent instrument of social reform.

How the rules of law work, not what they are on paper, is the core of the pragmatic approach to legal problems. This, of course, is very general. To concretise what they had in mind, realists turned to those sciences which had begun to explore human behaviour in society. In particular they turned to economics, criminology, general sociology and psychology, and sought to utilise them for the science of law.

To study the law as it works and functions means investigating the social factors that make the law on the one hand and the social results of law on the other. Thus the realists' movement sets out to see what law is really like, by linking it at both ends, so to speak, with the facts of social life. In a wide sense it thus represents a sociological trend in jurisprudence; it accepts in principle—or rather it implies an acceptance of—Ihering's conception of the law as a means to an end. But it is not principally interested in elaborating the ends and purposes of the law.

Therefore only one of the principal spokesmen of American realism in jurisprudence[9] has put forward a theory at the end of law, which is in essence a vindication of Bentham's Hedonism.

[9] F. S. Cohen, *Ethical Systems and Legal Ideas* (1933).

But he does not consider the acceptance of this or any other theory of the ends of law as essential to the realistic approach. For the realist movement is not a philosophy of law, it is a modern method of approach which wants to find out what the law is, not what it ought to be. In exploring the law it is positivist, and puts its faith in science. In both these respects it agrees with the adherents of analytical jurisprudence. But instead of the single avenue of logic, realists seek to utilise the multiple avenues which modern science has opened or is opening up, for a more exact and detailed knowledge of the many factors that compose modern life.

The law is both a result of social forces and an instrument of social control. Accordingly, the field covered by the programme of realist jurisprudence is almost unlimited. Human personalities, social environment, economic conditions, business interests, current ideas, popular emotions, all these are both makers and products of the law as it is in life. It therefore is quite true, as one of the leading realists has said, that the essential feature of realist jurisprudence is "a movement in thought and work about the law."[10] As characteristic of this movement, Llewellyn enumerates a number of points, of which the following are most important:

(1) There is no realist school; realism means a movement in thought and work about law.

(2) Realism means a conception of law in flux and as a means to social ends, so that any part is to be examined for its purpose and effect. It implies a concept of society which changes faster than the law.

(3) Realism assumes a temporary divorce of IS and OUGHT for purposes of study. Value judgments must always be appealed to in order to set an objective for any inquiry, but during the inquiry the description has to remain as largely as possible uncontaminated by the desires of the observer or by ethical aims.

(4) Realism distrusts traditional legal rules and concepts in so far as they purport to describe what either courts or people are actually doing. It accepts the definition of rules as "generalised prediction of what the courts will do." In accordance with this belief, realism groups cases and legal situations into narrower categories than was the practice in the past.

(5) Realism insists on the evolution of any parts of the law in terms of its effect.

[10] Llewellyn, "Some Realism about Realism—Responding to Dean Pound," 44 Harv.L.Rev. 1222 (1930-31).

To these points of programme correspond certain lines of approach, of which Llewellyn mentions in particular the following:

(1) A "rationalisation" which does not take the lawyers' arguments at their face value but rather as the art of the trained craftsman to make a decision plausible after he has reached it.

(2) To discriminate among rules with reference to their relative significance.

(3) To replace general legal categories by specific correlations of fact-situations.

(4) This approach involves a study of personal as well as of quantitative factors in the law. By the study of the personality of judges as well as by statistical inquiries into the remedies available in certain situations, realism hopes to predict with more certainty what the courts will do after it has shattered the traditional belief in certainty by its attack upon the logical consistency and water-tightness of the legal system.

All this leads to the conclusion that there must be much greater emphasis on the social effects of law, and of legal decisions in particular, in relation to the particular part of the community which is affected. Lastly, the realist approach agrees with the more radical sociological doctrines and the *Freirechtslehre* that there is a much larger field of free play for the judge in deciding cases than traditional jurisprudence allows. It follows from the power of selection between conflicting precedents and the ability of the lawyer to find an adequate reason *ex post* for any decision.

The borderlines between the functional or realist jurisprudence on one hand and sociological jurisprudence on the other are thus not very clear. Another leading realist defines as the realm of functional jurisprudence the "definition of legal concepts, rules and institutions in terms of judicial decisions or other acts of state force," and as the realm of sociological jurisprudence "the appraisal of law in terms of conduct of human beings who are affected by the law."[11]

He is aware, however, that both movements are in part complementary and in part overlapping, while both "spring from a com-

[11] F. S. Cohen, "The Problems of a Functional Jurisprudence," 1 Mod.L.Rev. 5, 8 (1937).

mon sceptical, scientific, anti-supernatural functional outlook."[12]

That the realist movement in jurisprudence forms, in a broad sense, part of the sociological movement is certain; on the whole, it appears indeed to be complementary to that aspect of sociological jurisprudence which we have described as "sociological idealism"; for it limits itself to a scientific observation of the law in its making, working and effect where the sociologically minded idealists like Pound, Cardozo, Gény, Heck, set out to define the ends of law.

American realism is, in its juristic foundations, the counterpart of the Continental movement of which Ehrlich is the principal exponent. The characteristic difference lies in the different emphasis given to the decision of the law courts. The American realists, like all Anglo-American lawyers, are inclined to place the decision of the law courts in the centre of the law and indeed concentrate the definition of the law on decisions of courts, whereas Ehrlich devotes his principal attention to what he calls: "The living law," that is to say, the body of rules of conduct and habits most of which never come before the courts. The historical and systematic background of lawyers under the two systems plays its part in this difference of approach.

The programme outlined by the realist movement is vast. Only a small portion of the potential field open to a functional investigation has as yet been covered. Much of the attention of realist jurists, as of all sociologists, has been devoted to the question of how to apply a scientific method of observation to the study of law. The relation between natural and social sciences has been one of the principal problems of scientific method ever since the social sciences became conscious of themselves.[13] The answer given to this question by Neo-Kantian philosophy and, in the field of jurisprudence, by Stammler, Kelsen and Radbruch has been discussed in another part of this book. Realists approach the same problem from a different angle, by examining the practical question how far the scientific experiment on which natural sciences rely is applicable to social science in general and to the law in particular.

That social facts are not susceptible to experimental precision in the same degree as natural facts, does not prevent fact study in the

---

[12] *Id.* at 9.
[13] See a fuller discussion above, p. 49 *et seq.*

law from providing infinitely more reliable data than the vague generalisations hitherto prevalent.[14]

The result is that facts must be studied in relation to valuations, ends, purposes. For example, such notions as "monopoly," "competitive régime," "fair and reasonable price," which are essential for legal interpretations of the Sherman Anti-Trust Act, must be ascertained by reference to the results of economic science.[15] Whether an employer is likely to get an injunction in a dispute with his employees must be ascertained not simply by reference to standard phrases such as "freedom of property" or "freedom of contract," but by finding out exactly what the judges concerned have decided in similar situations, or what they are likely to decide in view of their upbringing and interests. If a statute gives a magistrate discretion to substitute educational methods for the punishment of juveniles, the desirability of choosing the one or the other must be studied by analysing the effects of either on the criminality of juveniles in similar circumstances and comparable situations.

These are but a few examples of the tasks that lie ahead of the realists. Some of them have been tackled. It is mainly to statistics, psychology, criminology, economics and general sociology that realists have turned to investigate specific aspects of the law at work. The clearest achievement so far has been the use of statistics as an auxiliary instrument to test the working and the effects of the law. The use of statistics makes it possible, for example, to collect relevant data on the way how different magistrates deal with drinking offences or applications for injunctions in labour disputes, or to compare the attitude of trained judges with that of juries in specific matters.[16] Characteristic of the psychological approach are the inquiries undertaken by Haines, Schroeder, Rodell and others into the personal histories of judges as an aide to the prediction of their likely reaction to particular problems. The decisive change in the attitude of the U.S. Supreme Court towards social legislation, since

[14] M. Cohen in *Social Sciences and their Interrelations* asserts that the significance of social facts cannot be ascertained without reference to socal ideals, and opposes Max Weber, who insists that the scientific study of the social sciences must be restricted to the study of the actual causes of social phenomena. It appears that Cohen misinterprets Weber's scientific relativism. Weber does not eliminate values from sociological research, but denies that the choice between conflicting social ideals is a scientific matter. Radbruch has applied this thesis by investigating legal systems and concepts with reference to their ultimate ideals. This is quite in line with what Cohen demands. See also above, p. 191.

[15] For practical illustrations of these problems, see below, p. 482 *et seq.*

[16] *Cf.*, for example, Oliphant, "Facts, Opinions, and Value-Judgments," 10 Texas L.Rev. 127, 129 (1932).

the replacement of judges during Roosevelt's presidency, or the vacillations of the High Court of Australia between Commonwealth supremacy and state immunity, between a *laissez-faire* interpretation of the Australian Constitution and an interpretation more favourable to economic planning, shows the relevance of such investigations.

How much room and need there is for a more extensive use of social statistics by the lawyer is illustrated by one of the most important Supreme Court decisions of recent years. In *New York v. U.S.*, the issue was whether a state was liable to pay a Federal tax on the sale of mineral waters where the state itself owned and operated the mineral waters. In the dissenting judgment delivered on behalf of himself and Black J., Douglas J. saw in the application of Federal taxing power to state enterprises a threat to state sovereignty. In emphatically denying that exemption of states from Federal taxes would harm essential Federal functions, he said that a proper inquiry would reveal that the extension of state economic and social activities had greatly increased the general welfare of citizens and thus the potential yield for Federal taxes. If, instead of a judicial guess, accurate social statistics were used to show the interrelation of national income and public enterprise in various fields, the decision of this, as of other vital constitutional issues, would still be fundamentally directed by ideological considerations, but the issues would be greatly clarified, and the area of "hunches," prejudices, guesses, ideological preferences would be reduced. Ideology would operate against the background of scientifically established facts.[18]

Jerome Frank in his well-known work, *Law and the Modern Mind* (1930), set out to analyse the law from a psycho-analytical point of view. In the traditional teaching and presentation of the law Frank discerns a desire for certainty which he likens to the infant's craving for infallible authority (father complex). Lawyers in general, and judges in particular, have clung to the myth of legal certainty, by establishing a fictitious system of precedents or of complete codifications, hiding from themselves and others the fact that every case is unique and requires creative decisions. A similar myth surrounds the activities of juries. Analytical jurisprudence expresses this childlike desire for certainty and stability. Frank's

---

[17] 326 U.S. 572 (1946). *Cf.* below, p. 442 *et seq.*
[18] Even statistics are, of course, subject to widely differing interpretations. But they give an irreducible minimum of incontestable facts (*e.g.*, unemployment figures or tax yields). See further above, p. 53 *et seq.*

own ideal is the "completely adult lawyer" typified by Oliver Wendell Holmes.[19] Such a judge needs no external authority to support him, he has a "constructive doubt," so well developed in the natural sciences, which enables him to develop the law in accordance with advancing civilisation. Frank is well aware of the importance of the ideal element in legal development. But he rightly stresses the extent and importance of law-making which has little to do with legal principles and the reported decisions of higher courts, but results from the weighing of evidence, the evaluation of witnesses and other factors incapable of analytical subsumption or theoretical formulation. Frank has therefore suggested special training in fact-finding, evaluation of prejudices, psychology of witnesses, both for trial judges and prospective jurors.[20]

There have been recent investigations[21] of the interrelations between criminal law and crime. Others have examined business practice as a determining factor for decisions in commercial law. Others[22] again have studied the American Constitution, not as it stands on paper but as a living institution which gives certain possibilities of action and function to certain sections of the population. Thurman Arnold, in his *Folklore of Capitalism* (1937), has

[19] For a contrasting view, Llewelyn in *The Common Law Tradition, Deciding Appeals* (1960) defends the rationality of judicial decisions in the United States against what he terms "a crisis in confidence which packs danger." He discounts arguments that stare decisis is dead and predictability gone with it. By an examination of numerous factors in the system which render decisions made by appellate courts reasonable and stable, and of the technical tools for prediction and stability, he concludes that "the work of our appellate courts all over the country is reckonable . . . quite sufficiently for skilled craftsmen to make usable and valuable judgments about likelihoods, and quite sufficiently to render the handling of an appeal a fitting subject for effective and satisfying craftsmanship. (*Id.* at 4). See symposium, "The Common Law Tradition: deciding appeals, Wash. U.L.Q. 1 (1962).

[20] For a later formulation of the late Judge Frank's views, see *Courts on Trial*, 1949. In this work the emphasis on the uncertainties of fact-finding and trial procedure, as proof of the fallacy of "higher court" rules, seems to be carried too far. The legal process consists of both. Better fact-finding or the abolition of juries may be more important for the improvement of law than a better theory of precedent or of statute interpretation. But no modern society could operate without rule generalisation, at least as a necessary basis. The "upper court myth" deserves attack insofar as it pretends to teach the whole law. Such a belief was probably held by Langdell and some others, but it commends itself to few contemporary jurists. The reported cases must continue to serve as the material for legal generalisations which are an essential part of the law though not the whole of it.

[21] *e.g.*, by Michael and Adler, *Crime, Law and Social Science* (1933), by Sheldon and Eleanor Glueck in many works. *Cf.* also Hall, *Crime, Theft and Society* (2nd ed., 1952).

[22] *e.g.*, Llewellyn, 34 Colum.L.Rev. 1 *et seq.* (1934); Beutel, "The Presence of Organized Interests as a Factor in Shaping Legislation," 3 Southern Calif.L.Rev. 10 *et seq.* (1929); Arnold (Symbols of Government (1935)).

analysed the process by which powerful corporations are enveloped by the myth of the sacred right of the individual and thus enabled to carry out a policy of economic domination. The counterpart is provided by the searching analysis which Berle and Means have made of the economic, legal and social power of the corporation in modern capitalist society.[23]

These are but a few examples of the possibilities of realistic approach to the law. From the point of view of legal theory it is less important to give a complete catalogue of realistic studies of positive law than to assess the realist position in the history of legal thought.

The realist movement is firstly emphatically on the side of those who believe in science and thus in an objective criterion as a possible and also a desirable guide for the law. It is secondly empiricist in that it seeks a scientific guidance in observable facts. So great was the insistence of realists on the need for scientific fact study instead of loose generalisation, so violent their anti-metaphysical bias that it appeared to such authoritative critics as Roscoe Pound or Morris Cohen that realists believed in a solution of legal problems by this means alone, to the exclusion of legal ideals. The patent absurdity of such a proposition has been pointed out by these and other critics.[24]

But a great deal of self-searching and clarification has gone on within the realist movement, and more consideration has lately been given to the decisive importance of ultimate valuations and postulates for the approach to any legal problem.[25] The attempt to divorce as neatly as possible the IS and OUGHT of the law is part of this endeavour.

It is also recognised by some if not all realists that realist jurisprudence, forming part of a sociological approach to law, is not a substitute for but a supplement to analytical, historical and ethical jurisprudence.[26] This is a timely and necessary corrective to the exaggerations which have provoked the not unjustified if one-sided criticism of English jurists.[27] No one with the slightest

[23] Berle and Means, *The Modern Corporation and Private Property* (1932).
[24] Pound, "The Call for a Realist Jurisprudence," 44 Harv.L.Rev. 697 (1930-31); 27 Colum.L.Rev. 237 (1927).
[25] Llewellyn, "The Constitution as an Institution," 40 Colum.L.Rev. 581 (1940); McDougal, "Fuller v. The American Legal Realists," 50 Yale.L.J. 827 (1940-41).
[26] *Cf.* F. S. Cohen, 1 Mod.L.Rev. *op. cit.* at 5.
[27] *e.g.*, Allen, *Law in the Making* (5th ed.), 41 *et seq.* (but *cf.* the much more balanced criticism in the 6th ed. of this work. 41 *et seq.*; Goodhart in *Modern Theories of Law*, 1 *et seq.*; and, for an American attack, Fuller, *The Law in Quest of Itself* (1940).

experience of law at work, least of all Holmes J., the idol of realists, would minimise the immense function of analytical jurisprudence in the everyday administration of justice. The large majority of legal decisions and other practical legal problems are matters of routine in which precedent and the reliance upon analytical rules are sufficient to meet the situation. Even in the intensely political legal administration of totalitarian states this applies to the majority of cases. It is quantitatively a small but qualitatively a decisive number of legal situations which routine and analytical methods are insufficient to meet. The original gap between the realist movement and those who, in one way or another, emphasise the importance of the ideal element in the law is further narrowed by the later admission of leading realists[28] that the search for justice is a paramount concern of the lawyer.

Realist jurisprudence thus appears in its true perspective, namely as an attempt to rationalise and modernise the law—both the administration of law and the material for legislative change—by utilising scientific methods and the results reached in those fields of social life with which the social law is inevitably linked. The guidance must always come from the social ideals which direct a given legal order. But by the use of these scientific instruments the law can be made more rational, articulate, scientific, objective.

But if the aim is now tolerably clear, this is far less true of the ways and means. This appears to be largely the result of the divergent ways in which the different sciences may be invoked in aid of the law. One of the necessary objectives of law—this, at least, is beyond dispute—is certainty. Analytical jurisprudence seeks to achieve certainty by relying on an allegedly complete logical system. Realism uses psychology to demolish this myth of certainty, and the psychologists among the realists, like Jerome Frank, have, at times, appeared to build up this lack of certainty into a philosophy very similar to the *Freirechtslehre*. For what else is the "completely adult lawyer" but the wise and creative judge who, unfettered by paragraphs and precedents, finds justice through a clear and cool perception and valuation of the social issues at stake. The philosopher-king of Plato's *Republic* appears in the cloak of the modern lawyer.

On the other hand, the use of statistics, economics, criminology, etc., is meant to introduce a new certainty into the knowledge of

---

[28] Llewellyn, *op. cit.*, note 1. Frank, "Say it with Music," 61 Harv.L.Rev. 221, 935, note 40 (1948).

law: a certainty based on scientific experiment instead of a fallacious logic.

The realist approach to legal problems is thus essentially a ferment which can be used for very different ideologies. The whole of the realist approach appears to rest, however, upon an "initial hypothesis." The realist movement has arisen and can operate only where there is sufficient freedom in the play of social forces to make this scientific weighing possible in the administration of law; it therefore demands a society which admits objectivity, that is a fundamentally tolerant society. A totalitarian system has no room for realist jurisprudence.[29] For the political will of the legislator permeates every sphere of law with such force and exclusiveness that such factors as the economic play of forces, personal leanings, business habits, etc., are relegated to a very subordinate function, although they are not entirely excluded. Only where the legislator is comparatively passive and neutral in regard to the social forces at work in the society, can a movement like that of American realism operate and prosper.

THE SCANDINAVIAN REALISTS

Although the association of a particular movement in legal or political thought with national or regional characteristics is not often justified, it has been so in the case of the "American" realist movement, whose origin, philosophy and representatives are associated with a particular period and trend of American thinking. It is no less justified to speak of a modern "Scandinavian realism" in legal thinking, because modern Scandinavian jurists have developed a characteristic approach to law that has little parallel in other countries. Although the word "realism" has increasingly come to be associated with this modern movement in Scandinavian legal thinking,[30] this apparent similarity to the American realist movement is a purely verbal one. American realism is, as we have seen, the product of a pragmatist and behaviourist approach to social institutions. Lawyers have developed it, with a characteristic Anglo-American emphasis on the work of courts and judicial behaviour, as a corrective to the philosophy of analytical positivism which dominated Anglo-American jurisprudence in the nineteenth

---

[29] Larenz, *Rechs- und Staatsphilosophie der Gegenwart* (2nd ed., 1935).
[30] See Ross, *Towards a Realistic Jurisprudence* (1946); Dias, *Jurisprudence*, 484 *et seq.* (2nd ed. 1964).

century. They have stressed law in action, law as experience, as against legal conceptionalism. They have, however, been little concerned with the transcendental bases of law. While they have tended to agree with a relativistic philosophy of law, American realists have, with the exception of Felix Cohen, not sought to elaborate any philosophy of values. They have, in Llewellyn's words, assumed "a temporary divorce of IS and OUGHT for purposes of study."[31]

By contrast, Scandinavian "realism" is essentially a philosophical critique of the metaphysical foundations of law. Rejecting the down-to-earth approach and language of the American realists, it has a distinct Continental flavour, in its critical and often heavily abstract discussion of first principles. A certain unity of approach— not necessarily acknowledged by its exponents—is due to the influence exercised upon the leading contemporary representatives of Scandinavian "realism"—Olivecrona, Lundstedt and, to a lesser extent, Ross—by their teacher, Axel Hägerström.

With differences only in emphasis, all the above-mentioned jurists join hands in the total rejection of natural law philosophy and, indeed, of any absolute ideas of justice, as controlling and directing any positive system of law. In so far as they are articulate on legal values, the Scandinavian "realists" are of necessity relativists, *i.e.*, they deny that rules of legal conduct can be compellingly derived from immutable principles of justice.[32] The virtual absence of natural law thinking in modern Scandinavian jurisprudence is, no doubt, in part, attributable to the non-existence of any significant Catholic element in Scandinavia. For the mainstay of natural law philosophy—at least since the decline of eighteenth-century rationalism—has been the scholastic or neo-scholastic philosophy of the Catholic Church, and of the legal philosophers inspired by scholastic doctrine. The rejection of natural law would not, however, distinguish modern Scandinavian jurisprudence from the many other jurists of varying persuasions who equally reject natural law philosophy. The characteristic and valuable contribution of Hägerström and his disciples has been to probe beyond the

---

[31] See above, p. 296.
[32] See, for example, Ross, *On Law and Justice*, Chap. 12 (1959). Similarly, Castberg, *Problems of Legal Philosophy*, 112 (2d ed., 1957) who cannot generally be classed with the above-mentioned jurists, refutes "the belief in a 'natural law' in the sense of a complete, integral system of law," but he accepts, somewhat like Stammler or Charmont, a "natural law" in the sense of rules of ideal law, which are adapted to the changing conditions of life.

rejection of transcendental justice into the validity of the entire apparatus of "rights," "duties," "sovereignty," "commands," and other basic legal concepts which have formed the mainstay of analytical jurisprudence in the work of Austin and his Anglo-American successors as well as in Continental analytical positivism.[33] Although the analytical positivists, whether Austin or Binding, rejected natural law or any other super-positive ideas of justice, they substituted for such absolute imperatives, the sovereignty of the modern state, which demands unconditional obedience to its commands, and which by virtue of its supreme power, bestows rights and duties on its subjects. In this, Hägerström and his successors have detected a "surreptitious introduction of ideas taken from natural law."[34]

A criticism of a "collective" or "general" will, or of a "will of the state," as a mystical concept that tends to legitimise the omnipotence of those in command of the machinery of the state in a manner basically similar to natural law methods, is the most important critical contribution of this school of thought.[35] Up to that point, the Scandinavian jurists would seem to agree with Kelsen's critique of the hidden or disguised idealistic philosophies as well as with Duguit's and Kelsen's attacks on the "command" and "will" theories of state and sovereignty. But Kelsen's work is in turn subjected to severe criticism, on the ground that, by detaching the "pure science of law" from all social reality, he avoids the real problems of the existence and validity of law.[36] In the *Grundnorm* which, even though it is a mere logical construct, is, in the theory of the Vienna school, the source of validity and comparison for all subordinate legislative and other legal actions, Hägerström detects a kind of mystical quasi-theology, akin to the way in which, in ancient Rome, "the act of legislation was regarded as directly creating, in a mystical and magical way, the connection between legal fact and legal consequence which was expressed in words."[37] In fact, the *Grundnorm* theory is seen as a kind of natural law philosophy, emptied of its substance, and in this criticism Häger-

---

[33] See above, Chaps. 22, 23.

[34] Hägerström, *Inquiries into the Nature of Law and Morals*, 48 (ed. Olivecrona, trans. Broad, 1953).

[35] See Hägerström, *op. cit.*, Chap. II; Olivecrona, *Law as Fact*, Chap. I (1939).

[36] Hägerström, *op. cit.*, Chap. IV.

[37] Hägerström, *op. cit.* at 274. Hägerström's theory of the magical origin of the Roman concept of obligation is elaborated in his work, "Der römische Obligationsbegriff im Lichte der allgemeinen römischen Rechtsanschauung" (1937) in *Modern Theories of Law*.

ström would seem to join hands with a disciple of Kelsen,[38] though, from entirely different premises and with entirely different objectives.

But what do the Scandinavian critics put in the place of the whole structure of basic norms, commands, rights, duties, *et cetera*? They certainly do not deny either the validity or the reality of law as a body of "rules about force, rules which contain patterns of conduct for the exercise of force."[39] Even in the work of the most radical of the critics, Lundstedt,[40] it is assumed throughout that there is a "law," as a machinery that works, that is propelled by certain forces and that induces people to behave in a certain way, that remains apparently distinct from theology and morality, but also from mere administration.[41] But what is law, if it is neither the emanation of a natural order of things, whether imposed by God or reason, nor a system of commands issuing from a sovereign, whether in the psychological "command" version (Austin) or in the logical and hypothetical norm structure derived from a basic norm (Kelsen)? In denying the reality of "rights," the Scandinavian jurists agree with Kelsen,[42] as with Duguit[43] though from different premises. But they cannot substitute, like Kelsen, the hierarchical structure of "pure" norms, or, like Duguit, a quasi-natural law principle of social solidarity that makes individual rights both redundant and repulsive. Quite logically, the Scandinavian critics go further in denying the reality of "duties" as well as of "rights." For Olivecrona, who, in a lucid and concise work, has essentially illuminated Hägerström's ideas, any theory of a "binding" force of law is, whether in its natural law or positivist version, a form of transcendentalism.

Positive rights are no more real than natural rights, except that they have "a corollary" in an actual security and an actual power in consequence of the regular functioning of the legal machinery.[44] For the notion of rules of law as commands of the state (implying a fictitious general will) Olivecrona substitutes the concept of "independent imperatives." These cannot be defined as commands.

---

[38] Lauterpacht's essay on Kelsen as quoted above, at 286.

[39] Olivecrona, *Law as Fact* at 134.

[40] See Lundstedt, *Legal Thinking Revised* (1956).

[41] In Lundstedt's rambling and intensely polemic and badly organised work, it is sometimes difficult to see the differences between his approach and that, for example, of Pashukanis, for whom, in a Socialist community, all law becomes administration.

[42] Above, p. 280.

[43] Above, p. 232.

[44] Olivecrona, *op. cit.* at 119.

To those who take cognisance of the rules, the law-givers are for the most part entirely unknown. They have only the imperative statements as such before them, isolated from the law-givers, who may have died a hundred years ago. These commands are addressed to specific persons. Law is fact, a body of rules about the use of organised force, without which community life is unthinkable. It is obeyed by the fear of force rather than by the direct use of it because the rules of law are a body of "independent imperatives" representing the organised force in a community as long as they are effectively obeyed. There is, for Olivecrona, no real problem of a "final" explanation of the law.[45] The revolution is only one step in the development of the law. Without transcendental interpolations, the law can never be traced back to its "ultimate origin." When, through effective force and propaganda a new set of independent imperatives has established itself effectively in a society, a new channel has been given to a rebel, and that is the end of it.

The emphatic rejection of any metaphysical basis of law is shared by Alf Ross whose concept of the validity of law combines behaviouristic and psychological aspects:

"In the concept of validity two points are involved: partially the outward observable and regular compliance with the pattern of action, and partly the experience of this pattern of action as being a socially binding norm."[46]

The rejection of legal ideology in any form, including the whole concept of justice, has been carried to extreme length by the Swedish jurist, Wilhelm Lundstedt, whose main work has been published in English, shortly after his death in 1955, under the title of *Legal Thinking Revised*. As this title suggests, Lundstedt claims no less than that he has completely revised the foundations of legal thinking.[47] For Lundstedt, "law" is nothing but the very life of mankind in organised groups and the conditions which make possible peaceful co-existence of masses of individuals and social groups and the co-operation for other ends than mere existence and propagation.[48] This formulation does not differ greatly from the more tersely stated definition of the function of law by Olivecrona or, indeed, from the objectives of legal order as stated by

[45] *Id.* at 72 *et seq.*
[46] Ross, *Law and Justice*, 371 (1959).
[47] A corollary of this is his condemnation of almost everybody else, from the natural law philosophers to the representatives of *Interessenjurisprudenz*, American realists, Roscoe Pound, and nearer home, the "Dane," Ross.
[48] Lundstedt, at 72 *et seq.*

Soviet jurists. In his denunciation of the concepts of rights and duties, and the rejection of transcendental ideas of justice, Lundstedt is in accord with the other Scandinavian "realist" jurists. What Lundstedt means by his rejection of the "method of justice" which, in his opinion, characterises and condemns all traditional jurisprudence[49] is far less clear, for he often speaks throughout his work of the outstanding importance in legal machinery of the feeling "for the right and against the wrong," and of the "common sense of justice." "It is only as bridled and checked by the legal machinery that the feelings of equity and justice render to society their indispensable service."[50] The great mistake of traditional jurisprudence, according to Lundstedt, is to have regarded the sense of justice or right as inspiring and guiding the law, whereas in fact "the feelings of justice are guided and directed by the laws, as enforced, *i.e.*, as maintained."[51] Law at any particular time and in any particular society is determined by "social welfare," which Lundstedt defines in a great variety of formulations, spread throughout his lengthy and polemical tirade.[52]

As a guiding motive for legal activities, social welfare means, "in the first place the encouragement in the best possible way of that—according to what everybody standing above a certain minimum degree of culture is able to understand—which people in general actually strive to attain."[53] This includes such familiar values as the minimum requirements of material life, security of life, limb and property, the greatest possible freedom of action, "in brief, all conceivable material comfort as well as the protection of spiritual interests." This would appear to be very similar to the cataloguing of human wants and interests undertaken by Roscoe Pound or by the representatives of German *Interessenjurisprudenz,* but Lundstedt denies this vehemently, and he particularly criticises Pound for having established yet another legal ideology, whereas he, Lundstedt, simply wishes to establish "as a fact what can be observed in general, namely, that the overwhelming majority of

---

[49] *i.e.*, almost everybody except himself, his teacher Hägerström, and with some qualifications, Olivecrona.

[50] Lundstedt, *op. cit.* at 169.

[51] *Id.* at 144.

[52] The interpretation of Lundstedt's work, at least in English, is made much more difficult by the tortuous style of his writing, which contrasts with the lucid and clear style of Olivecrona and Ross who have been assisted by English editors or translators. However, Professor Broad has made Hägerström's difficult style of writing as accessible as is humanly possible to English readers.

[53] Lundstedt, *op. cit.* at 140.

human beings . . . wish to live and develop their lives' possibilities."[54]

The area of social welfare is described as "comprising the general spirit of enterprise and its postulate" and "a general sense of security." From this derive such postulates as "the common production of wealth and common exchange of commodities, the reliability of promises, the sense of safety to life and to limb, *et cetera.*"[55] The balance between these various interests has obviously to be struck differently at different times and under different circumstances—and the consideration of "social welfare" leads Lundstedt, for example, to accept strict liability in tort as against the supremacy of the principle of guilt—but in all these respects the philosophies of "social engineering" or "balancing of interest" as analysed elsewhere in this book[56] take no basically different position.[57] Put as briefly as possible, Lundstedt appears to say that the legal machinery, *i.e.*, the compound of legislative, administrative and judicial activities, must be determined without any preconceived ideology, by the best possible balance between competing social demands, deeds and aspirations of a certain community. There is little new in this except the author's claim to originality.

As is so often the case with intellectual criticism, the critical aspects of the Scandinavian "realist" movement are more significant that its positive achievement. Its main contribution has been to pursue the detection of open or hidden legal ideologies beyond the usual criticism of natural law doctrines into the positivist concepts of command, sovereignty, rights and duties.[58] By implication, rather than as a matter of articulate philosophy, the Scandinavian

[54] *Id.* at 140.

[55] *Id.* at 137 *et seq.*

[56] See below, p. 336 *et seq.*

[57] Lundstedt apparently misinterprets Pound's formulation of categories of interests as establishing a definite hierarchy. He says that "Pound's fundamental idea of law turns out to be the well-known legal ideology although expressed in a somewhat unusual way" (*Id.* at 351). The same may, however, be said with at least equal justification of Lundstedt's own formulations, except that they are far more difficult to follow.

[58] It should be noted, however, that Alf Ross, in his recent work, *e.g.*, *On Law and Justice*, Chap. VI, and "Tû-Tû" 70 Harv.L.Rev. 812, (1957), while joining in the denunciation of the fallacies of absolute concepts of "rights," has convincingly shown that "the concept of rights is a tool in the technique of presentation." In other words, it serves as a convenient "shorthand," a simplification of a multitude of conditioning facts and conditioned consequences, *e.g.*, in the description of "ownership." As long as we are aware that the "right" of ownership does not imply a claim derived from natural law or other transcendental ideas, it is a convenient and indeed indispensable tool of legal technique. In its absence, a cumbrous sequence of propositions would be needed to describe the legal aspects of what is summed up in "ownership."

"realists" have demonstrated that any legal order must be con-ditioned upon a certain scale of values, which can be assessed not in absolute terms but with regard to the social needs changing with times, nations and circumstances. Whether law is described as a "fact," as a "machinery in action," or in any other manner, it is directed to certain ends.

Utilitarianism, the Jurisprudence of Interests and
the New Legal Idealism

CHAPTER 26

LAW AND THE PURSUIT OF INTERESTS

BENTHAM'S UTILITARIANISM

IN one sense utilitarianism represents a reaction against the metaphysical and abstract character of eighteenth century political and legal philosophy. Bentham, its founder, devotes much of his work to violent attacks upon the whole natural law conception. But if he is impatient with the vagueness and the inconsistencies of the natural law theories, if utilitariansm represents one of the periodical movements from the abstract to the concrete, from the idealistic to the materialistic, from the *a priori* to the empirical, this movement at the same time expresses aims particularly characteristic of the nineteenth century.

Bentham's legal philosophy is a utilitarian individualism. His individualism inspired his numerous and vigorous legislative efforts, all directed towards the emancipation of the individual from the many constitutional restrictions and iniquities which impeded, in England at any rate, the free play of forces that was to give full scope to individual development. Once these iniquities (such as the "rotten boroughs") were removed and individuals had attained equality of position, legislation should withdraw and the free play of forces would serve the general interest best.

The same individualism permeates Bentham's utilitarian philosophy. To sum up the essence of this philosophy in Bentham's own words:

Nature has placed man under the empire of pleasure and pain. We owe to them all our ideas, we refer to them all our judgments, and all the determination of our life. He who pretends to withdraw himself from this subjection knows not what he says. His only object is to seek pleasure and to shun pain. . . . These eternal and irresistible sentiments ought to be the great study of the moralist and the legislator. The principle of utility subjects everything to these two motives.[1]

Pleasure and pain are Bentham's "Law of Nature." Utility he

[1] Bentham, *Theory of Legislation*, 2.

defines as expressing "the property or tendency of a thing to prevent some evil or to procure some good." Now good is pleasure, evil is pain:

> That which is conformable to the utility or the interest of an individual is what tends to augment the total sum of his happiness. That which is conformable to the utility or the interests of a community is what tends to augment the total sum of the happiness of the individuals that compose it.[2]

Thus good and evil are linked to pleasure and pain, and the task of law is to serve the good and avoid the evil, that is to serve utility. Pleasure and pain replace, for Bentham, such notions as justice and injustice, morality or immorality, virtue or vice. This sensualistic evaluation of life is somewhat modified, however, by Bentham's analysis of the types of pleasure and pain. Sense, riches and power are among the pleasures tabled by Bentham; but among others are friendship, good reputation, benevolence, knowledge and association. Pains, on the whole, are the counterparts of pleasures. The measure of pain either depends above all on their extent, and the individual's pain (therefore an evil to be avoided) may be one caused to him because of his relationship with or interest in the first sufferer.

Bentham is an individualist and an egalitarian. There is for him no myth of the *volonté générale* or of an organic community. The individual is an end in himself; every man counts for one, and the aim of law is the creation of conditions which make possible the maximum freedom of each individual so that he may pursue what is good for him.

But Bentham, the social and legislative reformer, is no anarchist. He knows that law must serve the totality of the individuals in a community. The ultimate end of legislation is to him the greatest happiness of the greatest number. As Hobhouse has pointed out,[3] the elaboration of this principle by Bentham was bound to result in the subordination of individual right to community needs. The greatest happiness principle is at the root of Bentham's decided opposition to any theory of inalienable natural rights. Article 2 of the French Declaration of the Rights of Man (1789) had declared:

> The end of every political association is the conservation of the natural and imprescriptible rights of man. These rights are liberty, property, security and resistance to aggression.

[2] *Id.* at 2.
[3] Hobhouse, *Liberalism*, 65 *et seq.*

Article 1 of the Convention of 1793 shifted the emphasis:

> The end of society is the common happiness. Government is instituted to guarantee to man the enjoyment of his natural and imprescriptible rights.

Bentham, whose prestige in revolutionary France as a rationalist and as a social and legal reformer was great, had mercilessly criticised the use of natural law phrases in the early drafts of revolutionary French Constitutions. The shift from the original insistence on natural rights to the paramountcy of social happiness is to a considerable extent due to Bentham's influence. Bentham was not altogether hostile to the recognition of permanent principles of law. In his essay on the "Influence of Time and Place in Matters of Legislation"[4] he admits that there are rules, such as the proper proportion between offence and punishment, between merit and reward, the classification of criminal offences, which, if they are just and proper now,

> would at any time have been so and will be so everywhere and to the end of time. . . . They will hold good so long as pleasure is pleasure and pain is pain . . . so long as difference of sex attracts, so long as neighbours need the help of neighbours.

Bentham here recognises certain natural law principles not far removed from those formulated by Aristotle and Grotius, under the thin disguise of his pleasure and pain philosophy, but this limited concession to natural law philosophy is insignificant compared with his insistence on the social purpose and subservience of law. This brings Bentham much closer to modern legal thought than to his contemporaries or to the predominant legal philosophy of the nineteenth century. Despite Bentham's personal inclination towards the sanctity of individual property and enterprise, he consistently refused to regard the right of property as a natural right and defined it as an expectation of enjoyment conferred by positive law.[5] Bentham also anticipated modern relativists in emphasising that the premises of any legal or political philosophy were a matter of faith and not themselves capable of deduction. In regard to his own utilitarian philosophy he said:

---

[4] Bentham, 1 *Collected Works*, 193.

[5] *Cf.* Bentham, *The Limits of Jurisprudence Defined* (Everett ed., 1945). This treatise, written in 1782 and only recently discovered by Mr. Everett among Bentham's unpublished manuscripts preserved at University College, London, reveals Bentham as one of the greatest analytical jurists of all time. See Friedmann, 64 L.Q.Rev. 341 (1948).

Has the rectitude of this principle ever been formally tested? . . . Is it susceptible to any direct proof? It should seem not; for that which is used to prove everything else cannot itself be proved; a chain of proofs must have their commencement somewhere. . . . To give such proofs is as impossible as it is needless.[6]

Is the happiness of the greatest number necessarily identical with the sum of the pleasures of each individual? Bentham knows that the unrestrained pursuit of happiness by each might well lead to a state of affairs where "*homo homini lupus.*" But his philosophy prevents him from finding a solution in such notions as justice, duty, virtue or subordination to the common good. The link he construes between the happiness of one and that of all is sympathy. Amidst unhappiness no one would be happy. It is painful and thus bad to be among unhappy people. Moreover, unrestrained egoism by one would justify similar behaviour by everyone else and thus reduce his own happiness.

Horribile dictu, we are more or less back to Kant and his definition of law. Only the result is not derived from the categorical imperative, but from the pursuit of pleasure. The practical problem remains: Is the individual or the legislator the best agent to produce the maximum happiness of all? Here we come to an apparent paradox. Bentham's faith was an individualistic one. As a representative of the rising English middle class he believed in individual initiative and freedom of action. He therefore was an ardent apostle of *laissez-faire* in economics.[7] He believed that if everyone looked after himself, the general good, that is the greatest happiness of the greatest number, would be secured.[8]

Yet Bentham was one of the most active and successful of social reformers[9] through the instrument of legislation, that is through measures by which the state regulates the conditions of life of all. Dicey has brilliantly analysed this paradox in his *Law and Public Opinion in England*. Bentham devoted his life to the removal of the numerous inequalities which hampered the rising English democracy, survivals from the age of feudalism and landed gentry.

---

[6] Bentham, *Introduction to the Principles of Morals and Legislation*, p. 84.

[7] *Cf.*, in particular, his pamphlet *In Defence of Usury*.

[8] A strange application of this creed is Spencer's assertion (*Social Statics*, Chap. 28) that epidemics were better than the curtailment of individual freedom through State Boards of Health.

[9] He was responsible for numerous, in some cases fundamental, reforms in electoral and constitutional law, poor law, criminal law, procedural law and the law of evidence. For a survey of the various aspects of Bentham's work, see *Jeremy Bentham and the Law: A Symposium* (1948).

He imagined that, once this task had been achieved, the law could withdraw, confine itself to a minimum of restraining activity. In his *Theory of Legislation* Bentham defines the main functions of law as being: to provide subsistence, to aim at abundance, to encourage equality and to maintain security. Of these, security is the most important, and it is this emphasis on the protective function of law which links Bentham with the analytical positivists, with whom he has otherwise little in common. It was in order to attain the second aim, equality of opportunity, that Bentham did so much to develop reforming legislation. He hoped that, once this reforming legislation had removed the many obstacles in the way of such equality, it would retire and leave the field to free individual enterprise and competition. But, by a strange irony of history, the weapon of legislation, which Bentham had so much helped to forge, was destined to be used more and more to restrict individual freedom in economic matters, as social problems and evils of undreamt magnitude compelled the state to abandon this passive attitude to economic and social problems and to introduce social and economic reforms through the instrument of legislation.

Much criticism has been directed against Bentham's allegedly hedonistic philosophy, his materialism and the faultiness of his premises. One of the first and greatest of his critics was Bentham's own disciple, John Stuart Mill. It is, however, easy to exaggerate the extent of this weakness. As has been shown, Bentham formulated in utilitarian terminology many maxims which metaphysical philosophers would have expressed in terms of duty and natural law principles. Bentham was not a great philosopher, but a great jurist and an even greater social reformer. Far more important than the theoretic weakness of his philosophy is the unity of thought between Bentham's first principles and his practical efforts as a legal and social reformer. Bentham laid the foundations for the predominant trend in modern legal philosophy by testing every legal action or principle in terms of the maximisation of pleasure and the minimisation of pain. In other words, he saw law as a balance of interests. This is particularly evident in Bentham's proposals on the reform of criminal law. For example, Bentham argues against the punishment of homosexuality because he thinks that the difficulties in tracing and accurately defining this offence, as well as the relatively small harm done to society by non-punishment, outweigh the interests of the community in punishment. Again, in his proposals for the reform of poor law which he worked out down to the smallest detail of architectural measurements and sanitation, Bentham consistently balances the interest of a free individualistic economy against the interest of society in usefully occupying paupers in industrial production.[10]

The main weaknesses of Bentham's work derive from two short-comings. One is Bentham's abstract and doctrinaire rationalism which prevents him from seeing man in all his complexity, in his blend of materialism and idealism, of nobility and baseness, of egoism and altruism. This leads Bentham to an over-estimate of the powers of the legislator and an under-estimate of the need for individualising discretion and flexibility in the application of law. Bentham believed in the possibility of complete scientific codification, once legislation was based on rational principles. So strong was his naïve belief in the universality of the scientific principles of codification that he worked with equal enthusiasm, and disregard for national or historical differences, on codifications for England, France, Russia and the South American republics. The same attitude of mind, reinforced by justified distrust of the judicial procedure in England at that time,[11] made Bentham an enemy of all liberal judicial interpretation. Yet the experience of codification in all countries has shown the need for an elastic and liberal judicial interpretation in aid rather than in defiance of the code.[12]

The second fundamental weakness stems from Bentham's failure to develop clearly his own conception of the balance between individual and community interests. Bentham believes that the interests of an unlimited number of individuals are automatically conducive to the interests of the community, but he nowhere really explains why this should be so. In his last great work, *The Constitutional Code*, Bentham resorts to a formula strongly reminiscent of Hegel:

Meantime, this function of interests, how can it be fixed? The nature of the case admits of one method which is of destroying the influence and power of whatever sinister interest the situation of the individual may expose him to the action of; this being accomplished, he will thereby be virtually divested of all such sinister interests; remains, as the only interest whereby his conduct can be determined, his

[10] Bentham's most important attempt in this direction is his pamphlet on *Pauper Management Improved*.

[11] Lord Eldon and the abuses of equity procedure were the targets of some of Bentham's most bitter and persistent criticism.

[12] *Cf.* below, p. 533 *et seq.*, and in particular the contrast between the Napoleonic Codes and the Prussian *Allgemeine Landrecht* of Frederick II.

right and proper interest, that interest which consists in the share he has in the universal interest, which is the same thing as to say that interest which is in accordance with the universal interest, taken in the aggregate.[13]

This delusion about the necessary identity of individual and communal happiness is reflected in some of Bentham's concrete proposals. In his *Theory of Legislation* Bentham expresses the belief that freedom of enterprise will automatically lead to greater equality:

> It is worthy of remark that, in a nation prosperous in its agriculture, its manufactures, and its commerce, there is a continual progress towards equality. If the laws do nothing to combat it, if they do not maintain certain monopolies, if they put no shackles upon industry and trade, if they do not permit entails, we see great property divided land by land, without effort, without revolution, without shock, and a much greater number of men coming to participate in the modern phase of fortune. . . . We are at no great distance from those ages of feudalism when the world was divided into two classes: a few great proprietors who were everything, and a multitude of servants, who were nothing. These pyramidal heights have disappeared or have fallen; and from their ruins industrious men have formed those new establishments, the great number of which tests the comparable happiness of modern civilisation.[14]

Consequently Bentham contradicts himself when weighing up the relative importance of self-interest and disinterestedness in public affairs. On the one hand, in his proposals for the reform of poor law, he advocates the establishment of productive centres of industry for the poor which are to be conducted according to commercial principles or, as modern protagonists would put it, according to the "profit motive":

> The notion which insists upon disinterestedness . . . as an indispensable qualification . . . in the instruction of a person bearing a part in the management of such a concern, is a notion respectable in its source but the most prejudicial in its tendency of any that can be imagined. . . . That principle of action is most to be depended upon, whose influence is most powerful, most consistent, most uniform, most lasting, and most general among mankind. Personal interest is that principle.[15]

On the other hand, Bentham proclaims the principle of disinterestedness for the reform of public administration. This leads him to propose not only general parsimony in public administration, but

[13] Bentham, *Constitutional Code*, 7.
[14] Bentham, *Theory of Legislation*, 128.
[15] Bentham, *Pauper Management Improved*, 55.

deliberate depression of public salaries and emoluments in order to exclude the motive of self-interest in the public service. Yet Bentham clearly assigns to the state the task of preventing the accumulation of wealth in the opulent few at the expense of the many. While, in his earlier *Theory of Legislation*, he apparently thought that equality would come automatically, in his last work he seems to acknowledge the necessity of state action:

> The principle of equality requires that so far as may be, without taking away the inducement to productive industry and frugality, the opulent few should be prevented from doing injury to the indigenous many, by means of the power necessarily and properly attached to opulence . . .hence, opportunity should be taken of breaking down large masses into smaller ones.[16]

Bentham thus prevented himself, by his individualist economic philosophy, from realising the full dynamic of his own thought on legal and social reform. He attempted to stabilise the respective spheres of private interests and public administration at a level which was soon made illusory by the development of modern industrial society. Given the identical postulate of a society of free men living in a condition of equality of opportunity, Bentham shared with many Marxists the illusion of an automatic and necessary development of society towards a certain goal. He marked out but failed to solve the problem how far the state would go to ensure, by deliberate and planned action, the attainment of equality of opportunity without the destruction of fundamental freedoms.

Stripped of all technicalities and accidentals, Bentham's significance in the history of legal thought can be summed up in the following points.

(1) He links philosophical premises with practical legal propositions.
(2) He places individualism upon a new materialistic basis.
(3) He relates and subordinates the rights of the self-contained individual to the happiness of the greatest number of individuals—all with equal claims—living in a community.
(4) He directs the aims of law to practical social purposes instead of abstract propositions.
(5) He lays the basis for a new relativist tendency in jurisprudence which later will be called sociological jurisprudence

---

[16] Bentham, *Constitutional Code*, 34 (1830).

and relates law to definite social purposes and a balance of interests.

(6) He sees a paramount object of law in the guarantee of security, a function developed, to the neglect of others, by analytical positivism.

(7) He stresses the need and develops the technique of conscious law-making by codification as against judicial law-making or evolution by custom.

John Stuart Mill

John Stuart Mill's part in legal theory lies in his investigations on the relations of justice, utility, individual interests and general interest.[17] It was too naïve an assumption of Bentham's to believe that there was no conflict between individual and general utility. Indeed, he half-heartedly arrives at a utilitarian version of Kant's formula of the aim of law, but from his point of view it remains quite unconvincing why the individual should restrain his unfettered pursuit of happiness, in the interest of the other members of the community. The notion of sympathy half covers an admission that there are higher and lower values in social life and the lower has to yield to the higher. Bentham derides justice and similar notions. Mill, on the contrary, investigates the nature of justice and its relations to utility. He rightly perceives that traditionally the eternal notions of justice and injustice are opposed to the shifting and less noble notions of utility and interest. He rightly observes that in fact nothing has been more unstable and controversial than the meaning of justice.

What Mill himself attempts is a synthesis between justice and utility. The link is, somewhat surprisingly, the sentiment of justice. It means in essence the individual feeling of right which would in itself lead the individual to resent and desire retaliation for anything disagreeable to him, tempered and "moralised" by the social feeling:

> Just persons resenting a hurt to society though not otherwise a hurt to themselves, and not resenting a hurt to themselves however painful, unless it be of the kind which society has a common interest with them in the repression of.[18]

[17] Mill, *Utilitarianism* (1863). His earlier book, *On Liberty* (1859), is still more strongly under Bentham's influence.
[18] Mill, *Utilitarianism, op. cit.* at 48.

Accordingly Mills adapts Kant's categorical imperative by saying that our conduct should be such that all rational beings might adopt with benefit to their collective interest. The "animal desire to repel or retaliate a hurt or damage to oneself" is widened and thereby "moralised" so as to include all persons. Individual self-assertion and consciousness of the general good then combine in the sentiment of justice. This association between the individual and the general good leads Mill to a theory of punishment not very different from Hegel's. In thinking of the general interest the criminal himself is led to consider his crime as an evil. For Hegel punishment is the negation of the crime and thus expresses the rational will of the criminal himself. And natural law reminiscences come to our minds when we read:

> Our notion, therefore, of the claim we have on our fellow-creature to join in making safe for us the very groundwork of our existence, gathers feelings around it so much more intense than those concerned in any of the more common cases of utility, that the difference in degree becomes a real difference in kind. The claim assumes that character of absoluteness . . . which constitutes the distinction between the feeling of right and wrong and that of ordinary expediency. . . .

This is how Mill links justice with general utility, and it is evident that the approach of this disciple of Bentham's differs very much from that of his master. The emphasis shifts from the individual to the general interest, and it is in reality duty rather than right, or self-seeking interest, or pleasure, which underlies Mill's conception of the law.[19] But the conflict between self-interest and general good is eliminated (in theory) by playing off the intellectual against the animal instinct in human nature. This means, once more, going back to Aristotle and, strange bedfellows as they may seem, the utilitarian Mill and the metaphysician Hegel reach amazingly similar conclusions in eliminating the dualism between individual and social interest, by sublimating the individual's will and his sentiment for justice. Mill is not, however, led to glorify the state, like Hegel.

RUDOLPH VON IHERING AND THE FOUNDATION OF SOCIOLOGICAL JURISPRUDENCE

Ihering's utilitarianism is, in many ways, a distinct advance from

---

[19] Lorimer describes Mill's philosophy as "transcendental eudaemonism." in his *Institutes of Law*, 48 (1875).

English utilitarianism, and his legal philosophy as developed mainly in his principal work, *Der Zweck im Recht* (1877-83),[20] is altogether one of the most important events in the history of legal thought.

Ihering's system develops aspects of Austinian positivism and combines them with principles of utilitarianism as established by Bentham and developed by Mill. It also makes an important contribution to the clarification of the specific character of law as being a form of volition.

The work of Ihering shows clearly the many advantages which a professionally trained lawyer with philosophical understanding enjoys in the approach to problems of legal theory, as compared with philosophers whose legal philosophies form but a part of a more comprehensive system.

Ihering came to develop his legal philosophy through an intensive study of the spirit of Roman law, the result of which he laid down in a brilliant work.[21] Reflections on the evolution of Roman law and the genius of Roman jurisprudence led Ihering to detest more and more what he came to style *Begriffsjurisprudenz* (jurisprudence of concepts). The study of Roman law taught him that its wisdom lay not so much in the logical refinement of concepts as in the moulding of concepts to serve practical purposes. Through that study Ihering became strongly aware of the paramount necessity for law to serve social purposes. Thus Ihering became a utilitarian. The philosophical basis of Ihering's utilitarianism is the recognition of purpose as the universal principle of the world, embracing inanimate as well as animate creation. The opposition between causality and volition, made fundamental by the Neo-Kantians, is overcome in Ihering's system by this notion of purpose dominating matter as much as will, each in its own sphere. The purpose of human volition is not the act itself but the satisfaction derived from it. Thus the debtor pays his debt, in order to free himself from it.

The purpose of the law is for Ihering the protection of interests, and in the definition of "interest" he follows Bentham by describing it as the pursuit of pleasure and the avoidance of pain. But individual interest is made part of a social purpose by connecting one's own purpose with other peoples interests. By converging interests for the same purpose co-operation is brought about. Commerce, society and the state result from this.

---

[20] See also *Der Kampf ums Recht* (1873).
[21] Ihering, *Der Geist des römischen Rechts* (1907).

Ihering has here arrived at the problem which faces every legal philosopher: whether reconciliation between individual and collective interest is possible, and how it can be brought about. Ihering finds the answer by means of the principle of the levers of social motion. In these levers he combines egoistic and altruistic motives. The existence of society is made possible by a combination of these. The egoistic levers are reward and coercion. The desire for reward produces commerce and the threat of coercion makes law or state possible. Thus Ihering joins those to whom coercion is an essential element of law and state alike.[22] The altruistic or moral levers of social motion are the feelings of duty and love. The four combine to make society possible, and the object of society is to secure the satisfaction of human wants.

The totality of these wants Ihering divides into three categories:

(1) Extra-legal (solely belonging to nature) offered to man by nature with or without effort on his part (*e.g.*, produce of soil).

(2) Mixed-legal, *i.e.*, conditions of life exclusive to man. In this category are the four fundamental conditions of social life, *viz.*, preservation of life, reproduction of life, labour and trade. These are specific aspects of social life, but independent of legal coercion.

(3) In contradistinction, the purely legal conditions are those which depend entirely on legal command, such as the command to pay debts or taxes. No legislation, on the other hand, is needed for such matters as eating and drinking, or the reproduction of the species.[23]

The realisation of the social purpose, *i.e.*, the conditions of social existence, may be pursued by morality, ethics or law. The characteristic approach of law is by means of the power of the state, which exercises external coercion.

It is this method, not the content of law, which is permanent and stable. The content of law, Ihering insists, not only may but must be infinitely various. Purpose is a relative standard, and accordingly law must adapt its regulations to the varying conditions of people, according to the degree of civilisation and the needs of the time. Thus Ihering is bound to oppose the idea of natural law

[22] On this aspect of Ihering's theory, see further, above, p. 260.
[23] Modern states have, however, legislated on all these matters. See also Plato's teaching, above, p. 8.

as giving certain permanent and universally valid contents to law:

> The idea that law must always be the same is no whit better than that medical treatment should be the same for all patients.[24]

Thus Ihering foreshadows the later Neo-Kantian distinction between form and matter and at the same time justifies the elasticity of the sociological approach to law.

But if law is coercion, how can it coincide with the pursuit of individual interest? Ihering's answer is that the basis of all legal measures is undoubtedly man, whether the measures belong to private, criminal or public law. But social life adds to man as a simple being man as a social being, as member of a higher unit (state, church, associations). The jurist, correspondingly, must conceive a higher legal subject, society, as standing above the particular individual. Thus the individual is enabled to desire the common interest, in addition to his own. Accordingly, the law never secures the good of the individual as an end in itself, but only as a means to the end of securing the good of society (*e.g.*, the right to reparation in the case of wrongful injury). It follows that Ihering is opposed to Kant's atomistic conception of society which sees individuals as living "in the manner of cages in a menagerie, that the wild beasts may not tear each other to pieces."[25]

Property, for example, exists not solely for the owners, it also exists for society. The law must try to reconcile the interests of the two. This leads Ihering to justify expropriation or legal restriction imposed upon the exercise of individual property rights. Expropriation solves the problem of harmonising the interests of society with those of the owner.[26] Ihering was the first jurist to develop a theory of balance of purposes or interests. His classification of the three main groups of interests—those of the individual, the state and society—was later adopted and developed by Roscoe Pound.[27]

To conclude the summary of Ihering's investigations with his definition of law, as it follows from the foregoing deduction:

> Law is the sum of the conditions of social life in the widest sense of the term, as secured by the power of the state through the means of external compulsion.[28]

---

[24] Ihering, *Law as a Means to an End*, 328. (Hussik, trans. 1924.)

[25] *Op. cit.* at 399. On the other hand, in his *Kampf ums Recht*, Ihering insists that the law is made and develops through the individual's fight for his right.

[26] *Law as a Means to an End, op cit.* at 391.

[27] *Cf.* below, p. 336 *et seq.*

[28] *Law as a Means to an End, op. cit.* at 380.

Criticism

With Ihering utilitarianism has, in substance, ceased to mean the pursuit of individual pleasure and becomes the balance between individual and communal interest. In this respect Ihering's system represents a further step away from Bentham, in the direction shown by Mill. Through the development of this idea of balance as the purpose of law Ihering has become the father of modern sociological jurisprudence. He prepares the most elastic legal technique required to meet new and changing legal problems by his fight against the "Jurisprudence of Concepts." Moreover, his insistence that law is realised through struggle and self-assertion has effectively opposed the romantic conception of an unconscious manifestation of the *Volksgeist* through the law.

By insisting at the same time on coercion as the characteristic of law and making the power of the state the instrument of the law, Ihering has created the essential foundations of a modern jurisprudence, suitable for the practical lawyer, because it was in much closer contact with the social realities of the nineteenth and twentieth centuries than Kant's idealism or Savigny's romanticism.

But the eternal problem of the conflict between individual and collective interests Ihering has not been able to solve any more than other legal philosophers. In an attempt to find harmony, Ihering goes some way towards an organic conception of the state and of corporate personality, seeing man in a twofold role. But he gives no satisfactory answer to the question why altruistic utilitarianism should harmonise with individual utilitarianism. In fact, both often although not invariably conflict. Can it really be seriously said that expropriation harmonises individual and collective interests? In actual fact, is subordinates the one to the other and which predominates is a matter of conflicting political beliefs. Modern sociological theories accordingly like to speak of the task of law as that of creating a just balance between conflicting interests.[29]

[29] See below, Chap. 27, especially pp. 327, 332 *et seq.*, 336 *et seq.*

CHAPTER 27

THE NEW LEGAL IDEALISM

LEGAL THEORY AND SOCIAL PROBLEMS

WHAT may quite appropriately be styled as sociological idealism is largely the legal philosophy of the modern lawyer. The history of legal thought had previously been predominantly a branch of general philosophy. For Aristotle, the Stoics, scholastic philosophy, Spinoza, Kant, Fichte, Hegel, Hobbes, Locke, Rousseau, legal philosophy is a part of their general system of philosophy. It is derived from certain general premises, and when it comes to details, as in Hegel's system, his legal philosophy often betrays his lack of acquaintance with the positive law and its problems. The representatives of modern sociological idealism, on the other hand, are all lawyers who, from the systematic study or the practical administration of any particular branch of the law, arrive at certain problems the solution of which they seek by a legal theory. To take but a few names, Pound, Gény, Ehrlich, Kantorowicz, Heck are or were professors of civil law; Holmes, Cardozo and Gmelin were distinguished judges. While the thorough acquaintance with the actual problems of law is a common feature of all modern legal theory, the representatives of sociological jurisprudence are mostly students of private law. It is connected with this fact that their theories are concentrated on the problem of balancing conflicting interests. For the civil lawyer is more than any other concerned with the solution of conflicting claims and interests between which he seeks to find a just balance. The constitutional and criminal lawyer is apt to see legal problems more directly as an aspect of the relations between authority and subject, between community and individual. The answer to these questions is naturally found by a subordination of one to the other, rather than by an adjustment of conflicting interests.[1]

---

[1] But see, for an earlier application of this method to criminal law, Bentham's views on the punishment of homosexuality (above, p. 316). *Cf.* also p. 334 *et seq.*

It is no accident that the jurists who have put the concepts of duty and state in their relation to the individual in the centre of their studies, have been constitutional lawyers such as Duguit, Hauriou, Jellinek and Kelsen.

Even where the professional lawyer turns legal philosopher he is apt to formulate a general legal philosophy largely from the angle of that particular branch of the law with which he is familiar.

To formulate the end of law in terms of balance between conflicting interests in itself indicates a further characteristic of this trend in jurisprudence. While all its exponents are aware of social evolution and change, and of the responsibility of the lawyer in keeping a proper relation between law and social change, they preserve at the same time the political neutrality which positivism had taught the lawyer, an attitude made possible by and dependent on the existence of a constitutional separation of powers. Balancing interests means to approach them with perfect impartiality, considering them as equivalent in principle and finding the proper adjustment from the facts and circumstances in the given case. Private property and respect for one's neighbour's freedom of person, sanctity of obligations, freedom of enterprise, responsibility for one's employees, all these and many other interests are considered as basically equivalent and must be balanced from case to case. Public interests are thrown in, as one of the factors to be considered, but without being given priority or any other definite rank. Consequently the representatives of this trend of social jurisprudence, appropriately termed *Interessenjurisprudenz* in German legal science, claim that, being independent of any particular *Weltanschauung*, they can provide a working basis for the lawyer under any legal system. What Kelsen's pure theory of law claims to achieve from a formal point of departure, this *Interessenjurisprudenz* intends to achieve by a proper consideration of the relevant social factors which the lawyer has to take into account in arriving at a solution. It is therefore the practical lawyer's philosophy of law, for the legislator is, of course, free to consider the various social interests in a sovereign manner and with direct reference to one political ideal or another. It gained ascendancy in the first decade of the twentieth century, when in all countries within the orbit of Western civilisation social evolution proceeded rapidly, but the stream had not yet grown into the torrent of social revolution that later on upset the nice balance of constitutional powers, and with it the neutral position of the lawyer. It is the common social and political background which is the principal explanation for the almost simultaneous development of the most important sociological theories in different countries, in defiance of the much exaggerated difference in the technical legal structure of Continental systems on the one hand and the Anglo-American law on the other.[2] To describe all these theories and their exponents in detail would require a treatise for itself. The essential features of all these theories are so similar that it may suffice to give an account of the most outstanding theories as they have been developed in French, German and American jurisprudence, principally during the first two decades of the twentieth century.

Francois Gény

Gény is one of the first and also one of the most important leaders in the fight for a new sociological conception of the law. It forms a part of a comprehensive legal theory, perhaps the most elaborate legal theory ever developed from the angle of the practical lawyer. For the query from which Gény started was a practical one, when in 1899 he published his *Méthode d'interprétation et sources en droit privé positif*: What, in the light of almost a century of legal experience, was the position of the lawyer and the judge in particular in regard to the *Code Civil* and other codifications of French law? At that time analytical jurisprudence was everywhere in full blossom. The complete logic of the law, based on the all-comprehensiveness of the provisions of the code, relegated in the eyes of analytical jurisprudence the task of the lawyer to that of interpretation according to strict logical principles. Gény, looking at the development of French law in the judicial interpretation of the code, delivered a powerful challenge to this theory. He realised what is now beyond doubt and argument, that judicial interpretation of the code civil had been a much more creative activity than that. Gény demonstrated that the judicial function in interpreting the code required an investigation of the realities of social life, some but not all of which can be discovered by means of analytical legal methods.

Against the then prevailing faith in written law as the sole source of all law, Gény puts as three additional sources: (1) Custom; (2) Authority and tradition, as developed by judicial decisions and doctrine; (3) Free scientific research.

[2] *Cf.* below. Chap. 33.

Custom has been neglected in the enthusiasm for codification and rationalisation of law. Judicial development and juristic teaching has greatly developed and, in fact, modified the principles laid down in the codes. But when all this is taken into account, there remains a wide field of problems where freedom to choose between different solutions is left to the judge. The guide to the solution of these problems is the *libre recherche scientifique.* It has to base itself on three principles as governing legal rules: (1) Autonomy of will; (2) Public order and interest; (3) Just balance of conflicting private interests.

On the whole, freedom of contract is the guiding principle, but this is subject to the overriding principles of public order, to be found by scrutinising the principles of political organisation and of the economic order in which the legal system operates. It is the task of free scientific research to guide the judge in the solution of juridical situations, which reduce themselves to a matter of conflicting interests.

As to the direction of this guidance, the following formulation shows Gény's thinking to be parallel to those of German and American contemporaries opposed to purely analytical interpretation:

> The principle of . . . equilibrium of interests concerned must be the guide of courts in all those cases where there is no sufficient and valid agreement between the parties, so that it becomes necessary to establish authoritative rules of conduct. . . . Estimate their respective force, weigh them in the scales of justice, so as to give preponderance to the most important of them, tested by some social standard and finally bring about an equilibrium.[3]

Gény also anticipates the famous provision of the Swiss civil code of 1907 by directing the judge to solve a question for which the text of the code and the traditional methods of construction give him no clear solution, according to the same principles as the legislator would apply.

From this problem, which confronts every modern civil lawyer who is aware of the tide of social forces and conflicts from which the law cannot hold aloof, Gény developed in his later work, *Science et technique en droit privé positif* (4 vols., 1914-24), a complete legal philosophy. Here Gény applies to the law the classical distinction between thought and will, knowledge and action, which accordingly has two spheres: science and technique. The

---

[3] Gény, *Science of Legal Method,* Modern Legal Philosophy Series, 35.

realm of science is the objective knowledge of those social realities which supply the law with its social material. This material is given, the lawyer cannot alter it. To this material the lawyer applies his technique, the specific art of the lawyer. It is this technique which for the lawyer is a field of creative action. This distinction is Kantian in so far as it applies the essential distinction between pure and practical reason, between thought and will. It differs, however, decisively from the Neo-Kantian development of this distinction. Gény, who has given a penetrating criticism of Stammler's theory,[4] does not restrict the law to form which regulates changing matter. On the contrary, the social matter with which the lawyer operates is as essential a part of legal science as the legal form which is part, but by no means the whole, of juristic technique.

Gény derives the foundation of this distinction from a combination of modern sociological tendencies with the *Philosophie Nouvelle,* of which Henri Bergson is the acknowledged leader. It emphasises the importance of creative intuition to supplement intellectual rigidity, the need to see the phenomena of life in their living unity, instead of dissecting them in categories, in sequences of causes and effects. The intellect is thus part of a deeper and greater consciousness of life, from which it draws an urge to transform itself into action, instead of being content with a notional analysis.

It is within the framework of the social matter which provides the material for legal action that Gény develops his theory of natural law. Natural law to Gény comprises those immutable and universal factors with which the law must necessarily operate. They are thus the basis of any positive law. Gény divides them into four categories, which he calls *donnés*:

(1) *Le donné réel.* It consists of the physical and psychological realities such as the facts of sex or climate, religious traditions, social habits of the people.

(2) *Le donné historique.* It consists of all those facts, traditions, circumstances of environment which mould those physical or psychological facts in a particular manner.

(3) *Le donné rationnel.* It consists of those principles which derive from the reasonable consideration of human relations. This embodies most of the principles of the classical natural

---

[4] In Appendix 1 to Stammler's *Theory of Justice*, in Modern Legal Philosophy Series.

law, the fundamental postulates of justice such as the sanctity of human life, the development of human faculties and more specifically such strongholds of liberal creed as freedom of thought and inviolability of the person.

(4) *Le donné idéal.* It provides a dynamic element, as it embodies the moral aspirations of a particular period and civilisation. It is a result of intuition rather than of reason and, for this last of the four principal social data, Gény admits that it overlaps to a considerable extent with the sphere of technique.

By means of juristic technique (*Le construit*) the lawyer moulds the given material so as to make it correspond to the needs of social life. Gény enters into a very detailed analysis of the various elements and parts of this juristic technique.

What Gény means by this analysis of the legal process may be illustrated by the example of the legal rules for the proof of paternity (*Recherche de paternité*). From the *donné réel* the legislator takes the fact that the conception of a born infant must have been no more than ten months and no less than six before its birth. It is a principle of natural justice (*donné rationnel*) that the father should share the responsibility for the child. On the basis of these data a particular law construes actions against the father and usually operates with certain time limits as well as certain judicial presumptions of paternity which enable the judge to arrive at a practical conclusion which would otherwise be difficult. Gény himself chooses the institution of marriage as one in which all the four *donnés* operate: natural facts of sexual relationship, the historical institution of marriage, certain elementary principles of justice demanding a permanency of relationship between man and woman, that is marriage but not necessarily monogamous marriage: finally, the current ideas on the relations of husband and wife which mould the legal institution of marriage in accordance with the social needs of the time.

Gény is well aware that his distinctions cannot possibly operate as neatly in reality as on paper, but he considers them as a general working basis which provides an explanation for the unfolding of the legal process and the functions of the various legal organs. Gény's theory represents a sociological counterpart of the *Stufentheorie* of the Vienna school. He shows that at every stage of the legal process there is and must be creative activity; but there is naturally less scope for the judge than for the legislator. For the judge and indeed any practical lawyer the given law is a *donné*, that is social material on which he can operate with the means of juristic technique, where the legislator is free to choose from an infinitely wider field.

In any conflict between natural and positive law the lawyer is, in principle, bound by positive law. But Gény does not altogether oppose disobedience to positive law in certain extreme cases, *viz.*, where the law is contrary to good sense or where it would mean flagrant injustice. Preferably such disobedience should be by legitimate means, such as are or rather were provided by the remedies before the civil and administrative tribunals: but Gény thinks that, in the "case of crying abuse of legislative power, there should be the 'extreme and desperate sanction' of insurrection, in resistance to the oppression of despotic laws." In other words, in extreme cases, natural law would legitimate rebellion.[5] But Gény does not become more specific, no more so than his compatriot Duguit, who arrives at similar conclusions.[6]

It appears that here the limit of juristic deduction and guidance is reached. In the absence of a superior authority which sanctions the breach, disobedience to positive law is revolution, and natural law supplies once again the ethical legitimation for such revolution.

Neither Gény nor Duguit, nor any one else has found an answer to the problem, how the law can be broken in the name of the law. What Gény calls natural law, Duguit calls the reaction of social solidarity against any violation. Jellinek calls it the *Normative Kraft des Faktischen* and Kelsen the "Minimum of Effectiveness" of a *Grundnorm*. Different words for the same problem, neither provable nor answerable in terms of legal argument.[7]

GERMAN "INTERESSENJURISPRUDENZ"

While, in France, Gény and a number of other jurists gave powerful expression to the need for a new approach to law, after a century's experience of legal codification, in Germany a similar movement sprang up very soon after the introduction of the New German Civil Code of 1900. Certain gaps in the Code and new social developments soon emphasised the need for a creative inter-

[5] 4 *Science et Technique*, ss. 288-300.
[6] Notably in Duguit, 3 *Traité de Droit Constitutionnel*, § 98 (2d ed. 1921-1925).
[7] See further, on the problem of resistance in the name of a higher law, below, p. 350 *et seq.*

pretation by the practical lawyer. At the same time a number of general clauses in the Code, such as those interpreting obligations in accordance with good faith (*Treu und Glauben*), those declaring an abuse of rights illegal, those invalidating contracts which are contrary to morality (*gute Sitten*) and many others pointed to a similar necessity. The only jurist who in Germany, at that time, attempted to combine philosophy and sociological jurisprudence was Stammler,[8] whose share in the development of sociological jurisprudence has, however, been paid little attention as compared with his philosophy. The greatest impetus for a sociological approach to law came from a school of younger jurists, both academic and practical lawyers, and most though not all of them were civil lawyers.

Ehrlich and Kantorowicz led the fight for a sociological approach to law in Germany.

In 1906 Ehrlich published *Soziologie und Jurisprudenz,* and Kantorowicz (under the pseudonym of Gnaeus Flavius) *Der Kampf um die Rechtswissenschaft.*

These were mainly devoted to a vigorous attack upon the purely analytical interpretation of law then prevalent. The insufficiency of the analytical interpretation of legal institutions was also demonstrated by Nussbaum, in his *Rechtstatsachenforschung* (1914), and his subsequent studies of mortgages, usufruct and various types of financial transactions which illustrated the need to supplement the conceptual analysis of legal institutions by a study of their economic and social functions.[9]

The following statement by Kantorowicz shows an approach to legal problems very similar to that formulated a few years later by Roscoe Pound:

Let him . . . (*i.e.,* the reader of any section of the German Civil Code) ask himself with respect to each statement, what harm would social life undergo if instead of the statement the opposite were enacted. And then let him turn to all textbooks, commentaries, monographs, and reports of decisions and see how many questions of this type he will find answered, how many he will find even put. Characteristically also, statistics upon civil law are almost wholly wanting so that we can be sure of almost nothing as to the social function of civil law.[10].

On the whole this movement leaves philosophy alone and con-

---

[8] *Cf.* above, p. 179 *et seq.*
[9] *Cf.* above, p. 302 *et seq.*
[10] Kantorowicz, *Rechtswissenschaft und Soziologie,* 8 (1911).

centrates on the problem of legal interpretation. Its programme can be summarised in the following formulation of one of its leading representatives.[11]

> The new movement of *Interessenjurisprudenz* is based on the realisation that the judge cannot satisfactorily deal with the needs of life by mere logical construction. The legislator wants a protection of interests. He wants to balance the interests of life which struggle with each other. But he knows that he cannot capture the manifoldness of life and regulate it so completely that logical subsumption draws a proper line in each case. The legislator can realise his intentions and satisfy the needs of life only if the judge is more than a legal slot-machine functioning according to the laws of logical mechanics. What our law and life need is a judge who assists the legislator as a thinking assistant and who does not only pay attention to words and commands, but enters into the intentions of the legislator and gives expression to the valuations of law, even for these situations which the legislator has not specifically regulated, by examining himself the interests involved. It is the task of legal science to facilitate the judge's task by preparing a proper decision through an investigation of the law and the relevant situation of life. In such cases it should openly acknowledge its method of finding the proper norm and not disguise it by the fiction of legal deductions. The primacy of logic is thus replaced by the primacy of an examination and valuation of life (*Lebensforschung und Lebenswertung*).

A growing and powerful movement in German jurisprudence has worked on these lines, primarily in the interpretation of problems of private law, but more recently with an extension of the same approach to criminal law and public law.[12]

At the same time the decisions of the law courts themselves, including the German *Reichsgericht,* showed a growing application of the method of *Interessenjurisprudenz* in preference to *Begriffsjurisprudenz.* Just as the French courts had developed a number of important new legal institutions from very scanty statutory material, so the German Supreme Court developed some most important doctrines from some of the general clauses of the civil code. In criminal law this approach had less latitude, since, prior to National Socialism, criminal statutes had to be interpreted strictly in accordance with the principle of *nulla poena sine lege.* The principal scope for a judicial balancing of conflicting interests in criminal law lies in the discretion given in choosing between the

---

[11] Heck, *Begriffsbildung und Interessenjurisprudenz,* 4 (1932).

[12] Of those who have applied the sociological method to criminal law, the most important is Hegler, and in constitutional and administrative law, the same substitution of *Interessenjurisprudenz* for *Begriffsjurisprudenz* is powerfully represented in the works of Triepel, Thoma and others.

statutory minimum and maximum punishments for a particular offence. In administrative law, on the other hand, interpreted in Germany, as in France, by a special hierarchy of administrative tribunals, discretion and the balancing of different public and private interests is a paramount consideration.

It should be noted that *Interessenjurisprudenz*, developing the ideas of Ihering, considers the balancing of interests as the paramount task of law and legal science and is emphatic in including in the interests to be balanced not only private, but also public interests, the satisfaction not only of material needs but also of ideal needs. As Heck has stated specifically,[13] the word interest is to be understood in the widest possible sense, and includes ideas. It is this very equivalence of public and private, of material and ideal purposes, which provoked the wrath of National Socialist (Neo-Hegelian) lawyers, who postulated a strict hierarchy of values, with state interests paramount.

The sociological movement in jurisprudence, as represented in legal science as well as in the development of German judicial interpretation of codes, should be clearly distinguished from analytical jurisprudence on one hand and from the free law movement on the other. Like the parallel movements in France, the United States and in other countries, it does not disparage the force of logic, of custom, of history. But it fights against the exclusive consideration of any one of these factors and of a purely logical completeness of the law in particular, and it emphasises as the ultimate task the balancing of interests. The theoretical neutrality which it observes in the balancing of the interests at stake is best expressed in the following words of a German judge who belongs to this movement:

> The will of the state . . . is to bring about a just determination by means of the subjective sense of justice inherent in the judge, guided by an effective weighing of the interests of the parties in the light of the opinions generally prevailing among the community regarding transactions like those in question. . . . In weighing conflicting interests, the interest that is better founded in reason and more worthy of protection should be helped to achieve victory.[14]

Fundamentally therefore this movement does not wish to provide the judge or administrator with a particular solution. It wants to supply him with the necessary material for his decision, to make

[13] *Op. cit.* 40.
[14] Gmelin, in *Science of Legal Method*, 131.

articulate the many different values and interests which float about, mostly inarticulately, in the statutory provisions from which the decision is to be drawn, to classify and arrange them properly so that the judge can find his decision more clearly and with a clear perception of the human interests at stake. But in being creative he must not overstep certain definite limits. He must not decide according to his own unfettered belief as to what is best. He must keep in line with the fundamental division of powers in the constitutional modern state and not usurp the function of the legislator except where the legislator gives him scope and authority to do so. The representatives of sociological jurisprudence suspect arbitrariness and anarchy in any idea of letting the judge decide freely what is good or bad in the particular case. His freedom is limited, but nevertheless real.

SOCIAL ENGINEERING: ROSCOE POUND AND HIS SUCCESSORS

How much more important the social forces which mould the law are than the technical legal expression is evident from the strikingly similar development of an *Interessenjurisprudenz* by American jurists against the background of a very different legal system, training and tradition. The programme and conclusions of American sociological jurisprudence have been most fully elaborated by Roscoe Pound.[15]

In a now classical formula Pound has described the cardinal task of modern thought about law as being that of "social engineering."[16] In many writings Pound has attempted to facilitate and substantiate this task of social engineering through the formulation and classification of social interests, the balancing of which results in legal progress. While the foundations of Pound's approach have remained unchanged, the catalogue of interests has undergone some modification in his later writings.[17]

Pound classifies legally protected interests in three main categories: public interests, social interests and private interests.

---

[15] In "Spirit of the Common Law" and in "A Theory of Social Interests," in Papers and Proceedings of the American Sociological Society, quoted from Hall, *Readings in Jurisprudence*, 238 *et seq.* (1938).

[16] *Cf.* Pound, *Interpretations of Legal History*, Chap. 7.

[17] For Pound's more recent formulations, see in particular *Social Control Through Law* (1942); "Survey of Social Interests" Harv. L. Rev. 1 (1943); "Individual Interests of Substance" 59 Harv. L. Rev. 1 (1945); and 3 Jurisprudence, Part 4 (1959).

The main public interests are, first, the interests of the state as a juristic person in the maintenance of its personality and substance, and secondly, the interests of the state as a guardian of social interests.[18] Of individual interests Pound enumerates three: interests of personality, interests of domestic relations and interests of substance. Interests of personality include the protection of physical integrity, freedom of will, reputation, privacy, freedom of belief and opinion. They would cover such branches of the law as the criminal law regarding assault and battery, the law of defamation, principles of contract or the limitations of the power of the police to interfere in meetings, processions, privacy of property, etc. The interest in domestic relations mainly concerns the legal protection of marriage, maintenance claims and the legal relations between parents and children. They cover such problems as the parental right of corporal punishment, parental control over the earnings of children and the powers of supervision of the juvenile courts over the legal relations between parents and children. Interests of substance include the protection of property, the freedom of succession in testamentary dispositions, freedom of industry and contract, and the consequent legal expectation of promised advantages. Pound also includes the right of association although one would expect this to be an interest of personality rather than an interest of substance.

Finally, Pound enumerates six paramount social interests.

First, the social interest in general security. This includes the interest in the legal protection of peace and order, of health and safety, of security of transactions and acquisitions.

Secondly, the security of social institutions covers the protection of domestic relations and political and economic institutions long recognised in legal provisions securing the institution of marriage or protecting the family as a social institution. Such problems as the balancing of the sanctity of marriage against the right of divorce, or the undesirability of actions between husband and wife against the general right to claim damages for wrong done, or the balance between the protection of established religious institutions and the claim to freedom of belief, come under this general heading. Within the interests in the security of political institutions such

---

[18] Stone, in *Social Dimensions of Law and Justice*, 171 *et seq.* (1966) has convincingly shown that these so-called public interests resolve themselves into either social or individual interests or in the attempt of the state to balance these interests against each other. To put it differently, the "public interest" results from the shifting balance between the other categories of interests in the light of changing policies and valuations.

matters as the guarantee of free speech are to be weighed against
the interest in the fundamental safety of the state.

Thirdly, the social interest in the general morals concerns the
protection of society against moral disruption. Provisions against
corruption, gambling, blasphemy, the invalidity of transactions
contrary to good morals, or the stringent provisions regarding the
conduct of trustees, come under this heading.

Fourthly, the social interest in the conservation of social resources
is described by Pound as "the claim or want or demand involved
in social life in civilised society that the goods of existence shall
not be wasted."[19] The law as to riparian rights or things of common usage, and the modern tendency to deny legal protection to
"abuse of rights" fall under this category.

Fifthly, there is the social interest in general progress:

that is, the claim or want or demand involved in social life in civilised
society, that the development of human powers and of human control
over nature for the satisfaction of human wants go forward; the demand that social engineering be increasingly and continuously improved; as it were, the self-assertion of the social group towards higher
and more complete development of human powers.[20]

This category is both the vaguest and the most controversial of
all. In Pound's own view it comprises four major policies, *viz.*,
freedom of property, free trade and protection against monopoly,
freedom of industry and the encouragement of invention. Pound
himself admits that some of these policies have had to give much
ground in recent legislation and judicial decisions, and the fundamental assumption that these four policies are in themselves
guarantees of general progress depends on certain basic political
and economic beliefs. Pound includes in the same category the
interest in political progress, through the protection of free criticism, fair comment, freedom of education and others.

Lastly, there is the social interest in the individual human life:

the claim or want or demand involved in social life in civilised society
that each individual be able to live a human life therein according to
the standards of the society.[21]

It is this interest which Pound describes as "in some ways the
most important of all." It is recognised in the legal protection of

---

[19] Pound, *Survey of Social Interests*, 57 Harv. L. Rev. 26 (1943).
[20] *Id. at* 30.
[21] *Id.* at 33.

free speech or freedom of vocation as well as, with changing strength and emphasis, in freedom of industry.

Some modern jurists have further elaborated or varied Pound's basic classification. Thus Stone[22] builds up on Pound's classification except for the elimination of the category of public interests as a separate category. Paton[23] also analyses law on the basis of interests, dividing them into social and private interests.[24]

What is the value of such classification? In the first place it pursues a line of thought originated by Ihering and Bentham, that is the approach to law as a means to a social end and as an instrument in social development. In the second place, such a classification greatly helps to make inarticulate premises articulate, to make the legislator as well as the teacher and practitioner of law conscious of the principles and values involved in any particular issue. It is thus an important aid in the linking of principle and practice.

It is, however, equally essential to realise that any such classification is in the nature of a catalogue, to which additions and changes have constantly to be made, and which is neutral as regards the relative value and priority of the interests enumerated. As soon as the interests are ranked in a specific order or given any appearance of exclusiveness or permanence, they lose their character as instruments of social engineering and become a political manifesto. Pound himself has inserted a certain evaluation by describing the interest in individual life as the most important of all. There is, however, as Pound himself recognises, the danger of an implicit evaluation in the grading of interests as either individual, public or social. What is an individual and what is a social interest is itself a matter of changing political conceptions. Many interests come under different categories. The protection of inventions by exclusive patent, for example, may be an individual interest of person-

---

[22] Stone, *Social Dimensions of Law and Justice*, Chaps 3-5 (1966).
[23] Paton, *Textbook of Jurisprudence* 112 (2nd ed.).
[24] Paton's classification, which he himself regards as tentative, is as follows:
   "(a) *Social interests*
       1. The efficient working of the legal order.
       2. National security.
       3. The economic prosperity of society.
       4. The protection of religious, moral, humanitarian and intellectual values.
       5. Health and racial integrity.
   "(b) *Private interests*
       1. Personal interests.
       2. Family interests.
       3. Economic interests.
       4. Political interests."

ality as well as a social interest in economic progress. It is not only the enumeration of interests as such but also their respective weight which is a matter of changing political and social philosophies. Pound's paramount four legal policies for the protection of general progress, for example, would today be hotly contested both in practice and theory. Freedom of property is subject to increasing limitations according to the prevailing social philosophy and ranging from the transfer of the means of production to the community to preventions of the abuse of rights. The degree to which patents should be protected is a subject of much controversy in view of the danger of the exclusive right of the patentee being used for sterilising inventions rather than for economic and social progress. A conservative legal order would emphasise most strongly the freedom of individual rights and of established institutions. A totalitarian system would suppress or severely restrict the interests of personality in favour of the interests of the state. The very conception of neutrality in the catalogue of interests, the evaluation of which depends on changing political and social systems, is characteristic of a liberal approach.

Pound has also made an attempt to define the main legal values of "civilised" society. While the very notion "civilised" includes an element of personal evaluation it is clear that the values of civilised society are not absolute postulates, independent of time and social experience, but postulates "of civilised society in our time and place." In 1919 Pound gave the following summary of the jural postulates of civilised society for the purpose of systematic exposition of private law[25]:

I. In civilised society men must be able to assume that others will commit no intentional aggressions upon them.

II. In civilised society men must be able to assume that they may control for beneficial purposes what they have discovered and appropriated to their own use, what they have created by their own labour, and what they have acquired under the existing social and economic order.

III. In civilised society men must be able to assume that those with whom they deal in the general intercourse of society will act in good faith and hence

   (a) will make good reasonable expectations which their promises or other conduct reasonably create;
   (b) will carry out their undertakings according to the expectations which the moral sentiment of the community attaches thereto;

[25] Pound, *Introduction to American Law* 36-44 (1919).

(c) will restore specifically or by equivalent what comes to them by
mistake or unanticipated or not fully intended situations whereby
they receive at another's expense what they could not reasonably
have expected to receive under the circumstances.

IV. In civilised society men must be able to assume that those who
are engaged in some course of conduct will act with due care not to
cast an unreasonable risk of injury upon others.

In civilised society men must be able to assume that those who maintain things likely to get out of hand or to escape and do damage will
restrain them or keep them within their proper bounds.

A distinguished philosopher, writing in 1926, regarded these
postulates as being of absolute value and establishing "the liaison
between philosophy and the science of law."[26] Pound himself,
writing in 1942,[27] felt compelled to admit that the civilisation
of our time demands some further propositions. Among them he
counts the claim of the job-holder to security in his job,[28] the duty
laid upon an enterprise in industrialised society to bear the burden
of the human wear and tear.[29] Finally, he sees the emergence of a
postulate that the risk of misfortune to individuals is to be borne
by society as a whole. Even with these amendments, many contemporary jurists, philosophers and politicians would regard Pound's
formulation of the legal postulates of our civilisation as inadequate.
Be that as it may, the formulation of any particular series of jural
postulates at a given time must always be kept separate by the
sociological jurist from the evaluation of law in general terms of a
balance of social interests.

Little is gained by an over-elaborate enumeration of catalogues
of interests. The main and more urgent problem is that of the
method by which the lawyer can arrive at a balancing and evaluation of such interests. In the Anglo-American sphere of jurisprudence it is Justice Cardozo who, by his investigation of the nature
of the judicial process, has attempted to elaborate the problems
involved.

His attitude corresponds closely to that which Gény and the
majority of the exponents of *Interessenjurisprudenz* in Germany
had developed from certain theoretical premises. It emphasises the

[26] Hocking, *The Present Status of the Philosophy of Law and of Rights*, 299-
305.
[27] Pound, *Social Control Through Law* (1942).
[28] Pension rights or legal provisions against unjustified dismissal would substantiate this postulate.
[29] This is exemplified by the provisions on workmen's compensation or the
duties under *Wilsons'* case or the rule of *Rylands* v. *Fletcher*; see p. 490 *et seq.*

need for judicial awareness of the social values and interests at stake, but limits the freedom of the judge to the comparatively restricted, though important, field which remains when the more definite sources of law-finding have been exhausted. Cardozo's conclusions are well summarised in the following words:

> Logic, and history, and custom, and utility, and the accepted standards of right conduct are the forces which singly or in combination shape the progress of the law. Which of these forces dominate in any case must depend largely upon the comparative importance or value of the social interests that will be thereby promoted or impaired. One of the most fundamental social interests is that law shall be uniform and impartial. There must be nothing in its action that savours of prejudice or favour or even arbitrary whim or fitfulness. Therefore in the main there shall be adherence to precedent. There shall be symmetrical development, consistently with history or custom when history or custom has been the motive force, or the chief one, in giving shape to existing rules, and with logic or philosophy when the motive power has been theirs. But symmetrical development may be bought at too high a price. Uniformity ceases to be a good when it becomes uniformity of oppression. The social interest served by symmetry or certainty must then be balanced against the social interest served by equity and fairness or other elements of social welfare. These may enjoin upon the judge the duty of drawing the line at another angle, of staking the path along new courses, of marking a new point of departure from which others who come after him will set out upon their journey.
>
> If you ask how he is to know when one interest outweighs another, I can only answer that he must get this knowledge just as the legislator gets it, from experience and study and reflection; in brief, from life itself.[30]

Even Cardozo's searching and balanced investigation fails to make the major problem of judicial interpretation entirely articulate. The increasing complexity of modern legislation and social problems raises some fundamental problems as to the position of the legal interpreter in political and social development. They will be the subject of a special discussion.[31]

FREE LAW THEORIES (FREIRECHTSLEHRE)

Sociological jurisprudence in the sense characterised above was not the only reaction against the predominance of analytical jurisprudence. A more radical reaction was represented by a movement, theoretically articulate mainly in Germany, which, in Hegel's term-

[30] Cardozo, *The Nature of the Judicial Process* 112 (1921).
[31] See below, Chap. 32.

inology, might be described as the antithesis of analytical jurisprudence, with sociological jurisprudence forming the synthesis. This
movement does not, like sociological jurisprudence, merely doubt
the completeness of legal logic, but denies its existence altogether.
In its scepticism about the analytical explanation of law and the
legal process this Continental movement is the counterpart of the
American realist movement in jurisprudence; but where American
realists concentrate on the analysis of the law as it works in fact,
leaving aside what it ought to be, the *Freirechtslehre* has a definite
idealistic bend. It discards legal logic as a fiction and an illusion,
but it is not content to analyse the legal process as a matter of
social reality. It has a philosophy and ideology of its own, that of
the creative lawyer who, free and untrammelled by *Paragraphen-
recht,* finds the law in accordance with justice and equity. Few
adherents even of this rather radical movement have gone as far as
to allow the judge complete freedom. But they want the judge to
alter the law (having in mind mainly statute law as it prevails in
Continental systems) where the letter of the law would not be in
accordance with certain fundamental principles and demands of
justice. They have thus anticipated in theory what has become
reality in the administration of justice under National Socialism.
Both the frequent practice of German law courts, under the Nazi
régime, of ignoring a specific and unambiguous provision of a
statute where it was not in accordance with National Socialist principles and the power given to the judge by a law of 1935 to inflict
punishment without a statutory provision where to do so is in
accordance with "the healthy instinct of the people" represent a
possibly unexpected application of the postulates of the *Freirechtslehre.*

Of its principal exponents we might mention Ehrlich, Stampe,
Ernst Fuchs and Hermann Isay. Ehrlich[32] postulates the free finding of the law in all cases except those relatively few where the law
is so clear that the need is not to be found. Stampe[33] demands a
judicial right to alter the law where the law has produced what he
calls a general calamity (*Massenkalamität*). Fuchs' radicalism is
influenced by the scepticism caused in the minds of observers
through judicial developments in Germany after 1918. A body of
judges who on the whole disliked the principles of the democratic
republic, had developed many judicial doctrines of a strongly poli-

---

[32] Ehrlich, *Freie Rechtsfindung* (1903).
[33] Stampe, *Freirechtsbewegung* (1911).

tical character of which the judicial right to examine the constitutional validity of statutes and the doctrines developed by the Supreme Labour Court about the community of risk between employer and employees may be mentioned. This led Hermann Isay, among others, to deny altogether that judicial law finding was based upon a rational process.[34] The finding of the law according to him is an intuitive process directed by certain sentiments and prejudices while the logical argument is substituted as an afterthought for the intuitive process and serves as a make-believe towards the other world. This attitude, closely akin to the scepticism of the extreme representatives of American realism, could be turned to different accounts. It certainly made it appear doubtful whether the unfettered discretion of the judge was the best alternative to a rigid obedience to the written law. But the freedom of the judge towards the written law could be and was used successfully once the question of political allegiance of judges as of any one else was cleared beyond doubt by the regimentation of National Socialism.

Recently, a new version of *freie Rechtsfindung* has been presented by Georg Cohn.[35] Rejecting the traditional jurisprudence of "norms" and "concepts," the author demands that law should be found in the individual case without any ties of norms or rules. Despite the fashionable name of "existentialism," this is a new version of *freie Rechtslehre,* and it suffers from the same illusion: that law can be made without any norm, be it policy of a statute, of precedent, or even of a "sense of justice" which must be based on some scale of legal values.[36]

It is an illusion frequent among German exponents of the *Freirechtslehre* that the English judge has that majestic freedom from the fetters of the statute law which the Continental judge lacks. In reality the obstacles presented to a progressive development of the law in the English system of precedent are considerably greater than those existing under codes which either contain general clauses or, like the Swiss code, specifically instruct the judge to develop the law in case of need.[37]

[34] *Rechtsnorm und Entscheidung,* 19.

[35] Cohn, *Existentialismus und Rechtswissenschaft* (1955).

[36] See the criticism of Kelsen, "Existentialismus in der Rechtswissenschaft," 42 *Archiv für Rechts- und Sozialphilosophie,* 161 (1956).

[37] See in greater detail, below, p. 535.

A Critique of the Search for Absolute Legal Values

CHAPTER 28

IDEALS OF JUSTICE

RATIONALISTIC, METAPHYSICAL AND INTUITIVE IDEALS
OF JUSTICE

IDEALS of justice have been formulated by legal thinkers who reject natural philosophy. Kelsen has attempted to reduce the many doctrines of justice to two basic types: a rationalistic and a metaphysical one, the former being represented by Aristotle, and the latter by Plato.[1] He describes the rationalistic type as the one which tries to answer the question of justice by defining it in a scientific or quasi-scientific way—in a way based on reason. The metaphysical type, on the other hand,

believes in the existence of justice, but considers it as a quality or a function of a super-human being whose nature—and that means whose quality and function—are not accessible to human cognition. Consequently, the realisation of justice is shifted to another world, beyond human experience; and human reason, essential for justice, is to submit to the immutable ways of God or the unfathomable decrees of Heaven.

This antithesis is probably an over-simplification. Scholastic legal philosophy, for example, or Hegel's philosophic system are both metaphysical and rationalistic. The principles of natural law are accessible to human cognition but derive from God's eternal reason. A fourfold division may give a clearer picture of the sources from which absolute ideals of justice are derived.

A theological basis provides the simplest, and perhaps the only genuine, foundation for absolute ideals of justice. The outstanding type of a legal philosophy which derives a complete set of legal principles from a religious foundation is the scholastic philosophy, especially in its neo-scholastic development. No less absolute in method and postulates is Hegel's deduction of specific legal prin-

---

[1] Kelsen, "The Metamorphoses of The Idea of Justice" in *Interpretations of Modern Legal Philosophies*, 390 (1947).

ciples from an absolute idea which is both metaphysical and rational.

The most important of the many legal theories that have based the knowledge of justice on inspiration and intuition—from Plato to Petrazhitsky—have been briefly surveyed in an earlier chapter.[2]

More important in the history of legal thought have been the various attempts to deduce principles of justice from a universal rational basis. All the rationalist theorists of natural law, from the Stoics to Grotius and the eighteenth-century philosophers, could proclaim principles of justice, such as the principle of *pacta sunt servanda*, or more controversial postulates, such as the right of property or of worship, as universal principles because they believed that nature contained universal principles of reason, that is to say, principles which direct human action in a certain sense. This supposition has been attacked by Hume's demonstration that reason is the slave of the passions which alone inspire human action.[3] More recent attempts to establish objective and universal principles of justice are therefore based on different premises. Foremost among them is Duguit's attempt to deduce generally binding principles of law from an allegedly observed and empirical fact of social solidarity, a short formula for the principles which hold modern society together. The fallacy of this attempt has been shown in connection with the discussion of Duguit's theory.[4]

RELATIVISM AND JUSTICE

The different schools of Neo-Kantian philosophers have realised the relativity of justice and the dualism between eternal justice and positive law. They have therefore divorced the idea of justice from positive law. Some have refused to study the varying content of the idea of justice as irrelevant to legal science (Vienna school),[5] alternatively they have formulated the main conflicting ideals of justice (Radbruch)[6] or attempted in vain to fill the formal idea of justice with a substantial content (Stammler).[7]

What emerges from all these varying attempts is the failure to establish absolute standards of justice except on a religious basis.

---

[2] See above, p. 84 *et seq.*
[3] See above, p. 129 *et seq.*
[4] See above, p. 233 *et seq.*
[5] Above, Chap. 24. See, however, Kelsen's recent classification of various ideas of justice in *Interpretations of Modern Legal Philosophy, op. cit.* at 390-399.
[6] See above, p. 192 *et seq.*
[7] See above, p. 179 *et seq.*

But religion is ultimately a matter of revelation and faith. The principles established by God must be believed in as part of one's religious faith. On the other hand, the philosophies which make knowledge of justice a matter of intuition are merely escapist. Their ultimate trust is not in everlasting principles of justice, but in the wisdom, goodness or the sheer power of men.

The recognition of this problem has induced modern sociological legal philosophers to formulate ideals of justice not in absolute terms, but as relative to civilisation. Notwithstanding all differences of philosophical premises, this is the link between the legal philosophies of Bentham, Ihering, Gény, Kohler, Holmes, Cardozo, Radbruch, Kelsen, Lundstedt, Morris Cohen and Pound.

POUND'S CRITIQUE OF "GIVE IT UP" PHILOSOPHIES

In recent years there have been many powerful attacks upon the whole philosophy of relativism. Some have, not surprisingly, come from Catholic jurists, but special interest attaches to the criticism of the pioneer of a relativistic sociological jurisprudence, Roscoe Pound.

Time and again Pound, in his later writings,[8] attacked what he calls "sceptical realism" or "give it up" philosophies. Although Pound has never clearly defined who is to be included in this description, it appears to be directed primarily at the "pure" science of law of the Vienna school, and at all those who define law as the

authoritative laying down of norms by the appointed agency of a politically organised society and enforcement of threats that, given a defined act or situation, neither qualified as good or bad, certain legal coercion will follow.[9]

Against the assertion of Kelsen that absolute ideals of justice and value lead to absolutism, Pound maintains that

absolute ideas of justice have made for free government, and sceptical ideas of justice have gone with autocracy. . . . If the idea is absolute, those who wield the force of politically organised society are not. Sceptical realism puts nothing above the ruler or ruling body.[10]

These various statements clearly indicate that Pound rejects relativist philosophies of law and favours a definition of law in terms of absolute justice. Yet he does not appear to have attempted

---

[8] *e.g.,* Pound, *Contemporary Juristic Theory* (1940); Pound, *Social Control through Law* (1942); Pound, *New Paths of Law* (1951).

[9] Pound, *Social Control through Law, op. cit.* at 28.

[10] *Op. cit.* 18-29.

such a definition himself. Nor is it conceivable how Pound could do so without contradicting the main principles of his own legal theory. His theory of social interests is based not only upon the relativity of values but on the need for their constant adjustment in accordance with social evolution. From time to time, Pound himself added some new legal interests to his former list.[11]

The spectre which haunts Pound is the service state, which he regards as destructive of liberty and as a harbinger of a "bureau state." The problem of how to reconcile freedom and welfare, law and administration is indeed a serious one,[12] but nowhere does Pound go beyond this brooding anxiety. He warns against the advent of the authoritarian state, but he does not discuss in practical and concrete terms where the line must be drawn between the "humanitarian" path and the "authoritarian" path. The legislator, the administrator, the jurist can only derive limited guidance from phrases such as these:

> What one must question is not state performance of many public services which it can perform without upsetting our legal-political, economic and legal order, but the idea that all public services must and can only be performed by the government—that politically organised society and that alone is to be looked to for everything, and that there is no limit to the services to humanity which it can perform.

The Judicial Scepticism of Holmes

As pointed out before[13] it is Oliver Wendell Holmes who has been the most influential exponent of relativism in the common law world, and violent attacks have recently been directed against his philosophy mainly but not entirely from Catholic quarters. The gist of these attacks, which range from serious criticism to downright abuse, is that Holmes recognises no absolute values, that he was a cynic who worshipped power, and denied truth and goodness. In one of the most extreme of the attacks,[14] Holmes is linked with Hobbes and Hitler. A more moderate critic, Lon Fuller, has criticised Holmes's acceptance of soldierly obedience expressed in a speech

---

[11] See above, p. 341.
[12] For a discussion of this problem see below, p. 422 *et seq.*, and in particular *Law in a Changing Society*, Chap. 16.
[13] Above, p. 196.
[14] Palmer (1945) 31 Am.Bar. Association Journal 569. For further references, see Howe, "The Positivism of Mr. Justice Holmes," 64 Harv. L. Rev. 529, 937 (1951).

in 1895.[15] If the theoretical writings and the memorial speeches of Holmes are open to many criticisms, his approach to the judicial function in a free and democratic society has been consistent. What has been the gist of this approach? It has, first of all, been a philosophy of humility. Holmes perceived the arrogance or the ignorance of many of his predecessors who had asserted their faith and their prejudices under the guise of objectivity. Against this, Holmes did not assert another dogmatic faith, but a philosophy of responsible and humble scepticism, based on a careful study of the problem involved and the scrupulous weighing of the conflicting values and interests at stake. He, secondly, showed his belief in democracy when he preached self-restraint for the one non-elected organ of the constitution, and respect, within the widest possible limits, for the will of the democratically elected legislator.[16] This approach is now accepted by the present Supreme Court, which exercises far greater restraint in the invalidation of legislation than its predecessors. Third and perhaps most important of all, Holmes accepted the burden of responsibility of the judge in a democratic society, the loneliness though not the isolation of those who must administer the law under a system which does not dictate beliefs and in which groups, individuals and conflicting interests have, within wide limits, the right of self-expression. Holmes's recent critics have reproached him for not professing to know what is "true, good and beautiful."[17] The foregoing survey of legal philosophies has shown that, when translated into concrete precepts, these terms are used for the advocacy of a particular political philosophy, of private enterprise or of Socialism, for a crusade against Communism or Fascism, for the defence of revolution or of reaction. The humility which Holmes practised on the bench might well be described as an eminently Christian virtue, his respect for the elected legislator as a profession of faith in democracy, his sense of responsibility and uncertainty as the hallmark of a mature society. Holmes's non-judicial defence of soldierly obedience, while

---

[15] "I do not know what is true. I do not know the meaning of the universe. But in the midst of doubt, in the collapse of creeds, there is one thing I do not doubt, that no man who lives in the same world with most of us can doubt, and that is that the faith is true and adorable which leads a soldier to throw away his life in obedience to a blindly accepted duty, in a cause which he little understands, in a plan of campaign of which he has no notion, under tactics of which he does not see the use."

[16] *Cf.* Frankfurter J. in *A. F. of L. v. American Sash and Door Co.*, 335 U.S. 538 (1948).

[17] *e.g.,* Henry Luce in *Fortune* (1951).

hardly relevant to this issue, indicates the romanticism of his earlier years, but it scarcely lies in the mouth of those who demand absolute and unquestioning faith in the truth as interpreted by the Catholic Church to criticise Holmes on this score.

The issue is indeed fundamental. If we believe in the free society, we must accept the burden of uncertainty, the consciousness of a choice which is often difficult and agonising, and which demands knowledge as well as a deep sense of responsibility. It is hard to understand how such an attitude can be confused with indifference to ethical values, while it is contemptible to compare it with the destructive nihilism of Hitler. The more radical of the recent attacks on Holmes indicate indeed a growing tendency towards orthodoxy, towards the intolerance of doubt which we condemn in totalitarian society, but often subconsciously accept in our own approach to the problems of life. This attitude has recently been characterised by another great American judge and jurist:

> We are in the distressing position of all who find their axioms doubted: axioms which, like all axioms, are so self-evident that any show of dissidence outrages our morals, and paralyses our minds. And we have responded as men generally do respond to such provocation: for the most part we seem able to think of nothing better than repression; we seek to extirpate the heresies and wreak vengeance on the heretics. . . . Happily there are a substantial number who see that, not only when they were first announced, but as they still persist, the doctrines that so frighten us constitute a faith, which we must match with a faith, held with equal ardour and conviction.[18]

RADBRUCH AND THE GERMAN REVIVAL OF "HIGHER LAW" PHILOSOPHY

A worthier source of attempts to reformulate absolute standards of justice, minimum values which no positive law should be allowed to violate, has been the reaction to the agonising experience of totalitarian justice. Under the Nazi régime, mass murders, the destruction of families, the deportation of millions, the vilest forms of human degradation, were sanctioned by the legal authority of the state, in the form of laws or orders which no parliament or public opinion was in a position to control. The most distinguished of all the exponents of a relativist legal philosophy, Gustav Radbruch, was driven by the impact of these experiences to postulate

---

[18] The Spirit of Liberty, *Papers and Addresses of Learned Hand* (1952).

at the end of his life a natural law philosophy which he had no time to elaborate.[19]

Radbruch's tentative suggestion is that where the violation of justice reaches so intolerable a degree that the rule becomes in fact "lawless law," the law has no claim to obedience. But Radbruch is conscious of the difficulty of drawing the line, except where there is not even the pretence of a formal ordering of relations. Aristotle's formula of justice says that those equal before the law must be treated equally. In the latter days of the Nazi régime, Hitler's oral pronouncements often overruled courts or statutes. Sheer chaotic arbitrariness undermined the hierarchical structure which even a positivist definition of law must regard as essential. Radbruch realised the need for legal security and certainty, and he felt that the task of nullifying statutes of the Nazi period as contrary to elementary justice should be reserved to a higher court or to legislation.

Radbruch's view was applied in some important post-war judgments of West German courts, of which the judgment of the Supreme Court for the Federal Republic of July 1951 is the most representative.[20] In that case, the defendant, a political Nazi official of middle rank, had been appointed in March 1945 as special commissioner to "fight defeatism and lift the will to resist." Upon certain information that the plaintiff and her husband kept a half-Jewess in their house to protect her from the Gestapo, and that they were preparing lists of party officials for the Allied forces, the defendant summarily arrested both, and when the husband tried to escape, shot him dead. Next day he certified that the husband had died as a result of sudden heart failure. The technical issue was whether the defendant was personally liable, in view of the temporary collapse of the German Reich as a legal entity. The jurisprudential issue was whether he could take cover behind the orders of the National Socialist Party, then an official organ of the state. The court conceded that normally the German Reich would be responsible. It denied the legitimacy of the defence that the so-called *"Katastrophenbefehl"* of March 1945 had made it obligatory for every armed German subject to shoot deserters without trial. The

[19] Radbruch, "Die Erneuerung des Rechts" 2 *Die Wandlung* 8 (1947); Radbruch, "Gesetzliches Unrecht und Uebergesetzliches Recht" (1946) 1 *Süddeutsche Juristen-Zeitung* 105. These have been translated and pieced together by Professor Fuller in his *Supplementary Readings in Jurisprudence*, 1951-52 (mimeographed).
[20] *Decisions of the Federal Court in Civil Matters*, Vol. 3, p. 94 *et seq.*

court specifically endorsed Radbruch's view that where a positive law altogether denied the principle of equality, it lost the character of law. It also dismissed the view of certain National Socialist jurists that any legally relevant declaration of Hitler which could conceivably be construed as a norm had the force of law. This the court described as "a degrading self-abandonment of the members of the legal community in favour of an autocrat, which is not worth serious consideration from the point of view of the rule of law."

The aforementioned judgment need not necessarily be justified in the name of higher principles of natural law. It is, at least in part, founded upon the evaluation of law as a formal order which needs a minimum structure, as it no longer existed in the final phase of the Nazi régime, and to that extent it could be acceptable to positivists such as Kelsen.[21] But the problem of natural law and higher justice arises more inescapably in some other German postwar judgments. Because they illustrate the whole problem of the tension between a positive law of unprecedented brutality and elementary ideas of justice, in a manner not likely to be easily repeated in history, these judgments deserve some closer analysis.

A group of cases, where wives had informed against their husbands—knowing that it would lead to their death or imprisonment —for remarks derogatory of the régime, is still relatively easy to solve.[22] Several Nazi enactments had made punishable "public" acts or utterances apt to weaken the German armed forces, the

---

[21] It seems to me that no more than this is implied in Professor Fuller's observation that "when a system calling itself law is predicated upon a general disregard by judges of the terms of the laws they purport to enforce, when this system habitually cures its legal irregularities, even the grossest, by retroactive statutes, when it has only to resort to forays of terror in the streets, which no one dares challenge, in order to escape even those scant restraints imposed by the pretence of legality—when all these things have become true of a dictatorship, it is not hard for me, at least, to deny to it the name of law" Fuller, 71 Harv. L. Rev. *op. cit.* at 660. That law must have a minimum rationality of structure, will be accepted by positivists and antipositivists alike. This leaves the higher law problems unsolved. See further above p. 19 *et seq*.

[22] See, for an example, the case reported in 64 Harv. L. Rev. 1005, and the discussion of this case between Professors Hart and Fuller 71 Harv. L. Rev. 618 *et seq*. (1958) 652 *et seq*. For surveys of German post-war decisions on this problem, see Bodenheimer, "Significant Developments in German Legal Philosophy since 1945" 3 Am. J. Comp. 379 (1954); Rommen, "Natural Law in Decisions of the Federal Supreme Court and of the Constitutional Courts in Germany" 4 *Natural Law Forum* (1959); von Hippel, *Id.* at 106. As Pappe points out "Validity of Judicial Decisions," 23 Mod. L. Rev. 260, 264, the report in the Harvard Law Review is not correct. The Court of Appeal held the Nazi law valid and the Federal Supreme Court, which, in an identical case, reversed the acquittal of the accused wife, left the question of its validity open. *Decisions in Criminal Matters*, Vol. 3, pp. 110-129 at p. 116. The validity of Nazi laws was, however, the issue in the decisions cited above, p. 351, n. 20, and below, p. 354, n. 26.

National Socialist régime, or the will to resistance. In 1944, a German soldier, on short home leave from the Russian front, had privately made derogatory remarks about Hitler and the Nazi régime to his wife. The latter, who had meanwhile engaged in other love affairs and wished to get rid of her husband, reported his remarks to the local Party leader. Although even the special tribunal informed her of her right to refuse testimony, the wife insisted on giving it, with the consequence that her husband was sentenced to imprisonment. She was later convicted by a post-Nazi court as being an accessory to the offence of false imprisonment. (In other cases, where the husband had been executed, the principal offence was murder.)

Few will disagree that, in cases of this kind, little pity need be wasted upon the informer wife. She had in fact exercised freedom of choice. Even if, contrary to the wording of the statutes, the husband's remark could have been construed as "public," it was clear that only the wife's determination to have him prosecuted could have produced any consequences outside the four walls of the private home. Even under the Nazi régime the legal institution of marriage was not formally destroyed—although it was under-mined in many ways. A wife made a free choice between the duties of loyalty to her husband and obedience to a law which, even though couched in possibly imperative form, was in fact permissive. Nor could the actions be construed as patriotic since they were clearly dictated by personal (and illicit) motives. But if there is little doubt about the moral merits of these situations, there is vast disagreement about the legal justification of the decision. In the above-mentioned controversy, Professor Hart, arguing in accord-ance with Austin's view that "the most pernicious laws, and there-fore those which are most opposed to the will of God, have been and are continually enforced as laws by judicial tribunals"[23] holds that the only proper procedure in this case would have been to make criminal legislation and punishment retrospective. "It would have made plain that in punishing the woman a choice had to be made between two evils, that of leaving her unpunished and that of sacrificing a very precious principle of morality endorsed by most legal systems."[24] Professor Fuller, on the other hand, agreeing with Radbruch and what he thought, on the basis of an erroneous report, to be the decision of the German court, seems to regard this as a

---

[23] Austin, *The Province of Jurisprudence Determined*, p. 185 (ed. 1954).
[24] 71 Harv. L. Rev., *op. cit.* at 619.

subterfuge, and squarely professes the view that a law, in order to be valid, must have an "inner morality."[25] Perhaps this conflict of view is more verbal than real. Obedience to a tyrannous and immoral law—however objectionable morally—will never be punished until and unless the objectionable order is overthrown and a new legal order substituted. When that is the case, the new law may be made retrospective, to satisfy the liberated sense of justice. Alternatively the new scale of values will express itself in a revolutionary new interpretation of legal standards by the courts (as in the aforementioned case). In substance, this is no less retrospective than a new law explicitly made so. But the retroactivity is disguised by the use of natural law formulas. Under either approach the ultimate question is a meta-legal one: was the conduct of the individual guided by a free choice between conflicting moral duties and principles? If so, punishment is morally justified, whether by way of an appeal to higher law ideas or through making a statute retrospective, contrary to general principles of democratic justice.

A deeper dilemma became apparent in the many cases where defendants—subsequently arraigned before Allied military tribunals or, in some cases, before German courts—had obeyed and abetted Nazi laws leading to the brutal extinction of millions of Jews, of political prisoners and others, under varying degrees of compulsion. In some German cases[26] Nazi officials had taken part as transport officers in the deportation of German Jews to places where they were subsequently murdered by the Gestapo. The court dismissed the plea of legality of orders under which the defendants had acted, by observations similar to those quoted earlier, namely, that laws denying altogether the value and dignity of human personality could not be regarded as law. But much as we may instinctively agree with the condemnation of those who took part, in however lowly a capacity, in the most gigantic, brutal and mercilessly organised mass murder of all times executed in the name of the sovereignty of the modern state, the dilemma remains: at what point does resistance to positive legal orders become more than an act of heroism—as it was in the case of the martyrs of the unsuccessful anti-Nazi *putsch* of July 20, 1944—and turn into a duty? It matters little whether we characterise this duty as a moral or a legal

[25] As an actual solution of the informer cases, Fuller agrees, however, with the retroactivity suggestion, not because it would be "the most nearly lawful way of making unlawful what was once law," but because it would symbolise the sharp break of values.

[26] *e.g.*, 2 *Supreme Court Decisions in Criminal Matters*, 234.

one. It is only when the odious order has been overthrown and a new legal order, guided by different values, been established in its place, that any duty can be made effective. And, whether we make punishment retroactive or appeal to higher principles—which have now become respectable but were high treason under the previous order—the problem is basically the same.[27]

The War Crimes Tribunals—both of Nürnberg and of the various occupation zones—were able, to some extent, to evade the problem by basing themselves on the London Charter—which for courts acting under Allied Military Government was the highest positive law. Yet they could not evade the dilemma of weighing, in the scales of justice, the compulsion of the defendants to obey cruel laws under often very drastic censure, or to risk unemployment, imprisonment or even death for the sake of higher principles. Among the many cases of doctors, industrialists, officials, judges, who were prosecuted under the Nürnberg Charter, perhaps the most poignant is the so-called "Justice" trial.[28] For here, civil servants and judges, men trained to obey and apply the law, were prosecuted—and most of them convicted—of having assisted in the making and execution of inhuman Nazi laws.[29] In the "Justice" case, most of the defendants had gradually slithered into their acts of connivance, *e.g.*, in the working out of the various Nazi decrees —as part of their official duties. They were not martyrs, and some of them no doubt enjoyed the opportunities of promotion created through the elimination of Jews and politically objectionable competitors. Nazi laws ranged from the merely unpleasant to the gigantically brutal legalisation of mass murder. Everybody who works and eats under such a régime takes part in it—some more actively than others. No doubt a collective act of mass defiance at the beginning of the Nazi régime could have stopped it. As it was, millions became individual accomplices. Some braved unemployment, some even death. The law is not, however, generally concerned with the highest standards of morality but with the minimum standards that can be made the norm of a general conduct. To some extent, the Allied post-war legislation attempted to cope with this problem by imposing sanctions ranging from death

[27] See further 64 Harv. L. Rev. 1284 (1954); and 35 N.Y.U.L.Rev. 1026 (1960).
[28] 3 *Trials of War Criminals before the Nürnberg Military Tribunals*, (1951).
[29] In particular, the so-called *Nacht und Nebel* decrees, which empowered the Gestapo to take away civilians of occupied countries accused of resistance activities for secret trial by special courts, without any normal trial, information of the relatives, and by the legitimised application of the refined terror which distinguishes modern dictatorship from those of older times.

and imprisonment for life to confiscations of property and inability to hold responsible jobs, according to the degree of participation and hierarchy in the Nazi structure. But even the mildest of sanctions —all of which collapsed when the programme was half executed— implied some measure of duty to resist the Nazi order—retrospectively. Despite his movement toward some acceptance of natural law at the end of his life, Radbruch was well aware of the dilemma.[30] He thought that only in extreme cases should obedience to positive law be held to have been illegal and that it should be reserved to special courts to do so.[31]

CRITIQUE OF NATURAL LAW APPROACH TO THE CONFLICT OF VALUES

How much does natural law help us in the solution of these conflicts? Reluctance to acknowledge as law a decree commanding the execution or degradation of millions of innocent people impels a desire to establish minimum standards to which a positive law must comply. But as soon as we go beyond generalities, such as the condemnation of laws offending human dignity, we feel uncertain of the point where moral indignation produces legal condemnation. Perhaps we should try to assess in practical terms how far a belief in absolute values of right and wrong, or good and evil, can lead us in the solution of legal problems.

The great majority of scholastic philosophers believe that the concept of the "common good" gives us a practical guide. We can agree that man is (or at least should be) a rational being endowed with the capacity of distinguishing between good and evil. We can deduce from that the basic postulate of human dignity.

---

[30] *Cf.* Fuller, *op. cit.* at 655.

[31] The danger of a theory postulating disobedience to positive law in the name of a higher duty will perhaps be more apparent to Anglo-American readers against a more familiar background than that of the Nazi régime. During the Congressional hearings directed by the then powerful Senator McCarthy against the Army the following remarks were reported (*New York Post*, June 17, 1954):

"St. Clair: You wouldn't want any employee of the Army to violate an order of the President of the United States?

"McCarthy replied that during the Nürnberg Trials of war criminals it was established that no man could use an order of a superior as an excuse for his actions. He insisted any individual who knew that Communists had been wrongfully cleared and restored to secret work was bound to give that information no matter if he lost his job."

For the possible application of these judgments to United States military action in Vietnam, see now "Lawyers Committee on American policy towards Vietnam," *New York Times*, January 15, 1967 and *contra* Moore, "The Lawfulness of Military Assistance to the Republic of Vietnam, (1967) 61 A.J.I.L. 1.

This might enable us to judge the mass extermination of human beings in gas ovens, whether or not sanctioned by decree, as "statutory lawlessness," though it is hardly necessary to invoke natural law to condemn the mass slaughter of helpless human beings. Murder is generally taken to be a crime in positive international law.

But how much further does the concept of human dignity take us in determining what is right and wrong without denying the very freedom of human conscience which this idea is meant to assert? Pacifists may well contend that compulsion to serve in the armed forces and to kill other human beings is contrary to human dignity, but others regard the duty to serve one's country as an overriding value.

The official doctrine of the modern Roman Catholic Church, from *Rerum Novarum* (1891) onwards, and of most neo-scholastic philosophers, is that the right of private property is a dictate of natural law. But St. Thomas Aquinas and Suarez strongly deny the natural law character of the right of private property and regard it (rightly as I believe) merely as a matter of social utility.[32] Catholic doctrine regards birth control as contrary to human nature and law, but this is not the doctrine of the House of Lords[33] and of many legal systems and conscientious human beings who regard birth control as an essential condition of the survival of the human race. The principle of the equality of all human beings is a noble one, but it is certainly not universally supported by biologists. How far is it to be carried? Are unequal pay for men and women, or legal restrictions on foreigners, offences against natural law?

Since Grotius many regard the duty to keep promises as a principle of natural law. But how far does this enable us to decide to what extent commercial or government contracts, which often give unilateral rights of terminating a contract, or statutory discharges of contracts, for example, in the case of nationalisation of an industry, offend against natural law?

When faced with the solution of concrete legal problems, we find time and again that natural law formulas may disguise but not solve the conflict between values, which is a problem of constant and painful adjustment between competing interests, purposes and policies. How to resolve this conflict is a matter of ethical or political evaluation which finds expression in current legislative policies and to some extent in the impact of changing ideas on

[32] See above, p. 110 *et seq.*   [33] *Baxter v. Baxter* [1948] A.C. 274.

judicial interpretations. And, of course, we all have to make up our minds as responsible human beings and citizens what stand we will take, for example, in the tension between state security and individual freedom. The danger is that by giving our faith the halo of natural law we may claim for it an absolute character from which it is only too easy to step to the condemnation or suppression of any different faith.[34]

It is possible to work out minimum standards and values which will be acceptable to various people, political philosophies and ethical codes of the contemporary civilised world, without engaging in dubious controversies how far nature commands certain ways of behaviour. As has been shown, the scale of values adopted by the more moderate neo-scholastic legal philosophers does not differ greatly from the scale of values adopted by non-scholastic legal philosophers, and by the theory and practice of modern democracies. The present efforts to establish closer associations among the nations of the West, through such organisations as the North Atlantic Treaty Organisation or the Council of Europe, will promote the process of clarification of common values. A European court for the protection of human rights has been established. The pursuit of common standards of justice in the fields of individual rights, of social welfare of the freedom of group life and other matters, is likely to prove more fruitful than the mantle of natural law which can fit well only those who accept the revelation of principles of conduct through the commands of God as interpreted by the Church, or who believe in universal reason. Such a theory will always divide rather than unite, especially as the predominant doctrine of natural law means an acceptance of Christian beliefs. But it has never been more important that East and West should work out together common principles of legal behaviour. This is certainly possible, but not on the basis of scholasticism or of any other specifically Western philosophy. Hindus, Buddhists and others can well agree with the West on principles of peace, justice and human dignity, but their outlook on the purpose of human life and its role in the universe is often different from that of the West. Even the distinction between men and animals—basic in Western philosophy—can hardly be accepted by Buddhism, which believes that a living being can move from one form of existence to another. The differences extend to the relative value of thought and action, to the relation of individual and society, and to many

[34] See O'Meara, "Natural Law and Everyday Law," 5 Natural L.F. 83 (1960).

other religious and philosophical questions. The time is past when Western beliefs can be regarded as a measure of all things. Nor will the natural law hypothesis aid much in the solution of the agonising problem of the limits of obedience to positive law. Those who resist repulsive laws out of a sense of moral responsibility will be punished under the law which they fight if their rebellion is unsuccessful. Such was the fate of the German rebels of July 20, 1944. Their moral sense will be elevated into positive law if their rebellion succeeds, or is subsequently legitimated.[35]

VALUE CONFLICTS AND UNIVERSALLY VALID INSIGHTS

Legal theory can fulfil a particularly important task by distinguishing in every legal problem or situation those factors which reflect conflicting values and those which are capable of objective analysis. The respective weight of these factors varies from case to case. Some legal problems are dominated by conflicts of values; in others this conflict is of relatively minor significance.

The necessity of assessing in any legal situation the "inarticulate premise," of separating ideology from science, of evaluating the conflict of interests, has been brought home to contemporary jurisprudence, though from very different angles, by the work of Holmes, Radbruch, Kelsen, Pound, Hägerström and others. We can, however, utilise other aspects of legal theory in order to narrow down further the irreducible minimum of conflicting valuations. A valuable contribution to this approach has been made by Gény's natural law theory,[36] which distinguishes the stable from the variable elements of a given legal situation. His distinction between *"le donné rationnel"* and *"le donné idéal"* is not far removed from the approach of modern phenomenological jurists, who believe that certain legal categories such as contract, property or personality, have certain immanent values, which are objectively and universally valid. From phenomenological premises,[37] some legal

---

[35] Natural Law has also been rather loosely invoked in justification of civil disobedience by Negroes to racially discriminatory laws in the United States (*e.g.*, by Martin Luther King in his Letter from "Birmingham Jail" (1963)). Insofar as State laws are resisted on the ground that they are in violation of the provisions of the U.S. Constitution against racial discrimination, peaceful disobedience may be legitimated as obedience to the higher positive law of the Constitution. But where the matter is one of ultimate State jurisdiction, or the Supreme Court has refused to intervene, resistance, however justified morally, is a revolutionary act designed to upset the existing legal order.

[36] See above, p. 330.

[37] See above, p. 203 *et seq.*

philosophers, such as Reinach, Coing and Fechner, have developed a number of legal principles derived from the essence or nature of legal concepts and institutions. For example, a commercial transaction, a marriage, a civil service status, are all supposed to have a certain minimum of characteristic elements which are valid everywhere and at any time. An illustration of this approach can be found in the opinion of the West German *Bundesgerichtshof*[38] on the correct interpretation of the legal status of the married woman during the interregnum when the relevant provisions of the Civil Code of 1900 had ceased to be law but the new statute which was designed to implement the equality principle of the Bonn Constitution of 1949 had not yet been passed. The court declared it to be one of the "facts of nature" (*Natur der Sache*) that the man, as head of the family, represents it towards the "outer world" (*nach aussen*), while the wife devotes herself to its "internal order" (*innere Ordnung*). In related branches of human knowledge, similar ideas have been used to develop a scheme of typical economic structures which appear and reappear in life in varying mixture,[39] or typical forms and structures of human qualities such as the "religious man," the "theoretical man," the "economic man," etc.[40]

This approach has something to contribute to a fruitful and constructive discussion of complex legal problems. It can help to sort out a healthy and justifiable minimum of universal standards from sweeping theories of natural law.

We speak, for example, of the "rules of a game." Instinctively we agree on certain rules such as equality of conditions for competitors or the need for impartial adjudication. Agreement on such minimum standards makes it possible for the United States, Soviet Russia, Great Britain, Mexico, India and a host of other countries to compete together in the Olympic Games although many of these countries are deeply divided on basic questions of personal and political life. The same demand led to the so-called rules of natural justice in English administrative law.[41] Philosophers may argue whether such insights are prompted by intellect or instinct. The jurist can accept these minimum rules as essential to the concept of a game. This leaves a great deal of scope for sharply conflicting motives, purposes and values. For the totalitarian state, such as Soviet Russia or Nazi Germany, success in the Olympic Games is a

---

[38] B.G.Z. 11, App. 34 (1953).
[39] *Cf.* Eucken, *Grundlagen der Nationaloekonomie* (6th ed., 1950).
[40] *Cf.* Spranger, *Lebensformen* (6th ed., 1927).
[41] *Cf.* above, p. 134.

political task, part of the realisation of the state which the individual must serve unconditionally. For many other nations, such as Britain, the "sport" idea still prevails over that of national competition or a political struggle. Agreed standards derived from the nature of a game enable the nations to compete, but divergent ideals prevent co-operation or agreement in the wider ethical or political realm.

In a more specifically legal field, the concept of contract appears essential to any developed legal system. Socialist legal systems have not been able to dispense with it any more than capitalist and liberal systems.[42] A *quid pro quo*, a reciprocal exchange of give and take inherent in Aristotle's "corrective justice" underlies such wider divergent notions as *causa* and consideration or the various contracts of Roman law, but the universal qualities of contract cannot tell us whether breach of contract should be dependent on fault or merely on the fact of non-performance, nor can it tell us whether frustration should be a good cause for discharge, or what the measure of damages should be where the non-delivery of a particular piece of machinery at a specified time has caused the loss of speculative profits. All these are questions which have to be solved with the help of further considerations. The impact of war or economic dislocation, the prevalence of a "private enterprise" or a "socialistic" type of economic thinking, current concepts on individual fault and responsibility—these and other factors will decide under what circumstances a contract may be discharged or what the measure of damages should be. Again, there may be a general concept of delict arising from an injury done without legal justification to the protected interests of another person. But whether such an injury should be regarded as a crime or a tort, or both, is a matter of historical and social development. Whether a private remedy should depend on fault or not is a matter strongly dependent on changing moral ideas and social conditions. Whether inability to replace a sunken dredger owing to lack of capital should be at the risk of the wrongdoer or the injured party[43] or whether damages for loss of expectation of life should distinguish between a Rockefeller or a Ford and an unemployed labourer,[44] must depend on the economic conditions and the social ideas prevalent

---

[42] It is, of course, a different question how far contract is the essential legal instrument of a particular society. It is obviously of greater significance in the commercialised society of the twentieth century than in the static and more self-sufficient society of the Middle Ages.

[43] *Liesbosch Dredger* v. *Edison* [1933] A.C. 499.

[44] *Rose* v. *Ford* [1937] A.C. 826; *Benham* v. *Gambling* [1941] A.C. 157.

in the society in which the situation occurs. The minimum of common elements is more limited and the divergence of social ideas more important in the concept of marriage. To the Catholic, no union other than the permanent union of one man and one woman can be a marriage, with consequences which are far-reaching as regards divorce, the recognition of polygamous unions or of legitimacy. Other civilisations and legal systems tolerate or even encourage polygamous unions. Between these extremes, contemporary English law, for example, is based on the monogamous idea of marriage, but recognises, for purposes of conflict of laws, the legitimacy of other unions.[45] Again, anthropologists will have little difficulty in demolishing the above-quoted view of the German Supreme Court about the "natural" division of functions between husband and wife (and so, perhaps, will modern American husband's). The conflict of values is even greater, and the minimum of necessary concept more restricted, in such fields as constitutional law. The idea of a federation implies that there is some distribution of powers between a central authority and the members, but it can say nothing on the political or social balance between these two: the doctrine of the "implied immunity" of the states, which was once predominant in American and Australian law, and recently revived in several decisions,[46] or the relation between provincial powers and the federal reserve power under the British North America Act, are not necessarily inherent in the concept of federalism, but are specific interpretations of political factors in which one value is given preference over another (state sovereignty over central power, or private right over planning).

Such analysis could be applied to almost any legal situation. Legal theory, supporting itself by philosophy at one end and political theory at the other, can break the complex situation down into its constituent elements; it can and must separate the ideal from the technical factors, the valuating from the analytical components, the elements which divide from those which unite. The result of such a process will be a clearer and more honest appreciation of juristic problems, but not a master solution which, under some spurious formula, can pretend that it has found the absolute answer.

---

[45] *Sinha Peerage Claim* [1946] 1 All E.R. 348; *Baindail* v. *Baindail* [1946] P. 122.
[46] *Cf. Commonwealth of Australia* v. *Bank of N. S. W.* (1950) 79 C.L.R. 497, also in [1950] A.C. 235; and the dissenting judgments in *New York* v. *United States* 326 U.S. 572 (1945).

UNIVERSALITY AND CLEAVAGE IN CONTEMPORARY THEORIES
OF JUSTICE

If legal philosophers were less wrapped up in their own nomen-
clatures, less easily convinced that their own systems offer a
radically new solution, instead of a modest addition to the formulations of age-old problems, the links between the various modern
legal theories would become far more apparent. The legal theories
carrying the banner of "social engineering," "existentialism,"
"phenomenological jurisprudence," "integrative jurisprudence,"
"egological jurisprudence," etc., often create a deceptive impression of uniqueness and novelty. Probably, only the two extremes of
legal ideology are separated, in their basic assumptions, from the
rest. On the one hand, we have the rather small band of extreme
natural law philosophers, who claim that a natural order—both
revealed and provable—establishes that, for example, private capitalism is good and socialism is bad, that birth control and divorce
under any circumstances are bad, or that freedom of opinion, as
understood in modern democracy, is to be condemned. On the other
hand, the more extreme versions of totalitarian legal philosophy,
as developed in the later stages of the fascist and national socialist
régimes, deny the basic value of the human personality as such.

Outside these extremes, there is a far greater degree of common
aspirations than generally realised or admitted. The basic autonomy and dignity of human personality is the moral foundation of
the teaching of modern natural law philosophers, such as Maritain,
Rommen or d'Entrèves.[47] It is also the basic philosophy of the
existentialists, who have gradually moved away from the assumption of the hopelessly lonely individual in a hostile world to the
realisation that the individual can find fulfilment only in the
constant constructive tension between his own "becoming" and
the order which not only permits him to develop himself, but to
do so in communication with others. The axiology of the modern
Wertphilosophie also postulates the individual, and his phenomenological experience of values. On the other hand, its order of values
is not an immutable, static hierarchy of things that are good, and
others that are less good or evil, but a scale of value experiences

[47] In "The Case of Natural Law Re-examined," 1 *Natural L. F.* 49 (1956)
d'Entrèves, while defending natural law, pleads for focussing attention "on what
unites us, rather than on what separates us," on the basis of the "unity that reflects what is common to human beings as human beings."

which direct the choice between alternative decisions and actions. In this, the philosophy of values seeks to provide an ontological basis for the decisionism of the existentialist and relativist philosophers, who recognise the conflict of values, and the need to choose between them, but despair of any scientific criterion by which the choice can be guided. At this point, the more pragmatically oriented theories of "social engineering" and *Interessenjurisprudenz* supply important guidance to the choice between alternative values. They do not do so in terms of natural law, but in the articulation of the concrete values and interests, as they were expressed in a constitution, in a civil or criminal code, in a specific statute, and in the decisions interpreting any or all of them. And if "integrative jurisprudence" means that the evolution of the law is determined, not only by the basic scheme of values, but by social and juridical facts, and received tradition,[48] it seems to restate what is accepted by every worthwhile legal theory: That law is not pure theory or ideology nor, on the other hand, a mere accumulation of facts and factual decisions, but the product of a constant tension and interpenetration of legal ideals and social data, which become concretised in specific norms, ranging from general statutes to administrative regulations and judicial or administrative decisions of concrete cases.[49]

Behind it all lies the realisation—which only the two extremes described above cannot accept—that the values of human dignity and the development of the individual personality do not present us with ready-made solutions. They cannot give the safety provided, either by infallible and absolute tests of Good or Evil, or the absorption of the individual in a totally conditioned society directed by a pseudo-godlike master. The agony of the decision, the conscious choice between values which—like the claim to security from treason of the organised community and the claim to individual freedom of conscience and opinion—have equal intrinsic value, but have to be adjusted in a concrete situation—is the noblest heritage of *homo sapiens*. Legal philosophy can aid in the choice: it cannot and should not eliminate it.

[48] Hall, *Studies in Jurisprudence and Criminal Law* Chap. II (1958).
[49] d'Entrèves, "The Case for Natural Law Re-examined," *op. cit.* at 49.

PART THREE

LEGAL THEORY
AND
CONTEMPORARY PROBLEMS

Section One

Legal Theory of Modern Political Movements

CHAPTER 29

SOCIALIST AND COMMUNIST THEORIES OF LAW

MARXIST THEORY

THE contribution of theoretic socialism to legal theory has been comparatively slight. This is largely due to two theories of orthodox socialism, both of which discouraged thought on the constructive function that the law might exercise in socialist society. The first is Marx's famous pronouncement:[1]

The totality of these relations of production constitutes the economic structure of society, the real foundation on which rise legal and political superstructures, and to which correspond definite forms of social consciousness.

The second is the theory[2] that the whole idea of law is linked with the state and is thus a means by which those who control the means of production maintain their control over those which they have expropriated. With the passing of the ownership of the means of production into the hands of the community, the individual will be emancipated and state and law alike, justified only by the need of compulsion, will wither away.

In this sweeping form both theories are not only misleading but act as a bar to constructive thinking on the function of law in a socialist community. Certain correctives to both these over-simplified theories are found in the later work of Marx and Engels themselves. In the first place it is important to note that Marx and Engels envisage the abolition of the state as an historical institution used for the suppression of the working class by the owners of the means of production: but they do not think of the abolition of all organisation and government.

The government of persons is replaced by the administration of

---

[1] In Introduction to *Critique of Political Economy.*
[2] Formulated, for example, in Engels' *Origin of the Family, Private Property and the State,* 63.

367

things and the direction of the processes of production. The State is not abolished; it withers away.[3]

In the second place Engels, in his later work, recognised the reality of the influence exercised by ideological superstructures such as law once they are established. "Such ideological superstructures have a tendency to detach themselves from their economic origin and react in turn upon the economic basis of society."[4]

Both these factors, the necessity of organisation and direction after the abolition of capitalist society, and the ideological importance of the social superstructures, call for further and deeper reflections on the function of law in the socialist state.

Neither Marx nor Engels found time to develop a legal theory of socialism. The orthodoxy of the lesser pupils delayed constructive thinking for a considerable time.

The conception of law as a superstructure seemed to deprive it of any autonomy.[5] On the other hand, the conception of law as an instrument of suppression barred the way for a socialist ideal of law.

Both conceptions have, to some extent, been rectified by modern socialist jurists. Towards the end of the nineteenth century, some socialist lawyers began to investigate the extent to which the recent Continental codifications of civil law had neglected the recognition of the right of labour, as compared with the right of property.[6] But by far the weightiest contribution to the problem of the relation between economic conditions and legal institutions from a Marxist point of view has come from the Austrian Socialist, Karl Renner.[7]

RENNER'S ANALYSIS OF PROPERTY IN CAPITALIST SOCIETY

Renner chooses the legal institution of ownership as the basis of an investigation of the extent to which the legal order corresponds to the social function of an institution. Renner first corrects the orthodox Marxist position and, at the same time, rejects Stammler's view by contending that legal institutions are neither automatically determined by the economic substrata nor a mere form super-

---

[3] Engels, *Anti-Dühring* 308-309 (English ed. of 1942).

[4] *Cf.*, in particular, Engels in a letter to Conrad Schmidt of October 27, 1890.

[5] Stammler, in his first work, *Wirtschaft und Recht*, opposed to the Marxist conception that of the relation between law and economics as of form and matter.

[6] *Cf.*, in particular, Menger, *Bürgerliches Recht und die besitzlosen Volksklassen*.

[7] Renner, *The Institutions of Private Law and Their Social Function* (English ed., 1949, by O. Kahn-Freund).

imposed upon it. In fact, they stand in the middle between the process of making the law and the social function of the law. Society produces certain ways of life in a process of permanent change and evolution. When they have reached a certain state of definiteness, the legal institution takes shape. It maintains itself in the rigidity inherent in the legal form, while the continuous evolution of society produces a gradual change in the function of the legal institution. Eventually, the tension between form and function becomes so great that the society forms new law, and the same process starts again. Legal science accordingly has to cover three stages: the formation of law, its formulation as a norm (the field of jurisprudence), and the social function exercised by the norm. It is on the last that Renner concentrates. The following is an outline of his deduction.

Originally, in medieval society, ownership, which in law means the absolute power of disposing of a thing, symbolises a unit of which the family farm is typical.[8] It comprises a complex of things, not only the house, the implements of work, stock, etc., but also the place of work and production, the place of consumption, the market and the family. In that stage, the legal conception of ownership represents, on the whole adequately, its economic substratum. But economic evolution gradually alters the function of ownership. When ownership of a complex of things, now regarded as capital, no longer coincides with the substrata of personal work,[9] it becomes a source of a new power of command. Marx had articulated the underlying thought:

> The capitalist is not capitalist because he directs (the work), but he becomes an industrial commander, because he is a capitalist. Industrial command becomes an attribute of capital, as under feudalism the power of command was, in war and in the law, an attribute of ownership of land.[10]

By means of this power, the capitalist exercises a quasi-public authority over those who are tied to him by the contract of service. The juristic institution is still the same as at the time when the worker also owned the means of production, but its function has changed. The owner of certain things can use his ownership to control other persons. Legally this is done by the use of ownership

---

[8] Economists describe the stage as that of *"Haus- und Eigenwirtschaft."*

[9] The identity of ownership and personal labour dominates the views on private property of Locke, Kant, Hegel, the American Constitution and Catholic jurists.

[10] *Das Kapital*, I, 297.

as the centre of a number of complementary legal institutions (*Konnexinstitute*), such as sale, loan, tenancy, hire and, above all, the contract of service. By means of the latter the worker agrees to hand over the substrata of work to the owner of the capital. Formally this contract, an institution of private law, is concluded between equals. In fact the liberty of those who do not own the means of production is confined to a certain choice between those to whom they are compelled to transfer, by contract, their share of the product. Behind the fiction of equality there stands the reality of the capitalist, exercising a delegated public power of command. The real expression of this power is not to be found in the contract of service, but in the internal rules regulating the conditions of work.

Another change of function takes place. The unity of ownership, typical of the former economic conditions, is broken up as specialisation in the various functions of ownership develops.

Property now becomes a source of power (control of factories), profit (owning shares in undertakings), interest (lending capital), rent (letting property), and so forth. At the same time the legal ownership ceases to represent the real control of the thing. The complementary legal institution assumes the real function of ownership, which becomes an empty legal form. Thus the owner of a completely mortgaged property is the legal owner, but the economic function of ownership is in the hands of a mortgagee.[11] The principal shareholder in a company, who controls the undertaking legally, merely owns some documents and certain claims against the company which formally has full ownership. In all these cases the *Konnexinstitut* has taken over some of the functions of ownership. Thus it becomes possible to expropriate without formal expropriation. Because of the complementary functions of the contract of service, the workers' share in the product which, according to certain legal theories, gives the title to ownership, can never be actual. By means of the contract of service, the right to appropriate is once and for all conferred on the owner of the material.

To sum up, ownership has ceased to be what it was. While remaining, in legal form, an institution of private law implying the total power of doing with the thing what one likes, it has in fact become an institution of public law (power of command), and its

---

[11] English law, before the property legislation of 1925, expressed this relation, but now is assimilated to Continental laws by limiting the mortgage to a right in the mortgagor's property.

main functions are exercised by complementary legal institutions, developed from the law of obligations.

The law eventually takes account of this change of function by giving property an increasingly public law character. Private ownership in public means of transport, for example, develops into what in Continental jurisprudence is expressed by *Anstalt,* and in English jurisprudence by "public corporation." The conditions of work become the object of collective agreements which are subject to public law. Renner asks socialists to abandon their passive attitude towards the law and to create the legal norm which adequately expresses the trend of social development. It is a significant departure from the original Marxist thesis when he declares that socialism, the cry for conscious regulation of human relations, demands the legal norm adequate to society.

Renner's analysis is an outstanding contribution to what in America is often described as functional jurisprudence, from Marxist premises. Modern developments in industrialised countries have largely vindicated his thesis. The National Socialist German Labour Law of 1934, which appointed the owner or managing director of a business or industrial undertaking as leader of the workers, is an illustration. The extent to which the controlling power of the capitalist has passed into the hands of the state marks a further stage in social and legal development. Renner's study has certainly contributed to the shattering of the superficial opinion that the legal norm has no creative force of its own, but is merely an appendix of economic conditions.

The theory that law, like the state, is an instrument of capitalist oppression and therefore disappears in a society where ownership of the means of production has passed into the hands of the community, has been developed by the Soviet Russian jurist, Pashukanis.[12] Pashukanis maintains that all real law is private law. It is under the guise of civil relations, as between equals, that those in control of the means of production exercise their power over the others.[13]

The development of public law is nothing but an unsuccessful attempt of capitalist legal science to transfer the notions and categories of law to an alien sphere, which does not really tolerate law. In a socialist community there is no scope for an autonomous

---

[12] Pashukanis, *Allgemeine Staatslehre und Marxismus* (German ed., 1927)
[13] This is parallel to Renner's thesis.

body of private legal relations. All order proceeds from the community and in the interest of the community. All law, therefore, becomes administration. But the essence of administration is discretion and utility, not a body of fixed legal rules.

In a modern socialist state, such as Soviet Russia, compulsion of the citizen is an essential factor. As long as there is no complete identity of law and moral consciousness legal sanctions are indispensable. On the other hand, the Soviet Constitution of 1936 recognises individual rights as the counterpart of legal duties.

Once it is recognised that the law, although a result of social forces, is at the same time itself an active agent in the shaping of social conditions, it is obvious that a legal philosophy can be built upon socialist ideals just as on any other political ideology. This is clearly stated by Radbruch.[14] The empirical aspect of Marxist analysis and, in particular, the mental confusion caused by the belief in the inevitability of the dialectic development towards socialism, has obscured but not altered the fact that socialism is a call for justice. Redbruch shows that it has been prepared by what he calls "Social Individualism," the demand to translate more political liberty, the creation of liberalism, into the social and economic sphere, and thus to mould the law in a way which would prevent formal equality from producing social inequality. Social individualism or, as others would call it, social reformism, attempts this by a mitigation of the inequality caused through capitalism, that is by protecting the economically weaker part. The whole trend of social legislation over a century (social insurance, unemployment assistance, factory Acts, workmen's compensation, collective agreements about wages and working hours, etc.) is an application of this principle. Juristically, Radbruch characterises this as a typical instance of equity, which tempers abstract justice. We might add that the various theories which see the balancing of social interests as the end of law, are also an application of the ideology of social reformism.

Socialism, on the other hand, demands a law which eliminates the causes of social inequality by abolishing private ownership of the means of production. Radbruch insists, however, that in terms of legal philosophy, socialism is an individualist philosophy; for the development of the individual is its goal. Socialism wants "an

---

[14] *Lehrbuch der Rechtsphilosophie* (1932). *Cf.* also Vinogradoff, 1 *Historical Jurisprudence*, 79 *et seq.* (1923).

association in which the free development of each is the condition of the free development of all."[15]

The function and purpose of law in a socialist society has ceased to be a matter of mere theoretical speculation. In our own generation several states are attempting to shape and adapt their law to socialist economic planning. The two great experiments differ decisively in their legal and political background.

SOVIET LEGAL THEORY AND PRACTICE

After more than four decades of a socialised economy the function and purpose of law in Soviet Russia is still a matter of doubt and uncertainty. This is due to the coexistence of at least five major trends which partly reinforce and partly conflict with each other.

Firstly, Soviet legal thought in the earlier revolutionary phase was largely dominated by Marxist formulas as restated in Lenin's *State and Revolution*, written on the eve of the Soviet Revolution. It assumed the withering away of state and law, both being identified with capitalist society and therefore with a specific ideological content.

This line of thought is supplemented by another which has survived the early Marxist phase of the Soviet Revolution: the concept of "revolutionary legality."[16] This means in essence the right of the new ruling class to exercise the coercive power of the state for the suppression of their opponents. It survived as late as 1938 in the definition by the then Procurator-General and later Foreign Minister of the Soviet Union, Vishinsky,[17] of law as:

the corpus of rules of behaviour expressing the will of the ruling class, established by legislation, and also of custom sanctioned by the state and secured by its coercive power in order to protect, to strengthen and to develop such social relations as are favourable for the ruling class.

The subservience of law to politics inherent in the suspension of rights and legal guarantees during a period of revolutionary transition has been largely perpetuated in the Soviet state by the establishment of a political dictatorship which consolidates the one-party system and the concept of political justice. The political control over the state is exercised by one party which occupies all

---

[15] Marx and Engels, *Communist Manifesto.*
[16] This is excellently analysed by Jones, *Historical Introduction to the Theory of Law*, Chap. 11.
[17] Quoted in Schlesinger, *Soviet Legal Theory*, 243 (2nd ed. 1950).

key positions and functions as watchdog in the state which it controls. As in Fascist systems, the effect of this political dictatorship is not so much seen in the day-to-day administration of law or in the published reports of cases as in the extent to which legal issues are removed from the normal and public administration of justice and subjected to a secret political and uncontrolled procedure behind closed doors. In continuance of a legal tradition established by Peter the Great,[18] the Procurator-General of the U.S.S.R. exercises a general supervisory power "to ensure the strict observance of the law by all Ministers and institutions subordinated to them, as well as by officials and citizens of the U.S.S.R. generally.[19] This ubiquitous, unique and very real function of the Procurator-General has been explained as an aspect of the parental character of Soviet law.[20] In civil and criminal cases it often operates in favour of the individual. The Procurator-General frequently brings the decisions of lower courts before the Supreme Court of the U.S.S.R. either on his own accord or on the petition of an aggrieved party. But he can also use that power to infuse the views and policies of the political authorities into criminal prosecution and the administration of justice in general. Article 5 of the Fundamentals of Civil Legislation of the U.S.S.R. of 1961[21] protects civil rights only in so far as they are not exercised "in contradiction to their purpose in socialist society in the period of communist construction." Above all, judges are not irremovable. The people's courts, which are responsible for the bulk of judicial work on the lower levels are elected and thus subject to the same political supervision as all elected organs in a totalitarian system.[22] The people's courts are elected by direct vote of the population for a term of five years, and the Supreme Courts of the U.S.S.R. and the Union Republics are elected for terms of five years by their

[18] *Cf.* Berman, *Justice in Russia*, 240-241 (rev. ed. 1963).

[19] Constitution of the U.S.S.R., Art. 113, See Hazard, *Soviet System of Government* (3rd ed. 1964) for text of Soviet Constitution as revised to 1964.

[20] Berman, *Soviet Criminal Law and Procedure* 109-117 (1966).

[21] The same article is reproduced in the Civil Code of the Russian Soviet Federated Socialist Republic (R.S.F.S.R.) of 1964. For the relationship between Union law and Union Republic Law see the discussion of federalism in the U.S.S.R. in Berman, *Soviet Criminal Law and Procedure* 13 (1966).

[22] Berman observes: "The provision of the 1960 Law (of the R.S.F.S.R.) that judges shall be 'independent and subordinate only to law' (Article 7) like the parallel provision of the U.S.S.R. Constitution signifies only that there should be no outside interference in the trial of a particular case; it is not intended to insulate judges against general policies of the Communist Party expressed in 'campaigns' against particular types of criminal activity and in party directives on law and law enforcement." *Id.* at 102.

respective Supreme Soviets. There are thus many channels through which politics can be directly injected into the administration of the law.

However, the pervading nature of political control has been formally tempered, in the recodifications which began in the late 1950s, by such actions as the dissolution of the U.S.S.R. and R.S.F.S.R. Ministries of Justice.[23] Now the U.S.S.R. Supreme Court and those of Union Republics are empowered to issue "guiding explanations," namely, to give directions as to the interpretation and application of the law, as well as to supervise the lower courts, a task formerly in the hands of the Ministry of Justice. Even more important, Article 12 paragraph 3 of the 1964 R.S.F.S.R. Code of Civil Procedure is entitled: "Adjudication of Cases on the basis of law in force." It states: "In the absence of any law regulating a contested relation the court shall apply the law regulating analogous relations, and in the absence of such law the court shall proceed from the general principle and meaning of Soviet legislation."[24] This appears to be a far cry from the 1923 Code: "If there is no legislation or regulation for the decision of the dispute the court decides, guided by the general principles of Soviet legislation and by the general policy of the workers and peasants government.[25]

A fourth factor has vitally influenced the Soviet attitude to law since the early revolutionary days. As the Soviet Union consolidated itself into a stable and authoritarian state, the need for the rehabilitation of law became stronger. The restoration of law was needed for two purposes: on the one hand, the state authorities needed law as an authoritative instrument of the organised coercive power of the state. History has shown that even the most dictatorial government, once stabilised in power, prefers the appeal to law to the naked reliance on force. On the other hand, the Soviet state, having achieved its main social revolution through the transfer of the means of production to the state or to collective entities controlled by the state, needed a measure of legal protection for its citizens. The Constitution of 1936 specifically sanctions private property in the attributes of personal life, as distinct from control over the means of production. Such protection includes, houses, tools, a limited number of livestock, savings, maintenance claims, etc. The development of the Soviet state thus needed simultaneously the

---

23 For statutes see Berman, *Id.* at 104 ns. 7, 8.
24 Article 12 of the Fundamental of Civil Procedure of the U.S.S.R., 1961.
25 Article 4, Code of Civil Procedure of the R.S.F.S.R., 1923.

restoration of law as an instrument of authority and the limited restoration of law as a protector of individual rights. For example, the renewed regard for personal property is shown by the increase in the penalty for theft from three months to two years.[26] There has, as a matter of fact, been a general lessening of the disparity of punishment between political and economic crimes and crimes against individuals. This trend must be seen, however, in terms of the restoration of individual guilt in the traditional type of crime. The notion of the criminality of acts contrary to the economic regime of the state is still intact, although the penalties for such crimes as speculation[27] have been greatly decreased since the period in the early 1960s when there was a return to very harsh criminal and administrative penalties. Further, the early revolutionary conception of the treatment of juvenile delinquency,[28] which was succeeded by a restoration of criminal liability for children over twelve, has been modified to 16 generally, a median which approximates the solution in most legal systems.[29]

The interest of the state in stability and order is also shown by the complete abandonment in recent years of the free dissolubility of marriage in favour of a strict and costly judicial divorce procedure.[30] The consolidation of the Soviet state, its industrial and scientific progress and increasing prosperity have strengthened internal pressures for some adjustment of police state methods in favour of individual rights and liberties. This coincides with the rise of a new educated middle class, composed of scientists, engineers, industrial managers, authors and others influential in Soviet society. The result has been, since Stalin's death, a gradual reduction of the powers of the M.V.D., the dissolution of forced labour camps and, generally, some shift towards "legality" as understood in western legal systems.[31] Thus the power to punish by analogy,[32] reflecting the concept of the 1926 Criminal Code that the terms "socially dangerous act" and "crime" are synonymous, eroded over

[26] Crim. Code of R.S.F.S.R., 1960, as amended 1965, Art. 144.

[27] *Id.*, Art. 154.

[28] "Juvenile crime is a concomitant of capitalism. In a Socialist society there will be no place for juvenile crime", Juvenile Delinquency, Moscow, 1932 quoted in Kiralfy, "The Juvenile Law-Breaker in the U.S.S.R.," 15 M.L.R. 472 (1952).

[29] Article 10, Criminal Code of the R.S.F.S.R., 1960 as amended 1965.

[30] Berman, *Justice in the U.S.S.R.* 336 *et seq.* (rev. ed. 1963).

[31] See Hazard 8 Am. J. Comp. L. 72 (1959).

[32] Article 16 1926 Criminal Code: "If any socially dangerous act is not directly provided for by the present Code, the basis and limits of responsibility for it shall be determined by application of those articles of the Code which provide for crimes most similar in nature." (Quoted in Berman, *Soviet Criminal Law and Procedure* 26 (1966)).

the years,[33] has been abolished. The 1960 R.S.F.S.R. Criminal Code states in Article 3: "Only a person guilty of committing a crime, that is, who intentionally or negligently commits a socially dangerous act provided by law, shall be subject to criminal responsibility and punishment."[34]

The four previously mentioned factors are characteristic of specific aspects of a revolutionary authoritarian and totalitarian state rather than of socialist society in general. It is the fifth and last factor which goes to the root problem of law in a socialist society. As the means of production passes into the hands of the state, economic planning by the state absorbs by far the most important sphere of law. Planning replaces free commodity exchange. State-controlled agencies deal with each other as the instruments of a national economic plan and not as autonomous individuals in a free economy. Contract and the transfer of property survive in so far as they are convenient instruments of economic planning but not as institutions inviolate in themselves.

The conflict between the necessity to subordinate civil rights and the security of legal transactions to the national economic plan, and the need to re-establish contract, property and other legal institutions in order to ensure efficiency and stability of administration in the nationalised enterprises, has produced the most important contribution of Soviet jurisprudence to legal thinking. Since 1923 industrial, commercial and other organisations—including certain government departments—entrusted with managerial and economic functions have been constituted as juridical entities. They receive a charter which lays down the functions and powers of the corporation in the manner familiar to non-socialist systems.[35] Many of these corporations are concerned with manufacture, purchases, sales and contracts of services on an immense scale. The management is given a large degree of autonomy, including the power to make contracts. It is obvious that no enterprise, socialist or otherwise, could function efficiently unless it could rely on the sanctions of contract. Whether the defendant be a private corporation or a state trust, it must be held accountable for failure to supply promised goods or for defects of quality. On the other hand, ability

[33] *Id.* at 26, 27, 28.   [34] See also Articles 6, 7.
[35] *Cf.* Hazard and Weisberg, *Cases and Readings on Soviet Law,* 280-284. The status of state enterprises of all kinds is now regulated by a Statute of 1965, which affirms their legal personality and generally strengthens their property rights. The Russian Civil Code of 1964 has new rules for the adjustment of the tensions between autonomy of contract and supervening planning directions. See Kiralfy, "The New Civil Code of the R.S.F.S.R.," 15 I.C.L.Q. 1116 (1966) at 1121.

to perform is, in the completely planned society, particularly dependent on circumstances outside the control of the parties. The planners at the centre may divert supplies or ration materials because of a change in priorities which may be due to military, economic or political reasons. In order to resolve this constant conflict between contract and planning, Soviet law has established a special system of commercial courts (Gosarbitrazh) to settle disputes between state enterprises. The importance of these institutions is apparent from the fact that in 1938 they litigated over 330,000 cases.[36] The Gosarbitrazh are subordinated to the administrative authorities of the territory in which they operate, and ultimately to the Council of the Ministers of the U.S.S.R. The decree establishing them in 1931 stated that the Gosarbitrazh "shall be guided by the laws and dispositions of the central and local organs of state power and also by the general principles of the economic policy of the U.S.S.R." Since then, authoritative commentators have repeatedly stressed their obligation to apply the law of contract strictly, although always with regard to the economic policy of the government. The reported cases[37] make it quite clear that state enterprises are not lightly excused from the performance of contractual obligations on the ground of circumstances beyond their control. It is, in fact, a paramount aspect of Soviet legal policy that the efficiency of the management of state corporations should be controlled by strict legal accountability. This is reinforced by a characteristic feature of the Soviet system and of the Gosarbitrazh in particular. The sanction for default may consist not only in damages or specific performance, but also in penalties and a report by the court to its superior administrative authority. Report of neglect may lead to the confiscation of assets, the withholding of credits, the dismissal of the management. This reveals a characteristic feature of a fully socialised law. The institution of contract is taken over from capitalistic systems and preserved, but for different purposes. It is predominantly a means of ensuring efficiency in the carrying out of the national plan. Therefore public and private law sanctions, criminal and civil law, are mixed and the court fulfils administrative as well as judicial functions. This links up with the concept

---

[36] Berman, *Justice in the U.S.S.R. op. cit.* at 124 *et seq.* The 1960 Statute on State Arbitrazh (Gosarbitrazh) both increases the scope of its administrative activity and systematises its operation. *Id.* at 127-128. No general statistics for post-war years are available.

[37] *Cf.* in particular the collection made by Berman, *Commercial Contracts in Soviet Law* 35 Calif. L.R. 191 (1947).

of economic crimes which plays an outstanding part in the Soviet criminal code and the practice of Soviet law. A typical provision is Article 100 of the Criminal Code of the R.S.F.S.R.:[38] "An unconscientious attitude towards his duties on the part of a person charged with protection of state or social property, resulting in the stealing, damaging or destroying of such property on a large scale, in the absence of the indicia of an official crime, shall be punished by deprivation of freedom for a term not exceeding two years or by correctional tasks for a term not exceeding one year, or by *social censure*." Again, Article 157 of the Criminal Code provides that, "Issuing for sale in trade enterprises, repeatedly or in large amounts, goods known to be of poor quality, non-standard, or incomplete, by the manager of a store, depot, warehouse, or section by a marketing specialist or specialist in sorting spoiled goods, shall be punished by deprivation of freedom for a term not exceeding two years, or by correctional tasks for a term not exceeding one year or by a fine not exceeding 100 rubles or by deprivation of the right to occupy the offices listed.[39] In the socialist state, bad management is not just a private matter for the parties concerned; it directly affects the national plan, the flow of production and the distribution of assets. The reward of profits or the threat of bankruptcy cannot suffice. The state is directly concerned in economic efficiency; it bestows legal autonomy on its enterprises only in order to control the conduct of business more effectively.

On the other hand, a great part of Soviet law as it affects the average citizen is not very different from the law of present-day England, France or the United States. Soviet citizens can own property within the limits assigned by the Constitution. They can protect their inventions by patent, their authorship by copyright, leave their property by will. They suffer accidents in the streets or in factories; they buy and sell goods within the limits assigned by the planning programme; they may be dismissed from their employment or fail to receive the wages promised to them by contract. In all these fields—which concern either the mutual relations, rights and duties of individuals or their claims as individual citizens against public authority—Soviet law provides an elaborate hierarchy of courts, of quasi-judicial and administrative authorities and a

---

[38] Criminal Code of the R.S.F.S.R., 1960 as revised in 1965 as translated in Berman, *Soviet Criminal Law and Procedure* 191 (1966). The last clause, with emphasis added did not exist under former law. The term "social censure" is defined in Article 33 of the Criminal Code.

[39] *Id.* at 206.

respect for individual rights comparable to that of non-socialist systems. Since the publication of much up-to-date material on Soviet law,[40] there is no longer any excuse for believing that law in the Soviet state is simply a sham. Within the limits assigned to it by Communist political philosophy, and the overriding demands of the state, it is real. The Civil Code of 1964, is, like the 1923 Code which it succeeds, predominantly akin to the structure of Western Codes. Such problems as the question of individual guilt in criminal law, of fault as a basis of tort liability, of illegality or impossibility in contract, of unjust enrichment, constantly arise in Soviet law and are dealt with by arguments familiar to other legal systems. Socialist ideology accounts for certain particular features. Article 127 of the Criminal Code makes criminally punishable: "The failure to render aid which is necessary and is clearly required immediately to a person in danger of death, if such aid could knowingly be rendered by the guilty person without serious danger to himself or to other persons."[41] Under Article 49 of the 1964 Civil Code when a contract, "made for a purpose known to be contrary to the interests of the socialist state and society and there is intent on the part of both parties . . . all that was received by them under the transaction shall be collected for the benefit of the state." A similar provision governs situations of unjust enrichment.[42] But such peculiarities do not point to fundamental differences. Modern English and American law, for example, has steadily moved towards a greater legal recognition of the moral duty to come to the rescue of persons in danger.[43] A more important difference between Soviet law and the law of contemporary democratic societies is revealed in the function of collective labour contracts. These exist in Soviet law as they do in American, English or German law, but in Soviet law the collective agreements, based on model contracts established for an entire industry, are not seen as the adjustment of the interests of conflicting groups but as a con-

---

[40] *Cf.* in particular the works by Gsovski, Hazard and Weisberg, Berman, Schlesinger as quoted in the bibliography to this chapter, below, p. 589.

[41] Article 128 provides for similar penalties for failure to assist sick persons. Translation of text in Berman, *Soviet Criminal Law and Procedure* 197-198 (1966). Formerly the same rule was applied specifically in cases of the legal duty of a swimmer to assist a drowning person by use of Article 130 of the Soviet Constitution which enjoins every citizen, "honestly to perform public duties, and to respect the rules of socialist intercourse."

[42] Article 473 para. 4 of the Civil Code of the R.S.F.S.R., 1964. On the extent to which this is applicable to relations between state enterprises, see the decisions and articles quoted in Hazard and Weisberg *op. cit.* at 239-241.

[43] *Cf. Haynes* v. *Harwood* [1935] 1 K.B. 146.

venient way of formalising the relations between management and labour within the framework of a national plan.[44] This again may become a difference of degree rather than of fundamentals. Under the impact of the social welfare philosophy, as well as of the defence needs of a perpetually mobilised society, the democratic states find it more and more difficult to leave collective bargaining entirely a matter between employers and labour. Reluctantly they are driven to emphasise the state interest in these agreements in a variety of ways.[45] On the other hand, Soviet law protects the individual rights of the worker strictly and by an elaborate procedure; it is in the interest of a Communist, as well as a Fascist or a democratic society, that the worker should be protected in his claims to wages, pensions, holidays, and that he should have safeguards against unjust dismissal. A totalitarian society must, if anything, strengthen the protection of these rights for, as it deprives the individual of all rights to autonomous political and social organisation, as it makes him a cog in an immense machine, it must on the other hand give him security; as it restricts the mobility of labour, it must reinforce stability of employment. In all these respects, Communist and Fascist law closely resemble each other.

It is not surprising that the vast and novel nature of the experiment, as much as the conflicting character of the different trends in social evolution, are reflected in the vacillations of Soviet legal theory. The theory of Pashukanis mentioned above[46] was at least definite in its definition of law as an instrument of commodity exchange between equal parties in a capitalist society, which eliminated law from socialist society altogether, replacing it by administrative discretion and utility. This, from the opposite point of departure, comes near to the views of modern critics of the Western world, which decry the arbitrariness of administrative discretion in a world of growing state power and hold up the rule of law in its established sense as a protector of individual rights. It is this parallel which partly accounts for the condemnation of Pashukanis' theory. The other reason is the previously mentioned policy of the Soviet state to re-establish the authority of law. But no satisfactory alternative to Pashukanis' theory has been found. Soviet legal theory has not abandoned established legal concepts and categories such as crime, guilt, civil law, administrative law.

[44] *Cf.* Aleksandrov writing in 1948, as quoted by Hazard and Weisberg, *op. cit.* at 144.

[45] For a survey, see *Law in a Changing Society*, Chap. 4.

[46] See above at p. 371.

It is struggling with the need to reassess the meaning of these categories in a socialist society. Schlesinger[47] enumerates at least six major attempts to redefine the sphere of civil law. They waver between formal and substantive definitions. Some are meaningless, such as Mikolenko's definition of civil law as the method used for the enforcement of civil rights. Others link civil law to the regulation of property regulations. The real problem of law in a socialist state is that stressed earlier. As the major sphere of social life passes from the private to the public sphere the ensuing relations must be governed by a system which combines certain forms of civil law with the substance of public law. A new balance between security, which characterises private law, and controlling utility, which characterises public law, must be sought. The working out of a satisfactory theory of Soviet law has, however, been made increasingly difficult by the fear of deviationism. A doctrinaire tyranny compels every Soviet jurist to justify his theory by the writings of Marx, Lenin and Stalin. Successive purges have shown that they have not always been successful in this attempt, but one certain result of this development has been the growing sterility of Soviet jurisprudence. There is an unquestionable decline in the quality of thought from the earlier work of such jurists as Stuchka and Pashukanis to the tirades of Vishinsky. The earlier Soviet jurists are still linked with the Western tradition of jurisprudence even where they fight its ideas. The later Soviet jurisprudence increasingly turns into political pamphleteerism.[48] It is likely that the relaxation of the police state methods of the Stalin period and the resumption of intellectual contacts with the West will bring continuing improvement in the quality of legal thinking.

Three major spheres of law are crystallising in the socialist Soviet state. The most important is the sphere of economic and property relations between the agents of state enterprise, in industry and farming. The second sphere concerns the relation between the state and the citizens. Most of the relevant principles are embodied in the Constitution of 1936. They include such matters as the right and duty to work, the guarantee of a minimum standard of living, the right to social security and rest. These legal relations have not the character of protected civil rights and duties in the established sense of Western law. Unlike constitutions of the

---

[47] Schlesinger, *Soviet Legal Theory* (2nd ed., 1950). For a more concise statement of legal problems see the same author's article, 6 Mod. L. Rev. 21 (1942).
[48] *Cf.* the collection of texts in *Soviet Legal Philosophy* (ed. Hazard, 1951).

Western type, such as the American, the Australian, or the new West German Constitution, they provide no protection or method of enforcement through legal procedure. On the whole, these so-called rights and duties are a formal indication of the principles of which the state is built. They form the basis for law rather than law itself. Lastly, a group of legal relations remains which closely corresponds to those in non-socialist societies, *i.e.*, the sphere of protected private rights and obligations. Among them are claims arising out of accidents, claims for maintenance, actions for divorce, claims arising out of wills, the recovery of stolen property, damage claims of all sorts. It is in this sphere, administered by the civil courts, that the general concepts of contract, tort, property, possession, crime, can survive to a much larger degree. But the relative importance of this sphere of law in society in relation to the whole is much smaller in a socialist than in a capitalist society; for the conduct of the major part of the economic life of the nation is removed from it.

LEGAL THEORY OF SOCIAL DEMOCRACY

It is not easy to state the legal theory of contemporary social democracy in general terms. From originally Marxist premises, the social democratic movement developed gradually, from the rejection of the revolutionary postulates of the Marx-Engels-Lenin theory of Communism, to a "revisionist" philosophy of gradual introduction of socialism into the life of a nation by constitutional means. This meant an attempt to blend the principles of political democracy with those of economic socialism. This evolution proceeded, quite independently, on the Continent, under the doctrinal leadership of such men as Jaurés, Bernstein and Kautsky, and in England, where socialism was less inspired by Marxist doctrine than by non-conformists religious leaders, practical philanthropists, the cooperative movement and trade unionism. In most countries of the Western world, social democracy is represented by a major parliamentary party, which in turn is linked with the trade union movement. Since the end of the First World War, the democratic socialists have often formed governments, singly or in coalition. The legal and political philosophy of social democracy has undergone corresponding modifications which have removed it further and further from the original theory of Marxism. Moreover, the major social democratic parties of the Western world—such as those of Great Britain, Sweden and Western Germany—differ from each other in philosophy and emphasis.

In Sweden, where a social democratic government has been in power for several decades, public ownership of the means of production is of little importance. The major emphasis has been on public investment planning, and the building of a social welfare state, with a highly developed national health service and a multitude of other social services. In Great Britain, where a Labour government, between 1945 and 1951, had the opportunity to implement at least some principles of moderate socialism, the two major pillars of legislative policy were the introduction of comprehensive public welfare institutions—such as a national health service and a comprehensive system of social insurance—and the nationalisation of basic industries in the form of semi-autonomous public enterprises. The latter aspect implied at least a partial retention of the original socialist ideology under which the means of production should be owned by the public. But although the public monopolies, constituted as statutory corporations in the fields of coal, electricity, gas, atomic energy and public transport, have remained generally untouched by subsequent Conservative governments the further nationalisation of industries and services has been virtually arrested and is unlikely to be revived, short of revolutionary upheavals.

The public corporations are legal persons with all the rights and liabilities of commercial companies. They are subject to commercial accounting and auditing, but they are managed by boards appointed by the competent Minister who represents the Government and is responsible to Parliament. Their capital is provided either through stock issued with a Treasury guarantee or by Government stock. The public corporations are instruments of national policy in so far as the Government, through the competent Minister, can give directions, and the Minister is responsible to Parliament. They thus become part of the national economic plan, like the Soviet trusts. But unlike the latter they are fully autonomous in their legal existence and conduct of affairs; their transactions are overwhelmingly with private law companies or with each other. On the whole, the British nationalised industries have fitted without any fundamental changes into a system in which public and private enterprise as well as public and private law are closely mingled. This is so largely because on one hand British public opinion has long accepted the need for Government direction and public enterprise in some fields, with the result that freedom of contract and property have long been modified by many public law controls, and on the other hand the public corporations have operated within a private enterprise law system and the framework of the common law.

The socialisation of certain basic utilities or industries, or of other sectors of the economy—sometimes in the form of public corporations, sometimes through semi-autonomous government departments, or sometimes through commercial companies in which the state owns a controlling interest—is now a universal phenomenon. Thus, in France, the basic utilities, and certain selected manufacturing industries, were nationalised after the Second World War, in a manner somewhat comparable to the British development. In Italy the state controls shipbuilding, metallurgy, mineral resources and other basic sectors of industrial life, through state-owned holding companies which operate networks of subsidiaries. In India, the railways, aviation, the steel and oil industries, and other basic sectors of economic life are owned by the State. Even in the United States—the chief pillar of a private enterprise ideology —the generation of electric power is to a large extent controlled by the Federal government, whereas in states such as New York a large number of semi-autonomous public authorities account for a substantial portion of economic life. Like all other industrialised countries, the United States has also adopted many aspects of the social welfare state, such as unemployment insurance, old age pensions and medical care, financed by taxes and other social contributions.

Social democratic theory has therefore lost much of its distinctiveness, with respect to the role of public enterprise in a mixed economy. Since public enterprises, especially in the public utility sector, exist in every legal system, the question at what point the predominance of public over private enterprise justifies the characterisation of "socialist" is essentially one of degree. Moreover, as the example of Sweden shows, it is not always necessary to operate public enterprises, for the state to exercise basic control over the economy. This can be done through a multitude of devices such as public investment planning, foreign exchange, import and industrial licensing controls, which play a dominant part in the economy of the developing countries.

What is essential to the conception of a social democratic, as distinct from a Marxist legal system, is that any degree of transfer of the means of production under public control must go hand in hand with the democratic values, parliamentary democracy and individual liberties, whether they are secured by constitutional guarantees or by the tradition of the common law.[49] Moreover, the public economic sector must coexist with the private economic sector. This may produce many delicate problems of adjustment, such as the problem of fairness of allocation between public and private enterprise in a scarcity economy, or the question of preferences in distribution of orders or the use of services, where public and private enterprise coexist in a particular field, such as aviation or road transport. In a mixed economy, it will probably have to be regarded as part and parcel of a social democratic legal ideology that public and private enterprise should be treated as equals. This may mean the creation of administrative and judicial organs to safeguard the application of equal standards.

[49] See, on Radbruch's philosophy of socialism, above, p. 192 *et seq.*

CHAPTER 30

NEO-SCHOLASTIC DOCTRINE AND MODERN
CATHOLIC LEGAL PHILOSOPHY

RESTATEMENT OF THOMISTIC PRINCIPLES BY THE
CATHOLIC CHURCH

LIKE most great intellectual creations, and like its counterpart, Dante's universal empire, St. Thomas' system illuminates the twilight of the society which it orders. But while the rise of the modern national state and of new social forces destroyed the medieval structure of Europe, the Catholic Church survived and, after centuries, under the challenge of modern nationalism and the industrial revolution, redefined its beliefs. In this attempt, initiated by Leo XIII, in a series of Encyclical Letters, St. Thomas' system and the doctrine of natural law are the principal guides. In almost all essentials (with the important exception of the doctrine of property) the scholastic system is preserved by modern Catholic doctrine. In regard to the relations between Church and state, concessions had to be made, and the main development lies in the elaborate definition of the social creed of modern catholicism, in the light of new social and industrial developments. But it is a development, not a modification, of Thomistic principles.

This Catholic doctrine commands the allegiance of hundreds of millions. In some cases it is also the official doctrine of the state. Thus the Constitution of Eire is explicitly based on the Catholic doctrine of law and state.[1] Again, the family law of many predominantly Catholic states, like Eire, Italy, Quebec or most of the Latin-American republics, is dominated by Catholic doctrine on divorce, legitimacy and other matters. In other legal systems, conflicts between the law of the state and the law of the Church may arise for the individual Catholic.[2]

Briefly, the following are the principal creeds which modern

---

[1] The same was true of the defunct Austrian Constitution of 1934.
[2] See below, p. 393.

official Catholic doctrine has developed from scholastic premises: [3]

(1) All law emanates from natural law, itself a product of divine reason, although certain laws of civil authorities derive only remotely from natural law.

Every positive law, from whatever lawgiver it may come, can be examined as to its moral authority in the light of the commandments of the natural law.[4]

But modern Catholic doctrine, in the days of the omnipotent state, is more cautious in the assertion of the legal invalidity of state law contrary to the law of nature. For though such laws are declared to be "incapable of sanctioning anything which is not contained in the eternal law"[5] and another Encyclical[6] even proclaims that "laws only bind when they are in accordance with right reason, and hence with the eternal law of God," the emphasis in modern conflicts is on the immorality, not the invalidity of such laws.[7]

(2) The state has the duty to keep the community in obedience by the adoption of a common discipline and by putting restraint upon refractory and "viciously inclined men," and to decide many points which the law of nature treats only in a general and indefinite way.[8] It is certainly held inferior to eternal law as interpreted by the Church and comes after, not before, man. But its actual power is greatly strengthened by the Catholic condemnation of violent resistance and revolution. Resistance to authority is sin, though authority should conform to the law of God. But this condemnation has been considerably modified where the interests of the Church itself have been involved in the issues of civil war. In the Spanish Civil War of 1936 the Catholic Church openly supported the insurgents, and in 1937 the apostolic letter to the Mexican episcopate stated that

if ever that authority should rise up against justice and truth to the extent of destroying even the very foundations of authority, it would be impossible to condemn a movement in which citizens were to unite to defend the nation and themselves, by lawful and appropriate means, against those who make use of the civil power to drag the nation to ruin.

---

[3] For a collection of texts and documents, see Oakeshott, *Social and Political Doctrines of Contemporary Europe* (1939).
[4] Papal Letter to the Church in Germany, 1937.
[5] Encyclical *Libertas* (1888).
[6] *Rerum Novarum* (1891).
[7] Papal Letter to the Church in Germany, 1937.
[8] Encyclical *Libertas* (1888).

(3) Of individual rights modern Catholic doctrine unreservedly recognises the right to worship. But freedom of speech and of the press is recognised only with considerable reservations.

The excesses of an unbridled intellect, which unfailingly end in the oppression of the untutored multitude, are no less rightly controlled by the authority of the law than are the injuries inflicted by violence upon the weak. . . . In regard, however, to all matter of opinion which God leaves to man's free discussion, full liberty of thought and speech is naturally within the right of every one.[9]

Official Catholic doctrine has also been a consistent and strong supporter of the right to private property, as a direct emanation of the law of nature as ordained by God.[10] The justification of the natural right to property is closely akin to that used by Locke and Hegel. As has been pointed out earlier,[11] the "natural law" approach to the right of property is a substantial and deliberate—though unacknowledged—departure from the philosophy of St. Thomas for whom the justification of private property had an essentially utilitarian basis, and who maintained that property must be used for the common good. The contemporary doctrine of the Catholic Church on this subject shows a certain modification of the philosophy of property—expressed in the Encyclical *Rerum Novarum* of 1891, and corresponding to the then predominant philosophy and practice of economic liberalism and capitalism. In the Encyclical *Quadragesimo Anno*, Pope Pius XI[12] had already stressed that "property is not unchangeable," and that its forms, modalities and purposes must vary with the times. In a speech of October 14, 1955, Pope Pius XII developed the distinction between unchangeable and changeable natural law and pointed out that changes of economic and social conditions had always, in legal history, required adaptations of the changeable aspects of natural law. This doctrine is particularly applicable to the relation of private property and public welfare. It is Pope John XXIII's Encyclical

---

[9] Encyclical *Libertas* (1888). For a restatement of the Catholic position on censorship, in particular of the Index of Prohibited Books and the so-called Twelve Rules, see Connell, "Censorship and the Prohibition of Books in Catholic Church Law," (1954) 54 Colum. L. Rev. 699. The justification is simply that the Church has received from God the right to teach officially the truths of religion and morality and the right to legislate on matters pertinent to the spiritual welfare of those subject to its jurisdiction (*ibid.* at p. 707).

[10] "The State acknowledges that man, in virtue of his natural being, has the natural right, antecedent to positive law, to the private ownership of external goods." (Eire Constitution, Art. 43.)

[11] See above, p. 110 *et seq.*

[12] See especially sect. 49.

Mater et Magistra of 1961[13] that spells out and modifies the contemporary attitude of the Church. Although the natural right to property, including ownership of means of production, is reaffirmed, the task of the State in insuring that property is used for the common benefit is far more strongly emphasised. "The leadership of the State has to insure that the planning of the directors of leading enterprises, especially of all those that are of decisive importance for the entire national economy, do not in this or that respect go contrary to the requirements of the common welfare. As experience shows, these problems exist irrespectively of whether the capital necessary for the big enterprises is in public or private hands."[14]

In contrast to the unconditional condemnation of socialism in all forms by previous Encyclicals, *Mater et Magistra* leaves far greater scope to public property and public enterprise. "It appears to be a characteristic of our time that State and other public property increases all the time. The reason for this, among others, is that the State, for the sake of the public welfare must undertake ever increasing tasks . . . only then should the State and other public institutions increase the extent of their property when the rightly interpreted public welfare clearly demands it; any excessive restriction or, what would be worse, complete displacement of private property, should be avoided."[15]

Given the immense variety of conditions in the different states, and especially in the economically undeveloped countries, to which the developed countries "should not impose their own style of life,"[16] the philosophy of *Mater et Magistra* leaves wide scope to the many different economic and social systems, from essentially free enterprise to essentially state-directed systems, short only of the complete abolition of private property.

(4) Of institutions within the state, the family is recognised as inviolable and sacred. The family is a society ordained by God and independent of the state. The procreation of children is regarded as an essential and God-ordained aspect of family life; hence the Catholic Church would emphatically reject the conclusion reached by the House of Lords some years ago,[17] that insistence on the part of the wife on the use of contraceptives did not amount to

[13] See especially secs. 104 to 121. See also Pope Paul VI, *Populorum Progressio* (March 1967) secs. 23, 50, 51.
[14] Sect. 104 (author's translation from German text.).
[15] *Id.* at sect. 117.   [16] *Id.* at sect. 170.
[17] *Baxter* v. *Baxter* [1948] A.C. 274.

wilful refusal of intercourse and therefore did not entitle the husband to a decree of nullity. Consistent with this attitude the Catholic Church condemns the use of contraceptives altogether as contrary to the institution of the family, and thus to natural law.[18] Official doctrine goes so far as to regard the life of the unborn child as more important than the life of the mother where one or the other has to be sacrificed.[19] The uncompromising hostility of the Church to any form of birth control other than abstention has become an international social problem of the utmost gravity, at a time when the present world population of three thousand million is likely to double by the year 2000 and to produce widespread famine and misery. This fact, together with the inconsistencies of the present official doctrine and the availability of an anovular oral pill has caused considerable dissent among Catholic clergy and scholars, and led the Ecumenical Council of 1965 to order a re-examination of the Catholic doctrine. It might have been expected that the Church would bless the procreation of children through artificial insemination as between husband and wife, where, for reasons beyond the control of the spouses, they are unable to procreate children in the natural way. Yet the Catholic Church stands alone among official Christian religions in the unconditional condemnation of artificial insemination, not only by the semen of third parties (A.I.D.)—a practice that causes great practical as well as theoretical problems, of adultery, legitimacy, tort, liability, succession and the like[20]—but also between husband and wife (A.I.H.). In an address to the Catholic Union of Midwives of October 1951,[21] the late Pope Pius XII, while reaffirming the procreation of children as the primary end of marriage, said that artificial insemination would be converting "the home, the sanctuary of the family, into a mere biological laboratory." By this strange emphasis on the sexual act rather than the more spiritual aspects of marriage,

[18] Recent Papal Encyclicals have reaffirmed this position while permitting the deliberate avoidance of conception through the selection of "safe periods" for sexual intercourse. On ethical grounds it is difficult to appreciate this differentiation. If marriage is the God-ordained instrument for the procreation of children, then any deliberate regulation of sexual intercourse in such a manner that pregnancy is avoided must be an unethical interference with the course of nature, whether or not mechanical means are used. See *Populorum Progressio* (1967) sect. 37.

[19] *Cf.* Pius XII, in his address to the Catholic midwives of October 1951: "If, despite all efforts, it is impossible to save both . . . nothing remains but to bow respectfully before the laws of nature and the dispositions of Divine Providence."

[20] On these, see among others Tallin, *Artificial Insemination*, 34 Can. Bar Rev. 1, 166 (1956).

[21] Reproduced in *Moral Questions Affecting Married Life* (The Paulist Press).

which would seem to be ennobled by the desire to have children despite the absence of sexual satisfaction, the Church seems to relapse into the more primitive biological conception of natural law as *"quod natura omnia animalia docuit."*

(5) The greatest advance—not in principle, but in detail—upon Thomistic thought is the emphasis on a just wage, "agreed freely and not insufficient to support a frugal and well-behaved wage-earner."[22] This follows from the human dignity of labour and the duty imposed by God on those in high places to be just and charitable towards their servants. In modern industrial society, the predominant form of regulation of a "just wage" is, of course, the collective agreement. The Catholic Church has, however, been hesitant and ambiguous in its attitude towards the principle of collective bargaining. While Catholic trade unions, which fully supported collective bargaining, prospered, for example, in pre-Nazi Germany,[23] the Church was driven by its hostility to any form of class struggle to bless officially the corporative philosophy of state adopted by Mussolini's Italy and Franco's Spain.[24] As the labour legislation of both these régimes meant the abolition of free trade unions, and of any process of genuine collective bargaining between employers and workers' organisations—for which an officially sponsored and state-directed system of division of the national economy into "estates" and "corporations" was substituted —the Church thus identified itself with an extremely reactionary and authoritarian form of labour organisation.

(6) Racial differences and persecutions are condemned as against the law of God which embraces all mankind.

On the whole, modern Catholic doctrine has tended to lessen the tension between the law of the Church and the law of the state by confining its authority to the moral rather than the legal sphere. Yet conflicts may arise for Catholic judges and other lawyers where Catholic doctrine sharply deviates from the law of the state. In recent years the Catholic Church has been explicit in the reformulation of legal doctrine. Sometimes the Church has gone so far as to authorise resistance against positive law, in particular in the case of laws directed against the Church itself.[25] In November

---

[22] Encyclical *Rerum Novarum* (1891). It should be pointed out that well-organised Catholic trade unions have supported collective bargaining both under the Weimar Republic and in the present Federal Republic of Germany.

[23] They are today officially, but not socially, merged with the more powerful Social Democratic trade unions.

[24] See Encyclical *Quadragesimo Anno* (1931).

[25] See above, p. 388.

1950, Pope Pius XII issued a decree in which he outlined the principles which are to guide Catholic judges in the administration of the law. This decree emphasises that a Catholic judge cannot evade responsibility for his decisions by reference to the will of the legislator. It also instructs him not to apply intrinsically immoral laws. Perhaps the most important and the most difficult of the Papal instructions is that a Catholic judge, except for reasons of the greatest importance, should not pronounce a civil divorce decree for a marriage which is valid in the eyes of God and of the Church. In predominantly Catholic countries which do not know statutory causes of divorce, a conflict between the law of the state and Catholic law will not often arise, but in other countries difficult situations may occur. Is a Catholic judge to refuse a divorce decree when the law of the land commands it? Is he to award a decree of nullity on the petition of either spouse if the other spouse insists on the use of contraceptives?[26] Should he interpret the law in a divorce action in such a manner as to avoid a divorce decree?[27] The Papal Decree was interpreted by Vatican commentators as meaning that Catholic judges should avoid presiding over divorce courts whenever possible. Such a solution is not always feasible, especially where the judges take duties in rotation. This reassertion of the positive authority of Catholic law in preference to the positive law opens up great problems. If the conflict is not usually as acute as it might be in theory, it is due to a more elastic practice.

NEO-SCHOLASTIC NATURAL LAW THEORIES

Modern natural law doctrines of Catholic origin correspond closely to the doctrine of the Catholic Church. They are derived from the same scholastic basis. While modern religiously based doctrines of natural law are almost entirely of Catholic-scholastic persuasion, a significant defence of natural law from a Protestant point of view, can be found in Emil Brunner's *Justice and the Social Order* (1945). Justice is seen as an imperfect reflection of God's love in the world of human institutions. While there are certain immutable principles of justice established by creation, true justice is "the

---

[26] *Cf. Baxter* v. *Baxter* [1948] A.C. 274.
[27] This is suggested by the dissenting judges in *Fender* v. *St. John Mildmay* [1938] A.C. 1.

O*

precept of the order of creation" accommodated to concrete historical circumstance.[28]

Cathrein[29] derives natural law from Christian revelation and reaffirms the scholastic doctrine with a rigour far exceeding that of the modern Church, by declaring that all positive law contrary to natural law is void. Accordingly, the judge is to disregard positive law where it is "manifestly unjust." What that means to Cathrein is evident from the large proportion of his work which he devotes to the justification of private property as an exigency of human nature, which alone is morally just, guarantees order, liberty and peace, compels man to work and is in harmony with family interest as well as the progress of civilisation. Once again, natural law ideology thus covers a specific political and social faith.

A number of modern French jurists, notably Renard and Delos, have combined Hauriou's theory of the institution with a Catholic conception of natural law. To them the institution is the embodiment of objective order which is part of the order of God. In the institution, individual voluntarism, expressed in contract, merges in a cause, thus reconciling social and individual needs and realising human nature in God's plan. Other writers, like Le Fur, emphasise the harmony of the universe, against such jurists who, like Radbruch, stress antinomy and conflict of ideals in legal theory, as in life altogether. In practice this harmony means anti-revolutionary and, in particular, anti-Communist principles.

The significance of these theories lies in the affirmation of the social discipline of modern society (from the institution it is not far to the corporate state) and of the anti-revolutionary character of the scholastic conception of the universe. In all practical questions these writers agree with the official Catholic doctrine. Renard[30] expressly states that the Encyclical *Quadragesimo Anno* reconciles common good and social justice and thus realises natural law, which is "justice associated to the contingencies of each historical *milieu*." Despite different premises there is also spiritual affinity with Duguit's belief in an objective order coupled with the praise of service for a collective (in the name of social solidarity). A theoretical rapprochement is effected when Duguit's pupil and successor, Bonnard, makes of his master a defender of the French

---

[28] *Op. cit.* at 210.
[29] *Recht, Naturrecht und positives Recht* (2nd ed., 1909).
[30] Renard, *L'Institution*, 108.

natural law tradition and proclaims himself an adherent of natural law.[31]

In recent years there have been a number of restatements and reformulations of the modern Catholic doctrine of natural law. Among the most influential are those of Maritain[32] and Rommen.[33] The experiences of the Nazi régime and the tragedy of the Second World War may largely account for the attempt of both these authors to restate the Catholic doctrine of natural law in terms many of which non-Catholics can accept; yet the point of departure of both these authors is Thomistic. The basis of natural law is reason, and understanding of the true essence of things. "For the rational, free nature of man this signifies: act in accordance with reason; bring your essential being to completion; fulfil the order of being which you confront as a free creature."[34] The primary norm, according to St. Thomas, is to do good and to avoid evil. Both authors concede that natural law can only determine certain general principles of which the most fundamental is the dignity of man. Again they are in accord with St. Thomas in allowing wide scope to the "variable conditions of social life and the free initiative of human reason, . . . which natural law leaves undetermined."[35] Both Maritain and Rommen oppose the omnipotence of the state and advocate within limits the pluralistic society, in which Churches, minorities, corporations and other groups have the right to free existence and development. They also affirm the right of private property. It is demanded by natural law because it is a guarantee of human dignity, but Rommen allows wide scope to different social and political systems:

Natural law . . . does not demand the property and inheritance institutions of feudalism, or of liberalistic capitalism, or of a system in which private, incorporated and public forms of ownership exist side by side. These are positive law determinations which spring from the diversity of peoples which change with the socio-economic evolutions.[36]

Such a definition does not exclude either the American or the Soviet economic system, for the latter recognises both private

[31] In *Mélanges Hauriou*, 31; *Revue International de la Théorie du Droit*, 1, 1928-29.
[32] E.g. Maritain, *The Rights of Man and Natural Law* (English ed., 1943); *The Man and the State* (1951).
[33] Rommen, *Natural Law* (English ed., 1947).
[34] Rommen, *Id.* at 178; similarly Maritain, *Man and the State*, at 94.
[35] Maritain, *Id.* at 97.
[36] *Id.* at 235 *et seq.*

property and the right of inheritance.[37] In accordance with American doctrine both authors postulate the equality of races and nations and the development of a world society overcoming nationalism. The Protestant legal philosophy of Emil Brunner goes even further in regarding "planning in the service of freedom and in the service of the welfare of the community"[38] as required by a Christian order.

Another notable, though hardly successful, attempt to harmonise the scholastic belief in the superiority of immutable laws of nature (as interpreted by neo-Thomistic doctrine) with the recognition of the monopoly of organised civil society to establish rules of conduct sanctioned by public compulsion is that of Dabin.[39] His definition of the law is essentially positivist: "The sum total of the rules of conduct laid down, or at least consecrated by civil society, under the sanction of public compulsion, with a view to realising in the relationships between men a certain order—the order postulated by the end of civil society and by the maintenance of the civil society as an instrument devoted to that end."[40]

Dabin also acknowledges, in elaboration of a distinction made by St. Thomas himself,[41] that many positive laws, while serving society, have no particular moral significance: *e.g.*, conveyancing or traffic rules. Yet, in the same work, Dabin claims that "natural law . . . dominates positive law in the sense that, while positive law may add to natural law or even restrict it, it is prohibited from contradicting it."[42] Again, the statement that immoral legal rules must be "condemned"[43] as contrary to the public good fails to make clear what "condemnation" means in practical legal terms.

[37] Maritain is on more slippery ground when he states that nationalisation should remain limited "to those public services so immediately concerned with the very existence, order or international peace of the body politic that a risk of bad management is a lesser evil than the risk of giving the upper hand to private interests." (*Man and the State*, at 21). He also commits himself to the view that the state has skill and competence in administrative, legal and political matters, but is dull, awkward, oppressive and injudicious in other fields. It is difficult to see what natural law has to do with all this, and by what criteria it enables us to assert dogmatically that the management, for example, of Imperial Chemical Industries, is of necessity superior to that of the National Coal Board.

[38] Brunner, *Justice and the Social Order*, 182 (trans. Hotlinger, 1945).

[39] Dabin, *La Philosophie de l'ordre juridique positif* (1929); Dabin, *Théorie générale du droit* (1944), trans. in *The Legal Philosophies of Lask, Radbruch and Dabin* (1950).

[40] *Id.* at 234.

[41] *Cf.* above p. 109.

[42] *Op. cit.* at 419 *et seq.*

[43] Among "unjust" laws, Dabin mentions laws sanctioning perjury, anti-racial laws, or laws prohibiting religious or industrial associations. *Cf.* Dabin, *Ordre juridique positif, op. cit.* at 676-712.

If, as it appears to do, it means that such rules should be repealed, this hardly distinguishes his theory from any non-scholastic theory of justice.[44]

The idea of the corporation as the harmoniser of individual and community is the platform on which as divergent doctrines as those of Hegel, Gierke, Del Vecchio, Duguit, Renard, meet those of modern Catholicism and Fascism. This may give us an explanation for the apparent ease with which the sternly Catholic régimes of Franco's Spain and Pétain's France were able to collaborate not only with the not very Christian, though not openly anti-Christian, régime of Mussolini's Italy, but with the definitely anti-Christian order of Hitler's National Socialist Germany. The Catholic Church itself must be and appears to be divided in its sympathies. Its authoritarian, anti-liberal and anti-Communist principles, coupled with its interest in the maintenance of Catholic institutions in such countries as Spain, France, Italy, Mexico, pull it towards Fascism. Its Christian doctrines, respect for family life, rejection of race doctrines and respect for order and law in international relations pull in the opposite direction.

The legal doctrine of Catholicism is deeply grounded in religious philosophy. It is fortified by one of the most powerful philosophical systems ever thought out, and by a continuous tradition of many centuries. Yet it must be evident from the foregoing analysis that the most absolute law, when translated into practical precepts by an institution immersed in human conflicts, loses its absolute character and ranges itself in the struggle of conflicting ideas and values.

[44] Dabin's ambiguity in this respect has been criticised by Roubier, *Théorie Générale du Droit*, 215 (2nd ed.) and by Patterson, *Jurisprudence*, 355 *et seq.* (1953).

CHAPTER 31

LEGAL VALUES OF MODERN DEMOCRACY

THE beliefs and thoughts that guide the legal philosophies of Socialism, Fascism and Catholicism are based on certain clear-cut and essentially single-purpose principles. An analysis of the legal values of modern democracy is a more complex task; for it is a more comprehensive and flexible creed, the condensation of a long historical development, which comprises the essence of most of the great legal theories of Western civilisation; and it is still in a state of flux. The main forces in the development of modern democratic thought have been the liberal idea of individual rights protecting the individual, and the democratic idea proper, proclaiming equality of rights and popular sovereignty. The gradual extension of the idea of equality from the political to the social and economic field has added the problems of social security and economic planning. The implementation and harmonisation of these principles has been and continues to be the main problem of democracy.

A discussion of the principal legal values of modern democracy can be grouped round four themes of legal theory:

(1) The legal rights of the individual.
(2) Equality before the law.
(3) The control of government by the people.
(4) The rule of law.

Although closely interlinked, these four themes each describe a distinct trend of thought in political and legal theory.

RIGHTS OF THE INDIVIDUAL

The evolution of the individual as the ultimate measure of things, and the consideration of government and authority, not as a divine right or an end in itself but as a means to achieve the development of the individual, can be described as the basic political and legal ideal of modern Western society, and as a universally accepted standard of democratic society. The development of the individual

398

to his full potentialities is an old idea, inherent in Athenian democracy, and fully developed in Stoic philosophy. It is given a new and deeper foundation through the Christian conception of a direct spiritual relation between God and the individual.

But the conception of a society based on definite rights of the individual citizen is a relatively modern one, developed in reaction, first against the medieval order of society and, secondly, against the absolutist government of the modern state, in the seventeenth and eighteenth centuries. It finds expression in the legal philosophy of Locke, the French Declaration of the Rights of Man, and the American Constitution. This trend of thought[1] postulates specific inviolable individual rights: the integrity of life, personal liberty and property.[2] Right, not duty, is stressed, and also the individual as a self-contained unit resisting the intrusion of government.

But a new trend greatly modifies this uncompromising individualism. The French Convention of 1793 stipulates "common happiness" as the aim of society; Kant defines law as "the aggregate of the conditions under which the arbitrary will of one individual may be combined with that of another under a general inclusive law of freedom." Bentham postulates the greatest happiness of the greatest number as the purpose of law, and this leads him to a definition of freedom similar to Kant's.[3] The American Constitution, on the other hand, preserves the unmitigated emphasis on individual rights with results of deep significance for American social and legal development.[4] The relation of the rights of the individual to those of his fellow individuals in the community has gradually led to a profound modification of the legal values of modern democracy. It has increasingly tempered individual right by social duty. Democracy has not accepted the elimination of rights; it has not recognised Comte's and Duguit's "right to do one's duty" as the only right. Duguit's postulate has, in fact, as shown before,[5] been the forerunner of Fascist legal principles. But democratic communities have universally, though with varying speed and intensity, accepted the principle of social obligation as limiting individual right. On the other hand they are in process of extending the sphere of individual rights beyond the original

[1] See above, Chaps. 10 and 13.
[2] The Declaration of 1789 speaks of: liberty, property, security and resistance to oppression.
[3] Above, p. 315.
[4] Above, p. 136 *et seq.*
[5] Above, p. 234 *et seq.*

trinity of life, liberty and property. This process is best described in conjunction with the specific individual rights which constitute the legal pillars of individual freedom.

Freedom of Contract

The substitution of freedom of contract for "status" conditions, as developed by Maine, is an essential legal aspect of individual freedom; but in this matter the need to balance one citizen's freedom with that of his fellow citizens became particularly urgent as industrial development led to a glaring discrepancy between formal freedom and actual lack of freedom on the part of "the greatest number." The application of the Benthamite principle has led to the gradual modification of individual freedom of contract, through a multitude of restrictions which have been analysed earlier in this book.[6] The state makes protective laws and attaches statutory obligations to the individual contract; inequality of bargaining is mitigated by freedom of association in trade unions which contract on behalf of the individual. But a crisis is reached when employers' or workers' organisations claim the monopoly of fixing terms in an industry, to the extent of making employment dependent on membership of the organisation and acceptance of its terms. At this point freedom of contract gives way to equality of bargaining. The modern worker or employer, at least in the more strongly organised industries, has very little if any individual freedom of contract left. He is free vicariously, as a member of a powerful organisation whose strength reflects his economic, political and social status. For the vast majority this is, on balance, an improvement. They have given up a theoretical freedom for a material improvement, but, as will be shown below,[7] the disappearance of this freedom may become important to the individual worker who objects to union policy, who wishes to join a rival trade union, or who, for some other reason, clashes with union leadership. Reference has also been made to the tentative attempts made by both legislator and judiciary to protect a modicum of individual freedom by stronger legal supervision over the conduct of union affairs.

Another vital restriction of practical, as distinct from theoretical, freedom of contract is the increasing predominance of the standard contract in such matters as transport insurance and sale of mass-

[6] Above, p. 218, and in more detail, *Law in a Changing Society*, Chap. 4.
[7] See p. 484 *et seq.*

manufactured goods. This mainly affects the ordinary and un-organised consumer, who has not developed any counter-pressure corresponding to that of collective bargaining in industrial relations.[8] In certain fields, American courts have attempted to counter such lack of equality by holding that a party which exercises a practical monopoly of a certain service has a duty to render public service and cannot therefore arbitrarily refuse to enter into a contract. But this judicial doctrine appears to be confined to public utilities and compulsory insurance. Nor does the duty to enter into a contract create equality of bargaining power about the terms. Such control as exists comes through public law, in the form of statutory rates, administrative tribunals and other brakes put upon the power of the stronger party to impose terms upon the weaker.

Freedom of contract is still regarded as an essential aspect of individual freedom; but it has no longer the absolute value attributed to it a century ago.

Freedom of Labour and Association

Originally freedom of contract represented the emancipation of labour from the fetters of status; but as freedom of contract, owing to the inequality of bargaining position, came into conflict with freedom of labour, the law more and more emphasised the latter, if necessary, at the expense of the former. The position is well illustrated in English law, by the comparison between restrictive covenants made between business men who contract for the good-will as equals, and for a consideration, and restrictive covenants between employers and employees concerning the use of the latter's skill and labour. The former are prima facie valid, the latter are prima facie invalid. The reason, as developed from the *Nordenfelt* case[8a] onwards, is the inequality of bargaining position and the necessity to protect freedom of labour. The same idea is expressed in *Nokes'* case.[9] These individual efforts, however, can touch little more than the fringe of the problem. A more far-reaching and fundamental way of restoring effective freedom of labour lies in the gradual development of collective bargaining, in substitution for individual bargaining. This presupposed the removal of the fetters imposed on trade unions and freedom of association in general. In English law the original inequality as between business

[8] See in detail, *Law in a Changing Society*, Chaps. 4, 10.
[8a] Below, p. 482. [9] Below, pp. 491, 496.

and labour has gradually given way to a legal recognition of their right to combine, with the result that it is increasingly groups which contract on behalf of multitudes of individuals. As employers' and employees' associations acquire an increasingly monopolistic position, this means a lessening degree of individual freedom of contract. Very similar developments have taken place in other democracies, in particular in Germany under the Weimar and Bonn Republics, in France before 1940, and under the New Deal in the United States. For the vast majority of individuals the loss of individual freedom of contract weighs little as compared with the gain of increased bargaining power through group membership. The loss of this freedom is no worse than the corresponding loss of freedom suffered by millions of transport users, mortgagees, insured, who, while retaining theoretical freedom of contract, must sign standard contracts, the terms of which they have no power to influence.

A real dilemma arises, however, where employers' and employees' organisations, sufficiently powerful to control a particular industry, agree on the "closed shop" principle. This is likely to happen where either a cartel of manufacturers or a single public corporation (such as the British National Coal Board or Transport Commission) represent the employers, and a single trade union the vast majority of employees. Such a union will look with jealousy upon both rival unions and non-union labour. The economic advantages of such indirect compulsion will generally outweigh the corresponding loss of both individual freedom of labour and— where exclusive recognition is given to one trade union—of freedom of association. But the small minority to whom these freedoms matter more than economic advantage are faced with a grave choice. Although non-unionists reap many of the advantages of collective bargaining, a democratic scale of values demands the maintenance of these basic freedoms even if they do not matter to the majority. A well-organised trade union has little difficulty in securing a dominant position without compulsion. The transition, from a closed shop principle and compulsory terms bargained between monopoly organisations of employers and employees, to the corporate state is fatally easy. Only the addition of compulsory state arbitration is needed. For this reason public opinion in Britain has hitherto resisted any widespread adoption of this principle.

In the United States the union which, according to a ballot conducted by the National Labour Relations Board, can speak for the majority of workers in that industry was until recently given the right to make a collective contract for all workers, whether members or not. The threat to personal freedom becomes grave when a union in this position excludes any group or individuals affected by the contract from membership (*e.g.*, Negroes). Some states have enacted statutory guarantees against such discrimination. Courts have granted injunctions. A democratic evaluation certainly demands that group monopoly shall not deprive an individual of the right to work. It cannot allow a combination of the monopoly of contracting on behalf of a group with the power to prevent individuals from participating in contracts by which they are legally affected. The main threat to this freedom comes at present from the almost unchecked power of the trade unions to control the admission to, and expulsion from, membership with virtually no legal control. The great majority of unions have very summary rules about disciplinary procedure against a member.[10] Some provision is made for proceedings which ensure that a member shall be heard on any charge preferred against him, and for a fair trial, but even if these provisions are strictly observed, there is no guarantee that those who issue the judgment are not prejudiced; indeed, they are in many cases responsible for the charges in the first place. Both British and American courts have for many years adhered to the rule of non-interference with union affairs which they regard as private associations. With the increase of monopoly power on the part of many unions, many courts have attempted to revise this attitude.[11] Recent American judicial practice aims at the enforcement of minimum standards of fairness through orders of reinstatement or damages in the case of flagrant infringement of fair trial, of the members' freedom of political opinions and other offences of a similar fundamental character.[12] But the limitations of such judicial controls are obvious. They may be successful in reducing extreme abuses, but no order of reinstatement or for damages can restore the excluded member to the position he would normally occupy. Only in very few cases would a penalised member even go to court. Legal theory must take note of the fact that many organisations which are still in theory private, now exercise

[10] For a thorough survey of the American position which, in this respect, is not very different from the British position, see Summers, "Legal Limitations on Union Discipline," 64 Harv. L. Rev. 1049 (1951).

[11] See on recent British developments, below, p. 484 *et seq.*

[12] See *Law in a Changing Society*, Chap. 10.

in fact public or quasi-public power. It must respond to this change by a stronger measure of public control. As in the case of monopoly in business and industry, this may check and slow down the trend of developments, but it cannot reverse it or fundamentally alter its direction.

Another real threat to freedom of labour comes from the increasing practice of governments to direct and tie people to their jobs. For Fascism, the absolute control of labour is a principle; to democracy it is acceptable only as an emergency measure in times of extreme national crisis.

The Soviet Constitution (*cf.* Art. 118, Constit. of 1936) has included "the right to work, that is, the right to guaranteed employment and payment for their work in accordance with its quantity and quality" among individual rights. The right to work, postulated in 1800 by Fichte and, a century later, by socialist jurists such as Menger, is now increasingly recognised as an essential of democracy and is finding expression in new principles of public budgeting which take note of the state's duty to provide employment by public works in times of depression, or in the new British National Insurance Act which implies public responsibility for unemployment. This blending of liberal thought with socialistic principles was forecast by liberal thinkers such as Dicey and Spencer, who viewed it with alarm, and Green and Hobhouse, who approved it.

On the American continent, the principle of public responsibility for employment has been accepted more reluctantly, but it is now clearly recognised. In Canada, national unemployment insurance was introduced by a Constitutional Amendment in 1940. In the United States, unemployment insurance is now virtually universal through a combination of federal and state laws. Some recognition of public responsibility for unemployment is found in the constitution of a council of advisers on unemployment to the President. How far the state would go in the creation of public works and other measures to fight unemployment has not yet been tested because there has been no major depression since before the Second World War. It is very improbable, however, that any government, Republican or Democrat, would be permitted by public opinion to remain passive in the face of a major unemployment crisis. This is the result, not only of the greatly increased scope of legislative and administrative powers of government but also of a change in the attitude of the public which, regardless of political philosophy, no longer condones official passivity in the face of an economic crisis.

Freedom of Property

To Locke and the makers of the French and American Revolutions, to Bentham, Spencer and the whole earlier liberal movement, freedom of property or "estate" constituted a cardinal principle. The same, however, applies to Kant and Hegel (but not Fichte) and to Catholic legal theory, as expressed in the Papal Encyclical and, in its most uncompromising form, by Cathrein.[13] The justification for this theory was, with all these thinkers, the mingling of man's labour with an object; but the ideology persisted despite the increasing dissociation of property and labour. As Renner has shown,[14] property has, in modern conditions, often become a means of control over other people's labour and life. Another aspect of the same development is revealed by Thurman Arnold's "myth of corporate personality,"[15] the application of the original American constitutional idea of inviolability of property—conceived for the pioneer farmer and settler—to the modern company which controls vast resources and numbers of men, but counts, in law, as an individual. The recognition of freedom of property as a basic right would still be generally considered as a principle of democracy, as distinct from socialism, which recognises it only in so far as it does not convey power over the means of production, and subject to the needs of the community.

But modern democracy, by the same process which has led to the increasing modification of individual rights by social duties towards neighbours and community, has everywhere had to temper freedom of property with social responsibilities attached to property. The limitations on property are of many different kinds. The state's right of taxation, its police power, and the power of expropriation—subject to fair compensation—are examples of public restrictions on freedom of property which are now universally recognised and used. Another kind of interference touches the freedom of use of property, through the growing number of social obligations attached by law to the use of industrial property, or contracts of employment. These statutory obligations are supplemented by judicial developments, such as the manufacturer's liability to the consumer established in *Donoghue* v. *Stevenson* or the employer's liability to the employee established in *Wilsons'* case.[16]

[13] See above, p. 394.
[14] See above, p. 368 *et seq.*
[15] *Folklore of Capitalism* (1937); above, p. 138.
[16] See below, pp. 469, 490.

In most countries statutes and courts have supplemented each other in bringing about this gradual adjustment in the rights of property. In the United States, however, the earlier conception of property as an absolute right not conditioned by social duty has persisted longer than anywhere else. This is due largely to the support given by the Supreme Court, as interpreter of the Constitution, to a rigidly individualistic interpretation. Grants of title to land, and eventually all property rights, were elevated into inalienable natural rights, and the power of taxation and other legislative interference strictly limited.[17] The culminating point was reached in the conflict between Supreme Court and Congress over the validity of some parts of the New Deal legislation. But this becomes essentially an aspect of the right of free enterprise, a right associated with that of inviolability of property in the interpretation of the American Constitution, but resting on somewhat different premises.

The last world war brought many further inroads in the inviolability of property and restriction on its use. Many of these were lifted with the return of more normal economic conditions.

The degree of public control over private property depends largely on the stringency of economic conditions. Increasing prosperity and availability of consumer goods has led to a drastic reduction of economic controls, and a trend away from socialisation in Europe. But in the struggling new democracies such as India, poor in capital and developed resources, and jealous of their newly-won sovereignty, public planning and control over vital resources are regarded as essential. The Constitution of the West German Republic of 1949, which reflects a blend of American, British and post-war German ideas on the economic aspects of democracy, lays down that land, minerals and means of production may be socialised or be subjected to other forms of public control by a statute which also regulates compensation. Such compensation must balance the interests of the community and those of the individual and leave recourse to law open to the person affected. This still permits wide divergences of political and economic philosophy, but in the recognition of social control over property, including socialisation as a legitimate though not a necessary measure, it reflects the modern evolution of democratic ideas. Between the capitalistic democracy of the United States and the social democracy of India there are many shades and variations. But modern democracy looks upon the right of property as one conditioned by social responsi-

[17] See above, p. 136 *et seq.*

bility, by the needs of society, by the "balancing of interests" which looms so large in modern jurisprudence, and not as a preordained and untouchable private right.

Freedom of Enterprise

The more crucial aspect of the right of property is its use in the pursuit of commercial enterprise. The right to develop one's initiative and capacities in commercial enterprise is an important aspect of the freedom of personal development. The main problem arises from the fact that individual property, as distinct from individual labour, may be the means of power over men and institutions. This is the crux of Marxist analysis, as juristically developed by Renner.[18] Property may become the means of domination over fellow men, and thus the instrument of slavery. The problem of the use of freedom of enterprise in violation of the Kantian and Benthamite principle of harmonisation of individual freedoms is no less acute than the correction of the formal freedom of contract which led to a new form of slavery, by the "positive" freedom postulated by T. H. Green. There has been a wide variety of answers to this challenge. Totalitarian systems are not greatly concerned about the problem of monopoly because they can control it sufficiently, through direct or indirect political pressure. Soviet Russia maintains control over production through a series of major state corporations which have juristic personality, but operate under a general plan and are under the strict political control of the Communist Party. The Nazi government, which did not socialise industry, favoured monopolistic cartels in industry because the leaders of industry, voluntarily or under pressure, collaborated with the government, and large-scale enterprises are easier to direct in a totalitarian economy.

By contrast, modern democracies are experimenting with two very different ways of tackling the problem of concentration of economic power in private hands.

The United States enacted the Sherman Act in 1890 as a result of widespread agitation against the growing concentration of American industry. The Act made illegal "every contract, combination in the form of trust or otherwise, or conspiracy in restraint of trade or commerce" among the several states or with foreign nations. It also declared guilty of misdemeanour every person

---

[18] See above, p. 368 *et seq.*

attempting to monopolise or combining or conspiring with others to monopolise trade or commerce among the states, or with foreign nations. A full survey of the results of this Act, and of supplemental legislation such as the Clayton Act of 1914, after more than sixty years of operation would greatly exceed the scope of this book. The following brief survey is intended to give some indication of its general philosophy.[19] The sweeping clauses of the Act were restricted in the famous *Standard Oil* case of 1911,[20] by the judicial adoption of reasonableness as a test by which to judge the validity of acts of restraint. This considerably restricted the scope of the Sherman Act and turned it essentially into "a weapon to restrain abuse rather than to destroy the monopolistic power giving rise to the abuse."[21] Moreover, manufacturing trusts as well as mergers were for a considerable time exempted from the scope of the Act by judicial interpretation. During that time, many monopolies were consolidated through mergers, holding companies and other devices taking them out of the scope of the Act. On the other hand, labour organisations were generally regarded as prohibited attempts at combination without any test of reasonableness. In both respects there have been great changes. Labour unions have long become fully recognised as legitimate agencies of collective bargaining.[22] On the other hand, there has been a tendency in recent years to prosecute monopoly concentration as such, in disregard of the judicial restriction of "unreasonableness." The number of prosecutions by the Department of Justice has risen greatly. The judicial effects of this new policy have been considerable. Price maintenance agreements are generally held invalid as are tie-in sales and group boycotts. The control of patentees over their licensees has been circumscribed. Above all, section 2 of the Sherman Act has been reinterpreted in many decisions, so as to make the concentration of economic power illegal *per se*, without the restraining factor of "reasonableness."[23] The combined effect of these developments is considerable. On the other hand, modern defence needs have

[19] For some critical surveys and estimates see the comparative notes in 59 Yale L.J. 899 (1949-50), and Carlston "Antitrust Policy: A Problem in State Craft," 60 Yale L.J. 1073 (1951). Further, Friedmann (ed.) *Anti-Trust Laws* (1956). See also Report of the Attorney-General's Committee to study Anti-Trust Laws, 1956; *Law in a Changing Society*, Chap. 8, esp. p. 278 *et seq.*

[20] 221 U.S. 1 (1910).

[21] 59 Yale L.J. 899, 918 (1949-50).

[22] Reference has been made to the problem of restraining the abuse of monopoly control by unions over their membership; see above, p. 402 *et seq.*

[23] For references, see 59 Yale L.J. 919-920. The leading case is *U.S.* v. *Aluminium Co. of America* 148 F. 2d 416 (1945).

accentuated a powerful technological trend towards increasing concentration and standardisation of resources. Only the greatest and wealthiest industries can maintain the necessary equipment for constant technological research and progress. And where the anti-trust division fights concentration, the defence authorities often prefer contractors who can mass-manufacture tanks or aeroplanes to standard design. The ideology underlying American legislation and judicial interpretation has not changed, at least officially. The replacement of competition by concentration is regarded as inherently bad. This assumption has been occasionally questioned, as, for example, in a famous dissent by Brandeis J.:

> The refusal to permit a multitude of small rivals to co-operate, as they have done here, in order to protect themselves and the public from the chaos and havoc wrought in their trade by ignorance, may result in suppressing competition in the hardwood industry. These keen business rivals, who sought through co-operative exchange of trade information to create conditions under which alone rational competi-tion is possible, produce in the aggregate about one-third of the hard-wood lumber of the country. May not these hardwood lumber concerns, frustrated in their efforts to rationalise competition, be led to enter the inviting field of consolidation? And if they do, may not another huge trust with highly centralised control over vast resources, natural, manu-facturing and financial, become so powerful as to dominate competitors, wholesalers, retailers, consumers, employees and, in large measure, the community?[24]

Recently, weighty American criticism has been voiced against some basic assumptions of the anti-trust philosophy. Kenneth Galbraith (*American Capitalism*, 1952) sees a corrective to the abuse of economic power in the "countervailing power" which powerful groups in different, interdependent sectors of the economy (producers, wholesalers, retailers, etc.) exercise in relation to each other. Adolph Berle (*Twentieth Century Capitalism*, 1954) regards the modern corporation as ennobled by its public "conscience" and the quasi-diplomatic functions it now exercises in international relations (*e.g.*, in the Iranian Oil Agreement of 1954). A far more radical attack is that of David Lilienthal (*Big Business*, 1953), who regards Big Business not only as "an efficient way to produce and distribute basic commodities" but as "a social institution that promotes human freedom and individualism." Progress, to the author, the chief architect of the Tennessee Valley Authority, is dependent on big-scale enterprise, mainly private, but sometimes

[24] *American Column and Lumber Co.* v. *United States* 257 U.S. 418 (1921).

public, while government has enough powers to control abuse by means other than the costly and laborious splitting up of efficient enterprises.

The legal checks on monopolies or restraint have certainly retarded, and in some cases prevented, a concentration of private economic power which might otherwise have reached unbearable proportions. In particular, the deterrent effects of publicity are powerful as long as a general attitude of mistrust of the economic combine prevails. Yet, concentration—though not monopoly—proceeds all the time.[25] Oil, steel, aluminium, chemicals, automobiles and aircraft manufacture, telephone and electronics, computer manufacture, to name but a few, are dominated by small groups of giant companies, most of them world-wide concerns. The philosophy of fighting economic concentration by legislative and judicial deconcentration is open to the challenge that it is neither effective nor unquestionable in its basic assumptions. The restoration of economic competition, even granted its effectiveness and soundness, requires a vast legislative and administrative apparatus. The Benthamite dilemma—the attainment of freedom of enterprise and equality through a legislative machinery which then becomes an instrument of the positive welfare state—reappears.

Yet the importance of maintaining some public control over economic concentration and restrictive practices is shown by the recent introduction of anti-trust legislation in some traditionally cartel-minded countries, such as Great Britain (Restrictive Trade Practices Act, 1956), or West Germany (*Wettbewerbsgesetz,* 1957). Neither of these laws is as radical as the American legislation; the objectionability of restrictive practices and concentrations is judged by the public interest.[26] But they indicate a definite policy of public control over private economic power.

Another attempt to curb the abuse of private economic power has been the reform of the English patent law by an Act of 1949, which confers stronger powers on the Comptroller of Patents, who may grant compulsory licences, or in extreme cases, revoke a patent where patent rights are abused or insufficiently used. What the practical effects of this reform will be remains to be seen.

---

[25] In 1947, 113 firms controlled nearly one-half the total capital assets of American manufacturing corporations, 19 major industries were concentrated to the extent of 85 per cent. or more in four companies (*New York Times,* December 5, 1949, and *Economist* 617 (1949), quoting report of Federal Trade Commission).
[26] For a fuller discussion of the relevant criteria, see Friedmann (ed.) *Anti-Trust Laws* (1956).

An alternative way of countering the abuses of economic power is the transfer of certain basic industries into public ownership through the legal device of the statutory public corporation, which has been done in a number of countries. The main features of this far-reaching experiment in democratic socialisation—which has been analysed elsewhere[27]—may now be accepted as a permanent part of the legal and constitutional structure of Britain or France. Its most important aspect is the unification and monopolisation of the basic public utilities (coal, electricity, railways, gas), under public ownership and management, which has to operate under the rules of the common law, subject to accountability and full legal liability, while responsible to Parliament. Freedom of private enterprise has been sacrificed to the principle of development and administration of basic necessities through the state, which subjects itself to the forms of private law.

Freedom of trade and private enterprise thus has ceased to be an absolute and unqualified right. In modern democratic society it is one of various alternative methods of economic activity, and it is everywhere subject to varying degrees of public control.

Freedom of the Person

Each of the freedoms discussed so far has been subject to the influence of changing social and economic conditions. Freedom of contract, property, trade and, to a lesser degree, labour, appear as more or less adequate instruments in the realisation of a more essential freedom and are justified only as long as they fulfil this purpose.

There is more absoluteness about the more directly personal aspects of freedom. The physical integrity of life and body is an essential aspect of all democratic constitutions and systems of law, and even those systems which, like English law, abstain from formulating any general constitution or catalogue of fundamental rights, are explicit about the safeguarding of personal liberty (habeas corpus). It is in their function as protectors of personal integrity that the independence of the judiciary and the "rule of law" gain their most essential and least controversial meaning. Since liberty cannot be absolute, but is qualified by the requirements of public safety, criminal law and other legal restrictions, the emphasis is on "due process of law," as a condition of its curtailment.

[27] See Friedmann (ed.) *The Public Corporation* (1954); Hanson (ed.) *Public Enterprise* (1955). See also above, p. 384 *et seq.*

Personal liberty involves more rights than individual bodily integrity. It includes, in the law of all modern nations, the protection of personal reputation, through the law of defamation; it includes the protection of family relations and of domestic life. A recent decision of the U.S. Supreme Court[28] has condemned a Connecticut statute prohibiting the sale of contraceptives as an illicit invasion of the right of privacy. But the most important aspect of individual liberty, though, at the same time, the one most difficult to define precisely, is spiritual and intellectual freedom. Its principal expressions are liberty of religion and thought and, as its media, liberty of speech, writing, printing, of peaceable association and discussion. Democracies may choose to guarantee these rights as *Grundrechte* in written constitutions, or they may, like the British legal system, choose to regard these freedoms as understood, except in so far as they are not specifically limited or excluded by law. The juristic difference is not great; for constitutional rights are subject to regulation and specification by law, and where they are expressed in unqualified terms (as in Article 125 of the U.S.S.R. Constitution) they usually constitute an expression of aspirations, but not enforceable rights.

The methods of protecting these liberties vary; but all democracies will agree on an irreducible minimum, which is best understood by the contrast to Fascist and authoritarian law. Some constitutions separate all religious denominations from the state (*e.g.*, the German Constitution of 1919 and the U.S.S.R. Constitution of 1936); others, like Great Britain, grant freedom of worship, but recognise one official religion with certain privileges; as long as this meant disqualification from office or educational advantages, as it did until well into the nineteenth century, freedom of worship was not real. Freedom of speech and Press is everywhere subject to the restraining laws of defamation or blasphemy, and to the requirements of public safety, but a system of state licensing of the Press, or the control of opinion by a Ministry of Propaganda armed with powers of coercion, is incompatible with democracy. Freedom of meeting and association is nowhere absolute; in England, for example, it is subject to many statutory and other legal limitations —especially since such decisions as *Lansbury* v. *Riley*[29] and *Duncan* v. *Jones*,[30] which greatly strengthen the preventive powers of the

---

[28] *Griswold* v. *Connecticut*, 381 U.S. 479 (1965).
[29] [1914] 3 K.B. 229.
[30] [1936] 2 K.B. 218.

police. The seemingly absolute guarantees of the First Amendment are considerably limited by the "clear and present danger" test.[31]

The revolutionary upheavals of the last fifty years have increasingly compelled modern democracies to face the problem at what point tolerance of freedom of opinion must give way to the defence of the democratic constitution against forces which aim at its destruction. The German Republic, established in 1919, certainly went too far in its tolerance of the barely disguised anti-democratic activities of the Nazi Party and its auxiliary organisations. Hitler's intention to destroy the democratic republic was shown clearly enough in his widely-known book *Mein Kampf,* and underlined by the creation of para-military organisations, which used force and intimidation to suppress opponents while the movement was still in opposition. Should the Republic have suppressed the Nazi Party altogether? There was no consideration of basic democratic philosophy which prevented it from doing so. The laws of treason and sedition are a necessary equipment of a democracy as much as of any other state. No government can be expected to watch preparations for its own destruction passively. The question which measures should be adopted is one of utility and practical politics. Experience shows that revolutionary movements prosper in the conspiratorial atmosphere of official suppression. In the circumstances, the Weimar Republic might well have saved itself by disbanding the Stormtroopers and other semi-military organisations of the Nazi Party without prohibiting the movement as such, or the free expression of its opinions. For the danger point is reached when democracies proceed from the outlawing of actions to the outlawing of dangerous or unpopular opinions. The Bonn Constitution of 1949 (Article 5) guarantees the right of the free expression and propagation of opinions "within the provisions of the general laws," but Article 18 provides that freedom of opinion and association may be forfeited by anybody who "abuses these rights to fight against the free democratic Constitution." Such forfeiture must be pronounced by the Federal Constitutional Court. The court also decides on the constitutionality of parties which "in their aims, or the conduct of their followers, purport to injure or abolish the free democratic Constitution or to endanger the existence of the federal republic" (Article 21). In October 1952 the Constitutional Court declared a neo-Fascist Party

[31] See above, p. 147.

unconstitutional and cancelled the parliamentary mandates of its members. A similar problem arose some years ago in Australia, when an Act outlawing the Communist Party and affiliated organisations was declared unconstitutional by the High Court of Australia.[32] The general problem of the borderline between the propagation of subversive opinions and seditious action arose in another Australian case where the court was equally divided on the question whether a Communist speaker who, in a public discussion meeting, had, in answer to a question, declared that in case of war "between Soviet Russia and American and British imperialism" Australian Communists "would fight on the side of Soviet Russia," could be convicted of sedition.[33] The casting vote of Latham C.J. confirmed the conviction, but the dissenting opinions of Dixon and MacTiernan JJ. seem more in accordance with democratic philosophy, in their emphasis on the distinction between incitement to action against the Constitution, and expression of an opinion on the action which certain people or organisations would take in certain contingencies. The majority opinion is, however, close to the majority opinion of the United States Supreme Court in the *Dennis* case,[34] which, in turn, was all but reversed in *Yates'* case.[35] This problem is not solved by the assertion that Communist philosophy as applied by Communist Parties throughout the world is in its very nature subversive and directed against democratic government. Democracies cannot apply the same methods as totalitarian societies. They can strike at any action directed against the state, but they must permit the expression of opinions in a lawful framework, however unpopular or objectionable these opinions may be.

All serious students of the problem of liberty have recognised that a degree of coercion is not only a necessary restriction of an individual's liberty for the sake of the liberty of his fellow citizens, but that coercion by the state may be an indispensable condition of effective, as distinct from purely nominal, liberty.

There is no true opposition between liberty as such and control as

[32] *Australian Communist Party* v. *Commonwealth,* 1951; *cf.* 24 A.L.J. 485. The majority of the court based its decision on the limitation of federal powers and refused to consider the Act as a legitimate exercise of the defence powers of the Commonwealth. For a full analysis of the whole development, see Beasley, "Australia's Communist Party Dissolution Act," 29 Can. Bar. Rev. 490 (1951).

[33] *Burns* v. *Ransley* (1949) 79 C.L.R. 101.

[34] Above, p. 148.

[35] 353 U.S. 346 (1957).

such, for every liberty rests on a corresponding act of control. The true opposition is between the control that cramps the personal life and the spiritual order, and the control that is aimed at securing the external and material conditions of their free and unimpeded development.[36]

This indicates the true test by which to distinguish liberating from oppressive control. Not all the freedoms discussed here are of equal value. Some are more fundamental than others. The more fundamental aspects of liberty are those which express and ensure "the highest and most harmonious development of man's powers to a complete and consistent whole" (Humboldt). The development of man's spiritual and intellectual faculties as a reasonable being, a creature who is not only matter but also spirit, is the dominant theme of Western thought, from the Athenians to the twentieth century. That is why the last-discussed personal liberties are the more essential and unchangeable aspects of individual freedom. Freedom of labour and enterprise form, in principle, part of this essential object of securing the maximum development of man's personality. But those freedoms which, because of their technical and commercial implications, have formed the particular preoccupation of the law—freedom of contract, property and trade—are of a less fundamental character.[37] They are concerned with "external and material conditions" and must therefore be tested by their capacity, at any given time, to ensure the development of man's essential freedom. Patently, the inalienable right of property, derived by Locke, Kant, Hegel and the makers of the American Constitution from man's right to the fruits of his toil, has little to do with the right of a modern corporation, clothed with legal personality, to control, in the name of individual liberty, the supply and price of a commodity vital to millions of consumers.

The adjustment between freedom and compulsion, between the rights of the individuals and the community, must therefore be a matter of changing needs and conditions. Legal theory can go no farther than lay down the general hierarchy of principles.

---

[36] Hobhouse, *Liberalism*, 147.

[37] This proposition is put forward independently of the question whether the U.S. Constitution knows "preferred freedoms" (see p. 149 *et seq.*). It would seem, however, that, while the rejection of the "preferred freedoms" doctrine can be based on principles of constitutional interpretation, its adoption can only be justified by recourse to basic principles of democratic, political and legal philosophy.

Equality

The doctrine of legal equality goes back to the natural law doctrine of the Stoics which, in the name of universal reason, postulates equality of individuals, races and nations. This was accepted by Roman jurisprudence, though sometimes with a distinction between the law of nature which postulates absolute equality, and the law of nations (*jus gentium*) which recognises slavery. Christian doctrine, too, is pledged to the fundamental equality of men, but in the scholastic and Catholic legal system this fundamental equality is subordinated to the acceptance of the existing social order as one ordained and to be borne—subject to certain principles of justice and charity. The modern postulate of legal equality dates from the era of the French and American Revolutions.

In a formal and general sense equality is a postulate of justice. Aristotle's "distributive justice" demands the equal treatment of those equal before the law. This, like any general formula of justice is, however, applicable to any form of government or society; for it leaves it to a particular legal order to determine who are equal before the law.

Equality in rights, as postulated by the great democratic charters, means the extension of individual rights, in principle, to all citizens as distinct from a privileged minority. Equality can never be absolute; it is qualified by natural inequalities and, in the formulation of Thomas Paine and the Declaration of 1789, by "public" or "common" utility. Certain natural inequalities, such as the differences in the legal status of infants and adults, or of insane and sane persons, do not touch the foundations of democracy. But most of the existing democratic systems preserve legal inequalities, contrary to the ideology of democracy.

Neither the limitation of franchise or other civic rights, nor legal inequality as between men and women or between white and black races, nor differentiations in the legal position of nationals and foreigners, are compatible with the basic legal ideals of democracy; yet all these inequalities still exist, to a greater or smaller degree. French democracy did not recognise women's franchise until after France's liberation from the Nazi régime; Swiss women still have no vote; Great Britain has only fairly recently abolished political and educational disqualifications due to religion; despite the guarantees of the Fifth and Fourteenth Amendments of the U.S. Constitution, Negroes remained effectively disfranchised and deprived of other basic rights, until Civil Rights Acts of 1964 and 1965, supported by a series of Supreme Court decisions which have struck down hosts of discriminatory State laws and practices began to use federal legal powers in support of equality. The status of married women, in England, reached full equality with that of their husbands only by an Act of 1935. Most Australian states still have upper legislative houses which, through an organisation of voting districts that greatly favours the country against the city vote, through property qualifications and other means, perpetuate stark inequalities. In the U.S. only a hotly debated Supreme Court decision of 1962[38] established the principle of "one man, one vote," setting into motion a nation-wide series of reapportionment and redistricting laws. Most modern democracies grant substantial equality in civil rights to foreign nationals (subject to certain restrictions, regarding, for example, the ownership of land or ships), but they are excluded from political rights. This is but another way of saying that the world is organised in a number of national states. The theoretical ideal of democracy—the equality of all men and races —is limited by a society for which the division into national groups organised in states is still the highest ordering principle. This discrepancy may eventually be overcome, or at least reduced, if and when a closer organisation of international society, through common judicial or, eventually, legislative institutions reduces the differences between nation and nation, and thus subjects their nationals to a greater measure of common law.

It is clear, however, that the principle of absolute equality between individuals of all classes and races cannot be understood in a rigid sense. The ideas of individual freedom and individual equality are correlated, and both have to be understood in a dynamic, not in a static, sense. Freedom means opening the road to the fullest development of personality, and equality means equality of opportunity for all to participate in such development; it means the abolition not of natural differences, but of the man-made differences inherent in the organisation of society. It is these which it is the task of law, in democratic societies, to remove.

Legislative developments in democratic societies have, during the last hundred years, gone far to remove the many obstacles in the way of such equality of opportunity. Equality of franchise and other civic rights is an illusion where property qualifications govern

[38] *Baker* v. *Carr* 369 U.S. 186 (1962).

its exercise, or widespread illiteracy would make its extension to everyone farcical. It is the immortal merit of Bentham to have stressed the necessity for the removal of inequalities in the opportunities of development as a condition of democratic development, while Mill has demanded the development of a sense of responsibility as a condition of equal political rights. Legislation cannot do it all, but it has a vital part to play. Such different legislative developments as the removal of legal obstacles to trade unions, the fight for women's franchise, the now successfully concluded struggle for constitutional amendments prohibiting state poll taxes in the United States, the British Education Act of 1944 widening the basis of general education, or recent Indian legislation directed against the rigid barriers of the caste system, constitute steps towards the same goal. They imply, not that men are or ever will be equal in faculties or attainments, but that the differences between them are not due to such attributes as race, wealth or nationality. Few men are leaders, but democracy believes that, given facilities of material and intellectual development, leaders may spring from any race, class or nation.

That the democratic ideal demands equality of rights can scarcely be doubted. But the association of liberal and democratic ideals is not uncontested. In a famous essay,[39] Troeltsch traces a difference between the French and the Anglo-Saxon ideas of progress. He includes equality of rights in the former, but not in the latter. This, according to Troeltsch, involves a deep division: "the division between democracy proper and a system which should be designated as liberalism rather than democracy."

There is much force in this contention. The French idea of equality has dominated French political development since the Revolution (though it has been considerably modified in de Gaulle's Fifth Republic), and deeply influenced American constitutional and legal principles.

The dominant factor in the British Constitution is the Cabinet, democratically constituted, but much more powerful in its relation with Parliament and the people than its American counterpart. The French constitutional revolution of 1958 has swung from a system that produced a chronically weak executive facing powerful but paralysingly divided parliaments, to a predominance of executive power which curtails the functions of parliament to such an

---

[39] "The Ideas of Natural Law and Humanity," Appendix I to Gierke, *Natural Law and the Theory of Society* (1934) (trans. Barker).

extent that contemporary France may only doubtfully be characterised as a democracy.

Although a powerful tradition of English liberal thought, from Bentham and Mill to Green, Hobhouse and Barker, has coupled liberal and democratic principles, an important school of thought rejects this partnership. Burke, the greatest opponent of the French Revolution, has found support among historical jurists. Maine's theory about the evolution from status to contract was a contribution to liberal thought; but he also derived from his study of legal evolution an opposition to democracy[40] which another distinguished legal historian has more recently affirmed. In a criticism of the democratic liberal thought of Barker,[41] the late Sir William Holdsworth[42] roundly condemned the development which, since the Reform Act of 1832, has extended franchise and other rights from what he considers the more enlightened classes to all. Accordingly, he rejects the conception of equal educational opportunity as a step towards political responsibility, in favour of a class of leaders educated in Britain's public schools.

This is not the place to discuss the political merits of this contention. The argument is political and historical, not legal. The implementation of this political ideology would, however, lead to a different set of legal values from that which stresses equality as the corollary to freedom. It would justify the division of the electorate into classes, and discrimination as regards rights and duties and, on the whole, promote a legislative trend contrary to that which, in the last hundred years, has increasingly determined British political and legal development.

GOVERNMENT OF THE PEOPLE

Individual rights and equality do not sufficiently characterise democracy. They may exist under a benevolent despotism. In modern democracy both ideals find their highest fulfilment and justification in the citizen's right to participation in government, the "Government of the People" (Lincoln). This, in modern states, means representative government through elected deputies.

The great problem of democratic political and legal thought has been the reconciliation of popular will with individual rights and,

---

[40] Maine, *Popular Government* (1884).
[41] Barker, *Reflections on Government* (1942).
[42] Holdsworth, "Professor Barker's Reflections on Government," 59 L.Q.Rev. 33 (1943).

in particular, of the rights of the majority with those of the minority. The possibility of conflict is apparent in the social contract theories of Locke and Rousseau.[43] If the will of the majority or the *volonté générale* is the supreme law, individual rights cannot be inalienable. The difficulty of reconciling both has involved Locke and Rousseau in contradictions. From the many studies of the problems of representative government, three main ideas have emerged which indicate a way out of the dilemma: one is the idea of proportional representation, championed by Mill and many later liberals. It ensures representation, in proportion to its strength, to every group and shade of opinion, down to very small units, and it thus goes far to give every individual a voice in the affairs of the community. Its obvious danger, as shown by the fate of the German Constitution of 1919, is an excessive number of small parties, which frustrates stable and effective government and encourages political blackmail. It is significant that British constitutional law, with its traditional emphasis on representative leadership rather than absolute equality, has so far refused to adopt the principle of proportional representation, although this involves much injustice to any political group other than the two principal parties which form alternative governments.[44]

The second idea is that of a protection of minority rights, intimately linked with that of "inalienable" individual rights. The nature and extent of these rights has been discussed above. Most modern democracies give them legal force by incorporating them in a written constitution. This does not make them inviolable; for no constitution is unalterable. But amendments are usually subject to a special procedure, either a plebiscite or a qualified majority in Parliament. Where the constitution is federal it is usually necessary for both chambers to pass the amendment with a qualified majority. The American Constitution has provided further safeguards for individuals and minorities, first, in subjecting the acceptance of commitments by foreign treaties to a qualified majority in the Senate; secondly, by allowing an action before the Supreme Court to test the violation of any right guaranteed by the Constitution.

The British Constitution does not know any formal protection of individual or minority rights; nothing prevents the majority from

---

[43] Above, pp. 122 *et seq.*, 125 *et seq.*

[44] The present electoral law in West Germany adopts the British principle, tempered by a limited concession to the proportional principle for "reserve" lists.

getting any law passed in Parliament (witness the recurrent suspensions of habeas corpus); individuals and minorities are protected by convention and tradition, backed by public opinion, and by a parliamentary system which recognised an organised minority as essential (symbolised by the appointment, in 1937, of a salaried Leader of the Opposition).

While this tradition is as effective as any formal declaration of rights in a strongly cemented and long-established political community, formal legal protection will be indispensable for any international legal organisation, which cannot build on such tradition and where discrimination against national, racial and religious minorities will constitute a formidable problem. This, indeed, was attempted, though only partly and with insufficient legal sanctions, in the Treaty of Versailles.

The third idea is the extension of individual participation in government from the national sphere, where, in modern conditions, it can only be indirect, through elected representatives, to the regional and local sphere, where it can be direct. The many new responsibilities which, with the extension of social, health, educational and other services, will devolve on regional and local authorities, will increase these opportunities. At present the participation of the average citizen in government is largely confined to occasional voting. While the Constitution of the Soviet Union is clearly undemocratic in so far as it allows only one privileged party as the expression of organised political opinion, it is at present ahead of many parliamentary democracies in the degree of active participation by the average citizen of all callings and races in the manifold tasks of self-government. The opportunities for delegated tasks of self-government are, of course, vastly increased by the greater scope of state activity and public responsibility. Thus, the new British education system and National Health Service, while introducing a uniform system for the whole country, at the same time impose new delegated and executive responsibilities upon regional and local authorities. The Acts setting up public corporations for the conduct of nationalised industries create consumers' advisory councils which the board or the Minister must consult. The spirit of enterprise which, in a capitalist society, finds its main outlet in private economic activity, is, in a socialist community, transferred to industrial management, social work and other tasks carried out on behalf of the state. Modern democratic societies find themselves today in an intermediate position.

Freedom, Planning and the Rule of Law

It has previously been shown[45] that it is impossible to lay down absolute principles of justice which under the name "rule of law" could claim universal validity. It is, on the other hand, both possible and necessary to formulate the principles of the rule of law as it is understood in modern Western democracy.

The democratic rule of law implies, first, the principle of equality before the law. It excludes the autocratic and totalitarian principle which, in the name of divine right, of inspired leadership or of power pure and simple, exempts individuals and groups from the law of the land. The creation of a privileged class like the members of Nazi organisations, subject to party tribunals, is repugnant to democracy. The inevitable corollary of a rule of law is a separation of judiciary and executive. *Nemo judex in causa sua!* But Dicey's contention that the "rule of law" does not permit of a separate system of administrative justice is today discredited even for English law. As the administrative activities of the state multiply, both the multitude and the character of the legal problems arising demand a type of jurisdiction and judges qualified to deal with disputes usually fundamentally different from the private law case. In all Continental countries this has led to a separate system of administrative tribunals which leaves to the agencies of government a good deal of discretion, but subjects them to liability where they infringe rights. The borderline between discretion and infringement is not always clear and distrust of any distinction between governors and governed has led some Continental jurists, like Kelsen, to reject the theoretical distinction between ordinary and administrative justice. But the alternative, in Great Britain and the U.S.A., has been the haphazard springing up of numerous semi-judicial administrative bodies with judicial powers which are, in personnel and method, closer to actual administration than the continental tribunals which, at least on the higher levels, enjoy complete judicial independence.

Administrative justice as developed in Continental laws is far from being the last word in democratic justice. But it cannot be maintained that the present-day common law system in England is a more democratic alternative, even though the historic anomaly of Crown immunity from jurisdiction has at last disappeared.[46]

---

[45] *Cf.* in particular Chap. 28.

[46] On the problem of administrative law and justice, see *Law in a Changing Society*, Part Four (Chaps. 11-13).

Nor can any particular form of constitutional government be regarded as the only true embodiment of the rule of law. A written constitution as the supreme law of the land appears as the legally clearest and most satisfactory embodiment of democratic legal principles. It is found indispensable in federal constitutions as a safeguard of state and minority rights; this would also apply to a more closely knit international community; but the unchecked legal supremacy of British Parliament has not led to dictatorship, while some written constitutions have quickly crumbled before political revolutions. The embodiment of judicially protected individual rights in the American Constitution has not prevented restrictions on freedom of thought, speech and association more severe than in contemporary Britain which has no such constitutional guarantees.[47] Again, the American Constitution regulates the relations between executive, legislature and judiciary differently from the British. It gives to a law court a supervisory function which, as shown above,[48] cannot help having deep political implications, and it isolates legislative and executive from each other, instead of the British method of constituting government as an executive committee of the majority in Parliament. Modern democracies also differ widely in the organisation of the administration of justice. In Continental democracies, a ministry of justice is in administrative control of the entire judicial machinery, and also the central agency for the drafting of legislation. In Britain, these functions are divided between the Lord Chancellor's secretariat, the parliamentary draftsman and *ad hoc* law revision committees. In 1965 the process of law revision was given institutional continuity, through the creation of Law Commissions for England and Scotland.[49] In the United States, the Attorney-General's Department exercises some of the functions of a ministry of justice, together with numerous congressional committees and *ad hoc* commissions.[50] Each of these national institutions has certain merits and

---

[47] Even more telling is the fate of the "entrenched clauses" in the South Africa Constitution Act, 1909. When the South African Court of Appeal held, in 1952, that the Union Parliament could not override these clauses—protecting certain voting rights of the coloured people by the requirement of a two-thirds majority for any amendment—by a Bill passed by a simple majority, Parliament, by an ordinary Bill, set itself up as "High Court" in constitutional matters. When the court declared this Bill invalid the Malan government "packed" the Senate so as to obtain the necessary qualified majority.

[48] p. 136 *et seq.*

[49] See below, p. 511 *et seq.*

[50] The States of New York and California have permanent law Revision Committees.

deficiencies and may be in need of reform, but they are all compatible with democratic ideas.

The other pillar of the rule of law, cardinal to all democratic thought, is the principle of equal individual responsibility. In Bentham's terminology, everybody counts for one. This does not exclude legal differences arising from the exercise of functions. Officials are, as such, nowhere in the same legal position as individuals. It does exclude, for example, the retrospective punishment of actions. It does exclude the exemption of individuals or classes from legal responsibility and, on the other hand, punishment or persecution of individuals by virtue of their membership of a specific race, religion or other group characteristics.

The democratic conception of the rule of law balances individual rights with individual legal responsibility. This accounts for such rules as the responsibility for damage done by official acts to private citizens, or the principle of criminal liability based on individual wrongdoing by a person responsible for his action. The relation between individual right and individual duty is in constant development, and its forms vary from system to system.

The universal increase of planning functions and of public control over a growing range of social and economic activities compels a re-examination of the meaning of the rule of law in modern democracy. Is the planned society compatible with a system of law which upholds the essential foundation of the "rule of law" as characterised earlier on? Or is there an irreconcilable conflict between the two? Must it be either planning or law?

That planning is inconsistent with the rule of law has been contended by one of the most radical of modern anti-planners.[51] In his opinion planning implies a method of official action which makes it impossible for the citizen to foresee what may happen to him. This absence of foreseeability means a denial of the rule of law, which to him means that "government in all its actions is bound by rules fixed and announced beforehand—rules which make it possible to foresee with fair certainty which authority will use its coercive powers in given circumstances and to plan one's individual affairs on the basis of this knowledge."

This assertion is based first on a questionable view of the functions of the modern state, and secondly on untenable assumptions about foreseeability in an unplanned economic system.

[51] Hayek, *The Road to Serfdom*, Chap. 6 (1944).

There can be no doubt that effective planning does entail a degree of administrative action which cannot be determined beforehand. The compulsory acquisition of land for the purpose of road-making or the development of new towns, the closing down or amalgamation of redundant industries in a certain branch or area, the prohibition of certain transactions for overriding reasons of public policy, such as shortage of foreign exchange, or the cancellation of government contracts because of the cessation of the original need for making them, these and numerous other situations may and often do arise as a result of unforeseen and unforeseeable conditions. To deny public authority such powers means to deny the state the paramount responsibility for good government and the promotion of the welfare of its citizens.

In the words of one of the staunchest opponents of administrative arbitrariness, "to attempt a return to pure *laissez-faire*, to reduce the state to its old minimum functions of tax-gatherer, policeman and panoplied protector is really a rejection of the whole trend of modern civilisation."[52]

Another distinguished English lawyer[53] has, however, launched a far more uncompromising attack on the modern welfare state and its implications for the legal and constitutional structure of Great Britain. Professor Keeton strings together a number of frequently analysed phenomena: the increase of delegated legislative powers, the anonymous collective power of the civil service, and the corresponding decline of effective parliamentary control; the still chaotic state of administrative justice, as compared with the Continental system; the insufficiency of the powers of the courts to control the executive; the powers concentrated in the state, through such instrumentalities as the modern incidence of taxation, the fetters imposed on land ownership, and the control of many basic industries by government corporations. These and other factors bring, according to Professor Keeton, contemporary Great Britain to "the edge of dictatorship" and they lead it on the "road to Moscow." Since this attack, the limited progress of administrative justice (Tribunals and Enquiries Act, 1958) and the introduction in 1966 of an Ombudsman to make enquiries into complaints submitted through Parliament, have removed some dangers of administrative arbitrariness. But there is a more basic flaw in the reasoning of Hayek, Keeton and their school of thought.

---

[52] Allen, *Law and Orders*, 279 (1945).
[53] G. W. Keeton, *The Passing of Parliament* (1952).

It is usually overlooked by the upholders of this strict traditional sense of the rule of law that the elimination of private rights and interests by unforeseeable action and without compensation has constantly taken place under free enterprise and the unplanned society. The *Mogul* case[54] presents a celebrated example of the power of an economically stronger combine to destroy the legitimate business of a competitor without any legal sanction whatsoever. The legal interpretation of a patent as a right not only to use an invention exclusively but also as a power not to use it, has been responsible for the effective destruction of many legitimate interests and inventions. Powerful combines within an industry, by a syst... of pooling patents or cross-licensing, by their power to fright... ...m impecunious inventor out of litigation and thus to force hi... his invention, by their cartel agreements to restrict pro... ...er- provide some examples of the destruction of legitimate... ...lia- in the absence of public control.[55] It is to counter such p... udits, of individual liberties that private individuals and gro... most invoked the protection of the state, through anti-trust law... able tions on the abuse of patents, the enforcement of collective... in an industry, and many other means. The difference b... ...ed interference with private interests by public action and... — action is that the former is subject to some measure of... ...in political control and to far-reaching obligations of pec... ...e pensation, whereas the latter is not. It is only by the fam... ...sk as considering as good what has been familiar for gen... as bad what is new, that the one can be considered... ...y the other as non-law. The uncertainty and insecurity... chaser of a house which may later be condemned a... slum clearance scheme or acquired for town developm... different from the uncertainty of a business man who i... of business by a combine. But it is probably less iniqu... total effect provided that slum standards are laid down... by statute and regulation. In the case of the compulsory... of property, compensation must be paid. Even from th... view of the affected individual the situation is therefore l... than assumed by Hayek and his school of thought. There... the difference of ultimate value assumptions, *viz.*, the qu... whether the individual private interest should not be subject to

---

[54] [1892] A.C. 25.
[55] For details see Stone, *Social Dimensions of Law and Justice* 343 *et seq.* (1966) and references there cited.

428 Contemporary Problems

compensation by administrative tribunals, subject to an appeal to the High Court on a point of law.

Fourthly, the extension of governmental activities must be balanced by the removal of the immunities of government, and of public authorities in general, from legal responsibility corresponding to that of private subjects in similar circumstances. Recent legislative developments in the major common law jurisdictions have gone a long way towards this, by the abolition of most Crown immunities and the subjection of public corporations to private and public legal liabilities. But most of the fifty state jurisdictions in the United States still preserve government immunities, and such anachronisms as the presumption of immunity of the Crown from the statutes, or from penalties,[60] remain.

Finally, there remains the supervision of public authorities exercised by higher administrative authority and ultimately by Parliament. This supervision, working through debate, public and inspection and other administrative means, is ultimately the most important protection of the citizen, although it is certainly capable and in need of much improvement.[61]

In recent years, the institution of the "Ombudsman"—named after its Scandinavian model first introduced in Sweden in 1809, has gained wide international attention as a supplement rather than an alternative to a system of administrative justice. Generally, the Ombudsman is a public official of independent status, whose task it is to protect individuals against administrative abuses. The extent of his powers varies from country to country. They generally include the submission of reports and, in some cases, the initiation of prosecutions.[62]

It can therefore be confidently asserted that while the development of a planned society does demand a reconsideration of the adjustment between private rights and public powers, it is compatible with the preservation of fundamental democratic values and with of the rule of law.

We may conclude with a brief summary of what appear to be the essential legal values of modern democracy. The first is the

[60] Cf. Law in a Changing Society, Chap. 12.

[61] For a detailed criticism, cf. Allen, Law and Orders, Chaps. 5 and 6 (1945). For the control of public corporations, cf. Friedmann (ed.), The Public Corporation 576 (1954); Robson (ed.), Problems of Nationalised Industry Chaps. 5, 15 (1952).

[62] See for a comparative survey and analysis, Gellhorn, Ombudsman and Others (1966).

some degree of insecurity and sacrifice for the sake of such over-riding public interests as the control of national resources, national health standards or economic development.

There will always be differences of opinion on the relative spheres of private freedom of action and public control. But a return to the "night-watchman" state, to which Hayek's or Keeton's conception of the rule of law correspond, is far removed from the realities of modern democratic society, American, British, French or Scandinavian. The main problem is that of surrounding planning and administrative discretion with the greatest amount of

al safeguards compatible with the effectiveness of public con-
[56] Five general principles indicate the way in which the funda-
ls of the rule of law and of individual freedom may be
ed in a planned society.[57] In the first place there is adminis-
urisdiction designed to protect illegitimate interference or
f discretion by public authorities. The alternatives are a
lged system of administrative tribunals on the Continental
or a system which seeks protection for the citizen in the
ry jurisdiction of the ordinary courts or by a combination
istrative jurisdiction with appeal to the High Court on
law. The choice between these alternatives is a matter of
ministrative law, not of fundamental legal theory. Either
the essential liabilities of the citizen, as the experience
inental democratic systems has shown.[58]

the laying down of definite standards as a test for
ference with private rights can be extended. This applies
s of sanitation, of factory protection, as much as to the
n of conditions under which government departments
public authorities may cancel contracts.[59]

the principle of reasonable compensation for unfore-
erference with legitimate interests must be extended. It
ct been fully adopted in the recent series of British
ation Acts which provide for impartial assessment of

himself has, in a more recent work (*The Constitution of Liberty*, 1960)
r a general adoption of the Continental system of administrative justice.
es, however, that many of the "socialist" lawyers whom he regards as
ible for the "decline of the law" in Britain, have long advocated the
guards of administrative justice. On the considerable progress in the direction of administrative justice see *Law in a Changing Society*, *op. cit.* at 410 *et seq.*

[57] For a fuller treatment, see *Law and Social Change*, Part IV.

[58] For some constructive suggestions, *cf.* Allen, *op. cit.* Chap. 11, and Wade "The Courts and the Administrative Courts," 63 L.Q. Rev. 164 (1947).

[59] *Cf. The Standard Conditions of Government Contracts for Stores Purchases*, (1947 ed.).

recognition of individual personality, whose development is protected by individual rights. Of these rights those are the most essential which protect the essential personal faculties and spiritual values. Those which protect material conditions of existence rank lower and are subject to changing conditions of society. Freedom of worship and thought ranks higher than freedom of property.

Individual right is balanced by responsibility towards one's fellow citizens and legal responsibility for one's acts.

Democracy, secondly, demands legal protection for equal opportunity of development, regardless of personal, racial or national distinctions; but the latter postulate is as yet severely limited by the organisation of mankind in national states.

Democracy further enjoins the law to ensure to the individual the possibility of participation in government, through adequate representation and direct responsibilities.

It finally demands a system of law which puts no individuals or classes above the law, guarantees its administration without distinction of persons and expresses the principle that everyone counts for one in legal rules.

THE ROLE OF LAW AND THE FUNCTION OF THE LAWYER IN DEVELOPING COUNTRIES

A reappraisal of the role of law, and of the function of the lawyer is needed in the great majority of nations that have recently acquired political independence, because of a generally very low and static economic and social level. The characteristic feature of an undeveloped country is the stark gap between its economic and social state and the minimum aspirations of a mid-twentieth century state modelled upon the values and objectives of the developed countries of the West. All these countries have an overwhelming need for rapid social and economic change. Much of this must express itself in legal change—in constitutions, statutes, and administrative regulations. Law in such a state of social evolution is less and less the recorder of established social, commercial, and other customs; it becomes a pioneer, the articulated expression of the new forces that seek to mould the life of the community according to new patterns.[63] In this type of society—which the underdeveloped countries represent most radically, though by no means

---

[63] For a general discussion of the role of law as an agent of social change, see *Law in a Changing Society* chap. 1.

exclusively—it is essential to reassess not only the function of law but the role of the lawyer.

In the tradition of the West, the lawyer has contributed to the development of the legal system, and thus in some way to the development of society, mainly as judge, advocate, and scholar. He has also been concerned with legislative change—as a member of a law revision committee, a parliamentary or extra-parliamentary commission, as an expert in a government department, or as a parliamentary draftsman.

But generally, the lawyer in the Western world has been a defender of the established order and of vested interests, for the simple reason that in a society dominated by commerce and industry the individual and corporate owners of property have been the principal clients. Correspondingly, the role of the lawyer has been generally more important in the shaping of private than of public law. Private law was until recently the much more important and dynamic part of the Western legal systems.

With regard to individual liberties the lawyer, especially in criminal and administrative processes, has often been a vital defender of liberties against official arbitrariness.

The continuing importance of the lawyer's function as a defender of both personal and economic rights against arbitrary interference can hardly be exaggerated. In these days of right and left wing dictatorships, the frequent muzzling of the press and other media of information, the stifling of open discussion, and confiscations of both national and foreign property interests, the protection of the legitimate interests of the individual, and most especially of his personal liberties as expressed in the minimum requisites of due process, remains one of the most important and noblest of the lawyer's functions.

But it is no longer sufficient. If the lawyer continues to be identified, as he predominantly is at the present time, with the defence of the existing order and of vested interests, against the urgent needs and interests of societies that must lift themselves from poverty and stagnation to a radically higher level of economic and social development, often within a desperately short time, the lawyer will eventually be reduced to an inferior and despised status in the developing nations. The contemporary lawyer in all states, but most emphatically so in the developing nations, must become an active and responsible participant in the shaping and formulation of development plans. He must guide and counsel but also warn where necessary. He must acknowledge the drastically increased role of public law in developing societies, which usually have inadequate resources, a totally inadequate quality and quantity of responsible private venture capital, gross educational deficiencies, and insufficient technical skills and administrative experience. These nations must plan for their future; they must seek to use and develop their resources for the maximum benefit of the community, even where they admit and desire a large share of private investment and enterprise.

An all too frequent feature in developing societies is the presence of large private landholdings, often held by absentee owners, impeding the development of a healthy agricultural economy, whether based on a system of individual peasant holdings or on cooperative farming. Very often these large land areas will also be needed for irrigation or for industrial development purposes. On the other hand, an industrial development or resettlement scheme may affect not absentee landowners but working peasants and smallholders. In such situations, the political planners will tend, and justly so, to differentiate between the various types of interests affected, according to the social and economic equities. They cannot be expected to treat large absentee landholders, who have collected excessive rents—often through rapacious middlemen—for decades or centuries, in the same way as the working smallholder. The lawyer would traditionally be inclined to regard all vested rights as equally worthy of protection. It is precisely this attitude that would tend to bring him into disrespect in developing societies. On the other hand, the political planner, unaided by the lawyer, would tend to ride roughshod over any private interests that may stand in the path of rapid planning. It is the lawyer's task, not only to ensure a proper balance between these competing interests and a sense of distributive justice that should be sharpened by his legal training, but also to ensure that the minimum safeguards of due process be preserved in order to have these matters ultimately settled by an impartial authority. But, for example, to let the courts decide the adequacy of compensation offered for expropriations made in the public interest, presupposes a judiciary that is not in ideological opposition to the very principles of the new order. Such supposition may well be erroneous, as was illustrated by the conduct of the German judiciary during the Weimar Republic, and the treatment of the compensation aspects of land reform by the Indian High Court.

A related issue that has arisen quite often in recent decades and has been the predominant subject of debate among international lawyers and in the U.N. debates leading to the Resolution on the permanent control over natural resources, is the expropriation of foreign interests and their transfer into national, usually public, control. These matters also normally form part of the national development policies and planning processes. Here again it is of crucial importance that the lawyer should not identify himself one-sidedly with the defence of vested interests but should contribute actively, and with an understanding of the issues at stake, to the responsible development and regulation of the planning processes, and to the adjustment of the competing claims of the interests of capital exporting and capital importing countries.[64]

An ever increasing part of the work of the lawyer is neither litigation nor the resolution of disputes. It lies in the shaping and formulation of policies, in the exercise of legal powers, construc-tively establishing or altering the relations between private legal parties *inter se,* between public authorities and private parties, between governments and foreign investors, and the like. In the public international sphere this task consists increasingly—and most notably in the case of developing countries—in the formula-tion of economic policies expressed in accession to multilateral trade agreements (such as GATT) or the conclusion of bilateral treaties. In the latter sphere, a decisive difference exists between treaties concluded with a state trading nation and those made with a free trading nation. These are not matters of form only; they presuppose an appreciation of the role played by foreign trade in the national economic development. The implications of bilateral or multilateral trade agreements do not have only economic aspects; the decision, for example, whether a country like India or Tanzania should accede to GATT—a multilateral treaty aspiring to inter-national free trade, based on the principle of the most-favoured-nation clause—or whether it should enter into a bilateral trade agreement with the United States or the Soviet Union, implies policy considerations of profound political importance. Similarly, whether to permit a foreign oil company to construct an oil refinery and, if so, whether to give it a monopoly of the crude oil supply or

---

[64] See Friedmann, "Social Conflict and the Protection of Foreign Investment Proceedings," Am. Soc. Int'l Law 126 1963, and "The Changing Structure of International Law" chap. 12 (1964). An understanding of this need underlies the unjustly criticised decision of the *Supreme Court in Banco Nacional de Cuba* v. *Sabbatino* 376 U.S. 398 (1964) see below, p. 488.

of tanker transport; whether to keep basic industries and utilities under public national ownership or, for the sake of more rapid and skilled development, to grant privileges to private foreign entrepreneurs; whether to accompany such policy with special tax or other financial concessions, or modifications of import-export policy —these and a multitude of other questions vital in the life of any developing country today require a basic understanding of the political and economic issues involved. In all these questions, the lawyer must play an important, often a decisive, part. It is he who must draft the necessary legislation or the complex international agreements; it is he who will usually be the principal, or one of the principal, representatives of his country in international trade negotiations. It is he who must draft the applications for loans from national or international credit agencies such as the World Bank or the United States Agency for International Development, or formulate the modalities and conditions of joint business ventures, between his own government or a private enterprise in his own country on the one side, and a private enterprise or a foreign consortium, a foreign government, or a public international agency on the other side.[65] It would be as artificial as it would be wasteful of the still desperately scarce trained manpower resources of developing countries to believe that the lawyer should or could confine himself to the strictly legal issues, such as the validity of the contract or treaty revision clause, or the legal position of a minority shareholder under company law. Indeed, the "general counsel," a concept notably developed in the United States, implies far more than technical legal advice. The general counsel, both of public agencies such as AID and of private corporations, actively participate in the policies as well as in the ultimate formulation of international business transactions. In the case of transactions between developed and developing countries, legal counsel on both sides are inevitably involved in an intricate mixture of policy issues and questions of public law, private law, and administration. All this requires a type of lawyer, on both the public and the private level, who has a different approach and a different background of knowledge from his predecessors. He cannot be expected to be an expert economist or engineer, but he can be given an understanding of the basic issues.

---

[65] For example, the International Finance Corporation is now permitted and seeks to take equity participations in conjunction with loans granted for development aid.

Within the province of the law, there will have to be a shift of emphasis, and again particularly so in the developing countries. Since most of the important planning decisions, both nationally and internationally, involve the relations between governments and private legal subjects (corporate or individuals), and since many of the major planning decisions inevitably involve some interference with property and other private interests, a study of administrative law becomes increasingly important. But it has to be a concept of administrative law wider than a study of the procedural safeguards of the citizen against administrative power as is the almost exclusive preoccupation of administrative law in the United States. In the developing countries it must correspond more closely to the wider compass of the discipline as understood in England, and even more fully in France and other continental countries. *Droit administratif* comprises the totality of legal relations between public authorities *inter se,* and between public authorities and private subjects. As developed by the jurisprudence of the Conseil d'Etat and of corresponding continental tribunals, it involves not only the legal processes determining the limits of administrative discretion and the procedural safeguards of the citizen through judicial or quasi-judicial procedures; it involves also the study of the administrative contract as an important way of regulating the manifold relations between public authority and private citizens in the provision of supplies and services. This concept may have increasing significance to international transactions between governments and private foreign investors.[66] Internally, the function and status of the public enterprise is of crucial importance in almost all the developing countries which seek to combine the principle of public control over vital commodities and services with the retention of some freedom of movement and initiative in the development of resources and the conduct of business. Hence the significance of contemporary development corporations which are either public, mixed, or private corporations, but which almost inevitably involve a specific legal status, and special relations with the government. Understood in this wider sense, administrative law will be the principal instrument of adjusting the interests of the public, as represented by the government, and of the private citizens, as represented by contractors, foreign investors, and the like.

It is only by actively entering into this process by equipping

---

[66] See Fatouros, *Government Guarantees to Foreign Investors* (1962); Friedmann, *Changing Structure of International Law, op. cit.* at 200 *et seq.*

himself as far as possible with the outlook and knowledge required for this more flexible, and also far more responsible, function of the law in the developing countries of our time that the lawyer can hope to retain or even broaden the role that he has traditionally played in the countries of the Western world. It is only in this way that he can help to move the ideal of the "rule of law" from the static and defensive meaning it has tended to acquire in the Western world, and to adapt it to the needs and ideals of our time—which make economic and social development a paramount matter of public national and international responsibility.

Legal Theory, Public Policy and Legal Evolution

CHAPTER 32

LEGAL IDEALS AND JUDICIAL LAW-MAKING

IT is still a common practice among lawyers to look upon legal ideology as a useless speculation of theorists, irrelevant to the administration of law. Many are the contemptuous utterances of practical lawyers on legal theory as "metaphysical" speculation, but none perhaps is more sweeping than the dictum of Lord Sumner (then Hamilton L.J.) in *Baylis* v. *Bishop of London*[1]:

Whatever may have been the case a hundred and forty-six years ago, we are not now free in the twentieth century to administer that vague jurisprudence which is sometimes attractively styled justice as between man and man.

The vague jurisprudence which Lord Sumner had in mind was Lord Mansfield's conception of equity and natural justice as foundations of a principle of unjust enrichment. Lord Sumner's own attitude was, however, itself the profession of a particular juristic faith. Only a few decades later, the "vague jurisprudence" which Lord Sumner condemned has found increasing recognition by English courts, which have gone a considerable way towards acceptance of a principle of unjust enrichment, based on general equitable principles.[2] Legal positivists could delude themselves that they were not concerned with legal ideology. In reality these lawyers were legal philosophers, like everyone who has to solve legal problems, but their philosophy was often inarticulate. Such self-delusion makes it psychologically easier to mould the law in accordance with beliefs and prejudices without feeling the weight of responsibility that burdens lawyers with greater consciousness of the issues at stake.

The contrast may be illustrated by two judicial pronouncements. Lord Finlay observed in the case of *Crown Milling Co.* v. *The*

---

[1] [1913] 1 Ch. 127.
[2] *Cf.* Lord Wright, *"Sinclair* v. *Brougham"* 6 Camb. L.J. 305 (1938); Winfield, *Province of the Law of Tort* (1931); Friedmann, "The Principle of Unjust Enrichment in English Law" 16 Can. Bar Rev. 243, 365 (1938); with some reservations, Holdsworth, "Unjustifiable Enrichment" 55 L.Q. Rev. 37 (1939).

King[3]: "It is not for any tribunal to adjudicate between conflicting theories of political economy."

Armed with this pronouncement the learned Lord proceeded to give a judgment regarding the validity of a New Zealand marketing statute which upheld principles of extreme economic liberalism against state supervision.[4] Practically all English decisions which are concerned with matters of economic competition, *e.g.*, in conspiracy or in restraint of trade, display a similar outlook. Economic doctrines of far-reaching consequence, such as principles according to which price or market control or monopoly of production may be upheld, have been developed in a rather haphazard manner, without much consciousness of the economic and social problems at stake and with little, if any, scientific inquiry into such economic problems as that of a fair and reasonable price.[5]

This contrasts strongly with the following judicial pronouncement by Holmes J.[6]:

This case is decided upon an economic theory which a large part of the country does not entertain. If it were a question whether I agreed with that theory, I should desire to study it further and long before making up my mind. But I do not conceive that to be my duty, because I strongly believe that my agreement or disagreement has nothing to do with the right of a majority to embody their opinion in law. It is settled by various decisions of this court that state constitution and state laws may regulate life in many ways which we as legislators might think as injudicious or, if you like, as tyrannical as this, and which equally with this interfere with the liberty to contract. Sunday laws and usury laws are ancient examples. A more modern one is the prohibition of lotteries. The liberty of the citizen to do as he likes so long as he does not interfere with the liberty of others to do the same, which has been a shibboleth for some well-known writers, is interfered with by school laws, by the Post Office, by every state or municipal institution which takes his money for purposes thought desirable whether he likes it or not. The Fourteenth Amendment does not enact Mr. Herbert Spencer's Social Statics . . . Some of these laws embody convictions or prejudices which judges are likely to share. Some may not. But a constitution is not intended to embody a particular economic theory, whether of paternalism and the organic relation of the citizen to his state or of *laissez-faire*. It is made for people of fundamentally differing views, and the accident of our finding certain opinions natural and familiar or novel and even shocking ought not to conclude our

---

[3] [1927] A.C. at p. 394.

[4] For a similar judicial attitude, *cf.* the *Salt Case* [1914] A.C. 461.

[5] For prominent examples of this attitude, *cf.* the *Mogul Case* [1892] A.C. 25; the *Adelaide Steamship Case* [1913] A.C. 781; the *Salt Case* [1913] A.C. 461.

[6] *Lochner* v. *U.S.* 198 U.S. 75, 76 (1905).

judgement upon the question whether statutes embodying them conflict with the Constitution of the United States.[7]

The former of these judicial utterances expresses the opinion that the lawyer can solve legal issues which involve economic and social problems by a process of purely legal reasoning. The latter utterance reveals a deep appreciation of the interdependence between judicial and social and economic ideology. Holmes J. himself chooses a solution characteristic of a judge in a non-totalitarian country, who is aware of his social responsibility, conscious of the political problem before him in the form of a legal dispute, but convinced of his duty of impartiality in the balancing of social forces and equally convinced of the duty of the judge to leave the shaping of the political principles of society essentially to the proper legislative authority.[8]

A more precise analysis is, however, necessary and possible of the ways in which the practical lawyer may come into contact with legal theory.

The "practical lawyer" comprises every one concerned with the administration of law. Although the judge figures prominently, the legal adviser, whether in industry or before the court, and the administrator are practical lawyers in this sense. If it was ever possible to maintain a clear-cut distinction between law and administration, such distinction has become more and more relative as the modern delegation of law-making as well as of judicial or quasi-judicial powers to administrative organs mingles legislative administration and judicial functions.[9]

The Blackstonian doctrine of the "declaratory" function of the courts, holding that the duty of the court is not to "pronounce a

[7] For a lucid analysis of the conflicting trends and roles of the court, see Mason, *Security through Freedom* 115 *et seq.* (1955).

[8] *Cf.* the very similar language of Stone J. in *Morehead* v. *Tipaldo*, 298 U.S. 587, 636 (1938).

[9] The relativity of the distinction between law and administration has come to be more widely recognised with the growth of administrative law, on the one hand, and the increase of state activity, on the other. Where, as in Soviet Russia, the state becomes the principal agent of economic activity, relations between various state departments, or between the state and its citizens assume a correspondingly large importance. Pashukanis (*The General Theory of Law and Marxism*) concluded that "law" was confined to relations between citizens as equals, arising from commodity exchange, and that in a socialised system administrative discretion would completely displace law. In fascist states the concentration of law-making, executive and supreme judicial power in a dictatorial and uncontrolled government has, in a different way, completely blurred the border lines between law and administration. From a rather opposite standpoint Kelsen has emphasised the theoretical relativity of the distinction (*cf.* 51 L.Q. Rev. 521) as denoting mainly the difference in the amount of discretion used in the administration of the legal order.

new law but to maintain and expound the old one"[10] has long been little more than a ghost. From Holmes and Gény to Pound and Cardozo, contemporary jurists have increasingly recognised and articulated the lawmaking functions of the courts. The radical transformations which, for example, contracts, torts or family law have undergone at the hands of the courts have made it increasingly difficult to maintain the time-honoured fiction of the declaratory role of the judge. It is not, perhaps, surprising that it should have been abandoned more wholeheartedly in the United States than in England. The profound effects, in all walks of life, of the interpretations of the Constitution by the Supreme Court—a Constitution which has in theory remained almost unchanged and yet governed the legal life of the country for almost two centuries—have long created in the United States a picture of the judge and his function very different from that traditionally cherished in England.[11] The celebrated dictum that "the Constitution is what the courts say it is"[12] has, if anything, been reinforced by the momentous decisions rendered by the Court during the last decade in such matters as school segregation, voting rights, and the redrawing of election districts. In England it may be that sheer respect for tradition, or perhaps a lingering love for the role of fiction as a major agent in legal evolution, are responsible for the survival of an increasingly untenable doctrine, which was, moreover, never adopted by some of the greatest of British judges from Holt, Mansfield and Blackburn to Wright and Atkin.

Judicial Law-Making in Contemporary Jurisprudence[13]

In 1923 Roscoe Pound, in an analysis of the theory of judicial

[10] Blackstone, *Commentaries* 69 (15th ed. 1808).

[11] The need to adapt the received common law of England to the diversity and dynamism of American conditions also tended to depreciate legislation and elevate the formative functions of the Courts. "This depreciation of the statute book was promoted by the preeminence of case-made, judge-made law in the formative first half of the nineteenth century; and this was reinforced, first, by the office-apprentice system of legal education, and then by the spread of the case method in the law schools." Hurst, *The Growth of American Law*, 186 (1950).

[12] Charles Evans Hughes, later Chief Justice of the United States, in an address to the Elmira Chamber of Commerce, 1907 (*Addresses of Charles Evans Hughes 1906-1916*, 185 (2nd ed.).

[13] This book is not concerned with the process of judicial reasoning and lawmaking in its entirety. On the many complex factors of personality, fact-finding, jury behaviour, subconscious prejudices, etc., much valuable work has been done in recent works by Jerome Frank, Llewellyn, Lasswell, McDougal and others. The present book is concerned with one of the elements, the impact of articulate or inarticulate legal ideas upon the judicial process. That it is a very important element is hardly contested.

decision,[14] described the following as the picture which the modern jurist had to draw for the assistance of the courts:

(1) To paint a process of legal social engineering as a part of the whole process of social control; (2) to set off the part of the field of the legal order appropriate to intelligence, involving repetition, calling for rule or for logical development of principle, from the part appropriate to intuition, involving unique situations, calling for standards and for individualised applications; (3) to portray a balance between decision of the actual cause and elaboration of a precedent, in which, subsuming the claims of the parties under generalised social claims, as much of the latter will be given effect as is possible; and (4) to induce a consciousness of the role of ideal pictures of the social and legal order both in decision and in declaring the law. Indeed the last is the item of most importance.

In the same article Pound stressed that legislation, common law, administrative and judicial justice demanded different types of social engineering. He considered certain subjects such as property and commercial law as more susceptible of legislative formulation than, for example, the law of torts or fiduciary duties.

Two factors are particularly relevant to Pound's statement. One is the dependence of scope and extent of legal idealism on the political structure of the system in which it operates. The other factor is the unprecedented advance of social service legislation in the common law systems, especially in England, and the consequent intermingling of "political" law and "lawyer's" law. Both these factors call for a critical examination of Pound's thesis.

JUDICIAL ROLE IN THREE TYPES OF LEGAL SYSTEMS

Three types of legal systems must be distinguished for the purpose of this analysis. The first is totalitarian society. As shown in previous chapters,[15] it is characterised by close subservience of the judicial machinery to the dominant political ideology. This operates more strongly in some fields of law than in others. Both the Nazi and the Soviet régimes retained many traditional concepts of civil law, but ensured its subservience to political ideology by the selection of the judiciary and by the destruction of effective guarantees of independence. In Nazi Germany the bulk of civil and commercial law remained intact, but in all cases of ideological importance the courts

---

[14] Pound, "The Theory of Judicial Decision," 36 Harv. L. Rev. 940, 958 (1923).
[15] See above, p. 373 *et seq.*

distorted the existing statutes for new political purposes whenever necessary.[16] In the field of public and criminal law the intrusion of political ideology is more direct and absolute. While Nazi Germany preserved the bulk of the existing system of law, other than constitutional law, twisting it to new purposes and sidestepping it wherever necessary, Soviet Russia introduced a new code of civil law. Both yielded to the necessity of establishing a sphere of relatively secure rights even in a society of political absolutism. This explains the attempts of both German and Soviet courts to reestablish the certainty of legal concepts and institutions against sheer utility and arbitrariness. It explains, for example, the attempt of the Soviet Supreme Court to restore the conception of individual guilt in criminal law, and the parallel refusal of the German Supreme Court to convict outstanding enemies of the Nazi régime in all cases. But in either case ordinary justice is subject to being overruled by administrative action, although it seems that recent Soviet law reforms have somewhat reduced the scope of administrative interference with legal process.[17] Moreover, the bulk of the judiciary in both cases has complied with an essentially political interpretation of law. In this type of society the judge is indeeed rather free from the rule of statutes and codes and from all written texts. He is enslaved instead to the political dictates of his superiors, and the sanction for non-compliance is severe. When, under the law of 1935, a German court convicted an accused because his act was contrary "to the healthy instincts of the people" it acted as a direct mouthpiece of the political executive. In totalitarian systems this is underlined by the power not only of superior courts but of the Ministry or Commissariat for Justice to give instructions of principle on the decision of cases.[18]

The second and third types are non-totalitarian systems. But with regard to the scope and character of judicial law-making, a basic distinction must be made between federal systems, in which a court is the ultimate interpreter of the Constitution, and other systems, in which the parliamentary law-giver is not subject to judicial control. Within the common law world, the former type is represented by the United States, Australia and Canada, the latter by Britain.

[16] See above, p. 343.

[17] Such as the arrest of Pastor Niemöller after his acquittal by the court, or the detention of hundreds of thousands of political or social opponents without trial in both Germany and Russia.

[18] *Cf.* above, p. 374.

JUDICIAL LAW-MAKING IN FEDERAL CONSTITUTIONS

Some account of the extent to which "higher law" ideas influence the judicial interpretation of a constitution has been given earlier.[19] But the problem goes deeper and further than the infusion of natural law ideologies into the interpretation of a constitution. The extension of planning and social service activities, and in particular the change in the scope and structure of commerce, has exposed constitutions and courts to a particular strain in recent years. This may be illustrated by some recent developments in the interpretations of the American, Australian and Canadian Constitutions.

Under art. I, section 8(1) the United States Congress has power "to lay and collect taxes duties imposts and excises to pay the debts and provide for the common defence and general welfare of the United States; but all these duties imposts and excises shall be uniform throughout the United States."

With the extension of social services and financial needs of all kinds, both federal and within the states, the problem has arisen whether state enterprises are immune from federal taxation affecting a particular industry throughout the United States. The original attitude of the Supreme Court formulated, for example, in *Ohio* v. *Helvering*,[20] was based on a distinction between the business and the "governmental" activities of the state. "If a state chooses to go into the business of buying and selling commodities its right to do so may be conceded so far as the federal Constitution is concerned; but the exercise of the right is not the performance of a government function" (*per* Sutherland J.). In the words of a contemporary American judge,[21] this meant that only such state activities were immune from federal taxation as were engaged in by states in 1787. It is obvious that such a conception was bound to become untenable. But the alternative approach is not easy. In the later case of *New York* v. *U.S.*,[22] the question arose whether the State of New York, in selling mineral waters taken from its state-owned and operated springs, was immune from a federal tax on mineral waters. The majority of the court held that the state was not immune from taxation. The different judgments fully reveal not only the dilemma of legal adjudication of vital political issues, but also the difficulty

---

[19] Above, p. 136 *et seq.*
[20] 292 U.S. 360, 369 (1933).
[21] Frankfurter J. in *New York* v. *U.S.* 326 U.S. 572 (1946).
[22] 326 U.S. 572 (1946).

of deciding which is the "reactionary" and which is the "progressive" view. Two of the majority judges, as well as the dissenting judges, exposed with equal force the obsolescence of the division between governmental and non-governmental powers, formerly adopted by the court. But from the same premise, Frankfurter J. drew the conclusion that no limitation could be implied on the federal taxing power, regardless of the type of activity in which a state was engaged, while Douglas J., for the dissenting judges, who was even more emphatic in saying that industrial and trading activities of a state were a legitimate government activity, concluded than any tax upon such activities implied an illegitimate limitation on the sovereignty of the state as guaranteed by the Constitution.

To say that the present tax will be sustained because it does not impair the state's function of government is to conclude either that the sale by the state of its mineral water is not a function of government, or that the present tax is so slight as to be no burden. The former obviously is not true. The latter overlooks the fact that the power to tax lightly is the power to tax severely. . . . The notion that the sovereign position of the states must find its protection in the will of a transient majority of Congress is foreign to, and a negation of, our constitutional system.

Four of the majority judges took an intermediate line by saying that the states certainly could not claim immunity even according to the now out-moded view of the court on the limits of proper government activity. But they admitted the possibility that federal taxation might be of such a character as to affect a state's performance of its sovereign functions even if it did not discriminate between state and private enterprise.

A later decision of the Supreme Court[23] gives an almost classical example of the conflict of judicial approaches to a problem of constitutional interpretation which involves an appreciation of social and economic policies. Under the Agriculture and Markets Law of the State of New York, the Commissioner had refused a licence for an additional milk distribution plant on the ground that the proposed expansion of the petitioner's milk distribution facilities would reduce the supply of milk for local markets and result in destructive competition in a market already adequately served. As so frequently in recent years, the court majority consisted of five justices, the dissenting minority of four. The approach to the problem revealed, however, three distinct philosophies. Jackson J., on

[23] *Hood* v. *Du Mond* 336 U.S. 525 (1949).

behalf of the majority, adopted what might be described as a fundamentalist approach. He regarded the New York law as a violation of the principle of free trade embodied in the commerce clause of the Federal Constitution.

This distinction between the power of the state to shelter its people from menaces to their health or safety and from fraud, even when those dangers emanate from interstate commerce, and its lack of power to retard, burden or constrict the flow of such commerce for their economic advantage, is one deeply rooted in both our history and our law.[24]

Our system, fostered by the commerce clause, is that every farmer and every craftsman shall be encouraged to produce by the certainty that he will have free access to every market in the nation, that no home embargoes will withhold his exports, and no foreign state will by customs or duties or regulations exclude them. Likewise, every consumer may look to the free competition from every producing area in the nation to protect him from exploitation by any. Such was the vision of the founders; such has been the doctrine of this court which has given it reality.[25]

Black J., with whom Murphy J. concurred, expounded the philosophy of the social welfare state. He regarded the majority view as an improper judicial interference with the legitimate regulating functions of government, and as a revival of reactionary philosophies.

The judicially directed march of the due process philosophy as an emancipator of business from regulation appeared arrested a few years ago. That appearance was illusory. That philosophy continues its march. The due process clause and commerce clause have been used like Siamese twins in a never-ending stream of challenges to government regulation.[26]

Both the commerce and due process clauses serve high purposes when confined within their proper scope. But a stretching of either outside its sphere can paralyse the legislative process, rendering the people's legislative representatives impotent to perform their duty of providing appropriate rules to govern this dynamic civilisation. Both clauses easily lend themselves to inordinate expansions of this court's power at the expense of legislative power. For under the prevailing due process rule, appeals can be made to the "fundamental principles of liberty and justice" which our "fathers" wished to preserve. In commerce clause cases reference can appropriately be made to the far-seeing wisdom of the "fathers" in guarding against commercial and even shooting wars among the states. Such arguments have strong emotional appeals and when skilfully utilised they sometimes obscure the vision.[27]

[24] *Id.* at 533.
[25] *Id.* at 539.

[26] *Id.* at 562.
[27] *Id.* at 563.

Frankfurter J., with whom Rutledge J. concurred, preferred to remand the case to the Supreme Court of Albany County for further fact investigation. His view—midway between the conflicting idealisms—represents the "balance of interests" approach.

I feel constrained to dissent because I cannot agree in treating what is essentially a problem of striking a balance between competing interests as an exercise in absolutes.[28]

As I see the central issue, therefore, it is whether the difference in degree between denying access to a market for failure to comply with sanitary or bookkeeping regulations and denying it for the sake of preventing destructive competition from disrupting the market is great enough to justify a difference in result.[29]

He thought that the facts before the court were insufficient to decide whether the action of the Commissioner had been on one side of the line or the other.

The three opinions in this case express at either extreme starkly conflicting philosophies of state power and individual economic freedom, as reflected in the American Constitution, and, between the extremes, a pragmatic approach in which the conflicting interests, policies and purposes of regulatory action are carefully weighed. Such conflicts are inevitable where independent judges have to interpret static clauses in a dynamic society. Indeed, such tensions are the life blood of democracy. Subservience to the dictates of government would be the price at which unanimity could be bought. For it is not only the conflict of values and philosophies in a free society which produces such clashes, but also the frequent divergence in the application of general principles to concrete issues. Where the power of government is divided between a federation and its member states, advocacy of planning or *laissez-faire* alone cannot decide the issue; for the further constitutional question arises whether in a federation there is an inviolable minimum of state powers which a federation cannot infringe by an expansive interpretation of taxing power, interstate commerce, and of other powers to which modern social conditions give a meaning vastly different from the time of the founding fathers. Moreover, judges in a free society will often deliberately check their own preferences because they regard even the appearance of a biased decision as

[28] *Id.* at 564.
[29] *Id.* at 570.

more harmful than a result which they personally disapprove.[30] Even when the issue of principle is clear, the question remains, as in *Hood's* case, how the exercise of a specific power should be classified. The discussion of principles can and must lead to a clarification of issues. It cannot eliminate the responsibility of decision in a given issue.

The expansion of the Federal legislative scope of power in the area of economic and social welfare has been achieved despite two basic arguments with which the Supreme Court has been faced. The arguments for restricting Federal powers based on theories of individual rights and resting mainly on economic substantive due process have been dicussed above and in a previous chapter.[31] Other arguments have been based on restrictive interpretations of the Commerce Clause[32] as well as of other Article I powers.[33]

Recent legislation by Congress in the area of racial discrimination has rekindled the issue of the permissible scope of Federal power based on the Commerce Clause and other Article I powers. The highly controversial public accommodations sections of the 1964 Civil Rights Act[34] are specifically based on powers derived from the Commerce Clause. This has been sustained by the Supreme Court in two decisions.[35] "The fact that Congress was also dealing with what it considered a moral problem . . . does not detract from the overwhelming evidence of the disruptive effect that racial discrimination has had on commercial intercourse." (Clark J. in the *Atlanta Motel* case.)

The High Court, which authoritatively interprets the Australian Constitution, is not hampered by the enactment of inalienable

---

[30] The High Court of Australia, in March 1951, by a majority of six to one, invalidated the Government Act outlawing the Australian Communist Party. None of the judges representing the majority could be suspected of any sympathy for the Communist Party, and some of them quite probably approved the political objectives of the Act.

[31] See above, p. 140 *et seq*.

[32] See *Hammer* v. *Dagenhart,* 247 U.S. 251 (1918) and *Bailey* v. *Drexel Furniture* 259 U.S. 20 (1920) which were unsuccessful attempts to use the Commerce Clause and the taxing power as bases for restricting child labor; *U.S.* v. *Butler* 297 U.S. 1 (1933); *Railroad Retirement Board* v. *Alton Railroad Co.* 295 U.S. 330 (1935); *Carter* v. *Carter Coal Co.* 299 U.S. 238 (1936).

[33] Article I, Section 8 of the United States Constitution contains the Commerce Clause which provides: "The Congress shall have Power . . . To regulate Commerce with foreign nations, and among the several states and with the Indian Tribes."

[34] 78 Stat. 241, 42 U.S.C.A. § 2000a-2000-6.

[35] *Heart of Atlanta Motel* v. *U.S.* 379 U.S. 241 (1964) (refusal to rent rooms to Negroes); *Katzenbach* v. *McLung* 379 U.S. 294 (1964) (refusal to serve food to Negroes).

individual rights and the "due process" clause of the American Constitution. But an ambiguously drawn provision of the Constitution has involved it in equally deep political and social issues. Section 92 provides that

On the imposition of uniform duties and customs trade and intercourse amongst the states whether by means of internal carriage or ocean navigation shall be absolutely free.

Does this mean freedom from state regulation or freedom in the volume of trade flowing between the states of Australia? The court has wavered between these two different interpretations and has not yet arrived at a clear line. In one of the few decisions of the Privy Council on the subject, Lord Wright exposed the ambiguity of the word "freedom."[36] He rejected the interpretation given in an earlier case by Dixon J.[37] that the words "absolutely free" mean an exclusion of all government control. But no clear alternative test was given. Subsequent cases, which have deepened the dilemma of judicial interpretation on profoundly political issues, include the validity of a Government air monopoly and the validity of a federal Act purporting to socialise banking through the compulsory acquisition by the Commonwealth of all the property and business of private banks. In the former case[38] the power of the Commonwealth Government to set up an Airways Commission, with the power to run its own air services, was confirmed as an aspect of the Commonwealth's power to legislate on interstate commerce; but the proposed monopoly was held to be an unconstitutional infringement of the powers of the states. In the latter case[39] the Act was partially invalidated as interfering with freedom of interstate commerce, notwithstanding the power of the Commonwealth to legislate on banking.[40]

How strongly judicial interpretation, especially in constitutional matters, can mould the seemingly plain text of a legislative document is shown by the fate of the famous sections 91 and 92 of the British North America Act of 1867, which still serves as the

[36] *James* v. *Commonwealth* (1936) 55 C.L.R. 1.

[37] *The Peanut Board Case* (1933) 48 C.L.R. 266.

[38] (1946) 71 C.L.R. 29.

[39] [1948] 2 Argus L.R. p. 89 *et seq.* For more recent decisions on this problem see Derham 6 *Res Judicatae*, 111-122 (1952).

[40] The approach of the court to problems of this kind has been criticised by a distinguished Australian statesman and social philosopher: Eggleston, *Reflections of an Australian Liberal* (1953). For a criticism of the court's positivism, see McWhinney, 1 Am. J. Comp. L. 36 (1952).

Canadian Constitution. Section 91 gives the Dominion Government power "to make laws for the peace, order and good government of Canada in relation to all matters not coming within the classes of subjects by this Act assigned exclusively to the legislatures of the provinces." Among the powers reserved to the provinces is the class of subject, "property and civil rights in the province" (section 92). The history of sections 91 and 92 and the opinions of most jurists and historians confirm that the general power of the Dominion was deliberately devised as a paramount power for the strengthening of the new federal authority. Not only did section 91 give the Dominion all residuary power but it also cut down the specific powers of the provinces through the enumeration of twenty-nine classes of subjects as illustrations of the scope of the federal general power. Two further classes were added to the enumeration of federal powers by amendments. In practice, the relationship between Dominion and provincial powers has been largely reversed ever since the Privy Council in the *Local Prohibition* case[41] held that the general power of the Dominion as distinct from the enumerations could never affect the sphere of any powers exclusively reserved to the provinces. The Privy Council and, following it, the Supreme Court of Canada also held that the phrase "property and civil rights" must be understood in the "largest sense."[42] Among the many dramatic consequences of this approach has been the invalidation of the so-called Canadian New Deal legislation, a series of statutes relating to minimum wages, limitation of hours of work, national unemployment and social insurance, and marketing regulations for natural products. All these statutes were thrown out on the ground that they were interferences with the exclusive power of the provinces to legislate in relation to property. In effect, judicial interpretation has thus assimilated the Canadian Constitution—where the Dominion is given the reserve power—to the Australian position where the states have the reserve power. The Dominion of Canada is no more, and perhaps even less, capable than the Commonwealth of Australia of enacting planning or social legislation. To some extent the courts have transferred a negative paramountcy from the Dominion to the provinces.[43]

But the dilemma is deeper than political idealism or prejudice.

---

[41] *Att.-Gen. of Ontario* v. *Att.-Gen. of Canada* [1896] A.C. 348.

[42] *E.g., Natural Products Marketing Act* [1936] S.C.R. 398.

[43] *Cf.*, on the whole development, Laskin, *Canadian Constitutional Law* (2nd ed. 1960).

Judges under democratic constitutions cannot go to the length of ignoring the written text, however obsolete or outmoded, without impairing all respect for the stability of law. Yet a static interpretation of an outmoded constitution would be equally fatal. In this dilemma the judges vacillate between a logical and a sociological, a static and a dynamic approach.

The dilemma can be lessened if courts follow the advice of Holmes J. that they should permit legislative policy to develop except where the plainest meaning of the constitution forbids it. But it cannot disappear where the ultimate interpretation of a political document is entrusted to a body of lawyers, however impartial and erudite, who cannot but hold the balance of political power in their unwilling hands. Their task is made more complex by the tension between the different organs of the state which time and again frustrates government under federal constitutions.

JUDICIAL ROLE IN THE BRITISH SYSTEM

The problem of judicial idealism is different and simpler where the check on the action of the government is not controlled by "abstract law" but by "a popular organ of government."[44]

In this type of society, classically exemplified by the British constitutional system, the judge is spared much of the dilemma which constantly confronts the judicial guardian of a written constitution. He is not compelled to adjudicate on legislative policy. He cannot question the validity of a statute. In the English legal system judicial creativeness flows through narrower channels. Thus, restrictive actions of various kinds, but mainly prerogative orders, enable the courts to restrain administrative arbitrariness. The actions of local authorities and other statutory bodies may be declared invalid if they are held to be unreasonable or an abuse of powers. The actions of Ministers may be held invalid where the Minister acts in a "quasi-judicial" capacity and offends certain principles of elementary justice. On the whole, the limited scope of these checks and the steadiness of long-settled constitutional tradition have preserved the British judiciary from the ideological warfare into which the American Supreme Court has at times been drawn. It has therefore given them a truer judicial independence than the theoretically more perfect system of checks and balances which

[44] *Cf.* Dickinson, *Administrative Justice and the Supremacy of Law,* 95 (1927).

characterises in particular the American Constitution. But the degree of judicial control is nevertheless influenced by the changing barometer of public opinion and social pressures. There have been occasional attempts to substitute the judge's own prejudice for the policy of the democratically elected authority. The outstanding example is probably the decision of the House of Lords in *Roberts* v. *Hopwood*,[45] where the House confirmed the district auditor's surcharge against the members of a borough council which had decided on a higher standard of wages than usual at that time, and on equal remuneration for male and female employees in exercise of their statutory authority to fix wages "as they think fit." Lord Atkinson's outburst against a council who "allowed themselves to be guided in preference by some eccentric principles of socialist philanthropy, or by a feminist ambition to secure the equality of the sexes in the matter of wages in the world of labour" compares with some of the more prejudiced approaches of the American Supreme Court to constitutional problems. The predominant attitude of British courts has, however, been one of restraint in regard to ministerial actions in exercise of their statutory powers.[46] In a series of decisions on the procedure of the Minister for Town and Country Planning in the approval of schemes for new towns, the House of Lords and the Court of Appeal have firmly refused to enter into a control of policy and administrative discretion by describing the Minister's action as "quasi-judicial" activities and thereby subjecting it to special principles of procedure. "Such justification (*i.e.*, of the Minister's action) must be called for by Parliament and not by the court."[47] But in a recent case, the Court of Appeal revived memories of *Roberts* v. *Hopwood* in holding an action by the Birmingham Corporation—authorised to charge such transport fares as it thought fit—in providing free transport at certain hours for aged people to be *ultra vires*.[48] More basic is the court's changed attitude towards the autonomy of private associations with monopoly power. Reversing a long tradition of non-interference in the affairs of "domestic tribunals," the Court of Appeal and the House of Lords have recently extended the legal

[45] [1925] A.C. 578.
[46] See, for recent surveys, Treves, "Administrative Discretion and Judicial Control," 10 Mod. L. Rev. 276 (1947); de Smith, "The Limits of Judicial Review," 11 Mod. L. Rev. 306 (1948); Wade, "The Twilight of Natural Justice?" 67 L.Q. Rev. 103 (1951).
[47] *Robinson* v. *Minister of Town and Country Planning* [1948] 1 All E.R. 851, 859, *per* Lord Greene M.R.
[48] *Prescott* v. *Birmingham Corpn.* [1955] Ch. 210.

supervision of decisions of trade unions[49] and even awarded damages to an unjustly expelled unionist.[50]

The conflict of approaches to the problem of legal development by judicial decision moves within a smaller compass in English as compared with American law, for the courts are not called upon to adjudicate upon the broad principles of a constitution. But within this smaller compass the problems are the same. There always will be dynamic and static periods, periods in which the urge for social reform predominates over the desire for stability and certainty, and other periods when extraordinary legislative activity and the restlessness of society produce a judicial reaction, and added emphasis on legal stability. There will always be the conflicts of judicial temperaments[51] as well as the inevitable divergences in applying any ideals and principles to a given fact situation. Such tensions are of the essence of law in a free society. It is neither possible nor desirable that any theory of judicial decision should attempt to resolve such tensions. What it can and must do for the legal practitioner, on the bench, at the bar, or in a government department, is to clarify the issue, to sort out the legal tools and instruments at their disposal. But their use in any given situation will always depend on the skill and wisdom of the user. Just as the excellent instruments supplied by modern technology are no substitute for the surgeon's skill and judgement, so legal theory can only prepare and sort out the instruments of legal decision.

INTERPRETATIONS OF STATUTES AND PRECEDENT

The major function of the judiciary lies in the interpretation of statutes and the application of common law precedents. In this field the problems are substantially the same for all common law jurisdictions. As a subsequent chapter will show, they are indeed not basically different in civil law jurisdictions.[52]

The English, as much as the American, Canadian or Australian judge, whether he interprets a statute or applies a common law precedent, is faced with the perennial problems: how to balance the need for stability and certainty, embodied in the principle of *stare decisis*, with the need for the constructive adaptation of the law to changing social needs; how to balance the certainty aimed

---

[49] *Lee* v. *Showmen's Guild* [1952] 2 Q.B. 329.
[50] *Bonsor* v. *Musician's Union* [1956] A.C. 104.
[51] For examples see below, p. 500 *et seq.*
[52] See below, p. 533 *et seq.*

at, if not always achieved, by a strict adherence to the letter of the law, with individual justice. The conflict can never be finally resolved. Changing climates of public opinion, fluctuations in the strength of political and social pressures, differences of personality, and the sheer limitless variety of individual situations calling for a solution, constantly pose the problem anew. Nor are they vitally different whether the problem at hand is the interpretation of a clause in a statute or an application of a common law precedent. Whether a court is to stand by its former interpretation of the statutory definition of an employee, or by a precedent defining the duties of an occupier towards a licensee, depends on considerations substantially similar in both situations.

But if there are no basic differences of principle, there are considerable differences in approach and method. A statute expresses a more or less general proposition, ranging from such sweeping clauses as the "due process" provisions of the American Constitution, to statutory definitions of a railway or of the control of one corporation by another for the purposes of taxation. The task of the judge is to find how far the facts before him can be fitted into the abstract and generalising definition of the statute. In common law cases, on the other hand, the sorting out process starts with the comparison of one set of facts with another set of facts. Even if the judge in either case is possessed by a strong desire to do justice rather than to be dominated by statutory texts or precedents, he will seek to attain his objective by different ways.

It is because of the differences of legal technique rather than of principle that the interpretations of statutes and precedents requires different treatment.

Principles of Statutory Interpretation

The English lawyer does not interpret general principles embodied in a written constitution, nor does he, apart from a few minor exceptions, interpret codes which, along with a comprehensive settlement of the law, instruct him as to the principles of interpretation. He does administer and interpret an increasing number of statutes; but, psychologically, if not statistically, these still appear as exceptions rather than as rule, and the theory of statutory interpretation is, accordingly, rather undetermined. For a consistent and constructive theory of statutory interpretation one would have to go back to Tudor times. The four rules of *Heydon's Case* (1584) give a clear basis for a broad and progressive interpretation which excludes neither parliamentary history nor the consideration of legislative policy. The "equity of a statute," as expounded by Plowden in his note on *Eyston* v. *Studd* (1574), contains a striking anticipation of modern principles of judicial equity:

And in order to form a right judgment when the letter of a statute is restrained, and when enlarged, by equity, it is a good way, when you peruse a statute, to suppose that the lawmaker is present, and that you have asked him the question you want to know touching the equity; then you must give yourself an answer as you imagine he would have done, if he had been present. . . . And if the lawmaker would have followed the equity, notwithstanding the words of the law . . . you may safely do the like. . . .

This is an almost verbal anticipation of the language used in the Swiss Civil Code of 1907.

It is in accordance with this attitude that Walmesley J., in the *Magdalen College Case* (1615), described the King, the legislator of his time, as the physician of his subjects "to cure their maladies and to remove leprosies among them."

The principles of the Tudor period, a time of strong government and active law-making, have, however, given way to a much narrower judicial and professional legal attitude towards the interpretation of statutes. It is not within the scope of this chapter to discuss the historical development in detail.[53] By the beginning of the twentieth century the rules of *Heydon's Case* had been substantially restricted by the development of the doctrine which excluded *travaux préparatoires* from judicial consideration and thus went far to prevent the judge from studying the disease which Parliament had set out to cure.[54] Even more important was the development of an attitude of jealousy rather than collaboration in the judicial approach to statute, expressed by many judges of the last rather than the present generation.[55]

This combination of conservatism, judicial jealousy and pro-

[53] On this, see Ll. Davies, 35 Colum. L. Rev. 518 (1935).

[54] Strikingly illustrated by the refusal of the court in *Salkeld* v. *Johnson* (1848) 2 Exch. 256 to consult the report of the Real Property Commissioners for the meaning of legislation based on the report.

[55] *Cf.*, for example, the dicta of Lord Halsbury in *Leader* v. *Duffy* (1888) 13 App. Cas. 301 and of Lord Sterndale in *Scranton's Trustees* v. *Pearse* [1922] 2 Ch. 87. But see, on the other hand, Jessel M.R. in *Holme* v. *Guy* (1877) 5 Ch.D. 905. For a detailed account of judicial destruction of a piece of social legislation, see Jennings "Judicial Process at its Worst" 1 Mod. L. Rev. 111 (1937) and, more generally, "Courts and Administrative Law" 49 Harv. L. Rev. 426 (1936); *Cf.* also Ll. Davies, *op. cit.*, and Allen, *Law in the Making* 6th ed. (1958) 488 *et seq.*

fessional specialisation was mainly responsible for the building of an impressive though deceptive façade of technical rules of statutory construction. The textbooks on this subject still bristle with such formulas as the *ejusdem generis* or the *expressio unius exclusio alterius* rule. Neither certainty nor consistency has resulted from this impressive technical apparatus.[56]

It certainly seems as if this predominant attitude of reserve if not jealousy is once more giving way to a more sympathetic and ideological approach towards statutory interpretation, an approach which marks a return to the principles of *Heydon's Case*. Thus Scott L.J. in *The Eurymedon*[57] supported an interpretation of the Maritime Conventions Act, 1911, by stating:

> The maintenance of uniformity in the interpretation of a rule of law after its international adoption is just as important as the initial removal of divergence, but never easy to achieve. From my experience of the views of Continental jurists about the proportional rule, I feel sure that the broad view of the proportional rule is their view; and if we maintain it here we shall help to preserve that international uniformity which was the object of the convention on collisions at sea. . . .[58]

In *Re the Regulation of Aeronautics in Canada*[59] Lord Sankey emphasised the need to go back to the words and the object of the Act itself rather than the decided cases.

In *Rose* v. *Ford*[60] Lord Wright observed that the construction of the Law Reform (Miscellaneous Provisions) Act, 1934, by the Court of Appeal,

> illustrates a tendency common in construing an Act which changes the law, that is, to minimise or neutralise its operation by introducing notions taken from or inspired by the old law which the words of the Act were intended to abrogate and did abrogate.

Lord Wright observed again, and more forcefully, in *Sumners* v. *Salford City Council*[61] on the construction of the Housing Act, 1936:

---

[56] Among the numerous discussions on this subject, see Radin, "Statutory Interpretations" 43 Harv. L. Rev. 863 (1930); Willis, "Statutory Interpretation in a Nutshell" 16 Can. Bar. Rev. 1 (1938); Allen, *op. cit.*, Chap. VI (V); Friedmann, *Law and Social Change*, Chap. 11.

[57] [1938] P. 61.

[58] This attitude stands in marked contrast to that adopted by Lord Esher in *Swindsen* v. *Wallace* (1884) 13 Q.B.D. 72 and Scrutton L.J. in *Gosse Millard* v. *Canadian Government Merchant Marine* [1928] 1 K.B. 717.

[59] [1932] A.C. 70.

[60] [1937] A.C. at 846.

[61] (1942) 59 T.L.R. at 80.

The section must, I think, be construed with due regard to its apparent object, and to the character of the legislation to which it belongs. The provision was to reduce the evils of bad housing accommodation and to protect working people by a compulsory provision. It is a measure aimed at social amelioration, no doubt in a small and limited way. It must be construed so as to give proper effect to that object.

In the field of constitutional law Lord Sankey's advice, in *British Coal Corporation v. The King*,[62] where the Statute of Westminster, 1931, was construed as including the right of the self-governing Dominions to abolish the prerogative appeal to the Privy Council in criminal matters, is dominated by a progressive and dynamic interpretation of constitutional statutes, in the light of political developments.

The same approach is even more evident in the opinion of Lord Jowitt L.C. in *Att.-Gen. of Ontario v. Att.-Gen. of Canada*.[63] In affirming the power of the Canadian Federal Parliament to enact that the jurisdiction of the Supreme Court shall be ultimate, the learned Lord Chancellor said:

Giving full weight to the circumstances of the union and to the determination shown by the provinces as late as the imperial conferences which led to the Statute of Westminster that their rights should be unimpaired, nevertheless, it appears to their lordships that it is not consistent with the political conception which is embodied in the British Commonwealth of Nations that one member of that Commonwealth should be precluded from setting up, if it so desires, a supreme court of appeal having a jurisdiction both ultimate and exclusive of any other member. The regulation of appeals is, to use the words of Lord Sankey in the *Coal Corporation* case,[64] a "prime element in Canadian sovereignty," which would be impaired if, at the will of its citizens, recourse could be had to a tribunal in the constitution of which it had no voice. It is, as their lordships think, irrelevant that the question is one that might have seemed unreal at the date of the British North America Act. To such an organic statute the flexible interpretation must be given that changing circumstances require, and it would be alien to the spirit with which the preamble to the Statute of Westminster is instinct, to concede anything less than the widest amplitude of power to the Dominion legislature under section 101 of the British North America Act.

In several wartime decisions concerning the interpretation of tax provisions both the House of Lords and the Court of Appeal

---

[62] [1935] A.C. 500.
[63] [1947] A.C. 503.
[64] [1935] A.C. 500.

pushed aside the verbal niceties in order to enforce the legislature's objective of spreading the burden fairly among the community, against ingenious evasion manœuvres of individuals. As Lord Greene M.R. put it:

> For years a battle of manoeuvre has been waged between the legislature and those who are minded to throw the burden of taxation off their own shoulders on to those of their fellow subjects. . . . It would not shock us in the least to find that the legislature was determined to put an end to the struggle by imposing the severest of penalties. It scarcely lies in the mouth of the taxpayer who plays with fire to complain of burnt fingers.[65]

Again, in a case where town planning policy clashed with the reliance of a private landowner on promises previously made by a public authority,[66] the Court of Appeal based its decision on the general objectives of a Town Planning Act:

> Is it likely that Parliament, . . . without express words to that effect would do anything so unusual, so explosive, as to enable a planning authority to do that which all the principles laid down and observed by the courts and the legislature in regard to statutory duties of this kind forbid, namely, to tie its hands and contract itself out of them?

But while the approach of English courts to statutes has on the whole changed from an attitude of hostile neutrality to one of sympathetic collaboration, this does not provide a general answer to concrete problems of statutory construction. A large majority of interpretation problems are predominantly technical. They turn on the definition of such terms as "bankruptcy" "railways," "production" or "shipping." The mischief rule is an invaluable aid to statutory interpretation, but the mischief or purpose of a statute is not always clearly apparent, or it looks different to different observers. If a statute establishes rent tribunals with power to adjust inequitable rents on application, one judicial interpreter may stress the objective of social justice against the sanctity of contract, another may do the opposite. In *R.* v. *Paddington and St. Marylebone Rent Tribunal*[67] the court obviously regarded the latter principle as paramount and accordingly gave a restrictive interpretation of the power to refer rent matters to the tribunal; although a block reference of rents for review by a local authority was within

---

[65] *de Walden* v. *Inland Revenue Commissioners* [1942] 1 K.B. 389, 397.
[66] *Ransom and Luck, Ltd* v. *Surbiton Borough Council* [1949] Ch. 180.
[67] [1949] 1 K.B. 666.

the terms of the statute, the court regarded this as a mala fide exercise of the powers.

As legislation covers an increasingly widening sphere of social relationships, its character becomes more and more complex. Together with a flood of statutes of all types there has been a wealth of judicial and academic studies of the problem of their interpretation, especially in American law. The results, however, become increasingly inconclusive.

In American law two factors above all make the problem more complex than in English law. One is the presence of the Constitution as the supreme statute of the land. Its interpretation is closely and immediately concerned with basic political values, such as the extent of civic rights, the limits of both federal and state regulative power in the light of the "due process" clauses, and other matters in which the technical legal factors are overshadowed by the political issues. The other fact is the sheer quantity of statutes which pour forth from the legislatures of the federation and of fifty state jurisdictions. It is not, therefore, surprising that in the pronouncements of judges and writers support can be found for almost any proposition ranging from orthodox adherence to the literal rule, to complete judicial freedom in the interpretation of statutes. The total effect, however, is unquestionably one of great elasticity in the interpretation of statutes. This may be illustrated by a few out of the innumerable relevant decisions.[68] Among the leading American decisions of recent years it is not easy to find many which openly support the literal approach as against a broader consideration of social objectives, legislative history and the balance of public interests. The Federal Kidnapping Act punishes anyone who knowingly transports or aids in transporting in interstate or foreign commerce "any person who shall have been unlawfully seized, confined, inveigled, decoyed, kidnapped, abducted or carried away by any means whatsoever and held for ransom or reward or otherwise, except, in the case of a minor, by a parent thereof." The Supreme Court refused to confirm the conviction of three persons who had conspired in inducing a mentally backward girl of fifteen to accompany them from one state to another for the purpose of a Mormon marriage in defiance of the orders of the juvenile authorities of the state of Utah.[69]

---

[68] For a full collection of materials, see Read, MacDonald and Fordham, *Cases and Materials on Legislation* (2nd ed. 1959).

[69] *Chatwin* v. *U.S.*, 326 U.S. 455 (1945).

The broadness of the statutory language does not permit us to tear the words out of their context, using the magic of lexigraphy to apply them to unattractive or immoral situations lacking the involuntariness of seizure and detention which is the very essence of the crime of kidnapping. Thus, if this essential element is missing, the act of participating in illicit relations or contributing to the delinquency of a minor or entering into a celestial marriage, followed by interstate transportation, does not constitute a crime under the Federal Kidnapping Act.

Even this interpretation was partly based on a consideration of the specific mischief contemplated by the Federal Kidnapping Act. Moreover, there is greater hesitation to give an extensive interpretation to a criminal statute. For even if the maxim *nulla poena sine lege* is far from absolute, it is still a guide of considerable importance.

On the other hand, recent decisions abound in which legislative purposes, the history of a statute, or considerations of fairness and justice have completely overshadowed grammatical or literal interpretations. In *Cabell* v. *Markham*[70] the court held that the Trading with the Enemy Act, as amended in 1928 and put into effect again in 1941, applied only to seizures made during the First World War, although its wording was not so limited. Judge Learned Hand declared:

Courts have not stood helpless in such situations; the decisions are legion in which they have refused to be bound by the letter, when it frustrates the patent purposes of the whole statute.

As Holmes J. said in a much-quoted passage from *Johnson* v. *United States*, 163 F. 30, 32; 18 L.R.A. (N.S.) 1194: "It is not an adequate discharge of duty for courts to say: We see what you are driving at, but you have not said it, and therefore we shall go on as before. . . ."

Of course it is true that the words used, even in their literal sense, are the primary, and ordinarily the most reliable, source of interpreting the meaning of any writing: be it a statute, a contract, or anything else. But it is one of the surest indexes of a mature and developed jurisprudence not to make a fortress out of the dictionary; but to remember that statutes always have some purpose or object to accomplish, whose sympathetic and imaginative discovery is the surest guide to their meaning. Since it is utterly apparent that the words of this proviso were intended to be limited to seizures made during the last war, and could not conceivably have been intended to apply to seizures made when another war revived the Act as a whole from its suspension, it does no undue violence to the language to assume that it was implicitly subject to that condition which alone made the Act as a whole practicable of administration.

---

[70] 148 F. 2d 737 (2d Cir. 1945).

The Supreme Court has in recent years repeatedly and openly overruled its own earlier interpretations of statutes. In *Helvering* v. *Hallock*[71] the court overruled its earlier decisions which for purposes of taxation had distinguished between a transfer of property in trust for a man's children or his wife with a possibility of reverter in case he survived them (non-taxable), and the gift of property to children for their life, with a remainder interest in case the children predeceased the donor (taxable). Frankfurter J., on behalf of the court, derided insistence on technical differences as against fundamental similarity of the two types of transaction.[72] In *Girouard* v. *United States*[73] the Supreme Court, against the dissent of the Chief Justice, reversed its earlier decisions which had denied admission to citizenship to an alien who refused to bear arms. It reinterpreted both the intentions of Congress and the general problem of conscientious objections to combatant service. In *Yates*[74] the court in all but name overruled its interpretation of the Smith Act, given a few years before in *Dennis*.[75]

The clash of philosophies, concealed behind different interpretations of a technical statutory term, is again illustrated in a more recent decision of the Supreme Court. In *U.S.* v. *Republic Steel Corp.*[76] the court split five to four on the question whether the term "obstruction" used in the Rivers and Harbours Act of 1890[77] prohibited the defendant and other companies from placing indus-

[71] 309 U.S. 106 (1940).

[72] This decision was the main theme of an amusing and instructive discussion between fictitious parties, in an article written by Baer and Washington 25 Cornell L.Q. 537 (1940). In that article a taxation lawyer deplores the instability and uncertainty created by the willingness of the Supreme Court to reverse itself. A law professor defends the need for judicial elasticity.

[73] 328 U.S. 61 (1946).

[74] 353 U.S. 346 (1957).

[75] 341 U.S. 494 (1951).

[76] 362 U.S. 482 (1960).

[77] The relevant section 10 of the Act provides as follows:

"That the creation of any obstruction not affirmatively authorized by Congress, to the navigable capacity of any of the waters of the United States is hereby prohibited; and it shall not be lawful to build or commence the building of any wharf, pier, dolphin, boom, weir, breakwater, bulkhead, jetty or other structures in any port, roadstead, haven, harbour, canal, navigable river, or other water of the United States, outside established harbour lines, or where no harbour lines have been established, except on plans recommended by the Chief of Engineers and authorized by the Secretary of the Army; and it shall not be lawful to excavate or fill, or in any manner to alter or modify the course, location, condition, or capacity of any port, roadstead, haven, harbour, canal, lake, harbour of refuge, or inclosure within the limits of any breakwater, or of the channel of any navigable water of the United States unless the work has been recommended by the Chief of Engineers and authorized by the Secretary of the Army prior to beginning the same."

trial deposits in a navigable river, with the result that the depth
of the channel was reduced. The majority (Douglas J.) held that
the United States was entitled to enjoin the respondent companies
from depositing industrial solids in a river emptying out of Lake
Michigan, unless they first obtained a permit from the Chief of
Engineers of the army. It interpreted "obstruction" as not limited
to some kind of structure, despite the enumeration of objectionable
activities in section 10 of the Act. In construed the Act as incorporating the broad purpose of securing navigation and commerce in
a vital waterway, and it found support in a number of previous
decisions for this broad construction. But the minority, in an
equally elaborate and learned dissent delivered by Harlan J.,
expressed the strong opinion that the statute had to be read in the
light of the exhaustive enumeration of particular types of obstruc-
tions, and in the historical context of the time and circumstances
in which it was adopted. It found as much support in previous
decisions for its own view as the majority did for the contrary
interpretation.

Behind the apparently technical dispute on the interpretation of
a neutral term such as "obstruction" lies a difference in philosophy
which is well formulated in Mr. Justice Harlan's dissenting opinion
for the minority:

> What has happended here is clear. In order to reach what it considers
> a just result the court, in the name of "charitably" construing the Act,
> has felt justified in reading into the statute things that actually are not
> there. However appealing the attempt to make this old piece of legisla-
> tion fit modern day conditions may be, such a course is not a per-
> missible one for a court of law, whose function it is to take a statute
> as it finds it. The filling of deficiencies in the statute, so that the burdens
> of maintaining the integrity of our great navigable rivers and harbours
> may be fairly allocated between those using them and the Government,
> is a matter for Congress, not for this court.

The present writer would tend to agree with the approach of the
majority. A realistic consideration of the legislative process,
especially in the United States, reveals the immense complexities
of statutory reform. In such a situation it behoves the court to
interpret a neutral but comprehensive technical term in accordance
with the broader objective of the legislation.

Another recent example of a policy interpretation departing
from the strict wording of a statute is a decision of the Appellate
Division of the New York Supreme Court, which upheld a wage

assignment by a husband to his divorced wife governed by a Massachusetts statute, which limited deductions from wage earners' salaries to ten per cent. The Court held that this was meant for commercial assignments, not for family obligations.[78]

Frankfurter J., in a much quoted paper,[79] summed up what is probably a representative view among contemporary American judges and jurists:

There are varying shades of compulsion for judges behind different words, differences that are due to the words themselves, their setting in a text, their setting in history. In short, judges are not unfettered glossators. They are under a special duty not to over-emphasise the episodic aspects of life and not to undervalue its organic processes— its continuities and relationships. For judges at least it is important to remember that continuity with the past is not only a necessity but even a duty. . . .

In some ways, as Holmes once remarked, every statute is unique. Whether a judge does violence to language in its total context is not always free from doubt. Statutes come out of the past and aim at the future. They may carry implicit residues or mere hints of purpose. Perhaps the most delicate aspect of statutory construction is not to find more residues than are implicit nor purposes beyond the bound of hints. Even for a judge most sensitive to the traditional limitation of his function, this is a matter for judgement not always easy of answer. But a line does exist between omission and what Holmes called "misprision or abbreviation that does not conceal the purpose." Judges may differ as to the point at which the line should be drawn, but the only sure safeguard against crossing the line between adjudication and legislation is an alert recognition of the necessity not to cross it and instinctive, as well as trained, reluctance to do so.

Rules and Decision

Any lawyer who expects from any set of rules an infallible guidance to the solution of the problems which life and law present in unending variety and complexity can only deduce from the foregoing analysis that many rules cancel each other out, that the result is a vacuum. Such a conclusion, however, would be due to a misapprehension of the judicial function in a free society. The great judges of all countries, and most articulately perhaps the

[78] *Downs* v. *Amer. Mutual*, 243 N.Y.S. 2d 640 (1963).
[79] Frankfurter, "Some Reflections on the Reading of Statutes" 47 Colum. L. Rev. 527, 534 (1947).

great American judges of the present century, have not discarded technical rules but they have been clearly aware of their limitations. They have looked at the issue and the statute before them and they have balanced verbal and grammatical texts against legislative history and social purposes, in varying mixture. This can hardly be otherwise, for statutes differ greatly, in scope, purpose, drafting and meaning. Sometimes legislative history is conclusive, more often it is not.[80] Some statutes have a clearly definable social purpose, others have not. It is easy to appreciate the social purpose of a specific law reform statute or of a housing Act. It is far more difficult to distil the social purpose of a broad constitutional provision, or on the other hand, of a technical statute dealing with trustee securities, depreciation allowances or currency restrictions.

It is, however, possible to get nearer to the clarification if not the solution of statutory problems of construction by differentiating between statutes and statutes, by recognising that a constitution poses problems different from a statute reforming the law on contributory negligence, or from a food and drugs Act.[81]

Yet no general theory could or should be a substitute for the discriminating wisdom applied to the solution of a particular problem. The acceptance of theoretical rules, literal or sociological, "golden" or plain, other than as technical aids can only lead to judicial self-deception or to mental slavery. It is the privilege and duty of judges and others exercising judicial functions in modern democratic societies to decide a situation unhampered either by the political dictation of a totalitarian government or the construction of technical rules. Yet these rules cannot be entirely discarded for without them we return to the chaos of "free" or "kingly" justice. Like Ulysses, the judge in interpreting statutes must steer between Scylla and Charybdis. The search for proper rules of statutory interpretation is part of the search for justice which is unending.

[80] On the exclusion of the use of legislative history in the British practice, see Allen, *op. cit.* at 487, 559.

[81] This need for a differential approach to the interpretation of statutes is discussed in *Law in a Changing Society*, 36 *et seq.*, and more fully in Friedmann, "Statute Law and its Interpretation in the Modern State" 26 Can. Bar. Rev. 1277 (1948). It has been criticised by Allen, *op. cit.* at 514, as apt to "add a series of ambiguous adjectives to the existing difficulties of interpretation." It is, however, strongly supported (independently) by Breitel, in "Courts and Law Making" in *Legal Institutions Today and Tomorrow* 16 *et seq.*, 29 *et seq.* (Columbia Law School Centennial Conference, 1959).

Precedent and Legal Development

That English lawyers have moulded the common law by the infusion of legal ideals, no one can doubt who compares, for example, the modern law of restraint of trade, or the employer's responsibility, or of charitable trusts with that of some centuries ago. The evolution of legal ideas has been so overwhelmingly unconscious and inarticulate that an analysis is no easy matter. Many are the pronouncements of eminent British judges that have emphatically disclaimed any function of the judge in the shaping of the law "as it ought to be."

Perhaps the most radical rejection of judicial law-making by a contemporary British judge is the speech made by the late Lord Jowitt, Lord Chancellor from 1945 to 1951, at the Australian Law Convention of 1951:

> It is quite possible that the law has produced a result which does not accord with the requirements of today. If so, put it right by legislation, but do not expect every lawyer, in addition to all his other problems, to act as Lord Mansfield did, and decide what the law ought to be. He is far better employed if he puts himself to the much simpler task of deciding what the law is. . . . please do not get yourself into the frame of mind of entrusting to the judges the working out of a whole new set of principles which does accord with the requirements of modern conditions. Leave that to the legislature, and leave us to confine ourselves to trying to find out what the law is.[82]

Lord Jowitt's view was no more than typical of that of the great majority of his brethren. Lord Porter,[83] Lord Simonds,[84] Asquith L.J. (as he then was)[85] and Lord Evershed[86] are among the many eminent judges who have sharply emphasised the role of the judge as one who ought to apply the law, just or unjust, as it is and not concern himself with the evolution of the common law on grounds of logic, systematic symmetry or justice. Among contemporary judges, Lord Denning stood almost alone for many years in pro-

---

[82] It is ironic that this observation was made in conjunction with the decision of the Court of Appeal in *Candler* v. *Crane, Christmas & Co.* [1951] 2 K.B. 164, and in undisguised opposition to the dissenting judgment of Denning L.J. (as he then was) who sought to obtain the result which the House of Lords itself has now affirmed in its decision on *Hedley Byrne* v. *Heller* [1964] A.C. 465, commented upon later in this chapter.

[83] *Best* v. *Fox* [1953] A.C. 716.

[84] *Scruttons* v. *Midland Silicones* [1962] A.C. 446.

[85] *Candler* v. *Crane, Christmas & Co.* [1951] 2 K.B. 164.

[86] Evershed, "The Judicial Process in Twentieth Century England," 61 Colum. L. Rev. 761 (1961).

claiming, in a series of important decisions as well as in his extra-judicial writings, the task of the common law as an instrument of evolution in accordance with the changing needs of society and the demands of justice.[87] It would appear that legal ideals have moulded the common law mainly through three channels: the development of precedent, the concept of public policy, and principles of general equity.

To the infusion of legal ideals into the judicial development of case law definite limits are set, on the one hand by the hierarchy of courts and on the other hand by the growing bulk of binding case law that leaves only a restricted number of blank spaces or loopholes. Nor does the modern system of law reporting allow to the creative-minded judge that freedom of discrimination between private law reports which Lord Mansfield used so generously. But, on the other hand, it is not as necessary that judicial freedom of development should exist over a quantitatively large area as that it should be able to work in qualitatively important marginal cases.

Seen from this angle the modern English judge has a considerable amount of freedom and, with the exception that the House of Lords until very recently considered itself bound by its own decision,[88] it is not the absence of such freedom so much as the haphazard, sporadic and, sometimes, tortuous way in which he must work that hampers him.

The principal ways of case law development in accordance with changing legal ideals appear to be the following:

(1) The judicial power of granting new remedies—as illustrated by the action of deceit granted in *Pasley* v. *Freeman*—has been

[87] Among his many judicial efforts in this direction, see *Robertson* v. *Minister of Pensions* [1949] 1 K.B. 227, one of several efforts to establish the validity of a promise regardless of consideration; *Bendall* v. *McWhirter* [1952] 2 Q.B. 466, an attempt to establish a new "equity" of the wife in the matrimonial home, a doctrine recently rejected by the House of Lords in *Nat. Prov. Bank* v. *Ainsworth* (below, p. 465 *et seq.*); and his dissenting judgements in Chandler's case seeking to establish liability for negligent financial statements, a doctrine adopted by the House of Lords in *Hedley Byrne* v. *Heller* (below, p. 172 *et seq.*), and in *Bonsor* v. *Musicians' Union* (claim for damages by an arbitrarily expelled union member against the union) also adopted by the House of Lords in *Bonsor* v. *Musicians' Union* [1956] A.C. 104. See further for a theoretical statement of his philosophy, "From Precedent to Precedent" (The Romanes Lecture 1959).

[88] In July 1966, the Lord Chancellor, in a non-judicial, *per curiam* pronouncement observed (in part) as follows: . . . Their Lordships . . . recognize that too rigid adherence to precedent may lead to injustice in a particular case and also unduly restrict the proper development of the law. They propose therefore to modify their present practice and, while treating former decisions of this House as normally binding, to depart from a previous decision when it appears right to do so.

stressed by Winfield[89] though this is not uncontested.[90] The border-line between the extension of an old remedy and the granting of an entirely new one is not always easy to draw. In *Candler* v. *Crane, Christmas & Co.*,[91]—which will be discussed further below—Denning L.J. squarely came down in favour of granting a new remedy, or boldly extending an old one when commonsense of social needs demanded it.

This argument about the novelty of the action does not appeal to me in the least. It has been put forward in all the great cases which have been milestones of progress in our law, and it has always, or nearly always, been rejected. If you read the great cases of *Ashby* v. *White*,[92] *Pasley* v. *Freeman*[93] and *Donoghue* v. *Stevenson*,[94] you will find that in each of them the judges were divided in opinion. On the one side there were the timorous souls who were fearful of allowing a new cause of action. On the other side, there were the bold spirits who were ready to allow it if justice so required. It was fortunate for the common law that the progressive view prevailed.

But the majority took a different, and more cautious view.

In the present state of our law different rules still seem to apply to the negligent mis-statement, on the one hand, and to the negligent circulation or repair of chattels, on the other, and Donoghue's case does not seem to me to have abolished these differences. I am not concerned with defending the existing state of the law or contending that it is strictly logical. It clearly is not—but I am merely recording what I think it is. If this relegates me to the company of "timorous souls," I must face that consequence with such fortitude as I can command (Asquith L.J.).

While the House of Lords, twelve years later, accepted the view of Denning L.J., it upset an even bolder judicial innovation of his, which the Court of Appeal had accepted. In *Bendall* v. *McWhirter*,[95] the court granted a deserted wife the right to continue occupation of a matrimonial home in which she had no legal ownership,[96] as against the husband's trustee in bankruptcy. This decision—specifically endorsed by the Royal Commission on Marriage and Divorce in 1956—was reversed by the House of Lords in 1965,[97] and with it its important ethical and jurispruden-

---

[89] Winfield, Law of Tort, 379 (5th ed.).

[90] Goodhart, "The Foundation of Tortious Liability," 2 *Mod.L.Rev.* 1 (1938).

[91] [1951] 2 K.B. 164 at p. 178.   [92] (1703) 2 Ld.Raym. 938.

[93] (1789) 3 Term Rep. 51.   [94] [1932] A.C. 562.

[95] [1952] 2 Q.B. 466, as modified in *Westminster Bank* v. *Lee* [1956] Ch. 7.

[96] *Bendall* v. *McWhirter* [1952] 2 Q.B. 466, as modified in *Westminster Bank* v. *Lee* [1956].

[97] *Nat. Prov. Bank* v. *Ainsworth* [1965] A.C. 1175.

tial rationale. Bendall had sought to cope with a situation that caused much hardship and bitterness in the postwar period, when there was both a high incidence of desertions, especially of "war-brides" by husbands, and an acute housing shortage.

The dominant "leitmotif" in the unanimous reversal by the House of Lords was undoubtedly that considerations of equity and mercy, or the desire to prevent social injustice, could not be allowed to disturb the well established though complex distinction between personal rights and rights in rem, of which interests in land form a prominent category. The desire to maintain the integrity of the legal system was reinforced by the commercial consideration that property encumbered with the somewhat uncertain and fluctuating "equity" of the deserted wife would be difficult to dispose of or could not easily be used in any commercial way.

Lord Wilberforce's judgment came closest to a consideration of the social and economic factors. Having referred to the "housing shortage which has persisted since the 1939 to 45 war," he pointed out that the great majority of cases in which deserted wives need protection fall under the Rent Restrictions Act, where the courts have held that a husband-tenant cannot put an end to the tenancy, so long as his wife remains on the premises. The rent restriction cases were distinguished from, and left undisturbed by, the present decision.

Lords Cohen, Upjohn and Wilberforce all expressed the view that the situation of the deserted wife—outside the realm of rent restriction legislation—was one for the legislator, rather than for the courts. Both Lord Cohen and Lord Upjohn underlined the desirability of implementing the recommendation of the Royal Commission on Divorce which was in accordance with *Bendall* v. *McWhirter*, while Lord Wilberforce made reference to the legislation prevailing in a number of states of the U.S.A. and Provinces of Canada, recognising a "homestead" right of the wife, *i.e.*, certain rights to the matrimonial home which are quite independent of legal title. In the opinion of the House of Lords such a law reform should be introduced by Parliament, not by the courts.

Entirely new actions will be rare in a highly developed legal system, where most major gaps have been closed and the legislator is increasingly active, but the degree to which the judge should supplement the process of legal change by bold extension will always depend on changing social conditions as well as on differences of tradition, outlook and temperament.[98]

(2) Of greater practical importance is the moulding of different and often scattered legal rules or remedies into a broad and comprehensive principle which combines restatement, remoulding and the making of new law. An outstanding example is the rule in *Rylands* v. *Fletcher*. It collected several cases of liability without fault which, in Dean Wigmore's language:[99]

> wandered about, unhoused and unshepherded, except for a casual attention, in the pathless fields of jurisprudence, until they were met by the master mind of Blackburn J., who guided them to the safe fold where they have since rested. In a sentence epochal in its consequences this judge co-ordinated them all in their true category.

As shown in another chapter, the fold has not proved permanently safe, but it certainly moulded the law for the next few generations, and it reshaped legal responsibilities in the light of new industrial developments.

In our own days *Donoghue* v. *Stevenson* has done much the same in another field. The leading judgments in that momentous decision are anxious to stress continuity of legal development[1] but nevertheless the decision of the House of Lords established in English law: (a) the legal separateness of a contractual relation A-B and a tort relation A-C; (b) a far-reaching responsibility of manufacturers and others, in similar positions, towards the public as a corollary of their control over products likely to affect the public.

(3) Though a long-established rule, even if not formally binding on the court, will not lightly be upset, this consideration will be overruled where demands of justice are felt to be weightier. Thus, the House of Lords, in the *Fibrosa case*,[2] did not feel deterred, by the fact that the rule in *Chandler* v. *Webster* was forty years old, from overruling it. But where the House of Lords itself has spoken before, the way for non-legislative reform may be barred. Today,

---

[98] In American law, where the sheer number of jurisdictions and decisions gives more scope for experimentation, there are some recent examples of new actions. In *Oppenheim* v. *Kridel* 236 N.Y. 156 (1923), the New York Court of Appeals granted a wife an action for criminal conversation against a woman who had had intercourse with her husband. In *Daily* v. *Parker* 152 F. 2d 174 (1945), the Second Circuit Court of Appeals granted an action for damages to children against a woman who caused a father to desert his family and to refuse to support them. The court specifically referred to a passage from Pound's *The Spirit of the Common Law* praising law-making by judicial decision in a period of legal growth.

[99] Wigmore, "Responsibility for Tortious Acts," 7 Harv.L.Rev. 441, 454 (1894).

[1] *Cf.* Lord Atkin's review of precedents.

[2] [1943] A.C. 32.

for example, the doctrines of common employment[3] or of *Sinclair* v. *Brougham*[4] are generally found irksome; but although the courts have whittled them down to a considerable extent, they have felt unable to abolish them.

(4) The irksome effect of binding precedent no longer in accordance with current legal ideals can, to some extent, be overcome by the technique of either ignoring or distinguishing precedent. The former device is not often applicable, in particular where the precedent is of high authority and cannot well be overlooked or be considered a "plainly unreasonable," but it is sometimes used. Thus, in *Craven-Ellis* v. *Canons*,[5] the Court of Appeal awarded the amount, contractually agreed upon as remuneration for the plaintiffs services to the defendant, in quasi-contract, as the contract between the parties was void. *Sinclair* v. *Brougham*, the authority of which should have been in the way of such a decision, was not referred to by counsel or court. In that way the court helped to spread the principle of unjust enrichment in English law.

The distinction of precedent, on the other hand, is a favourite judicial device of developing the law, though it has the grave disadvantages of uncertainty and haphazardness.[6] It takes three main forms:

    (a) the distinction of facts;

    (b) the relegation of objectionable judicial opinions to the position of *obiter dicta*;

    (c) the reliance on one or the other judgment where the authority of a precedent rests on a concurrence of judgments which arrive at the same result for different reasons.[7]

---

[3] Now abolished by an Act of 1948.

[4] [1914] A.C. 398.

[5] [1936] 2 K.B. 403.

[6] The extent and danger of these uncertainties is fully brought out in a critical analysis of recent cases by Paton and Sawer, 63 L.Q.Rev. 461 (1947).

[7] Stone in *Legal System and Lawyer's Reasoning*, Ch. 7 (1964) has made a more detailed examination of the ways by which law courts change and develop the law under cover of apparently logical conclusions and categories. He distinguishes the categories of meaningless reference, concealed multiple reference and indeterminate reference. An example of multiple reference is the rule in *Phillips* v. *Eyre* ((1870) L.R. 6 Q.B. 1), which lays down that for an action on a foreign tort to be entertained in England the act must be "not justifiable" by the *lex loci commissi*. There have been at least three different interpretations of this term "justifiability," but every one of them is treated as explaining the identical term. Again, the choice between competing subsumptions of a case under a legal category, such as the substitution of a negligence for nuisance, or of trust for contract, where an action would succeed under the one but not under the other category, contains an element of creative choice. Again, the concept of duty in

(a) Among the innumerable examples the somewhat strained distinction established by Lord Atkin, in his judgement in *Donoghue* v. *Stevenson*, between a considerable string of former decisions, and the case before the court may be mentioned;[8] it illustrates the numerous possibilities that exist for distinction, by speculating on omissions or ambiguities in a report, relying on one ground of a decision rather than another, referring to subsequent conflicting interpretations of a particular judgment, establishing minute differences of fact[9] or discounting reasonings which appear to be based on an erroneous interpretation of previous cases. It is no disparagement on the great speeches of the majority in the snail case to say that the precedents discussed would easily have borne an opposite interpretation—as they did indeed in Lord Buckmaster's dissenting opinion—and that the considerations which

negligence, or the test of obligations by the standards of a "reasonable man," are examples of a "circuitous" reference—it might more simply be called a tautology or a vicious circle. Lord Wright has expressed the same thought by characterising this process of judicial reasoning as a "proceeding on the basis of *idem per idem.*" As has been pointed out time and again, the "duty concept of negligence" is tautologous with the definition of negligence itself, and any decision that in one case a duty exists while it does not exist in another simply conceals the creative choice by the judge.

Despite Professor Stone's searching analysis I believe the distinctions made in the text to be sufficient for an understanding of the creative element in the judicial process. The essential question, from the point of view of legal theory, is the direction and limitation of creative development by this method. To this Stone gives no clear answer. See, for an attempt at a more precise formulation, below, p. 492 *et seq.*

In another recent analysis of the process of legal change through judicial decisions—those interpreting earlier precedents as well as those interpreting statutes —Edward Levi (*An Introduction to Legal Reasoning*, 1949) sees "reasoning by example" as the method by which important similarities and differences in the interpretation of case law, statute and the constitution of a nation are brought into focus. A certain new concept is suggested in court, but rejected until the idea achieves standing in the society. The courts eventually accept the new idea, reinterpret earlier cases, and tie the new concepts to others long accepted. Through subsequent cases the ideas are largely modified and broken down, through the process of reasoning by example. Then the whole process may be repeated. Levi illustrates this by tracing the evolution of the idea of liability for things dangerous *per se*, from *Dixon* v. *Bell* (1816) 5 M. & S. 198 to *MacPherson* v. *Buick* 217 N.Y. 382 (1916) and *Donoghue* v. *Stevenson* [1932] A.C. 562. Another example is the evolution of the judicial interpretations of the interstate commerce clause of the American Constitution, which has been used as a lever for a complete judicial revolution in regard to the constitutionality of child labour, minimum wage and other social legislation. Levi believes that the law eventually reflects new social theories, but that the contrast between logic and what the judges do in fact is false. Legal reasoning by virtue of its own logic is able to absorb new social theories when resolving the ambiguities of a particular case.

[8] [1932] A.C. 9, 587-597.

[9] *Cf.*, in particular, Lord Atkin's discussion of *Winterbottom* v. *Wright* (1842) 10 M. & W. 109, *Longmeid* v. *Holliday, Earl* v. *Lubbock* (1905) 1 K.B. 253 and *Blacker* v. *Lake & Elliott Ltd.* (1912) 106 L.T. 553.

weighted the scale were in the realm of certain broad principles of social justice.

(b) An interesting illustration of the attempt to discard an objectionable authority by relegating a judicial opinion to an *obiter dictum* is the judgment of Scott L.J. in *Haseldine* v. *Daw*.[10] The learned Lord Justice strongly felt that a tenant's visitor should be the landlord's invitee, not licensee; but the authority of the House of Lords, in *Fairman's* case,[11] was in the way. Scott L.J. proceeded, however, to dismantle the authority of that decision on the position of tenant's visitors, by reinterpreting three of the judgments which, he thought, were primarily based on the absence of negligence and not on the visitor's position as a licensee. Goddard L.J., through agreeing with the principle of Scott L.J., refused to follow him in this daring assault which was finally rejected by the House of Lords in *Jacobs* v. *L.C.C.*[12]

(c) The possibilities of relying on one or the other of different reasonings arriving at the same result are demonstrated by *Bell* v. *Lever*.[13] In that case, which exhibited wide divergences of views among the judges of the three instances, only two of the majority of three in the House of Lords decided that there was no fundamental mistake to avoid the contract, while the opinion of the third member of the majority was based on a different ground. Another well-known example of divergent reasonings is *Jones* v. *Waring & Gillow*.[14]

Finally, all these methods together were used by the House of Lords in the *Fibrosa case*,[15] to "conjure the *French Marine* case out of the way."[16] Differentiation of facts, reliance on *obiter dicta*, emphasis on divergences as to the *ratio decidendi*, all were ingeniously combined to get rid of a precedent which would have obstructed the desire of the House to abolish the rule in *Chandler* v. *Webster*.

In *Read* v. *Lyons*,[17] the House of Lords refused to apply the rule in *Rylands* v. *Fletcher* to an injury caused to a factory inspector by the explosion of a shell, the responsibility for which could not be ascertained. The House refused to regard *Rylands* v. *Fletcher* as a peg on which to hang a general principle of strict liability for

---

[10] [1941] 2 K.B. 350-352.
[11] [1923] A.C. 74.
[12] [1950] A.C. 361.
[13] [1932] A.C. 161.
[14] [1926] A.C. 670.
[15] [1943] A.C. 32.
[16] Glanville Williams, "The End of *Chandler* v. *Webster*," 6 Mod.L.Rev. 48 (1942).
[17] [1947] A.C. 156.

hazardous operations. More remarkable perhaps was the observation of Lord Macmillan, a member of the majority in *Donoghue* v. *Stevenson*, that

> your Lordships' task in this House is to decide particular cases between litigants and your Lordships are not called upon to rationalise the law of England. . . . Arguments based on legal consistency are apt to mislead, for the common law is a practical code adapted to deal with the manifold diversities of human life and, as a great American judge has reminded us, "the life of the law has not been logic; it has been experience."[18]

Similarly in *Searle* v. *Wallbank*,[19] the House of Lords refused to acknowledge any liability of the keepers of animals straying on the highway and causing damage, beyond negligence. Basing itself almost entirely on historical reasons, the House thus refused to bring this branch of the law into line with the general development of the legal responsibilities of owners towards users of the highway.[20] In *London Graving Dock Co.* v. *Horton*,[21] the House of Lords, against the strong dissent of Lords MacDermott and Reid, dismissed the action of a welder injured while working on a trawler under unsafe conditions against which he had often protested. The majority repudiated any general duty of care on the part of the invitor and thus threw into renewed confusion a subject for the rationalisation of which courts and jurists have long laboured.[22] It was technically as possible to construe from the cases a general duty of care towards an invitee as was the more restricted interpretation. Indeed, the Court of Appeal and two of the five judges of the House of Lords thought so. In taking the narrower view, the majority did not stand for a "non-ideological" against an "idealogical" view. The "inarticulate premises" of the majority was an almost fanatical resistance to a modest piece of rationalisation of the law which was, fortunately, achieved some years later by legislation (Occupiers' Liability Act, 1957). Emphasis on historical categories and distinctions, however outworn and unjust, even where the analytical position is open, is no more unprejudiced and "unideological" than the opposite attitude.

Very much in the same vein, the majority of the Court of Appeal had rejected, in *Candler* v. *Crane, Christmas & Co.*,[23] the attempt

---

[18] [1947] A.C. at p. 175.
[19] [1947] A.C. 341.
[20] See *Fleming* v. *Atkinson*, [1959] S.C.R. 573.
[21] [1951] A.C. 737.
[22] *Cf. Salmond on Torts*, Chap. 12, 13th ed. (Heuston, 1961).
[23] [1951] 2 K.B. 164.

by Denning L.J. to extend the principle of *Donoghue* v. *Stevenson* to the liability of a chartered accountant whose negligent report on the position of a company had caused damage to prospective investors.

It is therefore all the more remarkable—and an illustration of the vacillations of judicial philosophy—that the House of Lords, twelve years later, chose a case in which it could have been content to dismiss an action against a bank for negligent information on the financial solidity of a client, on the ground that the defendant had excluded liability for his information. The House, which did dismiss the action, nevertheless took this opportunity to overrule the doctrine of *Candler* in a series of elaborate, *per curiam* statements—which some critics have described as *obiter dicta*—affirming the principle of legal responsibility for negligently made statements causing financial damage, at least where there is a "special relationship."[24] The decision in *Candler* v. *Crane Christmas & Co.*[25] and the corresponding American decision of *Ultramares* v. *Touche*[26] had been widely criticised by English and American legal scholars. In an increasingly interdependent society, the consumer needs protection, and this protection the House now seeks to extend, from the manufacturer of standard products to the professional purveyor of information and advice, and correspondingly from physical damage to financial damage. The overall instrument is the action of negligence which has come to occupy an increasingly dominant position in the field of tort. But in responding to this need, the House of Lords not only exploded the cherished doctrine that judges do not make law or develop it in accordance with changing ideals; it also showed robust disregard for well established legal concepts—respect for which was decisive in the rejection of a wife's right in the occupation of the matrimonial home, in *Nat. Prov. Bank* v. *Ainsworth*.

Lord Devlin spoke of "categories of special relationships which may give rise to a duty to take care in word as well as in deed . . . not limited to contractual relationships or to the relationships of fiduciary duty but [including] also relationships which . . . are equivalent to contract. . . ." Insofar as this relationship may include not only bankers, stockbrokers, and solicitors, but also perhaps barristers and doctors functioning under the National Health

---

[24] *Hedley-Byrne* v. *Heller* [1964] A.C. 465
[25] [1951] 2 K.B. 164.
[26] 255 N.Y. 170 (1931).

Service, is this just an extension of the action for negligence in tort? Or does it mean something like an equivalent to the continental doctrine of *culpa in contrahendo* which has long extended liability in contract to the antecedents of the contract at hand?[27] Or is this a new category of liability, neither contract nor tort, but "equivalent to contract"? Does the decision purport to eliminate one of the most important remaining distinctions between common law and equity, *i.e.*, with regard to liability for innocent misrepresentation? Is *Hedley-Byrne* in effect a generalisation of the equitable doctrine of fiduciary or quasi-fiduciary duties towards persons not in contractual relations with the defendant, as it was developed by Haldane L.C. in *Nocton* v. *Ashburton*?[28]

The law-reforming zeal of *Hedley-Byrne* is not an isolated instance. In an earlier chapter we have discussed the sweeping use by the House of Lords of the old common law offence of "conspiracy to corrupt public morals" as an instrument of control over public morality—and that despite the applicability of statutory offences to the case at hand.[29]

It has generally been held to be a basic principle of English law, and indeed of the rule of law as understood in democracies, that criminal offences should be precisely defined and not be capable of indefinite expansion in a manner reminiscent of the notorious Nazi statute of 1935 which empowered the courts to punish according "to the fundamental conceptions of a penal law and sound popular feeling."[30] Moreover, in the field of criminal law, which attracts generally far more public and political attention than civil law questions, Parliament is not only in theory but in effect able to act. Although there is no codification of the criminal law in England, the whole sphere of criminal offences has long been

---

[27] See, on the scope of *culpa in contrahendo* in German law, Palandt, *Kommentar Bürgerliches Gesetzbuch*, Sec. 276, note 6. (24th ed. 1965.)

[28] [1914] A.C. 1932.

[29] In *Shaw* v. *D.P.P.* [1962] A.C. 220, see above, p. 45 *et seq.*

[30] It is noteworthy that both the Canadian Criminal Code of 1954 and the U.S. Model Penal Code specifically abolish the common law offence. Section 1.05 of the Model Penal Code says: (1) No conduct constitutes an offense unless it is a crime or violation of this Code or another statute of this State. The commentary is as follows: "Indeed, in England it seems fairly clear that notwithstanding *Rex* v. *Manley* [1933] 1 K.B. 529, the common law power would not now be exercised to declare conduct a misdemeanor, unless its criminality has been established by clear precedent. See Williams, *Criminal Law: The General Part*, 457 (1953). We should be even firmer in this view in the United States. A statute declaring conduct *contra bonos mores* would hardly satisfy constitutional requirements of specificity. See *e.g., Musser* v. *Utah*, 333 U.S. 95 (1948); *State* v. *Musser*, 223 P. 2d 193 (Utah, 1950). The concept has no greater merit when it rests upon the common law."

covered by statutes which have gradually replaced the older common law offences. The most ringing affirmation of the opposite view came from Lord Simonds, a former Lord Chancellor:

> . . . I now assert, that there is in that Court[31] a residual power where no statute has yet intervened to supersede the common law, to superintend those offences which are prejudicial to the public welfare. Such occasions will be rare, for Parliament has not been slow to legislate when attention has been sufficiently aroused. But gaps remain and will always remain, since no one can foresee every way in which the wickedness of many may disrupt the order of society. . . . Must we wait till Parliament finds time to deal with such conduct? I say, my Lords, that if the common law is powerless in such an event then we should no longer do her reverence. But I say that her hand is still powerful and that it is for her Majesty's Judges to play the part which Lord Mansfield pointed out to them.

This emphatic assertion of the function of the Courts as lawmakers came from the same judge who time and again had castigated, sometimes in scathing terms, the much more modest function of the courts of developing and clarifying the principles of civil liability, *e.g.*, in the following words:

> . . . [I]t would, I think, be to deny the importance, I would say the paramount importance, of certainty in the law to give less than coercive effect to the unequivocal statement of the law made after argument by three members of this House in Fairman's case. Nor, perhaps I may add, are your Lordships entitled to disregard such a statement because you would have the other otherwise. To determine what the law is, not what it ought to be, is our present task.[32]

A third, sweeping assertion of judicial ideology, virtually dismantling a vitally important statute and reviving a forgotten common law action, is discussed later, in the context of "public policy" as an instrument of judicial law-making.[33]

Recent Modifications of the Doctrine of Precedent

Some eminent contemporary judges have contended that the House of Lords is free to depart from precedent in matters in which public policy is concerned.[34] Such statements are based on a dictum by

---

[31] *I.e.,* the Court of King's Bench.

[32] *Jacobs* v. *L.C.C.* [1950] A.C. at p. 373.

[33] *Rookes* v. *Barnard* [1964] A.C. 1129. See below, p. 485.

[34] *Cf.* Sir Raymond Evershed M.R. in *The Court of Appeal* at 17; also Cohen L.J. "Jurisdiction, Practice and Procedure in the Court of Appeal," 11 Camb.L.J. 3, 11 (1951).

Lord Watson, in the *Nordenfelt* case,[35] that public policy decisions "cannot possess the same binding authority as decisions which deal with and formulate principles which are purely legal." The foregoing discussion has shown that the House of Lords has not in theory accorded itself such liberty, although it has been able to depart from precedent by various methods, where major public policy issues were at stake.[35a]

There has, however, been in recent years a partial but open departure from the strict rule of *stare decisis* on a lower level. Both the Court of Appeal and the Court of Criminal Appeal have substantially modified their earlier attitudes in regard to *stare decisis*. The Court of Appeal in 1944,[36] having reaffirmed that it was bound by its own decisions, defined certain exceptions as follows:

(1) The court is entitled and bound to decide which of the two conflicting decisions of its own it will follow.

(2) The court is bound to refuse to follow a decision of its own which, though not expressly overruled, cannot, in its opinion, stand with a decision of the House of Lords.

(3) The court is not bound to follow a decision of its own if it is satisfied that the decision was given *per incuriam*.

In addition, Lord Greene M.R. mentioned two further exceptions which may be regarded as adding to the list of qualifications:

Two classes of decisions *per incuriam* fall outside the scope of our inquiry, namely those where the court has acted in ignorance of a previous decision of its own or of a court of co-ordinate jurisdiction—in such a case a subsequent court must decide which of the two decisions it ought to follow; and those where it has acted in ignorance of a decision of the House of Lords which covers the point—in such a case a subsequent court is bound by the decision of the House of Lords.

This reformulation has considerably loosened up the rigidity of *stare decisis* on the level of the Court of Appeal, and of lower courts. Thus, in *R.* v. *Northumberland Compensation Appeal Tribunal*,[37] a divisional court of three judges presided over by Lord Goddard C.J. felt authorised by *Young's* case to disregard a decision of the Court of Appeal[38] which it considered to be inconsistent with two earlier decisions of the House of Lords. In *Gower*

---

[35] [1894] A.C. 535 at p. 553.

[35a] It is too early to say what effect the announcement of July 1966 (above, p. 464) will have in practice.

[36] *Young* v. *Bristol Aeroplane Co., Ltd.* [1944] K.B. 718. [37] [1951] 1 K.B. 711.

[38] *Racecourse Betting Control Bd.* v. *Secretary of State for Air* [1944] Ch. 114.

v. *Gower*,[39] the Court of Appeal criticised the standard of proof in adultery cases set up by an earlier decision of its own. Denning L.J. suggested no fewer than five reasons for disregarding the earlier decision.[40] In *Fitzsimmons* v. *Ford Motor Co.*,[41] the Court of Appeal overruled three prior decisions of its own, as inconsistent with a decision of the House of Lords which antedated two of the three overruled Court of Appeal decisions.

Various writers have discussed the uncertain implications of *Young's* case.[42] There is, as yet, insufficient evidence to support the claim[43] that the recent qualifications placed on the principle of *stare decisis* by the Court of Appeal "have completely changed the character of that rule in modern English law." But it is undeniable that the impact of the decision on the rule of *stare decisis* has already been considerable.

Precedent in the Criminal Law

In 1950 the full court of Criminal Appeal overruled an earlier decision of it own of 1939 on a question of bigamy, and laid down its own principles in regard to *stare decisis*.[44] The reasoning, as formulated by Lord Goddard C.J. for the court, is remarkable in its implications:

> This court . . . has to deal with questions involving the liberty of the subject, and if it finds, on reconsideration, that, in the opinion of a full court assembled for that purpose, the law has been either misapplied or misunderstood in a decision which it has previously given, and that, on the strength of that decision, an accused person has been sentenced and imprisoned, it is the bounden duty of the court to reconsider the earlier decision with a view to seeing whether that person has been properly convicted. The exceptions which apply in civil cases ought not to be the only ones applied in such a case as the present. . . .

The direct effect of this statement—the most open attack on *stare decisis* yet made by a modern English court—is, of course, limited to criminal cases, but the reasoning has wider implications.

[39] [1950] 1 All E.R. 804.
[40] *Ginesi* v. *Ginesi* [1948] 1 All E.R. 173. Among them were absence of full argument, failure to cite a decision of the House of Lords, and the refusal of the High Court of Australia to follow the previous Court of Appeal decision.
[41] [1946] 1 All E.R. 429.
[42] *Cf.*, among others, Goodhart, 9 Camb.L.J. 349 (1945), and Schmitthoff, "The Growing Ambit of the Common Law," 30 Can.Bar.Rev. 48, 58 (1952).
[43] Made by Schmitthoff, *op. cit.*
[44] *R.* v. *Taylor* [1950] 2 K.B. 368.

Some of the most important decisions involving the liberties of the subject, such as *Liversidge* v. *Anderson*,[45] have been civil decisions. Can it be seriously contended that expulsion from a trade union[46] or professional disqualification are of less fundamental importance to the individual concerned than conviction for a minor offence? Or is a distinction between major and minor criminal offences implicit in the reasoning of the Court of Criminal Appeal? Whatever the direct consequences of the decision, its motivation is a powerful attack upon the whole rationale of the doctrine of *stare decisis*. It openly admits that vital considerations of justice may be more important than past authorities.

Quite apart from *R.* v. *Taylor* precedent must play a role in criminal law somewhat different from the (civil) common law. The latter is essentially concerned with an adjustment of economic relations between two or more parties. Criminal law, on the other hand, lays down on behalf of the community at large a set of sanctions against the individual offender, ranging from monetary fines to long terms of deprivation of liberty and, in extreme cases, capital punishment. According to the scales of values generally predominant in civilised legal systems, this is a far more serious matter than the adjustment of financial losses, and the application of sanctions must therefore be surrounded with stricter safeguards against the extension of sanctions to the detriment of the individual.

One consequence is the general rejection in civilised legal systems of retroactive punishment.[47] Another is the objectionability of blank powers of judicial extension of criminal liability as granted by the notorious Nazi statute of 1935 which declared punishable acts "deserving of punishment according to the fundamental conceptions of a penal law and sound popular feeling." Hardly less objectionable is the carte blanche given to judicial extension of criminal offences in the much criticised dictum of Lord Hewart[48] that "all such acts or all attempts as tend to the prejudice of the community are indictable."[49] One of the most alarming aspects of *Shaw* v. *D.P.P.*—discussed earlier[50] is the revival of the similarly[51]

[45] [1942] A.C. 206.

[46] *Cf. Bonsor* v. *Musicians' Union* [1956] A.C. 104.

[47] For the justification of exceptions in cases where a particularly repulsive legal system has been overthrown, see the discussion between Hart and Fuller, in 71 Harv.L.Rep. *op. cit.* 615 *et seq.*, 648 *et seq.* (1958). And see above, p. 352 *et seq.*

[48] *R.* v. *Manley* [1933] 1 K.B. 529.

[49] The Canadian Criminal Code of 1954 has specifically abolished common law offences. See above, p. 473, n. 30.

[50] See above, p. 45.   [51] [1962] A.C. 220.

sweeping common law offence of "a conspiracy to corrupt public morals." On the other hand, an increasing proportion of modern criminal legislation is in the area of public welfare, transport, public health, and industrial safety. Here the still widely held view that because this is "criminal law," the maxim *nullum crimen sine lege* demands a "strict" interpretation of statutes, leads to a frustration of legislative policies.[52] It is based on an identification of two types of criminal law which share little but the name.[53]

The common law jurisdictions of the British Commonwealth have on the whole adopted the English doctrine of precedent but they have made considerable modifications. The Canadian Supreme Court has, after the abolition of appeals to the Privy Council, reaffirmed the strict principle of *stare decisis*—which it had laid down for itself in 1909.[54] Although the court has reserved for itself a liberty to reinterpret its own decisions as well as those of the Privy Council, it has not so far made use of this reservation. On the other hand, a number of provincial courts of appeal in Canada have shown considerably more independence towards strict *stare decisis* and have departed from decisions of the English Court of Appeal as well as from their own decisions in a number of cases.[55]

The Australian High Court has for many years past adopted a modified doctrine of *stare decisis*. It has recently reaffirmed[56] its liberty to reverse earlier decisions where they are manifestly wrong but at the same time the majority of the court asserted that it would not reverse "recent and well-considered decisions upon . . . a highly disputable question."

It is thus easier to point out the extent to which the courts can and do mould the law than to indicate a clear and consistent trend. There are certain broad limits which minimum standards of ortho-doxy set to judicial reform of the law. Within these wide limits the possibilities of judicial law-making are great, but the way in which they are used depends on a multitude of fluctuating factors, such as the pressure of social or political events, on personal background and constitutional framework, on the relations between legislator and judiciary.

---

[52] See Pound, "Common Law and Legislation," 21 Harv.L.Rev. 407, 383 (1908); Hall, "Strict or Liberal Construction of Penal Statutes," 48 Harv.L.Rev. 752 *et seq.* (1935).

[53] For a more detailed discussion, see *Law in a Changing Society*, p. 48 *et seq.*

[54] *Cf. Woods Manufacturing Co.* v. *The King* [1951] 2 D.L.R. 465.

[55] For references, see notes by Kennedy in 29, 30, 31 Can.Bar.Rev.

[56] In *Att. Gen. for N.S.W.* v. *Perpetual Trustee* (1952) 85 C.L.R. 189.

Public Policy

The "unruly horse" of public policy has influenced English law much more than is apparent to a superficial examination. It may indeed be described as the fundamental agent of legal development if we distinguish, with Professor Winfield,[57] the unconscious or half-conscious use of it which probably pervaded the whole legal system when law had to be made in some way or other . . . and

the conscious application of public policy to the solution of legal problems, whether it bore the name by which it is now known or was partly concealed under some other designation which, however, really expressed the same thing.

In the former sense public policy is but another name for the fundamental ethical, political and social principles which guide legal evolution, whether in legislation or legal administration, at any given time.

To give the concept even the semblance of a technical term and instrument in the hand of the lawyer it must be restricted to the narrower sense as defined by Lord Wright:[58]

. . . [T]here are considerations of public interest which require the courts to depart from their primary function of enforcing contracts and exceptionally to refuse to enforce them. Public policy in this sense is disabling.[59]

It is in this more specific, disabling sense that the concept of public policy appears and exposes some, but by no means all, of the ideological foundations of English law.[60] The other, "unconscious or half-conscious" part either merges into legislative policy, or it translates itself into a creative development of case law, or the application of general principles of equity.

The restricted scope of public policy in this professed sense is due to two paramount reasons:

(1) The traditional reluctance of judges, and of English judges in particular, to disclose or discuss openly the ideological assumptions underlying the administration of the law.

[57] Winfield, "Public Policy in the English Common Law," 42 Harv.L.Rev. 76 (1929).
[58] *Fender* v. *Mildmay* [1938] A.C. at 38; *cf.* also Lord Wright in *Legal Essays and Addresses*, 66-96.
[59] *Cf.* also Lord Sumner in *Rodriguez* v. *Speyer* [1919] A.C. 125.
[60] On the historical aspects, see Knight, 38 L.Q.Rev. 207 (1922), and Winfield, *op. cit.*

(2) The acceptance of separation of powers and the consequent reluctance to compete with the legislator in the application of legal policy.

That the danger of competing or conflicting competences is very real, is shown by the different position of the American Supreme Court which, as guardian of the Constitution, has decisively influenced American social policy for almost a century, but mainly in a negative, restraining way, and without the responsibility which the parliamentary law-maker has towards the electorate.

There is, indeed, in the predominant attitude of the English judiciary, as expressed by the majority of the judges in *Egerton* v. *Brownlow*,[61] or in many subsequent pronouncements,[62] an attitude of diffidence and self-restraint which has certainly contributed to spare Great Britain the grave social problems which the attitude of the Supreme Court has caused in the United States. The value of this achievement has, however, been impaired by the frequent lack of consciousness of the issues of legal ideology when they did influence judgements. This is particularly evident in the judgments concerning freedom of trade and competition.[63]

In this restricted sense public policy could not acquire a technical meaning before the eighteenth century; its modern role can hardly be traced back further than to *Egerton* v. *Brownlow*,[64] when the House of Lords decided to recognise a distinct principle of public policy as

a principle of law which holds that no subject can lawfully do that which has a tendency to be injurious to the public, or against the public good. . . .[64]

Since then there have been relatively few cases where public policy has been directly and openly used as an overriding principle which may invalidate a contract, will, trust or any legal instrument.

In terms of moral, social, or political principles the cases may be classed as follows:

(1) The principle of religious tolerance was recognised, in the light of an altered public policy, in *Bowman* v. *Secular Society*[65]

[61] (1853) 4 H.L.C. 1-256.

[62] *Cf.* Lord Halsbury in *Janson* v. *Driefontein* [1902] A.C. 484, and Lords Atkin, Wright and Roche in *Fender* v. *Mildmay* [1938] A.C. 1 *et seq. Cf.* Winfield, *loc. cit.* 91: "But for the House of Lords, public policy would have pretty nearly perished in *Egerton* v. *Brownlow*."

[63] *Cf. Law in a Changing Society*, 265 *et seq.*

[64] Lord Truro at 196.

[65] [1917] A.C. 406.

in regard to secular movements, and in *Bourne* v. *Keane*[66] in regard to Catholic masses.

(2) The integrity of political life was protected by *Egerton* v. *Brownlow*[67] and *Parkinson* v. *College Ambulance*,[68] which declared the purchase of honours illegal.

(3) The degree to which intercourse with enemies is prohibited in war, was treated by the majority as a matter not of strict law but of public policy in *Rodriguez* v. *Speyer*,[69] and consequently an enemy subject was allowed to be co-plaintiff in an action by a partnership dissolved owing to the enemy character of one of the partners.

(4) The question whether public policy, in regard to the reprehensibility of suicide, had changed sufficiently to allow the representatives of a person who had committed suicide to recover the sum for which his life was insured was answered in the affirmative by Swift J. in *Beresford* v. *Royal Insurance*, but in the negative by the Court of Appeal and the House of Lords in the same case.[70] Lord Wright succinctly brought out the limits set to judicial law-making by recognition of changing moral ideals when he said:

Opinions may differ whether the suicide of a man while sane should be deemed to be a crime, but it is so regarded by our law. . . . While the law remains unchanged the court must, we think, apply the general principle that it will not allow a criminal or his representative to reap by the judgment of the court the fruits of his crime.

(5) The extent to which the sanctity of the marriage tie prevented freedom of action where the spouses had obtained a decree nisi was decided in *Fender* v. *Mildmay*,[71] when a bare majority decided that a spouse, after the decree nisi, could make a valid promise of marriage. The divergence between the majority and the minority may be characterised as one of realistic and formalistic approach; for the majority emphasised the real termination of marital community against the continuation of a formal tie; but it meant also a victory of a liberal over a Catholic attitude towards the dissolution of marriage; for the minority—consisting of Lords Russell and Roche—obviously insisted on the formal aspects,

[66] [1919] A.C. 815.
[67] (1853) 4 H.L.C. 1.
[68] [1925] 2 K.B. 1.
[69] [1919] A.C. 116.
[70] [1937] 2 K.B. 197 and [1938] A.C. 586.
[71] [1938] A.C. 1.

because it disapproved any extension of the dissolubility of the marriage union, unless the law decreed it clearly beyond doubt. There was, however, no disagreement on the limits of judicial law-making by public policy. There is little between the views of Lord Atkin that

the doctrine should only be invoked in clear cases in which the harm to the public is substantially incontestable,

of Lord Wright that if

certain rules of public policy have to be moulded to suit new conditions of a changing world . . . that is true of the principles of common law generally,

and that it was

difficult to conceive that in these days any new head of public policy could be discovered,

and of Lord Roche that

now to evolve new heads of public policy or to subtract from existing and recognised heads of public policy, if permissible to the courts at all, which is debatable, would . . . certainly only be permissible upon some occasion as to which the legislature was for some reason unable to speak and where there was substantial agreement within the judiciary and where circumstances had fundamentally changed.

By far the most important aspect of conscious public policy had been its restrictive function in regard to covenants in restraint of trade and to the applicability of a foreign law in an English court.

(6) In the name of public policy the modern rules regarding the validity of covenants in restraint of trade have been developed from the *Nordenfelt* case onwards. They have led to the elaboration of three guiding principles:

   (i) Restrictive covenants arising from the sale of business good-will for good consideration are valid.[72] To that extent freedom of trade and freedom of contract work hand in hand.
  (ii) Where the restrictive covenant is "an embargo upon the energies and activities and labour of a citizen[73] it is void. Here freedom of labour prevails over freedom of contract.
 (iii) Agreements regulating production, prices, or imposing other restrictions in economic activity are valid, unless they unduly hamper freedom of movement of any of the parties. This

---

[72] *Maxim Nordenfelt* v. *Nordenfelt* [1894] A.C. 535.
[73] Lord Shaw in *Morris* v. *Saxelby* [1916] 1 A.C. 688.

rule follows from a series of cases of which *Evans* v. *Heath-cote*[74] on one hand and the *Salt case*[75] and *English Hop-growers* v. *Dering*[76] on the other hand are the most important.

Here freedom of contract prevails over freedom of trade, unless it amounts to an excessively severe restriction of freedom of movement.

All these rules are supposed to be subject to the overriding principle that the restraint must be reasonable towards the public.[77]

But there does not appear to be a single decision in which the public interest has been allowed to overrule the result reached by a consideration of the interests of the parties.[78] Identity of interest is presumed once the interests of the parties have been considered. In the *Salt* case a striking difference between the purchasing and selling price of a monopolistic salt combine evoked no different result or even an investigation of the interest of the public. Again, in a group of very recent cases,[79] the validity of agreements between petrol suppliers and dealers, by which the dealer undertakes to buy all his petroleum products from the particular supplier, were considered solely from the point of view of the parties.

In none of the cases was any attention given to the covenant issues involved and whether, in fact, the agreement operated to the detriment of the public. . . .[80]

As a result of this inadequate conception of public policy, the consumer or public has remained a vague shape and a passive spectator. The problem of economic control over private and group interests has largely passed from the hands of the courts to those of the legislator. Sometimes the remedy adopted is nationalisation of industries (as, partly, in Great Britain and France), sometimes it is anti-trust legislation, as adopted at the end of the last century in the United States and Canada, and, since the last world war in a

---

[74] [1918] 1 K.B. 418.

[75] [1914] A.C. 461.

[76] [1928] 2 K.B. 174.

[77] *Nordenfelt* case, *supra.*

[78] Except perhaps for the perverse decision in *Wyatt* v. *Kreglinger* [1933] 1 K.B. 793, where the court invalidated a pensions agreement against the wishes of the pensioner, in the name of public interest.

[79] *Petrofina* (Great Britain) v. *Martin* [1965] Ch. 1073, affirmed [1966] 2 W.L.R. 318; *Regent Oil Co.* v. *Aldon Motors* [1965] 1 W.L.R. 956; *Esso Petroleum* v. *Harper's Garage* [1965] 3 W.L.R. 469

[80] Whiteman, *Agreements in Restraint of Trade,* 29 Mod.L.Rev. 77, 82 (1966).

number of European countries (including Great Britain and West Germany).

In the British Restrictive Trade Practices Act of 1956 the public interest is the key criterion for the invalidation of restrictive agreements, and the Restrictive Trade Practices Court has made vigorous use of this test to invalidate a number of restrictive arrangements of major economic importance.[81]

(7) Recently, public policy has assumed new significance as a possible instrument of control over the disciplinary and quasi-judicial activities of groups which are in theory private, but exercise in fact complete control in important spheres of public and economic life. As late as 1951 the Privy Council reaffirmed[82] the position long taken by the English courts that any expulsion of a member of an association by a so-called domestic tribunal could not be challenged before the courts, even where the expulsion proceedings were tainted by bias, intimidation and absence of natural justice, if the procedure provided by the constitution of the association had been complied with. Shortly afterwards the Court of Appeal took an entirely different attitude in a case where a showman had been expelled from his guild, a registered trade union,[83] over a quarrel with another member regarding the occupation of a particular site. The Court of Appeal held the expulsion void because the committee had misconstrued the rules of the union in holding the plaintiff guilty of unfair competition. The court vigorously affirmed the judicial right of control over the conduct of proceedings by associations of this type.

> They cannot stipulate for a power to condemn a man unheard. . . . They can, indeed, make the tribunal the final arbiter on questions of fact, but they cannot make it the final arbiter on questions of law. They cannot prevent its decisions being examined by the courts. If parties should seek, by agreement, to take the law out of the hands of the courts and into the hands of a private tribunal, without any recourse at all to the courts in case of error of law, then the agreement is to that extent contrary to public policy and void. . . . (*Per* Denning L.J.)

A few years later, the House of Lords, contrary to its usual conservatism in the matter of precedent, reversed earlier cases and

---

[81] 4 & 5 Eliz. 2 c. 68; Stevens and Yamey, *The Restrictive Practices Court, A Study of the Judicial Process and Economic Policy* (1965).
[82] *White* v. *Kuzych* [1951] A.C. 585.
[83] *Lee* v. *Showmen's Guild* [1952] 2 Q.B. 329.

granted damages to a musician who had been expelled from the union in violation of procedure.[84] All the Lords robustly, though by different routes, found it possible to overcome the technical difficulty of the defendant's lack of legal personality, which has vexed courts in many countries. The American courts have, for many years, devised remedies in similar situations, by giving a liberal construction to such concepts as "property interest," "due process" or "natural justice."[85]

In *Rookes* v. *Barnard*[86] the House of Lords went much further in changing the law by judicial fiat. This decision has been described by one learned commentator[87] as "a frontal attack on the right to strike," and by another[88] as "a new extension of civil liability," which "reduced to insignificance the protections of the Trade Disputes Act 1906, which should have been a defence against it." None of the many commentators, whether favourable or opposed, has denied the profound impact on the legal position of trade unions in labour disputes of this decision. It held two fellow employees and a union organiser liable in damages to the plaintiff who had been dismissed from employment with the BOAC—without breach of contract—under threat by the defendants—acting on behalf of the union—of a strike in breach of a "no strike" agreement. The political significance of the decision is evidenced by the fact that in 1965 Parliament passed a new Trade Disputes Act which undoes most of the theory of the *Rookes* decision. From a jurisprudential point of view, the remarkable fact is that what was clearly a major policy decision, a deliberate and concerted effort on the part of the unanimous House of Lords to neutralise the essential provisions of the Trade Disputes Act of 1906 and to put a major legal obstacle—in the form of damage liability—in the path of typical union activities in a labour dispute, did not make any allusion to the policy issues. It is perhaps because of its outstanding social and political significance that the Law Lords chose to couch their judgments in analytical legal phraseology. The legal tools chosen to reach a decision were: (a) the revival of an all but forgotten tort of "intimidation," as distinct from "conspiracy": (this was necessary to bypass section 1 of the Trade Disputes Act

---

[84] *Bonsor* v. *Musicians Union* [1956] A.C. 104.
[85] For a more detailed discussion, see *Law in a Changing Society*, 322-339.
[86] [1964] A.C. 1129.
[87] Kahn-Freund, 14 Federation News, 30-42 (1964).
[88] Wedderburn, *Intimidation and the Right to Strike*, 27 Mod.L.Rev. 257 (1964).

under which an act done in pursuance of an agreement or combination shall "not be actionable unless the act if done without any such agreement or combination would be actionable"), (b) the neutralisation of section 3 of the 1906 Trade Disputes Act, which provides that an act "shall not be actionable on the ground only that it induces some other person to break a contract of employment or that it is an interference with the trade, business or employment of some other person. . . ." This, in view of the Court of Appeal, clearly disposed of the action against Silverthorne, the union organiser, who was not an employee of BOAC and, therefore, had no contract which he could threaten to break. But this was circumvented in the House of Lords by a variety of devices. Thus, Lord Reid said that each of the defendants while acting alone thought he could and intended to induce the BOAC employees to break their contracts by strike, whereas Lord Evershed maintained that while there was not a threat to procure a strike action, there was a threat that a strike by all the union members "would in fact occur." Lord Devlin hitched a conspiracy on to the tort of intimidation by arguing that the union member who was not an employee could be made liable as a party to a "conspiracy to intimidate," despite the absence of any contract on his own part.

It is difficult to believe that the decision of the House was not a clear and deliberate attempt to effect an important change in social policy through legal reinterpretation. It does, in fact, represent one of the periodical swings of the pendulum. It is a counterpart to the decision in the *Crofter-Harris Tweed* case,[89] which marked the highlight of a judicial acceptance of economic group pressures in labour disputes as a legitimate method in modern industrial society. It can be explained as a reaction to the greatly strengthened status of trade unions and to the arbitrariness often displayed by union organisers towards their own dissident members as towards other parties. In this respect, it may be seen as a continuation of the much less controversial decision in *Bonsor* v. *Musicians' Union*.[90] In *Stratford* v. *Lindley*,[91] the House of Lords went one step further, by holding that an embargo declared by the Waterman's Union on the handling of barges controlled by a company one of whose affiliates had concluded an agreement with a rival union, was not in "furtherance or contemplation of a trade dispute." This inter-

[89] [1942] A.C. 435.
[90] [1956] A.C. 104.
[91] [1965] A.C. 269.

pretation, again a radical reversal of a continuous string of contrary decisions, including that of the Court of Appeal in the same case, has been described by Professor Wedderburn as "astounding".[92] The changing attitude of the courts[93] reflects the grave problems created by the growing power of groups within the state: trade associations, trade unions and other corporate organisations, which are in theory private, but exercise in fact controlling powers that should be reserved to public authority.[94]

(8) All these various aspects of public policy, as well as some ethical principles of the common law, have contributed to develop the meaning that public policy has in private international law, as a criterion of the applicability of foreign law before a local court. Personal freedom, sanctity of private property, the monogamous character of marriage, freedom of trade, discrimination against illegitimate children, all these principles of the common law have been held to exclude a foreign law in the name of public policy,[95] which here becomes a reflection of all the general ideological foundations of English law, and thus has a far wider meaning and function than in internal law. Public policy plays yet another part in private international law. Frequently a court will reject the application of a foreign law and apply its own, not on grounds of public policy, but by the classification of a certain matter as one of procedure rather than of substance,[96] or by the interpretation of a foreign legal provision in the light of its own concepts rather than those of the foreign law,[97] or, simply, by the artificial extension of internal law as the law applicable to transactions which have no proper connection with it.[98]

The degree to which the court of jurisdiction should refuse recognition to foreign legal policies has acquired particular importance in regard to the numerous nationalisation measures of states that have undergone social and national revolutions. Public policy, as under-

---

[92] Wedderburn, "What is the point of Ultra Vires?" 29 Mod.L.Rev. 208 (1966).
[93] On the whole problem see Whitmore, "Judical Control of Union Discipline," 30 Can.Bar.Rev. 1, 617 (1952); Lloyd, "Judicial Review of Expulsion by a Domestic Tribunal," 15 Mod.L.Rev. 413 (1952).
[94] *Cf. Law in a Changing Society,* Chaps. 9, 10.
[95] For details, see Cheshire, *Private International Law,* Chap. VI (6th ed. 1961).
[96] *Cf. Leroux* v. *Brown* (1852) 12 C.B. 801.
[97] *Ogden* v. *Ogden* [1908] P. 46.
[98] This, juristically and politically, undesirable technique—which turns a great deal of *ordre public interne* into *ordre public international* has been trenchantly criticised, for English law, by Kahn-Freund, "Reflections on Public Policy in the English Conflict of Laws," 39 Grotius Soc., 38-83 (1954), and, for American law, by Paulsen and Sovern, "Public Policy in the Conflict of Laws" 56 Colum.L.Rev. 989-1016 (1956).

stood in the common law jurisdictions, generally concedes to a foreign state the right to nationalise foreign property, provided there is no discrimination against foreigners, as compared with nationals. But the political passions of the post-war period have often led courts to expand the application of nation public policy, by invalidating foreign "acts of state" injurious to the economic interests of the court's nationals. A remarkable exception to this trend, the U.S. Supreme Court's decision in *Sabbatino*[99] which refused to upset the firmly established "act of state" doctrine so as to invalidate the passing of title in a Cuban sugar shipment to the Republic of Cuba, as the result of a decree nationalising all U.S. owned sugar in Cuba, was reversed by Congressional action.[1] Whether confiscation without compensation, if applied equally to nationals and foreigners, should be held legal is controversial, though most Western writers answer in the negative.[2] British and American courts have, however, recognised the validity of confiscations with regard to property situated within the confiscating state, though not for property situated outside its territory.[3]

It is in this field that public policy has exceptionally been allowed to assume the revolutionary function of being enabling instead of disabling.[4] In *Lorentzen* v. *Lyddon*[5] Atkinson J. declared valid a decree of the Free Norwegian Government which requisitioned all Norwegian ships and put them under the control of a curator. "Public policy certainly demands that effect should be given to this decree." Instead of excluding an otherwise applicable foreign law, public policy here allowed foreign law to override the rule of English law that foreign confiscatory legislation has no extra-territorial effect. This decision was dissented from, and the more narrow function of public policy restated, by Devlin J. in *Bank voor Handel* v. *Slatford*,[6] where the recognition of any foreign legislation purporting to have effect over property within the

---

[99] *Banco Nacional de Cuba* v. *Sabbatino*, 376 U.S. 398 (1964).

[1] See Falk, *The Role of Domestic Courts in the International Legal Order* (1964); Friedmann, "National Courts and the International Legal Order," 34 G.W.L.Rev. 443 (1966).

[2] For recent discussions, see Wortley, *Expropriation in International Law* (1959); Fatouros, in Friedmann and Pugh (eds.), *Legal Aspects of Foreign Investment* 726 *et seq.* (1959).

[3] See *Luther* v. *Sagor* [1921] 1 K.B. 456; *Salimoff* v. *Standard Oil Co. of New York*, 262 N.Y. 220 (1933).

[4] Lord Sumner, in *Rodriguez* v. *Speyer* (1919) at p. 125, said that he had never heard of a legal disability being relieved in the name of public policy.

[5] (1942) 71 Ll.L.R. 197.

[6] [1951] 2 T.L.R. 755.

territory of the United Kingdom was rejected. Like Asquith L.J. in another recent case,[7] the learned judge restated the limitations of the use of public policy by the courts, and firmly rejected it as a "positive effort to give to an act validity which it would otherwise lack." Such a use, he thought, would force the courts into political considerations from which they should keep away.

The last mentioned decisions throw light on what one might call the "reserve" function of public policy. On the whole, public policy in the common law fulfils the limited function of supervising the validity of certain transactions, in the light of principles of interpretation adapted, from time to time, to "the changing needs of the community."[8] But more often than not the name of public policy is not used; it may have crystallised into a more definite rule of law[9] or the court may prefer to express new ethical or social principles in terms of general equity, or by the development of case law, in one of the ways analysed above. It is this indefinitive and haphazard nature of public policy as much as the distrust of a "mix-up" with politics and law-making that seems to produce an almost universal attitude of judicial caution. It is significant that as progressive a judge as Lord Wright shares, in this respect, the feelings of a judge as different in outlook as Lord Halsbury, not because he is unaware of the need to adapt the law to changing social needs but because he does not wish to operate with so vague a concept in the judicial development of law.

But it appears that in times of crisis, when political considerations are more apt than usual to intrude into the administration of

---

[7] *Monkland* v. *Barclay* [1951] 2 K.B. 252.

[8] Winfield, 42 Harv.L.Rev. 76 (1929).

In Continental systems of law the concept of *ordre public* is wider than that of public policy. *Ordre public* is applied in many areas of law, notably in contract law, as a standard by which the acts or agreements which offend the public order or good morals (*bonnes moeurs* in French law, *gute Sitten* in German law) may be set aside. Specific Code provisions, widely applied, may be found in Articles 6, 1131, and 1133 of the French Code Civil and Article 138 of the German Civil Code. *Ordre public* has another dimension unknown to the common law concept in that it is also the term by which the legislator designates whether a statutory enactment is imperative in the sense that no agreement may exclude it. *Ordre public* in that sense is positive law and not merely a negative standard by which permissible acts are measured.

In some Continental systems there exists a distinction between internal *ordre public* and external *ordre public international* in the area of private international law. The latter may generally be said to be the equivalent to public policy as it is known in the Anglo-American systems, though as restrictively applied. See Lloyd, *Public Policy, a Comparative Study in English and French Law* (1953); Gutteridge, *Comparative Law* 98-104 (2nd ed. 1949); Simitis, *Gute Sitten und ordre public* (1960); Malaurie, *l'Ordre public et le Contrat* (1953).

[9] *Cf.* the analysis of Lord Haldane in *Rodriguez* v. *Speyer, supra.*

the law, public policy can be used and extended to achieve a desired result.

GENERAL EQUITY

There remains the method of infusing legal ideals by means of general equity. The term "Natural Law" or "Natural Justice," more popular in former days, has fallen into disrepute and survives only in isolated portions of the English law.[10] Modern judges prefer such terms as "just and reasonable"[11] or "common sense and decency."[12] What is more important than terminology is the very definite swing of the pendulum from judicial contempt for "that vague jurisprudence sometimes attractively styled Justice between Man and Man"[13] or "well-meaning sloppiness of thought"[14] to an attitude much more reminiscent of that of Lord Mansfield.

Law is not an end in itself. It is a part in the system of government of the nation in which it functions, and it has to justify itself by its ability to subserve the ends of government, that is, to help to promote the ordered existence of the nation and the good life of the people.[15]

The common law of England has throughout its long history developed as an organic growth, at first slowly under the hampering restrictions of legal forms of process, more quickly in the time of Lord Mansfield, and in the last hundred years at an ever-increasing rate of progress, as new cases, arising under new conditions of society, of applied science, and of public opinion have presented themselves for solution by the courts.[16]

This consciousness of the creative function of judicial equity, fairness, common sense or justice has translated itself into numerous practical applications.

Such decisions as *Wilsons & Co.* v. *English*,[17] *Radcliffe* v. *Ribble*,[18] *Caswell* v. *Powell Duffryn*,[19] strengthen the social respon-

---

[10] Notably as a ground of reversing inferior judgments, by means of the Prerogative Orders, and of refusing the recognition of foreign judgments. In either case the high-sounding term conceals a very restricted principle of "due process." *Cf.* above, p. 134 *et seq.*

[11] Lord Wright, in *Brooks' Wharf and Bull Wharf* v. *Goodman Bros.* [1937] 1 K.B. 534.

[12] MacKinnon L.J. in *Heap* v. *Ind, Coope and Allsopp* [1940] 2 K.B. 476.

[13] Hamilton L.J. (Lord Sumner) in *Baylis* v. *Bishop of London* [1913] 1 Ch. 127.

[14] Scrutton L.J., in *Holt* v. *Markham* [1923] 1 K.B. 513.

[15] Lord Wright, "Precedents," 4 Toronto L.J. 247, 271-272 (1942).

[16] Scott L.J., *Haseldine* v. *Daw* [1941] 2 K.B. 343 at 350.

[17] [1938] A.C. 57. Birkett L.J. has described it as "perhaps the most quoted case in the courts today" (15 Mod.L.Rev. 279).

[18] [1939] A.C. 215.

[19] [1940] A.C. 152.

sibilities of the employer. The decisions on libel from *Hulton* v. *Jones*[20] to *Newstead* v. *London Express*[21] foster a tendency to discourage the publication of the more gossipy types of news by the Popular Press, by imposing a strict standard of liability. Decisions like *Haynes* v. *Harwood*[22] and *Hollywood Silver Fox Farm* v. *Emmett*[23] give expression to an attitude of greater helpfulness towards one's neighbour as against the rugged individualism of the former common law. A broad development of the torts of negligence, nuisance, and the rule in *Rylands* v. *Fletcher* shows a definite movement from the principle of individual fault towards strict liability as a corollary of social control.

In *Nokes* v. *Doncaster Amalgamated Collieries*[24] the House of Lords interpreted section 154 of the Companies Act, 1929, in the light of "rights of man," refusing to consider a miner in a company's employ as "property."

In *Hivac, Ltd.* v. *Park Royal Scientific Instruments*[25] the Court of Appeal decided a matter of great social significance when it held that an industrial competitor could be restrained from employing highly skilled specialist workmen in their spare time, but that in general a modern workman was free to use his spare time as he liked, being bound to the employer by free contract and not by feudal ties of loyalty.[26] General equity has played an important part in the development of the principle of unjust enrichment.[27]

The decisions of the House of Lords from *Allen* v. *Flood*[28] to the *Harris Tweed* case[29] and *Rookes* v. *Barnard*[30] show the influence of changing legislative and public opinion on judicial evaluation as regards the right of collective bargaining. The unsuitable category of malice is gradually replaced as a test of legitimacy by the broad evaluation of collective action as a means of furthering

[20] [1910] A.C. 20.
[21] [1940] 1 K.B. 377.
[22] [1935] 1 K.B. 146.
[23] [1936] 2 K.B. 468.
[24] [1940] A.C. 1114.
[25] [1946] 1 All E.R. 350.
[26] As the discussion between Kahn-Freund, "Spare Time Activities of Employees," 9 Mod.L.Rev. 145 (1946) and Lewis on the same subject, *op. cit.* at 280 shows, the decision bears not only on personal freedom but also on the extent of monopoly protection.
[27] *Cf.* Friedmann, "The Principle of Unjust Enrichment in English Law," 16 Can. Bar Rev. (1938), at 365.
[28] [1892] A.C. 25.
[29] [1942] A.C. 435.
[30] [1964] A.C. 1129.

the social and economic interests of a group.[31] Conversely, the growing power of quasi-private groups equipped with *de facto* monopoly powers in the labour market has produced the judicial revolution of *Bonsor's* case.[32]

LEGAL DEVELOPMENT IN THE CONTEMPORARY COMMON LAW

We have so far considered the various methods by which legal ideals are infused into the administration of law. But how does the practical lawyer obtain an assured knowledge and sense of the direction in which he is to develop the law? How does he get the knowledge which the Swiss Civil Code or Justice Cardozo ask him to acquire—the knowledge of an imaginary legislator? The growing articulateness of modern social life, and especially the speedier translation of new social policies into definite legislation, reduces the problem to somewhat smaller proportions. Legislation either takes charge of, or at least directs, a growing number of problems formerly left to the practical lawyer. Current discussions or summings up of public opinion through radio, press, Gallup polls, scientific congresses, and other media, translate trends of current thought into generally understandable language.[33] The judge can seldom be a pioneer in social progress. He must not walk either too fast or too slow. He cannot consider a single bold social innovation undertaken by a radical government as being an assured part of the social thinking of his generation and country. But he is no more justified in regarding principles accepted a century ago as being fixed for all time in the interpretation of the law. In trying to trans-

---

[31] For a detailed examination, see *Law and Social Change in Contemporary Britain*, Chap. 6; see also Stone, I *Social Dimensions of Law and Justice*, Chap. 7, Part II (1966).

[32] See above, p. 484 *et seq.*

[33] The problem is illustrated by the decision of the U.S. Court of Appeals, Second Circuit, in *Repouille* v. *U.S.*, 165 F. 2d 152 (1947). The Court had to decide whether an alien—the conscientious father of four other children—who had put to death a mentally and physically totally deformed son of thirteen—had "good moral character" as required by the Nationality Act for the granting of citizenship. With some hesitation, the majority (*per* Learned Hand J.) concluded that the standard must be the generally accepted moral conventions "current at the time" and that, despite the jury's verdict of manslaughter in the second degree and its recommendation for clemency, in the petitioner's trial, "only a minority of virtuous persons would deem the practice morally justifiable, while it remains in private hands, even when the provocation is as overwhelming as it was in this instance." But Frank J., in dissent, stated that "the correct statutory test . . . is the attitude of our ethical leaders," and that the district judge "should give the petitioner and the government the opportunity to bring to the judge's attention reliable information on the subject. . . ."

late social evolution into legal judgments, the judge must look for aid not only to jurisprudential thought but also to the multitude of other sciences which influence the law. This he cannot do unaided. He must, for example, weigh the state of modern medical research before deciding whether to accept blood group tests as evidence in maintenance actions, or other actions in which the proof of parenthood is relevant. He will also have to take into account medical and psychological research in decisions on mental instability or insanity, in both civil and criminal suits. The research of modern economists and statisticians on business cycles and national income curves has long been accepted as evidence of decisive importance in such matters as the fixing of a basic wage by the Australian Commonwealth Court of Arbitration. But in all these matters, the judge must tread carefully; he cannot follow his own economic or political or scientific views in advance of what he regards as reasonably well established in the light of current public opinion, the legislative policy not of a particular political party but of the major political parties of the country, and of contemporary scientific research.

The following summary may epitomise some of the major evolutions of legal policies as they are reflected in the contemporary law.

1. Legitimate activities of the state and other political authorities are no longer confined to the traditional functions of defence, foreign affairs, judicial administration and police. At least four major activities may now be added as within the scope of government functions in all contemporary democracies.[34] In the first place, the state is now expected to, and does, to a greater or lesser degree, dispense social services of many kinds. It is legitimately concerned with public works, unemployment insurance, pensions, repatriation grants, and a multitude of other services ranging over all fields of economic and social life. In the second place, the state is expected to safeguard the public interest by a reasonable balance between employers and labour, now organised in powerful groups which more and more substitute collective bargaining for the individual employment contract. The share of the state in the regulation of labour conditions is stronger in the United States and Canada than in Britain. In the former, labour relations boards exercise important supervisory and regulatory functions, in the latter the Govern-

---

[34] For a more detailed analysis, see *Law in a Changing Society*, 485 *et seq.*

ment interferes only in extreme cases, or for the protection of conditions in weakly organised industries.[35] In the third place, the state is expected to ensure the equal distribution of scarce resources, especially in times of emergency.[36] A corollary to this is the responsibility of the state for the conservation of national resources. Evidence for this can be found in the modern British legislation on Town and Country Planning, the New Towns Act, the Minister's power under the Agriculture Act to displace inefficient farmers, and in numerous American statutes concerning the conservation of water reserves or soil.[37]

Lastly, it is now recognised as legitimate that government may itself conduct economic enterprises of all kinds, as departmental activities, or through the semi-autonomous form of public corporations. This says nothing of the extent to which public enterprise is regarded as desirable or efficient. The statutory constitution, in Great Britain, the Commonwealth and many other countries,[38] of a great variety of public enterprises, is evidence of this agreed legislative policy. In the United States public enterprises of an industrial and commercial character are far more numerous than generally realised—quite apart from the famous Tennessee Valley Authority. In the State of New York, for example, over one hundred public authorities, with budgets totalling many billions of dollars, operate transport, power, harbours, highways, bridges, and other public utilities.[39] The Supreme Court, in overruling earlier decisions to the contrary in *New York* v. *United States*,[40] has clearly recognised that government enterprise is no less a legitimate function of government than other functions traditionally regarded as governmental. Again, a decision such as *Att.-Gen.* v. *Fulham Corpn.*,[41] where the statutory power of a borough council to establish a wash-house for the people was held to exclude the establishment of a municipal laundry, cannot now be regarded as good law.

---

[35] *Cf. Id.* at 105 *et seq.*

[36] Some extreme liberal economists still maintain that such matters as a soil conservation policy or the allocation of foreign exchange for essential foodstuffs in preference to luxury goods is unwarranted interference with economic freedom. It is safe to say that no major party in any modern democracy would now advocate such a view.

[37] *Cf.* for a collection of cases and materials, Simpson and Stone, *Cases and Readings on Law and Society*, 1047-1087 (1948).

[38] For comparative surveys, see Friedmann (ed.) *The Public Corporation* (1954), and Hanson (ed.) *Public Enterprise* (1955).

[39] Staff Report on Public Authorities in New York State, 1956.

[40] 326 U.S. 572 (1946).

[41] [1921] 1 Ch. 440.

2. The corollary to the vast expansion of governmental functions is the elimination of the legal privileges of the state developed in an earlier period, as a relic of history or against the background of a far more limited scope of governmental functions. In the British legal sphere, the immunity and privileges of government and public authorities in the matter of contract, tort and property transactions have been steadily reduced, although in most of the states, and to a lesser extent in the federal sphere, in the United States ancient immunities survive.[42] Thus the antiquated presumption of governmental immunity from liabilities imposed by general statutes still remains.[43] But for the independently constituted public corporations, such as the British Transport Commission, the principle of full legal responsibility, regardless of the public character of its function, has now been clearly established.[44] Recent British legislation shows a definite trend towards a more systematic structure of administrative justice.[45] In the United States the courts have tended to confine the operation of the doctrine of sovereign immunity to cases expressly required by statute. Suits have been permitted against administrative agencies. Thus, with the emergence of the state as a social service instrument, the trend of the law has been to avoid, reduce or discard the doctrine of sovereign immunity.[46] But in some recent cases[47] the irresponsibility of government has on occasions been reaffirmed. On the other hand, the United States has been able to sue one of its own agencies.[48] This indirectly recognises the transformation in the character of the modern state whose unity can be disregarded for functional purposes.[49] The whole problem of the liability of government and public authorities, as a corollary to their greatly increased functions, demands a clear evaluation of legal values, public opinion and legislative policy.[50] Judicial vacillations in this matter are largely due to the absence of clear and consistent thinking on these issues. The paradox has arisen that judges, profoundly distrustful of the increased activities

---

[42] For a detailed discussion, *Law in a Changing Society*, at 388 *et seq.*
[43] *Cf. Bombay Province* v. *Bombay Municipal Corporation* [1947] A.C. 58.
[44] *Tamlin* v. *Hannaford* [1950] K.B. 18.
[45] Tribunals and Inquiries Act, 1958.
[46] Note in 25 N.Y.U. L.Rev. 875 (1950).
[47] *E.g., Federation Crop Insurance Corpn.* v. *Merrill*, 332 U.S. 380 (1947).
[48] *U.S.* v. *I.C.C.*, 337 U.S. 426 (1949).
[49] *Cf.* also the Australian case of *Cain* v. *Doyle* (1946) 72 C.L.R. 409, and the discussion of the whole problem in *Law and Social Change in Contemporary Britain*, Chap. 12.
[50] *Cf.*, for an excellent comparative survey, Street, *Governmental Liability— A Comparative Study* (1953).

of the government, have reaffirmed its immunity even where precedent left them a choice.[51]

Discretionary power is not only vested in administrative authorities. Judicial discretion in such matters as the granting or forfeiture of bail, or the wide divergencies in the measure of punishment for a criminal offence—where the law only fixes maximum and minimum standards—calls for the formulation of equitable standards. The American Model Penal Code seeks to set standards of punishment. A recent decision of the New York Supreme Court (Appellate Division)[52] moves in the same direction by setting standards for the remission or forfeiture of professional bail suretyships. (A survey of 57 cases.)

3. The right of group organisation in the pursuit of political, economic, cultural or social principles is now fully recognised. This follows clearly not only from the trend of industrial legislation, with its recognition of collective bargaining agencies, but also from the trend of judicial decisions which has increasingly recognised the legitimacy of economic pressure.[53] There remains the problem of reconciling the protection of group action with the protection of individual rights. In the United States the exclusionary practices of the trade unions, particularly in regard to Negroes, have often brought the problem to the attention of both legislatures and courts.[54] In Great Britain the closed shop principles as such—seldom openly applied in industry—does not appear to have occupied the courts, but several recent British and Canadian decisions have been concerned with a similar problem in dealing with the limits of autonomy and immunity of trade unions or trade associations.[55] In other fields, British courts have repeatedly affirmed the freedom of the individual to dispose of his labour, although these decisions seldom touch the deeper issues of economic compulsion. Examples are the long line of decisions invalidating covenants in restraint of trade as between employers and employees, and the decision of the House of Lords in *Nokes* v. *Doncaster Amalgamated Collieries*,[56] where the House refused to include in an order made

---

[51] *Cf. Law and Social Change*, Chaps. 5, 12. *Law in a Changing Society*, Chap. 12.

[52] *People* v. *Peerless Insur. Co.*, 21 A.D. 2nd 609 (1964).

[53] See for a detailed discussion, Stone, *op. cit.* Chap. 7, and Friedmann, *Law and Social Change*, Chap. 6.

[54] *Cf.* Summers, "The Right to Join a Union," 47 Colum.L.Rev. 33 (1947).

[55] *Cf.* above, p. 484 *et seq.*

[56] [1940] A.C. 1014.

under the Companies Act for the amalgamation of companies the transfer of the contracts of personal service. A corresponding evolution is the increasing preoccupation with the quasi-public functions and powers of the modern corporation, and the ways in which the law can take account of this transformation.[57]

4. There has been a steady expansion of the principle of legal responsibility of those in control of an enterprise for those employed by it. It had led Roscoe Pound to formulate the principle of responsibility for the "human wear and tear" involved in the operation of an enterprise as an emerging jural postulate of our time.[58] In terms of creative judicial idealism the problem is, however, very complex. As has been shown earlier on,[59] the tendency of British courts to enlarge the legal duties of employers towards employees has recently suffered several checks, probably as a reaction to the growing legislative extension of statutory duties and social insurance. Moreover, judges may in some cases deliberately refuse to mitigate a social evil through judicial reform in order to compel the legislator to act. The problem is thrown into relief by the report of the Monckton Committee on Alternative Remedies[60] and the subsequent Law Reform (Personal Injuries) Act, 1948. Here again the problem of adjusting judicial and legislative development and legal policy leaves much room for judicial experimenting. The steady expansion of both social and private insurance in fields traditionally dealt with by the law of tort deeply affects the evolution of the law of tort, and legal philosophy. The greater the certainty of pecuniary compensation for accidents, through either private or social insurance, the smaller is the need for an extension of personal liability. Fault liability may re-establish itself as a test by which to judge either the recovery of insurance from the author of the accident or as a measure of criminal liability. Where the victim's interests are sufficiently looked after by insurance, fault liability may again come to the fore, and a tort action can reacquire an admonitory character which it had largely lost in the move towards the extension of the liability of those in charge of enterprises as against the insured member of the public. This appears already to be recognised in Scandinavian law and it

---

[57] See Berle, *The Twentieth Century Capitalist Revolution* (1954), and for a full discussion *Law in a Changing Society*, Chap. 9.
[58] Pound, *Social Control Through Law* (1942).
[59] See above, p. 470 *et seq.*
[60] Cmd. 6860.

is becoming an acute problem in the common law jurisdictions.[61]

5. The principle of sanctity of marriage is a field in which differences of opinion and belief have a somewhat wider range than in most other fields. The dissolubility of marriages is now a recognised principle of legal policy in Great Britain. It has been underlined by the Act of 1937, which creates certain additional grounds of divorce. But whether this should be considered as a minimum or a maximum is largely dependent on conflicting religious and ethical convictions, as is apparent from the case of *Fender* v. *Mildmay*.[62] In 1947, the House of Lords unanimously adopted the view[63] that insistence by the wife on the use of a contraceptive as a condition of sexual intercourse with her husband does not amount to wilful refusal to consummate the marriage. This view would be sharply rejected in those parts of the Commonwealth which, like Quebec, accept the religious and legal policies of Catholicism. The same clash of public policies occurs in regard to the dissolution of marriage in general. In the United States the different jurisdictions differ sharply, as regards grounds and ease of divorce, so that divorce decrees granted in some states will not be recognised in others. Catholic judges have been directed by the Church to avoid divorce decrees.[64] But the trend towards greater freedom appears to assert itself increasingly. This is shown by the remarkable liberalisation of the divorce law of the State of New York—where Catholic and Puritan influences are strong—in 1966. The new law—passed almost unanimously—introduces, *inter alia*, several new grounds of divorce—such as cruelty and desertion—and permits divorce after 2 years of separation.[65]

6. There has been an almost universal trend, inside and outside the common law world, towards the legal autonomy of women and legal equality of husband and wife. This finds expression in a multitude of developments: the political enfranchisement of women, and their increasing participation in public life; the gradual removal of restrictions on professional and business activities of women; the abolition of the husband's privileges in the education of the children, and the administration of communal marital property.[66]

---

[61] See Ussing, 1 Am.J.Comp.Law 358, 367 (1952). For a fuller discussion of the whole problem, see *Law in a Changing Society*, Chap. 5.

[62] [1938] A.C. 1.

[63] *Baxter* v. *Baxter* [1948] A.C. 274.

[64] *Cf.* above, p. 393.

[65] N.Y. Sess. Law 1966, ch. 254.

[66] See *U.S.* v. *Dege*, 364 U.S. 51 (1960) for a recent judicial application of this evolution.

This emancipation proceeds with unequal speed and intensity in different legal systems, depending on the strength of social traditions. But the trend is both unmistakable and universal, and it is now spreading from the Western sphere of law and the Soviet system to tradition-bound legal orders such as Hindu and Moslem law.[67]

7. The spreading abolition of legal impediments to freedom in sexual relations shows not only an advance in individual freedom but also a new social policy, with regard to birth control. A British Act of 1967—paralleled by the American Model Penal Code—has accepted the Wolfenden Committee's recommendation to abolish the criminality of private homosexual relations between consenting male adults. More importantly, Catholic and other opposition to birth control by contraceptives, based on natural law[68] is weakening—as shown by the discussion of the subject in the Ecumenical Council of 1965—in the light of the overwhelming danger to mankind's peace and well-being resulting from the catastrophic growth of the world population, estimated to reach 6 billion in the year 2000. In 1966, the U.S. government, for the first time, permitted the use of aid funds for the dissemination of knowledge of, and other forms of assistance to, birth control.

8. The principle of racial equality has become a major facet of legal policy, nationally and internationally. In the United States, the Civil Rights Acts of 1964 and 1965, which considerably strengthen federal enforcement powers, have at last begun to translate constitutional principles of equality of races into reality, in terms of voting rights, housing, transportation, education and economic opportunities. In Britain, in implementation of the Race Relations Act, 1965,[69] a Racial Discrimination Board has been set up to investigate, mediate and report on cases of racial discrimination. The international counterpart is the growing number and status, in international law, of many Asian and African states composed of peoples long subject to political, economic and social domination. The doctrine of white supremacy is now held and enforced only by South Africa, Rhodesia and, to a lesser extent, Portugal.

---

[67] For a fuller discussion, see *Law in a Changing Society*, Chap. 7, and for matrimonial property, the comparative surveys in Friedmann (ed.) *Matrimonial Property Law* (1955), Rouast (ed.) *Le Régime Matrimonial Légal dans les Législations Contemporaires* (1957). And see on recent French reforms, *infra* at p. 524 *et seq.*

[68] See above, p. 391.

[69] Race Relations Act, 1965, c. 73.

Limits of Judicial Law-Making and Prospective Overruling

The continuing validity of the basic separation of functions, in a modern legal system, between the legislative, administrative and judicial branches of government is no less important than the admission that the judicial branch does indeed play a vital part in the evolution of the law. By and large, legislatures must be responsible for the formulation of general principles of conduct which are of general, publicly promulgated and prospective applicability to a given community for an indeterminate number of situations; administrators must apply such general principles to more specific situations and often to specific groups within the community—even though administrative orders and regulations often have certain legislative aspects; and the courts must apply the prescriptions of legislators, or the generalised principles deduced from a series of precedents to individual disputes. Such a separation of functions is not confined to the democratic doctrine of separation of powers; it is part of the essential structure of any developed legal system.[70] In a democratic society, the processes of administration, legislation and adjudication are more clearly distinct than in a totalitarian society, where legislative and administrative procedures tend to merge and the judges are expected to be the executants of the political ideology of the government. But even in such societies, the three functions remain generally separate.

It is therefore a matter of both theoretical and practical importance to inquire into the limits of judicial lawmaking. Only when we have admitted that judges do make law, does it become necessary and possible to distinguish the characteristic aspects of judicial lawmaking from those of legislative lawmaking.

Legislative Inaction and Judicial Reform

The dilemma of the courts in deciding whether to reform the law, in the face of legislative inaction, has recently been succinctly formulated by a distinguished American judge:[71]

[70] For recent formulations of the essential structural requisites of a developed legal system, see H. L. A. Hart, *The Concept of Law*, 95 (1961), and Lon Fuller's requirements of generality, promulgation and prospective operation, which constitute the first three of his eight requirements of the "inner morality" of law, in Fuller, *The Morality of Law*, 41 (1964).

[71] Charles D. Breitel, *The Lawmakers—The Twenty-Second Annual Benjamin N. Cardozo Lecture*, 32, 38-39 (1965).

It is now a commonplace that courts, not only of common law juris-dictions but also those which have codified statutory law as their base, participate in the lawmaking process. The commonplace, for which the Holmeses and the Cardozos had to blaze a trail in the judicial realm, assumes the rightness of courts in making interstitial law, filling gaps in the statutory and decisional rules, and at a snail-like pace giving some forward movement to the developing law. Any law creation more drastic than this is often said and thought to be an invalid encroach-ment on the legislative branch. . . .

It is the failure or inability of the legislature to act where there is, nevertheless, a desperate need for creative lawmaking. . . . Whether it be deadlock or a refusal to face up to legislative or political hazards, there is often a deferral or refusal to act. Sometimes the reason is strongly based on the desire to permit the difficulties of the problem to be resolved judicially by an evolutionary case-by-case approach in the decisional process, at least for a time, until the question is ripe for legislative handling. Sometimes the reason is only the view that the common law solution is best because of nice technical distinctions and because the need for harmony with other rules of law is deemed para-mount. . . . These are some of the reasons which make for a strong lawmaking function in the courts, far beyond the interstitial and the gap-filling. These reasons, however, do not mean that it is all to the good and that courts are best equipped to perform the function. On the contrary, there are grave limiting factors: the limitations of judicial procedure, political dependence upon other branches of government, and the isolated nature of the judicial office.

It is a difficult question for a court to decide whether, in the face of continued legislative inaction, it should intervene to change a manifestly unjust and outdated legal principle, sometimes at the risk of stinging the legislator into retaliatory action, or remain passive. Certainly the answer cannot be given in terms of subject matter. The long overdue reform of the principles of liability of occupiers to visitors could easily have been carried out by the courts, by interpretations far less sweeping than those the House of Lords used in cases like *Bonsor* v. *Musicians' Union*[72] or *Rookes* v. *Barnard*.[73] In the end the law was changed by legislative reform.[74] Such questions as the joint liability of tortfeasors, the immunity of public authorities (in the United States) from liability for negligence, or the rights of a married woman to occupancy of a matrimonial home could be and have been the subject of judicial as well as legislative reforms. In 1959 the Supreme Court of Illinois decided

[72] [1956] A.C. 104.
[73] [1964] A.C. 1129.
[74] Occupiers' Liabilities Act. 1957.

that it was time to do away with the absurd rule of immunity of local authorities from liability for negligence, in a typical case where a bus driver employed by a local school authority had negligently injured children riding to school in the bus.[75] But although the court applied its new doctrine only prospectively,[76] the Illinois legislature was stirred into action and restored the old doctrine. The Supreme Court of California, which, in 1961, went even further by overruling the old immunity doctrine retroactively,[77] was somewhat luckier, in provoking a comprehensive study of the problem and an eventual legislative reform in 1963. There are those who would solve the dilemma by generally prescribing judicial inaction in the face of legislative inaction. This was propounded by Professor Henry M. Hart in a symposium on "Courts and Lawmaking" held in 1958 at the Columbia Law School:[78]

The Constitution of the United States and each of the state constitutions prescribe the ways in which bills shall become law. Failing to enact a bill is not one of these ways, even when a bill has been introduced and voted down. A fortiori, the failure to act is not an authorized way of making law when no bill on the subject was ever introduced in the first place. . . . A legislature is a deliberative body. It is an instrument for arriving at a consensus, not an instrument for recording a consensus previously arrived at, as if by some mysterious emanation from the electorate. To arrive at a consensus, the legislature follows an elaborate procedure of investigation and consideration eventuating in the approval of a particular form of words as law. For the courts to treat the legislature as making law by any other means is to treat this procedure and this agreement upon a particular form of words as mere froufrou—without any real function.

But two eminent judges are far less categorical: Judge Breitel, of the Court of Appeals of New York has observed:

Legislative inaction, total or partial, in a troubled area, may indicate a rejection of proposals; or it may indicate a warrant to the courts to exercise the traditional common law responsibility of piercing out,

---

[75] *Molitor* v. *Kaneland Community Unit District No. 302*, 18 Ill. 2d 11, 163 N.E. 2d 89 (1959). It should be noted that in the United States, the discredited doctrine of the sovereign's immunity from tort liability has, in application of the ancient decision of *Russell* v. *Men of Devon* (1788), 2 T.R. 667, been carried to much greater lengths than in England, where statutory public authorities, including school boards, have long been held subject to suit in tort.

[76] On the meaning of the principle of "prospective overruling," see below, p. 507 *et seq.*

[77] *Muskopf* v. *Corning Hospital District*, 359 P. 2d. 457 (Cal. 1961).

[78] *Legal Institutions Today and Tomorrow*, 46-47 (Paulsen, ed. 1959).

case by case, the necessary legal innovations. Unfortunately there is no rule of thumb to distinguish these contradictory indications; the only course is examination of legislative purpose by investigation of surrounding circumstances and the available legislative history.[79]

Chief Justice Traynor of the California Supreme Court writes:

> However timely an overruling seems, a judge may still be deterred from undertaking it if there are cogent reasons for leaving the task to the legislature. There are no ready lists of such reasons, and a judge has no absolute standards for testing his own. It is for him nevertheless to articulate the uneasiness he may feel about judicial liquidation of a precedent, however ripe it appears for displacement in the time and circumstances of the case that has brought it into question.[80]

Criteria for Limits of Judicial Reform

While the general proposition that, in the face of legislative inaction, the courts should also remain passive has proved unacceptable to courts of many countries, one observation in Professor Henry Hart's critique deserves further attention: "To arrive at a consensus, the legislature follows an elaborate procedure of investigation and consideration eventuating in the approval of a particular form of words as law." The nature of the judicial function imposes certain limits upon judicial reform. A few years ago, the present writer sought to formulate the basic limitation of judicial reform as follows:[81]

> Courts can and indeed are called upon to adjust rights and liabilities in accordance with changing canons of public policy. But because they develop the law on a case-by-case basis they can not as can the legislature, undertake the establishment of a new legal institution, "an elaborate procedure of investigation and consideration eventuating in the approval of a particular form of words as law."

Thus, courts can interpret the word "children" in wills so as to reflect contemporary views which no longer penalise illegitimate children. But they cannot establish new institutions such as adoption or legitimation. By contrast, it was suggested that courts were perfectly well equipped to abolish outdated distinctions such as

[79] Breitel, *op. cit.* at 12.

[80] Traynor, "La Rude Vita, La Dolce Giustizia; or Hard Cases Can Make Good Law," 29 U.Chi.L.Rev. 223 (1962).

[81] Friedmann, *Legal Philosophy and Judicial Lawmaking*, 61 *Colum.L.Rev.* 821, 839, 101, 119 (1961); reprinted in *Essays on Jurisprudence from the Columbia Law Review* (1963).

those between "governmental" and "proprietary" functions, between "invitees" and "licensees," or between "adminstrative" and "medical" acts as determining the liability or immunity of a municipal authority, an occupier, or a hospital.[82] On the other hand, it was suggested that the substitution of comparative for contributory negligence, however desirable and justified, could not easily be introduced by the courts because "the effective carriers of liability are, in the great majority of cases, the insurance companies, and not the nominal parties. Judicial reform would therefore affect the whole insurance rate structure."[83]

The view that the kind of law-reforming task which courts cannot properly undertake is that which requires basic institutional adjustments, is supported not only by Professor Henry Hart's formulation of "an elaborate procedure of investigation and consideration eventuating in the approval of a particular form of words as law,"[84] but also by Chief Justice Traynor, who, like Justice Breitel, is convinced of the need for major and continuous participation of courts in the lawmaking and law-reforming process, but agrees with the present writer "that the legislature is pre-eminently qualified to cope with such problems as contributory negligence. There are many such problems whose resolution entails extensive study or detailed regulation or substantial administration that a court cannot appropriately or effectively undertake."[85]

Yet, the distinction between institutional change and the adjustment of liabilities, as a general criterion for what it is proper and improper for a court to do, is too simple. Not only are there borderline cases, like *Bendall* v. *McWhirter*, where the Court of Appeal attempted to create a new *quasi in rem* status for the deserted wife, by constituting for her benefit an "equitable right" or at least an "irrevocable license" to occupy a matrimonial home despite absence of title.[86] There are also cases in which a court has—very much like a legislator—initiated a basic institutional change, and left it

---

[82] See, for examples of judicial reform in these fields, the decisions of the Court of Appeal in *Cassidy* v. *Minister of Health* [1951] 2 K.B. 343, and in *Razzel* v. *Snowball* [1954] 1 W.L.R. 1382; and the American decisions in *Bing* v. *Thunig*, 2 N.Y. 2d 656, 163 N.Y.S. 2d 3 (1957), and *Collopy* v. *Newark Eye and Ear Infirmary*, 27 N.J. 29, 141 A. 2d 276 (N.J. 1958).

[83] Friedmann, *Legal Philosophy and Judicial Lawmaking*, 61 Colum.L.Rev. 841 (1960).

[84] See above, p. 502.

[85] Traynor, *op. cit.* at p. 233.

[86] [1952] 2 Q.B. 466, as revised in *Westminster Bank* v. *Lee*, [1956] Ch. 7. The decision was overruled by the House of Lords in *Nat. Prov. Bank* v. *Ainsworth* [1965] A.C. 1175. See above, p. 465 *et seq.*

to legislators and administrators to elaborate the basic principles and work out the necessary institutional adjustments. This is more likely to occur in federal jurisdictions where a Supreme Court has the ultimate power of constitutional interpretation and thus a scope for lawmaking unrivalled in other types of legal systems. The interpretation of "due process" or "equality" or "freedom of commerce" clauses means in effect a power of almost unlimited sweep to lay down principles of legislation and administration, in accordance with changing ideas of public policy. Two famous recent decisions of the Supreme Court of the United States illustrate the magnitude of such lawmaking—and institution-creating—power.

In *Brown* v. *Board of Education*[87]—a decision that initiated a period of almost unprecedented legal and social change in the United States—the Supreme Court held the racial school segregation system prevailing in most of the Southern states to be unconstitutional, thus overruling its own earlier doctrine, that "separate but equal" facilities were compatible with the Constitution.[88] This decision set in motion a major reorganisation of school systems—far from completed—in which the Federal District Courts, enjoined by the Supreme Court to supervise and scrutinise the legislative and administrative changes, act as judicial executants of the Supreme Court decision. Although the court here did not "approve a particular form of words as law," it clearly set a new institutional pattern, leaving it to state legislatures and administrators to work out the details under the supervision of subordinate courts.

In *Baker* v. *Carr*,[89] the Supreme Court went perhaps even further in the ordering of new institutional arrangements. Here the court considered a suit by a group of Tennesseans alleging that they had been deprived of their federal constitutional rights by legislation classifying voters with respect to representation in the General Assembly. The court held these allegations to be justiciable, and a denial of the equal protection guaranteed by the Fourteenth Amendment. This decision—which has been bitterly attacked as an improper judicial interference in matters of political decision—set in motion a nationwide process of redrawing of both federal and state election districts. Again the court, in the course of decid-

---

[87] 347 U.S. 483 (1954), 349 U.S. 294 (1955). The Supreme Court remanded the implementation of its decision to the District Courts, setting as guide-line that: "in fashioning and effectuating the decrees, the courts will be guided by equitable principles."
[88] *Plessy* v. *Ferguson*, 163 U.S. 537 (1897).
[89] 369 U.S. 186 (1962).

ing a specific complaint, laid down a new principle of the most far-reaching institutional implications, leaving it to legislatures and administrative authorities to work out the details.[90]

In all these cases, the institutional and status change was initiated by the court, and it was left to the other two branches of government—the legislative and the executive—to elaborate the change.

More frequent—and perhaps more generally acceptable to jurisprudential thinking—is a give and take between courts and legislators, in the initiation and elaboration of law reforms. Thus, in the early twenties, when the German mark slumped to unfathomable depths, the law courts took the initiative in refusing to uphold currency nominalism in the performance of contracts. They were confronted with the fantastic inequities produced by the ability of landowners, insurance companies, or pension funds to pay off heavy debts at virtually no cost, while the creditors found the work and savings of a lifetime reduced to nil. The courts used a general clause of the German Civil Code, which prescribes that all obligations are to be fulfilled "in good faith," to lay down certain rough and ready principles of adjustment of obligations. But they were not in a position to prescribe a detailed scheme of revaluation, which entailed a great deal of actuarial, administrative, and institutional arrangements. This was later done by statute. Again, the series of Supreme Court decisions which reinterpreted the provisions of the U.S. Constitution with regard to civic equality, eventually resulted in certain institutional and procedural guarantees provided by the Civil Rights Act of 1965—which includes the appointment of Federal Registrars to supervise the fairness of registration of electors in the states.

While it thus remains generally true that courts are not equipped to engage in law reforms which entail institutional and administrative arrangements, this does not mean that courts do not at times initiate basic legal changes, through the reinterpretation of constitutions, or through bold judicial innovations, which lay the foundation for subsequent legislative changes.

[90] See *Reynolds* v. *Sims*, 377 U.S. 533 (1964) where the Supreme Court upheld District Court invalidations of six state reapportionment plans under the principle of *Baker* v. *Carr*. Harlan J. observed, in dissent, that "these decisions . . . have the effect of placing basic aspects of state political systems under the pervasive overlordship of the federal judiciary."

Prospective Overruling and Judicial Lawmaking

The significance as well as the peculiar characteristics and limitations of judicial lawmaking are brought out in a judicial doctrine which over the last thirty years has been increasingly applied and articulated in the American courts—both federal and state—but which appears to be virtually unknown outside the United States. This is "prospective overruling," *i.e.*, the overruling of a well-established precedent limited to future situations, and excluding application to situations which have arisen before the decision and are therefore presumed to be governed by reliance on the overruled principle.[91] As the Supreme Court of the United States pointed out in a recent decision,[92] which held that "the Constitution neither prohibits nor requires retrospective effect,"[93] and that it was therefore for the court to decide on a balance of all relevant considerations whether a decision overruling a previous principle should be applied retroactively or not,[94] prospective overruling is clearly not compatible with the Blackstonian proposition that courts do not "pronounce a new law, but . . . maintain and expound the old one." It implies a clear admission that courts do make new law, and the very posing of the question whether the new rule should be applied retrospectively or only prospectively indicates awareness of its legislative aspects. In the legislative process the problem of retroactivity is, of course, a familiar one, and it is generally, at least in criminal statutes, held to be incompatible with the principle of a democratic system of government.

Despite isolated earlier applications, the principle of prospective overruling gained a definite and respectable place in American

[91] In *Linkletter* v. *Walker*, 381 U.S. 618 (1965) (see below for facts) the rule established was applied to cases whose direct appeals were pending when the decision was made. The cut off point was finality of the conviction at the time the decision was made. However, in *Johnson and Cassidy* v. *New Jersey*, U.S. (1966) a stricter test is applied as the Supreme Court holds that the decisions in *Escobedo* v. *Illinois*, 378 U.S. 478 (1964) and *Miranda* v. *Arizona* U.S. (1966), (the latter of which states that a person held for a crime must be advised of his right to have counsel by the police at the outset of questioning) "should apply only to trials begun after the decisions were announced."

[92] *Linkletter* v. *Walker*, 381 U.S. 618 (1965).

[93] *Id.* at 629. The Court in *Johnson and Cassidy* v. *New Jersey*, U.S. (1966) added, "We here stress that the choice between retroactivity and non-retroactivity in no way turns on the value of the constitutional guarantee involved . . ."

[94] In *Linkletter* the issue was whether *Mapp* v. *Ohio*, 367 U.S. 643 (1961), which held that evidence illegally seized is inadmissible in a state criminal trial, could be applied retroactively to convictions obtained before this principle was judicially asserted. The court decided, essentially in the interest of "the administration of justice and the integrity of the judicial process," that the rule of *Mapp* should not be made retroactive.

jurisprudence through a decision of Mr. Justice Cardozo in 1932.[95] In that case the Supreme Court of Montana overruled a previous decision granting shippers certain rights to recover excess payments under a statute regulating intrastate freight rates. The Montana court held that the statute did not create such a right, but that the old rule should be applied to the *Sunburst* case and to other contracts of carriage entered into in reliance upon the earlier decision. The Supreme Court's decision, delivered by Justice Cardozo, is like the court's much more recent decision in *Linkletter*,[96] an example of the American judges' much greater readiness—as compared with their English brethren—to apply general considerations of legal philosophy to problems of the judicial process:[97]

We have no occasion to consider whether this division in time of the effects of a decision is a sound or an unsound application of the doctrine of *stare decisis* as known to the common law. Sound or unsound, there is involved in it no denial of a right protected by the federal constitution. This is not a case where a court in overruling an earlier decision has given to the new ruling a retroactive bearing, and thereby has made invalid what was valid in the doing. . . .

A state in defining the limits of adherence to precedent may make a choice for itself between the principle of forward operations and that of relation backward. It may say that decisions of its highest court, though later overruled, are law none the less for intermediate transactions. . . .

On the other hand, it may hold to the ancient dogma that the law declared by its courts had a Platonic or ideal existence before the act of declaration, in which event the discredited declaration will be viewed as if it had never been, and the reconsidered declaration as law from the beginning. . . .

The choice for any state may be determined by the juristic philoso-

---

[95] *Great Northern Railway* v. *Sunburst Oil & Refining Co.*, 287 U.S. 358 (1932).

[96] The opinion delivered for the court by Justice Clark refers to Sir Mathew Hale, Blackstone, Austin, Gray, Holmes, and Cardozo.

[97] See the observations made by Lord Evershed, M.R., in an article originally contributed to the *Columbia Law Review* (61 Colum.L.Rev. 761 (1961)), and reprinted in *Essays on Jurisprudence from the Columbia Law Review*, 69, 79 (1963):

Anyone in my country, as in the United States, who wishes to reflect on the broad problems of the law's philosophy and the judicial function in its exposition will without doubt turn to the writings and recorded lectures and opinions of the great American judges and law teachers of recent times. To these authorities all English lawyers, and particularly English judges, acknowledge their indebtedness. I have in the course of this paper made reference to notable living American authorities. But the names of American judges of not long ago are constantly in mind, names like Oliver Wendell Holmes, Harlan Stone, Louis Brandeis and, especially in this context, Benjamin Cardozo, whose lectures, *The Nature of the Judicial Process*, must always remain a classic—an assertion that is happily supported by the recent announcement of its publication in England. I have to confess that no English judge in modern times has provided any comparable work.

phy of the judges of her courts, their conceptions of law, its origin and nature. We review not the wisdom of their philosophies, but the legality of their acts.[98]

Since *Sunburst*, courts and commentators have been feeling their way as to the merits as well as the limits of the "prospective over-ruling" principle. Any decision that, for example, widens the legal responsibility of an employer to an employee, through the narrowing of the scope of common employment, or the broadening of the responsibility for independent contractors, alters the law and upsets somebody's expectations. Whether and when there is scope for a "prospective overruling" must therefore be a matter of degree. In the careful analysis of a recent commentator,[99] as followed by a recent Supreme Court case,[99a] the five values—of stability, protection of reliance, efficiency in the administration of justice, equality, and the image of justice—have to be balanced against each other. In the first place, it is obviously necessary to distinguish criminal law decisions from decisions in matters of civil liability. In matters of criminal law—except, probably, those allocated to the general field of "public welfare offences," which are essentially in the nature of administrative sanctions and therefore subject to different juris-prudential considerations[1]—the defendant should not be prejudiced by retroactive legislation. The principle of *nullum crimen sine lege* is generally held to be part of a liberal and democratic system of values. By contrast, an improvement in the criminal defendant's position does not meet with this objection. This is the rationale of the decision of the Court of Criminal Appeal in *R. v. Taylor*,[2] which permits departure from precedent (in that case on the question of bigamy) where the effect is to narrow the scope of the crime, not to widen it. The same reasoning induced the Supreme Court in *Mapp v. Ohio*[3] to apply the benefit of the new rule making certain evidence illegal in Miss Mapp. But counterbalancing considerations of security and efficiency in the administration of justice made the court refuse to apply the rule retroactively to convictions already obtained. Such a compromise inevitably causes inequality of treatment, as between

---

[98] 287 U.S. 358, 364-365 (1932).
[99] Currier, *Time and Change: Prospective Overruling in Judge-Made Law*, 51 Va.L.Rev. 201, 234 (1965).
[99a] *Johnson and Cassidy* v. *New Jersey*, 384 U.S. 719 (1966).
[1] See the basic decision of the Supreme Court of the U.S. in *Morissette* v. *U.S.*, 342 U.S. 246 (1952), and the discussion in *Law in a Changing Society* at 197.
[2] [1950] 2 K.B. 368.
[3] Above, p. 476.

those who happen to have been convicted before the enunciation of the new rule and the others, including the defendant at bar.[4]

In civil matters, "prospective overruling" has hitherto been predominantly applied to cases involving the ending of municipal and charitable immunities from tort liability.[5] The reason is that, in this type of case, public authorities and institutions are involved, and that the ending of traditional immunities may provoke public and legislative opposition.[6] Prospective overruling in civil cases also raises another problem: If the rule is only applied to future cases, excluding the case at bar, prospective plaintiffs will generally have little incentive to bring an action. Except for the relatively rare instances of test cases or actions brought by public authorities, plaintiffs bring actions in their own interests and not for the sake of clarification of legal principle. In some cases, such as the Illinois court's decision in *Molitor*, this difficulty was met by extending the benefit of the new rule to the plaintiff, on the ground that the public authority had taken out adequate insurance and could not therefore be prejudiced by reliance on the overruled immunity rule.

Clearly, prospective overruling, while a welcome acknowledgment of the lawmaking function of courts, opens up as many difficulties as it solves. It must remain confined to relatively few situations, of exceptional importance.[7]

It is unlikely that English courts—still much more strongly wedded than American courts to the Blackstonian doctrine—will adopt, *eo nomine*, any theory of "prospective overruling." But the House of Lords, in one of its recent major lawmaking decisions, found another way of doing virtually the same thing. In *Hedley Byrne*,[7a] the House of Lords could have been content to dismiss the action on the ground that the defendants had excluded any legal responsibility for their statement. It chose instead to enunciate, in

---

[4] See, for a searching analysis of *Linkletter* and its implications, Mishkin, The Supreme Court: 1964 Term—Foreword, The High Court, The Great Writ and Due Process of Time and Law, 79 Harv.L.Rev. 56 (1965). *Cf.* "Comment, Linkletter, Shott and the Retroactivity Problem in Escobedo," 64, Mich.L.Rev. 832 (1966).

[5] See Currier, *op. cit.* at 213; Mishkin, *op. cit.* at p. 71.

[6] This is indeed what happened in *Molitor* (Illinois) and in *Muskopf* (California), although in the latter case the end result was legislative reform broadly in accordance with the new judicial principle.

[7] See Mishkin, *op. cit.* at 61, who, after having pointed out the problems that a generalised application of prospective ruling would present to the "essential function of courts which requires that the normal mode of judicial operation be retroactive," suggests that these difficulties "do not constitute a barrier to occasional, sporadic, and unpredictable resort to such prospective limitation. But they do exert substantial force against any generalised or regularised invocation of such power."   [7a] See above, p. 472 *et seq.*

a series of elaborate opinions, a future principle of responsibility for financial statements negligently made under circumstances in which third parties can reasonably be expected to rely on them. The decision thus operates in effect as a "prospective overruling."

Alternative Roads to Legal Reform

In conclusion, reference may briefly be made to two alternative ways of lessening the problem of judicial lawmaking. One is the expanded use of the declaratory judgment. Many years ago the late Sir Ivor Jennings[8] pointed to the importance of declaratory judgments, especially in the ascertainment of the legal powers of public authorities.[9] Some years later, the present writer suggested that the declaratory judgment "may well develop into one of the most important means of ascertaining the legal powers of public authorities in the intricate mixture of public and private enterprise which is becoming a distinctive feature of both British and Australian life.[10] But while local authorities can obtain clarification of important legal issues by such means, and while public prosecutors can, within limits, emphasise issues of public interest in the selection of cases for prosecution, the ordinary civil litigation still depends upon the interest of a particular plaintiff in risking the expense and delay of a civil action to obtain a certain result. To some extent, representative lawsuits, *e.g.,* an action against a local authority brought on behalf of a group of residents or taxpayers, may mitigate the chanciness of such procedure as a means of developing the law. But in most civil actions, the prevalence of the litigation function between particular parties will restrict the lawmaking function of the courts; and, as we have seen, the rule of prospective overruling can at best have limited application.

Apart from the declaratory judgment, it is recourse to a more systematised form of legislative law reform that can ensure a more methodic procedure of law revision, especially in the field of "lawyer's law." This is the purpose of the new Law Commissions for England and Scotland.[11] Law revision committees in Britain

---

[8] Jennings, "Declaratory Judgements Against Public Authorities in England," 41 Yale L.J. 407 (1931).
[9] As noted earlier, the major field of application of prospective overruling in the United States has been the immunities of public authorities and charitable hospitals, apart from issues of criminal procedure in the federal sphere.
[10] Friedmann, *Law and Social Change in Contemporary Britain* (1951), at 218. See now, for a comprehensive analysis, Zamir, *The Declaratory Judgement* (1962).
[11] Law Commissions Act, 1965.

and in some American jurisdictions have been responsible for a number of important reforms in the field of lawyer's law since the mid-thirties.[12] But the activities of *ad hoc* law revision committees have, on the whole, remained too sporadic to be adequate for the increasingly complex and pressing business of legal reform. The more important law reforms, such as the reforms of divorce law and of criminal procedure have generally been entrusted to *ad hoc* law revision committees (as has until now been the case in England). The most important institution in the United States concerned with law reform is the American Law Institute—a highly respected non-governmental permanent institution, supported by all branches of the legal profession. The Institute has a small permanent staff aided by a director of high legal renown.[13] Although the task of the American Law Institute is the "restatement of the law," *i.e.,* the reformulation of the various branches of the law, in the form of model codes, uniform codes, and systematic restatements,[14] it has been a major agent of reform. The process of codification and systematisation involves change as well as clarification. Moreover, the model codes often embody major reforms, such as the abolition of the criminal offence of homosexuality between consenting adults in the Model Penal Code—very much on the lines of the recommendations of the Wolfenden Committee and the recent British legislation on this subject. The model codes and uniform codes are the product of many years of preparation and successive drafts in which the academic legal community plays a prominent part. The Uniform Commercial Code—designed to be adopted without any substantial change, so as to insure uniformity of commercial transactions—and the Model Penal Code designed as a model for state legislation which may adopt some but reject other parts—are perhaps the best known examples of systematic reforms already adopted by a number of states and likely to be adopted by many more.[15] The semi-official activities of the American Law Institute are the nearest parallel to the recent British legislation in the field

[12] New York and California. On the New York Law Revision Commission, which has remained a body of rather minor significance, see MacDonald, "The New York Law Revision Commission, 28 Mod.L.Rev. 1 (1965).

[13] At present this is Professor Herbert Wechsler of the Columbia University School of Law.

[14] An example of the latter is a recent restatement of the "Foreign Relations Law of the United States" (1965).

[15] The National Conference of Commissioners on Uniform State Laws has participated in the formulation of the Uniform Commercial Code. Its primary function—like that of the Canadian Commissioners on Uniform laws—is to encourage the adoption of uniform laws in the various states.

of law reform. The great advance of the Law Commissions Act lies in the establishment of a body of full-time and high-level Law Commissioners whose task it is "to take and keep under review all the law . . . with a view to its systematic development and reform, including in particular the codification of such law, the elimination of anomalies, the repeal of obsolete and unnecessary enactments, the reduction of the number of separate enactments and generally the simplification and modernization of the law." For this purpose an elaborate procedure of preparatory studies and channels of communication with the Lord Chancellor and Parliament is provided. It is too early to say whether the hope expressed in some quarters will materialise that this new machinery, "if effectively used, should enable rules of law, as well as those of common law, equity and of the statute book, devised to meet the requirements of earlier ages in which needs were different, to be changed or moulded so as to provide a flexible and suitable system for our own day, and, indeed, for periods to come."[16] What cannot be doubted is that only a procedure of this kind can lessen the judicial dilemma: *i.e.,* either to continue to apply outmoded and inequitable rules, prolonged by prevalent legislative lethargy in the field of "lawyer's law," or to engage in law-creating activities which must be sporadic, depend on the initiative of individuals, and create the dilemma here surveyed of doing either too little or too much.

CONCLUSIONS

The picture of the impact of social engineering and of legal idealism which Roscoe Pound has asked the jurist to draw for the practical lawyer is thus a much more complex one than is apparent from most current discussions.[17] The following tentative conclusions may sum up the thoughts developed in this chapter:

(1) In all but totalitarian societies the social engineering function of the judge is determined and confined by the need to balance legal stability and certainty against the development of law as an instrument of social evolution.

(2) In the democratic societies, to which an independent judiciary is essential, a further limitation is introduced where law courts are the ultimate interpreters of a written constitution. While the pre-

---

[16] Chorley & Dworkin, The Law Commissions Act 1965, 28 Mod.L.Rev. 674 (1965).
[17] Including the discussion in the first edition of this book, Chap. 23.

dominant trend of recent years is not to interfere with modern legislative policy through a rigid and only superficially objective interpretation of the constitution, the plain words of constitutional texts often erect insuperable barriers.

(3) In legal systems where the ultimate control of legislative policy in a political organ, the function of the judge is relatively simpler. In his auxiliary function, as interpreter of political statutes and as arbiter over administrative actions, the task of the judge is to leave policy to the elected organs of democracy and to interpret such policy intelligently. This means a restrictive interpretation of such checks as violation of natural justice, unreasonableness, *ultra vires*, etc.

(4) In the interpretation of precedent and statutes the judicial function can and must be a more positive and constructive one. An intelligent interpretation of statutes, which aids, instead of frustrating, legislative policy, is dominated by the same principles which indicate judicial restraint in the invalidation of statutes or acts of government. The development of the law through the flexible interpretation of precedent may be helped by the statement made by the Lord Chancellor on July 26, 1966 that[18] the House of Lords would, in future, not feel strictly bound by its own previous decisions.

(5) The growing use of law, as an instrument of social control and policy, in modern society, is gradually reducing the sphere of "lawyer's law" and, with it, the primary creative function of the judge in common law systems, while it increases the importance of a constructive judicial development of law, in the auxiliary function of interpretation of statutes and judicial restraints on administrative action.

[18] See above, p. 464, n. 88.

CHAPTER 33

ENGLISH, AMERICAN AND CONTINENTAL
APPROACHES TO LAW

A COMPARISON between the two trends of legal thinking, method and practice which, in a very general way, are described as Anglo-American and Continental jurisprudence, is certainly a matter of great importance. Legal theory cannot achieve its principal object, self-reflection, without rising beyond the limitations of one-sided legal training; the practitioner, when confronted with a conflict of laws, often has to compare the legal notions and institutions of different nations; a workable system of international law must blend the methods and outlook of different national legal systems.

Between English and American law there are many and even fundamental differences. So there are between the principal Continental systems. Nevertheless, it is possible to contrast in a broad sense Continental and Anglo-American law. Historical development emphasises the outward difference. English law, through geographical circumstances and the continuity of political and social evolution, has largely developed on a line of its own, and in its turn formed the basis of American legal evolution. Although American law has become increasingly independent, the common basis of both systems, namely the common law of England and a judicial theory built on a precedent system, still preserves a fundamental unity which is evidenced by the persuasive authority enjoyed by decisions of one country in the other, and by the continuous exchange of legal ideas. On the other hand all Continental codifications, most of them less than half a century old, owe their inspiration to the principles of the Napoleonic codes. They are largely influenced by the reception of Roman law, and thus by a common background of legal notions and institutions as well as by similar conceptions of law-making and law interpretation. Moreover, there has been much conscious imitation and mutual influence among the various Continental codifications. The oldest of the present-day civil codes, the French Civil Code, has been kept in tune with the more modern codifications through the breadth of its principles as well as the creative work of the French judiciary and the academic lawyers.

GENERAL DIFFERENCES

The differences of principle between the English and American systems of law, as they stand today, might be summarised as follows:

(1) The supreme law in the United States is a written law, the American Constitution, which prevails over any ordinary statute. There is no supreme law in England, where the law-making power of Parliament is unlimited.[1]

(2) Through the frequent need for interpretation of the Constitution, American judges have been faced much more than English judges with vital problems of public policy, and in particular the conflict between vested right and social state policy. Such matters, as Lord Macnaghten observed in the *Nordenfelt case*,[2] do not fit well into the precedent system. The existence of a Federal and fifty judicial systems, making strict adherence to a single judicial hierarchy impossible, and the rapid economic expansion of the United States compared with the gradual evolution in England, may account in large part for the difference between precedent as found in the United States and in England. American judges may be conservative, as the majority of the Supreme Court, which for many decades consistently opposed and invalidated social legislation in the name of natural law, or progressive, as its present majority and many other American judges, but in either case the attitude towards the binding force of precedent is a much freer one than in English law. The difference has been analysed by Professor Goodhart.[3] But his view of the English position must be read subject to the very noticeable change which has since taken place.[4]

(3) The need for systemisation of the law has been felt earlier and more urgently in the United States, owing to the mass of legal material which threatened to become unmanageable. Apart from a certain number of actual codifications in different states, the

---

[1] Australia and Canada (except Quebec) have the English common law system. But both are federations and have written constitutions authoritatively interpreted by law courts. Their constitutional law is, in this respect, much closer to the American than to the British system.

[2] *Nordenfelt* v. *Maxim Nordenfelt Guns and Ammunition Co.* [1894] A.C. 535.

[3] *Essays in Jurisprudence and Common Law*, 50 *et seq.* (1931).

[4] *Cf.* the analysis above, p. 474 *et seq.*

unofficial codification of the different branches of law has proceeded far, notably through the authoritative *Restatements* issued under the auspices of the American Law Institute, and its model codes in such fields as commercial and criminal law which many of the American States have adopted. Previous case law on the subject is generally employed to cover gaps and to provide needed interpretation for the provisions of the legislation.

Subject to these differences, one may still speak of "Anglo-American jurisprudence."

The principal factors which have tended to direct the development of Anglo-American and Continental law into different channels are partly of a technical character, that is, related to the structure of the law, partly of a sociological character, that is, deriving from the function and scope attributed to the law by the social order.

It is the technical side which has hitherto been almost exclusively emphasised by jurists. We may classify the principal aspects of this alleged structural difference as follows:

(1) Continental jurisprudence has been decisively influenced by the reception of Roman law; Anglo-American law has not. Instead it is largely the product of gradual historical growth and therefore still shows considerable elements of feudalism. It is for this reason that Scottish law might be ranked with Continental rather than with the English system, because of the affinity in legal method and theory.

(2) All Continental systems are essentially codified;[5] Anglo-American law is still based on the common law.

(3) From this follows a different approach to problems of legal interpretation. Judicial decisions in Continental systems are not primary sources of law, but only a gloss on the law. On the other hand, in Anglo-American law, precedent is one of the principal sources of law.

(4) It is an aspect of the contrast of inductive and deductive approach that Continental systems, proceeding from general rules to individual decisions, establish general legal principles, whereas Anglo-American law centres round a decision of individual problems and builds up the principle, from case to case. Such principles as there are, have been developed from a gradual adjustment to practical requirements.

---

[5] Except for the Scandinavian countries which still live largely under partly systematised customary law, but appear to be moving towards codification.

(5) As a corollary to this difference in legal development, Anglo-American legal thinking gives a predominant place to the law courts, whereas Continental jurisprudence thinks of law not only in terms of litigation but largely in terms of its general function.

(6) The dualism of common law and equity in Anglo-American law is unknown in Continental systems, where equity is a principle of interpretation applied to any legal question, but not a special body of law.

(7) All Continental systems distinguish in substance and procedure between private law and administrative law. The former deals with legal relations between subjects, as equals, the latter with legal relations between authority of all types and the subject.[6] Anglo-American law has, until recently, rejected this dichotomy and has adhered—at least in theory, to the principle of the equality of all before the law.

(8) The more abstract and generalising approach to law of Continental jurisprudence has been conducive to the development of legal philosophy, whereas the pragmatic and empiricist character of Anglo-American law has had the opposite effect. Hence the pre-eminence in Anglo-American law of the analytical school of jurisprudence, compared with the infinite variety of Continental legal theories.

An examination of these principal points of difference reveals that they have either been very much exaggerated in the first place or have recently lost much of such importance as they may once have had. Moreover, a comparative consideration of Scottish law might well help to form a bridge between the systems and methods of Anglo-American and Continental jurisprudence. For Scottish law, while being linked to English law through centuries of political union and common life, as well as by a common supreme court of appeal, the House of Lords—which always contains a proportion of Scottish judges—has developed from sources and on lines very different from English law and exhibits many characteristic features of Continental law.[7] The following seem to be the principal reasons:

---

[6] Public authority comprises the state itself, local authorities and other bodies entrusted with the exercise of public functions.

[7] *Cf.* McGillivray (ed.), *Sources and Literature of Scots Law* (1936). On the intermediate position of *stare decisis*, see now Smith, *The Doctrine of Judicial Precedent in Scots Law* (1953). And for an excellent restatement of modern Scottish law, Smith, *Scotland, The Development of its Laws and Constitution* (1962); Walker, *The Scottish Legal System* (2nd ed. 1963).

(1) Scottish law, like Continental law, has been directly influenced by Roman law, which is even now referred to as a principal source.

(2) Scottish legal education has been directed, much more than English legal education, towards the study of other systems and been influenced by study at Continental universities, particularly between the sixteenth and eighteenth centuries.

(3) The Scottish intellect is much more inclined towards abstract and systematic thinking than the English intellect.

(4) Scottish law knows no separate administration of equity. As regards at least four of the above-mentioned principal points of difference, Scottish law must therefore be ranked with Continental rather than English jurisprudence.

LEGAL CONCEPTS

Property Law

A comparison of legal notions and institutions seems to show that the contrasts are still strongest in the law of property. Roman and Continental laws distinguish between movable and immovable property according to the nature of the object; Anglo-American law distinguishes between personal and real property, according to the action by which the property could be recovered. It is a relic of feudalism that there is theoretically no full private ownership of land in Anglo-American law, although in England the distinction has lost what practical importance it still had by the real property legislation of 1925.[8] Of some practical importance, however, is the possibility of different degrees of property in Anglo-American law. A 999-year lease is a type of property although less comprehensive than full ownership. Again, ownership is divided between the trustee and the beneficiary under a trust. This is impossible in Continental law where the *fiducia*, necessitated by modern company developments, can only be explained as a type of agency, or as a personal obligation.[9] Certain civil law systems, however, which operate in common law surroundings, have found it necessary and possible to assimilate the trust concept to the unfamiliar atmosphere

---

[8] *Cf. American Law Institute's Restatement of Property*: "Freehold Interests."
[9] But see Bolgar, "Why No Trusts in the Civil Law?" 2 Am.J.Comp.Law 204 (1953), on the division of ownership in the older Roman law (*dos*) and an explanation why trust or *fiducia* could be absorbed in Roman, Dutch and Quebec law. The rigid "absolutism" of ownership was, according to this author, introduced into Continental law only by the "Code Civil."

of a civil law system. The Civil Code of Quebec,[10] in 1888, incorporated a chapter on *fiducie*. Its application is, however, limited to gifts and wills. In the field of family and succession law, the *"fiducie"* does not, however, appear to have become of any importance comparable to that of the trust in family and succession matters in the common law systems.[11]

The Anglo-American difference between various degrees of property (and the inclusion of a long-term lease as a type of property in particular) on one hand, and the Continental differentiation between property and limited rights in a *res aliena* on the other hand, is responsible for many substantial legal differences. Mortgages in the form of leases are, of course, unknown to a system which does not have a long-term lease as a form of ownership. But such differences have ceased to be of major importance, in the same degree as the long-term lease had ceased to represent feudal tenancy in more than a purely formal sense. Moreover, the reduction of the status of a mortgagee from a nominal owner of the mortgaged land to the owner of a right in a mortgagor's land, and the introduction of the charge as an alternative form of mortgage have substantially approximated English law to the current Continental legal forms of real property.[12]

To be sure, English and American conveyancing still differs in hundreds of large and small technicalities from conveyancing in Continental countries. Many of these differences are either derived from professional tradition or are a survival of feudal institutions. On the whole, they refer to technicalities of conveyancing and succession rather than to fundamentals. The general introduction of a land register on Continental lines would substantially reduce differences and assimilate the principles of conveyancing. The great success of the limited introduction of the land register shows that the opposition against its general adoption is due not to legal

---

[10] Another example is the law of Panama. *Cf.* 33 J. Comp. Leg. 25 (1951).

[11] For an analysis of the position of the *"fiducie"* in the civil law of Quebec, *cf. Curran* v. *Davis* [1933] S.C.R. 283, where the Supreme Court of Canada decided that the *"fiducie"* was a genuine importation of the English law of trust into the civil code, not a mandate or a contract as suggested by many writers. Therefore acceptance by the beneficiary was not required and the trust could not be unilaterally revoked after acceptance by the trustee. But the same decision also shows that a civilian system cannot adopt the "dual ownership" conception, in the absence of equity; the beneficiary's status is akin to that of a creditor. The fullest discussion of the subject is by Faribault, *La Fiducie* (1936).

[12] In American law the position is not uniform. In the majority of states the property owner retains the legal title, in a minority the mortgagee acquires it (lien theories and title theories).

reasons but to political and professional opposition. Scottish law has long known a land register. As early as the fifteenth and sixteenth centuries the Scottish Parliament recognised the need for an authentic register of all rights in land, and notaries kept protocol books in which they entered notes of sasines and instruments. A complete system of land registration has long been in operation.[13] Even more significant is the success of the Torrens system, which comes close to the Continental systems of registration of title and transactions in land. This was first introduced by an Englishman in South Australia in 1857, and it has spread from there over the whole of Australia, New Zealand and most of Canada.

As for the rules of succession, such difference as they still represent as compared with Continental systems is of the same order as that created by the trust. The devolution of property to an administrator of the estate entrusted with its administration and distribution for the benefit of others is unknown to Continental systems, as is the whole institution of trust. Maitland relates that Gierke told him once: "I do not understand your trust." Most Continental lawyers will sympathise with Gierke. The dualism of legal and equitable ownership has a certain parallel in Roman law, but not in modern Continental systems. The use made of the institution not only in the law of property, but as a substitute for corporate legal personality and as the legal backbone of unincorporated associations, reveals a considerable difference in legal thinking, of which Maitland has given us a brilliant and profound account.[14]

Corporate Personality

In Maitland's analysis, this difference stems from the contrast between a conception of rights and duties in terms of individuals and a propensity for the construction of abstract entities. The Anglo-American lawyer does not conceive of an endowment fund or a charity or an institution devoted to certain purposes as of something with an existence and personality of its own. He thinks of the property behind it and allocates rights and duties to certain persons according to their share in the administration and enjoyment of such property. The Continental lawyer, on the other hand, has no difficulty in elevating such institutions to independent legal

[13] See the Land Registry Act, 1808.
[14] *Selected Essays in Anglo-American Legal History*, Chaps. 3-5.

existence. If recent developments, particularly the increasing importance of holding companies, have produced a considerable discussion of the *Treuhand* concept in Continental systems, it could not assume the same function as in English and American law, it could only be conceived as a type of agency. This difference of approach, which reveals itself in many other aspects of the law, is responsible for certain differences in the conception of corporate personality in Continental and Anglo-American systems. In accordance with the greater scope given to corporate personality (but also with the greater inclination to philosophical speculation) the Continent, and Germany in particular, has produced a great variety of theories of juristic personality, while English and American law, without giving much attention to theory, have been content with the fiction theory as a working proposition. Maitland disturbed this state of affairs when he made known and explained Gierke's organic theory. The other German theories were so much linked up with the existence of impersonal juristic entities, like charities, that they were without interest to Anglo-American lawyers.

The pressure of social and economic developments has, however, considerably narrowed the gap between the American and Continental conceptions, with the result that the contemporary position is very different from that analysed by Maitland. In Great Britain and Australia, for example, the company limited by guarantee is now increasingly used for the incorporation of charitable purposes. Its status is not unlike that of the German *Stiftung*. In the United States and Canada the foundation, which is almost invariably incorporated, is now the normal legal form in which major charities are established. The main reason for the phenomenal growth of foundations is the desire to escape the heavy succession duties, to make provision for family members and to retain control of a family business.[15] The combination of modern big business and welfare state policies has greatly influenced the social as well as the legal concepts still prevalent half a century ago.

More deeply, however, than by those theoretical discussions, English and American law have been affected by modern economic developments common to all industrialised countries. Gierke's theory was based upon Germanic village communities, medieval guilds and similar truly corporate entities. But such a theory hardly fits the modern holding company, the one-man company and the

---

[15] On the whole development, see *Law in a Changing Society*, p. 288 *et seq.*

thousands of juristic persons which have no corporate life whatsoever. Again, the fiction theory cannot answer the need, felt in all
modern societies alike, of "piercing the veil" of juristic personality
and looking at the purposes which it pursues. The result is that
those who administer the law, whether as judges, as revenue
authorities, or as administrators, in civilian and common law
systems alike, have had to discard all known theories of corporate
personality, and to relativise the conception of juristic personality,
respecting it for some purposes, disregarding it for others, in
accordance with the nature of the problems before them: the
frustration of tax evasion, the consideration of the real purpose of
a transaction as against its legal form, the disguise of the controlling hand through subsidiary companies. German and American
law, for example, have gone very similar ways to solve this problem, despite the difference of legal systems and conceptions
of corporate personality.[16] Thus, in this matter, as in so many
others, new social problems have obliterated old technical distinctions.

Criminal Law

In criminal law the many differences of terminology and historical
development have not been able to obscure the similarity of social
and legal problems which face the different systems. A comparative
study of the problems of *mens rea*, of attempted crime, of criminal
negligence, of the distinction between criminal law in the old sense
and the modern administrative criminal law—the latter largely laid
down in statutes concerned with social administration and based on
very different principles from the other body of criminal law—reveals an astonishing similarity of legal problems, although the actual solutions by various systems may, of course, differ.[17]

Family Law

Family law is a subject intimately concerned with historical
traditions, with social habits and institutions of a country, and
many differences still exist in that field among the various countries.
But such differences do not arise essentially from a contrast between
Continental and Anglo-American jurisprudence. The principal

[16] *Cf.* in greater detail, below, Chap. 34.
[17] See, for a comparative discussion, *Law in a Changing Society*, Chaps. 11-13.

institutions of family life, like the monogamous marriage, the relations between parents and children, guardianship, adoption and the legal autonomy of married women, are now essentially common to all countries within the sphere of Western civilisation.

Such fundamental differences as exist are based first on religious principles, notably the attitude towards divorce adopted in Roman Catholic countries on one hand, and non-Catholic countries on the other; in the second place, conflicts in matters of family law arise from the conflict between domicile and nationality as determining principles in different countries.[18]

A most striking illustration of the ways in which, from completely different starting-points, the common law and the civil law systems are coming closer to each other, under the impact of new ideologies and influences, is provided by matrimonial property law. The common law systems are based on separation of property, and, with the help of equity, have gradually arrived at legal equality (and separateness) in the property and management status of husband and wife. The civil law systems (including South Africa, Quebec, and seven of the western and southern states of the United States) have community property systems, with preponderant powers and privileges for the husband. The former have recently moved towards certain community concepts, either by homestead legislation or by judicial reforms.[19] The latter have gradually emancipated the married woman, but the German *Gleichberechtigungsgesetz* of 1957, has largely abandoned the community system for the separate property system, while retaining certain community features,[20] in the event of the termination of the marriage. More recently, the comprehensive French statute, amending the civil and commercial codes, which came into effect on February 1, 1966, has drastically modified the traditional community property system as well as broadened the legal status of married women with respect to their capacity to manage their assets and to exercise a profession.

---

[18] The countries of the British Commonwealth and the U.S.A., where many different states and legal systems live under a common political allegiance, choose domicile as a principal point of contact by which to judge relations of family status. Continental countries, unitary in character, generally choose nationality. The difference is of a political rather than of a technical legal character.

[19] See above, p. 465 *et seq.*, and, more fully, Kahn-Freund and Dean in *Matrimonial Property Law*, 295, 326 (Friedmann ed. 1955).

[20] See the comparative analysis in Friedmann *op. cit.* 439 *et seq.* See Leyser, "Equality of the Spouses" under the New German Law, 7 Am. J. Comp. L. 276 (1958).

Under the amended system, unless the parties enter into a contractual arrangement before the marriage, only the property acquired by the spouses, jointly or separately, during their marriage is to be considered within the property community (*communauté des aquêts*). All other assets of the wife are to be managed by her as separate property. Further, the husband's right and power to manage the community assets have been severely limited.[21]

Contract and Commercial Law

Modern conditions of trade and industry have had an assimilating effect upon those legal institutions which are most concerned with them. Certain institutions of commerce have always been largely international. This is true of maritime law in particular, and this is one part of English law upon which Roman law has had a direct influence. It is from that branch of the law that Lord Mansfield took many of the principles by which he hoped to reform and modernise English law.[22] An institution like salvage has been universally known for many centuries, and in that matter English and American law adopt, like Continental law, the principles of *negotiorum gestio* which they otherwise reject. Negotiable instruments are essentially international institutions, and if both Britain and the United States have so far refused to participate in the international codification of the law for bills of exchange, the reason is not a fundamentally different conception of the function of the bill of exchange but a difference in a number of points of positive law, over which no compromise could be obtained.[23] Similar considerations apply to the international codification of sale of goods. However, both Britain and the United States participated in the discussions of the Hague Convention of 1964 to implement the Uniform Law on the International Sale of Goods, and Britain has signed the Convention. The laws of England and the United States

---

[21] Law No. 65-570 of July 13, 1965, effectuating a reform of the matrimonial regimes, Bull. Legis. Dalloz, 422, 1965. See Brown, *The Reform of French Matrimonial Law*, 14 Am. J. Comp. L. 308 (1965).

[22] The Maritime Law (Convention) Act of 1932 and the Carriage by Air Act of 1932 are examples of international conventions in matters of international commerce which have bridged a difference between the systems; in the case of these conventions, by an adaptation of English law to the Continental law of apportionment in cases of contributory negilgence.

[23] The main differences relate to acquisition of title through forgery, the position of holders in due course and bearer bills, apart from many questions of formalities. See Gutteridge, "Unification of the Law of Bills of Exchange," *Brit. Yb. Int'l L.* 13 (1931).

on one hand and of Continental countries on the other certainly differ in important points of positive law,[24] but this does not affect the growing similarity of the principles by which the sale of goods is dominated in all these countries. Much as the terminology may differ, such fundamental problems as mutuality of obligations, the passing of risk from vendor to purchaser, breach of contract, impossibility of performance, etc., arise in a substantially similar way in all countries.[25]

Much has been made of the alleged difference between the Continental cause and the Anglo-American consideration. No doubt at one time—when consideration was taken seriously as an element of contract, and not subject to the innumerable exceptions and qualifications which today make it mainly a matter of concern for the student of law—the difference was considerable. Anglo-American law, for the valid making of a contract, requires something additional to the consent of the parties, but today the difference is certainly one of rather small proportions. Stripped of all details it amounts to no more than this:

In contracts not made under seal, English and American law require consideration generally,[26] whereas Continental systems do not require evidence of a valid cause. They presume a contract to be complete when there is consensus between the parties. If there is absence or failure of *causa*, and one party has performed, this party may recover on the ground of unjust enrichment. The same, however, is true in English and American law in all those cases—summed up in Continental systems as lack or failure of *causa*—which support an action for recovery on the ground of mistake, failure of consideration, etc. The notion of *causa* is more comprehensive, but that is a difference of degree rather than of kind. The only further difference is that a good *causa* is a little wider than a good consideration, since it includes a moral cause (such as gratitude) whereas consideration does not.[27] Even these remaining points of difference would be eliminated by an adoption of the

[24] In particular on the question of completion of the contract, *i.e.*, on the theory of offer and acceptance, complicated by the doctrine of consideration and the question of remedies for breach of contract, interpellation, specific performance. See Gutteridge, An "International Code of the Law of Sale" *Brit. Yb. Int'l L.*, 86 (1933).

[25] See, *The Sources of the Law of International Trade* (ed. Schmitthoff, 1964); Friedmann, *The Changing Structure of International Law*, 170-175.

[26] The Uniform Commercial Code now provides that modifications of a sales contract do not need consideration to be binding, provided the Statute of Frauds is satisfied. 2-209 (1958).

[27] For details, see Friedmann, 16 Can.Bar.Rev. 243, 261 *et seq.* (1938).

Report of the English Law Revision Committee which suggests that consideration should be reduced to a matter of evidence in oral contracts (writing replacing consideration), and that moral consideration should be recognised as valid in law. This, it may be noted, brings English law back to the ideas of Lord Mansfield who, in the second half of the eighteenth century, strove to bring English law closer to those parts of other systems which, especially in the light of international commercial experience, seemed to express generally recognised principles.[28] Had Lord Mansfield's attempt been successful, the gulf between Continental and Anglo-American systems would probably never have reached any considerable proportions.

Scottish law has always been closer to Continental than to English law. In Scottish law an obligation may arise from mere consent, without consideration. The undertaking to keep an offer open without consideration for example is binding in Scottish, void in English law.[29] The principles of restitution are based on *causa*, not on consideration, in Scottish law.[30] Scottish law has, accordingly, recognised the principles of unjust enrichment and *negotiorum gestio*, both of which are only very incompletely recognised in English law.[31]

Law of Torts

The most interesting point of comparison is perhaps the law of tort. At a primitive stage of legal development, delict and crime are closely akin and even indistinct. Intimately connected as both are with the habits of the people, they strongly express national or racial characteristics. As in criminal law, the problems of modern society have, however, brought about a remarkable measure of similarity in the development of delictual liability. At the present time, between Anglo-American systems on one hand and Continental ones on the other, there is still a substantial divergence in form, but a very much smaller one in substance.

In all modern Continental codes we find a general principle of delictual liability, usually considerably developed by creative

---

[28] *Cf.* 1 Mod.L.Rev. 99 et seq. (1937).
[29] Contrast *Littlejohn* v. *Hawden* (1882) 20 S.L.R. 5 with *Dickinson* v. *Dodd* (1876) 2 Ch.D. 463. *Cf.* Gloag and Henderson, *Introduction to Scottish Law*, 39 (6th ed., Jibb and Walker eds. 1956).
[30] *Cantiare San Rocco* v. *Clyde Shipbuilding Co.* [1924] A.C. 226.
[31] See below, p. 553.

judicial interpretation.[32] English law, on the other hand, started from certain specific actions in tort, which were gradually extended, by means of the Statute of Westminster *de consimili casu*, by numerous judicial fictions—a prominent instrument of legal development in English legal history—and occasionally, as in the cases of *Pasley* v. *Freeman*[33] or *Rylands* v. *Fletcher*,[34] by the creation of a new action.

Until recently there could, however, be no doubt that no action in English or American law could be based on a general principle of liability. But the situation is rapidly changing, owing to a number of factors, of which the most important one is probably the unprecedented development of the action of negligence—a result of the vastly increased contacts and frictions of modern industrial society. Negligence is framed in general terms, and this tort has tainted an increasing number of other tort actions dealing with similar situations, in particular the torts of *Rylands* v. *Fletcher*, nuisance, those based on the keeping of animals, fire or other dangerous things, and trespass committed on or off the highway.[35] Eminent authors, like Pollock, Winfield and Stallybrass,[36] as well as distinguished judges, and in particular the House of Lords, have gone a long way towards formulating general principles of tortious liability, in the process of adaptation of this branch of the law to new social requirements. American law has led English law in that development, and it is sufficient to refer to the American Restatement on the law of tort, or to the American decisions which have exercised a considerable influence upon the framing of the principles of *Donoghue* v. *Stevenson*[37] and of *Haynes* v. *Harwood*.[38] English and American law are at least on the way towards the establishment of a general principle of delictual liability for unlawful interference with a protected interest, and the more modern actions in tort are being

[32] Art. 1382, *Code Civil*; Art 823, German *BGB*; Art. 41, Swiss *Obligationenrecht*; Art. 1151 Ital. *Codice Civile*. *Cf*. Walton, *Delictual Responsibility in the Modern Civil Law* (more particularly in the French Law) as compared with the English Law of Torts. The Scottish legal concept of reparation—the obligation resulting from a wilful *delict* or negligent *quasi-delict* comes close to Continental notions. Gloag and Henderson, *op. cit.* at p. 394.

[33] 3 T.R. 51.

[34] (1868) L.R. 3 H.L. 330.

[35] For details, compare Winfield, "Nuisance as a Tort," 4 Camb.L.J. 189, 194 (1930-32); Friedmann, "Modern Trends in the Law of Torts," 1 Mod.L.Rev. 39 (1937).

[36] As editor of Sir J. Salmond's *Law of Torts*. Salmond himself, at an earlier period, took the opposite line. *Cf*. also Goodhart, "The Foundation of Tortious Liability," 2 Mod.L.Rev. 1 (1938).

[37] [1932] A.C. 562.

[38] [1935] 1 K.B. 146.

extended so as to justify such a principle, at least to a considerable extent, although at present with a great amount of overlapping.[39] As to the type of protected interest, a comparison between the principles of Continental codifications and Anglo-American law reveals that protection centres, in all alike, around life, liberty, honour and the basic property rights. To the latter are being added, by statutory reforms or judicial interpretation, quasi-propietary rights, like copyright, patents and trade marks.

As for the principle underlying liability, both groups of systems have moved along similar lines, owing to ethical and social influences common to the whole of Western civilisation. For the nineteenth century, liability in tort was essentially the penalty of fault to be found in the individual tortfeasor. Practical necessities forced all systems alike not only to seek evidence of fault in conduct rather than a state of mind, but increasingly to shift emphasis, in the law of tort, from moral blame to social responsibility. Thus, in Germany, in addition to the general principle of tortious liability for wanton or careless injury to person or property, special statutes have created strict liability for motor-car drivers, keepers of animals, etc., and similar statutes or judicial developments are to be found in all modern legal systems. French courts have imposed strict liability on the motor-car keeper through an extensive interpretation of Articles 1382, 1383, *Code Civil*. In English law there are the Workmen's Compensation Acts, now replaced by the National Insurance (Industrial Injuries) Act, 1946, the numerous statutory duties imposed upon employers and many other strict obligations. But more significant perhaps is the gradual change in the basic meaning of tortious responsibility, and above all an extension of the conception of negligence which makes it hardly distinguishable from strict liability. Thus the development, in French law, of responsibility for *le risque créé*, in English law, of the manufacturer's liability under *Donoghue* v. *Stevenson* (following American precedents, *cf. American Restatement of the Law of Torts*, "Negligence," s. 395), the extension of the conception of "things dangerous in themselves," in accordance with the infinite potentialities of the use of things through modern science, the widening of liability in nuisance, and *Rylands* v. *Fletcher*, all point to an increasing importance of social control rather than moral turpitude as the outstanding though not the exclusive principle of

---

[39] For a brilliant survey of the development of the English law of tort up to 1948, see C. A. Wright, 26 Can.Bar Rev. 46 (1948).

tortious liability under modern conditions.[40] Since the reasons for this are common to all countries which have factories, motor-cars, aeroplanes, millions of working people without other capital than their working skill, and other industrial and social conditions which leave less and less freedom of movement to the average individual, the law has had to be adapted to these new tasks whatever its technical structure. This is also true of the increasingly important problems of the relationship between tort liability and insurance. The question how far the advance of comprehensive motor-car insurance as well as of social insurance affects the place of the law of tort, and whether it may justify a return to *mens rea*, has been discussed for English, American, Soviet and Scandinavian law.[41] This discussion has revealed few if any differences between the approach of Anglo-American and Continental jurisprudence. Consequently, in this branch of the law, the difference between Anglo-American and Continental systems is rapidly shrinking. Less affected by these developments[42] is that group of torts which deals with wrongs to possession and property, and is, in essence, a part of the law of property.[43] This part of the law of tort is diminishing in quantitative importance compared with that part which reflects the changing needs of modern society.

It would be beyond the scope of this chapter, to follow up in detail the various legal developments, statutory and judicial, within the different systems of law. But the foregoing observations may have been sufficient to vindicate the suggestion—important for the comparative study of law—that historical and technical differences in the structure of different systems of law have to be studied against their sociological background. The largest differences surviving from the very different origins of the Anglo-American and Continental systems of law appear to be in land law—because of its commercial immobility[44] and historical association with feudalism —and in family law, to the extent that religious, ethical and social principles and habits still influence it. They become weaker where the influence of international commerce (mercantile law, contract)

---

[40] For a more detailed survey, see *Law in a Changing Society*, Chap. 5.

[41] *Cf. Law in a Changing Society*, Chap. 5, Hazard, 65 Harv.L.Rev. 545 (1951); James, 27 N.Y.U.L.Rev. 539; Ussing, "The Scandinavian Law of Torts, Impact of Insurance on Tort Law," 1 Am.J.Comp.L. 359 (1952).

[42] Except for trespass on and off the highway which is assimilated to negligence.

[43] *Cf.* Pollock, *Torts*, 256 *et seq.* (1951).

[44] Which is rapidly disappearing as land is commercialised. Even the seemingly indestructible rule in *Cavalier* v. *Pope* [1906] A.C. 428 was finally disposed of in the Occupiers' Liability Act, 1957.

or the parallel pressure of social developments is weightier than technical legal differences.

EVIDENCE AND PROCEDURE

The differences between Anglo-American and Continental principles of evidence and procedure are important and, in some respects, spectacular. Generally, Continental methods emphasise more strongly the legal value of utility. The state takes a more active part in the exploration of truth, both in civil and criminal matters. Anglo-American law, on the other hand, emphasises security, and the individual litigant or defendant not only has more elaborate safeguards, which not infrequently lead to the acquittal of obviously guilty persons, but also takes a bigger part in the course of the proceedings. Another important difference results from the Continental institution known as *Juge d'instruction* in France and as *Untersuchungsrichter* in Germany. On the motion, either of the prosecutor or the accused, a judicial inquiry may be held in major cases in order to clarify the facts. In certain cases it is compulsory. There has been much criticism in recent years of this institution, mainly because the proceedings before the *Juge d'instruction* are largely discretionary, and because he is, at least in German law, too strongly linked with the Public Prosecutor, who decides, upon the result of the investigation, whether to lodge an indictment or to drop the proceedings. There is however, little foundation for the view, widespread in American legal circles, that this institution necessarily weighs the scales against the accused.

Another difference exists in the conduct of trials and court proceedings. The Continental judge actively directs the trial and controls the evidence. The parties play a supplementary and subsidiary part. Anglo-American proceedings are dominated by the parties. Masters and judges have an essentially arbitral function, although modern English procedure gives considerable powers to the master in regard to the preparation of particulars by the parties. Cross-examination still dominates the proceedings. The Continental court is familiar with a case before the main trial which is consequently shortened and, in the case of civil proceedings, often a mere formality. Again, Continental systems are far more liberal in the admission of evidence. The "Best Evidence" rule, which so often excludes good documentary evidence in British procedure,[45] is

---

[45] Although it has been substantially mitigated, for civil proceedings, by the English Evidence Act, 1938.

unknown. Yet international proceedings have shown these differences to be far from unbridgeable. The Permanent Court of International Justice and its successor, the International Court of Justice, have had little difficulty in blending Continental and Anglo-American principles of procedure.[46] The Nuremberg trial of leading German war criminals was admittedly dominated by the desire to leave as few possibilities for escape as possible. Here the court relied to a large degree on documentary and secondary evidence, even in some cases where witnesses were available.[47] Otherwise, the proceedings constituted a skilful blend of Continental and Anglo-American principles. The form of prosecution and the status of prosecutors, for example, were closer to the Continental model, but cross-examination played an essential part. Even in this field, a predominantly technical one, the technical differences between the two systems, though important, are not decisive.

The Role of the Judge

A difference of far greater significance is that between the anonymous "bureaucratic" character of the Continental judgement, as against the personal and individual responsibility assumed by the Anglo-American judge. To some extent, this reflects the contrast between the civil service status of the Continental judiciary—the vast majority of the Continental judges are career judges—and the elevation of distinguished practitioners to the much more rarefied judicial office of the Anglo-American type. The practical and psychological differences are great. The clashes of views and personalities which come out dramatically in the judgements of British and American courts—particularly in those of the United States Supreme Court—occur in the Continental courts behind the closed doors of the conference room. The majority judgement is that of the court; dissents remain unreported, and a dissenting judge may have to write the judgement of the court. A powerful source of argument about the *ratio decidendi* is eliminated—as it is also with the judgements of the Privy Council. There could be no analysis of the judicial philosophy of the Continental brethren of Holmes or

---

[46] On the whole, the rules indicate a degree of initiative by the court closer to the Continental system. *Cf.* the provisions regarding the conduct of the case, preliminary documentary evidence, the ordering of expert evidence, refusal to accept further evidence, etc. *Cf.* ss. 48-54, Statute of International Court of Justice. See Rosenne, *The Law and Practice of the International Court* (vol. 2, 1965).

[47] *Cf.* Leventhal and others, 60 Harv.L.Rev. 857, 862, note 26 (1946).

Cardozo, Lord Blackburn or Lord Atkin. Their views are absorbed in the anonymous judgement of the court. The differences are too deeply rooted in social organisation and tradition to be capable of compromise. In the common law countries, dissenting judgements have often had an influence on legal development as great as, or greater than, the majority decision.[48] International tribunals have, in this respect, adopted the Anglo-American model, partly because their judgements are few and the judges sit as individual representatives and partly because national viewpoints and interests still diverge widely. The collective and anonymous rendering of judgements by the International Court of Justice, on a majority vote, might enhance their authority, but it is very unlikely in the present state of international relations. On the other hand, in the common law jurisdictions, the abolition of the dissenting judgement—or even of the concurring opinion—would deeply affect the traditional position of the judiciary and eliminate a characteristic instrument of legal evolution.

CODE LAW AND CASE LAW

At first sight the difference between a codified and a case law system appears fundamental. A code law states the law comprehensively, in general principles, and the finding of the law in an individual case is deductive, an application of general principles to particular facts. A case law system, on the other hand, develops tentatively, and truly casually; the principles crystallise slowly from decisions in particular cases, and the method of law finding proceeds inductively from the particular to the general.

These differences are, however, at the present day far more apparent than real. From different starting points, Continental and Anglo-American methods of legal development have come closer together. Again we can only summarise the principal developments:

After the distinct failure of some attempts at codification, notably the Prussian *Allgemeine Landrecht*, which hoped to solve all conceivable problems by thousands of minute provisions on every contingency, modern codes have preferred to state the law in general principles and to leave the solution of particular cases to the intelligence of those administering the law, and the formative

[48] Outstanding examples are the dissenting judgements of Holmes J. or Lord Atkin's dissent in *Liversidge* v. *Anderson* [1942] A.C. 206.

influence of public opinion. In no other way could the *Code Civil* have survived a century and a half of unparalleled social and economic revolution. The result has been, in all Continental countries, an amazing amount of judge-made law, which has supplemented and sometimes virtually superseded the provisions of the Code. Prominent examples, which could, however, be multiplied, are in France the development of a law of unfair competition from the general clause for delictual liability in Articles 1382, 1383, C.C., the imposition of strict liability upon the keeper of a motor-car, through an ingenious combination of two articles of the *Code Civil*, and the creation of the principle of strict liability as a counterpart of industrial control, a principle analogous to the rule in *Rylands* v. *Fletcher*, but much more broadly conceived, so much so that French legislation on workmen's compensation and accidents caused by civil aeroplanes only had to adopt the judicial rule.[49]

Germany presents many examples of judicial law-making of outstanding social and political importance. Among them is the development of the principle of revaluation, after the inflation which followed the First World War, by the German Supreme Court from a general clause of the Civil Code (section 242) which lays down that obligations must be fulfilled in accordance with good faith. Another, in a field only partially codified, industrial and labour law, is the doctrine of the *Betriebsrisiko*, according to which employers and workmen, forming a "working community" (*Betriebsgemeinschaft*), shared the risk of interruption of work caused by general strike and other circumstances outside the control of the employer, and the workmen therefore lost their claim to wages. This creation of the Supreme Labour Court partly anticipated the National Socialist conception of labour. Equally far-reaching and dramatic are the recent efforts of West German courts to develop principles of matrimonial law which would implement the constitutional precept of equality of the sexes. Article 3 of the Bonn Constitution of 1949 laid down that the old matrimonial law of the civil code would cease to apply on March 31, 1953 (in the expectation that by then the new family code would have been passed). No such code was adopted until 1957. During the interregnum the courts, in a creative exercise of the judicial function, applied the principle of equality to various matrimonial problems (*e.g.*, the equitable sharing of earnings where the wife worked in

---

[49] For details, see the comparative materials on French and German law in von Mehren, *The Civil Law System*, 339-464 (1957).

the husband's business). In a judgement on the constitutional validity of the above-mentioned provision of the Bonn Constitution the German Constitutional Court held that the principle of separation of powers did not stand in the way of the ability, and indeed the duty, of the courts, to adapt the law to new governing principles, where the legislator was under a temporary disability to effect the change. The court specifically referred to Article 1 of the Swiss Civil Code.[50] Moreover, large parts of the law, notably the *Droit Administratif* in France, are not codified and therefore entirely of judicial creation. The *Conseil d'Etat* has constructed the whole imposing edifice of French administrative law. Apart from such major judicial creations there are countless examples of judicial interpretations of statutes, in all Continental countries, which gave the statutory provision a meaning either not foreseen by, or openly antagonistic to, the opinions prevailing at the time of the Code, but in accordance with modern social developments or trends of public opinion. This attitude finds striking expression in Article 1, Swiss Civil Code, which directs the judge to decide as if he were a legislator, when he finds himself faced with a definite gap in the statute. The Italian Civil Code of 1942 has adopted a similar provision.

Despite this increase of creative judicial activity in Continental jurisprudence there has never been a theory of precedent analogous to the Anglo-American one. Courts may reverse their own opinions, or even dissent from a superior court in a new cause. The elasticity resulting from this method of social experimenting, of "trial and error," has been praised by Anglo-American lawyers critical of their own system.[51] But in practice the continuity of precedent is much more marked than in theory. First, there are provisions in some countries, as in Germany, which secure uniformity of principle in the Supreme Court by prescribing a plenary decision in case of dissent between different sections of the Supreme Court.[52] But above all there is the factual authority enjoyed by decisions of the higher courts, the futility of lower courts insisting on principles certain to be rejected on appeal, even if they feel strongly on the matter, and the reluctance of junior judges—in an elaborate hierarchy—to jeopardise their chances of promotion by obstinacy.

---

[50] Civil Decisions (BGZ) Vol. 11, Appendix P. 35 (1953).
[51] *Cf.* Goodhart, "Precedent in English and Continental Law," 50 L.Q.Rev. 40 (1934).
[52] *Cf.* German *Gerichtsverfassungsgesetz* (version of September 12, 1950), s. 136.

The need for a minimum degree of certainty in litigation is as urgent on the Continent as anywhere else, and consistency of judicial authority is a fact although one lacking in theoretical foundation. There is no theoretical objection in a court giving up a principle which it recognises as untenable. But this is, for human reasons as much as for any other, a rare occurrence, and in most cases, on the Continent as in England or the United States, statutory reform must remedy major legal evils.

Both the slavish obedience of Continental judges to codes and their freedom from precedent are largely a myth. In truth, while there is greater freedom towards the provisions of codes, there is also much greater respect for judicial authority than imagined by most Anglo-American lawyers.

In Anglo-American law the theoretical propositions are just the reverse. The judge is supposed to be essentially unfettered by statute, but hemmed in by precedent. Is he a king or a slave? Strangely conflicting opinions are held on this point on the Continent. Some Continental jurists have looked with envy upon the freedom with which the Anglo-American judge, unfettered by the dead letter of the law, can mete out justice in the individual case,[53] while others deplore the dead hand of an interminable string of antiquated precedents unfit to master new problems.[54] But among Anglo-American lawyers themselves opinions are highly conflicting. If the judge applies the law, and does not make it, as traditional doctrine has it, how can non-statutory law today be as fundamentally different even from that of a hundred years ago as it undoubtedly is? If the judge does, in fact, make new law, how does he do it? Is it according to well-established legal principles, or is it, as the American realists suggest, by an extra-legal choice between conflicting precedents, based on political, social or other non-legal factors?

Again, we shall have to assess the powerful influences which have altered the position in the Anglo-American legal system in recent years, which have mitigated the rigour of precedent in so far as it fetters legal development and, on the other hand, have altered the balance between statutory and case-made law.

In England and the United States the outlook on law is very much influenced by the autonomous training and tradition of the legal profession as compared with the Continent, where legal train-

---

[53] Adickes coined the term *"Richterkönigtum"* (regal judge).
[54] *Cf.* Gerland, *Englische Gerichtsverfassung.*

ing is often state directed. It is probably this fact which explains the disproportionate preponderance that case-made law still has in Anglo-American legal teaching over statute law. In the United States, increasing attention is now paid to subject-matters regulated by statute, such as tax law or labour law. The number of decisions based on statutory interpretation, in comparison with common law decisions, increases from month to month. Revenue law, workmen's compensation, transport and traffic regulations, insurance Acts, housing statutes, local government legislation, not to speak of war legislation, these and other statutory matters provide the majority of decisions: and in criminal law, even if we disregard the fact that all the main common law crimes are now codified, new statutory offences occupy more and more of the judicial work. On the basis of a statistical comparison there would today be little in the alleged contrast between the Continental and the Anglo-American position. The difference, such as it is, has two reasons:

First, many statutes are not codifications, nor comprehensive regulations, but merely remedy one specific defect, and leave the common law otherwise intact. Typical examples are the English statutes on gaming and the statutory reforms in the law of tort.

Second, and more important, is a widespread judicial attitude which regards statutory legislation as interference and accordingly pays comparatively small attention to the problems of statute law. This attitude has been responsible for an incongruous and unfortunate rule which has made judicial interpretation of statutes binding as precedent and thus transplanted the common law principle into an alien soil. This in itself has largely prevented English statute law from becoming a field for "trial and error." The gradual modification of this attitude and the present state of the problem of statutory interpretation has been discussed earlier in this book.[55]

In this respect, however, the differences between English law on the one hand and the law of those common law countries which have a written constitution are probably more fundamental than those between Anglo-American and Continental jurisprudence. The Supreme Court of the United States, for example, is predominantly engaged in the interpretation of the United States Constitution, that is, of a statute framed in the widest possible terms, in terms of fundamental rights. This gives the American as distinguished from the English courts the greatest possible freedom

---

[55] *Supra*, p. 452 *et seq.*

in making a law of their own, while calling it interpretation of the Constitution. Whereas Continental judges apply detailed statutory provisions, and English judges since Lord Coke have not attempted to supersede statute by a higher law, the American Constitution has enabled the Supreme Court to combine an almost unfettered legislative function—although one of a negative character—with the appeal to the written law. On the other hand, this position has made American judges more keenly aware of the problems of statutory interpretation.[56]

As Continental judges have freed themselves from a mechanical and literal interpretation of the statutes and have become aware of their share in the creation of law, so English and American judges are freeing themselves to a remarkable degree from the worst aspects of the binding force of precedent. Again the increasing pressure of new social problems has compelled judges to find ways of overcoming precedents, the application of which would be contrary to modern conceptions of justice. Sir William Holdsworth has pointed out[57] that English judges have never followed precedent as slavishly as recent textbooks on jurisprudence have made out. Current conceptions of the binding force of precedent are largely influenced by the positivism predominant in the ninenteenth century, which produced in all countries an exaggerated theory of the judge as someone who applies the law in accordance with principles of strict logic and does nothing else.[58] That also fitted in with the strict doctrine of the separation of powers.

Both in England and the United States several factors have contributed to a very substantial change in outlook and method. In the United States a social fact, namely the rapidity of industrial ex-

---

[56] English law forbids the judicial consideration of *travaux préparatoires*, which is well recognised in Continental systems. In the United States this rule has been virtually abandoned, and references to the legislative history not only of the Constitution but of ordinary statutes are very frequent. *Cf. Factor* v. *Laubenheimer*, 290 U.S. 276 (1933). But the English rule too is not quite as absolute as appears on the face of it. *Heydon's Case* (1584) enumerates among the four points to be considered in the interpretation of statutes the mischief for which the common law did not provide and the true reason of the remedy that Parliament has appointed. The difference between such statutory motives and purposes on one hand and parliamentary history on the other is often extremely artificial, as has been noticed, for example, in *Holme* v. *Guy* (1877) 5 Ch.D. 905. See also Allen, *Law in the Making*, 476 et seq. (6th ed.). English lawyers do not appear to apply the theory to international treaties or indeed to any case decided by international tribunals which often take preparatory material into consideration. The English rule has been severely criticised by leading English lawyers, such as Professors Gutteridge, H. A. Smith, Lauterpacht, Sir M. Amos.

[57] Holdsworth, "Case Law," 50 L.Q.Rev. 180 (1934).

[58] For an illustration of that method in commercial cases, see Chorley, "Liberal Trends in Present Day Commercial Law," 3 Mod.L.Rev. 272 (1940).

pansion, and a technical fact, namely the immense number of precedents, produced by the Federal as well as by fifty different state jurisdictions, made the old doctrine difficult to maintain. A product of these influences is the realist movement in jurisprudence which in its more extremist spokesmen discards the doctrine of precedent altogether and sees judicial decision as a result of a number of political, economic, psychological and other non-legal influences. In England the traditional approach is being modified more gradually, and without much theory. The doctrine of precedent still holds good for the great majority of cases. But in the higher courts at least the movement towards greater mobility is undeniable.[59] Although there are still numerous examples of precedents which only statutory reform can overrule, the position of the English and even more of the American judge, like that of the Continental judge, is nothing like as slavish as is often pretended.

During the height of the positivist and analytical approach to jurisprudence, judges in all countries, whatever their system, were inclined to minimise their creative function. Under the impact of new social problems and the number of new unsolved cases which defy exhaustive regulation by legislation, judges under both types of legal system became aware of their creative function. As has been pointed out in the previous chapter,[60] the extent to which the judges exercise their creative function fluctuates, but it is unlikely that there will ever be a complete return to the earlier attitude of innocence in regard to the relation of law and society.

ABSTRACT PRINCIPLES AND CONCRETE DECISION

There remains, more than any actual difference in the position of judges, a certain difference in the mental background. English and American judges, even when they make law and new principles, build them up from specific cases, where the Continental judge thinks of a general principle. There is probably a difference of political tradition behind it. English judges, and American judges in so far as they have developed English law, can look back on an uninterrupted development of many hundred years. They have been able to build the law up slowly, from case to case, and until recently in terms of forms of action rather than substantive principles. The latter only began to emerge slowly, at an advanced stage

---

[59] See, for detailed discussion, above, pp. 463, 474 *et seq.*
[60] See above, p. 500 *et seq.*

of development, when the growing mass of precedent became unmanageable and modern conditions demanded clearer and more rational principles. This whole development would have been unthinkable without the continuity of political and social evolution which no Continental country has enjoyed. Consequently, deliberate law-making, the assertion of legislative authority, especially when it followed upon a social revolution, produced on the Continent different methods of legal thinking, and a much greater emphasis on principles. The popular opposition of the abstract and theoretical approach of Continental lawyers and the common sense empirical approach of Anglo-American lawyers, though much exaggerated, is not entirely without foundation.[61]

There is no doubt, however, that, as Continental administration of justice has become more concerned with the justice of the individual case, so Anglo-American legal development has moved towards the formulation of broader principles. American law, stimulated by the increasing flood of precedents, has led English law, particularly through the highly important series of Restatements which, although no official codification, systematise the law in a manner analogous to Continental codification. A number of American states have actually codified their law. The increasing influence of law teachers upon legal development in the United States has reinforced this tendency. To mention one example, the law of quasi-contract owes its scientific existence to Professor Keener's treatise published in 1893. Moreover, a considerable proportion of high judges and law officials is now chosen from among academic lawyers. Chief Justice Stone, Justice Frankfurter, California's Chief Justice Traynor and Illinois' Judge Schaefer—all of whom have had considerable influence on the development of American law—were law teachers before becoming judges. In England too the trend towards systematisation is unmistakable, for example, in the gradual codification of company law. It is evident in all branches of the law. The law of tort is particularly interesting because that branch of the law is neither codified nor to any considerable extent regulated by statute.[62] English law courts in recent years have been able to develop that increasingly

[61] The contrast has been brilliantly—and with some exaggeration—formulated by Lord Macmillan in *Law and Other Things*, 76 *et seq.* (1937).

[62] Some important reforms, such as the apportionment of damages between joint tort-feasors and in cases of contributory negligence, or the abolition of the doctrine of common employment, have, however, had to be introduced by statute. They illustrate the limitations of law reform by judicial decision. (*Cf.* p. 503 *et seq.*)

important branch of the law largely, if not entirely, in accordance with social need, and have thereby avoided a flood of statutory interference. They have achieved this by abandoning procedural thinking and formulating broad principles of delictual liability. The work of such judges as Lord Blackburn, Lord Atkin, Lord Wright and Lord Denning is well known. There has been a great increase in the influence of legal textbooks which have attempted to extract principles from the mass of forms of actions and precedents.[63] English courts of law, and the House of Lords in particular, have mostly though not always[64] been wise enough to see that any other attitude would only have increased the domination of parliamentary legislation in a sphere always dominated by the law courts. The British Law Commission Act, 1965, has established a body of full-time Law Commissioners, whose mandate includes the systematisation as well as the modernisation of law. The result is that, much as concrete problems and solutions still differ, there is now much more similarity of principle and approach between the Continental and Anglo-American systems than formerly.

The comparison between the respective merits of the two methods is seldom untainted by hasty generalisation based on inadequate knowledge of the practical working of one or the other system, and even more by prejudice, professional or nationalist. It will be difficult to deny that in modern circumstances development of law through precedent is slow, costly, cumbrous, and often haphazard. It is therefore less suitable for a time of fast changes and restlessness such as ours. It is also dependent upon a continuity and steadiness of social conditions which may not last. Perhaps none but British judges could have worked it in such a way as to make it withstand, at least partially, the onslaught of centuries. Many present-day judges find that the only way of preserving the system is to take a bold attitude towards antiquated precedents, and to form the law in terms of broad principles. But others take the view that law reform should be left to the legislator. As a result the judicial approach to law reform, under a precedent system, is increasingly uncertain, and more influenced by changes in the judicial personnel than a code law system.[65] Consequently the

---

[63] Such modern textbooks as Cheshire's *Private International Law* (6th ed., (1956), Gower's *Company Law* (2nd ed., 1957) or Williams' *Criminal Law* (2nd ed., 1961) combine with a systematic exposition, a critical and constructive approach which is exercising considerable influence on the development of law.

[64] See above, p. 463 *et seq.*

[65] *Cf.* above, pp. 463, 469 *et seq.*

sphere left to judicial law-making diminishes steadily, even if it tries to engraft itself upon statutory interpretation.

Be that as it may, it is certain that whenever Anglo-American and Continental lawyers have co-operated in the development of international law by judicial decisions the alleged contrast of their systems has never proved a substantial obstacle, while the different judicial temperaments and methods of approach seem to have blended happily.

The emphasis, in English and American legal training and teaching, upon case law is responsible for one difference of considerable importance. Anglo-American legal thinking centres round the decision of cases, as if the legal life of the country were entirely or predominantly reflected in litigation. The theories and definitions of law of Salmond and Gray, of Holmes and the realist movement, all think of law essentially as what is laid down by the courts. Legal education in both countries is overwhelmingly a study of cases, or of statutes in the light of their judicial interpretation. This has grave consequences. For example, the law of contract as taught in England has only remote resemblance to the law of contract as it exists in the millions of transport, insurance, landlord and tenant, hire-purchase, employment and apprenticeship agreements, where terms are overwhelmingly standardised, and where the adjustment of the individual minds, which looms so large in textbooks, has little place.[66] The great majority of these contracts never come before the courts, nor do more than a very small fraction of the industrial agreements controlling production, prices and labour. Even if it is said that all these contracts, as well as the by-laws of corporations, are law only in so far as they would be sanctioned by the courts, the fact is that, since they hardly ever come before the courts, the theory of law remains untouched by them, and the time lag between social development and legal education is thus increased.

It may be attributed to the same cause that family law is still neglected in the systematic development of English and American law, although the subject is now taught at many of the major American and British law schools. What is known is mainly the law of divorce, that part of family life which comes before the courts, but which happily does not reflect the essential part of family life. All Continental codes, on the other hand, contain a

---

[66] *Cf.* in greater detail, *Law in a Changing Society*, Chap. 4.

section on family law which comprehensively regulates the main aspects of family life. We have here undoubtedly a difference caused by the fact that one system thinks in terms of cases, the other in terms of rules laid down in statutes. Here again, the gap is closing gradually. Civil law and common law systems alike are concerned with such problems as the change in the personal and property status of the married woman, or the problem of liberalisation of the grounds of divorce. The differences are caused by religious and social, not by technical factors.[67]

DUALISM OF LAW AND EQUITY

The development of the law through the dualism of common law and equity is undoubtedly a characteristic feature of the Anglo-American system, but the specific aspect which it has given to Anglo-American legal development is mainly a matter of history. From the time when equity hardened into a body of fixed legal rules supplementing the common law, the difference between the two branches of the law became mainly a matter of technique and professional tradition. The distinction between the Chancery Bar and the common law Bar is still jealously maintained in England, while New South Wales and a few of the United States' judicial systems (*e.g.*, Delaware) have even preserved equity courts. But no lawyer could afford to ignore either of the two branches, since such matters as the law of real property and the law of contract simply cannot be understood today without a knowledge of both systems. The insistence upon the continued separation of the two branches of the legal profession, even after the Judicature Acts, has, however, had a retarding effect upon the development of certain parts of the law. A prominent example is the law of quasi-contract, in which Lord Mansfield attempted to fuse legal and equitable principles. Professional conservatism killed his attempt, or at least delayed it until the present day. By overcoming this conservatism, American law was able to develop this part of the law to a very much greater importance. However, the separation of law and equity is now more a matter of professional etiquette than a matter of vital importance in either English or American law, while most American states have actually abolished the difference altogether.

---

[67] *Cf.* Llewellyn, in *Essays on Research in the Social Sciences*, 96-97; F. S. Cohen, in 1 Mod. L.Rev. 5, 24 (1937). See further, above, p. 523 *et seq.*

Continental systems do not know such dualism, and equity means, as it did for Aristotle, the application of equitable principles to correct and mitigate the harshness of legal rules. This, of course, is also known to Anglo-American law, but under a different name. What Continental systems do today, by the insertion of certain general clauses designed to ensure a broad-minded and equitable interpretation of statutory provisions against a too formalistic interpretation, was known to English law in the past as the "Equity of a Statute."[68] Today the word "equity" in that sense is not used so much as such formulas as "fair and reasonable," "what reasonable men would do," or sometimes "in accordance with natural justice." At the height of positivism, Lord Sumner scornfully rejected as out of date "that vague jurisprudence sometimes attractively styled justice between man and man."[69] He used this phrase in rejecting a principle of unjust enrichment. But only a quarter of a century later, the cautious recognition of such a principle was evident in such cases as *Craven Ellis* v. *Cannons*,[70] *Brooks Wharf* v. *Goodman*,[71] *Ministry of Health* v. *Simpson*,[72] and others, while it was openly advocated by a number of authors, among them Lord Wright and Professor Winfield.

Equity, however, is applied in many other cases. A few out of hundreds of examples are the mitigation of the strict rule of *Cutter* v. *Powell* and *Forman* v. *Liddlesdale* on *quantum meruit* in the case of *Dakin* v. *Lee*,[73] or the mitigation of the rule that contributory negligence is a good defence to breach of a statutory duty in cases of workmen working under pressure.[74] The "new equity" which the Court of Appeal introduced in 1952 to protect a deserted wife in her occupancy of the matrimonial house, is an unusual combination of general equity with the equity tradition of English law.[75] In these decisions equity is applied in exactly the same way

---

[68] Plowden's recommendation, that "it is a good way, when you peruse a statute to suppose that a law maker is present . . . and then you must give yourself such an answer as you imagine he would have done if he had been present . . . and if the law maker would have followed the equity, notwithstanding the words of the law, you may safely do the like," anticipates modern Continental codes although it goes farther than they do. *Cf.* Allen, *Law in the Making*, 373 (6th ed. 1958).

[69] See *Baylis* v. *Bishop of London* [1913] Ch. 127.

[70] [1936] 2 K.B. 403.

[71] [1937] 1 K.B. 534.

[72] [1951] A.C. 251.

[73] [1916] 1 K.B. 566.

[74] *Caswell* v. *Powell Duffryn Assoc. Collieries*, 55 T.L.R. 1004.

[75] *Bendall* v. *McWhirter* [1952] 2 Q.B. 466. Overruled in *Nat. Prov. Bank* v. *Ainsworth* [1965] A.C. 1175.

as by Continental judges. Nor would any modern administration of justice be conceivable without the application of equity. The assessment of damages by judge or jury, the choice between a fine and a term of imprisonment from the wide range of punishments between the statutory maximum and minimum, or the exercise of the prerogative of pardon, are among the many illustrations of the application of individualising equity. It means nothing else but the application of considerations of fairness and justice against the letter of the law. The binding force of precedent excludes it for English and American judges to some extent, but not much more than that. Scottish law understands equity essentially in the Continental sense. Stair[76] defines it as:

> the moderation of the extremity of written law and the whole law of the rational nature, for otherwise it could not possibly give remedies to the rigour and extremity of positive law in all cases.

This definition comprises both the Aristotelian definition of equity and the natural law ideal, which has influenced Scottish legal thinking considerably.[77]

There is no separate court of equity in Scotland. The court of Session exercises equitable jurisdiction as a nobile officium, which is directly deduced from Roman law and the office of the Praetor.[78] It enables the court to grant remedies similar to those developed by English equity courts. By means of its nobile officium the Court of Session has also developed a law of trusts. But apart from these and other specific equitable developments the court has the general function of administering all law in the light of equity, which is characteristic of the Continental understanding of that term.[79]

PRIVATE LAW AND ADMINISTRATIVE LAW

Since the work of Dicey, the contrast between Continental systems, which distinguish between administrative law and private law and have a separate system of law courts for each, and the Anglo-American system, which professes to know only one type of law, is familiar to Anglo-American lawyers. No doubt at one time this gave expression to a profound contrast in the attitude taken by the

---

[76] *Institutes,* iv, 3.
[77] *Cf.* Lorimer's *Institutes of Law.* Lord Mansfield, the greatest judicial exponent of natural law, was a Scots lawyer.
[78] Stair, *op. cit.*
[79] *Cf. Encyclopaedia of Laws of Scotland,* article "Equity," pp. 274-279.

two groups of legal systems towards the relations between authority and individual. The English system of equality of all before the law expressed the inherent Anglo-Saxon mistrust of a special law which might give privileges to public authorities against a private citizen. But it is commonplace today that this difference, so eloquently stated by Dicey, is in substance essentially a matter of the past, and that even in his own time it was only partly true. Dicey's doctrine has been so often criticised by jurists and constitutional lawyers[80] that no more than a general reference is needed. There is today a vast body of administrative law in both Britain and the United States, but it has not yet been given a definite place in the legal system whereas administrative law has long been recognised in many Continental countries. It consists of the increasing mass of statutes, orders, regulations, which deal with local government, social insurance and other social legislation, powers delegated to Ministers, ministerial committees, marketing boards, special tribunals, and last but not least, the growing number of public authorities which are independent corporations in form but fulfil a public function in fact, whether under complete government control or with a certain amount of independence. Such bodies as the British Broadcasting Coroporation, the Agricultural Marketing Boards or, in the United States, the Interstate Commerce Commission, the National Labour Relations Board, the Federal Power Commission, the New York Thruway Authority and hundreds of others are, in fact, bodies whose status is governed by public law and which would on the Continent come under administrative jurisdiction. In Britain the constitution of a number of public corporations which operate the nationalised industries and public utilities has greatly widened the scope and importance of public law. Yet there is little sign of a coherent system of administrative jurisdiction.

Numerous statutes, supplemented by Orders in Council, ministerial and other regulations, substitute, for the common law courts, different types of administrative tribunals, although in many cases the executive authorities themselves act as judges. In the United States the controlling power of the Supreme Court, as guardian of the Constitution and the fundamental rights of the citizen, makes it more difficult for such developments to go to the length of a

---

[80] *Cf.* Allen, *Law in the Making,* 507 *et seq.* ; Wade, in Introduction to Dicey, *Law of the Constitution* (10th ed., 1959); Jennings, *Law and the Constitution* (5th ed., 1959); Robson, *Justice and Administrative Law* (3rd ed., 1951); Griffith and Street, *Principles of Administrative Law,* 19-23 (3rd ed., 1963). See also *Law in a Changing Society,* Chap. 11.

curtailment of individual liberties. In Great Britain, Australia, Canada, New Zealand, and in the colonial jurisdictions, the power to do so is confined to the orders which the law courts may issue when an administrative authority or tribunal has acted *ultra vires* or against the principles of natural justice. The main control is exercised not through law courts but through Parliament, which controls the competent Minister or establishes special committees. Not the least important aspect is the filtration of public into private law. The rights and duties of public authorities are determined by a mixture of common law and public law principles.[81]

In the countries of the Anglo-American sphere of law, a deeply engrained individualism struggles against a growing mass of administrative rulings and authorities, whose activities are not subject to control by the ordinary courts. In countries with a written constitution the highest court attempts to maintain a precarious balance, as far as the text of the constitution allows it to do so (U.S.A., Australia, Canada, India, West Germany). In countries without a written constitution this task falls to parliament, as the supreme political control organ. Under both systems the fundamental problem is how to balance the guarantees against official arbitrariness with the need for greater administrative activity and authority which results from the growing function of the state in the regulation of social life. The principal difficulty in subjecting administration to some legal control seems to consist in the problem of finding some independent organ for control of abuse, without giving it a roving commission to enter the field of administration proper.[82]

This very problem has been the principal concern of the *Conseil d'Etat*[83] and other Continental administrative tribunals. The creation of a separate hierarchy of administrative courts has undoubtedly helped to clarify the division between the spheres of public and private law. A legal action must be allocated either to civil or to administrative jurisdiction. The separate publication of decisions by the administrative courts has greatly contributed to the development of a system of administrative law. In the common law countries, on the other hand, the growth of public law has been gradual and surreptitious. Many of the most important public law problems, especially those concerning the legal liability of public

---

[81] See for detailed analysis, *Law in a Changing Society*, Chaps. 4, 12.

[82] See the Report of the Committee on Ministerial Powers, 1932, and the R of the Committee on Administrative Tribunals and Inquiries (1957).

[83] *Cf.* Alibert, 3 Mod.L.Rev. 257 (1940). Hamson, *Executive Discretio Judicial Control* (1954).

authorities, arise in the course of common law actions. This is one reason why the establishment of separate divisions in the ordinary courts may be preferable to the establishment of a separate system of administrative courts. What common law and civil law systems share is a relentless growth of administrative law which demands some systematisation, although the form in which it proceeds may differ from country to country. But it is equally clear that the fundamental issue in all countries is not a technical, but a political one. No "scientific" administrative law can mitigate this fact. In the United States, for example, the fight against administrative discretion is largely the fight of anti-New Dealers against the New Deal. And National Socialism made the distinction of legal and administrative justice in Germany irrelevant.[84]

The reason is again one which transcends the technical differences between legal systems. It is, above all, the increasing measure of public control over the life of the community, over more and more matters which were formerly left to private activity, which in all countries creates an ever-increasing body of public law. The climax is reached in a country like Soviet Russia, where all essential social activities are controlled by the state. Accordingly, some Soviet jurists have argued that in a socialised state all law becomes administration, and law, as understood in Western countries, disappears.[85] An intermediate position exists in all other countries where the increase of state control over economic, social, cultural and other matters creates a corresponding development of legal relations largely different from the relations or notions of private law. Those countries which have a well-established system of public and administrative law find it easier to fit new relations of public law into the legal system. On the other hand, in a totalitarian system the difference between public and private law disappears because all laws become subject to political order and any legal guarantee of individual right disappears. In the Anglo-American world a rapidly growing body of public law waits for a proper place in the legal system. But there is certainly little if any differ-

[84] It is an interesting commentary on the change of juristic opinion in Britain that, of the four Allied Governments controlling Germany, the British Military Government was the most energetic in restoring, in the British zone of occupation, the former German system of administrative courts and in actually extending their jurisdiction by the introduction of the "general clause" according to which the citizen has an action generally in all cases of unlawful infringement of his rights by a public authority, and not only in specifically enumerated cases.

[85] Pashukanis, *Allgemeine Staatslehre und Marxismus* (1927). On the changes and vacillations in Soviet legal theory, cf. above, p. 381 *et seq.*

ence of legal principle left as betwen Continental countries on the one hand and Anglo-American countries on the other. Recent American and British developments indicate a trend towards a system of administrative justice, *e.g.*, in the recommendation of a general appeal on law and fact to an appellate administrative tribunal by the Franks Committee (1957) and the partial implementation of this Report in the Tribunals and Enquiries Act, 1958.

THE NARROWING OF THE GAP

From the discussion of every one of the principal factors which in the past have been alleged to constitute vital differences between Continental and Anglo-American jurisprudence certain conclusions emerge. Broadly speaking, the differences between the systems have either been eliminated, or have lost in significance to the same extent to which common social and political developments have affected countries living under the different systems of law, and as the need to face these problems has overshadowed the difference in legal technique. This teaches us one lesson which lawyers, in times of tranquility and stability, are only too apt to forget: that law is dependent on politics although there is great variety in the degree and form of this dependence. The basis of every legal system depends upon the principles which govern the social order of the country or countries in which it operates. The fact that countries like Britain and Germany both developed into highly industrialised and densely populated countries was bound eventually to have a bigger effect upon their law than the differences in legal tradition and technique, which undoubtedly existed. Notwithstanding all these differences they, like all other countries affected by the same developments, were compelled to produce an immense new body of social legislation, to increase administrative functions and authority, to make judges aware of the social and economic significance of the issues before them; they all had to create a new body of law based on social responsibility rather than individual fault, they had to protect the workmen against the dangers of modern industrial labour, the public against the risks of modern traffic, the consumer against the dangers of modern mass products.

Undoubtedly differences in legal tradition and technique have done much to make these developments occur with different speed and often in different forms. For example, Continental countries have less objection to comprehensive new legislation, whereas under the Anglo-American system courts and Parliament are rivals in the legislative process. But these differences are more and more becoming secondary in importance. In meeting new social problems, Continental countries were technically at an advantage because their legal systems are more the product of modern times and conditions. With the exception of the Napoleonic codes which —young in Anglo-American legal eyes—make up for their comparative age by the breadth of their principles, all Continental codifications date from the latter half of the last or from the present century. They were conceived and framed in awareness of the modern need for rationalisation of the law, and of the social significance of legal principles and administration of justice. Small wonder, therefore, that our discussion reveals a strong movement of Anglo-American legal development towards the Continental technique. It is interesting to note that most of the reports of the English Law Revision Committee, for example, have recommended changes in the law which would bring English law closer to Continental systems (*cf.* the reports on consideration, contributory negligence, joint tortfeasors). On the other hand, Continental property concepts are moving, especially in France, from the conceptual rigidity of the codifications to the more elastic property concepts of Anglo-American law. The introduction of a land register, the gradual recognition of a principle of unjust enrichment, the more friendly attitude taken by the law towards help extended to fellow citizens, all these examples point in the direction of a narrowing of the gap between Anglo-American and civil law systems. It is certainly true of the general tendencies in legal development: of the movement from thinking in terms of procedure to thinking in terms of legal principles, of the increasing weight of statute law in relation to non-statutory law, of the growth of administrative law, of the growing interest in the theory of law. Anglo-American legal traditions, professional particularities and characteristics of race and temperament, have certainly given this development a form largely different from the Continental one. But the increasing pressure of social and economic conditions is bound to reduce the importance of these factors in the law, as it has done in other walks of life.

DIVERGENCE OF SYSTEMS AND INTERNATIONAL LAW

Both the cardinal factors which our inquiry has attempted to bring out—the dwindling of technical divergences between Anglo-American and Continental jurisprudence, and the opening up of the new and deeper gulf between different legal systems according to the political and social principles underlying them—are strikingly illustrated by the development of international law since 1914. When the post-war wave of increased international collaboration, centring around the work of the League of Nations, the International Labour Organisation, the Permanent Court of International Justice, and laid down in numerous bilateral and multilateral treaties, brought about vastly increased legal contacts between different groups of legal systems, it was found that the differences between the Anglo-American and the Continental systems of jurisprudence hardly if ever impeded legal collaboration. But when the political and social revolutions of Russia, Italy, Germany and Japan produced a radical change in the principles of justice underlying the administration of justice in these countries, the resulting split destroyed the basis of international collaboration and law between the countries differing on those principles.

On the whole, international law, as it stood when the war of 1914 broke out, was not too much concerned with questions of municipal law. It was essentially a system of interstate relations, and its rules were confined to legal forms of a kind which are possible between states regardless of their internal social and legal structure. Recent developments however, have revealed a much greater connection between internal and international law, for a twofold reason: in the first place international law was based, partly expressly, partly tacitly, upon a community of fundamental legal values, the disappearance of which has made the continuing functioning of international law largely impossible. In the second place, the steady increase of state control over formerly private matters has produced a corresponding growth of public at the expense of private law, and thus a parallel problem in the international sphere.[86]

That certain legal principles and formulas can be applied in international law as common to all countries, both under the Anglo-American and the Continental systems of law, may be illustrated by the use made of four general legal principles of great importance in modern law[86a]:

---

[86] *Cf.* Friedmann, 19 Brit. Yb. Int'l L. 118 (1938).
[86a] The classical treatment of this subject is Lauterpacht, *Private Law Sources and Analogies of International Law* (1927).

(1) *Clausula rebus sic stantibus.* We are not concerned here with the mischievous use made of this formula as a pretext for the breaking of contractual obligations and full freedom of action. Although discredited in this way, the principle has a place in every important system of law, and in an international society which recognises the rule of law in principle, and seeks for a legal formula to direct the permanent change of conditions of society into lawful channels, it has certainly an important function to fulfill. The various legal systems, Continental and Anglo-American, have developed the principle, under different names. English and American law have developed the doctrines of frustration of contract and of supervening impossibility of performance, from the foundation laid in *Taylor* v. *Caldwell*.[87] German law courts have built up a similar doctrine from certain provisions of the Civil Code as to impossibility of performance, and the general clause directing judges to interpret contracts in accordance with bona fides. From this the German Supreme Court developed the whole doctrine of revaluation of obligations discharged during the German inflation, following the first World War. In France it fell to the *Conseil d'Etat*, in its development of administrative law, to create the doctrine of *imprévision*, as an exception to the principle of strict performance of contractual obligations. The doctrine of revision of contracts in accordance with this principle is also well known to Greek, Italian and Swiss law.

(2) The Anglo-American principle of estoppel expresses the idea that in law a person cannot deny the effect created by his own conduct upon other parties. The principle is often supposed to be a characteristic feature of Anglo-American law but, in fact, the same principle is well known to Continental systems as a type of *exceptio doli* (*venire contra factum proprium*).[88] The universality of the estoppel principle may become an important means of bridging the divergent views (mainly as between developed and underdeveloped countries) on the legal aspects of state promises given to foreign investors.[89]

(3) One of the concrete manifestations of natural law, to Roman

---

[87] (1863) 3 B. & S. 826.

[88] *Cf.*, *Restatement on Restitution*, s. 1, and a German monograph by Riezler, *Venire contra factum proprium*. See McGibbon, "Estoppel in International Law," 7 Int'l Comp. L.Q., 468 (1958).

[89] See further, *Law in a Changing Society*, p. 456 *et seq.*; Fatouros, *Legal Security for Investment* in Friedmann (ed.), *Legal Aspects of Foreign Investment*, 721 (1959).

lawyers, was the principle of unjust enrichment. It found expression in the various *condictiones*, certain rules as to the *peculium*, and in the maxim: *Jure naturae aequum est neminem cum alterius detrimento et injuria fieri locupletiorem* (D. 50, 17, 206). All Continental systems have embodied the principle in some form (*e.g.*, specific provisions in the German, Swiss, Italian, Spanish, Russian Codes, and an almost identical development by French courts.)[90] It is a principle particularly suitable for the solution of many problems where specific provisions fail, embodying as it does the rather elementary principle that none should enrich himself at another person's expense without lawful cause.

Positivist lawyers in England and the United States have in the past prided themselves on the fact that such a principle was unknown to English and American law. It can, however, be strongly argued that this is in fact not the case.[91] The various actions for money had and received, for *quantum meruit* and, in equity, certain principles of constructive trust and of restitution of property, have always been based on the idea of unjust benefit, although until recently, without any systematic cohesion. American law, however, following the investigations of Keener, Ames and others, has more boldly developed, from the same beginnings, a general rule very similar to the Continental one. English law has gone a considerable way towards the same goal, by a number of judicial decisions and with the support of such a principle by Lord Wright, Professor Winfield and others. The Anglo-German Mixed Arbitral Tribunal has repeatedly applied the principle as one of international law, and so has the award in the *Lena Goldfield Case* of 1930.[92]

(4) The principle of "abuse of rights" has attracted some attention, in legislation as well as in legal practice and theory, as one particularly suited to give expression to social duty in the exercise of private right. It is a very elastic principle and can, according to the political background, be stretched so as to nullify private right. It is contained in the law of countries with as widely differing social backgrounds as pre-Nazi Germany, Soviet Russia, democratic France and others. The absence of such a principle in English law

[90] *Cf.* David and Gutteridge, "Unjustified Environment," in 5 Camb.L.J. 240, 223 (1935).

[91] See Friedmann, "The Principle of Unjust Enrichment in English Law," Can.Bar.Rev. 243, 365 (1938); Dawson, *Unjust Enrichment* (1951).

[92] For a discussion of the uses of unjust enrichment as a general principle of law in contemporary international law, especially in the nationalisation of colonial properties in newly independent countries, see The Changing Structure of International Law, 206-210 (1964).

T*

has been based, above all, on the decision in *Bradford* v. *Pickles.*[93]
That decision, like others of the same period, no doubt gave strong
expression to the then prevailing individualism of the common
law. The decision is certainly still good law, and it stands in sharp
contrast to leading French decisions in similar cases; but the tendency expressed in *Bradford* v. *Pickles,* in the *Mogul* case,[94] decided
about the same time, and others, to give the widest possible freedom to the *homo economicus,* as long as he does not use means
specifically condemned by the law, is certainly weakening. Some
decisions on nuisance[95] have made the malicious use of the right
of property the test of nuisance, and the whole development in the
law of tort points to the strengthening of social responsibility as a
concomitant to the use of property.[96] The question at which point
the use of property ceases to be lawful is essentially a matter of
current social morality and public policy, much more than one of
technical legal structure. In so far as Anglo-American law differs
from Continental systems, it is because of a difference in social
policy. In many parts of the law the individualistic attitude of the
older common law is rapidly vanishing (nuisance, rescue cases,
responsibility of employers and manufacturers).

The Permanent Court of International Justice (*e.g.,* Judgement
No. 7) and other international tribunals have repeatedly applied
the doctrine of abuse of rights.[97] In international law the principle
would have a specially wide scope of application, as long as states
are left free to act as they like, unless specifically restricted. The
more fully the extent of the use of individual rights is regulated,
the less need there will be for the application of the general principle of abuse of right. Be that as it may, the principle is bound to
be applied by any system which wishes to restrict the excesses of
individualism. And the weight of academic legal opinion in England
seems to agree on the inclusion of the principle as part of a modern
administration of justice.

But while the steady assimilation of general legal principles
paved the way for a broader basis of international law, the working
of international law presupposes agreement on basic values. If

[93] [1895] A.C. 589.
[94] [1892] A.C. 25.
[95] *e.g., Christie* v. *Davey* [1893] 1 Ch. 316; *Hollywood Silver Fox Farm* v.
Emmett [1936] 2 K.B. 468.
[96] On the acceptance of the principle of abuse of right in American law, see
Prosser, *Handbook of the Law of Torts,* 412 *et seq.* (2nd ed., 1954).
[97] *Cf.* Lauterpacht, *op. cit. supra,* note 85; Schwarzenberger, *International Law,*
333, 344 (3rd ed., 1957).

states are to submit to a judgement on "denial of justice" to a foreigner, they must be able to agree as to the fundamental principles of justice, of fair trial and lack of arbitrariness. If they are to conclude an extradition treaty they must agree on the definition of a political crime. If they are to be bound by common rules of neutrality they must have commensurable systems of State control over private trade, lest there be complete absence of equality of treatment. If they are to be parties to an international labour convention they must agree on labour standards, and so forth.[98] Underlying it is the broad principle that, apart from purely technical matters such as postal conventions, international law—increasingly so, as more and more matters come under public control—demands broad similarity of social values. The existence of such similarity has made intense international collaboration in many fields possible for countries like Great Britain and France, despite the different structure of their legal systems. The absence of such a community has paralysed effective collaboration between Soviet Russia and the West in the United Nations. There are now certain signs that the magnitude of the danger resulting from the unchecked development of nuclear weapons and the race for control of Antarctica and outer space is creating a sufficient community of interest between the Soviet Union and the West to make certain agreements, and a measure of international co-operation, possible on the international control of nuclear explosions and co-operation in the Antarctic region. But these are essentially technical—though vital—matters not touching the divergences of political, social and cultural ideals.[99] It is the extent of community or clash of values, not of techniques, that will determine the rate of progress of international legal order. In this process comparative jurisprudence plays a vital role.

---

[98] *Cf.* the classification in 2 Mod.L.Rev. 208 (1938).
[99] For a discussion of the different levels of international law, see *Law in a Changing Society*, Chap. 15. *The Changing Structure of International Law* (1964), Chap. 6.

CHAPTER 34

CORPORATE PERSONALITY IN THEORY AND PRACTICE

THE principal theories of corporate personality have not been primarily concerned with the solution of legal problems. They have been concerned either with the philosophical explanation of the existence of personality in beings other than human individuals, or with the political interpretation of group personalities of different kinds. The latter type of theories, in particular, has exercised great influence on political theory and practice; but it has been of very limited use in the solution of problems of modern taxation, property transactions or company law.

THE PRINCIPAL THEORIES OF CORPORATE PERSONALITY

It will suffice briefly to restate the principal theories on corporate personality:

(1) The fiction theory, whose most famous exponent is Savigny,[1] and whose principal British advocate is Salmond,[2] regards the legal personality of entities other than human beings as the result of a fiction. "Real" personality can only attach to individuals. States, corporations, institutions, cannot be subjects of rights and persons, but they are treated as if they were persons.

(2) The concession theory though more closely linked with the philosophy of the sovereign national state than the fiction theory is, in some respects, a variant of it, for it asserts that corporate bodies within the state have no legal personality except in so far as it is conceded to them by the "Law," which means the state. This theory is also supported by most of the exponents of the fiction theory, such as Savigny, Salmond and Dicey.[3]

(3) The theory of the *Zweckvermögen*[4] declares that the property

---

[1] *System des heutigen römischen Rechts*, Vol. 2, p. 236 *et seq.*
[2] *Jurisprudence*, para. 113.
[3] *Law of the Constitution* (8th ed.), pp. 87-88.
[4] Associated with the names of Bekker, and, in particular, Brinz (*Pandekten*, Vol. 1, p. 196 *et seq.*).

of juristic persons may be dedicated to, and legally bound by, certain objects, but that they are subjectless property, without an owner. This theory also assumes that only human beings can have rights.

(4) Ihering's theory[5]—philosophically akin to the fiction theory—finds the subjects of the rights of the juristic person in those human beings who are really behind it—the members of a corporation, and the beneficiaries of a foundation (*Stiftung*) which is endowed with legal personality in nearly all Continental laws, although in Anglo-American law they receive different treatment through the concept of trust.

(5) The realist or organic theory, associated, above all, with the name of Gierke[6] and to some extent supported by Maitland,[7] is opposed to all the foregoing theories; for it asserts the real existence of legal persons as the source of their juristic personality. The corporate body is a *reale Verbandsperson*; it does not owe its personality to state recognition; it is not a fictitious legal creation, nor does personality reside in its component members or beneficiaries.

A brief analysis will reveal that all these theories have primarily political significance and that their usefulness for the solution of practical legal problems takes second place. The fiction theory proper is essentially the product of a philosophical conception: of the innate quality of the human person, which gives him *a priori* personality. In Savigny's words:

> All law exists for the sake of the liberty inherent in each individual; therefore the original concept of personality must coincide with the idea of man.[8]

It is therefore hardly correct to assert that "the fiction theory is not a theory at all" but "merely a formula."[9] In its pure form the fiction theory is politically neutral. Its offspring, the concession theory, is, however, an eminently political theory; its principal purpose has been to strengthen the power of the state to deal as it pleases with group associations inside the state. The state alone, though itself a juristic personality, is placed on the same level as the individual. Its personality is really beyond question, and it

---

[5] *Geist des römischen Rechts* (5th ed.), Vols. 2 and 3.
[6] *Das deutsche Genossenschaftsrecht*, 4 vols.; *Das Wesen der menschlichen Verbände* (1902).
[7] Introduction to Gierke's *Political Theories of the Middle Ages* (1900).
[8] *System des heutigen römischen Rechts*, Book 2, para. 60.
[9] Wolff, "On the Nature of Legal Persons," 54 L.Q.Rev. 494, 505 (1938).

bestows on or withdraws legal personality from other groups and associations within its jurisdiction as an attribute of its sovereignty. It is not surprising that the theory was found handy, for example, to justify the confiscation of Church property in the French Revolution and that it underlies the claim of any political dictatorship to prohibit freedom of association. The concession theory is, in fact, the necessary concomitant of any theory of unfettered state sovereignty. It has been shown in another chapter[10] that one of the principal weaknesses in Gierke's theory is his attempt to combine the reality of all corporate groups with the legislative supremacy of the state, by the questionable assertion that the state is a corporate being in itself but, at the same time, comprises, and therefore is superior to, all corporate groups within its sovereignty.

Brinz's theory of the *Zweckvermögen* is closely linked with legal systems which regard the institution of public law (*Anstalt*) and the endowment of private law (*Stiftung*) as legal personalities. For this type of *juristische Person* is not constructed round a group of persons, but round an object and purpose. The perpetuation of a purpose meant to be permanent—for example, a public college, or endowments of the type of the Carnegie Endowment, the Rhodes Trust or the Rockefeller Foundation—is not only a fascinating and fertile idea; it also leads straight to the political mysticism of Hauriou's *"Institution,"*[11] an idea personified so as to claim the loyalty of those who serve it. The link between this conception of *"Institution"* and the Fascist labour theory has been discussed elsewhere in this book.[12]

Anglo-American legal thinking has avoided both the advantages and the dangers of the legal personification of institutions and endowments by the use of trust. A sober property concept, with legal rights and duties arising between the trustees and the beneficiaries for the time being, it replaces the mysticism of an *Unternehmen* or an *institution* which absorbs and dominates the persons connected with it.[13]

At first sight the "Corporation Sole" seems to represent an idea similar to that of the *Anstalt*. But this moribund conception of a single person—such as the Postmaster-General—having legal personality by virtue of his office, has now less juristic and practical significance than the new type of public corporation, whose legal

[10] Above, p. 238 *et seq.*
[11] See above, p. 239 *et seq.*
[12] See above, p. 241.
[13] See above, p. 521 *et seq.*

personality, like that of the *Anstalt*, is not based on an association of persons but the institutionalisation of an enterprise.

The political aspects of the realistic theory far outweigh its purely juristic aspects.

It is closely linked with the "organic" interpretation of the state, the greatest and most powerful of all group associations. This interpretation which, from Rousseau's *volonté générale*, led to the ever greater glorification of the state, and the justification of its claim to absolute obedience of its subjects, in the theories of Hegel and the majority of the Neo-Hegelians,[14] is capable of two alternative developments. One is to assert the "real" character of every group association, with the result that the state is but one, albeit the most powerful, of corporate group personalities. This is the view professed by the Pluralists. The other alternative is that the state, a true Leviathan, engulfs and ultimately absorbs all other associations. This is the development which has, in fact, taken place in all "corporative" and Fascist states. The concession theory is the most suitable justification for this; for it limits the application of the realist or organic conception to the state and subjects all intermediate associations to subordination in the name of the fiction theory.

In vain did Gierke and Jellinek attempt to combine nationalist and liberal ideals, the sovereignty of the state and the right of free association. Jellinek sought to save the right of free association by the "self-limitation" of the state, just as, by the same theory, he wished to combine national sovereignty with international law, while Gierke construed a hierarchy of "real" group persons, of which the state is but the highest and largest. But, as shown below,[15] these compromises are fragile, in logic as in fact.

LIFTING THE VEIL OF CORPORATE PERSONALITY

The ubiquitous use of the limited company in modern commercial life[16] has been the cause of important judicial developments, which also illuminate the nature of legal personality.

---

[14] See above, p. 174 *et seq.*
[15] p. 575 *et seq.*
[16] The problem is now thoroughly discussed in Gower, *Modern Company Law*, Chap. 10 (2nd ed., 1957). For American law, see 18 *Law & Contem. Prob.*, 473 (1953), and see the comparative treatise by Serick, *Rechtsform und Realität juristischer Personen* (1955). Further: Cohn and Simitis, "Lifting the Veil in the Company Laws of the European Countries," 12 Int'l & Comp. L.Q. 189 (1963).

From a practical point of view these cases fall into three groups:

(1) Cases in which it becomes relevant to analyse the "character of a corporate person."
(2) Cases in which the interpretation of a legal obligation or transaction makes it necessary to look at the human individuals covered by the mask of a juristic person.
(3) Cases in which the device of corporate personality is used fraudulently, in particular for the evasion of tax obligations.

These groups present essentially different aspects of one problem: to what extent it is necessary and permissible to "lift the veil" of legal personality, in order to look at the real persons, purposes, intentions covered by the legal form?[17]

The legal problems which have arisen are strikingly similar in countries with as different systems as Great Britain, U.S.A. and Germany.

(1) Two well-known examples are the English *Daimler* case[18] and the American case of *People's Pleasure Park* v. *Rohleder*.[19] In the former a company incorporated in England was held by the House of Lords to be an enemy company for the purpose of "trading with the enemy," because all its shares, and thus the effective control, were in enemy hands. In the latter case the Supreme Court of Appeal of Virginia decided that a covenant providing that title to land should not pass to a coloured person or persons, was not violated where a lease was given to a corporation all the members of which were Negroes. In the former decision the "curtain" was lifted, in the latter it was not. In a more recent decision the House of Lords has again applied the "control" test, deciding that a "commercial residence," *i.e.*, the place where the directors habitually meet, determines the enemy character of a corporation.[20] The United States, which in the First World War had refused to "lift the veil," applied this method more and more during the Second World War, with respect to the enemy character of corporations,

---

[17] On the basis of a study of recent German developments, Serick, *op. cit.*, at 202, concludes: (1) that the corporate form may be disregarded where it is abused for illegal purposes. (2) That human qualities (such as colour, race, enemy character) may be attached to corporate persons where this is compatible with their purpose. (3) That the corporate form may be disregarded, where it disguises the real persons behind it, provided this is relevant to the norm in question.
[18] *Daimler Co.* v. *Continental Tyre Co.* [1916] 2 A.C. 307.
[19] 61 S.E.R. 794 (Virg.).
[20] *V/O Sovfracht* v. *Van Udens Scheepvaart* [1943] A.C. 203.

and it now seems to be firmly established.[21] German Nazi legislation in many instances applied its anti-Jewish measures to companies or other juristic persons defined as "Jewish" by virtue of Jewish participation in capital or management. Correspondingly, the post-war restitution laws were, in certain cases, applied to juristic persons which had been prejudiced as such.[22]

(2) A famous example is the sale, by the sole shareholder of a limited company formed for the purpose of owning and administering land, of the shares. Is this sale to be interpreted as a sale of land, or can the seller avoid obligations arising from defects or incumbrances, by framing a sale of land as a sale of shares? The German Supreme Court has consistently decided that the contract is, for the purpose of claims against the vendor, to be regarded as a sale of land.[23] Many recent English cases have brought up similar problems, with varying results.

The leading case is still *Salomon* v. *Salomon*,[24] which refused to identify a company with its controlling shareholder, so that the latter could claim the preferential rights of a bondholder against the company which was, in reality, himself, to the detriment of genuine creditors. The spirit of this decision which, in Gower's words, has put an "Iron Curtain" between the company and its members, still hovers over recent English decisions, and it appears to be recognised as an authority by American courts. Thus a parent company was not held entitled to deduct its subsidiary's trading losses as a revenue expense from its taxable income,[25] or to claim an insurable interest in the latter's property.[26] On the other hand, a company which takes a lease of premises as residence for its controlling director and shareholder will not have the protection of the Rent Act, for an artificial person cannot be in residence.[27]

But a number of decisions have boldly lifted the veil of corporate personality. Thus, a company was treated as a member of a trade association though, strictly speaking, it was not the company, but

---

[21] See Domke, "The Control of Corporations," 3 Int.L.Q. (1950); *Uebersee Finanz-Korporation* v. *McGrath*, 343 U.S. 205 (1957).

[22] See Serick, *op. cit.*, at 162 *et seq.*

[23] *Cf.* Wolff, *op cit.*, n. 9 above at p. 557, 513.

[24] [1897] A.C. 22.

[25] *Smith, Stone and Knight* v. *Birmingham Corp.*, 161 L.T. 371.

[26] *General Accident Corp.* v. *Midland Bank* [1940] 2 K.B. 338.

[27] *Lee* v. *K. Carter* [1949] 1 K.B. 85 (C.A.). On this "boomerang" effect of corporate entity, see Kahn-Freund (1943) M.L.R. at p. 56.

In *Re F. G. (Films), Ltd.* [1953] 1 W.L.R. 483, the court refused to recognise a film made by a small British company controlled by a U.S. company as "British."

the nominee who was registered as a member[28]; the Privy Council held a valid covenant in restraint of trade to be violated where the covenantors had acquired a controlling interest in a competing company.[29]

The result, at least in English law, is inconclusive. Sometimes the strict formalism of *Salomon's* case prevails, sometimes corporate form is disregarded and the economic purpose of a transaction analysed.

(3) Cases where the corporate form has been used for fraud and, in particular, for tax evasion, are, in principle, a specific category of the kind of situations analysed under (2). But owing to the stronger impulse not to allow incorporation to be used for fraud or tax evasion, legislative and judicial trends have been more consistent. The main instrument of fraud is, of course, the one-man company; the relations between principal and subsidary, or between holding and affiliated companies also figure prominently in legal cases. Thus, a German statute of 1919 makes the sale of shares of a one-man company owning land subject to the same tax as is due by the sale of land itself. The Fundamental Tax Law of 1919, by a general formula, enables the judge to counter transactions whose main object is tax avoidance. German law courts have applied this principle fairly resolutely. A number of English statutes also give powers to disregard the corporate entity where it is used as a device for tax evasion.[30] The courts, owing probably to the *Salomon* case, have been vacillating. On one hand. the Privy Council has disregarded corporate form in refusing to treat a transaction between a parent company and its subsidiary as a sale for the purposes of a Canadian taxing statute[31]; on the other hand, the Canadian Revenue was not held entitled, "in the absence of fraud or improper conduct," to treat two closely associated companies as one for the purpose of fixing the proper amount of depreciation allowance.[32] A significant advance towards "lifting the veil" was made in the *Malvern* School case[33] where the court held that a company (for purposes of exemption from the development charge under the Town and Country Planning Act) held property on charitable trusts if all its shares were so held and its governing body

[28] *Liverpool Corn Trade Ass.* v. *Hurst* [1936] 2 All E.R. 309.
[29] *Connors Bros.* v. *Connors* [1940] 4 All E.R. 179.
[30] *e.g.*, Finance Acts 1937, s. 14; 1938, s. 41; 1939, s. 38.
[31] *Canada Rice Mills* v. *R.* [1939] 3 All E.R. 991.
[32] *Pioneer Laundry* v. *Min. of Nat. Revenue* [1937] 3 All E.R. 555.
[33] *The Abbey Malvern Wells, Ltd.* v. *Ministry of Town and Country Planning* [1951] Ch. 728.

were the trustees. But in *Ebbw Vale U.D.C.* v. *South Wales Traffic Board*,[34] where a transport company was wholly owned by the British Transport Commission, the Court of Appeal took the very formalistic view that a service supplied by its subsidiary was not a service provided by the Transport Commission. A decisive advance towards the "piercing the veil" theory, and away from the *Salomon* case, was made through the adoption of the test of effective control as against legal form, in the new British nationalisation statutes, which define identity or separation of corporate bodies by the effective dependence which follows from control, through shareholdings or control of board appointments.[35] The Companies Act, 1948, ss. 150-153, prescribes group accounts for holding and subsidiary companies, so as to give a true view of the financial situation of the group.

American law has had to face all these problems earlier and on a vaster scale, owing mainly to the scope of business enterprise and its use of the limited liability advantages of the corporation. The juristic result is not much more definite than in English law. The cases in which the courts may choose to disregard corporate entity were summed up as early as 1912 by Professor Wormser[36] as being the use of the corporate device to defraud creditors, to evade existing obligations, to circumvent a statute, to achieve or perpetuate a monopoly, or to protect knavery or crime. To these a second group of rather miscellaneous cases may be added where the corporate form will be disregarded "when it is necessary to promote justice or to obviate inequitable results."[37] It is certain that, with the help of these principles, the veil of corporate entity is often pierced; but it remains a matter of uncertainty and individual judicial discretion, when this is done. Where incorporation is clearly used to evade a statute or another public obligation, courts will now usually pierce the veil, as in *U.S.* v. *Lehigh Valley Railroad Co.*[38] where a railway company attempted to evade a statute prohibiting the transport of coal mined by the transport company itself, by acquiring all the shares of a coal company whose coal it was carrying. It is more difficult to determine the limits up to which incorporation may be used by an individual to shield behind the

[34] [1951] 2 K.B. 366.
[35] *e.g.*, Thirteenth Schedule to Transport Act, 1947. See also s. 154, Companies Act, 1948.
[36] Wormser, "Piercing the Veil of Corporate Entity," 12 Col.L.Rev. 496, 517 (1912).
[37] Fuller, 51 Harv.L.Rev. 1373, 1402 (1938).
[38] 220 U.S. 257 (1911).

limited liability of a corporation. In the vast majority of cases, incorporation effectively limits liability; a sole shareholder may claim against the company, like any other creditor, in accordance with the *Salomon* case; but there are many cases in which the real identity has been judicially recognised. Thus the principal shareholder of a company was held liable for breach of an employment contract which he had made individually, as the business had continued on the same lines and on the same personal basis.[39] Parent corporations have been held liable for the debts of subsidiaries where the resources of the latter were grossly inadequate for the normal strain of business.[40] A U.S. District Court held that a complaint which alleged that 100 corporations each owning two taxicabs and carrying the minimum amount of insurance required by state law were formed to defraud the public gave sufficient grounds to state a claim against the individual stockholders.

"The sanctity of a separate corporate identity is upheld only insofar as the entity is consonant with the underlying policies which give it life. . . ."[41]

One-man companies have been held to be bound by the contracts of their sole shareholder as *"alter ego."*[42] In some actions against a one-man corporation, the sole shareholder was permitted to set off a private claim against the plaintiff.[43] The testamentary disposition of corporate property by a sole shareholder has been given effect where the incorporation was merely a business expedient for individual operations and corporate existence would not survive the testator.[44] A debt due to the parent company from its subsidiary was postponed and made junior to the rights of outside stockholders in the subsidiary, on the ground the two companies formed a combined enterprise and the contribution made by the parent, though in form a loan, was in fact an equity investment.[45] More recently a group of individuals, who had formed a corporation for the specific purpose of purchasing controlling interests in a number of banks, were held personally liable for the judgement obtained

---

[39] *Wittman* v. *Whittingham*, 85 Cal.App. 140.

[40] Cases in Latty, *Subsidiary and Affiliated Corporations*, 110 *et seq.* (1936).

[41] *Mull* v. *Colt Co.*, 31 F.R.D. 159, 166 (1962). But see, for a contrary decision, where the defendant was the principal shareholder of 10 "two cab" corporations, *Walkovszky* v. *Carlton*, 19 N.Y. 2d 414 (1966).

[42] Cases quoted in Warner Fuller, *loc. cit.* p. 1388, note 58.

[43] Fuller, *loc. cit.* note 86.

[44] See cases quoted by Fuller, note 101.

[45] *Taylor* v. *Standard Gas and Electric Corp.*, 306 U.S. 307 (1939); (Deep Rock case).

by the receiver against one of the banks, which had failed.[45a]

Such cases are countered by countless others, where the corporate form is upheld against attempts to "lift the curtain." A recent American survey of the liability of a corporation for acts of a subsidiary or affiliate[46] concludes that:

the law will generally treat an effectively formed corporation as a distinct legal entity. In certain cases, however, the liability of a corporation may be fully transferred to a controlling individual stockholder, or to a corporation controlled by substantially the same interests.

This survey criticises the failure of consistency and reasoning in the decisions so that there is little predictability.

The conclusion on the meaning of corporate personality, as formulated by an American jurist in 1938, could equally apply to any other modern legal system:

The emphasis . . . is progressively less and less upon the corporation as having a preordained nature and more and more upon the underlying social, economic and moral factors as they operate in and through it.[47]

It is indicative of the relativist approach to the problem that the corporate fiction is disregarded for certain purposes only, against those who wish to use the corporate form as veil, but that they themselves are not allowed to discard the corporate form for their own benefit. Thus, the House of Lords decided in *Macaura* v. *Northern Assurance Co.*[48] that a corporator holding all shares has no insurable interest in chattels belonging to the company. The German Reichsgericht has held that a trade mark registered in favour of a company cannot be used by another company, all the shares of which belong to the first company.[49] A U.S. Court of Appeals held that the sole owner of a corporation was not entitled to refuse to produce corporate records subpoenaed by the Internal Revenue Service on the basis of his personal constitutional privileges under the Fourth and Fifth Amendments.[50]

CRIMINAL LIABILITY OF CORPORATIONS

Finally the problem of criminal liability of corporations illustrates the increasingly relative and functional interpretation of corporate

---

[45a] *Anderson* v. *Abbott*, 321 U.S. 349 (1944).
[46] 71 Harv.L.Rev. 1122 (1958).
[47] Fuller, "The Incorporated Individual," 51 Harv.L.Rev. 1373.
[48] [1925] A.C. 619.
[49] 114 *Civil Decisions*, 278. [50] *Hair Ind. Ltd.* v. *U.S.*, 340 F. 2d 510 (1965).

personality.[51] In a number of recent cases, contrary to earlier authorities, corporations have been held criminally liable for the actions of certain persons acting on their behalf. Thus, in *D. P. P.* v. *Kent and Sussex Contractors, Ltd.*[52] the transport manager of a company had sent in false returns for the purpose of obtaining petrol coupons. The Divisional Court held that the company, "by the only people who could act or think for it," had committed the offence. The Court of Criminal Appeal, in *R.* v. *C. R. Haulage, Ltd.*,[53] held a company guilty of common law conspiracy to defraud where its managing director and nine other persons had conspired to charge another company for a quantity of goods in excess of that which was in fact delivered. In a third case, *Moore* v. *Bresler, Ltd.*,[54] a company was convicted for acts committed by the secretary of the company who was a branch manager, and the branch sales manager, which were not authorised by the directors. The leading American case is *U.S.* v. *Dotterweich*,[55] where both the corporation and its president were convicted for adulteration of drugs (Food, Drug and Cosmetics Act) by a strongly divided court. In principle, therefore, the imputability of a crime, other than a purely administrative offence, to a corporation has now been admitted in several decisions. But which test is to determine when the corporation itself becomes involved? The test accepted in German law, and approved by Lord Haldane in *Lennard's case*,[56] is the distinction between those who are the *alter ego* of the company or, in German legal terminology, its *Organe*, and those who are merely employees or servants.[57] The border-line cannot always be a clear one. In a commercial company, for example, it is not easy to decide whether the management, the shareholders' meeting, the board of directors, or all or some of them acting in conjunction, represent the company. This problem must be answered by the court pragmatically, from case to case. In a different manner, the problem of criminal liability of a corporation arose in the Australian case of *Cain* v. *Doyle*.[58] Here the question was whether the Crown, in right of the Commonwealth

---

[51] This has been very ably discussed by Welsh, "The Criminal Liability of Corporations," 62 L.Q.Rev. 345 (1945).
[52] [1944] K.B. 146.
[53] [1944] K.B. 551.
[54] [1944] 2 All E.R. 515.
[55] 320 U.S. 277 (1943).
[56] *Lennard's Carrying Company* v. *Asiatic Petroleum Co.* [1915] A.C. 713.
[57] "The Model Penal Code (Draft No. 4) of the American Law Institute adopts the term "high managerial agent" for policy-making officers.
[58] (1946) 72 C.L.R. 409; the case is fully discussed in *Law and Social Change*, Chap. 5.

of Australia, could be indicted for an offence under a repatriation Act specifically declared applicable to the Crown. The majority of the court held that the Crown could not commit a crime against itself and declined to hold it indictable, but a dissenting minority saw no reason why the Crown, within the limits of practical possibility, should not be held accountable under the provisions of a statute, for example, by the imposition of a fine.

The conclusion of *Welsh* is that

where the only punishment which the court can impose is death, penal servitude, imprisonment or whipping, or a punishment which is otherwise inappropriate to a body corporate, such as a declaration that the offender is a rogue and a vagabond, the court will not stultify itself by embarking on a trial which, if the verdict of guilty is returned, no effective order by way of sentence can be made.

This obviously would not apply to fines imposed on the Crown or any other corporation. The general conclusion is that a corporation can be indicted but that whether the criminal act of an agent can be imputed to the company must depend upon

the nature of the charge, the relative position of the officer or agent, and the other relevant facts and circumstances of the case.[59]

Thus far it is obvious that a strongly formalistic and rigid interpretation of the corporate form is increasingly giving way to a more sociological and relativist interpretation. It is particularly marked in cases where the corporate form is apt to be used as a device to frustrate the public interest in the collection of taxes or the statutory restraint of abuses; it is, on the whole, more clearly marked in Continental and American as compared with English legal development, owing probably to the authority of the *Salomon* case; but the tendency is universal.

THE UNINCORPORATED ASSOCIATION AND CORPORATE PERSONALITY

The basis of the distinction between incorporated and unincorporated associations would, at first sight, appear to consist in the very fact of legal personality. Yet in English law, on a closer analysis, the distinction appears very fragile.[60] Unincorporated associations

---

[59] *Op. cit.* note 51, above
[60] The notion that there are but two kinds of suitable entities in law, the "individual human being and the corporation" has been criticised by Professor Ford in his valuable study of "Unincorporated non-Profit Associations," 115 (1959).

of a "quasi-corporate" type, such as trade unions, have been declared liable for torts of their servants by the *Taff Vale* case,[61] which thus blurs the distinction between the corporation—liable, at any rate, for the *intra vires* torts of its servants—and the unincorporated association, not so liable. In a later case[62] Scott L.J. suggested that a trade union had all the powers of a *persona juridica* except those solely characteristic of a natural person, and those expressly expected by the creating statute. And in *Bonsor* v. *Musicians' Union*,[63] the House of Lords adopted some robust constructions to award the plaintiff damages against his union, an unincorporated association. In two very recent decisions, a trustee savings bank was held to be suable as a "quasi-corporation"[64] and the Central Council for University Admissions (U.C.C.A.), an unincorporated association, as a "separate entity" for the purposes of the Landlord and Tenant Act, 1954.[65] In the United States the courts have often granted remedies against unincorporated unions, which for certain purposes are expressly deemed to be legal persons.[66] An unincorporated association may not sue or be sued in its own name; a representative action is permitted, actively and passively, by Ord. 16, r. 32, but the courts do not easily admit the "common interest" which must be proved to bring or defend a representative action on behalf of the members. Members of unincorporated associations, such as clubs, are only bound to the extent of their express or implied contractual commitments[67]; but the submission, by a joining member, to standard rules embodied in the contract, achieves substantially the same result as the submission of a member of a limited company to the memorandum and articles of association. The internal autonomy of an unincorporated, as of an incorporated, association in regard to the treatment of its members is complete, subject only to a right of interference by the courts, where "natural justice" is violated.[68] Unincorporated, like incorporated associations, have a "reputation"; registered trade unions and friendly societies can sue and be

[61] [1901] A.C. 426.

[62] *N.U.G.M.W.* v. *Gillian* [1946] K.B. 81.

[63] [1956] A.C. 104.

[64] *Knight and Searle* v. *Dove* [1964] 2 Q.B. 631, 643.

[65] *Willis* v. *Assoc. of Universities of the British Commonwealth* [1965] 1 Q.B. 140.

[66] See the discussion in Summers' "Legal Limitations on Union Discipline," 64 Harv.L.Rev. 1049 (1951).

[67] *Wise* v. *Perpetual Trustee* [1903] A.C. 139.

[68] *Weinberger* v. *Inglis* [1919] A.C. 606; *McLean* v. *Workers' Union* [1929] 1 Ch. 402. On recent decisions extending judicial supervision, see p. 484 *et seq.*

sued in defamation.[69] Ordinary unincorporated societies cannot use the representative action of Ord. 16, r. 9, but a libel directed against the society may be a ground of action for the members, jointly, or in some cases individually.[70]

Nor is there any objection, in principle, to the indictment of unincorporated associations. Thus, the Road Traffic Act, 1934 (section 26), defines as "society" "any association of persons whether incorporated or not."[71]

The difficult question of the property of the unincorporated association, which in theory cannot be held by the association as such, is solved by vesting the property in one or several trustees.[72] It is true that an unincorporated association cannot be held liable for the torts of its agents; but the liability of the corporation, too, is severely limited by the *ultra vires* theory which still prevails.[73] On the whole, subsequent developments have underlined Maitland's dictum that

it would not . . . be easy to find anything that a corporation could do and that is not being done by this *nicht rechtsfähiger Verein*.[74]

Were it otherwise the Inns of Court and many famous clubs could hardly continue to be unincorporated, although charitable and non-profit-making associations now increasingly prefer incorporation as companies limited by guarantee, or, in the United States, as foundations. Maitland concluded that "morally there is most personality where legally there is none."[75] It would, perhaps, be truer to say that legal personality is not absolute, that it can exist to a smaller or greater degree. The commercial partnership

---

[69] See discussion and cases quoted in Gatley, *Libel and Slander* 460, (3rd ed.).

[70] *Cf.* Lloyd, *Law of Unincorporated Associations*, 155 (1938).

[71] But see *Wurzel* v. *Houghton Main Delivery Services* and *Wurzel* v. *Atkinson* [1937] 1 K.B. 380.

[72] The trust device is not entirely satisfactory in all cases, as compared with the *Ansalt* as a juristic person. In the *Free Church Case* [1904] A.C. 515, the trust deed, in the view of the majority of the Lords, prevented the property from being used in accordance with the will of the majority of the living members of the Church. "The dead hand of the law fell with a resounding slap upon the living body of the Church" (Maitland). The trust device is adequate for property matters, but it fails to give expression to the needs of a living institution behind the trust deed.

[73] Although it is convincingly attacked by Salmond (10th ed., s. 15). In German law, the distinction between an "Organ" representing the juristic person and a servant, acting within limited authority, serves to make both incorporated and unincorporated associations liable for torts. Salmond uses the same distinction for English law. This view finds strong support in Lord Haldane's speech in *Lennard's Co.* v. *Asiatic Petroleum Co.* [1915] A.C. 713.

[74] Maitland, *Selected Essays*, 194 (1936).

[75] *Id.* at 201.

of German law, for example, is, in certain respects, treated like a juristic person; it can make contracts with a partner, sue and be sued by him, become bankrupt. English law, too, though less emphatically, treats the partnership as distinct from the partners by allowing, for example, actions between the partnership and a partner. The Ghana Company Act of 1964 establishes an incorporated partnership, a suitable legal form for the many small and personal business enterprises prevailing in many less developed countries.

The relativity of corporate personality, both in quantity and quality, thus is demonstrated by the modern treatment of incorporated associations as well as the status of unincorporated associations. "Between the two extremes of an unincorporated club or society and the corporation there are many hybrids which, though formally unincorporated, possess a greater or lesser number of the attributes of a corporation."[76]

Is it possible to deduce any general principle from this bewildering variety of empirical solutions to a very complex problem? Berle sees the unifying principle in the concept of "economic enterprise."[77]

Whenever corporate entity is challenged the court looks at the enterprise. . . . The nature of the enterprise determines the result, negativing the corporate personality or any other form of organisation of that enterprise. . . . The courts disregard the corporate fiction specifically because it has parted company with the enterprise-fact for whose furtherance the corporation was created; and having got that far, they then take the further step of ascertaining what is the actual enterprise-fact and attach the consequences of the act of the component individuals or corporations to that enterprise-entity, to the extent that the economic outlines of the situation warrant or require.

Wedderburn,[78] after an analysis of the many recent English decisions which have treated unincorporated associations as legal entities, asks whether the time has not come "for the 'representative action,' the unincorporated 'association,' the 'entity,' the 'quasi-corporation,' the 'near-corporation' . . . to be covered by a general statute concerning procedure and rights in respect of actions by and against all 'bodies' which are not within the conventional boundaries of corporations"?

---

[76] Gower, *op. cit.* at 61. And see Ford, *op. cit.*, passim.
[77] Berle, "The Theory of Enterprise Entity," 47 Colum L. Rev. 343, 348 (1947).
[78] "Corporate Personality and Social Policy: The Problem of the Quasi-Corporation," 28 Mod. L. Rev. (1965).

CORPORATE PERSONALITY—THEORY AND REALITY

What is the relation of these important juristic developments to the theories of corporate personality?

The adherents of the fiction theory can point to the absurdity of a "group will," a "collective consciousness" in the case of the thousands of one-man companies or other companies founded merely for the purpose of trading with limited liability. But realists can point to the extent to which unincorporated associations, such as many trade unions, clubs, colleges and guilds, with a strong corporate life, enjoy legal personality, despite the absence of formal incorporation; a fact which discredits, in particular, the concession theory.[79] Does the inquisitiveness which induces modern courts, in so many countries, to "lift the veil" of corporate personality, confirm the fiction or the organic theory? It confirms and repudiates both. It may be said that the corporate form is treated as mere fiction, to be used or discarded at will. It is equally true that this development means the recognition of the social reality behind the juristic form. Finally, the theory of the *Zweckvermögen* recognises the reality of the permanence of an impersonal institution, devoted to a particular objective, beyond the coming and going of members and executives, and this is certainly as true of the Carnegie Endowment or the Rhodes Trust as it is of the Zeiss works (constituted as a *Stiftung*). It has also been shown[80] that the company limited by guarantee in modern English law and the foundation in modern American law increasingly fulfil the purposes of the *Stiftung*.

While each of these theories contains elements of truth, none can by itself adequately interpret the phenomenon of juristic personality. The reason is that corporate personality is a technical legal device, applied to a multitude of very divers aggregations, institutions and transactions, which have no common political or social denominator, whereas each of the many theories has been conceived for a particular type of juristic personality.[81] None of them foresaw the extent to which the device of incorporation would be used in modern business.

Modern jurists seem increasingly inclined to overcome the dilemma, by reducing the concept of juristic personality to a technical

---

[79] This is overlooked by M. Wolff, in his defence of the fiction theory, "On the Nature of Legal Persons," 54 L.Q. Rev. 505 *et seq.* (1938).

[80] Above, p. 569, *Law in a Changing Society*, p. 288 *et seq.*

[81] *Cf.* now Serick, *op. cit.* at 222: "The juristic person of civil law is what the legal order makes of it."

device. Some analytical jurists, like Kelsen[82] and Kocourek,[83] stress the technical and relative character of the concept of personality. Others stress the distinction between physical and juristic reality.

The conception of corporate personality expresses a juristic reality, . . . nothing more and nothing less, although its reality is, nevertheless, rooted in its reference to the world of empirical fact.[84]

Legal personality . . . is a juristic creation . . . but it does not follow that it is not something real. . . . If we ascribe reality to the general body of law, . . . we must equally ascribe it to the essential elements of law . . . thought and willed into permanent being by the same agency.[85]

"Analogy with a living person and shift of meaning are . . . of the essence of the mode of legal statement which refers to corporate bodies."[86]

The result teaches an important lesson: it is not that legal theory is irrelevant to legal practice, but that the legal theory and the legal practice of corporate personality have developed independently of each other. The task of legal theory is to explore the ultimate foundations of legal systems and institutions, and to pursue them into the manifold practical and specific situations and problems that arise. In a totalitarian system the concession theory obviously has much greater force than in a liberal system which allows freedom of association. The organic character of the state is largely dependent on the function which it exercises in society, just as the medieval guild and the limited company are not social or legal phenomena of the same order.

---

[82] *Cf.* above, p. 280.

[83] Kocourck, *Jural Relations*, p. 57 *et seq.*

[84] Hallis, *Corporate Personality*, 240.

[85] Barker, Introduction to Gierke, *Natural Law and the Theory of Society*, p. lxxvi.

[86] Hart, "Definition and Theory in Jurisprudence" 70 L.Q. Rev. 37, 59 (1954).

Legal Theory and International Society

CHAPTER 35

STATE SOVEREIGNTY AND INTERNATIONAL ORDER

THE desire and struggle of man for a law which is impartial and objective is as old and persistent as the desire of those who hold the power to use the law as an instrument of domination. Many controversies fought out under the name of such principles as state supremacy, the rule of law, or the natural rights of the individual have, in fact, been struggles between rival organisations and interests for power.

The copious literature on the subject has, to no inconsiderable extent, been caused by a desire of most legal writers to hide the essentially political character of the questions behind legal argument. There have been those writers who set out to prove the absolute sovereignty, first of a monarch, later of the state; there are those on the other side, who have fought the law-making monopoly of the state on behalf of corporate bodies within the state, such as estates, churches, corporations. Again, other writers have proclaimed inalienable rights of the individual against all interference by authority; finally, the fight between national and international sovereignty is a persistent theme of juristic controversy.

A brief survey of the principal theories will show the relation between legal theory and political ideology.

PRINCIPAL THEORIES OF STATE SOVEREIGNTY

In various ways, but essentially with the same object, the doctrine of absolute state sovereignty has been put forward by Bodin, Hobbes, Ihering and a powerful school of modern jurists, especially in Germany.

The early writers state the principle ruthlessly and without compromise: in the nineteenth century a certain restraint is noticeable as liberal and constitutional ideas grow. Modern totalitarian doctrines revert to an uncompromising restatement of the older doctrine adapted to modern circumstances. Bodin, the founder of the modern doctrine of sovereignty, was mainly concerned with securing and consolidating the legislative power of the monarch in France against the rival claims of estates, corporations, and the Church. He largely identified, in accordance with the conditions then prevailing, the state with those in power. A state differs from other communities through the presence of *summa potestas*. This, although inherent in the nature of the state, rests in the individuals who in fact possess supreme power. One aspect of sovereignty is the power to make law as a means of making the sovereign's will effective, and Bodin therefore largely equates law with statute. Like all champions of state power, Bodin denies custom the force of law until it has received the confirmation of the sovereign.

Stripped of some medieval accessories Bodin's theory is re-affirmed by Hobbes and strengthened in so far as Hobbes recognises no limitation at all upon the absolute law-making power of the sovereign. No principle of natural law, but only the ability to govern effectively limits the absolute power of the ruler.

Austin, by clarifying the concepts both of sovereignty and of law, and by his sharp distinction between the science of legislation and the science of law, formulated the legal philosophy of the modern national state, with its claim to undisputed sovereignty. Ihering linked the power of the modern state firmly with the notion of law when he defined the latter as "Security of the conditions of social life procured by the power of the state." Building on Ihering, the majority of jurists, in the latter half of the nineteenth century, parallel with the powerful expansion of a new nationalist German state, developed the doctrine of absolute state sovereignty but tried to blend it with the equally powerful doctrine of the *Rechtsstaat* which protects individual rights and also favours restraint in international relations.

NATIONAL SOVEREIGNTY AND INTERNATIONAL LAW

The nineteenth century, while witnessing the triumph of the sovereign national state, also brought increasing international contacts, and thus made it more than ever necessary to establish international law on a firm basis. Customs and treaties, as the principal sources of international law in the absence of a sovereign international legislator, multiplied rapidly. But the question of legal supremacy, the juristic corollary to the political choice between an international society of sovereign and warring states, and an international community with authority over national states, remained to be solved.

The predominant, dualistic view argued that international and municipal law differed fundamentally, as the former regulated relations between equal and sovereign states without authority and power of enforcement, whilst the latter was concerned with relations between the state and the individuals subject to its authority. It follows from this doctrine that international law can never, as such, be part of municipal law, but must be specifically adopted in every case by the proper state authorities. It was inevitable that every advocate of this theory had to attempt a theoretical and political compromise between the sovereignty of the national state and the respect due to international law. Four well-known theories will be briefly discussed as representative of this trend of thought.

Jellinek[1] attempts a solution by the doctrine of the self-limitation of the state. According to this theory the sovereign state consents to observe the customary rules of international conduct on one hand, and the subjective rights of the subject on the other hand. In cases of conflict between state sovereignty and international order, Jellinek's theory is, however, bound to come down on the side of state sovereignty; for in the absence of a superior norm and authority, the state can revoke its voluntary self-limitations, internally by altering the constitutional functions of its organs, internationally by revoking its voluntary observation of rules of conduct. Only considerations of ethics or, more frequently, of balance of power and political tactics, may impose restraint.

Triepel[2] sees the validity of international law in the fact that the agreements made between states merge into an objective body of conventions, which states are then no longer free to repudiate. Anzilotti,[3] reviving in its essential features the theory of Grotius, without its natural law flavour, seeks to save the validity of international law by the universal recognition of the principle of *pacta sunt servanda*. Both theories go some way towards recognising a legal value superior to the will of states, but shrink from facing the full implication of a limitation of national sovereignty by international authority.

The most ambitious attempt at theoretical compromise, the theory of Del Vecchio,[4] admits that the freedom of will (an aspect of sovereignty) of the state seems to imply the negation of international

---

[1] *Allgemeine Rechtslehre* (1905).
[2] *Völkerrecht und Landesrecht* (1899).
[3] *Corso di diritto Internazionale* (3rd ed., 1928).
[4] *Lehrbuch der Rechtsphilosophie* (German ed., 1937).

law. But on the other hand, principles of natural law, that is reason, demand that men should associate with each other and recognise each other as equal. The same principle of reason, Del Vecchio argues, demands the mutual recognition of states as equals. Jumping from a logical to a sociological argument, Del Vecchio then asserts that real sovereignty can only exist if each state recognises the existence of others as equal. The actual collision between national and international law is glossed over by the argument that legal systems may have different degrees of "positivity," which apparently means effectiveness. Several systems have historical reality and this actual plurality defies the logical demand for unity. There is a logical inconsistency in this theory. In so far as reason demands international law, it must be superior over national laws, as Grotius had pointed out. But the justification of the coexistence of both national law and international law is possible only by the abandonment of logical argument in favour of an empirical estimate of power. For this alone is the meaning of "different degrees of positivity."

The theories justifying the coexistence of national sovereignty and international law have been attacked both from nationalist and internationalist quarters.

The nationalist theory is advanced by Erich Kaufmann,[5] who considers the binding force of international law as incompatible with state sovereignty and declares for the latter. This is essentially a continuation of the doctrine of Hegel, who considers that neither mankind nor a family of nations has reality. The state, to Hegel, is the ultimate unit, and nations join hands only through their contribution to world history. Neo-Hegelian legal philosophers, like Gentile, Binder, Larenz, reinforce the power of the state by the doctrine of the mission of the nation, for which the way had been paved by Fichte, Treitschke and Savigny.

The incompatibility of national sovereignty and international order, which Kaufmann had proved from a nationalistic angle, is argued for the opposite purpose, by the "monistic" school, led by Kelsen. In his *Problem der Souveränität*, Kelsen shows that the alleged differences of sources, spheres and objects in municipal law on one hand, and international law on the other hand, is a fallacy. Both have the same ultimate object: of regulating the conduct of individuals and of enforcing the legal order by sanction. Conse-

---

[5] *Clausula rebus sic stantibus und das Völkerrecht* (1911).

quently, there is a clear alternative between the supremacy of national and international law. There can either be a number of sovereign states, each claiming to be the highest authority, or an international authority, superior in law to the national states. Equality of states can only be derived from a superior authority.[6] Following Kelsen, Verdross[7] and Lauterpacht[8] have demonstrated the logical completeness of international law, even where it has not yet evolved a concrete rule, and Lauterpacht has proved the logical fallacy of the distinction between "legal" and "political" disputes —a distinction which affords a convenient disguise for liberty of action by any state which chooses to regard a particular dispute as "political" (*i.e.*, important) rather than "legal" (*i.e.*, not so important).

The proponents of this monistic theory have obscured their case by attempting to prove that the existing system of international law provides sanctions as weapons of authority in the form of war and reprisals,[9] surely the very symbols of international anarchy—or of international servitude,[10] or that English law, despite overwhelming authority to the contrary, incorporates international law as such.[11]

Both the League of Nations Covenant and the United Nations Charter, representing a society of nations that is aware of the need for international organisations but unwilling to surrender the essentials of national sovereignty are compromises.

The United Nations Charter starts with the ambiguous formula that the Organisation is based on the "sovereign" equality of all its members (Article 2). In so far as the Charter provides for majority decisions in the General Assembly by a simple, or, on "important questions" by a two-thirds majority of the members, it marks a definite advance over the unanimity principle of the League Covenant. But the powers of the Assembly include only "recommendations" with respect to the maintenance of international peace and security. The Security Council is the authority which determines the existence of threats to the peace or acts of aggression. Its decisions on matters other than procedural must

---

[6] For the details of Kelsen's doctrine, see above, Chap. 24.

[7] *Die Einheit des rechtlichen Weltbildes* (1923).

[8] *The Function of Law in the International Community* (1933).

[9] Kelsen, in the writings discussed above, p. 279.

[10] Verdross, *Die Verfassung der Völkerrechtsgemeinschaft* (1926).

[11] Lauterpacht, "Is International Law Part of the Law of England?," Grotius Society 51 (1939).

include the concurring vote of all the permanent members, *i.e.*, of each of the big Powers, although a party to a dispute endangering international peace and security must abstain from voting. This make decisions possible which condemn a big Power as aggressor. But such a decision would remain theoretical; for any enforcement action is subject to veto by a permanent member of the Security Council, whether a party to a dispute or not. Moreover, effective action depends on an integrated International Security Force, and negotiations for the establishment of such a Force have failed to produce agreement on the fundamental problems of an international command, international bases and effective international control over the Force. In the vital field of executive police action the principle of national sovereignty thus prevails. Nor is international sovereignty established in the juridical sphere. The jurisdiction of the International Court of Justice is no more compulsory than that of the former Permanent Court of International Justice.

Slight progress towards international sovereignty appeared to result from the "Optional Clause," by which over thirty states (not including the Soviet *bloc*) have bound themselves to submit certain categories of legal disputes to the International Court of Justice. However, the value of these declarations is largely neutralised by the reservation of disputes regarded as domestic, in the opinion of the signatory.

The split between the U.S.S.R. and the other permanent members of the Security Council which all but paralysed the Council, led to an increasing decision-making role of the Secretary-General and of the General Assembly. The "Uniting for Peace" Resolution of 1950[12] purports to transfer to the Assembly, by a qualified majority resolution, certain responsibilities for the maintenance of international peace and security where the Security Council fails to act because of lack of unanimity of its permanent members. In 1956 it was the General Assembly that set up the first of the U.N. peace-keeping forces in the Gaza strip; this was a vital element in the liquidation of the Suez Canal crisis.[13] But in recent years the flood of new members—mainly African states—has so much shifted the balance of voting power that the major members have tended to turn from the Assembly to the use of regional organisations or of individual force.

If the validity of international law—as a legal order, not a system

---

[12] U. N. Gen. Ass. Off. Rec. 5th Sess., Supp. No. 20 [A/1775].
[13] U. N. Doc. No. A/3290.

of "positive morality" (Austin)—is held to be predicated upon a clear legal supremacy of the international community over the nation states, the conclusion can only be that there is no international legal order in the present society of states. Neither in terms of the power of command of a defined sovereign, nor in terms of the sanctioning power, has the United Nations established the minimum elements of sovereignty. Nor can an answer be found in recourse to war, reprisals, or the attribution of "decentralised decision-making power" to the use of force by individual states in what they consider the implementation of the United Nations' purposes.[14] All such actions are in fact instances of the unilateral use of force, by the decision of individual or several states, which differ from the traditional assertion of sovereign prerogatives only in the attempt to cloak their actions with a mantle of collective security purposes.

The reality of international law can only be derived from its recognition, by the community of nations, as an obligatory system, and from the admission that the theory of absolute and unconditional sovereignty—developed for the municipal law of nation states over the last two centuries—does not necessarily apply to the condition of contemporary international society. International law will have to be sustained, as an imperfect system, lacking organised sanctions, but nevertheless real bceause "every actual state recognises that it does exist and that it is itself under obligation to observe it."[15] In H. L. A. Hart's rationalization, international law rests on a "primary rule of obligation, as distinct from the secondary rules of recognition"—a phase that it has not yet reached.[16]

The view that there can only be an unconditional alternative between national and international sovereignty, is closely linked, not only with that of a strict hierarchical norm structure but also with the punitive conception of law, that characterises the theories of Austin and Kelsen, and of most doctrines of analytical jurisprudence. But the growing importance of modern functional collaboration between states in matters of common concern has led to the establishment of international organisations to which the member states have transferred certain sovereign powers while retaining others. The clearest example of a partial transferral of

---

[14] This is for example the justification given for the U.S. intervention in the Vietnamese war, which is supported by reference to Article 51 of the Charter, but for which no U.N. authorisation has been given.

[15] Brierly, *The Outlook for International Law* 4-5, (1944).

[16] See Hart, *The Concept of Law*, Chap. X. (1961).

sovereignty is the structure of the European communities. They have been characterized by eminent international jurists as representing a "new system of law".[17] Although the communities are based on a multilateral treaty, they have certain powers which are not subject to unilateral revocation by the members, and decision-making authority which does not require unanimity. The constitution of the Netherlands—one of the member states—in an amendment of 1956, unambiguously stipulates the supremacy of community law over Netherlands law where the two conflict. And while there remain doubts as to the relation between general international law, community law and the national laws of the member states, there is virtual unanimity that the member states have transferred certain of their sovereign powers from themselves to an international institution.[18]

The weakness of the "monistic" theory, is that it stipulates the model of a sovereign equipped with the power both of command and of punitive sanctions, as the only type of legal order. But once we admit that there are different types of legal systems, with different degrees of authority and sanctioning power, we can accept international law as a weaker, but nevertheless real legal order, distinct in this and many other respects from the characteristics of a municipal legal system.

[17] Ch. de Visscher, *L'Interprétation Judiciare des Traités d'Organisation International*, 41 *Rivista de Diritto Internazionale* 177 (1958); see also Bebr, *The Relation of the European Coal and Steel Community Law to the Law of the Member States: a Peculiar Legal Symbiosis*, 58 Colum L. Rev. 767 (1958).

[18] See, for example, Reuter, *La Communauté Européenne du Charbon et de l'Acier* 44 (1953). And see for a more detailed discussion of the entire problem, *The Changing Structure of International Law*, *op. cit.* Chaps. 8, 9.

SELECTED BIBLIOGRAPHY

CHAPTER 2

The Republic of Plato (Jowett ed., 1901) or Everyman's Library (Lindsay, 1935).
The Laws of Plato (ed. England 1921).
Aristotle, *Politics* (trans. Jowett, Oxford University Press 1926).
Aristotle, *The Nichomachean Ethics* (Everyman ed.).
Barker, *The Political Thought of Plato and Aristotle* (1906).
Hamburger, *The Awakening of Western Legal Thought* (1942).
Cairns, *Legal Philosophy from Plato to Hegel* (1949).
Calhoun, *Introduction to Greek Legal Science* (1944).
Frank J., Book Review of *Introduction to Greek Science*, Calhoun 57 Harv.L.R.1120 (1944).
Jaeger, "In Praise of Law" (The Origin of Legal Philosophy and the Greeks) in *Interpretations of Modern Legal Philosophies*, 352. (Sayre ed., 1947)
Kelsen, "The Metamorphoses of the Idea of Justice," in *Interpretations of Modern Legal Philosophies* 390. (Sayre ed., 1947).
Jones, *The Law and Legal Theory of the Greeks* (1956).
Hamburger, *Law and Morals: The Growth of Aristotle's Legal Theory* (1951).
Stone, *Human Law and Human Justice*, Chap. 1 (1965).

CHAPTER 3

Fuller, *The Morality of Law* (1964).
Austin, *Province of Jurisprudence Determined*, Lecture 1.
Ross, *On Law and Justice* 59-64 (1959).
Hart, *The Concept of Law* Chaps. 6, 9 (1961).
Stone, *Legal System and Lawyers' Reasonings* 178 *et seq.* (1964).
Hart, "Positivism and the Separation of Law and Morals" 71 Harv. L. Rev. 593 (1958).
Fuller, "Positivism and Fidelity to Law—A Reply to Professor Hart", 71 Harv. L. Rev. 630 (1958).
Fuller, "Irrigation and Tyranny", 17 Stan. L. Rev. 1021 (1965).
Ginsberg, *On Justice in Society* (1965).
Kantorowicz, *Definition of Law* 43 *et seq.* (Campbell ed. 1958).
Frankena, *Ethics* (1963).
Christie, "The Notion of Validity in Modern Jurisprudence" 48 Minn. L. Rev. 1049 (1964).

Ayer, *Language, Truth and Logic* (2nd ed. 1946).
Nakhnikian, "Contemporary Ethical Theories and Jurisprudence" 2 Natural L. F. 4 (1957).
Russell, *Human Society in Ethics and Politics* (1954).
Hart, *Law, Liberty and Morality* (1963).
Devlin, *The Enforcement of Morals* (1965).
Bodenheimer, *Jurisprudence*, Chap. 13 (2nd ed. 1962).
Hart, "Definition and Theory of Jurisprudence" 70 L. Q. Rev. 37 (1954).
Villey "Law and Values: A French View," 14 Cath. U. L. Rev. 158-170 (1965).

CHAPTER 4

Nagel, *The Structure of Science* (1960).
Berns, "Law and Behavioral Science" 28 *Law and Contemporary Problems* 185 (1963).
Fuller, "Human Purpose and Natural Law"; Nagel, "On the Fusion of Fact and Values; A reply to Professor Fuller" in 3 Natural L.F. et seq., 77 et seq. (1958).
Vickers, *The Art of Judgment: A Study of Policy Making* (1965).
Hart, "Legal Responsibility and Excuses" in *Determinism and Freedom in the Age of Modern Science* (Hook ed. 1958).
Gluck, "Psychology and the Criminal Law" 12 *Mental Hygiene* 575 (1928).
Flugel, *Men, Morals and Society* (1945).
Sawyer, *Law in Society*, Chap. 11 (1965).
Patterson, *Law in a Scientific Age* (1963).
Miller, "Technology, Social Change and the Constitution," 33 G.W.L. Rev. 17-46 (1964).

CHAPTER 5

Friedmann, *Law in a Changing Society* Chaps. 1, 2 (1959).
Pound, *Social Control through Law* (1942).
Stone, *Legal System and Lawyers' Reasonings*, Chaps. 6, 7 (1964).
Stone, *Social Dimensions of Law and Justice*, Chap. 15 (1966).
Mannheim, *Man and Society in an Age of Reconstruction* (1940).
Simpson and Field, "Social Engineering through Law" 22 New York University L.R., 145 (1947).
Freund, "Social Justice and the Law" in Brant, R. B., *Social Justice*, 119-170 (1962).

CHAPTER 6

Windelband, *A History of Philosophy* (transl. Tufts, 1926).
Russell, *A History of Western Legal Philosophy* (1946).
Barker, Introduction to Gierke, *Natural Law and the Theory of Society* (1934).

Pound, *Law and Morals* (2nd ed., 1926).
M. Cohen, "Philosophy and Legal Science" in *Essays on Law and the Social Order* (1933).
Mitchell, "Social Ideals and the Law," 46 Philos.Rev. 113.
Kelsen, "Metamorphoses of the Idea of Justice," in *Interpretations of Modern Legal Philosophies* (Sayse ed. 1917).
Kessler, "Natural Law, Justice and Democracy," 19 Tulane L.Rev. 32 (1944).
Stone, *Human Law and Human Justice*, Chap. 8 (1965).

CHAPTERS 7-14

Aristotle, *The Nicomachean Ethics* (Everyman ed.).
St. Thomas Aquinas, *Summa theologica* (Part 2), London, Burns, Oates & Washbourne (1927).
Grotius, *De Jure Belli al Pacis* (Classics of International Law, No. 3).
Pufendorf, *De jure naturae et gentium* (Classics of International Law, No. 17).
Hobbes, *Leviathan* (Blackwell, Introduction by Oakeshott).
Hume, *Treatise of Human Nature* (Everyman ed.).
Locke, *Two Treatises on Civil Government* (Book 2) (Everyman ed.).
Cairns, *Legal Philosophy from Plato to Hegel*, Chaps. II-V, X, XI.
Bodenheimer, *Jurisprudence: The Philosophy and Method of the Laws*, Chaps. II, III (1962).
Jones, *Historical Introduction to the Theory of Law*, Chap. 4 (1940).
Hall, *Readings in Jurisprudence*, Chap. 1 (1938).
Bryce, "The Law of Nature," *Studies in History and Jurisprudence*, Vol. 2, pp. 556-606.
Barker, Introduction to Gierke, *National Law and the Theory of Society* (1934).
Pollock, "The History of the Laws of Nature," in *Essays in the Law* (1922).
Haines, *The Revival of Natural Law Concepts* (1930).
Pollock, "Locke's Theory of the State," in *Essays in the Law* (1922).
Barker (ed.), *Social Contract*.
Holmes, "Natural Law," 32 Harv.L.Rev. 40 (1919).
Sabine, *A History of Political Theory*, Chaps 5, 8, 9, 13, 15, 23, 26, 29 (1937).
Corwin, "The 'Higher Law,' background of American Constitutional Law," 42 Harv.L.Rev 149, 365 (1929).
O'Sullivan, "A Scale of Values in the Common Law," 1 Mod.L.Rev. 37 (1937).
Troeltsch, *Natural Law and Humanity*. Appendix 1 to Gierke, *Natural Law and the Theory of Society*.
Constable, "Natural Law Jurisprudence and the Cleavage of Our Times," 39 Georgetown L.J. 365 (1950).
Hall, *Living Law of Democratic Society* (1949).
Patterson, *Jurisprudence*, Chap. 13 (1953).

Brunner, *Justice and the Social Order* (1945).
Rommen, *Natural Law* (1947).
Wu, *Fountain of Justice* (1955).
Lloyd, *Introduction to Jurisprudence*, Chap. 3 (2nd ed., 1965).
d'Entrèves, "The Case for Natural Law Re-examined," Natural L.F. (1956).
Stone, *Human Law and Human Justice*, Chaps. 2, 7 (1965).
Pound, "Natural Law and Positive Natural Law," 68 L.Q.Rev. 330 (1952).
Shellens, "Aristotle on Natural Law," Natural L.F. 72 (1959).
Ross, *On Law and Justice*, Chaps. 10, 11 (1959).
Hart, *The Concept of Law*, Chap. 9 (1961).

CHAPTER 15

Kant, *Philosophy of Law* (ed. Hastie, 1887).
Bosanquet, *The Philosophical Theory of the State* (1899).
Hobhouse, *The Metaphysical Theory of the State* (1918)
Croce, *What is Living and what is Dead in Hegel's Philosophy?* (1912).
Stace, *The Philosophy of Hegel* (1924).
Windelband, *History of Philosophy* (1926).
Berolzheimer, *The World's Legal Philosophies*.
Sabine, *A History of Political Theory*, Chaps. 30, 34 (1937).
Russell, *A History of Western Philosophy*, Book 3, Part 2.
Brecht, "The Myth of Is and Ought," 54 Harv.L.R. 811.
Cairns, *Legal Philosophy from Plato to Hegel*, Chaps. XII-XIV (1949).
Patterson, *Jurisprudence*, Chap. 14 (1953).
Friedrich, *Philosophy of Law in Historical Perspective* (1958).
Stone, *Human Law and Human Justice*, Chap. 3 (1965).

CHAPTERS 16-17

Stammler, *Theory of Justice* (trans. Hussik), 1925, with critical essays on Stammler by Gény (App. 1) and Wu (App. 2).
Ginsberg, "Stammler's Philosophy of Law," in *Modern Theories of Law* (1933).
Hussik, "Legal Philosophy of Stammler," 24 Colum. L. Rev. 373 (1924).
Sabine, "Stammler's Critical Philosophy of Law," 18 Cornell L.Q. 321 (1932).
Del Vecchio, *The Formal Bases of Law* (Modern Legal Philosophy Series, 1921).
Del Vecchio, *Justice, Droit, Etat* (1938).
Radbruch, in 20th Century Legal Philosophy Series, vol. 4, 47-224.
Jones, *Historical Introduction to the Theory of Law* Chap. 9 (1940).
Pound, "Fifty Years of Jurisprudence," 51 Harv.L.R. 444, 454-460 (1938).
Hall, *Readings in Jurisprudence*, Chap. 3 (1938).
Cohen, M. R., "On Absolutism in Legal Thought," 84 U. Penn. L. Rev. 681.

Holmes, "Natural Law," 32 Harv.L.R. 40 (1918).

Hartmann, *Ethics*, 3 vols. (tr. Coit, 1932).

Heinemann, *Existentialism and the Modern Predicament* (1953).

Recasens-Siches and Cossio, in *Latin-American Legal Philosophy* (20th Century Legal Philosophy Series, Vol. III).

Recasens-Siches, "Juridical Axiology in Ibero-America," 3 Natural L.F. 135-169, (1958).

Brecht, *Political Theory* Chaps. VI, VIII, (1959).

Strauss, *Natural Right and History* (1953).

Stone, *Human Law and Human Justice* Chap. 6, (1965).

Bodenheimer, *Jurisprudence: The Philosophy and Method of the Law*, Chap. IX, (1962).

CHAPTER 18

Savigny, *On the Vocation of our Age for Legislation and Jurisprudence* (trans. Hayward, 1831).

Maine, *Ancient Law* (ed. Pollock, 1906).

Dicey, *Law and Public Opinion in England* (2nd ed., 1914).

Pound, *Interpretations of Legal History* Chaps. 1-4 (1923).

Jones, *Historical Introduction to the Theory of Law* Chap. 2 (1940).

Hall, *Readings in Jurisprudence*, Chap. 2 (1938).

Kantorowicz, "Savigny and the Historical School of Law," 53 L.Q.R. 334 (1937).

Graveson, *Status in the Common Law* (1952).

Robson, "Sir Henry Maine Today," in *Modern Theories of Law* (1933).

Seagle, *The Quest for Law* Chap. 17 (1941).

Stone, *Social Dimensions of Law and Justice* Chap. 2 (1966).

Friedmann, "Some Reflections on Status and Freedom," in *Essays in Jurisprudence on Honor of Roscoe Pound*, 222-237 (1962).

CHAPTER 19

Barker, *Political Thought in England from Herbert Spencer to the Present Day* (1915).

Barker, Introduction to Gierke, *Natural Law and the Theory of Society* (1934).

Sabine, *A History of Political Theory*, Chap. 31.

Duguit, *Law in the Modern State* (transl. Laski, 1919).

Duguit, "Objective Law," 20 Colum. L. Rev. 817 (1920).

Duguit, "Theory of Objective Law Anterior to the State," in *Modern French Legal Philosophy* (1921).

Laski, "Duguit's Concept of the State," in *Modern Theories of Law* (1933).

Jethro Brown, "The Jurisprudence of M. Duguit," 32 L.Q.R.168 (1916).

Allen, *Law in the Making* (5th ed.), p. 561 *et seq.*

Hallis, *Corporate Personality* Parts 2, 3, 4, (1930).

Maitland, Introduction to Gierke, *Political Theories of the Middle Ages* (1900).

Jennings, "The Institutional Theory," in *Modern Theories of Law*, 68 (1933).

Stone, *Social Dimensions of Law and Justice*, Chap. 9, 11 (1966).

CHAPTER 20

Pound, "The Scope and Purpose of Sociological Jurisprudence," 25 Harv. L.Rev. 489 (1911).

Timasheff, *An Introduction to the Sociology of Law* (1939); "Growth and Scope of Sociology of Law" in Modern Sociological Theory 444 (1957).

Gurvitch, *Sociology of Law* (1947).

Friedmann, "Sociology of Law" 10/11 Current Sociology, No. 1 (1961-62).

Max Weber on Law in Economy and Society (trans. Shils, 1954).

E. Ehrlich, *Fundamental Principles of the Sociology of Law* (trans. Moll).

Stone, *Social Dimensions of Law and Justice*, Chap. 1 (1966).

CHAPTERS 21-24

Austin, *Lectures on Jurisprudence* (4th ed., 1879) (ed. Campbell).

Jethro Brown, *The Austinian Theory of Law* (1906).

Holland, *Elements of Jurisprudence* (10th ed., 1924).

Kocourek, *Introduction to the Science of Law* (1930).

Pollock, *First Book of Jurisprudence* (6th ed., 1929).

Eastwood and Keeton, *The Austinian Theories* (1929).

Salmond, *Jurisprudence* (10th ed. by Glanville Williams, 1957).

Gray, *The Nature and Sources of Law* (2nd ed., 1921).

Manning, "Austin Today," in *Modern Theories of Law* (1933).

Pound, "Analytical Jurisprudence, 1914-27," 41 Harv. L. Rev. 174 (1927).

Kelsen, "Pure Theory of Law,' 50 L.Q. Rev. (1934); 51 L.Q. Rev. 517 (1935).

Kelsen, *General Theory of Law and State* (1945).

Ebenstein, *The Pure Theory of Law* (1945).

Silving, "Law and Fact in the Light of the Pure Theory of Law," in *Interpretations of Modern Legal Philosophies* (1933).

Hart, "Definition and Theory in Jurisprudence" 70 L.Q. Rev. 37 (1954).

Dias, *Jurisprudence* (1957), Chaps. 14, 15 (2nd ed., 1964).

Lloyd, *Introduction to Jurisprudence*, Chaps. 4, 5 (2nd ed., 1965).

Pound, "50 Years of Jurisprudence," 50 Harv. L. Rev. 557-582 (1937).

M. Cohen, "Positivism and the Limits of Idealism in Law," 27 Colum. L. Rev. 237 (1927).

Hall, *Readings in Jurisprudence*, Chaps. 9-11 (1938).

Buckland, *Reflections on Jurisprudence* (1945).

Nakhnikian, "Contemporary Ethical Theories and Jurisprudence" 2 Natural L.F. 4 (1957).

Hart, "Positivism and the Separation of Law and Morality" 71 Harv. L. Rev. 595 (1958).

Fuller, "Positivism and Fidelity to Law" 71 Harv. L. Rev. 630 (1958).

Pound, *Jurisprudence* Vol. V (The System of Law) (1959).

Kantorowicz, *The Definition of Law* (ed. Campbell, 1958).

Shuman, *Legal Positivism* (1963).

Hart, *The Concept of Law* (1961).

Stone, *Legal Systems and Lawyers' Reasonings*, Chaps. 1, 2, 3, 4, 8 (1964).

H. L. A. Hart, "Kelsen Visited," 10, U. of Cal. L.A.L. Rev. 709-728 (1963).

CHAPTER 25

Pound, "The Scope and Purpose of Sociological Jurisprudence," 25 Harv. L. Rev. 489 (1911).

Weber, M., "Rechtssoziologie," in *Grundriss der Sozialoekonomik*, Abt. 3.

Ehrlich, *Fundamental Principles of the Sociology of Law* (transl. Moll 1936).

Holmes, "The Path of the Law" and "Law in Science and Science in Law" in *Collected Legal Papers* (1920).

James, *Pragmatism* (1925).

Dewey, "Logical Method of Law," 10 Cornell L.Q. 17 (1924).

Frank, *Law and the Modern Mind* (1930).

Frank, *Courts on Trial* (1949).

Pound, "The Call for a Realist Jurisprudence," 44 Harv. L. Rev. 697 (1930-31).

Llewellyn, "Some Realism about Realism," 44 Harv. L. Rev. 1222 (1930-31).

Kantorowicz, "Some Rationalism about Realism," 43 Yale L.J. 1240 (1931).

F. S. Cohen, "The Problem of a Functional Jurisprudence," 1 Mod. L. Rev. 5 (1937).

Goodhart, "Some American Interpretations of Law," in *Modern Theories of Law*, 1-20 (1933).

Llewellyn, "On Reading and Using the Newer Jurisprudence," 40 Colum. L. Rev. 581 (1940).

Fuller, *The Law in Quest of Itself* (1940).

Radin, *Law as Logic and Experience* (1940).

McDougal, "*Fuller* v. *The American Realists*," 50 Yale L.J. 827 (1940).

Hall, *Readings in Jurisprudence*, Chaps. 16-18, 21-25 (1938).

Patterson, *Jurisprudence*, Chap. 17 (1953).

Mendelson, "Mr. Justice Holmes—Humility, Skepticism and Democracy," 36 Minn. L.R. 343 (1951).

Olivecrona, *Law as Fact* (1939).

Ross, *On Law and Justice* (1959).

Hart, "Scandinavian Realism" 15 Camb. L.J. 233 (1959).

Dias, *Jurisprudence*, Chap. 19 (2nd ed., 1964).
Llewellyn, *The Common Law Tradition, Deciding Appeals* (1960).
Lloyd, *Introduction to Jurisprudence*, Chaps. 7, 8 (2nd ed., 1965).
Stone, *Human Law and Human Justice*, Chap. 9 (1965).
Hart, *The Concept of Law*, 132-144 (1961).

CHAPTER 26

Bentham, *The Theory of Legislation* (ed. C. K. Ogden, 1931).
Bentham, "Essay on the Influence of Time and Place in Matters of Legislation", *Works* (Bowring ed.).
Davidson, *Political Thought in England* (*Utilitarians from Bentham to Mill*).
Mill, *Utilitarianism* (Everyman ed.).
Ihering, *Law as a Means to an End* (transl. Hussik), 1924.
Barker, *Political Thought from 1848-1914*.
Hobhouse, *Liberalism* (1911).
Sabine, *A History of Political Theory*, Chap. 31 (1937).
Laski, *The Rise of European Liberalism* (1936).
Hall, *Readings on Jurisprudence*, Chap. 4 (1938).
Jennings, "A Plea for Utilitarianism," 2 Mod. L. Rev. 22 (1938).
Cohen, F. S., *Ethical Systems and Legal Ideas* (1933).
Stone, *Human Law and Human Justice*, Chaps. 4, 5 (1965).
Friedmann, "Bentham and Modern Legal Thought," in *Jeremy Bentham and the Law: A Symposium* (1948).

CHAPTER 27

Gény, *Method of Interpretation and Sources of Private Positive Law*, 2nd ed. (Engl. transl.) (1963).
Ehrlich, *Fundamental Principles of the Sociology of Law* (transl. Moll).
The Jurisprudence of Interests, Selected Writings of M. Rümelin, Ph. Heck, etc. (1943). Twentieth Century Legal Philosophy Series, vol. 2.
Pound, *Interpretations of Legal History*, Chap. 7.
Pound, "Survey of Social Interest," 57 Harv. L. Rev. 1 (1943).
Pound, "The Scope and Purpose of Sociological Jurisprudence," 25 Harv. L. Rev. 489 (1921).
Pound, "Fifty Years of Jurisprudence," 51 Harv. L. Rev. 777 (1937).
Cardozo, *The Nature of the Judicial Process* (1921).
Cardozo, *The Paradoxes of Legal Science* (1928).
Hall, *Readings in Jurisprudence*, Chaps. 8, 24 (1938).
Amos, "Roscoe Pound," in *Modern Theories of Law*, 86-105 (1933).
Wortley, "François Gény," in *Modern Theories of Law*, 139-160 (1933).
Paton, "Pound and Contemporary Juristic Theory," 22 Can. Bar Rev. 484.
Patterson, "Pound's Theory of Social Interests," in *Interpretations of Modern Legal Philosophies* (1947).

Stone, *Social Dimensions of Law and Justice*, Chaps. 3-5 (1966).
Pound, 3 *Jurisprudence* Part 4 (1959).

CHAPTER 28

M. R. Cohen, *Reason and Law*, Chap. 3 (1950).
Stone, *Human Law and Human Justice*, Chap. 7 (1965).
Allen "Justice and Expediency", Hocking "Justice, Law and the Cases" and Kelsen "Metamorphoses of the Idea of Justice" in *Interpretations of Modern Legal Philosophy.*
Friedmann, *Law and Social Change in Contemporary Britain*, Pt. IV (1951).
Cahn, *The Sense of Injustice* (1949).
Pound, *New Paths of the Law* (1951).
Hart, "Positivism and the Separation of Law and Morality," 71 Harv. L. Rev. 598 (1958).
Fuller, "Positivism and Fidelity to Law," 71 Harv. L. Rev. 630 (1958).
Yoffee and Tolstoy, "The New Civil Code of the R.S.F.S.R., a Soviet View," 15 Int'l and Comp. L.Q. 1090 (1966).

CHAPTER 29

Marx, *A Contribution to Critique of Political Economy.*
Lenin, *State and Revolution* (1918).
Laski, *The State in Theory and Practice* (1934).
Jones, *Historical Introduction to the Theory of Law*, Chap. 11 (1941).
Mirkine-Guetzevich, *La Théorie Générale de l'Etat Soviétique* (1928).
Pashukanis, *Allgemeine Staatslehre und Marxismus* (1927).
Oakeshott, *The Social and Political Doctrines of Contemporary Europe*, Chap. 3.
Gsovski, "Soviet Civil Law" (1948).
Schlesinger, *Soviet Legal Theory* (2nd ed., 1950).
Stone, *Social Dimensions of Law and Justice*, Chaps. 10, 15 (1966).
Renner, *The Institutions of Private Law and their Social Function* (1949). (Introduction by O. Kahn-Freund.)
Hazard and Weisberg, *Cases and Readings on Soviet Law* (mimeographed ed., 1951).
Hazard (ed.), Introduction to *Soviet Legal Philosophy* (1951).
Juins, *Soviet Law and Soviet Society* (1954).
Berman, *Justice in the U.S.S.R.* (1964).
Hazard, *The Soviet System of Government* (3rd ed., 1964).
Berman, *Soviet Criminal Law and Procedure* (1966).

CHAPTER 30

Oakeshott, *Social and Political Doctrines of Contemporary Europe* (1939), Chap. 2.
Renard, *La Théorie de l'Institution* (1930).

Le Fur, *Les Grands Problèms du Droit* (1938).
Maritain, *Man and the State* (1951).
Rommen, *Natural Law* (1947 ed.).
Dabin, in *The Legal Philosophies of Lask, Radbruch and Dabin*, 20th Century Legal Philosophy Series (1950).
Powers, *Papal Pronouncements and the Political Order* (1952).

CHAPTER 31

Denning, *Freedom under the Law* (1949).
Stone, *Human Law and Human Justice* 99 et seq. (1965); *Social Dimensions of Law and Justice* 111-118, 619 et seq. (1966).

CHAPTER 32

Devlin, *Samples of Law Making* (1962).
Cardozo, *The Nature of the Judicial Process* (1921).
Pound, *Law and Morals* (2nd ed., 1926).
Allen, *Law in the Making*, Chaps. 4, 5, 6 (v) (6th ed., 1958).
Stone, *Social Dimensions of Law and Justice*, Chaps 4, 14 (1966); *Legal Systems and Lawyers' Reasonings*, Chaps. 6, 7 (1964).
Paton, *Jurisprudence*, §44 (2nd ed., 1951).
Patterson, *Jurisprudence*, Chap. 19 (1953).
Levi, *Introduction to Legal Reasoning* (1949).
Read, MacDonald and Fordham, *Cases and Materials on Legislation* (2nd ed., 1959).
Pound, "The Ideal Element in American Judicial Decisions," 45 Harv.L.Rev. 132 (1932).
M. Cohen, "Positivism and the Limits of Idealism in the Law," 27 Colum.L.Rev. 243 (1927).
Mitchell, "Social Ideals and the Law," 46 Philosoph.Rev. 113.
Lord Wright, *Legal Essays and Addresses*, 66-98 (1938).
Winfield, "Public Policy," 42 Harv.L.Rev. 112 (1932).
Pound, "A Survey of Social Interests," 57 Harv.L.Rev. 1 (1944).
Lord Wright, "Precedents," 8 Camb.L.J. 118 (1942).
Goodhart, "Precedent in English and Continental Jurisprudence," 50 L.Q.Rev. 40 (1934).
Willis, "Statute Interpretation in a Nutshell," 16 Can.BarRev. 1 (1938).
Friedmann, "Judges, Politics and Law," 29 Can.BarRev. 871 (1951).
Marsh, "Principle and Discretion in the Judicial Process," 68 L.Q.Rev. 226 (1952).
Mason, *Security through Freedom* (1955).
Lloyd, *Public Policy* (1953).
Berle, *The Twentieth Century Capitalist Revolution* (1954).
Friedmann, *Law in a Changing Society* (1959).
Fuller, "Reason and Fiat," 59 Harv.L.Rev. 376 (1946).
Lloyd, *Introduction to Jurisprudence*, Chap. 10 (2nd ed., 1965).
Dias, *Jurisprudence*, Chaps. 3-7 (2nd ed., 1964).

Hart, *The Concept of Law*, Chap. 7 (1961).
Breitel, "Courts and Law Making," in Legal Institutions Today and Tomorrow (1959).
Traynor, "La Rude Vita, La Dolce Giustizia or Hard Cases Can Make Good Law," 29 U.Chi.L.Rev. 223 (1962).
Currier, "Time and Change: Prospective Overruling in Judge-Made Law," 51 Va.L.Rev. (1965).
Mishkin, "Foreword—The High Court, the Great Writ and Due Process of Time and Law," 79 Harv.L.Rev. 56 (1965).
Breitel, "The Lawmakers," [Association of the Bar of the City of New York (1965)].

CHAPTER 33

Gutteridge, *Comparative Law* (2nd ed. 1949).
Allen, *Law in the Making*, Chaps. III-VI (6th ed. 1958).
Lawson, *The Rational Strength of English Law* (1951).
Lawson, *A Common Lawyer Looks at the Civil Law* (1953).
Lauterpacht, *Private Law Sources and Analogies of International Law* (1927).
Lauterpacht, *The Function of Law in the International Community* (1933).
Goodhart, "Precedent in English and Continental Law," 50 L/Q.Rev. 40 (1934).
Gutteridge, "The Abuse of Rights," 5 Camb.L.J. 22 (1935).
Gutteridge and David, "Unjustified Enrichment," 5 Camb.L.J. 204 (1935).
Walton, "Delictual Responsibility in Civil Law," 49 L.Q.Rev. 70 (1933).
Radbruch, "Anglo-American Jurisprudence through Continental Eyes," 52 L.Q.Rev. 330 (1936).
Maitland, Selected Essays, Chaps. 3-5.
Friedmann, "The Principle of Unjust Enrichment," 16 Can.BarRev. 243 (1938).
Cohn, "Precedents in Continental Law," 5 Camb.L.J. 366 (1935).
Schwarzenberger, 1 *International Law* (3rd ed. 1957).
Schlesinger, *Comparative Law, Cases and Materials* (2nd ed., 1959).
David and de Vries, *The French Legal System* (1958).
Von Mehren, *The Civil Law System* (1957).
Dawson, *Unjust Enrichment* (1951).
Von Mehren, "The Judicial Process: A Comparative Analysis," 5 Am.J.Comp.L. 197 (1956).
Bolgar, "Why no Trusts in the Civil Law," 2 Am.J.Comp.L. 204 (1953).
Langrod, "Administrative Contracts: A Comparative Study," 4 Am.J.Comp.L. 325 (1955).
Catala and Weir, "Delict and Tort: A Study in Parallel," 38 Tul.L.Rev. 663 (1964); 29 Tul.L.Rev. 701 (1965).
Von Mehren, "Civil Law Analogues to Considerations," 72 Harv.L.Rev. 1009 (1959).

Dawson, "Negotiorum Gestio: The Altruistic Intermeddler," 74 Harv.L.Rev. 817, 1073 (1961).

Szladits, *Guide to Foreign Legal Materials: French-German-Swiss* (1959).

Rudzinski, "The Duty to Rescue—A Comparative Analysis," in *The Good Samaritan in the Law* (Radcliffe ed., 1966).

CHAPTER 34

Maitland, *Selected Essays* (1936).

Barker, Introduction to Gierke, *National Law and the Theory of Society*, s. 5.

Hallis, *Corporate Personality*, Introduction and Part 1, Chap. 1; Part 3, Chaps. 1, 2, 4.

Douglas and Shanks, "Insulation from Liability through Subsidiary Corporations" 39 YaleL.J. 193 (1939).

Berle, "The Theory of Enterprise Entity" 47 Colum.L.Rev. 343 (1947).

Wolff, "The Nature of Legal Persons," 54 L.Q.R. 494 (1938).

Gower, *Modern Company Law*, Chap. 10 (2nd ed., 1957).

Cohn and Simitis, "Lifting the Veil in the Company Laws of the European Countries," 12 Int. and Comp. L.Q. 189 (1963).

Welsh, "The Criminal Liability of Corporations," 62 L.Q. Rev. 345 (1945).

Lloyd, *The Law of Unincorporated Associations* (1938).

Ford, *Unincorporated non-Profit Associations* (1959).

CHAPTER 35

Cohen, *Recent Theories of Sovereignty* (1937).

Lauterpacht, *The Function of Law in the International Community* (1933).

Keeton, *National Sovereignty and International Order* (1939).

Sabine, *A History of Political Theory*, Part 3 (1937).

Kelsen, *General Theory of Law and State* (1946).

Friedmann, *Law in a Changing Society*, Chaps. 9, 14 (1959).

Jessup, *Transnational Law* (1957).

Friedmann, *The Changing Structure of International Law* (1964).

Hart, *The Concept of Law*, Chap. 10 (1961).

Bodenheimer, *Jurisprudence: The Philosophy and Method of Law*, 227-231, 259 et seq. (1962).

Brierly, *The Outlook for International Law* (1944).

Stone, *Social Dimensions of Law and Justice*, Chap. 7 (1966).

The Corporation in Modern Society (Mason ed. 1960).

INDEX OF AUTHORS

This index is limited to those authors and judges whose views are quoted or discussed. References in black *type indicate the place where the principal account of a theory is given.*

GENERAL INDEX

Black *type indicates the place of the main discussion.*